FIFTH EDITION

Administrative Procedures for the Canadian Office

Lauralee Kilgour
Northern Alberta Institute of Technology

Edward Kilgour
AT&T Canada

Sharon Burton
Brookhaven College

Nelda Shelton
Tarrant County Jr. College

Lucy Mae Jennings
Emeritus, Munroe Community College

Prentice Hall Canada Career & Technology
Scarborough, Ontario

Canadian Cataloguing in Publication Data

Main entry under title:

Administrative procedures for the Canadian office

5th ed.

ISBN 0-13-013573-9

Second ed. published under title: Secretarial procedures for the automated office/Lucy Mae Jennings, Lauralee Kilgour. Third ed. published under title: Administrative procedures for the Canadian Office/Lauralee Kilgour, Lucy Mae Jennings.

1. Office practice. 2. Office procedures. I. Kilgour, Lauralee G. (Lauralee Gail), 1953– .

HF5547.5.J465 2000 651.3'74 C99-931543-9

Prentice-Hall, Inc., Upper Saddle River, New Jersey
Prentice-Hall International (UK) Limited, London
Prentice-Hall of Australia, Pty. Limited, Sydney
Prentice-Hall Hispanoamericana, S.A., Mexico City
Prentice-Hall of India Private Limited, New Delhi
Prentice-Hall of Japan, Inc., Tokyo
Simon & Schuster Southeast Asia Private Limited, Singapore
Editora Prentice-Hall do Brasil, Ltda., Rio de Janeiro

ISBN 0-13-013573-9

Vice President, Editorial Director: Laura Pearson
Acquisitions Editor: David Stover
Developmental Editor: Marta Tomins
Production Editor: Alex Moore
Copy Editor: Shirley Corriveau
Marketing Manager: Sophia Fortier
Production Coordinator: Wendy Moran
Cover Design: Alex Li
Cover Image: Peter Coates
Page Layout: Debbie Kumpf

Original English-language edition published under the title *Procedures for the Automated Office* by Prentice-Hall, Inc., Upper Saddle River, NJ, 07458. Copyright © 1998, 1994, 1990, 1986.

6 7 8 9 10 11 12 05 04 03 02

Printed and bound in the United States

This book is dedicated to the memory of Newton Hunter Ross
Lauralee Kilgour

Contents

Preface

The fifth edition of *Administrative Procedures for the Canadian Office* is an essential text for students studying professional office procedures. It is specifically designed to prepare students for entry into the contemporary Canadian work force and to act as the best possible tool for an instructor offering classes in progressive office practices.

In order to support the students' learning in the most effective way, *Administrative Procedures for the Canadian Office* has a myriad of quality features. For example, the text includes **Working Papers** both on disk and on hard copy so that students can conveniently complete assignments either on paper or on the screen. Each chapter contains a set of practical **Challenges** that relate to lessons learned in the chapter. The disk contains a number of **Hotlinks** and each chapter offers a list of **Web Links** that encourages students to learn more through the Internet.

Each chapter displays a **Graduate Profile** of a successful Office Administration graduate from a Canadian college. These graduates act as role models for students, encourage them to succeed at college, and to achieve their professional goals. An extensive **Glossary** of terms, **Perspectives** articles, and photos enhance the fifth edition.

The fifth edition has been revised to include the most current and appropriate information available to students. Each chapter also contains a ***Pro-Link***, a short list of interesting and entertaining information that pertains to the chapter. As well, **quotations** from Canadian office administration graduates offer seasoned advice and motivation throughout the chapters. New and enhanced information on office technologies, office politics, letter styles, and nonverbal communication adds to the effectiveness of the text. Additional figures in this edition demonstrate the concepts and aid in the students' understanding. This text is written from a Canadian perspective but it includes information on handling international clients that is critical to doing business in the new millennium.

The comprehensive scope of the text, ranging from human relations to continuing professional growth, promotes positive attitudes about office procedures, technical expertise, and a career as an office professional. Emphasis is given to the topics of teamwork, communication, office politics, human relations, professional growth, quality management practices, an environmentally conscious workplace, and information technology in the office. The text places importance on time management and efficient office practices such as e-mail, voice mail, and electronic document creation. Of course, the essential skills associated with teamwork are emphasized throughout.

Each of the 16 chapters is self-contained and may be studied in any order. The complete text may be used for an Office Procedures course, or individual chapters may be used to supplement or reinforce other courses.

At the end of each chapter, the **Question for Study and Review** and the **Spelling Reinforcement** support factual review of the chapter's content. The **On-the-Job Situations** and **Special Reports** provide students with an opportunity to think critically, problem solve, and participate in constructive classroom interaction. The **Production Challenges** and **Working Papers** encourage students to apply the knowledge they have gained. The fifth edition of *Administrative Procedures for the Canadian Office* is a highly flexible and valuable tool for both students and instructors.

We would like to thank the following reviewers who evaluated the manuscript at various stages and all of whom offered valuable suggestions: Nancy Barry, Georgian College; Christine Berkhout, Niagara College; Jane Brooks, Sheridan College; Diane Blaney, Capilano College; Adrienne Goeldner, The Toronto School of Business; Dana Heddle, The Toronto School of Business, Mississauga; Doreen Hounsell, Cabot College; Peggy Hudson, Seneca College; Cris Jensen, Ontario Business College, Belville; Janice Linton, Toronto School of Business; Asima Macci, The Career College, Calgary; Ann McIntyre, George Brown College; Jim Miles, Fanshawe College; Petra Pemberton, Algonquin College; Kathy Rhodes, Durham College; Jackie Sawasy, Kwantlen College; Beth Shewkenek, Saskatoon Business College; Alice Szajber, Mohawk College of Applied Arts and Technology; Nancy Wallace, Canadore College; Peder Wilson, Vanier College.

In addition, we would also like to thank Dorthy Haines, Kathy Magee-Elgert, and Lee Voyer for their constructive feedback.

Lauralee Kilgour
Edward Kilgour
Kilgour@v-wave.com

Acknowledgments

Without the co-operation of many organizations, the fifth edition of *Administrative Procedures for the Canadian Office* could not have been written. We wish to thank the following for their contributions:

Air Canada

Association of Administrative Assistants

Association of Records Managers and Administrators

AT&T Canada

Bell Canada

Canada Post Corporation

Canadian Airlines International Ltd.

Canadian Transportation Agency

Canon Canada Inc.

Datavue Products

Edmonton Public Library

Federal Express Canada Ltd.

International Association of Administrative Professionals®

International Business Machines Corporation

Kardex®

NAIT Learning Resources Centre

National Association of Legal Secretaries®

Northern Telecom (Nortel)

NorthwesTel

Pitney Bowes

Rogers Cantel Inc.

Royal Bank of Canada

Shaw-Walker Company

Sheaffer-Eaton, Division of Textron Inc.

Steelcase Inc.

Thomas Cook Travel Canada Ltd.

Unisys Canada Inc.

U.S. Defense Mapping Agency

Xerox Canada Ltd.

3M Canada Inc.

The photographs provided by International Business Machines Corporation are reproduced by permission. Unauthorized use not permitted.

Most Perspectives articles have come from *OfficePRO* magazine, the official publication of the International Association of Administrative Professionals. Permission to reproduce these articles is gratefully acknowledged. The International Association of Administrative Professionals (IAAP) sponsors Professional Secretaries Week. To order *OfficePRO* or to become a member of IAAP, contact IAAP, P.O. Box 20404, Kansas City, MO, 64195-9966, 816-891-6600 Ext. 235.

PART I
THE WORKING ENVIRONMENT

INTRODUCTION

A Career as an Office Professional

Outline

Learning Outcomes

At the completion of this chapter, the student will be able to:

1. Describe current office trends.
2. Explain why some professional office workers prefer titles other than "secretary."
3. Define the role of the administrative assistant.
4. Describe ways the administrative assistant uses electronic equipment to accomplish the job.
5. Plan and keyboard a chronological vacation request list.
6. Prepare a requisition for supplies.

WHAT'S HAPPENING?

No professional environment has taken on greater changes in the last five years than that of the business office. This means that people working in this environment have to be cognizant of the change and ready to adapt. If you don't adapt and simply rely on what you've learned in the past, your technical skills will become obsolete and your attitude will likely be considered inconsistent with the corporate vision.

Here is a description of the current office trends that office professionals need to adapt to.

1. There's a new attitude in the office. The administrative assistant is no longer a subordinate who simply follows directions given by the manager. Administrative assistants are considered full team members whose skills are absolutely essential to the operation of the business. The role of an administrative assistant is not one that just anyone can fill. It is a highly specialized role where both advanced technical training and human relations skills are paramount. The administrative assistant's role is that of a contributing team member who must make valuable decisions within the realm of her/his authority.
2. The level of skill and responsibility has changed. Administrative assistants use sophisticated hardware and software and coordinate a myriad of details. They are expected to handle people as deftly as they handle computers. In fact, many administrative assistants perform what a decade ago were considered strictly managerial responsibilities. The gap between management and administrative assistants is closing. As an example, managers may spend time focused on business strategies based on Internet research and graphs prepared by administrative assistants. In the future office, keyboarding letters and paper filing may be the least of what administrative assistants do.
3. Working hours have become very flexible. The concept of working 9 to 5 Monday to Friday is disappearing. With computer networking many office professionals perform some of their responsibilities from their home computer on a Saturday or Sunday or even at 4:00 a.m. on a weekday. Flexible time works well for parents who want to shift their working day to meet family needs. The mode of working from home and having flexible hours means that employees have become managers of their own time. Self-discipline for these office professionals is an essential skill.
4. Companies have become more employee-friendly with wellness programs and quality management programs that require input and recommendations from the staff. So office specialists cannot simply bring problems to the attention of management. Instead they are required to bring recommendations and solutions to the table.
5. Office specialists have the opportunity and need to become entrepreneurial. Where once we settled into long-term employment with benefits and eventual retirement, we now see more short-term contracts available and less jobs with company benefits. Therefore, the administrative assistant must be constantly ready for change, in search of new assignments, and ready to upgrade technical expertise. Fortunately, the skills of an administrative assistant lend themselves to entrepreneurial work, giving assistants the ability to open their own business offering office support to individuals or corporations.
6. Technology will continue to remove routine tasks from the office. Instead, administrative assistants will take a higher level of responsibility.
7. The practice of payment for actual work performed as opposed to payment for a job title is popular. Many Human Resource departments rate each task listed on each separate job description. Each task is given a score based on importance and difficulty. Therefore, two administrative assistants from the same office but performing different responsibilities will receive different rates of pay.

The future is bright and the opportunities are infinite. Office professionals should always be looking for new opportunities, responsibilities, and possibilities.

WHAT DOES YOUR TITLE MEAN?

As the role of the secretary became more diverse, the title also changed. For years the term **secretary** was often inappropriately used to refer to office workers handling repetitive and simple tasks. The term was originally intended to refer to people requiring more complex organizational and supervisory skills.

Many secretaries have become dissatisfied with this misuse of the title and, as a result, are insisting on titles that distinguish them from office workers who perform routine tasks. A wide range of titles are currently being used. Some of these titles are *executive secretary*, *executive assistant*, *office coordinator*, *office specialist*, *administrative assistant*, and *office professional*. Usually the word "administrative" in a job title denotes a higher level of

Electronic equipment has automated procedures at all levels of the office.

Courtesy of International Business Machines Corporation. Unauthorized use not permitted.

responsibility than does the word "secretary." "Executive secretary" denotes a secretary who works directly for an executive.

Operators who do word processing are sometimes called word processing specialists or document preparation specialists.

It is interesting to compare the use of the term "secretary" in Japan. Most office professionals in Japan are called assistants; however, these assistants would like to be called secretaries. The position of secretary is a top management position that is often very influential. One of the earliest uses of the word "secretary" came from the Roman Empire, where the secretary was a close confidant to the Emperor.

However, in Canada the general title "secretary" is still applied to a large number of office professionals who should be called "executive assistant" or some other more descriptive/appropriate title. For these office professionals, the issue of which title ought to be used is a sensitive one. Changing a title to *executive assistant*, *office coordinator*, or similar can sometimes mean changing salary, status, and opportunity.

The desire of Canadian secretaries to have their title changed is understandable, but in some ways also unfortunate. It is understandable that they wish to be distinguished from the many office workers who mistakenly hold the title *secretary* and yet perform routine tasks. But, it is also unfortunate, because *secretary*, in its true meaning, is a title that designates a career to be very proud of.

To eliminate confusion, the term *administrative assistant* has been used throughout this text to designate all classifications of office professionals.

WHAT IS THE ROLE OF AN ADMINISTRATIVE ASSISTANT?

Today's office is a dynamic place to work. Electronic equipment has automated procedures at all levels of the office; the microcomputer and the Internet have forced dramatic changes in the office. Advanced information technology enables office professionals to perform their jobs better and faster than ever before. However, the computer is only a tool—one that helps make the administrative assistant more efficient. Having strong technical skills is not enough; without effective management and people skills, the administrative assistant will be unsuccessful.

Modern technology has led the way for the revolution known as the **Information Age**, in which there is an abundant and rapid flow of information available for decision making. The administrative assistant must provide the human element in the rapid and unceasing flow of information in today's business world. Clearly, communication is an important part of every administrative assistant's role.

The Information Age has made the administrative assistant's profession one that is exciting and challenging and that requires fine-tuned technical, administrative, and human relations skills. Administrative assistants are the lifeblood of an organization. They are information and people managers, and no company could be successful without them.

Dynamic Communications

The communications functions in an office demand that an administrative assistant have excellent technical as well as personal skills. Because there is a constant demand for information to flow faster, the administrative assistant must use high-tech skills and automated tools to be productive and efficient.

The following are examples of how administrative assistants use electronic tools to stay efficient.

1. Send and receive facsimiles.
2. Use an electronic calendar to select a date and time for a meeting.
3. Use a word processor to merge variable information, such as names and addresses, with a standard document that is being sent to all the clients or customers of a company.
4. Compose and send mail to electronic mailboxes.
5. Use an electronic database and the Internet to collect data for a monthly report.

PERSPECTIVES

Administration 2000

By Nancy Miller

Another look at the workplace of the future as we move closer to the new millennium.

In the future, office professionals will face continuous challenges—changing technology, new working relationships, and increased demands. As well, their jobs will expand through their employers who desperately need them but are not always enlightened enough to support them.

Human resource managers at large Fortune 100 companies most frequently ask the following questions about their administrative support staffers: What skills do office professionals need in the future? How do I motivate my current office professionals to learn new skills? How do I find the right employees for my changing needs? The answers to these questions offer insight into how you should plan your career as an office professional.

Let's look at skills first. Office professionals must continue to build skills in three competency areas.

- **Computer Literacy:** All employees of the 21st century organization will be heavy users of computers and networks. You must be more proficient in using emerging technologies than your bosses. They will look to you to help them. By the way, your ability to use the Internet as a research tool to help your management team is essential in the future office.
- **Soft Skills:** The office will require all office professionals to demonstrate professionalism in the midst of constant change—dealing with diverse issues, and solving unique problems. Hence one's flexibility and adapability will be key to survival in the future. Beyond this, many additional business skills are going to be prerequisites in the future workplace. These include customer service; written and oral presentation abilities; negotiation and conflict resolution; project management; procurement and contract management; interviewing, hiring and training; and financial management.
- **Company Specific Knowledge:** Office professionals should place a high priority on understanding the nature of their employer's business. Who are the customers? Suppliers? Competitors? What are your company's main products or services? How is the company organized and where are the different locations? What are the internal services the company offers that you can use to better support your management team? In other words, your internal stock value with your employer goes up by virtue of how much you know beyond your typical administrative duties. This also gives you a broader perspective of what other departments do. You could ultimately find your next career move within the company by your knowledge of other departments and functions.

Motivating you

Employers are increasingly challenged with how to motivate their employees to learn new things. Barriers to learning that employers often sense of their employees include no need to learn, no payoff, no fun, no urgency, no direction, no resources, no support, and no time. These could be valid. Or not? Many office professionals are willing and able to learn, but management does not always make learning a priority. The business deadlines of the day take precedence over continuous learning. This will always be the case. Therefore, you have to take charge of your own career development and continuous learning.

Of course, there are innovative employers out there who do value learning and continuous education. Companies like IBM, Hewlett-Packard, and Toyota are standouts with their commitment to enhancing the skills of the office professional. They offer traditional training, on-line training programs, and other opportunities for office professionals to further their skills development.

Office professionals' leading sources of job dissatisfaction are "lack of opportunity," "excess workload," and "(lack of) training/education," according to recent Norrell Corp. research of more than 3,000 office professionals. In the context of the future workplace, this means that many office professionals could reach the point of frustration and decide to leave their employer or even the profession. Employers must focus on their valuable resources: office professionals who are ready, willing, and able to move to the next millennium.

Ideal 21st century employees

The final question of employers is: "How do I find the right office professionals for my changing needs?" Management, and more specifically the entire corporation, must make a commitment to continuous learning for all employees. By doing this, office professionals will have the opportunity to learn with their employers' support. But whether or not the employer makes continuous learning a priority, you must be committed to it. This will ensure your long-term viability in the future workplace.

Another way management can find the right employees is to begin considering the office professional position as an entry-level job into the corporation. Employees would come into the organization and have a customized "career development plan" or "career path" that will provide for their moving into other roles and departments during their career. This would clearly "upscale" the perceived role of the office professional who has the interest or skills to pursue areas beyond his or her current assignment.

Office professionals and employers have to work more closely in the next century to ensure they create a satisfying and productive relationship. You must demonstrate personal leadership and perseverance to "upskill" yourself. Encourage your employer and your peers to engage in a dialogue about the future and how you can best contribute to it. This will go a long way towards demonstrating the value that you bring to your company.

Nancy Miller serves as director of Administration 2000 at Norrell Corporation, provider of staffing and out-sourcing services.

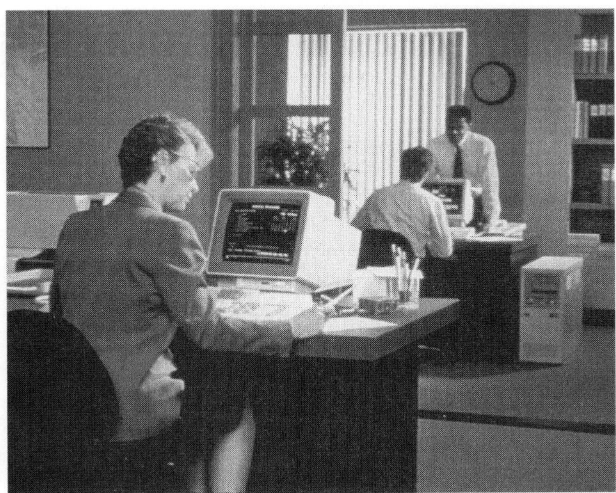

The administrative assistant provides the communication link between people and technology.
Courtesy of International Business Machines Corporation. Unauthorized use not permitted.

6. Use a copier to colour-copy, duplex (copy on both sides of the paper), collate, and staple documents.
7. Use a computer to locate an address in a records file.
8. Use "voice mail" to prevent telephone tag.
9. Query a computer index to locate a letter in a file, then make a copy and attach it to a letter in the incoming mail.
10. Revise a report using word processing software.
11. Search the company database for current facts to include in a speech.
12. Plan, design, and produce documents with desktop publishing software.
13. Prepare spreadsheets and graphs to be included in reports.
14. Investigate websites on the Internet.

Will There Be a Job for You?

There has always been employment for skilled office professionals. Today is no exception. The skills of an office professional are portable, flexible, transferable, and in demand.

Every office needs personnel who can handle computers, administration, and people. If you live in a community where employment is scarce, don't be discouraged. Remember that your skills are portable enough to keep you employed just about anywhere in the world. This gives you choices and opportunities. As well, professional office skills are required at every level in business and your skills are flexible and transferable enough to have you performing document processing in one job, selling office software in the next, training new office staff in another, or running your own business.

Statistics indicate that there may be less permanent jobs with benefits and retirement packages in your future. But on the other hand there will be more work assignments. This means that it will be necessary to keep your skills upgraded, be the best at your profession, and have an entrepreneurial spirit. This will be the winning formula for continuous employment.

AN OVERVIEW

Procedures for carrying out the varied responsibilities you will encounter in your office career are presented in this book. The subjects discussed and illustrated will enable you to learn the following:

1. How to be an efficient administrative assistant—organizing work, managing time, maintaining desirable attitudes, and setting priorities.
2. Electronic office concepts such as sending and receiving electronic mail; using the Internet, electronic calendar, voice mail, local area networks, on-line databases, computer-assisted retrieval, and desktop publishing; assisting with teleconferencing; managing records files with a computer; and caring for and storing magnetic media.

3. Procedures for preparing and processing written communications—transcribing, composing letters, processing incoming and outgoing mail, and preparing reports.
4. Procedures and guidelines for dealing with people—face to face in the office or in meetings, and over the telephone—and for making appointments and travel arrangements.
5. How to rely on modern office equipment—computers, copiers, facsimile machines, transcribing equipment—for effective job performance.
6. How to use published sources and databases for finding facts.
7. Information management—filing procedures, rules, systems, supplies, equipment, retention, storage, and retrieval.
8. Ways that banking services are related to office procedures.
9. The importance of a job campaign and ways to launch a successful one.
10. Suggestions for carrying out responsibilities as a supervisor.

Questions for Study and Review

1. Discuss four trends that are occurring in the office.
2. Why do many office workers wish to avoid the title of "secretary?"
3. How has the Information Age affected the role of the administrative assistant?
4. Suggest ten ways that an administrative assistant could use electronic equipment.
5. What steps can you take to ensure you will have continuous employment?

Spelling Reinforcement

abundant	confidant	facsimile	revolution
administrative	controlling	launch	routine
automated	distinguish	organization	sophisticated
classifications	entrepreneurial	processor	technology

On-the-Job Situations

1. The organization for which you work has invited a consultant to hold a seminar for administrative assistants on "The Dos and Don'ts of Electronic Messages." You had read the first announcement and had wished you could attend, but you did not apply because you had been on your job only one week. Today another announcement has been distributed, saying there is room for three more administrative assistants to attend. You have decided you are going to tell your manager you want to go to the seminar. Phrase the statements you will use when you make the request to your manager.
2. You work in a law office. More than 35 percent of the material you are asked to key is presented to you in longhand. You have severe difficulty reading the longhand of one word originator to whom you have been assigned. This word originator often sends you lengthy material. Because you have so much difficulty reading the word originator's longhand, your production is very slow. What should you do? What are some solutions to this problem?
3. You worked as an administrative assistant on your first job for four years before the organization merged with another organization. At that time, you were offered a job as a document specialist. You accepted it. You have been on this job one year and do not like it. On a daily basis, you spend between six and seven hours keyboarding; you are not getting experience performing a variety of office tasks. You have gone to personnel several times requesting a job similar to the one you had before the two organizations merged, but this type of position is not available. What are your alternatives?

Special Reports

1. Read and prepare a one-page summary of an article on office procedures and equipment in a current issue of *OfficePRO*.
2. Volunteer to be a class representative to visit a central office at your school. Find answers to questions such as these: How many administrative assistants work in the centre? What are the principal types of work performed by the centre? What equipment and software are used? What types of records are kept of the work performed? Report your findings to the class.

Production Challenges

In the production challenge(s) that end each chapter, imagine that you are an administrative assistant with

Millennium Appliances, Inc.
3431 Bloor Street
Toronto, ON M8X 1G4

You work for Mr. William Wilson, vice-president of marketing, and his four assistant vice-presidents:

Mr. J.R. Rush
Assistant Vice-President of Marketing
Eastern Region
Extension 534

Mrs. Linda Yee
Assistant Vice-President of Marketing
Midwestern Region
Extension 535

Mr. Sid Levine
Assistant Vice-President of Marketing
Northwestern Region
Extension 536

Ms. Charlene Azam
Assistant Vice-President of Marketing
Western Region
Extension 537

Most of your communications are with the following managers of the four regional sales offices and the two manufacturing plants:

Ms. Joanna Hansen
Manager, Sales Office
Eastern Region
197 Queen Street
Fredericton, NB E3B 1A6

Mr. John Reddin
Manager, Sales Office
Midwestern Region
3436 College Avenue
Regina, SK S4T 1W4

Mrs. Mary Karlovsky
Manager, Sales Office
Northwestern Region
9129 Jasper Avenue
Edmonton, AB T5H 3T2

Ms. Karuna Singe
Manager, Sales Office
Western Region
3152 45th Avenue W.
Vancouver, BC V6N 3M1

Mr. Raymond Jones
Plant Manager
Midwestern Manufacturing Plant
2202 Logan Avenue
Winnipeg, MB R2R 0J2

Mr. Eugene Liem
Plant Manager
Western Manufacturing Plant
836 Carnarvon Street
New Westminster, BC V3M 1G1

At your workstation you have a microcomputer. Your computer and those in the regional sales offices and manufacturing plants are connected to the Internet. This means that you can send (and receive) information instantaneously to (and from) these six locations.

Millenium Appliances, Inc., sells and manufactures its own line of innovative refrigerators, ovens, garbage compactors, freezers, dishwashers, microwave ovens, and clothing washers and dryers.

In-A Keyboarding Vacation Requests

Supplies needed:

- *Vacation Requests, Form In-A, page 377*
- *Plain paper*

You spent most of the first day on the job, Monday, May 12, in orientation sessions. Mr. Wilson introduced you to the employees in the Marketing Division, showed you the equipment available for you to use, and explained your duties. You also spent 30 minutes or more talking with each of the assistant vice-presidents of marketing, for whom you also work.

Mr. Wilson asked you to key the list of vacation requests in chronological order. He explained that he has not yet scheduled two weeks of his vacation and that he has a policy of not taking a vacation when any of the assistant vice-presidents of marketing are on vacation. He said a chronological list will quickly point out the weeks when he should be in the office.

You set up and key the vacation information on Form In-A. You place a hard copy on Mr. Wilson's desk or send it to him electronically.

In-B Requisitioning Supplies

Supplies needed:

- *Requisition for Supplies from Inventory, Forms In-B-1 and In-B-2, page 378*
- *Working Papers Disk, File In-B*

You had a note from Mr. Rush saying, "Please get me six ruled office pads, 21.5 cm x 28 cm, white."

You decided to check the supplies you had on hand and to requisition what you needed. The following supplies were low: ruled office pads, letterhead, self-stick notepads, index cards, and ballpoint pens.

All employees at Millennium Appliances, Inc., requisition office supplies from the Stationery and Supplies Department. Mr. Wilson had explained that you would sign your own requisitions for supplies. Your location is Office 216, Second Floor. The requisition number is 21.

Here is what you requested: six ruled office pads, 21.5 x 28 cm, white; one ream of letterhead; five packages of removable self-stick notepads, yellow, 76 x 127 mm; four packages of index cards, 7.5 x 12.5 cm, white; six ballpoint pens, black, fine point.

Keyboard the requisition.

In-C Correcting a Letter

Supplies needed:

- *Letter for Correction, Form In-C, page 379*

You were trying out your new software on your microcomputer, but you were not pleased with what you printed. The letter that you keyboarded is Form In-C. Mark the corrections needed on the lines provided.

World Wide Website

OfficePRO

http://www.iaap-hq.org/
This is the home page of the International Association of Administrative Professionals. It includes techniques, tips, and advice.

Human Relations

Outline

Learning Outcomes

At the completion of this chapter, the student will be able to:

1. Describe how setting goals and ground rules will promote effective teamwork.
2. Describe productive team behaviours and how to cope with nonproductive behaviours within a team.
3. Describe the desirable personality traits and attitudes of an effective administrative assistant.
4. Recognize behaviours associated with office politics.
5. Explain why change is inevitable in the office and how office professionals should cope with it.
6. State guidelines for dining etiquette during business luncheons.
7. Identify strategies for dealing with stress.
8. Recognize the appropriate types of humour to use in the office environment.
9. Prepare and summarize a time distribution chart.
10. Select the most appropriate common courtesies to use in a given situation.

GRADUATE PROFILE

Hilda J. Broomfield Letemplier
President

President, Pressure Pipe Steel Fabrication Ltd., *and* Vice-President of Finance *and* Administration Labrador Industrial Supplies Ltd., *and* Vice President, Northern Oxygen Ltd.

College Graduation:
Secretarial Science Program
Labrador Community College
Happy Valley—Goose Bay, Labrador
1992

Having earned a black belt in karate, Hilda Letemplier, an Inuit woman, knows the discipline required to be successful.

After graduating from the Secretarial Science program, she began working as an administrative assistant for Labrador College. She soon became president of Pressure Pipe Steel Fabrication Ltd. and four years later, co-owner and vice-president of finance and administration for Labrador Industrial Supplies Ltd. In addition, she presides as vice-president and co-owner of Northern Oxygen Ltd. Future business plans for all her companies include diversification and restructuring. Hilda reports that the potential for business growth in these three companies is unlimited. Besides running her own company, Hilda represents the Central Labrador Economic Development Board on the Institute for Environmental Monitoring and Recording and is a member of the Labrador North Chamber of Commerce. Her academic pursuits include a commitment to keep abreast of ever-changing computer and software technology. Despite her busy professional schedule, she also finds time to be an assistant karate instructor.

For her contribution to industry, Hilda was recently recognized in *Who's Who Among Top Executives*, published by Kaleo Publications. Hilda was a regional finalist for the Canadian Woman Entrepreneur of the Year Awards for 1997 in the category of Impact on the Local Economy.

"Whatever you do, give it 100 percent."

Her philosophy for success is to put 100 percent effort into everything she does. Hilda says that although in the early stages of your career, you may not believe that what you are doing is important, your efforts are appreciated, and in the long term you will reap the rewards.

Business offices are connected to virtually the entire world by the telephone, written communications, and telecommunication systems. Administrative assistants do not know what situations they will encounter until they answer the telephone, open the postal mail, access their electronic mail, listen to their voice mail, or greet callers at their desks. Even so, they are expected to respond in a manner that will keep, or make, friends for their organization.

Administrative assistants spend most of their time either directly in contact with people or producing and channelling information that will affect people. They assist their managers in collecting, analyzing, transmitting, and storing information. Much of this information will be transmitted and stored electronically, by computer. In addition, they use computers to communicate with others in the same building and nationwide, mostly within their own organizations.

To be an effective office professional your goal should be to leave a positive impression with every person you communicate with. In your professional activities, you will need to communicate effectively with colleagues, management, customers, potential customers, and friends of the organization.

You cannot depend on knowledge and skills alone for success on your job. Your performance as an excellent office professional is largely dependent on your effective communication skills and your ability to work cooperatively with others.

If you think in terms of what you can contribute rather than of what you can get, you will earn greater acceptance on the office team. As an administrative assistant, you will perform a lot of detailed work. Remember that this work is essential to the quality of the overall team project; in that sense, the role of the administrative assistant is a central one on the office team.

BE A TEAM PLAYER

Teamwork is replacing individual work as the basic building block of organizations. Teamwork is viewed as an effective and efficient way to accomplish work, to build harmony in the office, to increase individual and group knowledge, and to strengthen the organization. In fact, employers value team skills so highly that they search for new employees who can contribute to the corporate team just as much as those who can contribute independently.

As an office professional, grasp every opportunity to work in a team. This will increase your knowledge, job satisfaction, and your value to the company. Take full responsibility for your part of the workload and for any problems that arise within the team. Strive for excellence and be enthusiastic about your team responsibilities. When the team is successful, every individual will be successful.

> *"To have a successful office team, you must respect co-workers' opinions."*
>
> Jennifer Hazelton, Graduate
> Nova Scotia Community College
> Burridge Campus

Many employees are forced to belong to teams as a condition of their employment. However, the best teams are comprised of people who have volunteered because they see the work to be achieved as important. The benefits to teamwork are numerous:

- An effective group can accomplish more work than an effective individual.
- Teams provide social interaction.
- During stressful periods of work, the team will provide emotional support for its members.
- As team members share information, the knowledge and experience of the team members grows.
- The company values employees who contribute to the organization's goals and decision making through teamwork.

Good teamwork consists of clear and full communication as well as trust. A successful team will be one that keeps all its members as well as management informed. A high level of disclosure leads to trust between team members and between management and the team. Trust is essential if the team members and the team as a whole are to be **empowered**.

One of your responsibilities on the team is to help all other team members feel that their contributions to the team are equally valuable. Offering courtesy and respect to all other team members will ensure this.

You should deal with your team members in the same way you deal with your customers. In fact, your fellow team members are your internal customers, in the sense that they are the receivers of your work and your team contributions.

As you contribute effectively to the team effort, your membership on other teams will become a desirable commodity. By contributing on more teams, your knowledge, responsibility, and career will expand.

Ground Rules

It is imperative to establish what will and will not be considered acceptable practice and behaviour within the team. Therefore, one of the formative tasks a team faces is the setting of ground rules. All team members must participate in this. The rules are not set until **consensus** is reached within the team. Agreeing on ground rules is not always a quick and easy task; often, one or two team members will disagree with what makes perfect sense to other team members. However, each team member has equal status and reaching a consensus on the rules will result in a cooperative effort for the team's project. Although reaching a consensus may be very time-consuming, the long-term results are worth it.

Refer to the section "Team Meetings" in Chapter 11 for examples of ground rules.

Setting Team Goals

Often a team is brought together without clearly understanding why. One of the best ways to begin a team's first meeting is by taking an informal survey regarding why everyone is a team member. Each individual member should state what he or she believes the purpose and expected outcome of the project is. Most often, there will be considerable diversity in the responses. Therefore, the team leader should make it very clear what the goals and expected outcomes of the team will be. How the team members will reach those goals and expected outcomes should be a team decision.

Once established, these goals should be formalized in a document and each team member should be given a copy of that document.

Productive Team Behaviours

Some of the many team behaviours that lead to productivity are:

- treating every member with the greatest respect
- basing decisions on fact rather than opinion
- communicating in a clear and honest style
- balancing participation between all team members at meetings
- staying on topic and not allowing digressions during meetings
- seeking creative ways to solve problems through brainstorming

- summarizing decisions at the end of team meetings
- committing to do equal work
- believing that every member has talents that will contribute to the team's work
- not personalizing criticism of the project; remember, it's a team effort.

Become a role model by displaying these positive team behaviours. In return, you will earn the respect of your team members.

Avoiding Nonproductive Behaviours

No matter how well intended your team is, unproductive behaviours may still exist. The following are descriptions of some of the nonproductive behaviours encountered in many teams. Also provided are some suggested remedies.

1. **Dominating or Reluctant Team Members.** When one or more members of a team monopolize discussions, or when you have a member who is reluctant to discuss the team's issues for whatever reason, you need to work at balancing the participation. While treating all members with courtesy and respect, you should point out the ground rule whereby you agreed to balance and share the team discussions. As well, you could encourage a balanced discussion by interjecting with comments such as "Carole, thanks for sharing that information. Rima, we haven't heard from you. What are your feelings on the ...?"
2. **Lacking Direction.** When team members lack direction, the team flounders: members do not know how to get started or what the next step should be. If the team establishes an action plan in the early stages of the process, the members will find it easier to stay on track. As well, a method of project planning such as a Gantt chart will help team members stay focused and ensure that they complete tasks on time. Refer to the section "Complete a Task" in Chapter 2 for further information on developing a Gantt chart.
3. **Digressing.** Not staying on topic is a common team problem. When the topic starts to drift, tactfully make the team aware of it, and ask the members to focus on the topic at hand.
4. **Quarrelling.** When two or more team members begin to argue, the other team members are left feeling uncomfortable, and frustrated by the team's lack of productivity. If this should occur during your team work, act as the mediator. Mediation may take the form of speaking privately to the members involved; however, if you have already established ground rules, you might simply compare their behaviour to the ground rule discouraging that behaviour and remind them that their actions are unproductive. Remember, however, that the disagreement may be deeper than it seems at first glance. Have these members had difficulty working together before?
5. **Discounting.** People sometimes discount the work and opinions of others through their unkind criticism, lack of attention, poor body language, and so on. However, every person deserves respect and attention. If you sense that some of your team members are being discounted, go to their support. Comments that show consideration and attention are not difficult to give. These are the same gestures you would appreciate from others. In the hustle and pressure of trying to meet deadlines and quality expectations, it is sometimes easy to slip into this unproductive behaviour yourself, without even realizing you are offending others. Be aware of this possibility and continue to apply diplomacy in all scenarios.

> ***pro-Link***
>
> Like any relationship, the manager/assistant relationship will have its ups and downs. Here are some positive points to help you deal with a manager who shouts and uses profanities.
>
> - This is unacceptable behaviour but the yelling may have nothing to do with your performance. Most people shout to vent built-up frustration from a variety of sources.
> - Keep calm and use a warm tone in your voice.
> - Think of a parent–child relationship and, without being condescending, deal with the situation like a clever parent.
> - Don't get engaged in the shouting or the expletives.
> - Let the manager know this behaviour is not appreciated, but don't show that you are rattled or distressed. Stay on top!

WHAT ABOUT OFFICE POLITICS?

Office politics can be defined simply as actions taken by office employees to influence others for personal objectives. Depending on how you react to office politics, they can either work to your advantage or your disadvantage.

These attempts to influence others are often exhibited in some of the following ways:

- **Withholding or Selectively Sharing Information.** If an employee chooses to pass along damaging information, it can seriously affect the careers of other employees. Or if accurate information is withheld from an employee, that person may perform poorly on the job.
- **Creating Political Networks.** When a person cultivates a relationship with someone for the purpose of getting advancement in the office, gaining information, getting approval on a project, or many other personal objectives, this is referred to as political networking. If you are excluded from the office social network, you may become quite powerless.
- **Accusing Other People.** Sometimes one employee will repeatedly place blame on a particular employee. This action might be to target the person in a position that is wanted by another employee. Eventually management may be convinced that this employee being blamed is detrimental to the staff. In this case, the accused person may lose his/her job leaving the job open for the accuser.
- **Forming Groups.** How often have we heard the expression "power in numbers"? When two or more people with a common purpose join together to force a change in the office, they are acting politically. This group may attempt to change office procedures or even to change management decisions.

Being able to recognize office politics is important. But for many people, this skill is acquired only with some first-hand experience. If you become politically involved in your company for the good of others, especially your co-workers or subordinates, you will be favourably recognized. An example would be creating a political network that allows you to become close with management personnel. Your association with management may get your department an increase in budget.

"I have learned to steer clear of office politics. When I am at work, I focus on the work and let everyone else deal with the politics."

Tammy Fredericksen, Graduate
Nova Scotia Community College
Akerley Campus

Subsequently, that budget increase might create some new work in your department allowing your co-workers to keep their employment. On the other hand, the people who lose at the game of office politics or are the victim of another person's political gain will view office politics as unfavourable.

Whether you approve of office politics or not, they do exist. The best policy is to stay away from politics that will adversely affect others. However, some healthy political maneuvers that bring success to your team and are not at the expense of others are characteristic of good leadership.

ATTITUDE IS EVERYTHING

Projecting a pleasant personality is easy when things are going right. But to be successful in business, you must be able to maintain your composure when things are going wrong: to say "no" tactfully, to soothe the feelings of an irate customer, to be considerate and tolerant of someone who is inconsiderate of you, and to exhibit poise under extreme pressure.

People who are successful in business cultivate attitudes and traits that contribute to their success. Having succeeded in coping with one difficult situation, you will be able to apply that experience in coping with the next difficult situation.

Show Your Human Side

A cheerful "Good morning" is viewed by many as mere ceremony, but such ceremony is highly desirable when coupled with sincerity and an optimistic approach to life. Take the initiative to speak first; call others by name. Make an effort to get acquainted with as many co-workers as possible.

To be an approachable person, you should be pleasant, courteous, responsive, and understanding. Listen attentively when someone is talking with you. Be responsive to what is going on around you. Treat others as you wish to be treated. Avoid being condescending when giving instructions. *Suggest rather than command. Request rather than demand.*

Be considerate of others in all the things you do, both large and small. Show your thoughtfulness by doing the following:

1. Stop at another administrative assistant's desk when you must go in to see his or her manager.
2. Wait your turn to use the office copier.
3. When you must interrupt someone, time the interruption so that the person is at a stopping point when you bid for attention.
4. Remember that everyone has personal interests and pursuits. These might include an interest in family, continuing education, leisure activities, and so on. Remembering to inquire about these nonbusiness topics shows a sense of maturity as well as diplomacy.

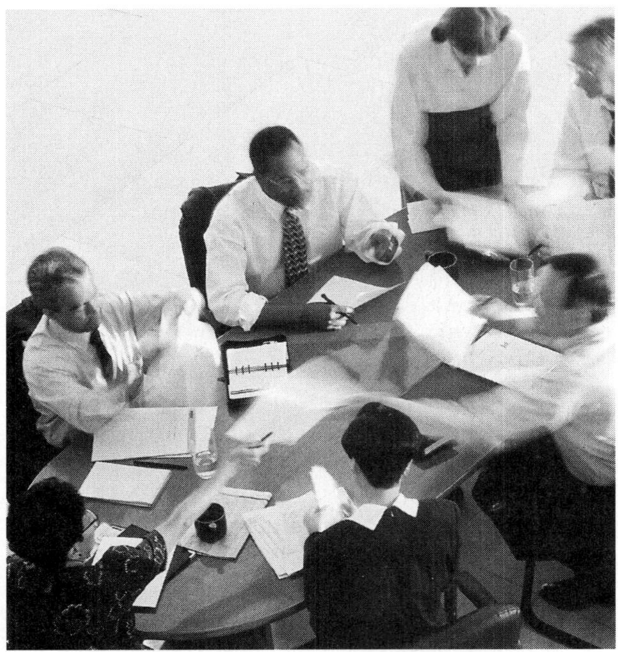

Figure 1-1 Good teamwork consists of clear and full communications.
Courtesy of International Business Machines Corporation. Unauthorized use not permitted.

Respect the rights of others. Knowing what *not* to say is as important as knowing what to say. Be very careful when discussing sensitive subjects such as religion, money, morals, or politics; you don't want to risk offending a co-worker. You can gain the trust of others by never talking about anyone. Be especially careful not to make remarks about co-workers and polite enough not to pry into personal affairs.

Remember that the little things do count. You can create a pleasant, businesslike atmosphere by your rapport with employees at all levels and with outsiders who come to your office or call on the telephone. Be consistent as you show your human side. Besides creating a pleasant atmosphere, your thoughtfulness will help you enjoy your relationships with others.

Adapt to New Management

You should anticipate being administrative assistant to several individuals during your career. Under the traditional arrangement of one administrative assistant for each manager, the administrative assistant often was promoted with the manager. Today this rarely happens.

Your challenge is to prove yourself in a variety of situations. Do not expect your second manager to be like the first one—no two managers are exactly alike.

The qualities that successful managers possess are difficult to define. True, many possess similar qualities, but each manager moves through the levels of management in her or his own fashion. Good managers have a capacity for hard work and dedication to the job. They never seem satisfied with the status quo; in fact, they cannot afford to be.

You should learn the priorities, preferences, and work habits of each new employer and adjust your schedule accordingly. After you are well acquainted with your employer, you can make helpful recommendations.

Respect your manager. Managerial jobs encompass continual dealing with problems that are not easy to solve. This situation carries with it some degree of emotional stress. You can help by listening, offering solutions, and keeping the content of these conversations confidential.

Refrain from expressing your manager's opinions. In fact, *everything* that goes on in your office should be kept confidential. To gain the trust of your organization, your manager, and your co-workers, do not discuss, mention, or refer to office business. Obviously, when there is an announcement, your manager is the one to make it. Refrain from giving your personal interpretation of a policy.

Be careful not to give away confidential information inadvertently to your friends and colleagues or to your company's competitors. Sometimes just one isolated fact obtained from you or one of your associates is all the additional information that a competitor is looking for.

You should be dependable and accountable for your work. However, at all levels of management, loyalty is rated as one of the most desirable traits an employee can possess. Being loyal means supporting the organization's policies and actions. Be careful not to criticize your company or its employees.

Being loyal to the organization's management can be difficult when you believe management is not working in the best interests of the organization. If you find yourself in this situation, be patient. Don't jump to conclusions! Make it a habit to never denounce anyone on your staff, including the management. Not all managers are good managers, and some do lose their jobs. Working for a manager who does not perform the job well will be difficult; however, by being tactful and tolerant you should be able to preserve your own job.

A promotion for you may mean moving to a new situation and working for new management. Be flexible. Be willing to accept change and to adjust to new situations. The more you demonstrate your ability to accept the challenges of your assignments, the more opportunities will come your way.

Establish Efficient Work Habits

You can boost your own morale by increasing your organizational skills and by managing your time and working efficiently. Follow the suggestions given in Chapter 2 for establishing efficient work habits.

Be a self-starter; that is, take the initiative to begin a task for which you are responsible. Do not wait for your manager to prompt you. You also need to be a finisher. If you have many tasks started and none finished, your workload will seem heavier than it actually is. As you face an accumulation of unfinished tasks, you may become less efficient. If you fall so far behind in your work that you cannot catch up during regular hours, work overtime. As you lighten your load by moving the finished tasks forward, you will feel more relaxed and find it easier to cope and be effective.

The administrative assistant often sets an example for other workers in the office. You can help create a desirable atmosphere by having a perfect attendance record and by being prompt in arriving at work each morning and in returning on time to your workstation after breaks.

An administrative assistant has to learn how to work under pressure. One of the most difficult parts of your job will be learning to judge priorities. You will have to learn what degree of importance to place on each task and when to shift quickly to another task and apply the extra effort.

Timing is an important factor in success; a job must be performed not only well but also at the right time. To make time for rush work, and to feel that you are in control of your job, you should work willingly, consistently, and with enthusiasm.

Develop Self-Confidence and Composure

An administrative assistant who is self-confident relies on the strength of his or her own judgment and competence with very little aid from others. Be aware that **self-confidence** can be developed: as you perform a task or handle a situation well, you gain confidence that you can do so again.

A confident person maintains **composure**, which is a sense of calmness or tranquillity. He or she exhibits **poise**, which denotes ease and dignity of manner.

Believe in your abilities and remain in control of your reactions. Be consistent in maintaining your composure. There is no place in the professional world for a temperamental person. If your colleagues cannot rely on you to be cooperative and pleasant, they will avoid working with you. Your temperamental attitude will provide a serious barrier to effectiveness and cooperation in the office.

You cannot control all the circumstances that surround your work. Most of the daily happenings in the office—new problems, minor changes, major changes,

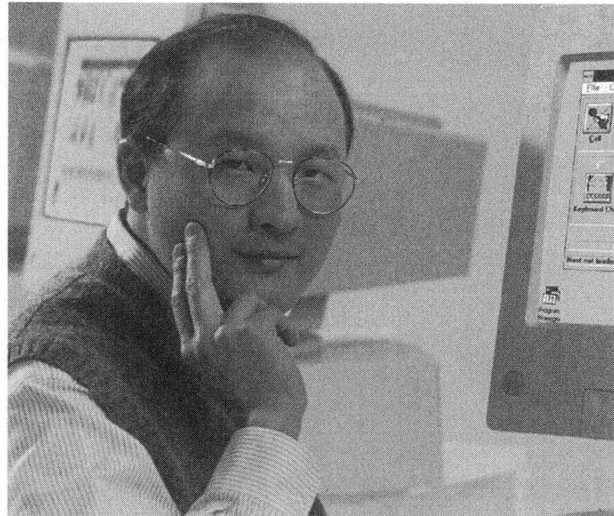

Figure 1-2 A confident person maintains composure even under pressure.

Courtesy of International Business Machines Corporation. Unauthorized use not permitted.

new situations, emergencies—are beyond your control. Even so, how you react to them *is* within your control. Be sure not to overreact turning challenges into problems.

The business world is demanding and fast-paced. To cope with it, proceed with assurance and keep cool. Learn to expect the unexpected. You must be able to produce accurate work under the greatest pressure. If you do not, you may find yourself moving in a frantic circle, which certainly will be an unproductive one.

At times you will get impatient. Don't show it! Sharpen your sensitivity to the needs of others. Exhibit your best manners. Be deliberate—avoid hasty comments or quick dismissals of suggestions. Distinguish between fact and fiction. Withhold judgment until you obtain all the facts.

Accept constructive criticism; in fact, welcome it. Have the courage to keep improving and to discuss problems that should be discussed. Good managers will offer constructive criticism because they want you to succeed. Follow through on these suggestions.

Develop a sense of humour and use it at the right time. Laugh at yourself, but laugh with others. Do not take yourself or your problems too seriously. Suggestions for practising humour in the workplace are discussed later in this chapter in the section "Handle Stress."

Rely on Your Strength of Character

Character denotes a pattern of behaviour. Strength of character is built upon the basic values of life.

A person who has strength of character has **integrity**, which is one of the most—if not *the* most—important traits a person can possess. Integrity encompasses sound moral principles, fairness, honesty, sincerity, and the courage to stand up for these moral precepts. A person who has integrity is truthful and refrains from twisting or withholding facts.

You will be respected if your dealings with others are fair, honest, and sincere. Not all aspects of business are as ethical as they should be. When you face a serious ethical situation, rely on your strength of character to make your own decision. Your only alternative may be to change employment. Whatever your decision, never cover for another person's transgression. You must be accountable for your actions.

Maintain an Optimistic Attitude

Consider your first full-time office employment as the beginning of your professional career. Learn and perform your first assignment to the best of your ability and never lose sight of the fact that you are on the path to professionalism.

Approach life and your job with a positive attitude, for attitude is a major determinant of behaviour. Count your accomplishments and your successes, not your defeats. Substitute determination for fear. Demonstrate a willingness to work and to perform new tasks. Strive to improve your job performance. Realize that the less supervision you need, the more responsibility you will get.

Motivation is related to your inner drives and no one else can really motivate you. You must choose to be motivated. Once you start to accomplish assignments in the office you will begin to feel dynamic, enthusiastic, and self-motivated. Be an enthusiastic participant and a morale builder. If you feel you are not being rewarded for your efforts, be patient. Promotions are earned long before they are awarded.

Set goals for yourself that will enable you to grow in knowledge, in your own abilities, and in your appreciation for life. To become a "pro," you must do more than work hard—you must work at the *right things*.

From time to time, take inventory of your needs and accomplishments. Set new goals and keep striving. Reaching your goals, no matter how small, will help you to maintain an optimistic attitude toward life.

DEAL WITH CHANGE

Change has become the expectation in the office. Change, both organizational and technological, is an important part of doing business. Why is change continuous, and how should you respond to this force?

Why Is Change Constant?

You cannot avoid change in the workplace. Changes come about rapidly because of the relentless updating of office technology, competition between companies, and the restructuring of organizations to become more efficient.

The rapid development of computers and software has enabled workers to produce more with greater speed and ease than in the past. Organizations keep replacing old equipment with state-of-the-art equipment. So accept the fact that the equipment and software you learn to operate today may be replaced by new technology tomorrow.

The pressure of competition has increased because of international trade. Telecommunications and the **Information Highway** have made competing in the **global marketplace** common practice.

Another major change has been the restructuring of organizations. Companies are constantly striving to outdo their competition, a process that involves combining or eliminating functions, and buying equipment that will improve their operations. All of this results in changes in procedures.

As well, company **mergers** and **buyouts** occur, resulting in a duplication of jobs and positions that must be addressed. In a merger, the two companies agree on the restructuring. In a buyout, one company buys out the other and there may be less agreement on restructuring.

How Should You React to Change?

Regardless of where you work, changes are inevitable. Anticipate them, and realize that change is the way of the future. Expect yourself to suddenly be using new equipment and new software, to be assigned an entirely new job within your organization, or to be looking for employment with another organization. Instead of wasting energy over changes you cannot avoid, direct your energy toward getting in step with the new arrangements. If an opportunity to use new equipment or software presents itself, or a chance to participate in further training or new responsibilities arises, grasp the opportunity. You should always welcome new possibilities for growth, since professional development prepares you for steady employment and improves your prospects for career advancement.

SOCIAL SKILLS

For the office professional, it's not enough to be just technically competent, an excellent office administrator, and a tactful communicator in the office. The

PERSPECTIVES

When Cupid Knocks

By Dennis M. Powers

Today's arduous work commitment doesn't leave much time to find romance—whether you're single, separated, or divorced.

Romance at the office is thriving. Despite personal career goals, sexual harassment fears, individual business climates, legal warnings, and opposing feminist philosophies, Cupid has won out for very simple reasons. Today's arduous work commitment doesn't leave much time to find romance—whether you're single, separated, or divorced. You're able to be with people of similar backgrounds and expectations, work closely with them, naturally find out about their likes and dislikes, do all this in a safe environment, and be paid for it.

As one who dated several men at her company says, "The easiest way to meet men is through your work. They can have similar interests and life goals. It beats fending off drunks at a sleazy bar or sifting through a dating service's videos. There's no question that work provides the dating service for the '90s.

Is it worth it?

If you're going to pursue an office romance, you need a good feeling at the very first that it has real possibilities, especially given the potential pitfalls. For example, Debbie, a 26-year-old assistant, was attracted to Pete who was higher up the pecking order. Her coworkers felt she was trying to move up the ladder by this route and didn't support her. "They actually undermined my work efforts once I started to date Pete," she explains. "I eventually gave up and both of us are now involved with others outside our work."

Another recalls: "I really liked Tim at first, but his mannerisms sometimes left me feeling uneasy. I decided that if this relationship didn't work out, that being in different buildings would be a definite plus. It was." If there is a breakup, it's obvious that seeing your ex every day could become a real bummer. Factor this in. Here are some other tips.

- **Don't date because you're afraid to say no.** And don't trade sex for power or any other perceived advantage—that isn't romance either. The great majority of romances aren't for power, because the individuals involved have more common sense. The problems happen when people get involved for the wrong reasons.

  Being together for the same romantic reasons is an important factor. If someone asks you out because they like you, that's one thing. However, if it's job related and the relationship ends badly, then that's another. It's when a relationship ends on a sour note with an impure or work-related motive that the real problems begin on either side. One person may be thinking "fling" while the other's thinking "honeymoon."

- **Check out the climate.** Find out how to work your relationship within the company's organizational climate and the specific paths to take. Remember that the firm's view can depend not only on its official and unofficial policies, but also on the approach taken by different managers. You need to understand the game there, as well as where both of you want to go in life. You must be honest with each other and share a strong commitment.

- **Assess the career pros and cons.** If you're in a lower-entry position, then there may be fewer career considerations. As your position moves higher up the chart, you may have more career factors to weigh. However, this can depend on where you work, so think ahead.

  For example, two employees began to work for a bank in different departments. They started dating, kept it to themselves, then made plans to marry. Just before announcing the date (and they could keep their present positions), both received promotions and were supposed to report to the same boss (now prohibited by their relationship). They rethought their strategy and the husband-to-be arranged a lateral transfer to another department. They announced their wedding after receiving the blessings of both bosses.

  Relationships today are jointly managed, which is a good habit to get into. "You need to decide on the rules before you become too involved," says someone who's been there. "For example, whose career is to be protected, and does it make any difference? Who transfers and stays? When should you tell the boss what's going on? How much work will be done at home? Dealing with these issues makes you a long-term item."

  In addition to the job considerations, any work brought home must be limited.

  Partnering also includes deciding on the exit routes if things don't work out. As one whose romance fizzled out says, "After two months, I knew that he and I weren't a good match. He didn't like my decision to end matters, but we had discussed what we'd do in that eventuality. We'd stick to work at the office, as best we could. It was tense at first and took time, but now he's with another person and all of this is behind us."

- **Keep your romance to yourself, even if the corporate climate is warm and receptive.** A recent *HR*

Management study concluded that two thirds of those in office romances did their darndest to keep it a secret. "It's safer to keep it to yourself. No one can get upset, no matter what happens later," says one now-married employee. "There can be no accusations of favoritism. And it is your own business."

As part of this, don't kiss by the fax machine. Forget the cute nicknames, neck massages in the elevator, or making out behind closed doors. Work is just that, so keep your work at work and your play at home.

Excerpted and adapted from The Office Romance: Playing with Fire without Getting Burned © *1999 by Dennis M. Powers. Reprinted by permission of AMACOM.*

responsibilities of many business professionals extend outside the walls of the office. Many administrative assistants find themselves entertaining customers of the company and most administrative assistants socialize with company personnel or customers outside the office. These social situations may require a new set of skills since it may be more difficult in some social situations to retain your professionalism. And in some circumstances you may even face ethical dilemmas. One of the more common dilemmas is office romance. The Perspectives article "When Cupid Knocks" provides an interesting view on how to handle intimate office relationships.

Knowing how to care for a guest, and displaying good manners at a business luncheon are desirable skills for any office professional. Management may expect you to take new employees or customers for lunch, or you might attend a business lunch for an association you belong to, or you may be attending a luncheon at a conference or business meeting. Whatever the occasion, you will want to make the right impression on your colleagues or guests.

Doing the Business Lunch

Entire books have been devoted to the subject of using proper manners. This short section in not meant to be a detailed guide; rather, the intent here is to help you avoid making mistakes in one of those areas where the greatest mistakes are often made—namely, the business lunch. The following are some simple but important guidelines for business dining.

1. When escorted by the restaurant host/ess to a table, your guest should walk ahead of you and behind the host/ess.
2. If you take a guest to a restaurant that has open seating, lead the way to an appropriate table.
3. Unless you intend to negotiate with your guest during lunch, offer your guest the best seat at the table; remember, your objective is to make your guest feel comfortable. Often the best seat is the one facing the main eating area. Never seat a guest so that he or she is facing the exit doors, or the kitchen or washroom doors.
4. Place your napkin on your lap only *after* everyone has arrived and is seated; once the meal begins, the napkin should not be placed on the table until the meal is finished.
5. Guests will get an idea of acceptable price range from the meal you suggest or order. Having your guest order first is a courteous gesture; however, unless your guest knows what you plan to eat, you may be placing your guest in an uncomfortable position.
6. When the server takes your order, refer to the other party as your guest ("I will let my guest order first," or "My guest would like to order ..." or similar). This is a clue to the server that you would like the bill brought to you.
7. Let hot food cool naturally; do not blow on your food, stir soup or coffee that is too hot, or fan your food. These activities are distracting and considered rude and unbusinesslike behaviour.
8. Begin eating only after everyone has been served. Often meals will arrive at the table a few minutes apart. It is considered rude to begin eating while someone is left sitting without a meal.
9. If you must reach for, say, a condiment or bread basket, offer the item to your guest before you serve yourself.
10. Table settings are often confusing, and leave a person wondering which glass or fork to use. The general rule for utensils is *outside in*. If there is a series of forks or spoons, simply begin by using the one on the outer edge of your table setting and work inward toward your plate. Your glass will be at the top of your knife on the right side of your plate; your bread and butter plate will be to your left.
11. Never chew with your mouth open or talk with food in your mouth. It's wise to take only small bites so that you can carry on a conversation.
12. If the need arises to remove something undesirable from your mouth (such as a seed, bone, or pit, or partially chewed food), you should use a

utensil rather than your fingers to catch the food. Lift your napkin to your mouth at the same time to curtain an undesirable scene at the table.

13. The proper way to eat any form of bread is to break it off as needed, into bite-sized pieces.
14. When you are finished eating, never remove or stack dishes for the server. You want to maintain a professional business image.
15. No primping at the table. If you wish to apply cosmetics, comb your hair, straighten your clothing or—worst of all—blow your nose, do so in the washroom.

Following these general guidelines will increase your confidence and pleasure at any business lunch.

HANDLE STRESS

Jobs in contemporary offices can be very stressful. But some people seem to thrive on **stress** while others crumble under it. The difference is that those who cope well with stress have control over their jobs. This control enables them to meet their own deadlines, as well as deadlines set for them by others. Having a positive attitude toward work helps people to deal with stress.

What Causes Stress in the Office?

What makes office work stressful? This question is difficult to answer since what causes stress for one person is quite stimulating to the next worker. However, the following is a list of reported sources of stress for some office workers.

- A number of office workers are hired to complete temporary assignments. In these cases, there is very little long-term employment security.
- Computer software and hardware change rapidly requiring constant retraining.
- Management styles and organizational structures are changing. Many companies have flattened their management and downsized their staff. In these cases, employees work under the constant threat of losing their employment.
- The responsibilities of office professionals have broadened and intensified.
- In order to keep up with the workload, many office professionals work through the day without taking a break for lunch.

Learn to Cope with Stress

People who have a lot of responsibility outside their employment may suffer from stress because they are trying to do too much—accepting responsibility for family and home, volunteering for community work, going to school, and so on.

Figure 1-3 Recognize when your co-workers are under stress.
Courtesy of Benjamin Ross Kilgour

To cope with stress, analyze what is happening to you. Often it is not the situation that causes stress but how you react to it and what you do about it. The duration of the problem can also produce stress.

A certain amount of stress helps us to stay alert, efficient, and creative. Here are some suggestions for coping with stress that becomes *too* great:

1. Recognize what your body is telling you, and recognize that anger and frustration are energy wasters. Keep notes on what is happening and the cause.
2. Organize your work and your time for the entire day. Assign priorities to your duties. Don't plan more than is possible to do in a day.
3. When faced with an overload of work, analyze it and discuss it with your supervisor. Offer solutions. By facing a situation, you will relieve stress and ensure that you don't become overwhelmed.
4. Don't be overly critical of your work and yourself; do *not* expect too much of others. Strive for excellence, but at times be pleased with an acceptable performance.
5. Slow down! You will accomplish more and also eliminate much stress by working at a comfortable pace—one that enables you to keep mistakes to a minimum, to relate well with others, and to avoid backtracking and revising.

6. Avoid taking on too much. Learn to say "no," but to say it tactfully. Don't hesitate to refuse outside organizations that ask you to do volunteer work. If necessary, hire help for home and family responsibilities.
7. Talk out your stressful problems. Find someone in whom you can confide—someone away from the job, someone who is a good listener. Simply talking out your problem can be helpful.
8. Eat nourishing food regularly and in moderate amounts.
9. Program relaxation into your schedule. Use lunch and coffee breaks to relax. Don't use these breaks to rush around on personal errands. During your breaks, be quiet, and practise relaxation techniques until you feel yourself relaxing. Use waiting time to relax. Allow yourself a quiet hour at home. Schedule some time for a hobby.
10. Get regular exercise. Exercise is one of the best ways to relax.
11. Escape to a movie, to your favourite TV program, to spend time with others, to do something for someone in need.

Practise Humour as Prevention

Work should be fun. If you dislike getting ready for work and going to your office each morning, it's time to take action. You can either terminate your employment or enhance your employment. When there is a healthy dose of humour in the office, productivity and enthusiasm increase. Humour need not detract from a professional atmosphere. In the correct proportion, humour can actually strengthen the professional environment.

Laughter promotes teamwork and reduces stress. Research indicates that laughter is healthy not only mentally, but also physiologically; laughter massages our internal organs. However, knowing when to refrain from using humour is paramount. Use your common sense to judge when and where humour is appropriate. Good timing and good taste are essential.

Assess your office and consider how to make the environment more enjoyable without losing the professional climate.

Here are some ideas to consider.

1. Purchase a joke book; occasionally select a joke. Key it up and send it to your manager and co-workers through **e-mail**.
2. Hold contests—for example, "The Month's Most Embarrassing Situation."
3. Hold an annual kick-off meeting where humourous awards are given to all staff members for any activities they participated in.
4. When a staff member has a birthday, prepare a cake with a humourous message. Invite the staff to share cake and coffee together for a few minutes.
5. At the annual Christmas party, exchange inexpensive but humourous gifts.
6. Once a year, select a good sport in your office and hold an annual roast. The staff will enjoy participating.
7. Watch for humourous articles in magazines and circulate them around the staff.
8. Share anything humourous that you have acquired. Humourous cards, books, and audio cassettes work well on a circulation list.

Questions for Study and Review

1. Describe the administrative assistant's role in forming the image of the organization.
2. Suggest three ground rules that may help make a team more effective.
3. What is the meaning of the term "consensus"? Why is consensus important to productive team activity?
4. Why should each team member receive a copy of the team's goals?
5. State five behaviours that would contribute to making an effective team.
6. State five nonproductive team behaviours and explain how you, as a team member, might influence a positive change in each of these behaviours.
7. Describe what creating political networks means.
8. Describe two reasons why a person might withhold or selectively share information in an office.
9. State three ways an office professional can show respect for co-workers.
10. State three ways an office professional can show respect for her/his manager or organization.
11. What attitude should you adopt when your management changes?
12. What office information should you consider as confidential outside the office?
13. What is meant by "taking initiative"?

14. What is meant by "maintaining composure"?
15. If an office professional has integrity, what traits might s/he display?
16. Why is change constant in the office?
17. As an office professional, how should you react to change?
18. Suggest ten guidelines you might follow when taking a guest for a business lunch.
19. State reasons why the work of an office professional may be stressful.
20. Suggest eight strategies you might employ to reduce stress.
21. What two factors should you weigh in determining whether humour is appropriate in the office?

Spelling Reinforcement

accomplishment	condescending	embarrassing	physiologically
accumulation	consensus	enthusiastic	potential
analyze	criticism	humour	priorities
character	desirable	judgment/judgement	sincerity
competence	eliminate	philosophy	temperamental

On-the-Job Situations

1. You are an administrative assistant in the purchasing department. Another administrative assistant, Janice McCall, is getting married on November 18. The purchasing department employs 12 office workers, two of whom are administrative assistants. According to a rumour, Janice is not coming back to work after the wedding, and two of the office workers want to apply for her position. They have come to you to find out if the rumour is true. You have not seen an official announcement about Janice's employment plans after she gets married. However, Janice did tell you that she does not plan to come back to work after the wedding. What should you say to your two co-workers?
2. You wanted your vacation during the last week in November, but you did not request it for that time because Bryan Irving, who does work similar to yours, had already requested vacation time during the last week in November. Yesterday Bryan cancelled his vacation for November because his personal plans fell through. The vacation schedule is approved six months in advance, but you still would like a vacation during the last week in November. Today is November 15 and you are thinking of asking for vacation time during the last week in November. Would you be justified in making this request now?
3. Five weeks ago you were promoted to administrative assistant for the Sales Department. There are 35 salespeople in the department, and you are having difficulty assigning priorities to your work. This morning one of the salespeople shouted, "You never get my work done by the time I need it. You are always doing work for Kristien and Adam." Kristien and Adam do give you more work than the other salespeople. You are aware that you have spent much of your time doing their work. What can you do to ensure that you allocate a fair portion of your time to doing the work of the other salespeople?

Special Reports

1. Interview an office professional who works for more than one person—several executives, everyone within a department, or everyone within a division. Request an interview and ask questions about how the office professional organizes and handles the work. Phrase your questions in advance. (This could be a class project.) Develop your questions carefully. As you formulate your questions, be sure to inquire about priorities for completing work, standards of acceptability, telephone and data management responsibilities, use of the services of others, problems encountered, and suggestions that might be helpful to you on the job. Do not limit your questions to the ideas given here. Report your findings to the class or to the instructor.

2. Think of someone whose personality you admire. Make a list of this person's personality traits that you like and then select the most outstanding traits and describe them in detail. Try to decide why these traits appeal to you. Do you think they would appeal to others? Write a memorandum to your instructor to share your ideas with the class.

Production Challenges

1-A Distribution of Time Spent for Week of May 19–23

Supplies needed:

- *Time Distribution Chart, Form 1-A-1, page 380*
- *Notes on time spent during week of May 19–23, Form 1-A-2, pages 381 to 383*
- *Working Papers Disk, File 1-A*

You decided that you could plan your work more efficiently if you kept a record of the demands on your time. You also wanted to know how much time you were spending working for each of your managers.

Your notes on the time spent are in Form 1-A-2. You have already prepared the Time Distribution Chart, Form 1-A-1. Under the heading Major Activities, use broad categories such as processing mail and word processing.

Processing the mail is for the group. You do not attempt to allocate the time spent processing the mail to the five executives. The time you spend on telephone calls each day is about evenly divided among the executives; therefore, you do allocate the time spent on telephone calls. You file only for Mr. Wilson.

Summarize the information given in Form 1-A-2. Enter the categories of duties performed in the Major Activities column of the Time Distribution Chart. Enter the total time spent on each activity in the appropriate columns of the Time Distribution Chart.

1-B Stress Management and Team Building Seminars

Supplies needed:

- *Access to the Internet*
- *Word processing software*
- *Plain paper*

Mr. Wilson is concerned about lack of teamwork in the office and what he perceives as a stressed staff. He has asked you to make two lists that will be circulated through the staff. Both rosters will list seminars or workshop names, dates, and registration fees. Prepare one list for Stress Management seminars and the other list of Team Building seminars.

Use the Internet for your research. Key the lists using word processing software and print the list on plain paper.

World Wide Websites

Stress Free NET

www.stressfree.com/

Features of this site include Ask the Psychologist, You Be the Therapist, the Answers Page, Model of Stress, Vulnerability Test, Stress Audit, Take Control Over Stress, Therapist Directory and Therapist Registry.

Business Etiquette

www.fredonia.edu/business/etiquette/links.htm

This site includes information on: Business Etiquette, Dining Etiquette, Introductions and Book Sites.

CHAPTER 2

Management of Work, Time, and Resources

Outline

Learning Outcomes

At the completion of this chapter, the student will be able to:

1. Define the concept of Total Quality Management.
2. Explain how Total Quality Management affects the work of an administrative assistant.
3. Explain the difference between working efficiently and working effectively.
4. Outline methods for working efficiently.
5. Assign priorities to the tasks of an administrative assistant.
6. Identify methods for managing a large project.
7. Identify ways of overcoming the habit of procrastination.
8. List the procedures that ensure accuracy when proofreading keyboarded work.
9. Describe ways to avoid interruptions and to handle interruptions without wasting time.
10. Suggest a systematic method of preparing for the next day's work.
11. Determine the normal working areas at a desk and the appropriate placement of equipment and supplies.
12. State suggestions for organizing both the office supplies and the workstation.
13. Suggest methods for practising environmental consciousness in an office.
14. Prepare a daily plan chart.

Administrative assistants work with a constant and rapid flow of information. Good organizational skills are a requirement for success in the workplace. To contribute to the processing of information, administrative assistants must be able not only to organize work and to manage their time but also to evaluate their effectiveness and efficiency and to look for ways to increase their contributions to the organization.

Methods of organizing work, managing time, and managing resources provide key indicators with which to measure your accomplishments each day, regardless of your long-term goals. This chapter identifies tools and techniques that may help you to become a more effective administrative assistant.

TOTAL QUALITY MANAGEMENT

As Canada moves into the twenty-first century, a business initiative has emerged that is shaping the practices and expectations of most, if not all, competitive organizations.

What Is TQM?

The *Quality* Initiative — making customer satisfaction the number one priority — does not, at first thought, seem to be significantly different from other customer-focused strategies. However, today an all-out quality commitment requires companies to eliminate wasteful practices and business methods, and to adopt an entirely new attitude.

Total Quality Management (TQM) is not new. In the late 1940s, Dr. W. Edwards Deming, an internationally renowned statistician and consultant, took his revolutionary management philosophy to Japan, where it became pivotal to that nation's successful economic recovery. Inspired by Japan's initial success, businesses worldwide have adopted quality management techniques in order to survive in the new marketplace. According to Dr. Deming, "The consumer is the most important part of the production line. Quality should be aimed at the needs of the consumer, present and future."

This statement forms the main principle of all Quality initiatives. In simple economic terms, we are all either producers or consumers, or both. Relating to the main principle is not difficult, but implementing it will be one of the challenges you face as an administrative assistant.

How Does TQM work?

There is no single formula that works for every organization; fundamentally, however, Total Quality Management makes all employees responsible for strengthening the competitive position of their company by improving its products and services. The optimization of labour, materials, and time is seen as the key to the success of the Total Quality movement; the assumption underlying this is that no customer is prepared to subsidize waste in these areas. Waste simply drives up the expense to the customer; inevitably, this results in loss of market share, profits, jobs, and ultimately the business itself.

The organization's suppliers of products also need to be aware of the Quality initiative. It should no longer be acceptable to deal with suppliers that are unreliable or

GRADUATE PROFILE

Rhonda Johnson
Manager, Customer Support and Administration

Advantage Energy Corporation

College Graduation:
Secretarial Arts Program
Southern Alberta Institute of Technology (SAIT)
Calgary, Alberta
1982

As if by design, Rhonda's training and academic success prepared her well for the challenges and dynamic environment of Canada's energy-sector hub of Calgary. This honours graduate from SAIT's Secretarial Arts program has applied her administrative knowledge and leadership skills to a career "in the oil patch" spanning a decade of personal continuous improvement.

Even before formal training, Rhonda taught herself Forkner Shorthand, a skill she still occasionally uses for messages, instructions, or meeting notes. Perhaps it was this early accomplishment that fashioned Rhonda's strategy for success—to seek continuous learning and development opportunities, and to accept change and the opportunities it offers. As a corollary, she cites the electronic office as, ". . . the *key driving force* behind the transition to more exciting, challenging, and self-gratifying roles for office adminisrators and assistants."

Her advice to new administrative assistants is just as pragmatic as she reflects on the contemporary environment in which she works. She says, "Be confident while maintaining a sense of humour; strive for excellence and not perfection; get and stay organized; learn to manage time and stress; and acquire a strong yet diverse skill set."

Rhonda has excelled in her professional and personal life holding various leadership roles both inside and outside of the office. In addition to her primary role and responsibility for the design and implementation of administrative processes and customer service, she has contributed to many quality teams as team leader, coach, and facilitator. Outside the office, she is a certified instructor and competitive bowler who somehow finds time to direct a youth bowling league!

"Be willing to challenge the status quo and to take low-impact risk."

shoddy. Depending on your responsibilities, you may wish to review your list of suppliers and develop an alliance with only one supplier for the benefit of cost, reliability, and quality.

In the office environment, TQM means that each employee is totally involved with office teamwork and focused on customer satisfaction. Employees at every level are encouraged to find new and innovative ways of doing their jobs more effectively, and to be flexible enough to assist others. You may be **empowered**—that is, given more autonomy and broader responsibilities—with the goal of simplifying office operations. You will be given responsibility for making decisions that affect your own effectiveness and performance.

You will be judged on your team contribution and on your innovation: If the filing system does not correspond to the operation—change it! If your colleague is having difficulty completing a project—help out! If a customer has a complaint—resolve it!

As an example, the administrative assistant may be invited to become part of a team that reviews the problem of products that aren't being delivered to the customer on time. The team would comprise employees who are directly involved in the delivery process under review. Each member of the team has equal responsibility and an equal voice in identifying all the steps and problems involved in the delivery cycle. Refer to the section "Team Meetings" in Chapter 11 for details of how to participate in a team meeting. The problem must be clearly understood and stated in written form.

"When dealing with office politics, I try to remain neutral."

Lisa Heron, Graduate
CompuCollege School of Business
Charlottetown

All the issues that team members consider important are recorded. Team members then prioritize (by vote) the stated problems. The problem that is deemed the most significant is the first one the team deals with.

This first-priority problem is then thoroughly examined. Each step of the current procedure is analyzed for its effectiveness and necessity. The process of examining the entire procedure will spawn improvements. Additionally, each member will feel that he or she has contributed to a solution for improving customer satisfaction.

This team problem solving approach is typical of process improvement activity that organizations are conducting as part of their Quality initiative. Let's review the approach as a sequence of events that might occur as a cross-functional team is formed to address the late delivery problem:

1. A team of employees who are directly involved in the order and delivery process is formed. This team may include the administrative assistant.
2. A team leader is selected to chair the meeting.
3. All input is documented by a designated recorder.
4. A facilitator may be involved to organize the team members' input.
5. The general problem is clearly defined during the first team meeting.
6. Each team member has an equal opportunity to state what he or she believes are the contributing factors to the general problem. This step, which allows the employees the freedom of open suggestion without criticism, is known as **brainstorming**. In this case, examples of contributing factors to the general problem may be:
   a. The person who places the orders is often away from work.
   b. When the orders are placed, the suppliers do not have ready stock; they must get stock from foreign markets.
   c. When suppliers deliver stock, it is sometimes in damaged condition, and therefore, must be reordered.
7. The team members now vote on what they believe are the most important specific problems (contributing factors). In this case, the most significant factor may be that the stock is often received in poor condition and must be reordered.
8. Next, each team member helps outline the exact steps that take place in the process. In the case of goods arriving in damaged condition, it may be discovered that the foreign suppliers are not packing the goods carefully enough.
9. As the process is completely identified, team members provide input about possible changes, until an improved process is developed. In this case, employees might suggest that proper packaging and careful handling of goods would expedite the delivery of the product to the customer.
10. The team will now make a delivery process improvement recommendation to their management.

It should be noted that there are no set rules for Total Quality Management; its principles are many and varied. But underlying them is this fundamental principle: continuous improvement and customer focus.

EFFECTIVENESS AND EFFICIENCY

For the administrative assistant, being effective and being efficient are equally important. However, these two qualities are often confused with each other. These terms, while interrelated, are separate and distinct. Effectiveness is often defined as *doing the right things*, efficiency as *doing things right*. These definitions may at first seem confusing; if so, the following section should clarify them for you.

What Is the Difference?

Effectiveness means producing a definite or desired result. **Efficiency** means producing the desired result with a minimum of effort, expense, and waste. While it is possible to be effective without being efficient, the cost of inefficiency is usually too great for profit-making organizations; they must couple efficiency with effectiveness.

Administrative assistants are appointed to specific positions, where they are responsible to one executive or to a group. Whether administrative assistants work for

pro-Link

Do time wasters plague you? Here are a few time wasters that can make you very ineffective and some sure-fire solutions to get you back on track.

- Defocusing from your work every time the phone rings?
  Solution—When you are doing work that requires focus, forward your telephone calls to your voicemail.
- Colleagues socializing at your desk?
  Solution—Change the direction that your desk faces, remove the chairs near your desk, acknowledge your colleagues but keep working when they come to socialize, and most important—let your colleagues know you are busy but you are looking forward to socializing with them at lunch.
- So much work that you can't complete anything?
  Solution—Set up a priority list and get at it!
- Afraid to delegate?
  Solution—Take time to give another person clear details of how to complete the work. Now live with the results! Remember you are not the only person who can do the job well!

PERSPECTIVES

The Quest for Quality

By Marlene Caroselli, Ph.D.

Here's how you can become a star player on your company's Total Quality Management team.

Total Quality Management—the latest managerial buzz-phrase or a time-tested philosophy? Common sense or complicated arcanna? Commonality of thinking or guru-grown separateness? What is this thing called "Quality"?

To each person who defines it, it means something different. The emphases shift from place to place; the adopted philosophy may belong to one guru or may be a combination of the best of each. To some people, the word "total" means "everyone in the organization is involved." To others, it means "quality applies to everything we do."

Some organizations are calling their quality efforts just "Total Quality." Others have substituted the word "leadership" in place of "management." Some firms have replaced the abbreviation TQM with their own adaptation, such as "c.m.i.—continuous measurable improvement." Some are calling what they do a program and others will not tolerate the use of that word.

And yet—despite the unique adaptations—there are some basic principles that underlie all the interpretations of this thing called "Quality":

- The desire to communicate closely with customers in order to meet their needs;
- The acknowledgement that teams are at the heart of improvement—their synergy brings about the improvement of work processes;
- The recognition that all work is process;
- The understanding that a process begins with input provided by a "supplier," and ends with an output, delivered to a "customer";
- The agreement that processes cannot really be understood or analyzed until they have been flowcharted;
- The need to measure in order to ensure improvement has really taken place;
- The belief that recognition, respect, and cooperation are the necessary conditions within which improvement can occur.

How do we stress that harmony is more beneficial to us all than competition? How do we overcome the perception that knowledge is power and the more knowledge I possess, the more power I will have over others?

Total Quality Management (TQM) encourages a logical look at problems that exist in the workplace. Until such problems are addressed honestly and openly, until they have been identified, and until individuals have expressed an interest in solving them, absolutely nothing will change.

There is a popular definition of "insanity" that many TQM-ers subscribe to: "Insanity is doing the same thing you have always done and expecting better results." If we continue communicating as we always have, then, quite simply, there will be no improved communication. To expect otherwise is insane.

Dig for data

Quality proponents advise having teams investigate the problems that exist. Teams should be composed of employees who have a genuine interest in the issue and/or some expertise in the area. Teams begin by brainstorming a list of possible reasons why a given problem has developed. They then isolate the causes they believe are most likely contributing to the problem. Once this is done, they can start collecting data to learn if those causes are true causes or perhaps mere symptoms. One source of data-gathering, for example, is a survey.

What if the survey results revealed that most employees felt a lack of information-sharing was the chief cause of poor communication in the work environment? What could a secretarial team do? Any number of things, including inviting a communications expert from a nearby college to address employees. Or, they could buy a book on the subject and summarize its content for the company newspaper. They could read and circulate articles, ask the training department to conduct classes, and so forth.

Everyone's a manager

Asked about the involvement of secretaries in corporate Quality [as it pertains to TQM] goals, Annette Worth explains: "I had to get involved! The Xerox Quality Policy states that Quality improvement is the job of every Xerox employee. Many secretaries don't consider themselves managers, but I have learned each employee's job is a business—and we are all managers of our own business."

Partnerships, clearly, extend beyond the internal opportunities to synergize. Worth offers this insider's view of how alliances can be strengthened with both internal and external customers.

- Fully satisfy requirements, but don't exceed requirements. Doing so could waste time and money. Compare this to a meal—too much is uncomfortable but not enough is not satisfying.
- Do it right the first time, or—for those who like acronyms—DIRTFT!
- Use the power of recognition—verbal recognition, thank you notes, small gifts, and other monetary rewards.

Worth relates that TQM has brought new definitions to old terms. Until 1983, she says, she relied upon her own definition of "quality": "neat work, no mistakes, work done on time."

"Then in 1983 Xerox changed my understanding of the definition of quality. Our Quality Policy states, 'Quality means conformance to customer requirements, internal and external. Quality means providing our external and internal customers with innovative products and services that fully satisfy their requirements.'

"By the way, we define 'customer' as 'the next person (or group) in the work process, the receiver of my output and the one who actually uses it.' So I learned that very often my manager is my customer, and to achieve quality, I must understand and satisfy all of his or her requirements."

Increase your effectiveness

Annette Worth of the Xerox Corporation offers these suggestions for becoming a "Quality Secretary."

- Utilize the creativity of every employee. It's important that you use your special skills, whatever they are.
- As far as a boss is concerned, never permit your manager to be caught unprepared! DO YOUR HOMEWORK. Remember, too, your manager needs answers, not questions on how to get her answers.
- Learn to prioritize projects. It's human nature to want to finish what we're working on at the moment, but sometimes we must put it aside—where we can find it later—in order to handle a higher priority task.
- Fully understand customer requirements, uncover the unexpressed requirements, anticipate the needs of customers.
- Use active listening skills. This means more than being quiet when someone else is talking. It's possible for you to give your best effort and produce an excellent output and yet be completely off target. Listen and test for understanding before you start.
- Follow up to ensure your customers have what they need. Besides fulfilling their requirements, you will let them know you care about the satisfaction they have after the sale, or after they have received their input from you.
- Organize, organize, organize! Sharpen your time-management skills.
- Avoid office politics/gossip.
- Leave prejudices behind when you join a team.
- Continue to grow and learn; enroll in seminars and company-sponsored training.
- Give status reports so your boss does not have to keep asking.
- Write everything down.

Handling conflict

Here are Worth's suggestions for handling conflict within the workplace, for changing hostile communication to more positive communication:

- Deal immediately with any negative situation.
- Use the behavior appropriate to the situation—we learn to do this in a training program titled "Interactive Skills." One example would be brainstorming, when all ideas are presented without judgment from others.
- Be patient—with yourself and with others—while the process is being learned. On my desk calendar there was a Chinese saying, "With time and patience the mulberry leaf becomes a silk gown."

Take action

Can secretaries effect positive change? Can they work with others—in teams or less formal partnerships—to improve processes, to enhance communication, to increase productivity? Of course they can! Here is further evidence from the Xerox Corporation:

As a result of [recent] cutbacks ... there were suddenly four secretaries to do the work that nine had been doing earlier ... To cope with this situation, the secretaries formed a Quality Improvement Team.

They addressed the problem using the Quality Improvement Process, found out what other groups were doing, compared support provided, and actually assigned certain tasks to their managers so the secretaries could continue to meet their customer requirements.

Their managers were involved and aware of the team effort and supported the plan. So, in appropriate cases, secretaries can, to a certain extent, manage their managers—for everyone's benefit.

Annette Worth recognizes her unique talents for increasing the quality of the work she delivers to customers. She also recognizes that every secretary possesses unique talents for improving quality.

Marlene Caroselli
The Center for Professional Development
324 Latona Road
Rochester, New York 14626
Phone: (716) 227-6512

one executive or for more than one, they must always do the following three things to organize their work so that they can perform efficiently:

1. Divide large projects into manageable segments of work.
2. Group related isolated tasks to reduce the time consumed in changing from one unrelated task to another.
3. Match the work to the time frames in which it must be performed, by classifying it as work that must be done today, work that must be done this week, or work that has no specific deadline.

Time Management involves developing work habits that result in maximum efficiency; acquiring knowledge, skills, and equipment to extend performance beyond present capabilities; controlling attitudes and emotions that have a tendency to steal time; and developing an effective reminder method for following through on each task at the appropriate time. Acquiring knowledge, maintaining a positive attitude, and controlling emotions were discussed in Chapter 1. Work habits and effective reminder methods are discussed here.

BE THE BOSS OF YOUR OWN TIME

There is no single "right way" for managing time on the job. The rules are often job-specific and change from organization to organization. Exactly what constitutes successful time management is difficult to define without reference to specific examples from the working world. There is no doubt that effective employees establish recognizable work *patterns*, but no two employees necessarily follow the *same* pattern. Nevertheless, the ideas presented in this chapter can be used as a guide to establish your own work habits and time management techniques. It is important to remember, though, that this is only a guide. You will have to work hard and think about how best to adapt these rules and suggestions to your own situation.

For example, balancing family responsibilities and work responsibilities is a significant challenge to many administrative assistants. Organizations are developing employee-friendly policies and support systems that provide flexible work schedules and permit more work-at-home and telecommuting options.

In a type of schedule redesign known as **flextime**, employees work a set number of hours each day but vary the starting and ending times. Flextime allows management to relax some of the traditional "time clock" control of employees' time. Similarly, working from home and telecommuting present an extraordinary opportunity to be the boss of your own time (see Perspectives, page 30).

Learn the Job

Organizing work is just one aspect of the overall management function. Management expresses its objectives—the work to be accomplished—in terms of long-range, intermediate, and short-range goals, and executives focus their attention on meeting these overall objectives of the organization.

In any given week, executives may focus their efforts on specific long-range goals, but they cannot ignore all short-range goals during that same period of time. If they devote too much time to day-to-day operations, they may neglect the more dynamic aspects of their work. Thus, in any given week executives schedule their time to complete the work at hand and to move toward accomplishing intermediate and long-range goals.

Before you can organize work, you must know what your goals are. Organize your day's work so that it dovetails with that of your manager; do not expect your manager to adjust to your work schedule. At first, concentrate on learning; be cautious about taking initiative until you understand what is expected of you.

Someone will explain your new role to you. This might be the administrative assistant you are replacing, or your supervisor. During this orientation, listen, take notes, and ask questions that will increase your understanding of what is being explained. Be alert to procedures you must follow; where the information, supplies, and other items you will need immediately are located; what are considered priority items; and your manager's preferences. Try to remember the names of the people you meet and what they do.

Every day, make an effort to learn more about your role and exactly how your manager prefers the work done. Learn the job not just for the current week and the next but for from three months to a year in advance. Become familiar with the information in your office. For example:

1. Carefully study all the instructions left for you by the previous administrative assistant.
2. Check on the different kinds of stationery and forms in your desk and determine when each is to be used.
3. Read instruction sheets that have been prepared for certain tasks you are to perform.
4. Study the office procedures manual, if given one.
5. Find out what is in the active files.
6. Refer to the directory of the organization to learn the names of the executives and other employees and their titles.

PERSPECTIVES

Flexibility the Name of the Game

By Betty Holcomb

Working mother

As a managing director at Merrill Lynch, Susan Scherbel knows she has it good. She works full time, but no one clocks her hours; in fact, no one even monitors where and when she gets her work done.

She now shows up in the office only when it's absolutely essential.

How did she cut such a good deal? With her background as an attorney with a wide-ranging knowledge of both corporate taxes and the tax aspects of employee benefit plans, she brings an expertise to many deals that virtually no one else on Wall Street has.

"I'd like to think that I'd have this arrangement no matter what, but I wouldn't bet the mortgage on that. The truth is the more indispensable you are, the more you can distinguish yourself, and the more likely it is that you can gain some flexibility and still move ahead."

That's excellent advice, according to consultants and academics who advise companies on flexible work arrangements.

Though some companies have begun to create new ways to work, most still measure employees the old-fashioned way, by the clock.

"Many managers still think if they can see your face, you're productive," says Marcia Brumit Kropf, vice-president at Catalyst, a New York City think-tank dedicated to advancing women in the workplace. "That's not true, of course. Just being there does not mean someone is productive."

But as Kropf and other consultants have learned over the years, it takes a big effort to move managers out of this old mindset. So what's a parent to do?

As Scherbel's experience shows, even in the most demanding, time-intensive careers, there are strategies for achieving success when you work flexible hours or must leave promptly each day. We surveyed readers and talked to the experts to come up with tactics for not only surviving, but thriving if you work with clock watchers.

✔ **Make yourself indispensable.** As Scherbel found, companies will go the extra mile for you if you have an important skill that no one else has. Toni Thompson an occupational therapist and mother of two accomplishes the same thing in another way. "I take on projects that no one else wants to do. I am developing a reputation as the one you can count on," she says.

Others say that they volunteer for special committees, especially those that mean working with other departments.

✔ **Showcase your productivity.** Of course, it won't help to have a talent or an expertise unless you make people aware of it. "I never really used to strut my stuff," says Thompson. "Now I make a point to talk up the committees I'm on and the projects I'm doing." Not only that, but Thompson is also quick to praise her co-workers' contributions as well. "I highlight other people's work, and that way, I show that I am contributing and also a team player who appreciates other people's productivity."

✔ **Choose the right priorities.** Productivity only counts when you're doing the right stuff. Spending hours on tasks that don't move the firm's main agenda forward is a waste of time. If the company's goal is to create a top-of-the-line digital camera or to make milk the most exciting drink in the grocery store, then that should be your priority as well.

If you aren't sure what your boss's priorities are, find out. "It's critically important to sit down with your manager and have clear objectives," says Joy Bunson, senior vice-president of organizational development at Chase Manhattan Bank. "Once you can focus on outcome, face time is less important."

At times, having the right priorities means adapting to your supervisor's habits and personality quirks. "My boss is a morning person," says one mom. So she does her best to make sure she's on time in the morning. "If I stay after 5 because I came in a bit late, it doesn't matter to him. It's more important that I am here on time."

✔ **Keep the focus on work.** Make sure that everyone knows you're committed to working hard during office hours. Many moms note that they don't waste time socializing during office hours; many skip lunch to make the most of their time. "I let my co-workers know that I do have deadlines," says Tanya Mahoney, a fundraiser for American Red Cross. "If there is a project looming, I let them know that I am not to be bothered, that my immediate project is the task of the day." With that kind of clear-cut dedication to getting the job done, co-workers are less likely to question your commitment or productivity.

✔ **Speak up when you have a problem.** If you have a conflict that makes it impossible to arrive on time or forces you to leave a little early, talk to your supervisor. Otherwise, you're likely to be seen as someone who does not care about your work.

"It's important to have an open conversation with your boss," says Kropf. Frame the issue professionally. "You might say, 'I know the standard schedule is to be here at 8:30, not 9, but that isn't working for me. I don't want you to think I'm late because I don't care. I want to be a good performer, and I'm hoping that we can come up with a mutually agreeable solution."

You can then suggest options, such as skipping lunch or staying a little later.

✔ **Take advantage of technology.** If you leave at 5, that doesn't mean you can't still be in touch with co-workers and your boss. Use a cell phone, voice-mail, e-mail, whatever it takes to stay on top of business that must be done after you leave the office. "I use my cell phone to attend meetings after 5 p.m. or before 9 a.m.," says one mother. That way, her boss and co-workers don't think of her as "leaving early;" instead, they see that she makes every effort to be a team player.

Susan Scherbel is evidence that a change is already under way. "When I first started working at home, I tried to keep the arrangement quiet," she says. But now she's extremely comfortable with it, especially since Merrill Lynch has touted the arrangement in company newsletters and to the media. Her schedule is now considered a model, a harbinger of the future. "I hope that's true," Scherbel says, "because it seems to be a win-win for everybody."

Betty Holcomb is the author of Not Guilty! The Good News About Working Mothers *(Scribners, 1998).*

When you report to work, the former administrative assistant may not be there to train you. Perhaps there will not be a procedures manual describing your duties. In this situation your manager will direct you. You will have to rely heavily on your resourcefulness and use good judgment in seeking and finding answers. Keep in mind that you cannot perform at maximum value to the organization until you fully understand the scope of your manager's job and yours.

Assign Priorities

Setting **priorities** will be the most challenging part of organizing your work and assigning your time to the given tasks.

Although you are guided by general policies about priorities, you will need to make judgments concerning performing the work in the most beneficial way for others and for the organization. Performing the work in the order in which it is submitted to you will not always be feasible because some tasks will have more pressing deadlines than others. An example of a low-priority item is a memorandum written only as a matter of record. It can be keyed and filed at any time.

The time demands of executives and others for whom you work will be the overriding factor in how you divide your time. When you are working for two executives, one may have a lot of work for you and the other very little. When you work for a group, it may be made up of salespeople who are out of the office much of the time. Each one may have only a small amount of work for you, but each one will expect you to do her is his work on the day he or she is in the office. Under this arrangement, you will be ahead if you prepare a schedule a week in advance showing who will be in the office on which days of the week. This information may not be easy to obtain, but it will be helpful when it comes to answering the telephone and anticipating your own workload.

Eventually you will learn how much time you will need to devote to performing each person's work. For your own use, keep a record of how you spend your time. Prepare a **time distribution chart,** as shown in Figure 2-1. The time distribution chart is designed to show the distribution of work and time for several workers performing related office tasks; however, with minor changes it can be used to show the distribution of time and duties performed by one worker for several others. At the top of the columns, write the names of the executives and others for whom you perform work. Enter the time used and a brief description of the task performed in the columns below the names.

After keeping the charts for several weeks, total the time used on behalf of each person and compute percentages. Your analysis will give you some estimate of how much work to expect from each person, and it will reflect what you are doing that could be channelled elsewhere. When you have so much work to be done that some of it must be reassigned, your charts will be especially helpful to your manager in deciding which duties can be handled by someone else.

When you work for executives of equal rank, one will be displeased if her or his work often has to wait while you perform the work of another. Be discreet in sharing your time. Do not impose repeatedly on the executive who is the most understanding. And do not try to smooth out disagreements among executives of equal rank concerning demands on your time: either say nothing at all or tactfully suggest that they work it out among themselves. But *do* make helpful suggestions. For example, could they possibly give you routine reports to key on Thursday instead of Friday, when others are back in the office and requesting your help?

Most administrative assistants who work for groups comprised of employees of different ranks give highest priority to the work of the top executive in their group, second priority to the executive next in rank, and so on. This arrangement may ensure you of a good relationship with your manager, but it may also create problems, particularly if some of the employees in the lower ranks feel that they can never get their work done on time or at all. Eventually they will complain. Avoid this

Figure 2-1 Time distribution chart.

Dorothy Auvigne

Week of: 20— 03 23

TIME DISTRIBUTION CHART

MAJOR ACTIVITIES	Napoli	hrs.	Carson	hrs.	Jones	hrs.	Parker	hrs.	Ramos	hrs.	For Group	hrs.	TOTAL
Mail											Open and distribute	1 1/2	1 1/2
Research	Internet	1 1/2			Internet	1/2							2
Keyboarding	Letters	1/2	Report	1/2			Letters	1/4	Memos	1/4			1 1/2
Setting Appointments	By electronic calendar	1/2					Telephone and in person	1/2					1
Payroll											Time sheets, distribute cheques	1/2	1/2
Misc.											Handle calls	1/2	1/2
TOTAL		2 1/2		1/2		1/2		3/4		1/4		2 1/2	7

problem by learning how to assess the urgency of the work of the top executives in the group. You will discover that some of their work can wait. Make your own judgment without discussing it with anyone and proceed with performing the tasks. However, when your work is backed up to the extent that it must be discussed formally, the top executive has the responsibility of assessing the total workload and determining the need for extra help.

Some employees, in an effort to gain priority for their requests, will label all requests RUSH. In each case you will have to judge what is a rush item and what is not. When you sense that these employees are under a lot of pressure, you might occasionally prevent a disruption by giving priority to their work; however, this practice must not become the norm. By giving priority to executives who mark all items RUSH, you are encouraging this behaviour at the expense of other executives' work. Those executives who decrease the stress in the office by practising effective time management should not be penalized. You will have to deal with this issue in a diplomatic way. The best advice is to collect facts before you approach the problem. How many rush items are you receiving? Which executives are giving you the rush items? What are the rush items? Exactly what dates are you being given the rush items, and when are the deadlines? The time distribution chart will assist with collection of this data.

Now that you have a better understanding, discuss the situation with the executives involved. Ask what they see as a resolution to the problem and always be prepared to offer your own solution. Remember that complainers receive no respect, but problem solvers do.

You can maintain more control over your work schedule by relying on your own judgment about the order in which work should be done, instead of trying to follow rigid rules. Your judgment must be good, and you will need to be as concerned about your rapport with the members of the group as you are about the quality of the work you perform.

Some administrative assistants aspire to work for only one executive. There are advantages and disadvantages to such a situation.

Advantages of Working with Only One Executive

1. You are often viewed as having more status within the company.
2. You do not have to adjust to conflicting management styles.
3. Your manager has a clearer idea of your time constraints. Where several executives share the same assistant, the executives often are not aware of pressures being placed on you by their colleagues.

Disadvantages of Working with Only One Executive

1. Your responsibilities may be more routine. Where an assistant works for more than one manager, the assistant often receives a greater variety of projects to complete. Remember—the more experience you receive, the more marketable you become.
2. An assistant who works for only one manager gains business contacts from only that source. If you work for a number of managers your chances of networking are improved; this, of course, could improve your future employment opportunities.
3. Working for only one executive may not allow you to practise your organizational skills to the same degree that working for multiple executives would.

The preference is a personal one. Both positions may require equal challenges. If the challenges do not present themselves, find them!

Adopt a Flexible Plan

Highly effective people recommend planning work and then following the plan. Therefore, to discharge efficiently the variety of duties that you will encounter, plan your work. However, adopt a flexible plan. Use your plan as an overall guide, but do not become discouraged when you cannot follow it closely.

One of your major responsibilities is to save your manager's time. To do this and to meet his or her deadlines, you must learn to make the best possible use of your own time. Perform as much of your manager's work as you can, decrease interruptions or at least schedule them, and assist your manager by collecting and verifying facts and assembling materials that he or she will need to accomplish the plan. To enable your manager to perform with maximum efficiency, tackle the most pressing or important job first and keep adjusting your plan so that you can meet the deadlines.

You can learn the order of priorities in two ways: by listening to your manager's requests and by noticing and keeping a record of the time schedule on which information flows in and out of the office. For example, know when routine reports are due and how much in advance to request work from service departments, learn mail pickup and transportation schedules, and be cognizant of the most convenient times to reach executives by telephone.

You must recognize that your work schedule truly is not your own. Your work schedule is governed not only by your manager's objectives and deadlines but also by the built-in schedules for the flow of information in your organization. For example:

- You may plan to devote the morning hours to starting a lengthy assignment only to discover that your manager wants you to work on something more urgent.
- A telephone call from corporate head office requesting critical information may take precedence over everything else.
- The deadline for sending the departments weekly and monthly revenue report is based on a routine and defined schedule.
- Whenever an associated department with which your work is interrelated changes its schedule, you must adjust your schedule to accommodate theirs.

Manage Details

You, like every other administrative assistant, will be faced with the problem of keeping up with numerous details, for in office work there is no way to escape the myriad of details. In fact, you will be forced to devise methods for managing them. Not only must you record them, but you must record them immediately and then put them in a form that will enable you to locate and use the information when you need it.

To capture details, use notebooks or forms. Use a separate notebook or form to record telephone dialogue or voice mail messages and subsequent action or conversations. Use another notebook or form to record reminders to yourself of action you must take; this is commonly referred to as a **To Do List**. Refer to Figure 2-2.

The computer may also manage details and reminders. Forms and simple templates are readily available in most word processing applications enabling administrative assistants to store the recorded detail in electronic format. The advantage of electronic format is that the detail is easily changed or modified, and that its distribution to other staff is made simple.

Figure 2-2 To Do List.

TO DO
TODAY

Date Sept. 5	Completed ✔
–Order new cartridges for laser printers	✓
–Call cellular phone suppliers	☐
–Review prices for ergonomic chairs	☐
–Arrange T.Q.M. meeting	✓
–Evaluate software for notebook computers	☐
–Arrange software training for staff	☐
	☐
	☐
	☐

To decrease the time you spend recording certain kinds of information, design a form in which you key and duplicate the constant information and leave space to write in the variable information. Forms bring related information together in one place and prompt the user to record all the essential facts. The Mail-Expected Record, discussed in Chapter 6, are examples of forms you can make.

Recording facts as soon as they become available to you is an important aspect of capturing details. You will discover that the practice of "do it now" is in conflict with the concept of grouping tasks to save time and energy; nevertheless, you need to capture details at the precise moment they arise in order to keep up with them.

Actually, the means you devise for keeping up with details can vary from task to task according to the work involved and your personal preferences. That being said, recognize in all your work

- the importance of having some method for capturing details.
- the need to be consistent in following your method.

You can use check marks, initials, codes, and symbols to indicate the status of each detail that you want to capture. For instance:

1. The date stamp you place on a piece of incoming mail will tell you that you have already seen it.
2. The check mark by the enclosure notation on the file copy of a letter will remind you that you did include the enclosure.
3. The electronic date and time stamp attached to a computer file will indicate when the file was last updated.

In addition, if you are consistent in using each type of notation to convey its respective meaning, the absence of an appropriate notation will alert you to give attention to that particular item.

When you encounter a new task, spend a little time deciding how you are going to manage the details and then be consistent in doing so.

Details arranged in the chronological order in which they were originally recorded usually are not in their most usable form. Details must be arranged so that they can be located quickly. The arrangement can range from indexing on cards to computer information search tools.

Organizing the details you need to keep, such as the names of new contacts, telephone numbers, changes of address, and schedule changes, can be done with great efficiency with a computer as you only need to record it once. Not everything you jot down needs to be transferred; this is especially true of reminders of things to do. Cross out the reminders as you complete the tasks, but go over your list carefully and transfer the reminders of tasks yet to be done to your To Do List for the following day. You may also want to transcribe detailed instructions that you have in your notebook and place them in your office procedures manual.

Control a Large Project

When you start a large project, you will need to allocate some time each day for planning and controlling. The following suggestions should help you manage a large project.

1. Determine what the desired goal is. Know exactly what you are to accomplish. Being unsure about the goal is a real time waster.
2. Write down the target date.
3. Divide the project into manageable segments and then, as far as it is possible to do so, work with one segment at a time.
4. Set completion dates for each segment of the project; as you progress, check the dates to ensure that you are on schedule.
5. Check out all the supplies you will need; have a few extras on hand of supplies that are quickly used.
6. Locate the equipment you will need to complete the project.
7. Delegate some of your regular duties to make time for working on the project.
8. If you will need the services of others, either within or outside the organization, contact them at the beginning to find out about scheduling. Determine what you will have to do to meet their schedules.
9. Determine what data you will need, how to obtain them, and when.
10. As soon as you begin the project, make copious notes in longhand in a large bound notebook.
11. Divide the notebook into segments, matching the segments of the project.
12. As you plan for each segment or part of a segment, list everything that must be done. Keep adding to your list at random.
13. As you complete each item, mark a line through it. Circle in a different colour the items still to be done. Do this very carefully—the most helpful part of your notes will be the notations about unfinished items.
14. When you have completed an entire segment, write COMPLETED at the top of the corresponding page in your notebook.
15. When you make a change, be sure to make it everywhere the change occurs.
16. Separate the in-progress segments so that you can add to them or reorganize them with ease.
17. Carefully recheck all the circled items to be sure that nothing has been left undone.

Work at One Task at a Time

Schedule your work so that you can keep at one task until you finish it or until you get to a logical stopping place, such as a new subheading. If a stopping place does not exist, try to work at one task for two hours or, at the very least, one hour. Jumping from one task to another is confusing. Furthermore, reviewing work to figure out where to begin and recalling what has and has not been done results in wasted time and energy.

As you work, thoughts about other duties will come to mind. Write down each usable thought on your To Do List and continue to concentrate on the work at hand. Learn how to handle interruptions and shift back quickly to the immediate task; coping with interruptions is discussed in the section "Excuse Me!" found later in this chapter.

Form the habit of working at an uncluttered desk. On the immediate work area of your desk, put out only

"Smile .... It works wonders!"

Susan Muise, Graduate
Nova Scotia Community College
Burridge Campus

the materials you need for the task on which you are working. Since you can give attention to only one main task at a time, put the other work aside, carefully organized and labelled. Stacking work on top of work in a disorganized way leads to confusion; it is how papers get lost and nerves become frayed. The time you spend organizing work in progress will not be wasted. When you put aside everything except the task on which you are working, you will feel more relaxed and able to focus upon it.

Start the Day with a Difficult Task

Begin your day in an unhurried way so that you will not need the first 30 minutes at the office to "pull yourself together." If you commute and often find yourself worrying about your transportation being late, try to improve your day by taking an earlier bus (or train, or subway, or whatever it is you use). If you drive to work, allow yourself an extra 5 or 10 minutes to get a head start on the morning rush hour. Arrive early, and go over your plans for the day (which you prepared the day before), and then tackle a task that requires concentration and effort on your part. Tackle either a task that is difficult or one that you dislike. It will seem easier when you have energy and your mind is clear.

Make the first hour one of accomplishment, not one in which you simply get ready to work. Perhaps your first tasks will be to listen to your voice mail, to take down messages or to read your electronic mail. As soon as you finish these regular duties, start a challenging task. Of course, there will be times when you use the first hour to complete unfinished work from the day before.

Some office workers claim that they perform best early in the day; others, in the afternoon; and still others claim that they concentrate best very late in the day. In fact, psychologists have confirmed that every person has her or his own preferred work cycle. If you consider yourself an afternoon performer, use your afternoon hours for your most creative and challenging work, but force yourself to make the first hour a brisk one. Workers who waste time getting started are only putting themselves under unnecessary pressure to accomplish their work in what remains of the day. At any rate, do not use the beginning of the day to perform those easy tasks that can provide relaxation at intervals during the day.

Group Similar Tasks

You can save time and energy by not shifting from one task to another. For example, replenish your supplies once a week or less often. Avoid making a trip to the supply cabinet every day. If supplies are delivered to you, fill out one requisition for all the supplies you will need for several weeks.

Different tasks require different degrees of concentration and, in turn, different speeds. Therefore, in order to control your pace, group together the tasks that require the same degree of concentration. Letters to grant appointments and to make routine requests are favourable in tone, usually short, and easy to write. Group these letters and compose them rapidly, then use a slower pace to compose a disappointing letter requiring a long explanation.

In addition, group tasks to increase effectiveness. For example, making a telephone call should not be a routine task to be sandwiched between other work in an offhand way. A telephone call conveys an impression of the organization to the receiver. By grouping your telephone calls, you can give them your complete attention and project your personality in a thoughtful, businesslike way.

Avoid Procrastination

Procrastination is an unproductive behaviour pattern that causes you to delay working on your most important assignments and to focus on tasks that aren't priorities. We all procrastinate to some degree at certain times; but to some people it is a habit. To break the habit of procrastination, you must first gain an understanding of your behaviour and then work to overcome it. You can gain a better understanding of this behaviour by:

1. admitting that you are procrastinating.
2. asking yourself what types of projects cause you to procrastinate. Some office workers might see a major project as a horrendous task, while others might find the daily routine tasks too much to face.
3. asking yourself why you avoid these projects or tasks. Are you bored with the routine or afraid of the challenge? Are you avoiding interaction with certain office workers or authority figures? Do you fear failing at greater responsibility?

After answering these questions, you will be better prepared to overcome this unproductive behaviour. The following tips will help you avoid procrastination and become more productive.

1. Ask yourself what the worst thing is that can happen while you perform this task. Once you think it through, you will find that the risk created by the project is not that great; in fact, the benefits of completing the project will far outweigh the difficulties.
2. If the project is large, divide it into smaller sections. Several small tasks always appear to be easier to accomplish than one large task. For more suggestions, refer to the section "Control a Large Project" presented earlier in this chapter.
3. Reward yourself often. Allow yourself a break or a more pleasant task once you have completed a portion of the work. Small and frequent rewards work better for procrastinators than one large reward at the completion of a very strenuous task.
4. Ask yourself what the downside is of not completing the task on time—or worse, not

completing the task at all. Does not doing the project mean the loss of your job, a demotion, or the loss of respect from your peers and managers? This alone may encourage you to get started.

5. If you are a perfectionist, you may be avoiding a simple task because of your working style. Remember that not all work must be flawless. Working *smarter*, instead of *harder*, means recognizing the difference between work that must be perfect and work that can contain minor flaws, and acting on it.

Build Relaxation into Your Schedule

Most organizations provide a lunch hour and short morning and afternoon breaks during a regular work day. With these exceptions, employees are expected to perform efficiently throughout the day.

To maintain your best performance throughout the day and the week, experiment with alternating difficult and easy tasks to establish the best combination for conserving your energy. Observe which tasks consume a great deal of energy and which ones seem to require little energy. Rotate tasks that require a great deal of concentration and effort with tasks that require less thought and energy. Whether a task is difficult or easy for you to perform will depend on your ability, your experience in performing the given task, and your attitude toward it.

Performing an undesirable task requires an extra expenditure of energy. Repetitive tasks are often disliked. Here the dislike arises from the repetition rather than from the work itself. Fortunately, the computer and its various peripherals have introduced new and interesting methods.

Once you discover which tasks are easy for you, save them to perform between difficult tasks. Use them to provide relaxation as you work. Start your day with a difficult task and work at a vigorous pace. Keep at one task for at least two hours or until you reach a stopping place. Throughout the day, alternate difficult tasks with easy ones. When possible, also alternate sitting with standing tasks. When you cannot change the task, change your pace. After lunch and after your morning and afternoon breaks, tackle difficult tasks.

Save easy tasks for late in the day. When you are estimating the time needed for performing a long, complicated task, allow for a decrease in production as you continue working. You cannot expect to perform at your maximum rate for six or seven hours. Your productivity will be highest when you can keep fatigue to a minimum. Discover and maintain a pace that will make it possible for you to do your best work.

After you make your plan to alternate difficult and easy tasks, do not become frustrated when you cannot follow your plan. Work in a busy office rarely runs smoothly, even with the best planning. Deadline after deadline must be met. Peaks and valleys occur in all jobs; there is no possible way to avoid them completely.

Because of the pressure of work, you may forgo your morning or afternoon break and shorten your lunch hour. You will stick to the difficult task and postpone other work. You may be asked to work overtime, and others in the office may be asked to assist you. You may feel that you have no control over your work schedule. When you face these situations, evaluate your working plan. Establish the duration of the peak load, how often it will occur, and what you can do about it. Determine what preparation you can make in advance to lessen the peak load. If there is no let-up in the work, either you are not approaching your job in the right way or you need assistance. Discuss the situation with your manager, but be prepared to offer viable solutions.

Get It Right the First Time

To produce acceptable work on the first try, plan each task before you begin, focus on the exactness of the details as you perform, and then check each finished task for correctness and completeness before you release it.

Remember that waste results when a piece of work that could have been completed correctly on the first try must be redone.

Before you start performing a task, make sure you understand the instructions; then review the facts, visualize the work in its finished form, and make a plan. Spend sufficient time determining exactly what you are expected to do: do not guess. You will discover that the extra minutes needed to perform the task correctly the first time are fewer than you would spend redoing the task. Work at a pace that will result in the most productivity for you.

The speed with which business information flows, especially with the advent of computer networks, has placed a premium on accuracy. An error that has been released is difficult to retrieve. Problems created by errors that are released into the channels of information are not only time-consuming to correct, but can also result in losses to the organization. So check your work carefully. Be sure that every detail is correct and that each item is complete before you transmit it. On the job, you will discover ways to check the various tasks you perform to ensure their correctness. Develop your own check points and guidelines for each task. Here are a few guidelines that should be observed for checking printed work:

1. Edit the copy for meaning. At the same time, watch for typographical, spelling, and punctuation errors. Do this while the copy is still on the screen so that making corrections will be easy.
2. Go over the copy a second time, scanning it for figures such as dates and amounts of money. Then check their accuracy.
3. Use a calculator to check a long list of keyed figures that have been totalled.
4. When a long series appears in a paragraph, count the items and compare the number with the list in the original. Also count the items included in a tabulation.
5. When you are copying from keyboarded material that you must follow line by line for proofreading, use a ruler to keep your place if you do not have a copy holder with a line finder.
6. Always proofread the two-letter provincial abbreviations and the postal codes in addresses. One wrong stroke at the keyboard, if not caught, can mean a delayed letter.

Prepare in Advance

With the exception of routine duties, office work requires planning. The amount of planning time needed depends on how complicated the job is, the length of it, and whether or not the person doing the work has ever performed similar tasks.

Executives in successful organizations plan three to five years in advance. Managers at all levels plan at least one year in advance. Observe how your manager and others in your organization think ahead, and then apply some of their techniques to your own assignments. The time you spend thinking through what needs to be done will save you minutes and hours of redoing work.

Take time to study a job until you can visualize it to its completion regardless of how complicated or lengthy it is. People who work aimlessly seldom reach the goals toward which they should have been working. If necessary, ask yourself and others what the expected outcome of the specific assignment is. Do not hesitate to ask about the purpose of an assignment. When an assignment is new to you, you may find it difficult, if not impossible, to visualize it to its completion. If necessary, ask your manager to guide you.

Do not permit your thinking about a complicated task you must complete in the future to interfere with getting today's work finished. Do one job at a time. Schedule thinking time in the same way that you schedule time for word processing. Start by jotting down your thoughts at random. Organize them later. As you study the job, estimate the time needed to complete each part of it. Start with the completion date and work backward to the current date.

The most critical parts of an assignment are the ones that require other people—either to supply information or to actually perform certain tasks. Begin your preparation with the segments of the work that involve others.

Assume that you are compiling data for a report. Make a checklist of your needs. For instance, will you need special information or materials, such as the most recent figures from the accounting department, a comparative analysis from the statistical department, pictures to be taken by the audiovisual department, charts that must be reduced in size by the printing department, or the public relations department's approval for the illustrations to be included in the report? Make each of these requests as soon as you are certain of your needs.

As you prepare an assignment in advance, make your plan so carefully that you can put it aside and not think about it until you are ready to start. This is important, because thinking about an endless stream of work has a negative effect on a worker's performance. Label a folder for the assignment and put everything pertaining to it in that folder. Budget your time for completing the assignment. Allow some time for delays. Keep careful notes on what you have and have not done. Once you actually start performing the assignment, make a daily check of the work completed against the projected time schedule.

Figure 2-3 illustrates a Gantt chart. This chart is an excellent tool for comparing your planned work schedule against the actual time that is required to complete a task.

Complete a Task

You will be doubly rewarded when you stay with a task until it is complete:

1. You will feel satisfaction at having finished the task.
2. You will have saved time you otherwise would have lost checking up on where to begin.

Always think more about what you have accomplished than about what you still must get done. Enjoy the satisfaction that one naturally experiences from completing an assignment or reaching a goal. When you are working on a lengthy project that seems endless, break the assignment into segments that you can complete in a morning or an afternoon, or into even smaller parts that you can complete in an hour or two. Plan stopping places, and measure your accomplishment by the segments you have completed.

Figure 2-3 Gantt chart.

GANTT CHART

NAME OF PROJECT: Keyboarding Analysis NAME OF TEAM LEADER: Ilka Stiles

ESSENTIAL TASKS	CRITICAL DATES													
		May 01	May 03	May 05	May 07	May 09	May 11	May 13	May 15	May 17	May 19	May 21	May 23	May 25	
1. Design a questionnaire to examine the keyboarding equipment used in offices.	S														
	A														
2. Make appointments with admin. assistants to collect answers for questionnaires.	S														
	A														
3. Prepare and mail confirmation letters with attached questionnaires to admin. assistants.	S														
	A														
4. Interview admin. assistants to collect info. and questionnaires.	S														
	A														
5. Send each admin. assistant a thank you letter for his/her contribution.	S														
	A														
6. Collate, calculate and analyze the results of the questionnaires	S														
	A														
7. Prepare graphs to indicate results of information collected on questionnaires.	S														
	A														
8. Compose and edit report to describe the findings of the data.	S														
	A														
9. Keyboard, assemble and bind report.	S														
	A														
10. Submit report to general manager.	S														
	A														
	S														
	A														

S = Scheduled Time A = Actual Time

When you stay with a task until it is finished, you also decrease the risk of forgetting to perform part of it. If you must put work aside unfinished, make detailed notes of what still needs to be done. Make your notes carefully so that you can rely on them.

If there are numerous demands on your time, you may discover that you have many tasks started and none finished. If possible, do not start another one; instead, use your time to complete the ones you have started. However, if you meet callers and answer the telephone, you may have little control of your time. When you feel burdened by an accumulation of unfinished tasks and see no chance to catch up during regular hours, analyze your problem, discuss it with your manager, and consider the possible alternatives: Can someone relieve you of your routine work? Can someone assist you with the unfinished tasks? Should you work overtime?

Avoid Interruptions

Every challenging position that demands a variety of duties will be punctuated by numerous interruptions. There are ways of avoiding some interruptions.

1. Practise avoidance by organizing your work area so that it is less accessible to co-workers who wish to socialize during work hours. Try moving extra chairs away from your desk, or moving or angling your desk so that it cannot easily be seen by passers-by.

2. Interruptions are often caused by noise. You can avoid this type of interruption by having noisy equipment relocated away from your desk.

3. When you are working on a project that requires your full attention, ask another administrative assistant to handle your telephone calls; explain the urgency of your task to co-workers and then move to a location away from your desk.

Excuse Me!

Your success in coping with interruptions will depend on your attitude toward them and your ability to handle them and then resume work quickly.

You know that interruptions cannot always be prevented—the telephone will ring, a caller will walk in, a co-worker will ask you a question, your manager will need assistance. What you do not know is the precise moment when the interruption will occur.

Recognize that interruptions are a part of the job, and allow time for them in your planning. Keep a record of the number of telephone calls you receive in a typical day, the number of callers you receive, and the number of times you assist your manager and co-workers. Estimate the time consumed by these duties and determine how much time you have left for other tasks. Do not create your own frustrations by planning to accomplish more than you can get done.

> *"Avoid being a part of a clique."*
>
> Rhonda Sherb-Gillam, Graduate
> Nova Scotia Community College
> Akerley Campus

Do not resent interruptions. Keep calm; do not allow yourself to become upset. You will feel less frustrated if you know how much time you will need to perform each of your normal tasks. For example, keep a record of how long it takes to key a 2-page letter, to compose a 1-page memo, to develop a 12-page formal report, and to process the daily mail. This is useful information for future planning and scheduling. If you discover that you are running out of time to meet a deadline, decide for yourself which work can be postponed. Use your time for the priority item.

Give adequate time to handling each interruption. Do not appear to be rushed. Be courteous, but do not waste time because of an interruption. To reduce the time used for each interruption, proceed in the following way:

1. Mark your place as soon as you are interrupted—a light, erasable check mark in the margin with a soft-lead pencil will suffice.
2. Once you are interrupted, handle the interruption immediately if it can be dealt with in only a few minutes. If a co-worker asks for information, look it up and supply the information while the co-worker is at your desk. In response to a telephone call you can handle, follow through on the caller's request, even looking up information if you can do so without keeping the caller waiting a noticeable length of time. However, if the interruption requires prolonged attention, you may have to postpone action on it. Realize, however, that each time you must postpone following through on a request, you are creating a new item for your To Do List.
3. Quickly resume work where you left off at the time of the interruption. Do not encourage co-workers to linger in your office. Be courteous, but do not continue a telephone conversation beyond the time actually necessary to handle the call.
4. Avoid interrupting yourself because of lack of planning.
5. Keep a pencil in your hand, or keep your hands on the keyboard. These actions inform the visitor that you are eager to continue your work.
6. Do not get involved in office gossip. Small talk creates large interruptions.
7. When a co-worker drops into your office for a visit, stay standing. Often a person feels invited to sit if you are sitting. If the visitor sits down and you feel the need to sit, do so on the edge of your desk. This does not invite the visitor to become too comfortable.
8. When possible, hold meetings in another person's office. This allows you to leave as soon as the business is complete. Meeting with visitors in reception areas or conference rooms helps to keep the meeting short, since these areas often do not provide the privacy of an office.

When you must interrupt, be considerate of others. Wait until the other person is at a break in her or his work. Direct your questions to the correct person, and do not interrupt others unnecessarily. Do not ask others to answer questions if you can find the answers yourself by looking them up. Accumulate the questions you must ask your manager; then ask several at one time to cut down on interrupting her or him. A concise memo or electronic message enumerating your questions is an excellent way to avoid a direct interruption and to obtain a quick response.

Make a Daily Plan

At the end of the day review the work you must do the following day. Estimate the time each of your tasks will take and fit them one by one into time slots. Go through the same steps daily, and then leave your office with the satisfaction of knowing that your work is well organized for the following day. To prepare a systematic daily plan, you could proceed as follows:

1. Verify that everything you have entered into the computer during the day has been saved.

2. If you use an electronic calendar or desk calendar pads, make sure the appointment entries in your manager's calendar and yours are identical.
3. Go over your To Do List. If something on the list must be carried out the following day, enter it in your daily calendar. As you are planning your work, you will think of tasks that must be done sometime. Put notes about these on your To Do List.
4. Prepare a list of your manager's activities for the following day. Include on it all appointments, showing with whom, the purpose, the time, and where (if it is outside your manager's office). At the bottom of the sheet, add reminders of work your manager must complete during the day.
5. Locate the reports, correspondence, and other items you know your manager will need to refer to during conferences, or before he or she places a telephone call, writes a report, or carries out other responsibilities. Flag these with coloured stickers so that you can retrieve them quickly the following day. Likewise, locate the information you will need in order to proceed with your own work. Also make computer printouts of information you and your manager will need.
6. Complete your filing, and lock the files. As a part of your filing routine, transfer copies of completed work and the related supporting data from your work-in-progress folder to the file. All papers should be stored in cabinets, for protection from fire or perusal.
7. Clear your desk, putting everything in place.

The next morning:

1. Review the entries in your daily appointment calendar.
2. Place your manager's list of activities on his or her desk if you did not place them there the day before.

With this system, a few minutes after arriving at the office you should be working on one of your priority tasks.

Operate Within Easy Reach

Normal and maximum working areas at a desk have been established through motion studies. Materials and tools should be positioned within the normal working area if the worker is to attain maximum efficiency.

You can determine the *normal* working area of the desk for either the right or the left hand by swinging the extended hand and forearm across the desk. You can determine the *maximum* working area for either the right or the left hand by swinging the extended hand and the entire arm across the desk.

Before you begin a task at a desk or a table, place the equipment, supplies, and tools you will need in the normal working area.

Use the space in your desk to store supplies, stationery, and work in progress. Materials should pass across the top of your desk but should not be stored on it. Keep a minimum of items on top of your desk.

File all your work in progress together in one drawer, unless your manager is working on a project that generates so much paperwork that the materials must be subdivided into several folders. Allocate separate space in a vertical file drawer for a project of this magnitude. Never put a single folder of pending material in an unusual place—relocation of this material can lead to confusion and wasted time.

In case you might be absent, let your manager know where you keep the correspondence folder and other work in progress. If the work in progress is highly confidential, you may have to store it in file cabinets with special locks at night.

If you have a drawer that is not deep enough to hold file folders in vertical position, keep it empty. Use it as a temporary storage when you want to clear your desk to store the papers on which you are currently working—for instance, while you sort the mail or go to lunch.

Do not use sections of your desk for permanent storage. File copies of completed items immediately after completing an assignment so that you will not be searching in two places to locate one item. Furthermore, you will need the desk space to store the data for the new project you will be starting.

OFFICE ORGANIZATION

By organizing office supplies and the workstation, an administrative assistant can save a great deal of time, as well as save the company money. Following are some suggestions for getting the office supplies and workstation organized.

Organize the Office Supplies

1. Label the shelves where supplies are kept. This way staff members know where to look without interrupting you. This procedure also helps you keep track of supplies on hand.
2. Make sure that one person is responsible for controlling inventory and ordering supplies. This is a task that a senior administrative assistant will often delegate.

3. Develop your own requisition form. Keep these forms in the supply room. Staff will be expected to complete the form if they notice a product is running low. Be sure the form has room for a full description. Encourage the staff to fill in as much information as possible (descriptions, quantities, colours, sizes, unit numbers, and so on). This will simplify your work when it comes to completing the requisition for ordering.
4. Compose a list of all items you use on a regular basis. Include the item unit numbers, unit prices, descriptions, colours available, and so on. Post this list in the supply room along with a stack of the requisition forms you have developed. This is necessary if you expect staff members to partially complete the requisition forms.
5. Discourage staff members from placing verbal orders with you. This type of interruption can be very time-consuming: you must stop your work, listen to the request, write down the information, check the supplies, and perhaps get back to the staff members for further clarification. Insist that all orders are completed on requisition forms.
6. When staff members have rush orders, request that they fill in a requisition, mark it RUSH, and bring it to your desk.
7. Take inventory on a regular basis. Taking inventory once or twice a month on a designated day works well for most offices.
8. Before placing an order, compare prices between the office supply catalogues and advertisements sent to you. The office supply market is a competitive one, and you may be able to order your items on sale.
9. Ordering items in standard package sizes may save you money. Ordering items one at a time is short-sighted and expensive.
10. Do not over-order supplies, unless you are ordering supplies in standard-size packages. Too many supplies will cause confusion. Because space is often at a premium, excess supplies tend to create a storage problem. As well, some supplies have a shelf life: if not used before a certain date, they become less useful.
11. When you place an order, be prepared with all the required information. Having requisition forms returned or needing to make a follow-up telephone call to clarify an order will delay delivery.

Organize the Workstation

If your desk is cluttered it gives clients, co-workers, and managers the impression that you are disorganized. A cluttered desk is not necessarily a sign that you are busy; in fact a cluttered desk simply adds to your workload. It is essential that you purge any extraneous materials and then organize the materials you intend to keep.

Purge Unnecessary Items

One of the first steps to take in organizing your desk is to eliminate all that you don't need. Each time you pick up a document from your desk and wonder where to file it, ask yourself whether provincial legislation dictates that you must keep it. If not, consider the recycling box or the garbage bin.

If any of the following applies to a document, you have just cause to purge yourself of paper:

1. Another co-worker has filed it where you can access it if needed.
2. You will not really use the information, it is just *nice* to have. Remember that libraries have incredible amounts of reference materials that can be easily accessed.
3. The document is duplication. Once you get organized, one copy is all you need of any document.
4. The document is out of date. Newer information is usually better information. You can always get current information from the Internet, or from the reference section of the library. If the document pertains to your company, historical records may be kept in the central registry.
5. Chances are you will never find the time to read the information. If the information is "nice to know" rather than essential, rid yourself of it until you are organized.

You will find that you work much more efficiently after you have organized your desk.

Organize Necessary Items

Ridding your workstation of excess paper is only the first step in getting organized. The importance of a highly organized workstation cannot be emphasized enough.

One of the most frustrating time wasters is searching for information that has been filed incorrectly or has simply disappeared. Of course, employing the correct ARMA filing rules is imperative; these rules are discussed in Chapter 7. However, there is much more to organizing your workstation. When your workstation is highly organized, you save valuable time.

The following are some suggestions to help you get started:

1. If your workstation is currently in a cluttered condition, plan several uninterrupted hours you can use to attack the problem.

2. Once you have organized the workstation, take a mental snapshot of it and vow that you will never leave it disorganized at the end of the day. Start the day with a clear mind and a clear desk. Many offices now practise a **clean desk policy**, which stipulates that each evening employees must leave their desks in either a totally clear or very tidy condition.
3. If your office does not have a paper shredder, approach your manager about purchasing one. Employees are often reluctant to discard confidential material, so they let it accumulate in what eventually becomes a very thick folder tucked into a corner of the desk. Compact shredders can be placed on top of wastebaskets.
4. A basket placed in your workstation to hold work that is pending often becomes a storage bin. If you do not intend to work on a document immediately, file it in its appropriate labelled folder. Then place the folder in the file cabinet and make a comment in your calendar on the day this document must be dealt with. This way the phrase "out of sight—out of mind" will not apply.
5. Use one calendar for all your appointments. If you keep your personal appointments separate from your business appointments, you will constantly be referring to two calendars. This is a time waster and will result in disorganization. Take your calendar with you to every meeting and seminar you attend. Tuck your calendar into your briefcase at the end of each day so that you can continue to record personal appointments.
6. Learn to compose documents at your keyboard. By using a computer screen to compose documents, you avoid excess paper with letters and memos scratched on them. If the documents you compose can be mailed and filed electronically, you will never have to add a piece of paper to your filing cabinet.
7. Wherever you store information—drawers, cabinets, folders, baskets, and so on—affix a label that describes the type of information that should be stored in this location. While you are getting organized you will have stacks of paper. Organize them by placing a temporary label on the top of the pile. Not only will the labels assist you in locating information, but they will also assist others in your absence.
8. Attempt to follow this rule: *Never handle a piece of paper more than once*. At times this rule may be unrealistic, but it will force you to make a decision rather than procrastinate, then rehandle and reread a document.
9. Never use the surface of your desk as storage space. Your desk is a work area; you need all of it available to remain organized while you conduct your work.
10. Keep your computer reference information current. If names, addresses, and telephone numbers are indexed on your computer system, consider it a priority to update the system as often as possible. You cannot enjoy the efficiency of using a computer system unless it provides correct information.
11. Continually organize, purge, and alphabetize your filing system. When you discover a document out of place or out of date, take action immediately. Your filing cabinet is a work area you should take pride in. Refer to Chapter 7 for filing strategies.
12. Create a reference for frequently called telephone numbers. Place this reference list or fax nearby or code the numbers into the memory of the telephone or fax machine.
13. Place reference sources (books, CD-ROMs, diskettes) at an arm's length from your work area. These references should include a dictionary, a thesaurus, an administrative assistant's reference manual, procedures manuals, telephone directories, and the like. When you need these books you need them *now;* you should never have to look for any of them.
14. Paper clips are not a reliable tool for keeping pages together. In fact, your files should contain no paper clips. When you want to avoid pages being separated, staple them.
15. Do you really know what is in your desk and cabinets? Schedule 15 minutes every month to purge your current bookshelves, desk drawers, and cabinets. You must keep current with the contents of your workstation. Keep the wastebasket and recycling box handy; you should constantly purge your workstation of unwanted materials.
16. If there is a bulletin board in your workstation, be sure the information is current and well organized. If the bulletin board is not easy to use, it is just occupying space and adding to the office clutter. A bulletin board is sometimes an invitation to clutter; if not in use, you may consider removing the bulletin board.
17. After you take a telephone message, place the message in a designated location, off your desk. In this way you have dismissed the task immediately. You are then free to continue with your other tasks, and your desk is less cluttered.

18. Use coloured paper to coordinate your tasks. This will assist you in locating categories of information. Coloured paper draws attention. For example, you will be able to quickly spot blue telephone messages or green memos in a pile of white documents. Not only will the coloured paper help you get organized, but it will also draw the attention of others to requests for action or information that you place on their desks. Try using fluorescent-coloured paper when you want your interoffice requests to get immediate attention.
19. Keep the equipment you rely upon the most within easy reach; you should be able to slide your chair easily between the telephone, the computer, and facsimile machine, and so on.
20. Your workstation will require drawer space for office supplies. Store only a limited supply at your desk; store larger amounts away from your workstation in a supply cabinet. The small supplies you keep at your desk (stapler, tape, pens, clips, adhesive notes, and the like) can be stored with drawer organizers, which are sold at stationery stores. Letterhead, envelopes, forms, and other major paper supplies should be placed in drawer trays, not left out in visible stacks.
21. Your personal items need a place too; but do not crowd your desk surface with family photos. Leave the desk surface as clear as possible and place the photos on top of your **credenza** or filing cabinet. Coats and spare shoes should be stored in the coat room. Lunches and tea bags belong in the lunchroom. Awards belong on the walls. If your office contains plants, place small ones on the window ledge, credenza, and so on, and large ones on the floor. Keep personal items to a minimum. The workstation is professional space, not personal space.

THE ENVIRONMENTAL OFFICE

Administrative assistants can play an important part in making the office an environmentally conscious workplace. Consider the opportunities for recycling, reusing, and reducing that present themselves each workday.

Many organizations take their environmental responsibilities so seriously that it is often written into their Vision, Mission, and Values statements. Individual offices are similarly taking a more responsible approach to managing resources. Most companies are making a serious effort to recycle and reuse materials, reduce waste, and purchase products that have been recycled.

Become Part of an Environmentally Conscious Office

If your office has not yet committed itself to becoming environmentally conscious, you should initiate this change. Here are some suggestions:

1. First look at the coffee/lunchroom. Is the office still using paper or polystyrene plates and cups? If so, don't replace them when the supply is depleted. A set of reusable dishes is not expensive. Request that staff clean their own dishes after using them. Washing dishes is not the responsibility of an administrative assistant; recycling is everyone's responsibility!
2. Consider your duplication procedures. Are you still copying single-sided documents? You should duplex whenever possible.
3. When a number of office personnel need the same information, don't duplicate it. Place a routing slip on it.
4. Before you copy anything, check and double-check the document. This way, you won't have to discard a multiple set of documents if you find an error after the copying is complete.
5. When you must discard paper, ask yourself if the paper can be recycled. Special paper trays and bins for the collection of recyclable paper should be set around the office in convenient locations. See Figure 2-4, which shows the difference between a product that is recyclable and one that is recycled.
6. Facsimile cover sheets are often a waste of paper; they almost always end up in the wastebasket. Temporary adhesive fax-transmittal labels (see Figure 6-4 in Chapter 6) will often suffice. These small adhesive notes, approximately 8 by 8 cm, can be adhered to the first page of the fax, and are adequate when a lot of cover information is not necessary. They can be purchased in the form of adhesive pads in stationery stores.
7. It is easier to simply discard the used toner cartridges from copiers and printers than to return them to the manufacturer for recycling; however, discarding cartridges is a wasteful practice. Most manufacturers welcome the return of cartridges for recycling. In some cases, manufacturers and suppliers will refill your used cartridge and return the same to your office, thereby reducing costs and waste.
8. If a vending machine selling canned drinks is used in the office, place a box next to the

Figure 2-4 Signs depicting recycled or recyclable materials.

machine. Post a sign asking the staff to drop empty cans in the box. The cans will count up quickly. You can offer the cans or the proceeds from them to a local charity, or use the proceeds to buy the reusable dinnerware for your lunchroom.

9. When ordering office supplies, make a conscious effort to purchase recycled products; but keep in mind that the term *recycled* can be vague. Canadian manufacturers are now expected to publish the percentage of recycled material in the product along with the RECYCLED logo (see Figure 2-5). It is important to note that currently many copiers cannot handle paper that has a high percentage of recycled content; no doubt, manufacturers of copy machines will overcome this difficulty in the future. Nevertheless, most office needs (with the exception of copying) can be met with recycled paper.

If you cannot buy recycled products, buy those which are recyclable.

Your office personnel will have more ideas about responsible resource management that might pertain to your office. Continue to explore these options. Welcome their ideas and publish them in a monthly newsletter. Of course, the newsletter can be printed on recycled paper and rotated on a circulation slip. Remember, not everyone needs a separate copy.

Organize a Recycling Program

The above suggestions for becoming an environmentally conscious office will be important to your recycling campaign. If you wish to make the program a profitable one that is fully supported by all employees, the following procedures will assist you.

1. Get management to endorse your campaign. If you succeed in doing so, your company may make funds available and allocate staff to the new responsibilities created by this program.
2. Consider all possible office products you can recycle. Research the recycling market to see if there is a collector or buyer for this product. You may be able to make this program pay for itself. Note that some collectors *charge* you for the service of picking up your products, while others are willing to *pay* you for the used product.

Figure 2-5 Sample of product displaying percentage of recycled material.

This envelope is made of
100% recycled paper
and is recyclable

Cette enveloppe est
fabriquée de papier
100% recyclé et est
recyclable

3. Containers and signs will be required for collecting materials. If the collector will not provide containers and signs, you may be able to locate containers within the office and produce professional-looking signs on a desktop publishing system.
4. A manager or coordinator for this program will be essential. The major responsibility of this person will be to liaise between employees, management, buyers, and collectors. This person should develop procedures to be followed, put those procedures in place, and ensure that they are followed. Additional tasks that may be delegated are:
   a. setting up contracts with collectors and purchasers.
   b. researching each individual department to find out which products they use have potential for recycling.
   c. determining where collection bins will be placed.
   d. educating the staff about the importance of participation, the company's commitment to the program, and the procedures to be followed.
   e. placing posters on bulletin boards, or articles in the company newsletter. This program and the efforts supplied by employees deserve attention. Further promotion and recognition can be gained by contacting the local media.
   f. monitoring the program. Continual follow-up and monitoring will be necessary to ensure the success of the program. This can take the form of visually checking the recycle containers to measure their use, or even designing a feedback form so the employees may voice their opinions on the success of the program.

All offices, regardless of size or location, can institute a resource-recovery program. While it requires careful planning and monitoring, the benefits to the office and (especially) to the environment will far outweigh the efforts made.

Questions for Study and Review

1. Who has been credited with founding the Total Quality Management movement?
2. Explain why Canadian businesses are now adopting the TQM initiative.
3. How will TQM change the way the administrative assistant works?
4. Explain how customer complaints may be handled by a company practising TQM.
5. Distinguish between effectiveness and efficiency.
6. What effect will an executive's work preferences have on the way the administrative assistant's daily work is organized?
7. Who should establish an understanding of priorities with all the members of the office team?
8. List categories of information that an administrative assistant should concentrate on as the new job is being explained.
9. Suggest ways that an administrative assistant can take initiative in learning a new job.
10. Should all segments of the working day be structured? Explain.
11. Why should details be recorded immediately?
12. What are the advantages of keeping the work you have in progress carefully organized?
13. Describe how to get a head start on the day's work.
14. Give examples of similar tasks that can be grouped.
15. What can you do to stop procrastinating over a large project?
16. What does the phrase "work smarter, not harder" mean?
17. Describe how to organize work to conserve energy.
18. In order to get work right the first time, what should you do before actually performing the task?
19. What effect has computer technology had on accuracy?
20. Make a list of routine tasks that can be performed between major tasks.
21. What are the primary advantages of sticking with a task until it is finished?
22. How should you manage a lengthy assignment that continues for days or weeks?
23. Suggest three ways to avoid interruptions before they occur.
24. Suggest three ways to deal successfully with interruptions once they have occurred.
25. What is considered the normal working area at a desk?
26. Why should you discourage staff members from verbally placing supply requests?
27. Suggest five ways to determine whether a piece of paper should be discarded rather than filed.
28. Suggest five ways to demonstrate environmental consciousness in your office.
29. Suggest four ways to make a recycling program cost recoverable.

Spelling Reinforcement

admitting	concentrate	environmental	recognize
calendar	conscious	interruption	requisition
categories	deliberate	precedence	resourcefulness
chronological	effectiveness	procedures	systematic
cognizant	efficiency	procrastination	throughout

On-the-Job Situations

1. You have a new job. You have been working for three weeks. Each afternoon before leaving work, you carefully plan your work for the next day. You are having difficulty keeping up with your plan because the telephone rings continually. You seem to be spending a lot of time on the telephone. In fact, you are becoming frustrated because you must answer so many telephone calls. What are the solutions to your problem?
2. When you started working for Mr. Chow, he suggested that filing was a low-priority item and that you should let filing go until you do not have other work to do. You have followed his suggestion for four weeks, and the papers in your filing baskets are about to reach the ceiling. You never seem to find the time to file. The problem is compounded when Mr. Chow calls for a paper and you must go through the unfiled stacks to find what he wants. What can you do to solve your filing problem?
3. Your manager, Ms. Polowski, writes many reports. She usually works on the reports on Monday, Tuesday, and Wednesday. On Thursday morning she hands you enough material written in longhand to keep you keyboarding all day. The final reports are prepared by the word processing operators, who request that all material coming to them be keyboarded in rough draft form. They will not accept material written in longhand. On Friday as soon as the completed reports come back, you spend about two hours checking them to make sure they are accurate and that everything has been included. You enjoy keyboarding the drafts and proofreading the reports. However, you are becoming frustrated because you are letting your other work go. What are the solutions to this problem? What can you do to relieve your frustration?

Special Reports

1. How many unfinished projects do you have? Are you burdened with the thought that "everything is started and nothing is finished"? Make a list of your unfinished projects and tasks. Select the one you can finish in the least amount of time and complete it. Select another task that you can complete in a few minutes and then complete it. Notice how you lighten your load by finishing tasks. Use what you have discovered to remind yourself to finish tasks as soon as possible, thus leaving your mind free to tackle new assignments. Write a memorandum to your instructor about what you learned.
2. Are you using your time effectively? To find out, keep a record. Begin by keeping a list of minor tasks that you perform between major tasks. Leave space to the right of each item on your list. As you complete each minor task, jot down the date, the time, and the number of minutes used. For example, did you pay unplanned attention to the postage? Did you package up literature for transfer to another branch office? Did you search for stationery that was not to be found in the appropriate location? At the end of one week, analyze your list for similar tasks, for redundant tasks, and for those tasks that were the result of interruptions. Add the time spent for each category and then multiply the time by 52 for an estimate of the time spent in a year. Write a brief report for your instructor that summarizes your findings and suggests methods to manage your minor-task time more effectively.

Production Challenges

2-A Setting Priorities

Supplies needed:

- *Daily Plan Chart, Form 2-A, page 384*

The time is 0900, Monday, June 2, and you have enough work to keep you busy for one week. Mr. Wilson is leaving on a business trip at noon today. At 0800 Mr. Wilson dictated three letters and discussed with you work to be done in his absence.

Here are the notes you took during your conference with Mr. Wilson:

1. Send copies of the combined sales report for the week of May 19 to the four regional managers. (You will use a copier to make copies of the sales summary from a computer printout.)
2. Call J.R. Rush, Assistant Vice-President of Marketing, Eastern Region, Extension 534, and ask him to see David Walters, an out-of-town supplier, who had an appointment with Mr. Wilson for Wednesday, June 4, at 1000.
3. Transcribe the letter to Allen Fitzgerald. Mr. Wilson stressed that it must be mailed today. The letters to Nancy Evans and Robert Berger may be mailed tomorrow.
4. Make a daily digest of the incoming mail. Hold all mail for Mr. Wilson to answer. Call Mr. Wilson if something is urgent.
5. Write a letter to Nancy Cromwell, Regina, telling her that Mr. Wilson will accept her invitation to speak at the National Sales Conference in Regina on November 28 at 1430.
6. Rekey the last two pages of the talk that Mr. Wilson gave at the local Chamber of Commerce and send a copy of the talk to Art Winfield so that he will receive it by Friday afternoon. (Art Winfield has a local address.)
7. Call Mr. Levine, Assistant Vice-President of Marketing, Northwestern Region, Extension 536, to remind him that Mr. Wilson will be out of town for the week. Mr. Wilson counts on Mr. Levine to represent him when Mr. Wilson cannot attend weekly Executive Committee meetings, held every Wednesday at 1000.
8. Make copies of an article on time management and distribute them to the four assistant vice-presidents of marketing.
9. Call Creighton's Restaurant at 555-0611 to set up a luncheon meeting for Monday, June 9, at 1230 for 12 members of the planning committee for the November Sales Seminar.
10. Call Canadian Airlines International at 555-1414 to cancel Mr. Wilson's reservation to Vancouver on Wednesday, June 4.

The assistant vice-presidents have left the following work in your in-basket:

1. A six-page report written by Mrs. Linda Yee to be keyed in final form by Wednesday afternoon.
2. A note from Mr. Rush asking you to obtain on-line the sales figures for the four regions for the week of May 26. He wrote, "Please key the figures on cards so that I may refer to them in a staff meeting at 1000 on Tuesday."
3. A note from Mr. Levine asking you to copy the figures he has circled in red on the computer printout. He wrote, "I need this information by 1400 today (Monday). Just key them on a couple of cards."
4. A revised 12-page report written by Ms. Charlene Azam. She needs to receive the completed report on Friday to review it before she presents it to Mr. Wilson on Monday, June 9. (You stored the first draft of this report on a diskette. You will need to keyboard the revisions.)

Before you begin working on these tasks, take a Daily Plan Chart, Form 2-A, from your desk, write down the work to be done, and assign priorities to the items.

2-B Correcting Letters

Supplies needed:

- *Plain paper*

Correct the spelling and capitalization errors in the two letters. List the incorrect words, correctly spelled, on a separate sheet of paper. Keyboard the two letters in an acceptable letter style.

(Current date) Mrs. M.M. Freedman, Financial Manager, Super Stove Store, 4909–50 Avenue, Red Deer, AB, T4N 4A7. Each year Millennium Appliances, Inc., provides you with a complete anual statement of the debits and credits made with our company. However, the statement we are curenntly enclosing includes all tranactions that occured during this past year, with the exception of those for the month of September and October. (P) You will recall that during those months, we ofered our retail customers a 30 percent discount on all colored appliances. Unfortunately, however, we neglected to include this discount on our new computerized accounting system. Therefore, your statement does not reflect this discount; when this oversite is corrected, we will forward an updated statement to you. We expect to have your corected statement in the mail within the next too weeks. Please except our apologies for any inconvenience this may cause. (P) If you have any additional conserns about the statement, please call our office. We look forward to your continued business in the year a head. Sincerely, William Wilson, Vice President of Marketing.

(Current date) Miss Lori Anderson, 630 Beach Blvd., Hamilton, ON, L8H 6Y4. Thank you for submiting your oficial transcript and resume as applicant for the position of administrative assistent. (P) This year their have been many well qualified canidates expressing intrest in employment at Millennium Appliances, Inc. We have not fill all the positions for administrative assistents. Because of the definate promise you education and experience reflect, we know you have much to offer and employer. (P) In the mean time we shall keep your credantials on active file for six months in case another opening ocurrs for which you qualify. You intrest in applying for employment with our organization and your cooperation in submiting the neccesary information requested of you is appreciated. Cordially Yours, William Wilson, Vice President of Marketing.

World Wide Websites

Total Quality Management and ISO 9000 Resources on the Internet

http://fiat.gslis.utexas.edu/~rpollock/tqm.html
This site provides a series of Internet links that serve as a layperson's guide to Total Quality Management and ISO 9000 information.

Day-Timer

www.daytimer.com/
Day-Timer users gain access to free software, a time tip of the day, and technology products. They can also meet other Day-Timer users, and browse the Day-Timer store and Day-Timer Resource Centre.

Green Office Tips

www.greenworld.com.au/WasteR.html
This on-line newsletter explores green office practices and technology. It includes articles on office paper recycling, printer consumables, recycling floppy disks, and many other topics.

CHAPTER 3

Organization Structure and Office Layout

Outline

Organization Structure
Classifications of Authority
Line Organization
Line-and-Staff Organization
Participatory Management
Divisions of Work
Organization Chart
Informal Organization

Office Layout
Arrangement of the Open Office
Decor
Consider the Hi-Tech Office

Ergonomics
Furniture
Lighting
Acoustics
Position and Posture

Learning Outcomes

At the completion of this chapter, the student will be able to:

1. Compare the structure of line organization with the structure of line-and-staff organization.
2. Compare participatory management with the line-and-staff management style.
3. Interpret an organization chart.
4. Describe the physical features of the landscaped office.
5. Assess the advantages and disadvantages of working in an open office.
6. Describe how office ergonomics involve furniture, lighting, acoustics, and position of equipment in the office.

GRADUATE PROFILE

Greta Gould
Law Clerk

Martin & Hillyer Barristers and Solicitors

College Graduation:
Legal Assistant
Mohawk College
Hamilton, Ontario
1994

As a law clerk, Greta Gould is dependable, flexible, and dedicated to her clients' needs. She believes her most important responsibility is to develop a good rapport with her clients. "It is extremely important my clients trust me and feel that I am approachable. The law is very complicated and it is very important that my clients feel comfortable enough with me that they are at ease when asking about the process." Greta generally works with victims of motor vehicle accidents and medical malpractice where she must be compassionate and understanding of each individual situation.

By being a member of the Ontario Trial Lawyers Association, Law Clerks Division, Greta keeps current on legal practices and procedures. She must work independently with initiative and efficiency in order to meet the very demanding deadlines of her position. To meet her aggressive schedule, Greta organizes her office environment and her procedures. She relies upon e-mail to remain efficient and productive throughout the day and uses the computer to organize precedent documents so they are easily accessible.

Besides having a busy professional schedule, Greta finds time to volunteer in her community as an organizer for the Hamilton's Canusa Games and as an advocate for the needy.

Greta strongly believes in goal setting. Despite personal barriers as a student, she achieved an honours diploma and an award for overall academic achievement from Mohawk College. Following graduation, she quickly found a rewarding career where she continues to work with an appreciative and supportive employer. According to Greta "Never give up on your goals. Even when the odds are against you, your goals can be achieved."

"Focusing on the positive will result in greater productivity from any individual."

In any business, industrial, or institutional organization, a formal structure is established to designate authority and responsibility. Subdivisions of work are established for carrying out and coordinating the activities essential for meeting the objectives of the organization.

The people who handle the flow of paperwork that accompanies the activities of the organization have individual workstations or offices. The arrangement of the workstations contributes to the effectiveness of the flow of information; consequently, modern offices are carefully designed.

ORGANIZATION STRUCTURE

The traditional organization structure emphasizes people-to-people relationships. The modern concepts in organization structure, on the other hand, are centred on the flow of information and on the communications needs for decision making, and involve a systems approach to organization structure. Regardless of the approach used, chains of command, authority, and responsibility must be established.

Classifications of Authority

Three main types of authority can be found within a typical organization. The different types of authority exist to enable managers to perform their duties and are:

1. line
2. staff
3. functional.

Line managers are those who contribute directly to the organization's goals. They are said to have line authority which is an authority that follows an organization's direct chain of command. *Staff managers* provide advice and expertise in support of the line managers. They are considered to be contributing indirectly to achieving the organization's goals. Staff managers have staff authority.

A staff manager usually advises line managers and makes recommendations. However, line managers have the final say in accepting or rejecting the recommendations of staff managers.

Functional authority allows staff managers to broaden their authority to limited line authority relating directly to staff expertise. For example, the vice-president of Human Resources at Central Office may have functional authority over Human Resources personnel in regional offices. See Figure 3-1.

To recognize the chain of command in any organization, you need to understand how the authority has been established. You also need to recognize that an executive can have line authority, staff authority, or functional authority.

Line Organization

The oldest type of organization structure is **line organization**, which is based on line authority only. It is often referred to as the *military* model. Authority is delegated from top management to middle management. The middle managers are in charge of specific activities, and in turn delegate authority to supervisors who are in charge of workers carrying out their operational duties.

Line authority flows in a straight line from the president to the supervisor. If there are several top executives, the authority flows from the president to the vice-presidents to managers to supervisors. If the organization is a large one, probably more than one level of middle managers will be established.

The chain of command is easy to determine under line organization. However, line organization is used primarily by small businesses and units of government. Large companies and institutions are too complex to rely on line organization only.

Line-and-Staff Organization

The most frequently established formal structure is **line-and-staff organization**. Line-and-staff organization is effective because the staff managers are specialists in their areas and are available to assist and advise the line managers throughout the organization. Functions staff managers may serve include staffing (human resources), corporate accounting, and public relations.

Staff managers are influential in the decision-making process. Besides assisting and advising line managers and making recommendations, a staff manager may have line authority. Staff managers are often given line authority under the systems approach to organization structure.

However, line-and-staff organizations are often fraught with problems. Many staff positions are located in corporate headquarters and the perception of a typical line manager is that:

- Staff managers assume authority they do not have.
- Staff managers interfere with the *real work* being accomplished in the line organization.
- Staff management advice often causes conflict in *the front line*.
- Staff managers offer no support after they have made a strategic decision.
- Staff managers take credit for the results of a decision that line staff implement.

Conversely, staff managers often feel that they are experts in their field and may resent feedback when:

- Line managers reject the direction of staff managers.
- Line managers avoid interaction with the staff organization.
- Line managers adopt a "can't do" approach to staff organization recommendations.

Figure 3-1 Typical line and staff functions and functional authority.

Line Functions	**Staff Functions**	**Functional Authority** (examples)
Product Manufacturing	Public Relations	• Corporate Accounting asks all divisions for financial reports.
Sales	Corporate Accounting	• The Human Resource Department will facilitate the staff's performance management reports.
Marketing	Management Information Systems (MIS)	• Marketing Research may launch a new corporate-wide initiative.
Technical Support	Legal	
Finance	Human Resources	

- Line managers placate staff managers by acknowledging advice and recommendations but never implementing them.

The ability to recognize the authority that staff managers have will be an asset to you in your dealings with managers throughout the organization in which you work. However, recognizing the authority that staff managers have is not easy. Studying the organization chart will not reveal all you need to know. Be observant; watch for the functions for which the staff manager makes recommendations but does not have the final say.

Participatory Management

The concept of **participatory management** has existed for a long time, but in the past was used only on a small scale. In isolated situations, project teams have been formed, bringing together employees who have the skills necessary for specific projects.

Organizations today, in an effort to increase productivity and meet competition, are focusing on participatory management. This management style is in contrast to the traditional line-and-staff management style. Employees work in smaller units within large organizations and are encouraged to communicate with different levels of management. Employees are being asked for input about their areas of responsibility and often are brought together in conferences to discuss and offer solutions to organizational problems.

"I have an open door policy. I let people feel comfortable to come in and ask questions or ask for help anytime that they require it."

Karen Hodgson, Graduate
Okanagan University College

Under participatory management, each employee reports to someone in the formal structure.

You should be aware that opportunities to participate in group discussions and to offer suggestions may exist where you work, and that you should accept your responsibility in making valuable contributions.

Divisions of Work

Work is divided according to the main objectives of the organization, and then further subdivided into manageable parts. The parts may be called *divisions*, *departments*, *units*, or some other appropriate title.

The main activities being carried out govern the divisions of work. For example, a manufacturer of toys would be concerned with procurement of raw materials, the actual manufacture of the toys, and distribution and sales. Natural divisions of work would be purchasing, production, and sales. The production division could be subdivided according to the kinds of toys manufactured. The divisions of work in a hospital could be according to the services rendered—for instance, a cardiac unit, a dialysis unit, a plastic surgery unit, and so on.

Other work divisions are needed to support the main functions of the organization. Many organizations have a personnel department and a financial department. Service departments are needed to carry out support activities such as office operations, mail processing, data processing, security, and building maintenance.

Organization Chart

An **organization chart** is a graphic illustration of the formal structure of an organization. See Figure 3-2. To understand an organization chart, look for lines of authority, existing divisions of work, and the relationship of the work groups to one another. If an organization manual exists, descriptions of the work divisions and of the positions shown on the organization chart will be provided in it.

As an administrative assistant, you may be asked to update or draw an organization chart. Begin by preparing an outline showing those functions of work which are on the same management level, and those which are subordinate. To save time, get the outline and the draft of the chart approved by the proper executive before you print the chart in final form. Getting approval is important, because the organizational relationship thought to exist by those performing certain functions may not be the one that is intended.

When preparing an organization chart, you must be aware that managers are sensitive about where they are in the organization structure; this means that you may find a manager who is reluctant to discuss his or her location on the chart with you. If so, your manager or someone at a higher level of management should talk with that person. Other resources to aid in the construction of an organization chart may be the human resources department, or simply the organization's telephone directory.

The titles shown in an organization chart may be expressed as either functions or positions, but the form chosen should be used consistently throughout. Functions that occupy the same level of management should be shown on the same horizontal line, as illustrated by the vice-presidential positions in Figure 3-2. Line authority is indicated by solid lines. Staff authority is indicated by broken lines.

A crowded organization chart is difficult to read. You may have to prepare one chart to show the main functions and then provide supporting charts to indicate subordinate functions under each main function.

Figure 3-2 Organization chart.

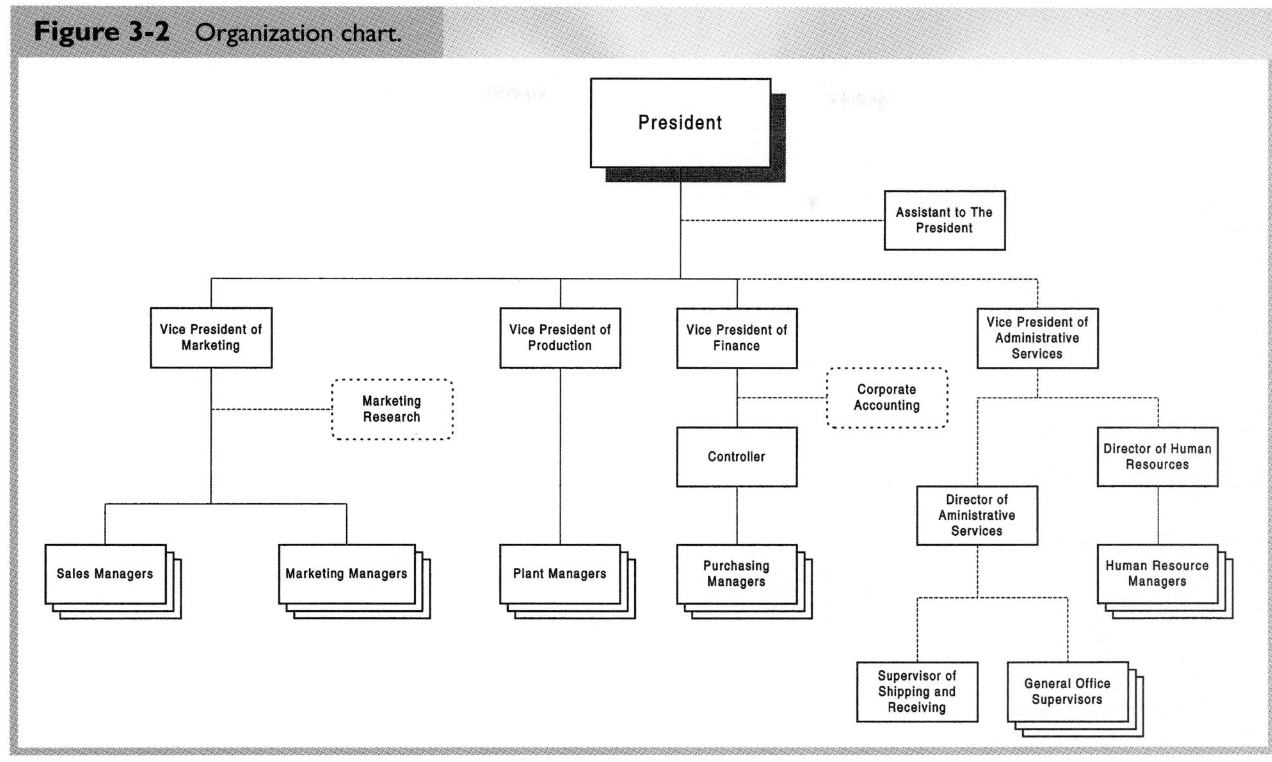

Informal Organization

Informal organization is a natural grouping of individuals according to personality preferences and interests. Informal organization is not created; it exists in every situation in which individuals are relating to one another.

Informal organization satisfies certain social needs; it also can become a channel of communication, referred to as the **grapevine**. The grapevine is used extensively where official channels are not meeting the organization's communication needs.

An informal leader usually exists within every informal organization. This leader is not designated—she or he becomes the leader as a natural outgrowth of the needs of the group. The group looks to the leader for guidance, and the leader is its spokesperson.

Managers in the formal structure need the support of the informal organization, and often use it as a supplementary means for carrying out the objectives of the organization, or for propogating information.

Managers can change formal organization because they created it. They cannot change the informal organization or make it go away. Wise managers will be aware of the natural groupings of individuals. Managers should be aware of the influence these groupings have on one another, and of the influence they have in furthering or impeding the objectives of the organization. Recognize that managers need the support of the informal organization but beware of your own involvement. Many office professionals are privy to confidential information that should not find its way to the grapevine. Unauthorized distribution of such information will be seen a serious violation of trust and professional responsibilities, and may result in dismissal.

OFFICE LAYOUT

In recent years the popular office layout has been the **open office**, designed without conventional walls, corridors, or floor-to-ceiling partitions. See Figure 3-3. The open office is often refered to as a **landscaped office** when it has a layout that has been well designed.

The open office concept grew out of the need for:

1. better work and communication flow
2. better and more flexible use of space
3. improved ventilation and lighting
4. a cooperative environment.

A well-planned design results in an attractive environment and improved employee morale. Also, open offices cost less to construct and reconfigure than enclosed offices.

Although the open office plan is popular, a compromise is usually made: the plan is designed to allow for both open and closed spaces. For personnel whose work

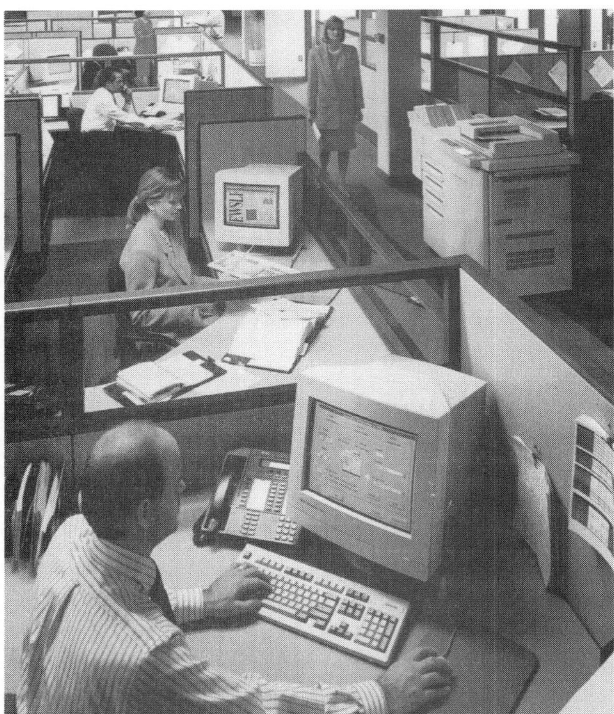

Figure 3-3 Open office layout.
Courtesy of Xerox Canada Ltd.

is of a confidential nature, or for personnel who need privacy in order to concentrate and be creative, the traditional private office is still more practical.

Arrangement of the Open Office

Offices of employees whose work is related because of the kind of information being processed are often located in the same proximity. This is especially true when employees are primarily dealing with hard-copy material such as drawings, pre-printed forms, or models.

Free-standing partitions are used to form individual **workstations**. The partitions usually do not go to the ceiling, but are high enough to eliminate distractions and provide some privacy. The worker has the feeling of being with others. In some offices, file cabinets and large plants are also used as space dividers.

The workstations are arranged at angles in various configurations, in contrast to the monotonous effect of rows of separate enclosed offices. The arrangement of the workstations follows the natural flow of the papers being processed. Workers who need to talk about their work are placed in close proximity to one another.

The supervisor may occupy a semi-private office in the area with the workers under his or her supervision. It is private enough for conferences, yet is arranged in such a way that the workers are in the supervisor's line of vision.

In a well-planned office, ample space is provided for easy movement from one workstation to another. Aisles follow the natural traffic pattern, which is usually not a straight line. Lighting, heating, air conditioning, and humidity are easier to control when the partitions do not go to the ceiling. The result is overhead lighting diffused over the entire work area. **Task lighting** may be used in addition to the ambient overhead lighting, to provide additional lighting where required. Better airflow and reduced energy costs should result from the open plan.

Decor

Colours that blend tastefully are used throughout each landscaped area. The colour scheme is harmonious, yet many contrasting colours are used to break up the monotony of look-alike stations.

The partitions may be curved, adding grace to the design. The wall-to-wall carpeting and the fabric surfaces of the partitions add elegance. Growing plants are placed throughout the area to provide privacy, individuality, and beauty.

Living decorations, such as plants and aquariums stocked with tropical fish, add to personal enjoyment and interpersonal needs during working hours.

Decorative appointments such as attractive light fixtures are also used. Because the decor of the landscaped area is artistically planned, it is aesthetically pleasing—an important factor in maintaining employee morale.

Consider the Hi-Tech Office

When electronic equipment is brought into the office, many problems accompany it.

The electronic equipment may not fit on the existing desks. If three pieces of equipment are needed—such as a keyboard, a computer, and a printer—more space may be occupied by equipment than previously, and the work area may become crowded. Purpose-built office furniture can be purchased to provide a more efficient use of available space.

Some electronic equipment also brings noise into the office; impact printers are especially noisy. However, sound hoods on impact printers can remedy this situation. Switching to laser or ink-jet printers will also reduce noise.

Research indicates that workers who spend long periods of time at a computer station may suffer from a number of health problems. Complaints arise about eyestrain, backaches, muscle tension in the shoulder and neck, and headaches. The greatest complaint of office workers has been about screen glare and reflection. Antiglare shields that fit over screens are available to combat this problem.

Figure 3-4 Lateral files adjacent to desk.
Courtesy of Shaw-Walker Company

However, **flat technology** monitors and nonglare treatments to screens have eliminated the need for these shields. Proper placement of the screen within the office and the use of adjustable window coverings also help to eliminate glare and reflection.

Most organizations recognize the importance of an environmentally friendly office; many work actively to improve conditions to make the office a better place to work. Management will often seek your advice in the design and optimal positioning of operational equipment such as computers, printers, and copiers. The proactive office professional will be prepared to make positive contributions to issues pertaining to office design and layout.

"I believe that you have to enjoy your job first to become successful."

Debbie Siscoe, Graduate
Nova Scotia Community College
Burridge Campus

ERGONOMICS

The science of adapting the workplace to suit the worker is called **ergonomics**; it was previously known as *human factors engineering*. The office environment should be as safe, healthy, comfortable, and productive as possible. Everything that affects the worker must be taken into consideration—furniture, lighting, amount of space, quality of air, heating and cooling, acoustics, and placement of the equipment in relation to the worker.

Furniture

Office furniture manufacturers have designed **modular furniture** to carry out the landscaped office concept. Modular furniture consists of separate components that can be fitted together in various arrangements to meet the needs of users.

pro-Link

The popularity of virtual offices—offices located wherever employees happen to be—has increased the number of office professionals who work outside the confines of the traditional office building. These telecommuters—travellers by way of telecommunications technology—must chose their workspace carefully. It is quite possible that you will become a telecommuter, perhaps working from home, so here are a few planning tips for *your* new home office:

- Locate the office as far away from temptation as possible: the cookie jar, the fridge, etc.
- Give yourself some business atmosphere; put a clock on the wall; provide yourself a coffee station, or a water cooler.
- Buy comfortable, purpose-built office furniture—you'll be spending a lot of time at the desk.
- Treat yourself to a decent sound system, but don't install a television.
- Make full use of available technology: a fast and capable computer, fax machine, telephone company services, or a wireless headset for example.
- Use your telephone company's voice mail and conference services—they appear more professional.
- Ensure you have adequate and timely support for the technology on which you will depend.

Modern desks are narrower than conventional ones, and have fewer drawers. Some of them resemble tables with modesty panels. The modern workstation usually provides more working space than that available in a conventional office. Modular furniture can be arranged in many different configurations, giving the worker additional space on one side of the desk, behind the worker, or both. Some desks are adjustable.

If the worker's duties change, creating a need for a change in working surface, the modular furniture can easily be rearranged.

The chair is one of the most important pieces of furniture in the office. A poorly designed or incorrectly adjusted chair can be a major contributor to physical discomfort. The height of the chair seat should be easily adjustable to accommodate the individual's height and size; the chair should provide adequate back support.

When the operator is seated, the angle at the knee should be 90°; thighs should be parallel to the floor;

most of the operator's weight should be supported by the buttocks, not the thighs.

Storage space may be integrated; easy-to-reach shelves can be added above the desk. Sometimes shelves are hung on a partition at the back of the desk. Credenzas can be included in the arrangement. However, storage space for files, or for manuals and books not currently in use, is not provided at a workstation. Separate work islands are often provided for processing mail, assembling materials, and performing other highly repetitive jobs.

Lighting

In addition to the diffused lighting over the entire area, referred to as **ambient lighting**, light fixtures are provided over individual workstations so that the intensity and direction of light for the worker's needs can be controlled. This is referred to as task lighting.

Windows are the greatest source of computer screen reflection and reading problems. A screen that faces directly into or away from a window can cause eyestrain. For this reason, windows should be covered by adjustable blinds. As well, antiglare shields that cover the screen and flat-technology monitors should be purchased to reduce or even eliminate glare.

Proper placement of lighting is also crucial; a light source directly behind the computer screen causes stress on the eyes of the worker, who must face the light source while using the terminal. The opposite case is also a problem: a light source directly behind the worker will result in direct glare on the screen. Generally, the best orientation for a light source is for it to shine over the left shoulder of a right-handed worker (over the right shoulder of a left-handed worker). The reason for this has to do with the shoulder action of the employee. A right-handed worker tends to lean forward in such a way that the right shoulder blocks light coming from the right side; this creates a shadow on the documents in front of the body.

Acoustics

Engineers must plan proper acoustical control so that sound does not disturb office work and conversations cannot be easily overheard.

Wall-to-wall carpeting, because of its sound-absorbing qualities, is used throughout the area. The free-standing partitions are covered with carpeting or fabric. Ceilings are equipped with baffles. Sound-reflecting surfaces are limited or avoided.

Although manufacturers are making office equipment that runs more quietly than earlier models, much more must be done to control noise in the office environment. **White sound**, a continuous masking noise that is evenly distributed, can be generated electronically. Floor-to-ceiling partitions are available to help combat the problem of office noise.

Position and Posture

In addition to the office environment, good work habits, correct keyboarding techniques and posture are important for prevention of **musculoskeletal** problems. Figure 3-5 illustrates proper posture at the computer, which can only be achieved with the correct positioning of equipment. Note that the chair and keyboard are set so that the thighs and forearms are parallel with the floor, and that the wrists are straight and level. If the table is too high to permit this, you should find an adjustable chair or you may need to put the keyboard in your lap.

While you are keyboarding, your wrists should not rest on anything, and should not be bent up, down, or to the side. Your arms should move your hands around instead of resting your wrists and stretching to hit keys with the fingers. When you stop typing for a while, rest your hands in your lap and/or on their sides instead of leaving them on the keyboard. Wrist rests are available and give you a place to rest your hands when pausing from keyboarding. They are not designed to rest your wrists while you are keyboarding.

In the illustration, you will note that the keyboarder is sitting straight, not slouching, and does not have to stretch forward to reach the keys or read the screen. A good posture isn't just about your hands and arms, but also about the use or misuse of your shoulders, back and neck. These areas may be even more important than what's happening down at your wrists.

Anything that creates awkward reaches or angles in the body may create discomfort. However, even a

Figure 3-5 Proper posture at the computer.

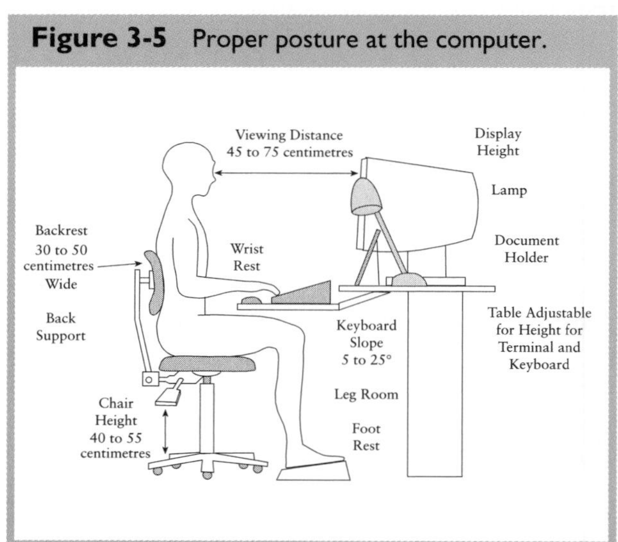

perfect posture may result in problems if it is held rigidly for long periods of time.

Here are basic tips to avoid discomfort while keyboarding:

- Relax.
- Use a light touch. Do not "pound" on the keys.
- Move and shift positions frequently.
- Wrists should not be bent to the side, but instead your fingers should be in a straight line with your forearm as viewed from above.
- Use an adjustable keyboard tray that permits optimal positioning, or tilt the back edge of your keyboard down and slightly away.
- Use two hands to perform double-key operations like Ctrl-C or Alt-F, instead of twisting one hand to do it.
- Move your whole hand to hit function keys with your strong fingers instead of stretching to reach them.
- Stretch and relax frequently. Momentary breaks every few minutes and longer breaks every hour or so work well.
- Hold the mouse lightly, do not grip it hard or squeeze it. Place it where you don't have to reach up or over. Place it close to the keyboard or learn and use keyboard equivalent commands.
- Keep your arms and hands warm. Cold muscles and tendons are at much greater risk for overuse injuries, and many offices are over-air-conditioned.
- Do not tuck the telephone between your shoulder and your ear so that you can type and talk on the phone at the same time. This common procedure aggravates your neck, shoulders and arms.
- Pay attention to your body. Aches and pains are your body's signal that it's in discomfort. Learning what is comfortable or awkward for your body before you're in pain may prevent injury.

Questions for Study and Review

1. Why is a formal organization structure established within businesses, industries, and institutions?
2. Compare line and staff authority.
3. How does line-and-staff organization differ from line organization?
4. Why is it difficult for an observer to determine the authority of a staff manager?
5. What determines the divisions of work of the productive operations of a manufacturing company?
6. What is an organization chart?
7. Describe how functional authority might help a staff manager who is located in the organization's head office.
8. What is meant by informal organization?
9. What is the grapevine? How can managers use the grapevine effectively?
10. Why should an administrative assistant be aware of informal organization?
11. Why should an administrative assistant be aware of the trend toward participatory management?
12. What is the open office designed to accomplish?
13. Describe the partitions in an open office.
14. Suggest three problems that accompany the introduction of electronic equipment into the office.
15. What is the meaning of the term *ergonomics?*
16. Differentiate between *task lighting* and *ambient lighting*.
17. Explain how noise can be controlled in the office.
18. Describe the proper physical position for a person seated at a keyboard.
19. Give four suggestions to avoid discomfort while keyboarding.

Spelling Reinforcement

acoustics
ambient
authority
configurations
credenzas
decor
distractions
emphasizes
ergonomics
government
guidance
influence
manufactured
modular
observant
organization
participatory
partitions
preferences
recommendations
reluctant
structure
subordinate
supplementary

On-the-Job Situations

1. Your manager, Mr. Wrigley, has 35 employees reporting to him. When he receives a memorandum from top management, he dictates portions of it, condensing much of the material, and asks you to keyboard and make copies of what he has dictated for distribution to the 35 employees. The employees often do not understand the summaries distributed to them and come to you for clarification. One co-worker, James Ellis, has demanded that he see the original memorandum. Should you show him the original memorandum or discuss the situation with Mr. Wrigley first? Why do you think Mr. Wrigley always rewrites the communications from top management before distributing them?
2. You work in an open office area. Your manager, Ms. Libby, said she would order a new desk for you. When you asked if you could have a conventional desk with many drawers, Ms. Libby said, "Let's talk about it." Later when she did discuss it with you, Ms. Libby said that you could not have a conventional desk and gave several reasons why. Should you have requested a conventional desk? What reasons do you think Ms. Libby gave?
3. One of your temporary administrative assistants, Marty Evans, is upset because she saw a memorandum written by a staff member in the personnel department recommending that all temporary workers throughout the organization be laid off at the end of September. You suggested that she talk with your manager, Mr. Roberts, before reacting to the memorandum. You tried to reassure her by saying you could not produce all the work that was stacking up on your desk. Were you justified in suggesting to Marty that she talk with Mr. Roberts? Explain. Who will make the final decision about Marty's employment?

Special Reports

1. How many levels of management exist at your college/school? If your college/school has an organization chart, study it and prepare a large one for the bulletin board. If there is no organization chart, draw one, using the titles listed in the college/school catalogue. If you encounter difficulty deciding who reports to whom, ask your instructor to obtain the information for you.
2. Write to an office furniture manufacturer. Request a brochure that is available on office furniture. Share what you learn from the brochure with members of the class.

Production Challenges

3-A A Personnel Problem

Supplies needed:

- *Plain paper*

Recently your office was redesigned and redecorated. The partitions that formed the private offices were removed, and a landscaped office design with smaller partitions and modular furniture was used. The office is beautiful. You work in a modular arrangement with Marge Stevens, administrative assistant in purchasing, and Ann Compton, administrative assistant in financial planning.

Marge and Ann spend much of their time talking. They remain at their workstations and shout over the "masking noise" in order to be heard. Their talking has decreased your productivity. The first week you tried to overlook the interruptions and worked overtime to keep up with your work. Later Mr. Wilson asked you to plan your work so that you would not have to work overtime. You did not tell Mr. Wilson why you were working overtime. The next day you asked Marge and Ann to refrain from talking so much, but they have ignored your request.

You are getting so far behind with your work that you are taking it home with you.

Today you again asked Marge and Ann to stop talking so loudly and so much. Ann retorted, "Don't be such a nag." You became so upset that you felt ill. You took the afternoon off. All afternoon you worried about your work piling up and your inability to concentrate while Marge and Ann are talking loudly.

What are the solutions to your problem? You decide that you need help with it. Jot down what you are going to do and what you will say.

3-B Proofreading

Supplies needed:

- *Draft on Aligning Copy, Form 3-B-1, pages 385 and 386*
- *Aligning Copy, Form 3-B-2, pages 387 and 388*
- *Common Proofreader's Marks, Appendix, page 471*

You work in the word processing centre and have recently been given the responsibility of proofreading all documents. One of the new word processing operators keyed and printed the two pages in 3-B-1. She submitted them to you for proofreading.

Compare 3-B-1 with 3-B-2. Mark the copy in 3-B-1 so that it is *exactly* like 3-B-2. Do not be concerned that something might be correct two ways. Circle the errors and return 3-B-1 to the operator to make the corrections. Remember that it is your job to find *all* the errors.

World Wide Websites

Center for Office Technology

www.cot.org/

This is an American coalition of employers, manufacturers, and associations dedicated to improving the office working environment and to promoting informed approaches to comfort and well-being issues associated with computers and office technology. The site includes sections on ergonomics, FAQs about VDTs, and publications.

Computer Related Health Hazards

www.yahoo.com/Health/Workplace/Computer_Related_Health_Hazards/Repetitive_Strain_Injuries/

This website features links to various sites concerned with repetitive strain injury.

DETAILS: Survival Kit for the Computerized Office

www.scdetails.com/

This site is maintained by Steelcase and the Ergonomics Consortium. It provides links to sections on physical trauma, eyestrain, and clutter, and gives hints and exercises.

CHAPTER 4

Computers and Office Applications

Outline

Computers

Basic Functions of a Computer
Operating Systems
Bits and Bytes
Application Programs

Computers in the Office

Ensuring Complete and Accurate Data Input
Providing Rapid Communications
Using Computer Storage
Increasing Your Productivity
Networking Computers
Internet Networking

Word Processing

Perspectives: "Give Yourself the Electronic Edge"
The Versatile Computer
Input for Word Processing
Impact of Word Processing
Word Processing Terminology

Desktop Publishing

Uses for Desktop Publishing
Importance of Learning Desktop Publishing
Desktop Publishing System
Other Desktop Publishing
Be Creative as a Desktop Publisher

Learning Outcomes

At the completion of this chapter, the student will be able to:

1. Explain the administrative assistant's role in using a computer in the office.
2. Identify possible methods of computer input and computer output that may be functional in the office.
3. Discuss applications software as it relates to word processing, spreadsheet, graphs, desktop publishing, electronic mail, and records management.
4. Describe ways to ensure accurate data input.
5. State why traditional paper filing systems are being replaced.
6. Explain how the administrative assistant can access the power of a mainframe computer even though his or her microcomputer is located remotely from the mainframe computer.
7. Identify tasks that are made possible by a local area network.
8. Describe the administrative assistant's role in desktop publishing.
9. Using word processing software, prepare draft and final-copy documents.

Graduate Profile

Eloise Durling
Information Technology Assistant

Safety Insurance Services (Atlantic) Ltd.

College Graduation:
Office Technology Program
Woodstock Community College
New Brunswick
1997

When Continuing Education is described as one of your organization's corporate values it suggests opportunity. For Eloise Durling it defined the opportunity to develop the strong curiosity in technology and automation that she acquired at Woodstock Community College.

Woodstock equipped Eloise with both the tools of an office professional and those of a technologist. After her administrative training in accounting, communications, and typing, she began working as an administrative assistant with Safety Insurance Services (Atlantic) Ltd. In this role, Eloise was only able to *operate* the general office systems and technology, but her training had provided a more in-depth knowledge of software and computer networks.

Eloise switched careers. She joined the Information Technology department as an assistant with the co-responsibility of maintaining the company's computers, network, and all other electronic equipment. That impressive charge includes all corporate information and data placed on the computers. Undeterred by this challenging role, she plans to begin her studies to achieve her Microsoft Certified Systems Engineer certificate and her Internet certificate—then move on to bigger and better things.

Not surprisingly, Eloise is assisting her organization to become "a paperless office." "Automation is making it easier to achieve our vision," she says. "Through the use of desktop scanners, faxing from individual stations, electronic upload and download, interoffice and Internet e-mail, the electronic office has definitely enabled us to be more productive and effective."

"Many times our success comes from the support of family, friends, instructors, and employers. To those people, I am thankful."

Never having touched a computer until attending community college, Eloise has surprised herself. She has not only succeeded in an entirely new discipline but is also living her dream career.

Because office automation is now widely accepted, it is essential that office employees gain an understanding of computer technology. Even more important to the administrative assistant is an understanding of how the computer's application software can provide productivity improvements.

There are two categories of computers that generally support office automation: mainframes and personal computers (PC). The mainframe computer is considered to be a computer with the capacity to process and distribute information fast and efficiently to multiple users. In contrast, the PC was designed for the use of one person at a time and can be found on desktops in most offices. When mainframes are used in the office, they act as central computers serving attached PCs with information and software. When connected together, the mainframe server, the PC, and **peripherals** of the PC are known collectively as a **network**.

Administrative assistants will experience benefits of the office network while processing and printing documents, maintaining a database, or simply sending e-mail. Office workers that operate from home (telecommuters) access common data through their PC that is connected to the office network by telephone line. The business traveller of a progressive office, will use a notebook PC (Figure 4-1) to **sign on** to the office

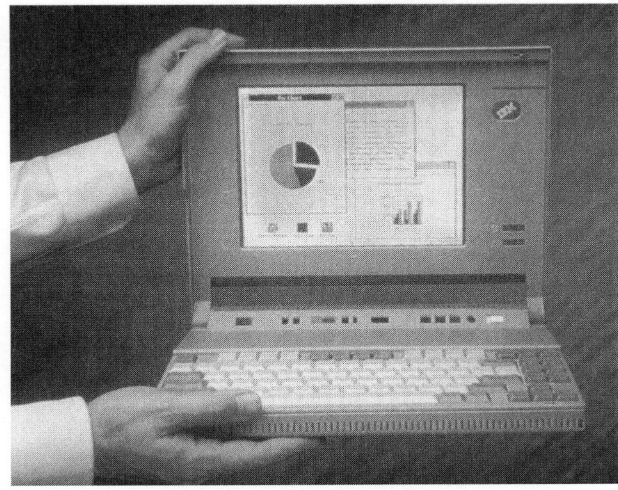

Figure 4-1 Notebook computer.
Courtesy of International Business Machines Corporation. Unauthorized use not permitted.

network from any place there is a telephone connection. Whatever the connection method, the office network provides office professionals with the opportunity

"The electronic office has enabled me to be far more productive."

Marian Vanderzouwen, Graduate
Fairview College

to share resources and remain productive wherever they work.

Office automation is a topic that embraces sophisticated technology. In this chapter, we focus on two elements of technology that the administrative assistant will use: the personal computer and selected application software.

This discussion is centred on the **desktop computer**, which can perform much the same functions as a mainframe but on a smaller scale. A mainframe can accommodate multiple users; a single desktop computer works with one user. Desktop computers are often called **personal computers** (PCs), or simply computers

COMPUTERS

Mainframes are typically found in a centralized area, in a closet, a separate room away from the main office, or a remote site, but always in a secured area to provide optimal conditions for serving the organization and its office professionals. By contrast, desktop computers (computers) are distributed throughout the organization for the use of those that require them. In most contemporary organizations, a computer can be found on every desk because every member of that organization is required to share, distribute, and contribute toward the accumulation of corporate information.

As an administrative assistant, you can anticipate not only having access to a computer but also to handling much of the important day-to-day information processing as part of your office duties. Understanding some technical terminology and concepts will be valuable for your role.

Basic Functions of a Computer

For all tasks that the computer is given, certain basic functions must be performed. See Figure 4-2. These functions are:

1. **Input**: Information is entered into the computer.
2. **Processing**: The computer works on the information in order to produce the desired results.
3. **Memory**: Programs and data are kept in this temporary storage.
4. **Output**: The result of the processing is sent out from the computer.

Figure 4-2 Input, processing, and output.

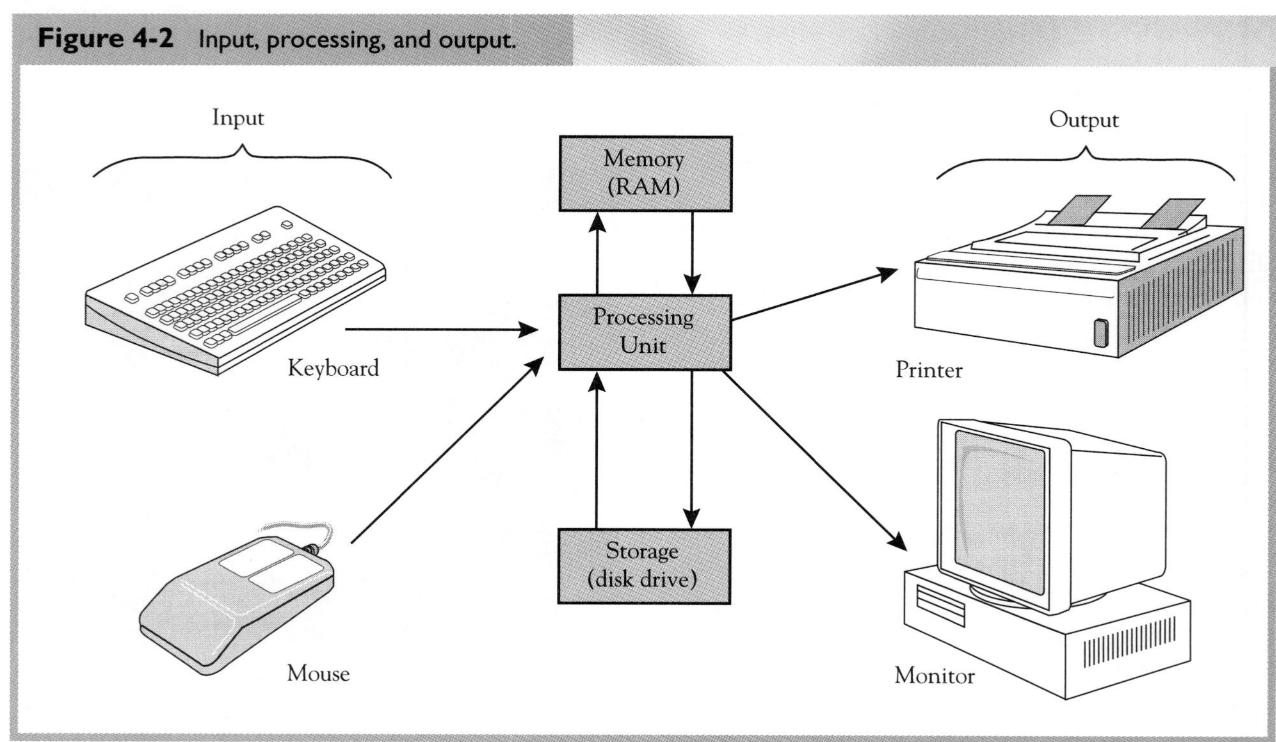

5. **Storage:** Application and other software are kept in this permanent storage (see Figure 4-7) ready for the operator's use.

Input

Information must be provided to the processing unit in a form that the computer can receive. Commonly used input devices are keyboards, mouses, scanners, and disk drives.

Voice recognition, which allows a person to verbally issue commands to a computer, is another form of input; however, it has limited commercial use. Voice recognition technology is most often found where repetitious and standard elements of information processing are required. For example, voice recognition may be used in a lawyer's office where the administrative assistant works with standard clauses or paragraphs for legal documents. It may also be found in an accounting office where the administrative assistant uses file numbers and common accounting functions to manipulate a spreadsheet. In each case, the voice recognition software has to be **voice trained** in order to recognize commands issued by the administrative assistant. While the manufacturers of some voice recognition systems claim their software does not need to be voice trained, these systems typically tend to be more specialized and need only a reduced vocabulary.

The computer **keyboard** is the most common device for inputting. Its appearance and arrangements are those of a typical typewriter keyboard. It is attached to the computer by a single cord, through which keyed information is passed to the computer.

The **mouse** is a small, hand-held device that allows the person using the computer to move the cursor on the screen and to make selections on the screen without ever touching the keyboard. It is most often used in Windows applications. Figure 4-3 illustrates a typical desktop computer with keyboard and mouse.

Scanners read textual and graphic information from paper (hard copy). This information may be sent to the screen, where it can be edited by the administrative assistant; or it may be sent to storage for future use. This method of inputting information and graphics can be a great time-saving device for the administrative assistant; it has the potential to save many hours of keyboard time. See Figure 4-4.

Processing

The **central processing unit** (CPU), commonly thought of as the brains of the computer, is a **microprocessor chip**. The commercial computer was made possible in 1971 by the introduction of a silicon chip that was smaller than a dime and contained 2,250 transistors. Chips today contain the equivalent of millions of transistors and can be found in many forms throughout the computer and its peripherals.

Figure 4-3 Typical desktop microcomputer with keyboard and mouse.
Courtesy of International Business Machines Corporation. Unauthorized use not permitted.

Figure 4-4 Page Scanner.
Courtesy of International Business Machines Corporation. Unauthorized use not permitted.

It is the CPU that seeks and interprets instructions from programs temporarily stored in memory. Based on its interpretation of the program instructions, the CPU directs all other functions of the computer, including the timing of input and output data. The CPU interprets millions of instructions and directions each second.

Memory

Memory is the place where data and the instructions—which tell the CPU what to do with the data—are stored.

The computer's memory is divided into **read only memory** (ROM) and **random access memory** (RAM).

ROM is where the manufacturer has placed permanent instructions. It holds the instructions the computer needs when it is first turned on. These instructions are commonly known as the **bootstrap** program. The process of first switching on the computer using these instructions is called **booting**. The user cannot change this program, and turning the computer off will not destroy it.

RAM temporarily holds the program and data currently being used. It is the working space in the computer. For example, if you create a word processed document using a keyboard, the document will be entered in RAM first.

Data in RAM must be *saved*—that is, moved into storage. Otherwise it may be lost when the computer is turned off. To use data that have already been saved, the user must reload the computer. The process is called *loading*.

Output

Two of the means of retrieving information from a computer are **video display terminals (screens)**, and **printers**. There is no output until the computer is instructed to display, print, or send it.

Audio response is a type of output in which the computer uses a sound to transmit the result. Audio response is widely used for music and voice simulation.

Data that have been entered can be displayed instantly on the screen, also called the **monitor**.

A hard copy of the output can be produced with the use of a printer. The most poplar forms of this peripheral are the laser printer and the ink-jet printer. Other forms include **plotters** and **postscript printers**, which generally have special uses.

The most common nonimpact printer is a **laser printer**. Refer to Figure 4-5. Laser printers use a combination of laser light and xerography and are similar to copiers. They make an electrostatic image and print an entire page at a time. Laser and inkjet printers have made **desktop publishing** possible because of the high quality of the reproduction. (Desktop publishing is discussed later in this chapter.) As well, they print without noise, making them popular in the automated office.

Storage

The capacity of the computer's memory is not large enough to store unlimited data internally. For this reason, computer data that should be kept permanently or for a period of time is stored on **diskettes**, hard disks, CD-ROMs, or tape.

Diskettes, also called **floppy disks**, come in several sizes and capabilities. When used in a computer, the magnetic diskette rotates inside its individual protective case. (Care and storage of diskettes is discussed in Chapter 7.)

Diskette and hard disk drives are options on many computers, but all computers have at least the hard disk.

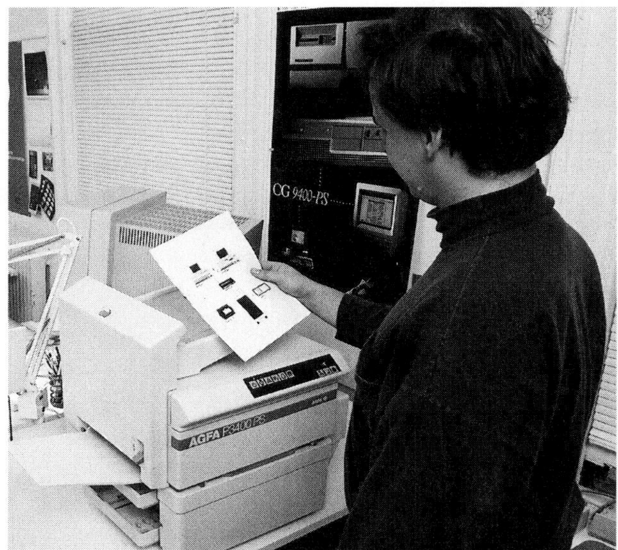

Figure 4-5 An administrative assistant using a laser printer.
Courtesy of International Business Machines Corporation. Unauthorized use not permitted.

Hard disks offer this advantage: they can store much larger amounts of information than a diskette can. Also, the length of time it takes to find data stored on a hard disk and to transfer them into memory is much shorter than when the data transfer is made from diskette.

The **compact disk** (CD-ROM)—is a newer generation of media available for the storage of even larger amounts of computer information. CD-ROMs are less susceptible than magnetic disks to temperature variations and mishandling. For a comparison of computer-based storage capacities, see the section "Using Computer Storage" found later in this chapter.

Operating Systems

The **operating system** gives fundamental operating instructions to the computer. It contains a number of internal commands needed to operate the computer. In some computers the operating system is on the disk with the application program and is automatically loaded before the application program. The operating system must be loaded into the computer's memory *before* the application program because the operating system is what enables the application program to make full use of the computer.

The application program must be compatible with the operating system of the computer being used. There are variations from system to system. PC DOS is written for IBM (International Business Machines). MS DOS is compatible with Microsoft application programs. Windows is an alternative operating system or operating environment in which application programs can run.

pro-Link

Confused by computer terminology? Here are some descriptions of commonly used terms that may, at least, put computer information terminology in perspective for you:

- A **directory** is a way to organize information. In your computer system, a directory contains a group of related *files* that are separated from other directories by a unique name. A familiar everyday example is the Yellow Pages telephone directory. Directories are also known as **catalogues** or **folders**.
- A **file** is a related collection of *records*. For example, you might keep a record on each of your customers in a file.
- A **record** consists of *fields* of individual data items, such as customer name, customer number, customer address, and so on. In this way, a customer record would contain all details of the customer.
- A **field** is an area within a record that has a fixed size. By providing the same *information* in the same fields in each record (so that all records are consistent), the customer file may be easily used by a computer program.
- **Information** is synonymous with **data**. Data is information translated into a form that is more convenient to manipulate by computers. It is often referred to in terms of *bits* and *bytes*.
- A **byte** is a unit of information that is eight *bits* long. A byte is the unit most computers use to represent one character such as a letter, number, or typographic symbol.
- A **bit** is the smallest unit of data in a computer. A bit has a single binary value, either 0 or 1. In most computer systems, there are eight bits in a byte.

Bits and Bytes

The computer's screen will often display the number of **bytes** (pronounced *bites*) available on the disk, or the number of bytes used to create a document. One byte can be compared to one character (a letter of the alphabet, a number, or a symbol). One byte can be broken down into eight **bits**. The word "bit" is a contraction of the term **bi**nary dig**it**. A bit is the smallest unit of information used by the computer.

When reference is made to a **kilobyte**, it means approximately 1,000 (1K) bytes or characters; a **megabyte** refers to 1,000,000 (1M) bytes; a **gigabyte** refers to 1,000,000,000 (1G) bytes.

Application Programs

Application programs, often referred to collectively as *application software*, are written to perform specific tasks such as word processing, graph and/or spreadsheet production, desktop publishing, and database management. Electronic mail requires its own application program.

A **spreadsheet** is an arrangement of columns and rows into which data is entered for analysis. One example of the use of a spreadsheet is the accountant's ledger. Business data worked out with a spreadsheet program can be transformed with the use of *graphics software* into graphs or charts.

Word processing and desktop publishing are discussed later in this chapter; electronic mail is discussed in Chapter 6; and records management and database management are discussed in Chapter 7.

Users of computers can gain the power of a mainframe computer even when the computer is situated a considerable distance from the mainframe. For this to be possible, the computer must be connected to a **modem**, which is a device used for changing the computer's signal into a signal that can travel over telephone lines. To use a modem, you must have access to a telephone line; you also need communications software. This arrangement of communicating is called **remote access.** Refer to Figure 4-6.

COMPUTERS IN THE OFFICE

Because the majority of the early changes resulting from the use of computers were in the area of financial operations, the role of the administrative assistant was not greatly affected by them. Today, because the computer is used for word processing, records management, and communications, it is widely used by office professionals.

The reliance on computers for decision making increases when managers begin applying them to tasks such as budgeting, scheduling, and general planning. The computer is a powerful tool for increasing productivity. More and more, administrators are relying on computers for planning production schedules, monitoring and controlling manufacturing processes, and analyzing sales reports. The administrative assistant who has learned how to analyze and interpret data will be an invaluable asset to any organization that uses computer processes.

"After having successfully completed my computer courses, I was determined have a good job with higher wages. I did it with a lot of hard work."

Nasheena Aziz, Graduate
Fraser Pacific College

Figure 4-6 A remote microcomputer on-line with a mainframe computer.

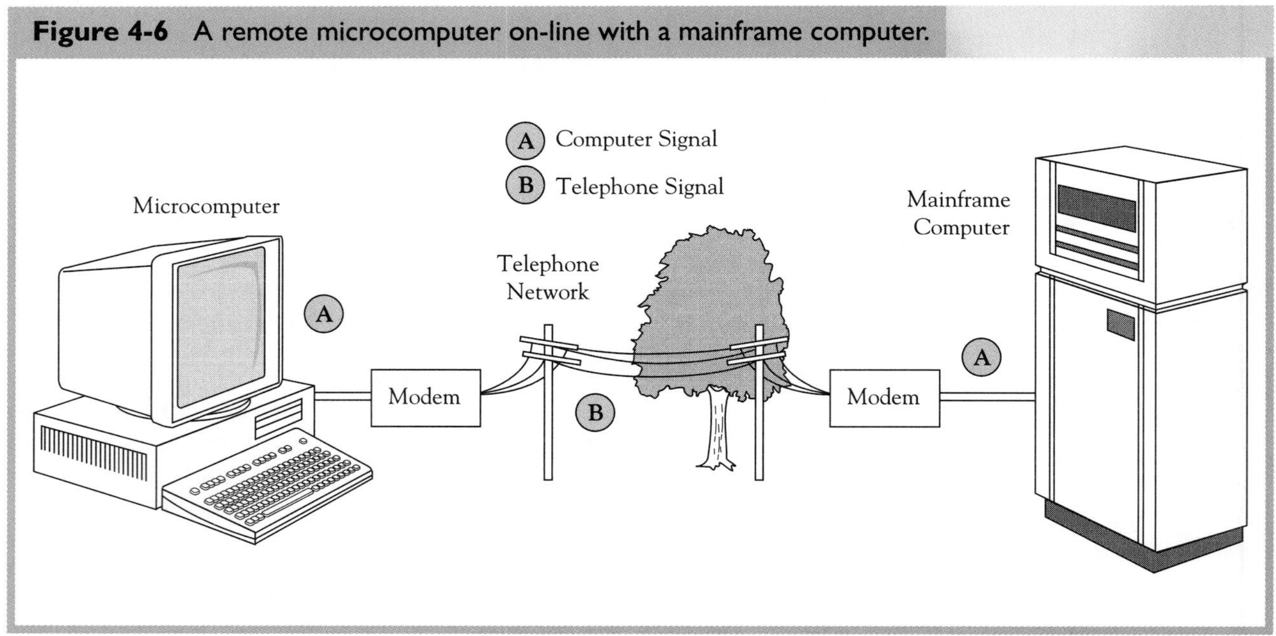

Ensuring Complete and Accurate Data Input

Most Canadians are familiar with the expression, "Garbage in, garbage out." This expression is particularly significant when applied to the use of computers. Basically, a computer is a collection of plastic, glass, silicone, and metal parts. Computer scientists and electronics engineers have assembled these parts to create a machine capable of taking in a list of instructions in the form of a program, and manipulating the associated input to provide accurate and complete results to the user. Input is information presented to the computer before processing. Advances in technology have increased the speed of information processing; at the same time, the use of computers throughout most organizations has increased the demand for accurate input.

Commercially manufactured computers and programs are designed to be reliable. Today it can be assumed that commercially manufactured computers and programs have been well designed, and tested carefully before they reach the marketplace. Clearly, accuracy and completeness of the input is the key to obtaining the desired results. If the user provides inaccurate or incomplete data input to the computer, inaccurate or incomplete output (results) will be produced.

Consider for a moment the speed at which a computer processes information (typically millions of instructions each second). Inaccurate input is processed and distributed so rapidly that the results may create long-term problems that are difficult to correct. In company terms, such problems have the potential to negatively affect the customer or financial records on which the company's survival depends. Often, when input is incomplete the computer is programmed to disregard the input. The practical results of incomplete input might be that a customer's order is not shipped, or that an employee's cheque is not issued. At the very least, some delay will almost certainly occur as a result of the incomplete transaction.

Data entry is often carried out from source documents. Source documents include orders, invoices, incoming cheques, time cards, and sales tickets. Source documents are often assembled in originating departments and then submitted for processing via computer by a data entry operator working either within the department or at a central location. Regardless of where the data entry operator is located, the originating department is responsible for ensuring the accuracy and completeness of the source documents before turning them over to the data entry operator. Similarly, the data entry operator is responsible for accurately transcribing source documents to the computer.

Sometimes there will be unusual transactions that are incompatible with your computer program. Someone in your organization may be assigned to work on these, processing them manually or translating them into acceptable source document format. The administrative assistant may be asked to perform this task.

Do everything you can to decrease errors in source document information. Keep a record of

- the frequency of errors
- the types of errors that occur
- the originator of the error.

Analyze the problem to determine

- how to decrease the frequency of errors
- how to eliminate errors altogether.
- how the process can be improved.

Your role as an employee and as an administrative assistant includes both preventing problems and attempting to resolve those which do occur. If the internal or external customer who has been a victim of a computer error calls you, be attentive to that customer's position. Demonstrate your commitment to customer support and your willingness to help correct the problem. Customer follow-up should be exercised any time there is an inconvenienced or dissatisfied customer. For the sake of retaining the customer's patronage, a written response or telephone call should be made by an appropriate company representative.

Providing Rapid Communications

Computers when appropriately connected, allow users to communicate with each other and with mainframe computers. Administrative assistants are among those who communicate with mainframe computers to obtain more information than is available on the local computer alone.

Several users may communicate with the mainframe computer simultaneously. The user contacts the central computer and then waits **on line** to use it; however, the computer operates so rapidly that the user is sometimes unaware of the waiting time. This is called **time-sharing.**

The on-line capability provides instantaneous updating of data known as **real-time** transactions. Processing takes place as the transaction happens. Commercial airlines' use of computer terminals for making airline reservations is one well-known example of time-sharing.

With an on-line inventory control system, the inventory balance is immediately available. A sales representative in a remote branch office can enter an order directly into the home office computer. An executive or administrative assistant can request desired data from remote computer files and receive an instantaneous response. The administrative assistant who has access to an on-line terminal will rely on it as an effective means of communication. For instance, if a customer calls about the status of its account, the administrative assistant can consult the computer and obtain virtually instantaneous information for the customer.

Using Computer Storage

Paper files are gradually being replaced by computer-based and computer-assisted filing systems. These new systems use media that require much less space than traditional, paper systems. A variety of computer-based storage media are now available. Typically, the choice of medium will depend upon availability and specific requirements. Figure 4-7 provides a practical guide to computer-based storage; it provides data both on media capacity and on the approximate equivalence in full pages of text.

Figure 4-7 Relative capacities of computer-based storage.

COMPUTER-BASED STORAGE	CAPACITY*	APPROXIMATE EQUIVALENT IN FULL PAGES OF TEXT
3.5 inch diskette	0.72 Megabytes 1.44 Megabytes	200 400
ZIP diskette	100 Megabytes 250 Megabytes	27,000 67,000
CD-ROM (writable)	475 Megabytes 650 Megabytes	131,500 180,000
hard drive	3 Gigabytes 17 Gigabytes	832,000 4,700,000

* In operation, 10 percent to 15 percent of the capacity of each medium would be used for directory and page-formatting information.

Both information access and retrieval speed are dramatically improved by these systems. However, the fact that they are susceptible to loss or damage is a definite disadvantage; the loss of information on one floppy disk could result in hours or even weeks of work. Consequently, duplex storage is essential. Computer-based storage can exist in many forms, as described in the next section.

Computer-based Storage

Data in process are stored in the computer's memory; this memory is sometimes referred to as *working storage*.

External computer storage is considered permanent and may be of several types, including

- diskettes, or zip diskettes
- hard disks
- CD-ROMs
- magnetic recording tape.

To retrieve information stored on any one of these media, the administrative assistant must use a computer that has the same media **interface**. This consideration is often referred to as the **compatibility** of media. It is important that the administrative assistant recognize that variation in storage media does exist. For example, if the administrative assistant receives data or information on diskette from an external source, the data may not be computer legible due to the incompatibility of the originating media.

Computer-assisted Storage

Computers are often used to help store information on noncomputer media such as microfilm or microfiche. While this form of storage may be assisted by the computer, other, optical-based equipment is used to retrieve the stored data.

Increasing Your Productivity

When you enter the job market, you will possess skills in keyboarding and word processing, and will know application programs for spreadsheets and desktop publishing. You may also have skills in database management, project management, and/or presentation management applications. Whatever your set of job entry skills, many opportunities to learn more on the job will be available to you. Be receptive to the challenges that come your way.

First, refine the skills you already possess. Accept change readily. When the computer you are currently using is replaced or upgraded, study the new manuals to become thoroughly familiar with the new computer. Be aware that improved software will make your job easier.

Learn new computer applications. Have a plan for professional growth on the job. Take advantage of in-house training sessions. Study manuals, read technical magazines, and attend night classes. Continually search for ways that the computer can help you perform your job. (See Figure 4-8.)

The speed with which the computer handles information will enable you to do more work in a day. Master the flow of information in and out of your office. Plan your work carefully; set priorities. Use the time you gain to think, to listen to customers' needs, to communicate, to solve problems, and to be creative.

Networking Computers

Many organizations use **local area networks** (LANs) for connecting their internal computers. LANs are designed not only to provide a means of communication between users of computers but also to facilitate the sharing of common documents, *hardware*, and *software*.

LANs typically connect computers that are in the same proximity. Fifteen hundred metres of cable, for all connections, is usually the maximum distance considered as the local area. The computers may be connected by coaxial cable (to permit higher transmission speeds) or by simple telephone cable. For enhanced capabilities, LANs can be connected to a mainframe computer. LANs can also be connected to other networks, such as a metropolitan area network (MAN), which, as the name implies, provides networking facilities within a town or city. In much the same way, a wide area network (WAN) provides networking facilities over a yet wider area perhaps an entire country, or even the entire world.

Through the use of networks, an administrative assistant can now

1. communicate with other employees through electronic mail or memo

Figure 4-8 Optical character reader scanning text to be placed on the computer screen for editing by the administrative assistant.
Courtesy of Unisys Canada Inc.

PERSPECTIVES

Give Yourself the Electronic Edge

By Stephanie Culp

Are today's high-tech wonders saving you time or wasting your time? Here's how to avoid the technology trap and use office electronics to your most productive advantage.

Today's conventional wisdom is quick to declare that if you want to save time and get organized, use high technology. Get a computer or a fax. Put a cellular phone in your car. Drag a mobile phone along with you all day so you never miss a call. High tech today means unsurpassed speed and maximum availability, which supposedly equals massive amounts of time saved. If you aren't on the electronic bandwagon, chances are you know someone who is, and that person is urging you to stop being such a dinosaur and get yourself upgraded electronically.

Availing yourself of all the electronic wonders on the market today—from special telephones to laptop computers—can indeed free your time. But there are pluses and minuses to consider when looking at electronic wonders as time-savers, because these machines can also be great *users* of time. If you make efficient use of technology, you will be able to save time; an overindulgence or over-dependence on machines, however, can wind up wasting far more of your time than those machines will ever save.

Regardless of the changes that occur almost daily in the world of electronics, some considerations need to be taken into account before you use machines to get organized. In addition to your budget, you might want to keep these pros and cons in mind as you turn to electronics to give you a time-saving and organizational edge that really will suit your lifestyle.

The multi-purpose computer

When used as a tool, the computer is an amazing organizational and time-saving machine for certain tasks. It is particularly good for word-processing, data storage, and accounting. Desktop publishing, too, has made self-publishing everything from fliers to reports laden with charts and graphics accessible to nearly all personal computer users.

The downside: An honest look at computers brings up some definite questions regarding how much time computers *save* and how much time they *waste*. While the temptation may be to emphatically endorse computers as a major time-saver, there are several pitfalls that can mean that you *waste* time on a computer. Here are some examples:

It's all too easy to think that a computer will solve all of your paper problems in the wink of an eye. Buy a computer, the thinking goes, and all of the mountains of paper in your life will be magically transformed into electronic data. Wrong. First, the data has to be *entered* by a human being onto the computer (and this might mean you). The papers will not beam themselves mystically onto the computer; the computer operator spends wads of time entering or scanning the information. This time expended is directly related to the size and number of piles of papers being computerized.

A computer makes it possible for you to access far more information than you need. Information anxiety can be quelled with a flip of the finger, which in turn starts the computer and the printer spitting out reports on everything from, say, the balance in your checkbook to how many widgets the plant sold in Siberia last Tuesday, to the names of all the dinosaurs that roamed the earth once upon a time. Along with all the extra information you can buy (such as encyclopedias on CD-ROM) you may get completely carried away, and add gobs of your own personal garbage. You spend days, weeks even, wasting time entering information you don't need to have computerized—from a recipe collection that you never use to an inventory of all the types of nails and screws in your workshop in the garage. This endless doodle is also known as GIGO—Garbage In, Garbage Out—and is an enormous waste of time.

If you have a computer, you may also belong to an on-line service that lets you "talk" to strangers over the computer. It's easy to get caught up in this, and before you know it, you're addicted—staying up until three in the morning to talk to someone with whom you have an on-line relationship.

Once you buy a computer, if the software doesn't already include one, you'll eventually come to believe that you must have games on the computer. Then you play the games when you should be doing something else.

A computer can lead you into the temptation to overdo. Where a two-page proposal may have been fine in the past, you now feel that a 12-page proposal, complete with charts and graphics, is in order. The truth is, the two-pager will probably still get you the job, but it's too late, you're well into creating 10 more pages and spending far more time than is necessary on the project.

A computer can be a perfectionist's handmaiden in compulsive editing and rewriting. A letter that you might have sent out with only one minor rewrite now gets rewritten four times before it passes your reluctant muster.

Adjustments can be endless with a computer. If you don't like the margins or tabs, it can take an unreasonable amount of time to get the computer to agree to, and accept the margins that you do want. (In the "old" days, you could have set the margins and tabs on a typewriter in about two seconds.)

Or you fiddle around with the fonts ad nauseam. You pick one for the title, one for the subtitles, one for the text, one for words requiring emphasis, and so on.

For some people, a computer is an invitation to futz around. *The Chicago Tribune* reported on a survey called the "PC Futz Factor" that was taken to see how people were really using the computer and software programs. Sponsored by SBT Accounting Systems in Sausalito, California, the survey results included these eye-opening "futz facts."

"The average office worker spends 5.1 hours per week futzing with the computer. Assuming there are 25 million office computer users in America, that means 5 billion hours yearly, representing wages worth $100 billion, or 2 percent of the gross national product."

Of that time, 19 percent was spent waiting for the computer or a co-worker to do something, 16 percent was spent helping co-workers, 17 percent was on checking or formatting output, 12 percent was on learning new software, 14 percent was on erasing files, 5 percent was installing software and 17 percent was "other."

According to the *Tribune*, "suspicions that the 'other' category represented time spent playing games could not be confirmed in follow-up interviews because the respondents were reluctant to discuss the issue."

The key to making electronic technology save time for you is to be selective about how much time you devote to that technology. And don't use time saved to then immerse yourself compulsively into even more technology that you don't really need. Use that time for yourself instead.

Reprinted courtesy of OfficePRO.

2. send draft copies of documents to individuals for validation or correction before committing them to final form
3. sequentially and electronically route a document for approval
4. co-author or co-edit large documents.

Internet Networking

The **Internet** is a global network of computer-based information available to anyone with a computer, a modem, and a subscription to an Internet Service Provider. More accurately, the Internet is a network of networks with international telecommunications facilities connecting them. By using a computer with a modem attachment, the user may connect to the Internet network. The user then has access to a vast selection of information and services. For more discussion of the Internet, see Chapter 9, "Telecommunications in the Office."

WORD PROCESSING

In many organizations today, text editing is one of the main administrative responsibilities. In preparation for your career, you need to acquire word processing skills and to learn about the capabilities of word processing equipment and software. Word processing may include creating, editing, storing, printing, and even transmitting documents to other word processing equipment.

The goals of organizations that install text-editing equipment are to increase productivity and to improve communications.

The Versatile Computer

When computers became an integral part of the office, they were used for word processing more than for any other application. But as the power and versatility of these machines has increased, so too has the number of uses to which they are put.

A variety of software applications have been developed for word processing. Each new version is an improvement on what was previously available. Also, computer hardware is continually being improved. These improvements in the computer and in word processing software have made the computer essential office equipment.

The computer's versatility is apparent in the range of software now available for business use: there is software on the market to handle spreadsheets, graphics, file and database management, telecommunications, accounting, and desktop publishing. Organizations use their computers not only for word processing but also for these other applications.

Input for Word Processing

Information in its original form is called *raw data*. Raw data for word processing can be any of the following:

- machine dictation
- person-to-person dictation
- longhand
- keyboarded rough draft
- form letters or documents—the word originator dictates the variables (addresses, dates, amounts of money, and so on)
- diskettes and disks on which information has been stored before processing
- **optical character recognition** (OCR) scans
- voice input devices.

Data from dictating machines, person-to-person dictation, longhand, and typewritten rough drafts, and variables for form documents, must be keyboarded.

The diskette or hard disk containing stored material must not only be compatible with the disk drive of the equipment being used, but must be in—or converted to—the correct data format for the word processing application in use.

An OCR reader scans materials that have been keyboarded with a font style the scanner can recognize. As the keyboarded material is scanned, it is transferred to the memory of a computer. See Figure 4-8.

Voice input is recognized, converted into bits and bytes, and presented as meaningful data to the computer.

Impact of Word Processing

The use of word processing for preparing documents has resulted in improved document accuracy and a decrease in the time needed to produce documents. The document originators (authors, dictators) are not reluctant to make revisions when they know that the entire document does not have to be rekeyed.

Administrative assistants enjoy working with word processing applications because most mundane tasks are eliminated. Word processing software can, for example, establish margins and tabs, paginate, assemble a table of contents, and tabulate end and footnotes. Merging variable information such as names and addresses with form letters is one of the most valuable word processing features that support the administrative assistant. This is sometimes called **mail merge**. The administrative assistant can keyboard and store the variables to be merged; the system can then produce hundreds of letters while the administrative assistant is doing something else.

Data can also be retrieved from a mainframe, stored on a diskette or disk to free the mainframe for other uses, and then merged with other stored information. The auto-features of word processing equipment enable the administrative assistant to set up statistical data in formal reports with ease.

Advanced word processing features allow administrative assistants to produce brochures, sales bulletins, and other documents with a variety of headings, columns, and designs, to standards that come close to matching those of professional printers.

You will need to plan your work carefully in order to increase your productivity. Be sure to save (transfer to a diskette or disk) what you have keyboarded. When you work with revisions, make sure that what is to be moved, deleted, added, or changed is clearly marked in the hard-copy draft. You need to understand and use proofreader's marks. The appendix illustrates the most commonly used proofreader's marks.

Word Processing Terminology

As so often happens with a technical discipline, word processing has developed its own terminology. It is vital to know these new terms since they will be a part of the office vocabulary used by other administrative assistants. Understanding word processing terminology will allow you to learn rapidly how to operate the software, to more easily follow a word processing procedures manual, and to converse with other office professionals.

DESKTOP PUBLISHING

Desktop publishing (DTP) refers to a class of sophisticated application programs that allow the administrative assistant to manipulate text, data, and graphics on a single page into a format suitable for publishing. Type sizes and typefaces are easily varied to produce a document with a professional appearance.

Uses for Desktop Publishing

Many administrative assistants are using DTP to produce a variety of documents. Once the administrative assistant masters the art of desktop publishing these specialized skills may be applied to nearly every document that crosses the desk.

Documents such as reports, memoranda, forms, procedures manuals, and advertisements are significantly enhanced by the use of desktop publishing, and therefore attract more attention than those produced by more conventional means. The administrative assistant is now able to create brochures, fliers, newsletters, and business cards in-house, without the expense and time delays that used to be unavoidable when private printing contractors were used. (See Figure 4-9.)

Figure 4-9 An administrative assistant uses technology and graphic software to produce a publication.

Importance of Learning Desktop Publishing

Mastering the skill of desktop publishing benefits the administrative assistant in a number of significant ways. The following list states some of these benefits.

1. DTP allows the user to exercise creative skills. A great deal of personal satisfaction is derived in this way. DTP brings enjoyment to what might have been a mundane task. For example, the addition of a graphic to a regular memo will add interest for both the administrative assistant and the recipient of the memo.
2. DTP increases the effectiveness of the document. The professional appearance will attract attention and increase credibility.
3. Illustrations and charts can be added to documents without difficulty. These deliver the message more clearly than words alone. The adage about a picture being worth a thousand words is no doubt applicable to desktop publishing.
4. The turnaround time is shorter when documents are produced in-house. Before desktop publishing, professional-looking documents could only be produced by sending the project out to a typesetter.
5. Professional documents can be prepared for less cost when the administrative assistant can produce them in-house.
6. Students who master the art of desktop publishing will have a competitive edge when applying for administrative assistant positions. Desktop publishing is a highly respected skill, and one that will impress prospective employers.
7. Administrative assistants who are adept at desktop publishing have greater career opportunities. Employers seek administrative assistants who have diverse software training. This asset will make the administrative assistant more valuable within the company, and more likely to be considered for promotions as they arise.

Desktop Publishing System

Since 1985, desktop publishing software has become increasingly sophisticated and complex. If the software is to perform effectively in an office environment, consideration must be given to the power and speed of the microcomputer system on which the software resides.

Individual DTP application documentation will prescribe specific hardware and software requirements. However, as a general statement, most DTP applications require as much working storage as possible, a fast microprocessor, and a good-quality printer.

At the time of publication of this textbook, the basic configuration for any standalone DTP computer system was:

1. A minimum of sixteen megabytes (MB) of random access memory (RAM).
2. A Pentium II (or equivalent) microprocessor running at no less than 300 megahertz (M/Hz).
3. A high-capacity hard drive (recommended: no less than 5 GB).
4. A PostScript laser printer.

A scanner or document reader can enhance a publication by permitting the user to include original text or graphics produced on other equipment, such as newspapers or photographs.

Other Desktop Publishing

Other forms of DTP may include drawing, charting (such as organizational charts, flowcharts, and productivity charts), and designing (such as **computer-assisted design**) applications. These applications are usually employed for specific purposes; also, they may require special system components, such as a plotter or a larger display screen.

It is recommended that system requirements (both hardware and software) be researched thoroughly before new applications are implemented.

Be Creative as a Desktop Publisher

The administrative assistant's role in desktop publishing includes numerous exciting tasks. Some of these are:

- designing the document's layout
- creating and/or keyboarding the text
- creating and/or accessing the appropriate graphics
- manipulating the text and graphics
- printing the final product.

Planning the document's appearance will require knowledge of design and layout as well as of advertising and public relations. The administrative assistant often works with printing houses by preparing a document for production, but usually does not have the sophisticated equipment to produce coloured and glossy pages.

The role of desktop publishing has, without doubt, provided the administrative assistant's career with challenge, creativity, prestige, and respect.

Questions for Study and Review

1. What are the four basic functions of a computer?
2. Which input devices are widely used in offices?
3. Distinguish between read only memory and random access memory.
4. Which printer prints an entire page at a time?
5. Define: laser printer, modem, software.
6. Name three types of external storage.
7. Which type of storage disk has the greatest capacity?
8. What is the function of DOS?
9. Define: bit, byte, character, megabyte, on-line.
10. How can you distinguish hardware from software?
11. Give three examples of application software.
12. Why has the computer placed such a premium on accuracy?
13. What are source documents? Why should they be checked for legibility, accuracy, and completeness?
14. Suggest ways you can learn about computers on the job.
15. What advantage does word processing provide word originators?
16. Name three examples of raw data.
17. How would you describe the Internet in terms of networking computers?
18. Consider yourself an administrative assistant who is seeking employment. What benefit will the acquired skill of desktop publishing provide you with?
19. What basic hardware is required to do desktop publishing?
20. Suggest four documents that the administrative assistant might produce on a desktop publishing system.
21. What is the administrative assistant's role in desktop publishing?

Spelling Reinforcement

accuracy	legibility	modem	sequential
centralized	mainframe	photosensitive	software
format	media	processing	sophisticated
instantaneous	megabyte	productivity	statistical
internally	memory	recognition	volatile

On-the-Job Situations

1. You are administrative assistant to the general sales manager in an organization that has four sales regions. You are responsible for seeing that the appliances requested by the regions are shipped promptly from the manufacturing plants. You operate a terminal that is connected on-line to the offices of the sales regions and the manufacturing plants. Recently the regions have been receiving the correct number of the appliances ordered but the colours have not been the ones that were requested. You analyze the input data that you have used for the past month. What should you look for in your analysis? What recommendations could you make to improve your accuracy?
2. You are teaching an assistant to input data. This week she has entered the input for all the orders. Every Friday the main computer prints a summary of all the orders for the week. This Friday the computer did not print the summary of your orders for the week. What do you do now to obtain a summary? What else should you do?
3. Your organization stores data on microfilm. One of your managers has asked you to verify data in a report she is preparing. The data you need have been stored on microfilm, and you must key the computer to locate the microfilm you need. The person in charge of microfilm retrieval is ill, and you do not know how to retrieve the data that you need. What should you do?

Special Reports

1. Interview an office worker who uses a desktop computer on line. How does the worker access the mainframe? Where is the mainframe located? What questions does the worker use to request data from the mainframe? Report what you learn to the class.

2. Inquire about the student record system at your school. Is a computer used to maintain the entire system or a part of it? If so, what data entry is used for students' schedules and for students' grades? How are the data stored? Report your findings to the class.

Production Challenges

4-A Preparing Final Draft of Material on Supervision

Supplies needed:

- *Draft on Supervision, Form 4-A, pages 389 to 396*
- *Common Proofreader's Marks Appendix, page 481*
- *Working Papers Disk, File 4-A*

Ms. Azam is assisting with a seminar on supervision for beginning supervisors. She is preparing some handouts for the attendees. Form 4-A is a draft of what Ms. Azam has written. Consider that you have already keyed the draft and stored it on disk. You gave a hard copy of the draft to Ms. Azam. Ms. Azam prefers to make all her notations concerning changes in the margins of the draft. You always read the changes and mark them in the copy before you begin inserting the changes on your computer. Perform this job in three steps.

1. Using (the draft copy) Form 4-A on page 389, the Common Proofreader's Marks Appendix on page 471, and your pen, carefully mark all the edits that Ms. Azam has indicated in the margins of Form 4-A.
2. Use the student Working Papers disk to open the document called 4-A.
3. Using your edited paper copy of Form 4-A, perform an on-screen edit of the document.
4. Print one copy of your final document. Give your instructor the printed copy of your final document as well as Form 4-A with the penned edits.

4-B Inserting Proofreader's Marks

Supplies needed:

- *Memorandum about Seminar, Form 4-B, page 397*
- *Working Papers Disk, File 4-B*

Using the proofreader's marks in the appendix, mark the memorandum on Form 4-B ready for processing. Check your copy to be sure that you have marked all the corrections needed. Next, keyboard the memo in final form.

World Wide Websites

Apple Canada

www.apple.ca/

This site contains information about Apple Canada, products, support, special communities, and Canadian resources.

Corel Corporation

www.corel.com/

Users obtain news and information on Corel products, service and support, and contests.

IBM Canada

www.can.ibm.com/

IBM provides company and product information, industry solutions, a What's New section, and other information.

NetworkMagazine.com

www.networkmagazine.com

This site allows users to examine product guides, tutorials, interviews, and test drives.

whatis?com™

http://whatis.com/index.htm

The page of **whatis.com** where you can find definitions and explanations of all technical terms and expressions.

PC Webopaedia—Desktop Publishing

webopedia.internet.com/TERM/d/desktop_publishing.html

This website presents a definition of DTP, and links to articles on ISPs, page layout programs, and offset printing.

PART II
OFFICE SERVICES

CHAPTER

Transcription and Reprographics

Outline

What Does It Take to Be a Transcriptionist?
Dictating and Transcribing Tips
Judging Priorities
Keeping Transcripts Confidential

Dictation and Transcription Equipment
Portable Equipment
Desktop Equipment
Centralized Equipment

What Are Reprographics?
Low-volume Copiers
Mid-volume Copiers
High-volume Copiers
Perspectives: "How to Choose a Copier"

Learning Outcomes

At the completion of this chapter, the student will be able to:

1. List the skills necessary to be a transcriptionist.
2. List tips for successful dictation and transcription.
3. Name ways that dictation equipment may be used in addition to dictating correspondence.
4. Discuss how to determine priorities for transcription of documents.
5. Discuss how to keep transcripts confidential in the office environment.
6. Differentiate between portable, desktop, and centralized dictation equipment.
7. Differentiate between the features of low-, mid-, and high-volume copiers.
8. Identify special features on reprographics equipment that would make the administrative assistant's job more efficient.
9. Transcribe correspondence and prepare envelopes for the correspondence.
10. Use the Internet to locate more information on office equipment.

GRADUATE PROFILE

Nicole Ronald, B.A.
Administrative Assistant

London Health Sciences Centre

College Graduation:
Medical Secretarial Arts—
Dictatypist
Fanshawe College
London, Ontario
1986

Nicole Ronald is a fine example of an office professional who believes that a solid education is the key to living a challenging life and having a successful career. After completing her Medical Administration diploma, she sought her certification as an ophthalmic assistant. With a goal to teach students in medical administration programs, Nicole earned her Bachelor of Arts degree. Relentless in her educational pursuit, and believing in lifelong learning, she is currently working on a diploma in Adult Education. In fact, Nicole has never taken an educational break; instead her career has included continual upgrading of her office administration skills. As both a medical administrative assistant and a college instructor, it is Nicole's contention that education is the key to successful employment. She believes that the more knowledge you have, the more indispensable you are.

In addition to her educational credentials, Nicole's human relations skills qualify her as a seasoned professional in the medical office. As she says, "When dealing with patients and their families, I have learned the importance of compassion and understanding. Those who are sick or dying don't always think rationally, and working in a physician's office you must learn to respect this."

"The more knowledge you have, the more indispensable you will be."

As a part of Nicole's administrative functions, she transcribes patient reports, business correspondence, and research. She states that one of her most important office functions is to make sure her transcription is error free. Simple transcription errors in a medical office can result in serious consequences for a patient.

Although transcription was once a popular method of producing documentation in most offices, it is now limited mostly to the medical and legal professions. The popularity and user-friendliness of word processing software and e-mail have made document production so much easier for executives that many find it just as easy to draft a document at a computer as they do to dictate into a machine. Long-distance dictation to a centralized dictation system was once considered very efficient; however, because many executives now travel with notebook computers that can be networked to the office, it has become just as efficient to send documents through the office network as to dictate them. Both dictating and transcribing documents require special skills.

WHAT DOES IT TAKE TO BE A TRANSCRIPTIONIST?

Transcription skill is a composite of many abilities. Your competence in transcribing will depend on your

- keyboarding skills
- facility with the English language
- knowledge of punctuation, spelling, and format
- desire to produce quality work
- knowledge of office procedures
- ability to make judgments
- work habits such that you spend most of your time actually producing output.

As an office professional, you will always be faced with meeting deadlines and setting priorities. In every case, prepare an accurate transcript with an adequate number of copies and properly addressed envelopes; assemble all the enclosures. When you submit correspondence for a manager's signature, you are saying that you have completed your task and that the correspondence is ready to be sent out.

> *"To encourage good office relations, always be on time for work and treat others as you would like to be treated."*
>
> Christine Scott, Graduate
> Toronto School of Business

Arrange your workstation so that the supplies and materials you need are easy to reach. These supplies will include

- a dictionary
- a reference manual
- correspondence that relates to the transcription.

When you are new to the position, check the office procedure manual, if one exists, to determine the document style to use. An organization that prepares an office manual or handbook usually requires that all employees within the organization follow the standard forms illustrated in the manual. Refer to Chapter 12, Reference Resources for information on how to prepare a procedure manual.

If a manual is not available and the choice is left to you, study the correspondence files to determine what style has been used in the past. For efficiency, most organizations use a block letter style, in which all parts of the letter begin on the left.

Prepare error-free transcripts. Make all your corrections on the screen before you print the document. Use your software to check the spelling of each document. Always run a spell check just before the final print; edits made after you check the spelling could leave the document with spelling errors. Also proofread for meaning. Watch for correctness in grammar. Avoid errors such as *hear* for *here* and *there* for *their*. If the document is long or difficult to comprehend, you may need to print all the pages and proofread the hard copy to catch all the errors.

PRO-LINK

pro-Link

Perhaps the most important objective of any written document is to communicate your message.

Here are a few ideas for one of your first tasks towards clarity of message—choosing a font from the myriad of fonts available in your computer:

- Keep it simple; don't be tempted to use obscure or elaborate typefaces.
- Don't use more than two typefaces in one document—it will begin to look unprofessional.
- Chose an appropriate typeface for your document—are you composing an invitation to a party or a business plan?
- Use only variations of your chosen typeface to make the message clearer—italics or bolding.
- Select an 11- or 12- point typeface. If the document is intended for older readers, consider a larger size, say, up to 14-point maximum.
- Maintain the same line spacing throughout the main body of your document.
- Consider reducing the point size of supporting information such as headers and footers.

Finally, date everything! Documents are often edited numerous times between management personnel and the transcriptionist. In the process of constant updating and editing, it may become confusing as to what draft you are working from.

Dictating and Transcribing Tips

Executives who use a machine to dictate correspondence should anticipate what information the transcriptionist needs and should record it at the appropriate location in the dictation. You can expect a good dictator to do the following things:

1. Give adequate information at the beginning of each item. This will include
   a. identifying the type of communication
   b. indicating rush items
   c. giving copy instructions
2. Spell names and unusual technical words.
3. Repeat amounts of money, dates, and other figures.
4. Speak distinctly and slowly, yet naturally.
5. Indicate specifically the enclosures you are to include.

Your success in transcribing from a machine will be governed by your transcription skills. Before you begin to transcribe, collect all the information you will need to produce the documents. This might include a complete file of previous correspondence, or simply a business card containing a person's correct address. Jot down any notes that may be helpful to you while you are transcribing. Never waste time by listening to the complete document before you begin transcribing. Thanks to the document-editing features of word processing, changes that the dictator makes pose no problem. Figure 5-1 shows a transcriptionist using software to edit documents.

Use the date you transcribe, not the date of the dictation, on all correspondence. If you sign the executives' names, use the date you transcribe; if you hold the correspondence for them to sign, use the dates they will return to the office. Also listen in the dictation for the words *yesterday*, *today*, and *tomorrow*. Change the sentences containing these words so that the transcripts will be accurate.

In addition to dictating correspondence, executives also use dictating equipment to

- remind themselves of conversations with customers or clients on whom they have called
- do research from company files for reports and presentations
- record information from newspapers and magazines

Figure 5-1 A medical transcriptionist uses software to edit documents.
Courtesy of Lanier Worldwide, Inc.

- have a verbatim record of an interview
- report trips, meetings, conferences, and sales
- summarize telephone conversations.

When executives use dictating equipment in these ways, transcribe their notes and put the notes on their desk.

Judging Priorities

Transcribe the rush items first. The usual order of priority for transcription is as follows: urgent letters, instructions to others, regular mail, interoffice mail, and rough drafts. However, the urgency of the situation dictates what you are to do first. You will rely on what the manager stresses, plus your own judgment, to know where to begin.

If part of the dictation is an instruction to place a call or send an e-mail, the earlier in the day you do it, the greater your chances are of reaching the person. Make urgent telephone calls or send urgent e-mails between transcribing rush letters, especially if you can make the telephone calls and e-mails and still get the rush letters ready for the next mail pickup.

Instructions to others should always be on your list of what to do first. Co-workers may be waiting for instructions to proceed with their tasks; their working day may be affected in some way by instructions from the manager. To help maintain a cooperative spirit, provide instructions to co-workers as quickly as you can, either by telling them directly or by sending electronic mail. If the instructions are for people who work both in and out of the office, make a special effort to get the instructions to them before they leave their desks.

Transcribe urgent letters as another top priority. You may need to tactfully interrupt the manager to get these urgent letters signed so that they can be faxed or couriered to their destination.

Regular mail is usually transcribed before interoffice mail because of the additional time needed for processing and delivery, but interoffice mail is just as important and can be equally pressing. If you cannot transcribe all the correspondence on the day it is dictated, you can often tell by the content which pieces must be completed the same day. Allow enough time at the end of the day to key a rough draft of a speech, report, or other material that your manager wants to take home to rework.

After reading this discussion on priorities, you might conclude that you are expected to complete all these tasks at once. However, as an office professional you will quickly learn how to prioritize your tasks so that you will be able to cope with work pressures.

Keeping Transcripts Confidential

You are responsible for keeping all dictation material confidential. Label a file folder FOR SIGNATURE and place correspondence in it while you are transcribing. Use a paper clip to fasten the file copy to the correspondence being answered and place both either behind the transcribed letter or in a second folder. With the folders closed, the correspondence will be out of sight of any person who comes to your desk. If you do not use folders, place the correspondence face down on your desk. If you should leave your desk, place the completed correspondence in a drawer.

Remember to protect the transcript when it is on the screen or being printed. The best way to do this is by closing the software window that displays your document.

> *"In the role of an office professional, confidentiality is essential. We should always remember that."*
>
> Heather Edwards, Graduate
> Sault College of Applied Arts and Technology
> Sault Ste. Marie

When the material you transcribe is highly confidential, keep paper copies in a locked file. When confidential information is stored on disks, the disks should be locked away just as confidential paper files would be. Where confidential information is stored on a hard disk that is shared by other employees, a password or access code should be used to protect confidentiality.

DICTATION AND TRANSCRIPTION EQUIPMENT

Dictating/transcribing machines have built-in features that make the equipment easy to use. The functions are controlled by microprocessor technology. Volume, tone, and speed controls enable the transcriptionist to adjust the playback. Instructions can be located quickly. Window displays or electronic index marks indicate the location of the instructions and the location and the length of each dictated item. A foot control allows the administrative assistant to use playback, fast forward, rewind, and adjustable automatic backspacing.

A wide range of dictation and transcription equipment is available, including portable, desktop, and centralized units.

Portable Equipment

Portable dictation technology uses microcassettes and a recording machine that is only slightly larger than the microcassette. The size of this device makes dictation very convenient for managers who travel. Figure 5-2 shows a pocket-size microcassette portable recorder.

Desktop Equipment

Once the tape has been recorded onto, the dictator gives it to the administrative assistant for transcribing.

The administrative assistant may use a desktop unit such as the one shown in Figure 5-3. This is a combination unit and may be used for both dictation and transcription. The microphone is used for dictation; the foot control and headset are used for transcription.

Figure 5-2 Portable dictation device.
Courtesy of Lanier Worldwide, Inc.

Centralized Equipment

Some large organizations use centralized dictation systems. A centralized dictation system makes it possible to dictate from any location using only a telephone.

When a centralized system is used, the administrative assistant can transcribe documents even while more dictation is being received. Flashing signals tell the transcriptionist when priority items have been dictated. The transcriptionist can then immediately transcribe the priority items before returning to the first item in the backlog of work.

These systems reduce the handling of cassettes and result in faster turnaround time for transcription.

Figure 5-4 shows the equipment necessary for a centralized dictation/transcription system.

Figure 5-3 Dictation/transcription unit (with microphone or headset).
Courtesy of Lanier Worldwide, Inc.

Figure 5-4 Centralized dictation/transcription system.
Courtesy of Lanier Worldwide, Inc.

WHAT ARE REPROGRAPHICS?

The term **reprographics** refers to reproduction processes from the highest-quality offset printing to the simplest photocopying. The reprographics industry produces a vast array of high-tech products; however, the reprographics equipment most often used by administrative assistants is copiers. For this reason, the following discussion will focus on copiers only.

Copiers quickly reproduce exact copies, one at a time, of original documents. However, many features and attachments may be added to copiers so that they do much more than copy the original image.

In general terms, copiers are used for printing multiple copies of paper documents and making transparencies that can be projected onto a screen.

Some copiers produce documents of such high quality that it is difficult to distinguish the copy from the original.

Copiers are classified as low-, mid-, and high-volume machines. The differences between categories are evident in Figures 5-5, 5-6, and 5-7.

Low-volume Copiers

Copiers are classified according to their use. Low-volume machines, called convenience copiers, are used in small businesses, or in decentralized areas to save the user travel time. These compact copiers have numerous features. Most low-volume copiers

1. reduce and enlarge documents
2. have easy to replace toner cartridges
3. have attachable sorting bins
4. have multiple trays to accommodate a variety of paper sizes
5. print up to 50 copies per minute
6. automatically feed documents
7. can print in colour
8. are user-friendly
9. scan documents and save them to a computer file when they are plugged into the office computer network.

Figure 5-5 Low-volume copier.
Courtesy of Canon Inc.

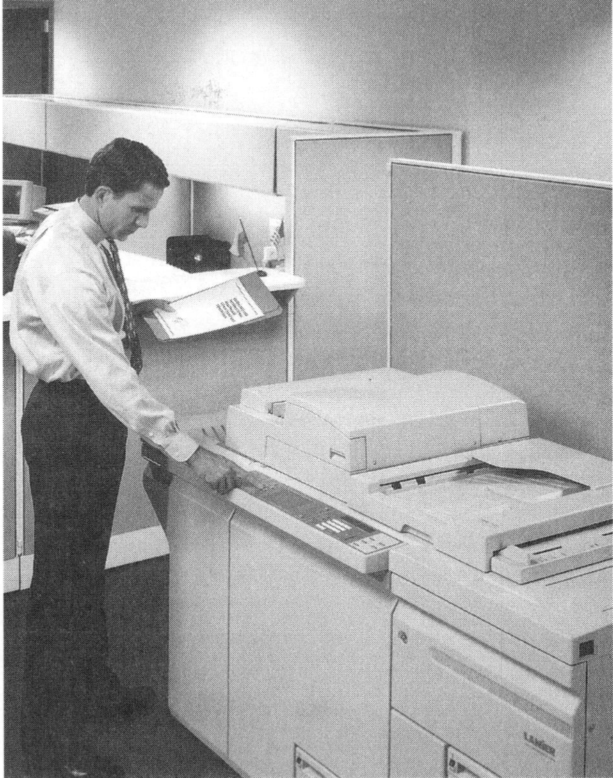

Figure 5-6 Mid-volume copier.
Courtesy of Lanier Worldwide, Inc.

Mid-volume Copiers

These copiers have all the features of the low-volume copiers, along with some additional features. Most mid-volume copiers

1. produce up to 135 copies per minute
2. accommodate more paper sizes
3. are able to copy on both sides of the paper (duplexing)
4. store multiple instructions
5. have remarkable colour features
6. sort and stack multiple copies
7. build booklets
8. staple documents
9. move the image to produce a binding margin
10. reduce and print as many as four images on the same side of the page

PERSPECTIVES

How to Choose a Copier

By Brian Merriman

Smart shopping begins with taking an inventory of your copying needs.

Most administrative assistants would undoubtedly agree that a copier is one of the most indispensable pieces of equipment in the modern office. It's also one of the most confusing to purchase.

After all, how do you know which model is right for your situation? Is it a desktop unit, capable of handling about 100 copies a day? Or a feature-laden workhorse designed to make 5,000 copies daily? With such a large variety of copiers on the market, how do you make a smart business decision?

Industry experts recommend taking an inventory of your copying needs before starting the purchasing process. Think about your current copier situation. Ask your employees or co-workers to spell out which features could make their jobs easier. Next, take a close look at your current copier's instruction manual—what features never get used?

Use the following checklist to gather the necessary information before you contact an office equipment dealer.

1. What size copies will you need?
   - ✔ Letter-size?
   - ✔ Legal-size?
   - ✔ Larger?
2. Are there any special sizes or kinds of documents you'll be copying?
   - ✔ Larger than legal size (11 x 14 inches)?
   - ✔ Up to 11 x 17 inches?
   - ✔ Larger than 11 x 17 inches?
   - ✔ Books?
   - ✔ Photos?
   - ✔ Transparencies?
3. How many copies will your office be making each month?
   - ✔ Below 5,000?
   - ✔ 5,000-10,000?
   - ✔ 10,000-25,000?
   - ✔ 25,000-50,000?
   - ✔ 50,000-100,000?
   - ✔ Over 100,000?
4. How many different people will use the copier?
5. How will you use the documents?
   - ✔ Internal use
   - ✔ External use
6. What type of copies will you need?
   - ✔ Collated copies?
   - ✔ Stapled sets?
   - ✔ Two-sided copies?
7. What service needs do you have?
   - ✔ How fast will you need service when your copier needs repairs?
   - ✔ Do you want a service contract to cover parts and supplies as well as labor?
   - ✔ Do you want free loaners provided in the event of extra-long downtime?
   - ✔ Will you require training for your employees?
8. Do you want to trade in your old copier?
9. What is your price range?

Working with a dealer

Once you answer all these questions, you're well on your way toward purchasing a new copier. The next step is to work with a reputable office equipment dealer who can match your individual needs with the right copier.

For example, if you'll be making copies for external distribution—to customers and clients—you may need a copier that can handle precise details and graphics.

A reputable dealer can also look at your volume needs to determine if more than one unit is necessary to increase productivity and reduce waiting time.

How do you find a reputable office dealer? Ask your colleagues at other companies. Or look in the Yellow Pages for a well-established dealer in your area.

The demonstration process

After an office products salesperson suggests a copier to fit your particular needs, it's time for a demonstration. Be an active participant in this process. Use the copier yourself instead of just watching the salesperson demonstrate its features.

What should you look for? Ease of use is a major consideration. Look closely at the control panel. Are the buttons easily accessible and easy to use? Is it easy to run your applications? Load paper into the copier. Take a try at toner replenishment. Make sure that a jammed sheet of paper won't require a service call.

Service details

If everything works well during the demonstration, you've completed the most difficult steps involved in buying a copier. It's time now to discuss such details as warranties, service contracts, routine maintenance calls, supply deliveries, and, of course, pricing terms.

Before signing the sales papers, do a last run-through with your copier of choice. See for a second time how it handles a standard load of copying work.

Remember: This will be more than just another piece of office equipment. Your new copier will be a constant companion for you and your co-workers. All the preliminary purchasing steps you've taken will ensure you've made the right choice.

Figure 5-7 High-volume copier.
Courtesy of Xerox Canada Ltd.

11. eliminate printing found in the margins of the original document such as fax numbers found at the top or bottom of faxed documents
12. centre the image on the paper
13. have touch control screens.

High-volume Copiers

These copiers combine copy quality, speed, ease of use, and high productivity. High-volume copiers have many features. In addition to the features of the low- and mid-volume copiers, most high-volume copiers

1. produce up to 175 copies per minute
2. have paper trays that hold large supplies of paper
3. have faster and greater sorting abilities
4. bind pages into a book-style cover
5. insert tabs and cover sheets where programmed to do so
6. have outstanding colour processing.

Questions for Study and Review

1. Describe four abilities that your transcription skill will be dependent on.
2. List five tips that would assist a dictator.
3. List five tips that would assist a transcriptionist.
4. What precautions should be taken to protect transcripts of highly confidential information?
5. Describe an efficient method for keeping track of tasks you must complete pertaining to what you are transcribing.
6. Compare the advantages of centralized dictation systems with those of desktop units and portable units.
7. List five advantages that a mid-volume copier has.
8. List five advantages that high-volume copiers have over low-volume and mid-volume copiers.

Spelling Reinforcement

centralized	dictation	identifying	signature
competence	dictionary	pertaining	simultaneously
confidential	duplexing	prioritize	stationery
convenience	electronic	punctuation	temporarily
correspondence	equipment	reprographics	transcriptionist

On-the-Job Situations

1. You sent a confirmation e-mail of a meeting called by your manager. In the e-mail you referred to reports that your manager wanted the participants to review before the meeting. You sent the e-mail without electronically attaching the reports. What do you do now?
2. The company manager is on a business trip. While away, she dictated three letters into the centralized dictation system. You are to transcribe any letters and sign for her in order to get the correspondence in the mail as soon as possible. One of the letters is so garbled that you cannot understand any of it. What steps should you take to carry out the manager's request to get all this correspondence in the mail immediately?
3. You requested the reprographics department to make 500 copies of a handout, which your manager will distribute at a national convention next week. The handout is eight pages long. By mistake, you attached a draft of the handout to the reproduction requisition instead of the clean copy you had prepared. Even though "DRAFT" had been keyed on each page, the machine operator did not catch your mistake. He ran 500 copies of the pages you submitted and assembled them. Several of the pages had minor editing changes; the last three pages had numerous deletions and additions in longhand. You were not aware that you had sent the wrong revision of the handout until the 500 copies were delivered to you. What do you anticipate happens next? What will you do?

Special Reports

1. Interview an administrative assistant and ask the following questions about transcribing.
   a. Do you use a desktop unit or a centralized system?
   b. Does your manager use a portable, a desktop, or a centralized unit for dictating?
   c. How do you prepare copies for the documents you transcribe?
2. Prepare a short report on the latest copiers or dictation/transcribing equipment by consulting magazines on office products.

Production Challenges

5-A Transcribing Letters and Making Copies

Supplies needed:

- *Working Papers Disk, File 5-A*
- *Letterhead for Millennium Appliances, Inc., Forms 5-A-1, 5-A-2, 5-A-3, and 5-A-4, pages 398 to 401*
- *Photocopier*
- *Eight No. 10 envelopes*

Your instructor will dictate letters to you (or will give you a tape of the letters) for Mr. Wilson's signature. Transcribe the dictation, making one copy of each letter for the files. If you require samples of acceptable letter styles, refer to Chapter 13, "Personal and Written Communication Skills." Use a copier to make any additional copies if they are needed. By using a copier, instead of printing on plain paper from a computer printer, your copied document will show the letterhead.

Address an envelope for each letter to be mailed. Refer to Chapter 6, "Incoming and Outgoing Mail," if you require instructions on preparing envelopes. Refer to Chapter 13, "Personal and Written Communication Skills," if you require instructions on copy notations. On letters with multiple copy notations, place a check mark by each name as you key the envelope. Use these letters for Challenge 5-B.

5-B Presenting Transcribed Letters for Signature

Supplies needed:

- *Letters transcribed in 5-A*
- *Envelopes addressed in 5-A*
- *File folder*

Arrange the letters and envelopes in a folder for Mr. Wilson's signature. Since Mr. Wilson often makes notations on the file copy, include the file copies in the folder. When the letters and envelopes are returned to you, fold the letters and insert them into the envelopes. For confirmation on how to present these letters, refer to Chapter 13, "Personal and Written Communication Skills."

World Wide Websites

Canon INC.

www.canon.com/
The Canon INC. home page features global links.

Pitney Bowes

www.pitneybowes.com/
The Pitney Bowes home page includes product and software solutions, and a What's New section.

Xerox Canada

www.xerox.ca/
This site contains information on the complete line of Xerox products, supplies, and solutions.

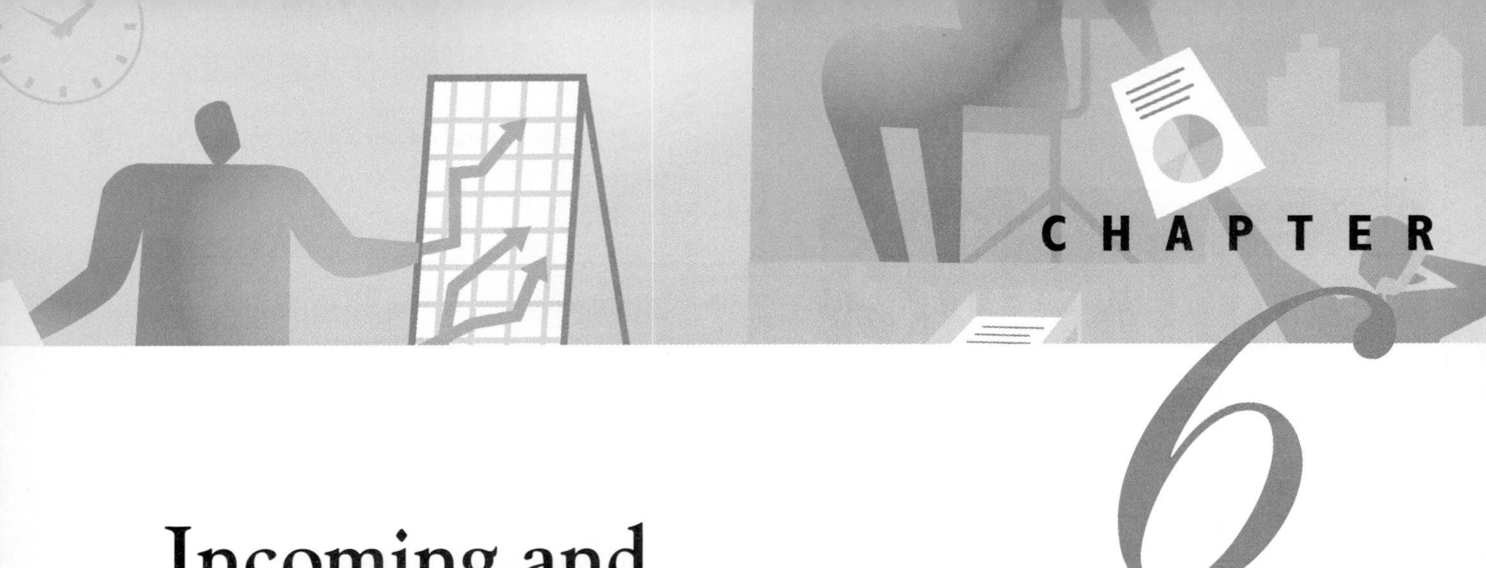

CHAPTER 6

Incoming and Outgoing Mail

Outline

Handling Office Technology
Electronic Mail
Electronic Bulletin Boards
Facsimile
Perspectives: "On Hold, On-Line, and On-Demand"
Telegram
Electronic Money Transfer
Envoypost
Electronic Lettermail
Electronic Admail
Omnipost
Voice Mail
Technology Tips

Handling Incoming Mail
Sorting Mail
Opening Mail
Inspecting the Contents
Date-Time Stamping Mail
Reading and Annotating Mail
Presenting Mail
Handling Packages, Publication Mail, and Admail
Distributing Mail
Answering Mail in the Manager's Absence

Handling Outgoing Mail
Types of Domestic Mail
Supplemental Services
Dangerous Goods
U.S. and International Mail
Proper Addressing
Metered Mail
Other Delivery Options

Exceptions
Redirecting Mail
Changing an Address
Returning Undelivered Mail
Refusing Mail

Learning Outcomes

At the completion of this chapter, the student will be able to:

1. Identify the benefits of electronic mail.
2. Compare different methods of technology-based mail.
3. Explain the procedures for processing incoming mail.
4. Prepare a routing slip.
5. Describe the duties involved in answering mail when your employer is absent.
6. List the categories of domestic mail and give an example of what might be included in each.
7. Describe the special mailing services available from Canada Post Corporation (CPC).
8. State what items are prohibited from being mailed.
9. List postal services that exist for international mail.
10. Demonstrate proper envelope addressing.
11. Describe methods of delivery that are options to those offered by Canada Post Corporation.

Graduate Profile

Patricia Shaheen
Administrative Assistant to the Dean of Business and Agriculture

Saskatchewan Institute of Applied Science and Technology (SIAST)

College Graduation:
SIAST Palliser Campus
Moose Jaw, Saskatchewan
1991

A strong work ethic and a 100 percent commitment to task are vital ingredients of this Moose Jaw native's lifestyle. As a part-time farmer and senior administrative assistant to the provincial dean of the Business and Agriculture Division, Patricia's activities are well planned and effective. In her professional role, she developed a unique easy-to-learn/easy-to-access system that provides the basis for rigorous filing and archiving.

Such organization and attention to detail permits Patricia to focus on her primary responsibilities of keeping the office running smoothly and maintaining the dean's complex schedule. Her diligence is rewarded by the dean's confidence in her work but more, she was recently recognized with a special SIAST Palliser Campus award for service, personality, and job performance. Clearly, this is testimony to her work ethic and commitment.

Patricia's personal growth commitments extend to continuing education where she studies computer software, professional development, and is an active member of Toastmasters International. She has also shared her expertise by developing and teaching professional subjects such as "computers" and "minute taking."

"Learn from those who have more experience."

This gregarious mother of two provides leadership, guidance, and motivation to other support staff and in so doing models her own philosophy of dedication and learning from experience.

Whether you are an administrative assistant in a large organization or a small one, mail will arrive daily—probably more than once during each business day. Mail service is a prime means of moving information from one location to another.

Each mail piece represents a contact with someone outside or within your organization, and the promptness with which you and your manager answer the mail is an important factor in building goodwill and increasing profits for your organization.

> *"You should let employees know that they are doing a great job and that they are valued. Most people work harder if they feel they are valued and are an important part of the company."*
>
> Karen Hodgson, Graduate
> Okanagan University College

As administrative assistant, you may or may not have direct contact with the post office—this may depend on whether or not the organization for which you work has a central mailing department. Nevertheless, you should become knowledgeable about postal and shipping services, because as you prepare outgoing mail you will have to indicate how it is to be sent. Ask questions about available services in your location and watch for information about rate changes and new services.

As postal rates and services are subject to frequent changes, the administrative assistant will find it prudent to access Canada Post Corporation's (CPC) website (see end of chapter Web Links) or obtain CPC booklets from the local postal outlet that will provide current information.

While far from comprehensive, this chapter introduces alternatives and advice for dealing with selective technology-based mail services, incoming mail, and outgoing mail.

HANDLING OFFICE TECHNOLOGY

Electronic Mail

Because of its speed and accessibility, **electronic mail** (e-mail) is the most popular and cost-effective mail system found in business. It is a computerized mail service that enables users to transmit messages and documents over networks from one computer to another. In many companies, a private e-mail system known as an **Intranet** connects employees' computers together.

Figure 6-1 General mail services

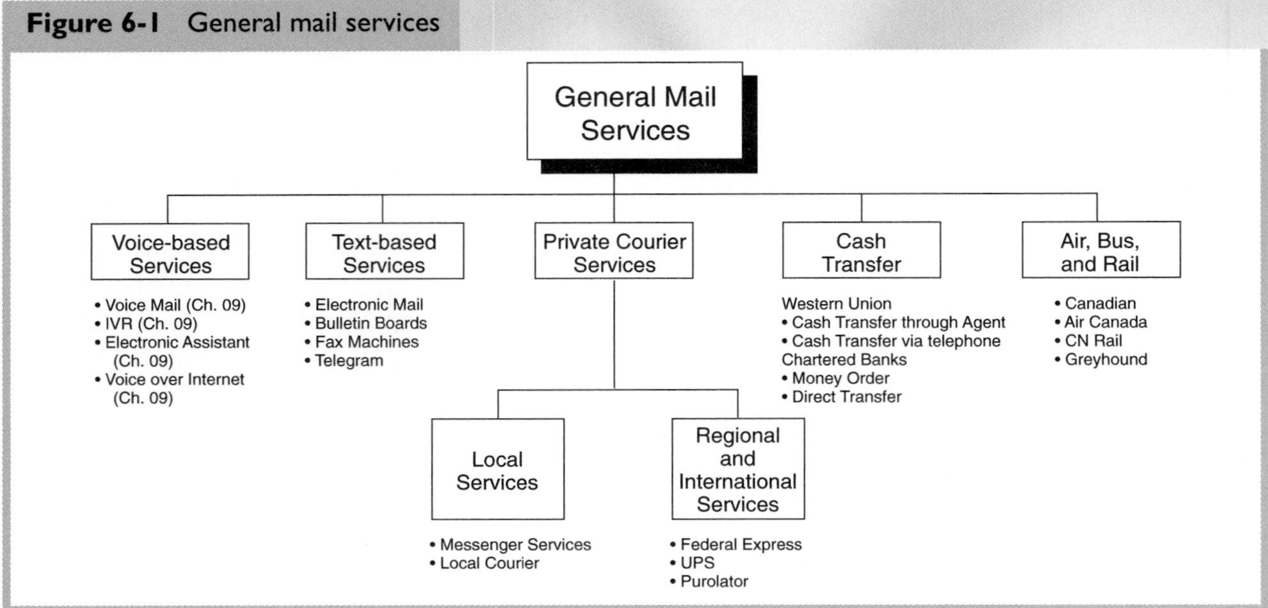

Companies may also subscribe to the larger, external **Internet** but in either case, employees are given a unique e-mail address to which both internal and external users can communicate.

E-mail is the backbone of many business communication systems. In a recent study of office workers' preferences, researchers found that in most situations, e-mail is favoured over paper-based letters and memos. Workers also preferred e-mail to paper-based requests for information, document drafting, and for coordinating activities.

E-mail systems vary widely both in configuration and screen appearance, but all have certain controls in common. Most commercial e-mail systems run within a **Windows** operating system in which controls and options are presented to the user in an **icon** format.

There are always at least two screens presented to the e-mail user, depending on whether the user is sending or receiving e-mail. If the user is *sending* an e-mail, the system will present the send screen, or **template**. See Figure 6-2A. Certain **fields** on the send template will already have information added, such as the date, time, and the sender's network address. These are already recorded by the operating system.

However, to prepare the message for sending, you must provide certain information. Specifically, you must enter:

1. The name or identification code of the intended recipient
2. The names and identification code of any users who are to receive a copy of your e-mail.
3. The subject title of your message, and
4. The message text.

Options such as, *mark as urgent*, *acknowledge*, or *cancel*, may also be selected from this screen.

When options (if any) are selected and the message is complete, the user may instruct the computer to "send" the message across the network to the addressee.

Similarly, when you read incoming e-mail, your message will be displayed in a message display template. See Figure 6-2B. The message will be received complete with:

1. The identification of the sender
2. The subject title
3. The date and time that the message was sent
4. Names of those that were copied on the message
5. The message's priority status
6. The incoming message itself.

The recipient is not given the option to directly edit incoming mail but typical options provided with incoming messages may be:

1. Reply—Reply to the originator using the same subject title
2. Forward—Forward this message to another user
3. Delete—Erase the message
4. Print—Print the message on your printer
5. File—Copy the message to a separate file (storage location).

The administrative assistant must quickly become familiar with the e-mail system in order to communicate

Figure 6-2A An e-mail message being composed for sending.

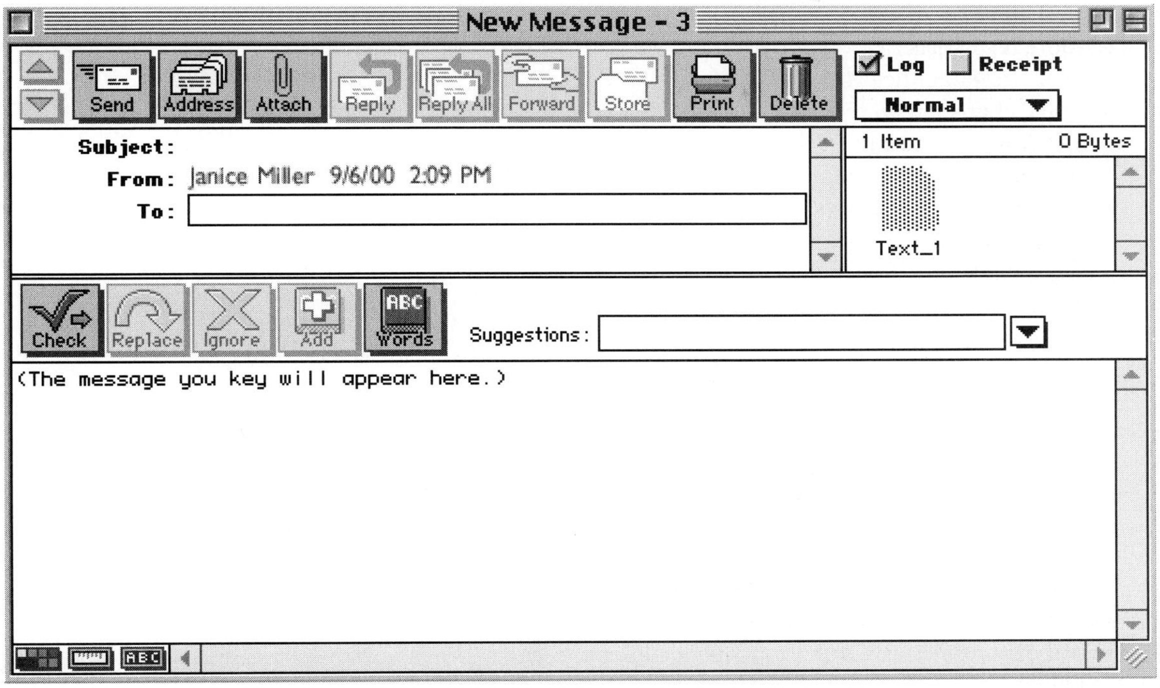

Figure 6-2B An incoming e-mail message.

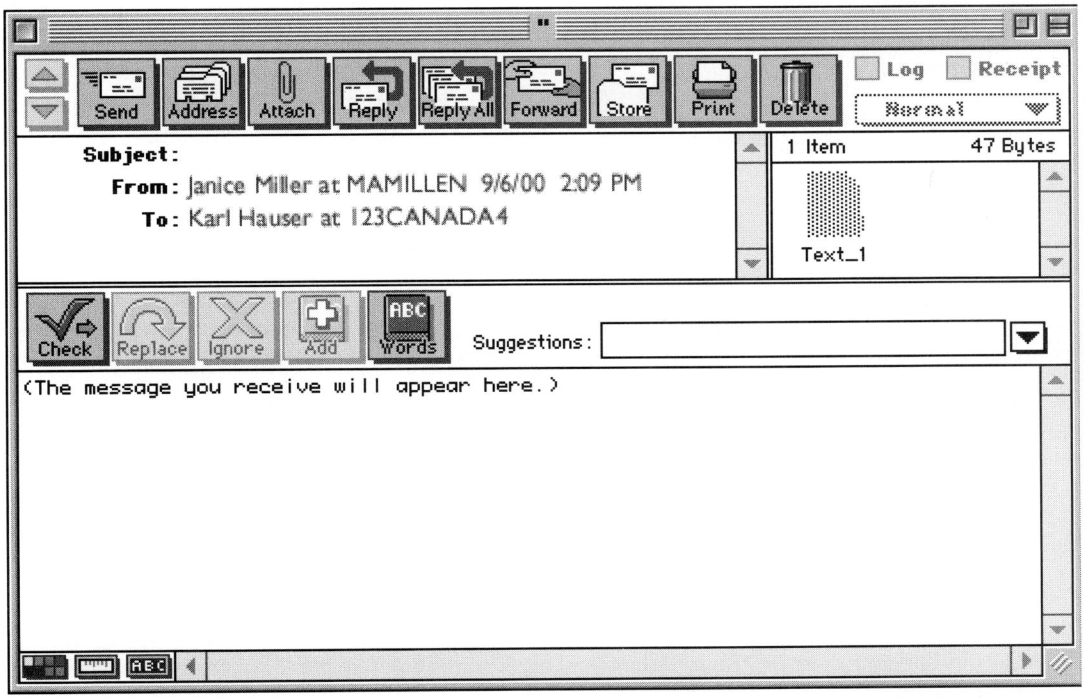

effectively. However, the Electronic Messaging Association predicts that in the year 2000, there will be 108 million e-mail users exchanging seven trillion messages a year. This unregulated exponential growth requires caution; it suggests that organizations and users need to implement guidelines. You may be required to join a committee charged with establishing e-mail usage guidelines for your organization.

Researchers have discovered that while the exchange of e-mail is becoming a way of office life, there is a surprising lack of concern over its risks. Unacceptable and inconsistent e-mail practices can develop into potential problems ranging from system overload to public relations and legal issues. Unless the organization has a policy in place, users may not know they are using e-mail incorrectly. Unintentional e-mail problems include overuse of messages, inappropriate length of messages, failure to credit the original author, impulsive or inappropriate use, poor communication, and a misunderstanding of the single-dimension aspect of e-mail.

> *"Tact, diplomacy, and good listening skills are essential for success."*
>
> Christine Scott, Graduate
> Toronto School of Business

The office professional should remember that while the printed word has long been governed by widely accepted rules, the guidelines for using e-mail are still evolving. To retain the meaning of the message and to ensure it will be read, remember to:

- Learn to use appropriately all the e-mail features.
- Clearly identify the subject so the reader can determine if the message is important. Be similarly clear and precise in your message.
- Avoid using bold, italics, fancy lettering as they may be misinterpreted by the reader as expressive or denoting urgency when none is intended.
- Avoid using special formatting. Special formatting commands in e-mail word processing programs are not universal and may be garbled during transmission to readers who do not have identical programs.
- Just as you would not send a printed document with spelling or grammatical errors, don't send e-mail with these mistakes either.
- Temper the speed and efficiency of e-mail by carefully proofreading every document for accuracy, tone, and content.
- Don't forward confidential mail to others without obtaining permission.
- Avoid sending highly emotional, sensitive or controversial information.
- Do not burden the receivers with unnecessary information. Use a more conventional method of communication for long, complex documents

Implementing suggestions like these will be easier if you remind yourself that a person not just a computer is on the receiving end of your electronic message.

Electronic Bulletin Boards

Much like their corkboard predecessors, **electronic bulletin boards** are public message centres that appear on computer networks. While e-mail is intended for addressed recipients, electronic bulletin board messages are intended for anyone and everyone with access to the network. The Internet has a collection of electronic bulletin boards, known as the *Usenet*, which are organized by subject categories. Electronic bulletin boards are also an integral part of such commercial networks as Telus Planet, Prodigy, America Online (AOL), and Delphi.

Facsimile

The **facsimile**, commonly known as the *fax machine*, is one of the most essential pieces of office equipment. See Figure 6-3. Fax machines can electronically send copies of original documents from one location to another. The fax machine will send almost any kind of hardcopy document—keyboarded text, charts, photographs, drawings, longhand messages, and so on. The document will be reproduced on paper at the destination fax or computer.

Facsimile may be the quickest way to get a document across the city, country, or even the world. The rates are more expensive than using CPC Lettermail service but less expensive than most courier services depending on the size of the document. The speed of

Figure 6-3 Facsimile system.
Courtesy of Pitney Bowes.

PERSPECTIVES

On Hold, On-Line, and On-Demand

By Kim Anderson and Scott Pemberton

As new rules define telephone and e-mail communication, you may be letting courtesy take a backseat to technology.

In survey after survey, the biggest complaint callers have about calling businesses is having to wait on hold.

Naturally, the best solution is to never put callers on hold. But anyone who has worked on the telephone for more than five minutes knows this isn't possible. So, when you have to put a caller on hold, always ask his or her permission. That will help callers feel like they have some control over the situation.

Be sure to check back with the caller every 20 to 25 seconds while she or he is holding. [Let the caller know you're still working on the problem.] If the caller doesn't want to keep holding, get the person's number and call back as soon as you have tracked down the information the caller needs. Finally, after returning to the call, always express your appreciation: "Thank you for waiting." Your gracious words may help defuse any anger the customer may have built up while on hold.

People's perceptions of you and your company often are formed the minute you answer the phone. Use that minute well.

Don't put anything in e-mail that you wouldn't want read over the loudspeaker throughout the company.

New technology has lessened the need for face-to-face or even voice-to-voice contact. E-mail, answering machines, and voice-mail, tools designed for convenience, have created less human communication. The problem is not even a new one. In fact, early developers of the telephone suspected it would be used only for business. They doubted people would want to talk socially on the telephone because it wasn't face to face.

With even greater electronic distancing since those first phones comes the danger that we will begin treating people less like human beings. Phone reps, who talk to countless customers every day but may never see one, can also let courtesy take a back seat to technology. How can you be sure you aren't letting technology take the "people" out of your everyday communication? Here are some helpful suggestions:

- Keep it personal. Technology may build distances, but those distances are not insurmountable.
- Respond to electronic messages. Nothing creates a bigger distance than the feeling that a business is hiding behind its technology.
- Keep technology in perspective. Remember, technology is only a tool.

The E-mail Advantage

Next time you're writing an e-mail message, keep in mind that, like written, telephone, or face-to-face communication, electronic correspondence requires common rules of courtesy and etiquette (or "netiquette"):

- Always be businesslike. A good rule of thumb is to never say anything in an e-mail message that you wouldn't say face-to-face
- Carefully consider who needs to receive your message. With e-mail address groups, a simple click of the mouse can send a message to an entire department or organization. But should you? It's inconsiderate and inefficient to transmit a message to an entire address group if it really needs to go to only two or three people. If you respond to a message that has been distributed to a group, think carefully about whether you need to reply only to the sender of the message or to everyone who received it.

Keep messages brief and to the point. E-mail is supposed to speed up communication, not slow it down.

- Keep messages brief and to the point. E-mail is supposed to speed up communication, not slow it down.
- Answer your messages promptly. If you have to check out some information, dash off a quick e-mail, letting the sender know you have received his or her messages and when you will have the information requested.
- Avoid sending personal messages. It's bad to use office e-mail for personal communication. Employers frown on the practice—they see it as a modern-day version of gossiping around the office water cooler.
- Be careful about sending confidential messages. The contents of the message may wind up in the hands of someone you don't want reading it.

Excerpted from Indispensible You! *by Kim Anderson and Scott Pemberton. Reprinted with permission from Dartnell Corporation © 1999, 360 Hiatt Drive, Palm Beach Gardens, FL 33418.*

facsimile transmission varies with the size of the page, the density of the image to be faxed and, of course, the level of technology of the facsimile machine sending and receiving documents. However, the sender can be sure that regardless of the distance, the document will reach its destination within seconds of being sent.

Facsimile transmission uses telephone lines to send documents—in fact, sending a fax is as easy as making a telephone call. Fax machines operate automatically, allowing you to send documents without first notifying the recipient. The general procedure is very simple:

1. Place the document to be transmitted in the sending fax unit.
2. Dial the fax number of the receiver.
3. Press the send button.

Each fax being transmitted should be accompanied by a cover page, called a **transmittal sheet**. The transmittal sheet gives full details of who the sender is and who the receiver should be. A full transmittal sheet is not always necessary; small adhesive sheets containing brief transmittal information may be adhered to the first page of the fax if space permits. (See Figures 6-4 and 6-5.) An office that sends numerous faxed messages and uses the small adhesive sheets rather than an entire extra page will realize cost savings.

If you work for a small company that does not own a fax machine, one can be leased. Many pharmacies, copy shops, and CPC outlets are equipped with fax machines for public use. Hotels will allow their guests to use their fax machines and often locate a fax machine in the lobby for public use. Most courier services are equipped with facsimile equipment that can be used for a fee.

While the most popular method of sending a fax is by fax machine, many residential computers, network computers, and a growing community of individual office computers have special software to enable the user to fax documents directly from their station. Any document composed on the computer can be faxed providing the computer has the special software, which emulates a fax. The software must be installed and the computer must be connected to the public telephone or cable network. A fax sent in this way can be addressed to another computer of a fax machine anywhere on the network. Conversely, any fax machine can send a fax to a computer that is connected to the public telephone or cable network and has the special fax software. The clear advantage of sending faxes from your computer is that no paper copy is necessary.

Feature-rich units are expected to become affordable for one-person offices. The newest and most advanced facsimile machines provide both cost and time savings to the office. The following is a discussion of some of their features.

1. **Dialing.** For fax numbers that are dialled frequently, the administrative assistant may program the telephone numbers into the machine's memory so that for future calls only one or two numbers need to be keyed. This is a real time-saver because it means that the sender of the fax does not need to look up and dial long number sequences.

   When the administrative assistant attempts to send a fax, and the receiving line is busy, the document may be left in the machine for transmittal when the line is free. The assistant may use the *automatic redial* feature to have the facsimile machine continually redial the number, and transmit when the line becomes available.

   Fax messages, like telephone calls, cost less to send outside business hours. For this reason, another popular feature is *delayed auto dialing*, whereby the administrative assistant can program the fax machine to send the message long after the staff have left for the evening. Leaving the hard copy in the machine is not always necessary, since some **high-end fax** machines can scan the document and electronically store it until the designated transmittal time.

2. **Security.** One of the problems with a basic fax machine is that documents transmitted via a fax may receive little or no confidentiality. Companies often avoid sending confidential information by fax, since the document may be read by whoever collects the printouts. However, more advanced and feature-rich machines have solved this problem. An advanced feature now allows the message to print only after the correct security code has been keyed. When sending a fax containing confidential information, the sender should telephone the receiving company immediately prior to the transmission and ask that the appropriate person wait at the fax machine for the transmitted document to arrive.

   Another precaution to take may be the inclusion of a *confidentiality request statement* at the foot of the cover sheet. See Figure 6-4. Caution should be used when using our example statement as it invites the non-intended recipient to phone collect. This statement could be taken literally for even non-confidential faxes. The administrative assistant may wish to modify the confidentiality request statement or have a separate set of fax cover sheets for critical and confidential faxes.

3. **Broadcasting.** An administrative assistant who often needs to send the same message to many

Figure 6-4 Fax transmittal sheet.

FAX *from* MA MILLENNIUM APPLIANCES, INC.

3431 Bloor Street, Toronto, ON M8X 1G4
(Tel) 416-795-2893 (Fax) 416-795-3982

DATE: ______________________ TIME: ______________________

NUMBER OF PAGES (Including Cover Sheet): ______________________

TO:

(Fax Number) (Telephone Number)

(Name) (Title)

(Company)

FROM:

(Name) (Title)

MESSAGE:

This facsimile contains confidential information. If you are a recipient of this facsimile but not identified in the address, please treat this communication as confidential and deliver it to the addressee. If the addressee is not known to you, kindly inform the sender by collect call as soon as possible. Thank you.

Post-it™ Brand FAX TRANSMITTAL MEMO / FEUILLETS POUR FAC-SIMILÉ 7671 | NO. OF PAGES / NBRE DE PAGES

TO: / À:	FROM: / DE:
CO.: / CIE.:	CO.: / CIE.:
DEPT.: / SERVICE:	PHONE #: / Nº DE TÉL.:
FAX #: / Nº DE TELECOP.:	FAX #: / Nº DE TELECOP.:

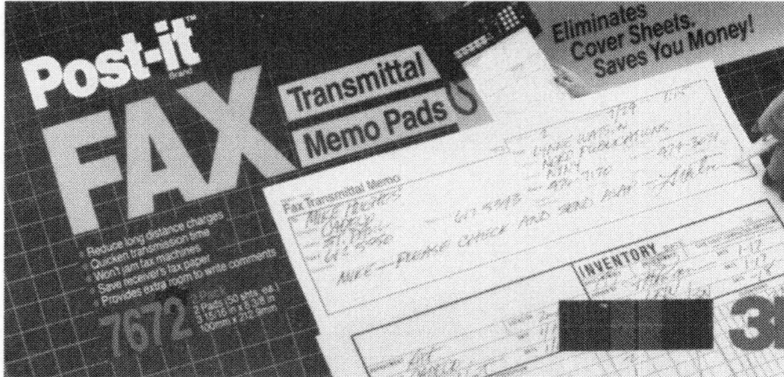

Figure 6-5 Adhesive fax transmittal memos.
Courtesy of 3M Canada Inc.

different offices would require a fax machine with the broadcast feature. The assistant would preprogram the fax numbers of the recipients and send the message only once. The same fax message would be sent to all the preprogrammed destinations at the time the assistant designated. The assistant need not be present when the fax is transmitted, since the facsimile machine can store the message in memory until the required transmittal time.

4. **Polling.** In an office where fax machines are connected to a network, polling may be required. This feature allows one fax machine to test others on the network for information. Users can store their messages on the fax network. The person waiting to receive the messages instructs his or her facsimile station to poll the other machines for facsimiles with the correct poll code. Where the correct code is found, the message is transferred to the polling fax machine. A head office wishing to pick up orders or check inventory from its stores, for example, may require the polling feature.

5. **Facsimile on Demand.** With this advanced feature, commonly broadcast faxes are held in memory at a central location. This central location is known as a repository. A potential recipient may dial into the central repository which is a central repository for many fax documents and, through the keypad, select a specific fax for return. For example, if an organization or a member of the public wanted to obtain a specific Legislative Bill from their Provincial Government Archives, they would first obtain the number of the government fax repository. An interactive voice response system (IVR) would coach the caller through a series of questions, including return fax number, document desired, and billing information. When complete, the document would be selected and faxed automatically to the fax number identified by the caller. One benefit of this system is that the expense is born by the person desiring the document, not by the creator of the document.

Telegram

The telegram is the oldest type of technology-based mail. Samuel Morse invented the telegraph and sent his first official telegraph message in 1844. As he tapped out the message *"What hath God wrought!"* it is unlikely that he envisioned the future developments of the telegram.

Telegrams are useful for emergencies, where the recipient has no access to e-mail or fax machine, or if an immediate response is necessary, say, to confirm a deal. However, the advent of high-speed telecommunications and the Internet has largely superseded the traditional telegram. Some private organizations maintain hybrid telegram services, which incorporate e-mail, or voice initiation and delivered by voice or an express delivery service. Similarly, a **Cablegram** is the international equivalent of the telegram. By visiting the Western Union website you may see examples and service commitments for one such telegram and cablegram provider. See end of chapter Web Links.

Electronic Money Transfer

If you wish to send or receive money over distance, it may be done though most chartered banks or through a Western Union agency. Most banks require a minimum of 24 hours to make the transfer; however, Western Union is more expeditious. In modern countries, transfers are almost immediate; however, in the worst case of a very remote location, the complete transfer and notification process might take as long as a few days.

There are more than 23,000 Western Union agencies in convenient locations around the world such as pharmacies, bookstores, grocery stores, and all Money Mart locations. The process for sending money via long distance is as follows:

1. The sender contacts a Western Union agency either by telephone or in person at a Western Union outlet.

2. The sender then tells the agent the exact amount of money to be sent, and gives the agent the recipient's name and address. Payment from the sender may be in the form of cash, certified cheque, or Visa or MasterCard. (These last two options allow the transaction to be made over the telephone.) If cash or a certified cheque is used, the transaction is completed in approximately five minutes; with Visa or MasterCard, the transaction should take less than one hour.
3. The Western Union office notifies a central Western Union agency in the destination city. It is then determined which outlet is most convenient for the recipient to pick up the money.
4. The sender contacts the recipient and tells her or him that the money has been sent, and where to collect it. The sender should also provide the recipient with the transfer number. When the sender prefers to have the destination Western Union office contact the recipient, it will do so for a fee. However, for security reasons, the only information provided during the telephone call from Western Union to the recipient is that a transfer has arrived. There is no discussion of the amount or of the identity of the sender.
5. When the recipient attempts to collect the cash, a screening process takes place. The recipient must present photo identification such as a driver's licence or passport. If the recipient has no photo identification, three pieces of identification issued by the government are requested—for example, a social insurance card, a birth certificate, and a health care card, or similar. If the recipient has been robbed and has no form of identification, Western Union will request that the sender of the money provide a code that the recipient will recognize. An example of this may be the middle or maiden name of a relative or even the family pet's name.

   The recipient must complete a receiving form that requires she or he to know the location from which the money was sent, the sender's full name, and the amount of money to be collected. Only after this information and a signature are provided will the money be released.

For full details of the money transfer process and other Western Union Electronic Message Services, the administrative assistant should call Western Union's North American toll free number at 1-800-235-0000, or visit their website. See end of chapter Web Links.

Envoypost

If you work on a computer that has access to the Envoy network, you can create a document and send it to a Canada Post Corporation (CPC) location. CPC prints the message, places it in an envelope, and physically delivers the message in the next scheduled Lettermail delivery. Envoypost messages can be sent to households and businesses within Canada.

Electronic Lettermail

For businesses that require high-volume (over 100,000 addressed letters each year) yet personalized mailings, CPC offers Electronic Lettermail. Examples of Electronic Lettermail applications include invoices and monthly bank statements.

The business organization provides CPC with a mailing list and an electronically stored message. In turn, CPC electronically transmits the messages along with the logo and signature of the business. When the electronic messages are received at the destination post offices, they are printed, inserted into envelopes, and delivered.

When this electronic option is used, messages are received more expeditiously than through the regular mail system.

Electronic Admail

Electronic Admail is the same process as Electronic Lettermail with the exception that the transmission is for high-volume (50,000 or more) mailings of advertising materials, notices, newsletters, and the like.

The message, logo, and signature are provided in electronic form along with a mailing list. The advertising materials are received at the destination post offices, inserted into envelopes, and delivered.

Omnipost

This bilingual delivery system marries the convenience of computer electronic mail or fax mail with the delivery of hard copy Lettermail. Letters are sent through e-mail or fax to the receiving postal outlet, where they are printed and delivered in one business day between most major Canadian cities. Because this service is electronic, it can be accessed 24 hours a day, any day of the week, from any computer where the user is an Omnipost subscriber. CPC bills the subscriber once a month.

Voice Mail

Because of its name, **voice mail** must be mentioned in this chapter. However, it is a telephone application and so will be explained in more detail in Chapter 9.

Voice mail is a form of telephone messaging. In its simplest form, voice mail allows callers to access or record voice information from a list of prerecorded options. However, voice mail technology is really much more than stated here. To better understand this technology, refer to Chapter 9, "Telecommunications in the Office."

Technology Tips

The Electronic Post Office

CPC's latest innovative postal service provides the ability to send and receive mail electronically. Mail, in this case, refers to invoices, forms and other correspondence that would normally be delivered as physical mail. The Electronic Post Office uses the Internet to deliver your mail to a secure **virtual** electronic post office box. Individuals and participating companies send mail to your electronic post office box just as they would send physical mail to a letter-mail box. The cost is free to the recipient, as participating companies that send letters, invoices, forms, and advertising will pay for the service.

You will choose the invoices you want to receive electronically from the list of participating companies. You may pay the bills in a number of ways; directly from your organization's bank account, a credit card, or by forwarding your invoices to your financial institution's banking facility.

All personal and confidential information remains secure by encrypted codes and passwords. Only the sender and the recipient are able to see the contents of your mail. The electronic mail is stored on CPC's own secured **servers** and not on public Internet servers.

From the participating company's point of view, the Electronic Post Office eliminates the cost of paper and postage. The company may also maintain accurate records of mail and invoices as they are already presented in electronic format.

"I'm confident in myself and my abilities and I'm not afraid to take risks when necessary."

Rhonda Sherb-Gillam, Graduate
Nova Scotia Community College
Akerley Campus

Electronic mail increases the flow of information in and out of the office. Since speed of communication is the main advantage of using electronic mail, the administrative assistant must be alert to e-mail that arrives on his or her system but is intended for someone else in the office. Deliver or transfer the e-mail without delay; however, if this type of e-mail is received frequently, delivery schedules should be worked out.

Electronic Lettermail and Omnipost may arrive in the regular mail and should be processed along with the other items. However, the fact that they are electronic mail indicates that there is some urgency for their receipt.

Facsimiles may be received at any time during the day or night. Those received at night should be processed at the beginning of the next business day. Others should be delivered to the recipients as soon as the facsimiles arrive or according to a designated schedule.

If you are responsible for collecting faxed materials, this information should not be left lying in the fax tray, for the following two good reasons:

1. The fact that it has been faxed and not sent through the regular mail system may indicate that it is urgent.
2. Many people avoid sending confidential materials via fax; even so, there is a chance that the information may be, if not confidential, at least sensitive.

Immediately after receiving a fax, advise the recipient that a fax has arrived, or deliver the fax to his or her office.

HANDLING INCOMING MAIL

Traditional incoming mail is very different than it was even a few years ago. With the popularity of the Internet and electronic mail, as well as voice mail, the administrative assistant is seeing, reading, and controlling less traditional mail now than ever before. Even so, every office still receives paper mail, and handling the mail is still a high priority on the desk of an administrative assistant. When the mail is handled accurately and expeditiously, other office employees are able to respond more efficiently to the needs addressed in the items of mail.

The information provided here on incoming mail is extensive. For an administrative assistant to perform all these steps would be too time-consuming. While it is not expected that every office will handle mail with this degree of care, the administrative assistant is certain to perform at least some of the steps listed below:

1. sorting mail
2. opening mail
3. inspecting the contents

4. date-time stamping mail
5. reading and annotating mail
6. presenting mail to the manager
7. distributing and routing mail.

Some large organizations still have their central mailing departments, although with the decreased volume of paper mail, one encounters fewer of these. Such departments are responsible for receiving *all* of the organization's mail and for routing it to the correct departments or individuals. Usually, the mailing department provides at least one pickup and delivery to each department every day. At one time, central mailing departments opened, date-time stamped, and distributed the mail. They rarely do so now; instead, recipients open their own mail, or the administrative assistant performs this task for the executives or for the whole department.

When the mail is delivered to one location, someone must sort the mail and deliver it to the appropriate workstations. If this task should be assigned to you, sort and make the deliveries at once so that other administrative assistants may start processing their own mail.

Sorting Mail

Mail may come to your desk unopened. When it does, read the information on the envelopes, and sort it into the following groups:

1. Mail sent with urgency (electronic or courier).
2. Lettermail, including bills and statements.
3. Interoffice mail.
4. Personal mail.
5. Newspapers and periodicals.
6. Booklets, catalogues, and other advertising materials.
7. Parcels.

The administrative assistant may have to sign for couriered mail and other insured and expedited pieces of mail before they can be received. Keep the priority mail separate from the rest of the mail, open it as soon as it arrives, and then put it on the addressee's desk in a way that calls attention to it. Priority mail refers to electronic mail, couriered mail, and all CP mail that is delivered via an expedited service.

In the stack of mail to be opened immediately, assemble Lettermail and interoffice memoranda. All interoffice mail is important. Each item either requires a reply or provides your manager with information she or he needs.

Do not open your manager's personal mail. Definitely do not open letters marked *Confidential*, *Personal*, or *Private*. Unless you receive explicit instructions to open them, place the personal letters on your manager's desk unopened.

Do not open, but quickly distribute, any mail specifically addressed to another employee in your work area. Any mail that has been delivered to you by mistake should be promptly forwarded to that person or returned to the post office.

You will have to decide whether mail addressed to an employee who is no longer with the organization is personal or business correspondence. If the letter appears to be personal, write the forwarding address clearly on the item and put it in the outgoing mail. If the letter is addressed by title to someone no longer with the organization, you can assume that it is a business letter. When you distribute the mail, deliver it unopened to the new employee who has this title or is responsible for the work implied by the title.

As you sort, put all circulars, booklets, advertisements, newspapers, and periodicals aside until you have opened and processed the more urgent mail.

Opening Mail

Before you begin opening the mail, assemble the supplies you will need: opener, date stamp, pencils, stapler, transparent tape, paper clips, your Mail-Expected Record, and your To Do List.

Slit the envelopes of all the important mail before you remove the contents from any of them. To reduce the possibility of cutting the contents, tap the lower edges of the letters on the desk so that the contents fall to the bottom.

Should you open a letter by mistake, seal the envelope with transparent tape, write "Opened by mistake" and your initials, and distribute or forward the letter to the addressee.

Inspecting the Contents

Be certain to remove *all* the contents from envelopes. A thorough inspection is necessary to avoid throwing enclosures out with the envelopes. Keep the envelopes until you are certain that all the enclosures and addresses are accounted for. Save the interoffice envelopes (sometimes called interdepartmental envelopes) for further use. See Figure 6-6.

Inspect each letter for the address and signature of the sender, the date, and enclosures. If the sender's address *or* signature is missing from a letter, look for the address on the envelope. If it is there, staple the envelope to the back of the letter. When a letter is not

Figure 6-6 Interdepartmental envelope.

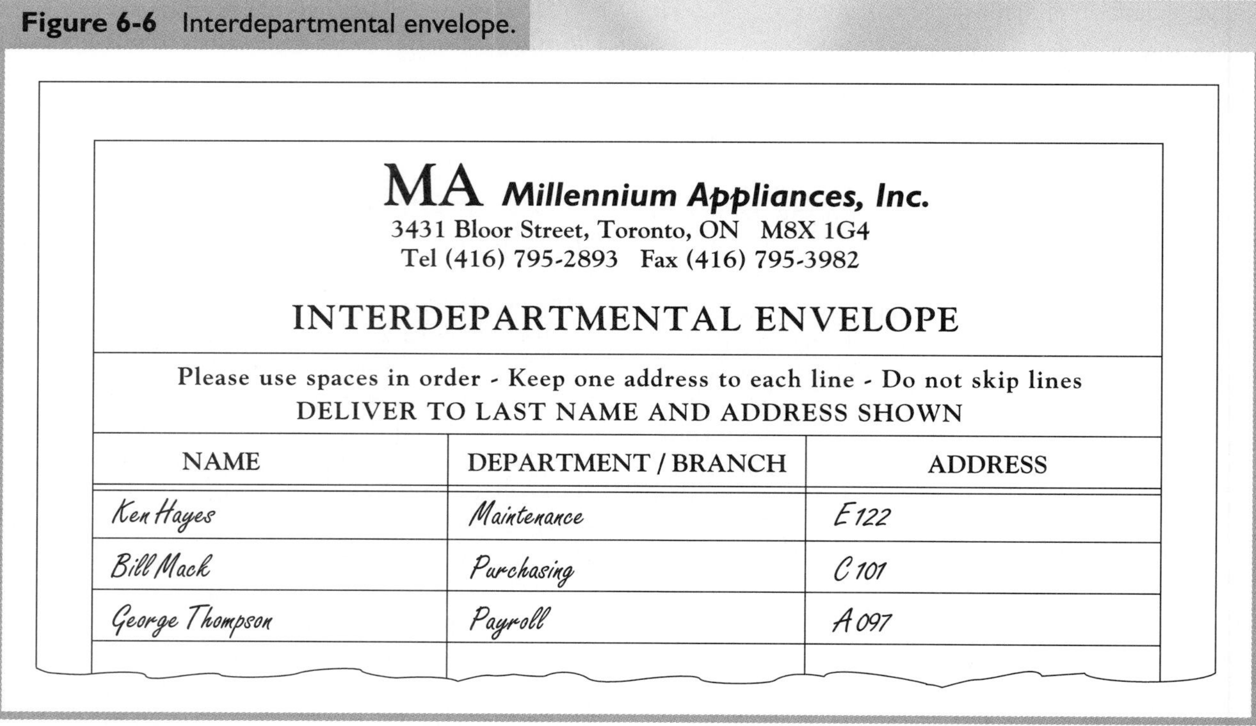

MA Millennium Appliances, Inc.
3431 Bloor Street, Toronto, ON M8X 1G4
Tel (416) 795-2893 Fax (416) 795-3982

INTERDEPARTMENTAL ENVELOPE

Please use spaces in order - Keep one address to each line - Do not skip lines
DELIVER TO LAST NAME AND ADDRESS SHOWN

NAME	DEPARTMENT / BRANCH	ADDRESS
Ken Hayes	Maintenance	E122
Bill Mack	Purchasing	C101
George Thompson	Payroll	A097

signed, the envelope may help identify who wrote the letter.

When a letter is not dated, write the postmark date on the letter and staple the envelope to the back of the letter. Also, if you notice a major discrepancy between the date on the letter and the date of arrival, staple the envelope to the letter.

Check the enclosures received against the enclosure notations. If an enclosure is missing, inspect the envelope again; if you do not find the enclosure, make a note on the face of the letter beside the enclosure notation that the enclosure is missing. Underline the reference to it and add a note in the margin. You will have to fax, or telephone, to request the missing enclosure; enter a reminder on your To Do List at once.

When appropriate, if enclosures are letter-size or larger, staple them to the back of the letter. Fasten small enclosures to the front of a letter. Use paper clips to temporarily fasten an item that a staple would mutilate—for example, a cheque or a photograph. Fold a small piece of paper over a photograph to protect it from the paper clip.

Date-Time Stamping Mail

The time of arrival of certain correspondence has legal significance. For example, the date a payment is received is a factor in allowing a cash discount; and a specific time of day is set for opening bids. When correspondence is received too late for the recipient to comply with a request, the date received is protection for the addressee.

Organizations do not prejudge which correspondence should be date-time stamped. With the exception of a few documents that should not be marred in any way, organizations stamp all incoming mail either with the date or with both the date and the hour of arrival. The entry is made in one of three ways:

1. by writing the date in abbreviated form, such as 9/21/—, in pencil
2. by stamping the word *Received* and the date with a mechanical date stamp, which must be changed daily
3. by stamping the minute, hour, and date of arrival with a date-time recorder. Mailing departments use a date-time recorder, which has a clock built in with the printing device.

Stamp or write the date received on each piece of correspondence in an area of white space at the edge. The same pieces of correspondence may come to your desk several times while they are in process. If you date-stamp all the mail as you read it, you will know as soon as you see the stamp that you have already seen and read a particular piece of correspondence. Consistently stamp booklets, catalogues, and periodicals on either the front or the back.

Reading and Annotating Mail

You can save a lot of time for your manager and yourself by marking and grouping correspondence according to the next step to be taken for each piece. You do this by reading the correspondence in search of the important facts, underlining key words and dates, and writing marginal notes. In some cases you will not know what the next step should be; in other cases your manager will not agree with your notations. Even so, by using good judgment you can organize the correspondence so that your manager can spend time on the letters and memoranda that truly need attention.

Some managers prefer that nothing be underlined or written in the margins of incoming letters. For this reason, get approval before you underline and annotate.

Read the correspondence rapidly, concentrating on the content and using a systematic method of making notes on which you can rely for following through. Develop a questioning attitude—one that will ensure that you pick out significant facts and help you decide what the next step should be. For instance, keep your eyes open for letters that

1. contain the date of an appointment that must be entered in the appointment calendars
2. mention that a report is being mailed separately
3. confirm a telephone conversation
4. request a decision that cannot be made until additional information is obtained.

Use a pencil to underline and make marginal notes. Underline sparingly; otherwise your attempt to emphasize will lose its effectiveness. Underline key words and figures that reveal who, what, when, and where.

Provide your manager with additional information in the margins. This is called **annotating**. Write small and make your notations brief.

Jot down what you would remind your manager of if you were talking to him or her about it. For example, if the letter is a reminder to send a booklet that was requested earlier and it has been mailed, write "Mailed" and the date of mailing. If an item referred to in a letter arrived separately, write "Received." See Figure 6-7 for an example of an annotated letter.

Annotating is preferable to verbally reminding your manager. The use of marginal notes eliminates interruption; as well, your manager is able to refer to those notes as she or he answers the correspondence. On the other hand, she or he might prefer that no marks be made on a letter—for example, in cases when that letter might be presented to a manager for consultation and action, or if the letter might be circulated. Marginal notes can confuse readers, and underlining can irritate the readers to whom a letter is circulated. Although your usual practice may be to underline and annotate, refrain from marking certain letters. When in doubt, do not mark them.

As you read correspondence, pay close attention to the items that require following up. Make the entries in the proper places in your reminder system. Your follow-up plan needs to be foolproof; do not rely on your memory. Enter the date of a meeting or the time of an appointment in both your manager's appointment calendar and your own.

Make a notation of anything being sent separately that you have not received. You can set up a Mail-Expected Record like the one in Figure 6-8.

As you discover that your manager will need previous correspondence, make a note in your To Do List to obtain it. As soon as you have finished reading the mail, obtain the earlier correspondence and attach it to the back of the respective incoming letters. However, do not delay getting the mail to your manager. You can obtain earlier correspondence, locate facts, and verify figures while your manager is reading the mail.

Be sure to enter reminders on your To Do List to write for missing enclosures. Occasionally the sender will discover that an enclosure was omitted and will send it separately. Unless an enclosure is urgently needed, wait a day to request it. At other times the enclosure will be needed immediately, and you will need to fax a message or make a telephone call to check on it.

If an enclosure is money, make sure the amount received matches the amount mentioned in the letter. When it does not, indicate the amount received and the difference in the margin of the letter.

Presenting Mail

When placing mail on your manager's desk, follow these simple rules:

1. Remember that the mail is a priority; act on it as quickly as possible.
2. Place the most urgent items on top and the least urgent items on the bottom. When items are couriered or faxed they may be urgent; however, you will need to determine this by reading the content. The longer you have worked for a particular organization or manager, the better your judgment will be in separating urgent mail from routine mail.
3. Mail should be placed in such a way that it is not visible to people visiting your manager's office in her/his absence. Often, you can protect the confidentiality of the mail by placing it in a large envelope or a folder.

Figure 6-7 Sample annotated letter.

MA ***Millennium Appliances, Inc.***
3431 Bloor Street, Toronto, ON M8X 1G4
Tel (416) 795-2893 Fax (416) 795-3982

06 September 20--

Mr. Kyle Rhodes
Manager, Sales Office
Millennium Appliances, Inc.
3152 - 45th Avenue
Vancouver, BC V6N 3M1

Dear Mr. Rhodes

NOVEMBER SALES SEMINAR

One of the speakers for the November Sales Seminar is in the hospital. Therefore, he will be unable to present a program for the Sales Seminar.

The members of the Executive Committee of the November Sales Seminar suggested that you would make an excellent speaker for the Seminar. You would receive an honorarium to cover any expenses you may incur. Your presentation would last approximately one hour and be shared with an audience of approximately 50 sales professionals. If you agree to speaking at the Sales Seminar, we will make arrangements for your accommodation at the Hilton Hotel where the Seminar will be located.

The dates for the Seminar are Tuesday, November 11 and Wednesday, November 12. We would ask that you present your topic twice, once on each day.

May we suggest that your topic relate to your successful methods of team building. I am enclosing a list of topics which will be used by other speakers at the Seminar.

Your acceptance of this invitation would be greatly appreciated.

Sincerely

J. Miller

Janice Miller
Chairperson, Sales Seminar

lr
Enclosure

No enclosure was sent.

You have a conference planned for Nov. 11, with H. Thomas and B. Ross.

Figure 6-8 Mail-expected record.

MAIL-EXPECTED RECORD			
EXPECTED FROM	DESCRIPTION OF DOCUMENT	DATE RECEIVED	FOLLOW-UP SENT
L. Crawford	map	Nov. 1	—
D. Duggin	photos	Nov. 16	yes — thank you
I.B.M.	brochures		
Unitel	annual report		

Handling Packages, Publication Mail, and Admail

Packages should receive priority over newspapers, periodicals, and advertising materials. Expedited parcels should receive the same priority as Lettermail. In some cases you will be watching for the arrival of packages. Packages that have letters attached or that are marked "Letter Enclosed" should be processed with the important mail. However, do not open a package or separate a letter from it until you have time to carefully check the contents against the packing slip or invoice. Always avoid opening a package with the intention of checking the contents later.

Your manager will want to know that certain items have arrived, but will be interested in seeing new items, not routine ones. For instance, if a shipment of a recently revised form arrives, your manager will want to know if what has been received is what was specified. Place one of the forms on your manager's desk. Store regular supplies in their proper places without your manager seeing them.

Unwrap newspapers and try to flatten them. On the front cover of newspapers and periodicals, affix circulation lists. Circulation lists are a type of routing slip. See Figure 6-9.

If the manager wishes to see the newspapers and periodicals before they are circulated to the rest of the staff, keyboard his or her name at the top of each list. Otherwise, names are commonly arranged in alphabetical order or according to the staff hierarchy.

As people pass the newspaper or periodical to the next person on the list, they should draw a line through their name on the circulation list.

Do not throw advertising materials away until your manager has had a chance to glance at them. Managers want to know about new products in their fields; perusing advertising materials is one way to become aware of what is new. If your manager tells you to screen advertising materials, be sure you clearly understand which items she or he has no interest in.

After your manager has seen the advertising materials, booklets, catalogues, and so on, you will have to decide what to do with them. Which ones should you keep? Which ones should you route to someone who has an interest in a particular subject? Which ones should you throw away? Ask your manager to initial anything that might be looked at again.

Do not clutter your correspondence files with advertising materials. Throw most ads away. For those you save, set up a separate file that you can go through quickly and update periodically. Advertising materials are usually not dated. However, if you date-stamp them, you can separate the old from the new by looking at the Date Received stamp. Replace old catalogues with new ones. If you keep many catalogues, work out a satisfactory filing system for them. Pamphlet and magazine files are available from manufacturers of filing supplies and are an attractive and organized way to file your catalogues, booklets, and magazines.

Figure 6-9 Routing or circulation slip.

ROUTING SLIP

SEQUENCE	TEAM MEMBER	DATE	INITIAL
4	J. Adams		
	A. Arnolds		
	K. Best		
	L. Davenport		
	M. Franzen		
3	L. Gatez		
	H. Hatherly		
1	E. Kaye		
	A. Kohut		
	L. Mann		
	J. Newman		
	L. Minchuk		
5	W. Roberts		
	K. Stansbury		
	B. Taylor		
2	C. Winters		

This routing slip was initiated on Feb. 2

Please return to J. Waye by Feb. 20

Distributing Mail

A manager distributes mail to others to

1. obtain information so that she or he can reply
2. ask someone else to reply directly
3. keep others informed.

Important mail can be delayed and can even get "lost" on someone else's desk. Nevertheless, top management expects mail to be answered. Your manager is still responsible for the reply to a letter even when the actual writing of it has been delegated to someone else.

As a general rule, your manager will make notations on letters or send memoranda asking others to provide information or to reply directly. Some managers attach "Action Requested" or routing slips as they read the mail so that they don't have to handle the same pieces of correspondence again. However, much of this responsibility can be handled by an administrative assistant. When given the responsibility for making requests, realize that a considerate tone will play a significant part in getting someone to comply. In contrast, a demanding tone will detract from your efforts and sometimes result in the letter getting "lost."

For informal requests for action, use an Action Requested slip similar to the one shown in Figure 6-10. For example, attach an Action Requested slip to a letter that has been misdirected to your manager and obviously should be handled in another department. Write the recipient's name, and check "Please handle."

Sometimes a letter requires two types of action, one of which your manager can handle and another that someone in another department must handle. When this situation arises, let the other person know precisely which part of the letter she or he is to answer. In the margin of the letter, indicate the part on which your manager will follow through.

Figure 6-10 Action requested slip.

ACTION REQUESTED!	
TO: Janice Miller	
FROM: Edward Kaye	
DATE: May 2	
✓	PLEASE RUSH - immediate action necessary!
	For your information; no need to return.
	Let's discuss.
	Note and return to me.
	Note and file.
	Please handle as you see appropriate.
	Please respond to this document.
	Your comments, please.
	Other –
COMMENTS: The Kentworth Project can't go ahead without the third communiqué. We need to push this through.	
Please complete action by May 2	

Decide whether the person who is to reply will require earlier correspondence. If you think she or he will need it, attach it to the letter being distributed.

To obtain information, you will be dealing with co-workers in numerous departments throughout the organization. Make an effort to get acquainted with them, at least by telephone. When you must obtain information from a service department, you should be aware of the work schedule followed by that department. Find out how much time must elapse between the time you place a request and the time the material will be ready. Often you will be pressed by a deadline, and you must communicate this. You may have to request special service in order to meet your deadline.

When you ask someone who is not following a predetermined schedule to assemble facts for you, request that the information be ready by a designated time. Suggest a realistic deadline. Often, work that can be done when it is convenient to do it gets relegated to the bottom of the stack.

Attach a routing slip to mail that is to be distributed to more than one person. A routing slip is a small sheet of paper on which are listed the names of the people to whom an item is to be distributed. Each recipient should initial and date the slip after she or he has seen the material, and then forward it to the next person on the list.

When mail is often circulated to the same people, the names can be pre-printed. On a pre-printed slip, you can change the order in which material is to be circulated by writing numbers in front of the names on the list. For an illustration, see Figure 6-9. Be sure to include "Return to" near the bottom of a routing slip.

When you distribute a letter, memorandum, or report to inform others, you will have to decide whether to attach a routing slip to the original listing the names of the recipients, or make a copy and attach a routing slip, or make a copy for each person on the list. When deciding, consider the important factors, such as the number of pages, whether each person on the list must be informed at the same time, your immediate need for the original, and the risk that the original will be lost

pro-Link

Did you know that many employers consider excellent communication skills as the single most valuable asset when seeking new employees? Did you also know that laliaphobia, the fear of speaking to groups, is considered as the number one phobia for many people?

So, it's essential that people studying to become office professionals learn how to be comfortable when presenting information verbally to groups. Here are a few great ideas to make your next group presentation feel easy.

- Are you enthusiastic about your topic? If not, don't do the presentation! Why should your audience be enthusiastic if the expert isn't?
- Can you make the topic come alive? If not, work at it! Have you ever had a teacher who could make an interesting topic seem dull? Have you had a teacher who can make a dull topic seem interesting? It's your choice!
- Remember, the format for any presentation is really easy:
  1. Tell them what you're going to tell them.
  2. Tell them.
  3. Tell them what you told them.

Now, just do that with enthusiasm and life!

while it is being circulated. Also consider paper wastage when you ask yourself how many copies are actually necessary.

Your records should show what information has been disseminated. When a circulated item is returned to you, staple the routing slip to the document. This makes a permanent record of who saw the item and the date she or he saw it. When you do not use a circulation or routing slip, and must make separate copies for each individual, write on your file copy the names of the people to whom you sent the item.

Answering Mail in the Manager's Absence

What happens to the mail when your manager is away from the office depends on his or her preferences and length of absence, and on the time and attention she or he can give—or chooses to give—to what is going on at the office while she or he is away.

You should process the mail as promptly when your manager is out of the office as when she or he is there. The first steps are always the same—classifying and sorting; opening, removing, and inspecting contents; date-time stamping; reading and annotating; and rerouting mail that does not belong in your department.

You will have the additional responsibilities of making a summary of all incoming Lettermail, answering and acknowledging letters yourself, and seeing that correspondence requiring immediate action receives it.

If your manager is away from the office for only a day or two, his or her preference probably will be for you to put aside all the mail you cannot answer. However, never put aside correspondence that must be handled immediately. If there is no one at the office who is authorized to reply to an urgent message, call your manager.

Send letters that require immediate action to the person designated to answer them; make copies of these letters and write the name of the person receiving each one on the letter itself. Put the copies in a folder for your manager marked *Correspondence to be read*.

Answer the letters that are within the scope of ones you can answer. Acknowledge nearly all the Lettermail not being answered immediately, indicating that your manager will be back in the office on a specific date and that the sender can expect a reply soon after she or he returns. Note and reply to the e-mail address (if any) on the incoming Lettermail. This form of response is expedient and can provide a concise record of your actions. If no e-mail address is evident, write a brief letter to explain the situation. The recipient of your acknowledgment will either wait for your manager's reply or contact someone else within your organization. You may say that your manager is on vacation, but do not say where. When your manager is on a business trip, remember that you would be giving out confidential information if you told where she or he is. (See Chapter 13 for examples of acknowledgment letters.)

Organize in folders all the business mail that accumulates during your manager's absence. Place the folders, along with your summary of the mail, on your manager's desk in the order listed below. Keep personal mail in a separate folder and put it on your manager's desk in a separate place. The folders might be labelled:

Correspondence for Signature—for letters you prepared for his or her signature.

Correspondence Requiring Attention—for all correspondence your manager must answer.

Correspondence to Be Read—for copies of letters you and others have answered, and copies of your replies. Often, as a courtesy, the people answering will send your manager a copy of their replies. When they do, staple these replies to the letters they answered.

Reports and Informational Memos—for all informational items.

Advertisements—for advertising brochures and other literature for your manager's perusal.

HANDLING OUTGOING MAIL[1]

Outgoing mail handled by Canada Post Corporation (CPC) may have a domestic destination, a U.S. destination, or an international destination. Domestic mail is mailable matter that is transmitted within Canada; this includes the ten provinces, Yukon, and the Northwest Territories. For information on Nunavut, refer to the "Proper Addressing" section of this chapter. Mail addressed to a point in any state of the United States, or to any U.S. territory or possession, is considered U.S. mail. Mail addressed to any destination outside Canadian or U.S. territory is considered International mail. These three destination groupings determine the cost of the mailing service. Of course, the size, weight, and delivery service required will also all have a bearing on the cost of the delivery.

CPC publishes brochures that provide rates and information for these three destinations. See Figure 6-12. However, because rates change rapidly, as do definitions of services, CPC now provides a toll-free number

FOOTNOTE

1 Information for the Handling Outgoing Mail section has been extracted from the *Canadian Postal Guide* and the *Canadian Addressing Standard: Delivery Needs Accuracy*, published by Canada Post Corporation.

Figure 6-11 Domestic business services.

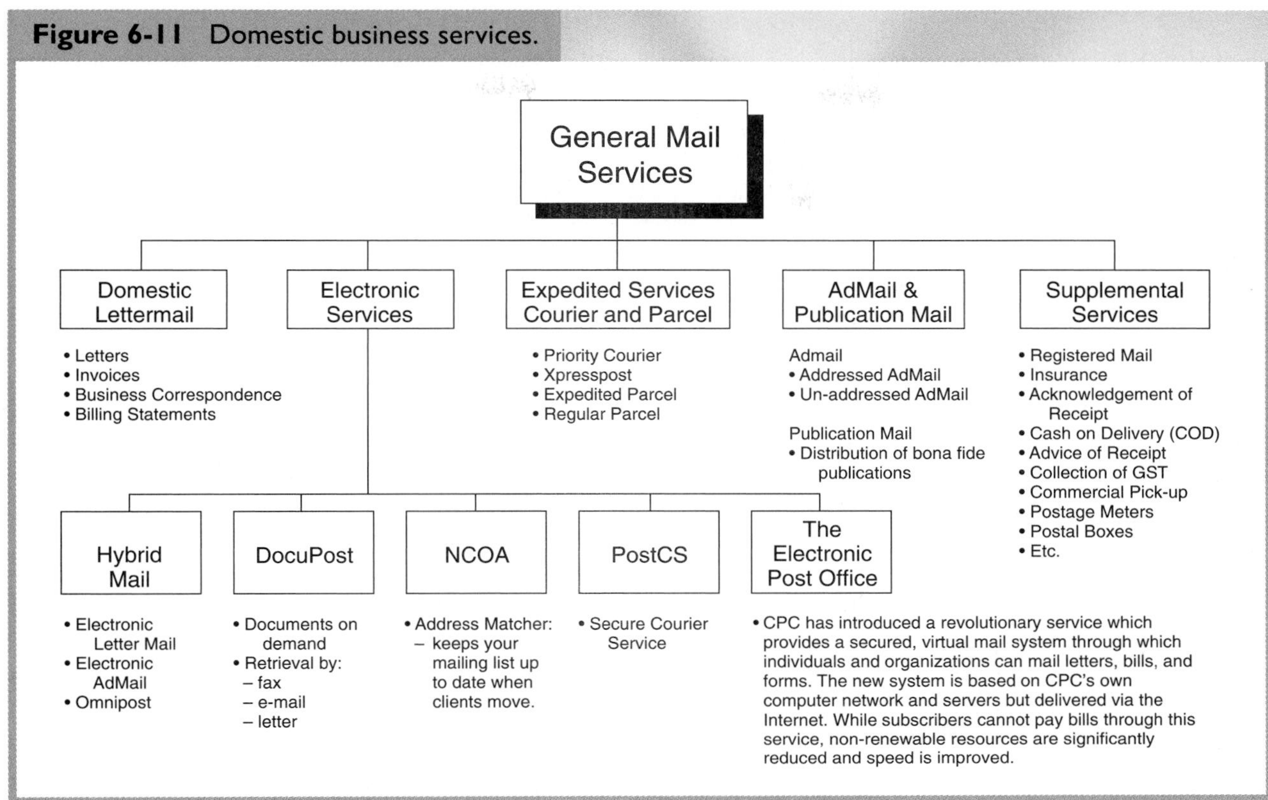

and a comprehensive website for Canadians to call. If you require the most current information on services provided by CPC to any destination, call 1-888-550-6333. If your office requires a printed document with detailed information and rates for all services available from CPC, the **Canadian Postal Guide** is available for reference at all Canadian postal outlets. Or, you may review and print it by contacting CPC's on-line information and services at website **www.canadapost.ca** or by writing to

Canada Post Corporation
2701 Riverside Drive Suite 410
Ottawa, ON K1A 0B1

Types of Domestic Mail

The basic types of domestic mail are Lettermail, Publication Mail, Admail, and Parcels. Your knowledge of available services should enable you to choose expeditious and economical means of sending mail.

Lettermail

Among the items classified as Lettermail are

- letters, postcards, or similar communications completely or partly keyed or handwritten
- receipts, invoices, or similar financial statements relating to a specified sum of money

Figure 6-12 Postal rates brochure available at CPC outlets.
Courtesy of Canada Post Corporation

- any other mail that the sender chooses to post at Lettermail rates of postage.

Lettermail items mailed without sufficient postage are returned to the sender. If the item has no return address, it is forwarded to the addressee for collection of the deficient postage and an administrative charge.

Publication Mail

To be eligible for mailing at the Publication Mail rate, a newspaper or periodical must be Canadian owned or controlled and published for the purpose of public dissemination. Most commonly, these publications include news, articles, and comments or analyses of the news. Publications that are focused on a particular topic may also qualify. A few of these topics are:

- religion
- academia
- science
- art
- public health
- and, articles of interest to a membership, special interest group, or association.

Publishers wishing to take advantage of this service must first:

- register with CPC
- prepare the publications in accordance with conditions specified by CPC
- prearrange the service with the postal outlet where the mailing will occur.

When you wish to mail a single copy of a newspaper, a magazine, or any other publication, you should do so by Lettermail.

Admail

Admail is advertising mail that is posted in Canada for delivery in Canada and that meets the conditions and requirements for such mail. There are two categories of Admail: Admail that is addressed and Admail that is unaddressed.

Unaddressed Admail is often referred to as householder mail. This unaddressed mail often contains samples, announcements, and promotional leaflets or brochures. CPC delivers unaddressed Admail between Monday and Friday only.

An administrative assistant who wishes to send out a bulk mailing should first contact the local post office for specific regulations and rates. If there is adequate volume, volume incentive rates will apply.

Parcels

Parcel service is used to send goods, merchandise, and so on. CPC will accept parcels within a broad range of sizes and weights. To be accepted, parcels must conform with the packaging requirements of the Corporation and must not contain dangerous or prohibited articles.

Parcel service includes:

1. **Commercial Parcels.** Commercial parcels are those the mailer has weighed and applied sufficient postage to, before bringing them to CPC for mailing.
2. **Counter Parcels.** Counter parcels are those parcels which the CPC counter staff must weigh and calculate postage for.

The minimum acceptable size for a parcel is a small packet; the maximum size depends on the length, width, and depth of the package. For exact specifications, check the website. Within certain limits, oversize items may be acceptable, but these may be charged higher rates. The maximum weight allowable is 30 kg. If you find it necessary to send a package exceeding the size or weight limits, you should consider alternatives to CPC. Among these alternatives are services offered by private courier companies, and by airline, train, or bus companies.

Sometimes special services are required. When this is the case, items usually sent as parcels may be sent Priority Courier. Refer to the next section of this chapter for more information on the Priority Courier service.

CPC publishes the brochure "Send your goods in a package they deserve" which recommends proper packaging methods for ensuring the safe arrival of goods. See Figure 6-13. Unless properly packaged, a parcel's contents could suffer damage; they could even cause harm to postal workers and damage other mail. Remember that a parcel containing damaged goods is a poor reflection on your company and also on the product it promotes.

You are not permitted to enclose a letter in a parcel; however, certain enclosures are acceptable. These include

- an invoice or statement of account relating exclusively to the contents
- a return card, envelope, or wrapper
- a card or slip of paper giving a brief identification or directions for the contents.

When a letter is enclosed or attached, it must be paid for at the Lettermail rate, and the item must bear the endorsement: *Amount includes Lettermail postage for letter attached/enclosed.*

Priority Courier

This is CPC's top-priority service. It is a guaranteed delivery service for urgent, time-sensitive items. Priority Courier items, deposited at a post office in any major Canadian location and addressed to another major

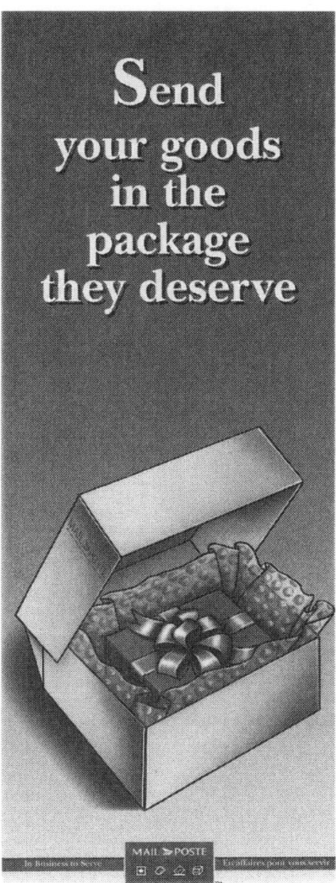

Figure 6-13 Proper packaging brochure.
Courtesy of Canada Post Corporation

Canadian location, will be delivered on the next business day. Although this one-day Priority Courier guarantee applies only to shipments within Canada, "Skypack," CPC's non-domestic courier service may also be used to send information to the United States or internationally.

The fee for Priority Courier covers $100 worth of insurance; additional insurance can be purchased up to a maximum of CDN$5,500. If you require further details, contact your local service and sales representative at CPC.

XPRESSPOST

This service combines speed with verification of delivery. CPC guarantees that XPRESSPOST will be delivered in one business day for local destinations and in two business days between major Canadian urban centres. It is intended to be faster than regular delivery and less expensive than Priority Courier.

It is available for both documents and packages up to 30 kg. Because an identification number and access code are printed on the sender's receipt, the customer may access information on the delivery status by using CPC's tracking system. Refer to the Registered Mail section for the toll-free numbers and Internet address.

Because XPRESSPOST envelopes are prepaid, they may be dropped in any street letter box. However, the money-back guarantee for expeditious delivery applies only when the XPRESSPOST is turned in to a CPC official at a postal outlet—not when it is dropped into a mailbox.

Supplemental Services

As an administrative assistant who prepares outgoing mail, you should know what special services are available from CPC and when to use them. The following is a discussion of some of the services that enable office workers to handle correspondence effectively and efficiently. CPC has an increasing number of services. If you require a service that is not discussed below, contact your local CPC sales and service representative or review CPC's website.

Registered Mail

Registered mail is an option with most of CPC's services. For an additional fee, registered mail provides delivery confirmation such as the date of delivery and the name of the person who received mail. It also includes a built-in insurance for loss or damage to the mail piece. Registered mail is coded with a red identification sticker and is available for letter, parcel, and courier services both domestically and internationally.

The senders receipt bears an identification number, which enables the sender to track the delivery status of the mailed item through either of CPC's inquiry services at:

- 1-888-550-6333, or
- **www.canadapost.ca**

Registered items must be turned in at an authorized postal outlet or given to a rural mail courier; they may not be dropped into a mailbox. On the delivery end, CPC must obtain a signature from the addressee or the addressee's representative before delivery is considered complete. The receiver may inquire as to the name and address of the sender but may not inspect the contents before accepting receipt of the item.

Insurance

CPC offers insurance on its distribution services. Coverage for loss or damage of CDN$100 is built in to the fee charged for registered mail but insurance is also available as an independent service for:

- *Xpresspost*
- *Priority Courier*, and
- parcel services.

This extra insurance is available in small increments. The fee will vary with the amount of **indemnity** coverage you purchase up to a maximum of CDN$5,000 in value. Insurance fees also apply to mail sent internationally or to the United States.

Articles to be insured must be handed in at the post office or given to a rural mail courier. They may not be dropped into a street letter box.

For insured items, a receipt for proof of mailing is always given to the sender. At the time of delivery of an insured article, the addressee (or representative) must sign for the article. However, the addressee may ask the name and address of the sender before signing for and accepting a registered article.

As with Registered Mail, the codes given on the sender's receipt permit the sender to access the tracking system in order to check the status of delivery. Refer to the previous section on Registered Mail for the correct telephone numbers and Internet address.

Acknowledgment of Receipt

Acknowledgment of Receipt (A/R) is included for Priority Courier service. For other services including XPRESSPOST and parcel services, A/R may be purchased. However, the automatic return of the A/R card is replaced by acknowledgment on CPC's tracking system.

In all cases, the signature copy of the receipt is available to the sender for an additional fee and will be forwarded by Lettermail or faxed within three days.

COD

By means of *collect on delivery* service (COD), the seller who wishes to mail an article for which she or he has not been paid may have the price of the article and the postage fee collected from the addressee when the article is delivered. COD articles must be sent at parcel rates. However, customers wishing to use the COD service for letter-size packages may pay XPRESSPOST service pus the COD fee.

CPC will collect payment up to $25,000 for a COD item; however, COD items over $1,000 must be picked up at a postal outlet. In this case, the addressee will be informed of the arrival of the COD item and of the amount that must be paid. Payment can be made only by cash or by certified cheque. Which method of payment is acceptable is determined by the sender of the goods, who indicates the preference on the original COD form. The CPC official acts only as a type of liaison in the transaction—delivering the goods, collecting the payment, and forwarding the money to the sender.

This service is available only for domestic mail. The item may be mailed at any postal outlet in Canada, and may be delivered to any postal outlet or mail delivery route in Canada.

Dangerous Goods

Articles or substances that could be dangerous to postal workers and postal equipment, or that could damage other mail, are prohibited from being mailed both domestically and to points outside Canada. It is an offence to use the domestic service to deliver:

- Explosives
- Flammable solids and flammable liquids
- Radioactive material
- Gases, oxidizers, and organic peroxides
- Corrosives
- Toxic and infectious substances
- Miscellaneous dangerous goods such as, asbestos, air bags, and dry ice.

A list of restricted items is available for international mail as well. If you are in doubt about any item you wish to mail, obtain a Dangerous Goods brochure (see Figure 6-14) or contact CPC at 1-800-267-1177 for a complete list of prohibited mail.

U.S. and International Mail

CPC offers a number of services for Lettermail, Admail, parcels, and other items subject to customs' clearance and duty.

SkyPack International Courier Service provides:

- Time certain delivery
- Origin to destination control of shipments

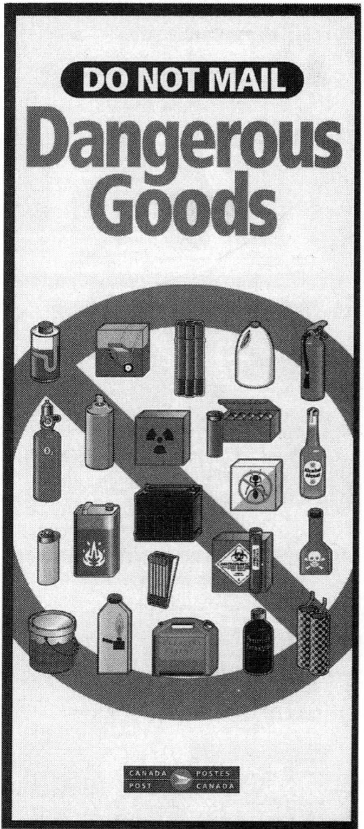

Figure 6-14 Dangerous Goods brochure.
Courtesy of Canada Post Corporation

- Worldwide "Trace and Track" facilities
- Prepaid products

For complete and specific details on these services and others available for U.S. and international mailings, you may consult The SkyPack International Customer Guide (Figure 6-15) or contact Customer Service at 1-888-550-6333 or www.canadapost.ca.

Proper Addressing

CPC uses computerized systems that can scan a wide range of addressing styles; this includes both handwritten and keyed addresses. To increase the speed and efficiency of mail handling, CPC has designed a consistent format for users. CPC requests that we use this *optimum* format whenever possible, but recognizes some other formats as acceptable for computerized scanning. This is especially important for mail addressed in some languages other than English. Especially important in Canada is the fact that the *acceptable* formats encompass the accents, upper- and lower-case characters, full spellings, and punctuation used in the French language. For the sake of brevity, this textbook will deal only with the optimum format as defined by CPC.

Figure 6-15 Skypack Courier brochure.

Distribution Services

CANADA POST POSTES CANADA

SkyPak™
International Courier
Customer Guide

international couriers

Courtesy of Canada Post Corporation

The following information is designed to help the administrative assistant properly prepare addressed mail. Properly addressed mail saves time and avoids errors in delivery. For further information on addressing mail, see Figure 6-16 and the Internet (see Web Link).

Address Format

The sequence of components for mail originating in and addressed to a destination within Canada is as follows:

ADDRESSEE INFORMATION
DELIVERY ADDRESS INFORMATION
MUNICIPALITY PROVINCE POSTAL CODE

1. The bottom lines of the address are the most critical, since the automated equipment scans from the bottom lines upwards.
2. Attention or information data must always appear at the top of the address block.
3. Addressee information, delivery address information, municipality, province, and postal code must always be the bottom three or four lines of the address block.
4. Address components and elements on the same line will be separated from each other by one blank space. The postal code, however, must be separated from the province by two blank spaces.
5. Where symbols exist for address elements, these should be used rather than full names.
6. Province and state names should always be written in the two-letter abbreviation format. Refer to Figure 6-21 for a complete list of these abbreviations.
7. All lines of the address should be formatted with a flush-left margin.
8. Upper-case letters are preferred on all lines of the address block.
9. Punctuation such as the number sign (#) should not be used as a delimiter between address elements. Use punctuation marks only where they are a part of the place name (for example, ST. ALBERT).
10. The name of the addressee is the last line scanned; this means that the automated equipment has already determined the destination before it reads the addressee's name. Therefore, punctuation is acceptable on this line. However,

Figure 6-16 Guidelines for addressing envelopes.

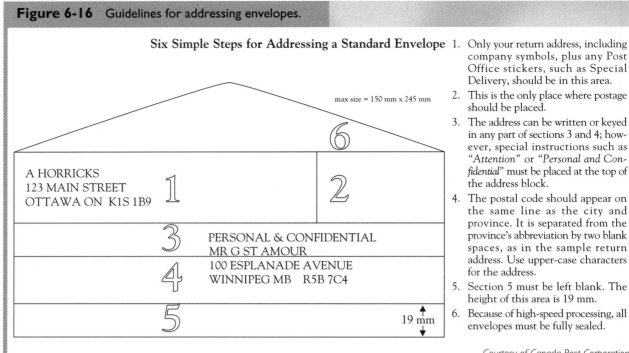

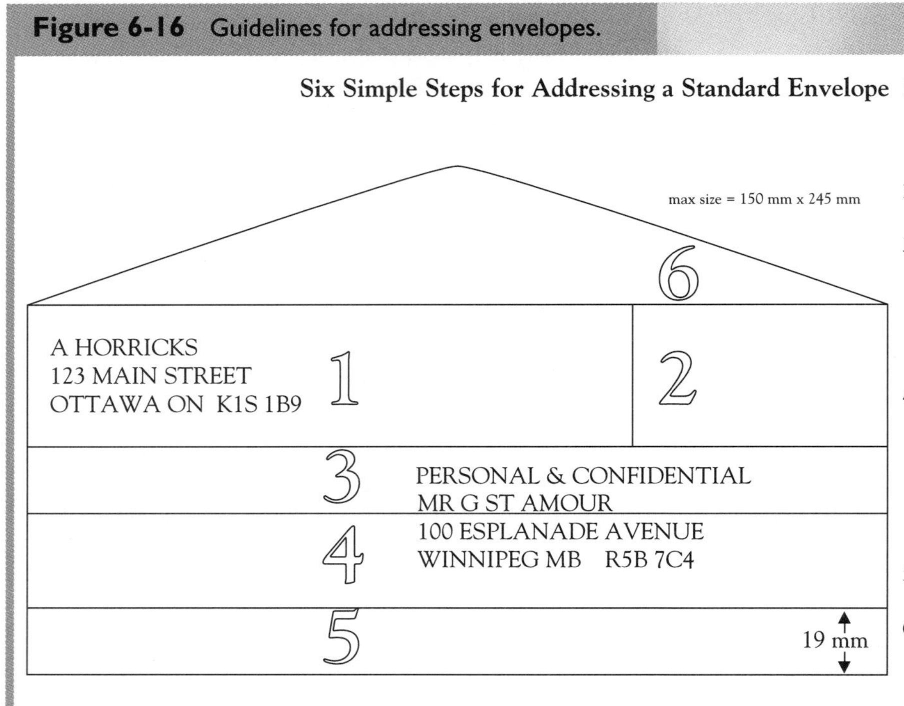

1. Only your return address, including company symbols, plus any Post Office stickers, such as Special Delivery, should be in this area.
2. This is the only place where postage should be placed.
3. The address can be written or keyed in any part of sections 3 and 4; however, special instructions such as *"Attention"* or *"Personal and Confidential"* must be placed at the top of the address block.
4. The postal code should appear on the same line as the city and province. It is separated from the province's abbreviation by two blank spaces, as in the sample return address. Use upper-case characters for the address.
5. Section 5 must be left blank. The height of this area is 19 mm.
6. Because of high-speed processing, all envelopes must be fully sealed.

Courtesy of Canada Post Corporation

for consistency this text will adhere to the rule of all capital letters, and no punctuation, except where these are part of the place name. Both of these are quite acceptable:

MR. W. ROSS
or
MR W ROSS

11. The return address should follow the same format as the main address. This is of little value in the original scanning for sorting and delivery of the item; remember, however, that if the address cannot be deciphered, the item may need to be returned to the sender. Use the same format, since the CPC staff are accustomed to it.

Non-Address Data

Non-address data refers to any additional information that you put on the envelope. This data should be located above all other lines in the address. Refer to the following sample.

ATTN: MR B CLARKE
MARKETING DEPARTMENT
IMPERIAL OIL LTD
PO BOX 9070 STN B
ST. JOHN'S NF A1A 2X6

Civic Addresses

In an English address the street type always follows the street name. See the complete list of symbols in Figure 6-17. In a French address the street type appears before the street name unless the street type is numeric, in which case the street type follows the street name. The street type should always be identified by the official CPC symbols. Two samples follow; in the first the French address has a street name, and in the second the street type is numeric.

B GUTHRIE
225 **RUE** FLEURY O
MONTREAL QC H3L 1T8

R MANN
2061 36E **RUE**
SHAWINIGAN QC G9N 5J9

Street Direction

Street direction, where required, should be identified by a one- or two-digit symbol, as shown below.

W WEEKS
548 GEORGIA ST **E**
VANCOUVER BC V6A 1Z9

For a complete list of CPC's street direction symbols, refer to Figure 6-18.

Figure 6-17 List of street types and corresponding symbols.

Street Type	Symbol
Abbey	ABBEY
Acres	ACRES
Allée	ALLÉE
Alley	ALLEY
Autoroute	AUT
Avenue	AVE (E)
Avenue	AV (F)
Bay	BAY
Beach	BEACH
Bend	BEND
Boulevard	BLVD (E)
Boulevard	BOUL (F)
By-pass	BYPASS
Byway	BYWAY
Campus	CAMPUS
Cape	CAPE
Carré	CAR
Carrefour	CARREF
Centre	CTR (E)
Centre	C (F)
Cercle	CERCLE
Chase	CHASE
Chemin	CH
Circle	CIR
Circuit	CIRCT
Close	CLOSE
Common	COMMON
Concession	CONC
Corners	CRNRS
Côte	CÔTE
Cour	COUR
Court	CRT
Cove	COVE
Crescent	CRES
Croissant	CROIS
Crossing	CROSS
Cul-de-sac	CDS
Dale	DALE
Dell	DELL
Diversion	DIVERS
Downs	DOWNS
Drive	DR
Échanger	ÉCH
End	END
Esplanade	ESPL
Estates	EST
Expressway	EXPY
Extension	EXTEN
Farm	FARM
Field	FIELD
Forest	FOREST
Freeway	FWY
Front	FRONT
Gardens	GDNS
Gate	GATE
Glade	GLADE
Glen	GLEN
Green	GREEN
Grounds	GRNDS
Grove	GROVE
Harbour	HARBR
Heights	HTS
Highlands	HGHLDS
Highway	HWY
Hill	HILL
Hollow	HOLLOW
Île	ÎLE
Impasse	IMP
Island	ISLAND
Key	KEY
Knoll	KNOLL
Landing	LANDING
Lane	LANE
Limits	LMTS
Line	LINE
Link	LINK
Lookout	LKOUT
Loop	LOOP
Mall	MALL
Manor	MANOR
Maze	MAZE
Meadow	MEADOW
Mews	MEWS
Montée	MONTÉE
Moor	MOOR
Mount	MT
Mountain	MTN
Orchard	ORCH
Parade	PARADE
Parc	PARC
Park	PARK
Parkway	PKY
Passage	PASS
Path	PATH
Pathway	PTWAY
Pines	PINES
Place	PL (E)
Place	PLACE (F)
Plateau	PLAT
Plaza	PLAZA
Point	PT
Port	PORT
Private	PVT
Promenade	PR
Quay	QUAY
Rang	RANG
Range	RG
Ridge	RIDGE
Rise	RISE
Road	RD
Rond-point	RDPT
Route	RTE
Row	ROW
Rue	RUE
Ruelle	RLE
Run	RUN
Sentier	SENT
Square	SQ
Street	ST
Subdivision	SUBDIV
Terrace	TERR
Terrasse	TSSE
Thicket	THICK
Towers	TOWERS
Townline	TLINE
Trail	TRAIL
Turnabout	TRNABT
Vale	VALE
Via	VIA
View	VIEW
Village	VILLGE
Vista	VISTA
Voie	VOIE
Walk	WALK
Way	WAY
Wharf	WHARF
Wood	WOOD
Wynd	WYND

Courtesy of Canada Post Corporation

Figure 6-18 List of street directions and corresponding symbols.

STREET DIRECTIONS AND SYMBOLS

English Street Type	Symbol	French Street Type	Symbol
East	E	Est	E
North	N	Nord	N
North East	NE	Nord-est	NE
North West	NW	Nord-ouest	NO
South	S	Sud	S
South East	SE	Sud-est	SE
South West	SW	Sud-ouest	SO
West	W	Ouest	O

Courtesy of Canada Post Corporation

Unit Designator

This designator indicates the type of unit, such as an apartment or suite, and should be identified by the official CPC symbol.

MRS A DALE
415 HERITAGE CRES **SUITE** 102
SASKATOON SK S7H 5M5

Where the number of characters is too long on a line, the unit information may be placed on a line by itself above the street information. Refer to the following example.

MME R HUGHES
UNITE 509
169 RUE NOTRE-DAME-DES-VICTOIRES
STE. FOY QC G2G 1J3

Unit Identifier

The unit identifier is the specific number of an apartment, suite, house, or building. It must appear in numeric format; therefore, you would never see an identifier written as SUITE TWO. Sometimes the identifier is alphanumeric, as in the next example.

MRS A DALE
415 HERITAGE CRES **SUITE 102A**
SASKATOON SK S7H 5M5

Where the unit designator is not stated in the address, the unit identifier may be placed before the street information. The proper separation between the identifier and the street information is a single hyphen. Refer to the example below.

MR W RIDDELL
104-2701 23RD AVE
REGINA SK S4S 1E5

Mode of Delivery

The mode of delivery refers to postal boxes, rural routes, general deliveries, and so on. The official CPC symbols should be used (see Figure 6-19). The numeric identifier is separated from the mode of delivery designator by one space. Do not use a number sign (#) before the mode of delivery identifier. Refer to the following examples.

MS B COLLINS
SS 4
SPRUCE GROVE AB T7X 2V1

MR BRIAN HUNTER
PO BOX 6001 LCD 1
VICTORIA BC V8P 5L

Postal Code

A unique alphanumeric code is used to identify the delivery address for a mail item. The address is not complete until the postal code is applied. The purpose of the postal code is to speed up delivery. The sequence for the characters in Canadian postal codes is letter, number, letter, space, number, letter, number.

Figure 6-19 List of delivery address symbols.

DELIVERY ADDRESS SYMBOLS

ENGLISH DELIVERY INSTALLATION TYPE	SYMBOL	FRENCH DELIVERY INSTALLATION TYPE	SYMBOL
Letter carrier depot	LCD	Poste des facteurs	PDF
Post office	PO	Bureau de poste	BDP
Retail Postal Outlet	RPO	Bureau auxiliaire	BA
Station	STN	Comptoir service postal	CSP
		Succursale	SUCC

ENGLISH DELIVERY MODE TYPE	SYMBOL	FRENCH DELIVERY MODE TYPE	SYMBOL
General Delivery	GD	Poste Restante	GD
Mobile Route	MR	Itinéraire motorisé	MR
Post Office Box (for lock box/bag service)	PO BOX	Case postale (pour service de cases postales/sacs)	CP
Rural Route	RR	Route rurale	RR
Suburban Service	SS	Service suburbain	SS

Courtesy of Canada Post Corporation

Since the postal code is read by a scanner, it is important that the characters not overlap each other or other parts of the address.

Canada has 18 postal code zones. The letter for each zone begins all six-character postal codes within that zone. The next two characters represent a region within that zone. The last three characters of the postal code identify a smaller section of the area. A correct postal code will lead the mail carrier to the correct side of a specific street, or even to an exact building. Canada's postal code zones are shown in Figure 6-20.

Postal codes are now available from a number of sources:

- Some telephone books publish the postal codes for all areas under the jurisdiction of the telephone book.
- Postal code software that has been recognized by CPC is available for purchase.
- The *Canada Postal Code Directory* is available by contacting the local divisional office of CPC. If you require the address or telephone number, simply call the toll-free customer service number, 1-888-550-6333.

The postal code should be placed on the same line as the municipality and the province unless the line is too long; in this case the code may be placed on the line below. Refer to the following examples.

MS DULAC
GD
COLD LAKE AB **T0A 0V0**

MARIELLE HOBBS
913 RUE DES MARRONNIERS
ST-JEAN-CHRYSÔSTOME-DE-LÉVIS QC
G6Z 3B1

The lists in Figure 6-21 show the preferred two-letter abbreviations for the provinces, territories, states, and districts.

Canada's New Territory

In 1993 the Inuit of Canada's North were granted self-government (which began in 1999) of a new territorial region, to be known as Nunavut. The area from the eastern Northwest Territories to the eastern Arctic above the 60th parallel constitutes the new territory. The six-digit postal codes will remain the same; the regional government in conjunction with CPC have not (as of the publishing date of this textbook) announced an official two-letter abbreviation for this new region.

Figure 6-20 Map of Canada showing postal code areas.

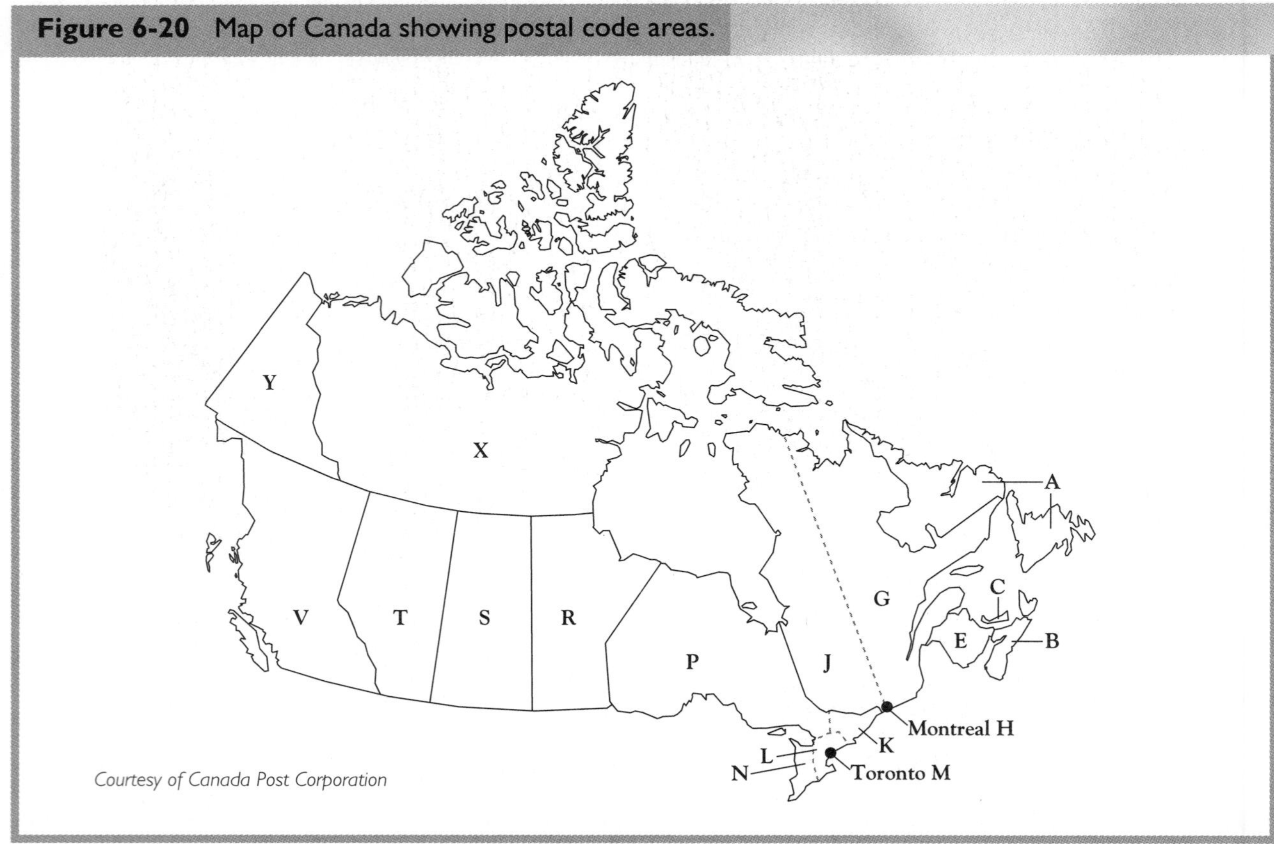

Courtesy of Canada Post Corporation

Country

The country name is used only on mail items to be delivered outside Canada. Use the official English- or French-language spelling for the country name. It should appear alone on the last line of the address block.

An administrative assistant may be called upon to prepare envelopes for delivery to foreign countries. For this reason, it is important to know the regulations that pertain to international addresses. CPC defines international mail as mail items addressed to countries other than Canada and the United States. During processing of international mail, CPC equipment reads only the country name. The official English- or French-language spelling for the country name is placed alone on the last line of the address block.

Canada carries on a great deal of trade with the United States; an administrative assistant in Canada may often have to prepare envelopes for delivery in that country. The CPC processing equipment reads the country name, municipality, state, and zip code. Therefore, the lines that include these pieces of information should follow the CPC regulations for envelopes being delivered in Canada. Other information in the address block is used by the U.S. Postal Service and should be prepared according to U.S. standards. The American standards are very similar to those used in Canada.

1. The full municipality name should be separated from the two-letter abbreviation by two blank spaces.
2. The zip code will appear on the same line as the municipality name and state abbreviation. Separate the state abbreviation from the zip code with two blank spaces.
3. The zip code will be either five or nine digits in length. When the zip code is nine digits, a single hyphen is used to separate the fifth and sixth digits.
4. The guidelines for names and street addresses in the United States are the same as those in Canada.

The following examples apply to mail prepared in Canada to be delivered to countries other than Canada.

MR THOMAS CLARK
17 RUSSELL DR
LONDON W1P 6HQ
ENGLAND

Figure 6-21 Two-letter abbreviations for destinations in Canada and the U.S.A.

CANADA
(Provinces and Territories)

Alberta	AB	Nova Scotia	NS
British Columbia	BC	Ontario	ON
Labrador (part of Newfoundland)	LB	Prince Edward Island	PE
Manitoba	MB	Québéc	QC*
NewBrunswick	NB	Saskatchewan	SK
Newfoundland	NF	Yukon Territory	YT
Northwest Territories	NT		

*Note that the province of Quebec uses QC as its official abbreviation. In the past, both PQ and QC were acceptable; however, this is no longer considered correct.

UNITED STATES
(States, District, and Territories)

Alabama	AL	Kansas	KS	Ohio	OH
Alaska	AK	Kentucky	KY	Oklahoma	OK
American Samoa	AS	Louisiana	LA	Oregon	OR
Arizona	AZ	Maine	ME	Palau	PW
Arkansas	AR	Marshall Islands	MH	Pennsylvania	PA
California	CA	Maryland	MD	Puerto Rico	PR
Canal Zone	CZ	Massachusetts	MA	Rhode Island	RI
Colorado	CO	Michigan	MI	South Carolina	SC
Connecticut	CT	Minnesota	MN	South Dakota	SD
Delaware	DE	Mississippi	MS	Tennessee	TN
District of Columbia	DC	Missouri	MO	Texas	TX
Federated States of Micronesia	FM	Montana	MT	Utah	UT
Florida	FL	Nevada	NV	Vermont	VT
Georgia	GA	New Hampshire	NH	Virgin Islands	VI
Guam	GU	New Jersey	NJ	Virginia	VA
Hawaii	HI	New Mexico	NM	Washington	WA
Idaho	ID	New York	NY	West Virginia	WV
Illinois	IL	North Carolina	NC	Wisconsin	WI
Indiana	IN	North Dakota	ND	Wyoming	WY
Iowa	IA	Northern Mariana Islands	MP		

Courtesy of Canada Post Corporation

KARL HAUSER
LANDSTRASSE 15
4100 DRUSBURG 25
ALLEMAGNE

MR B ROSS
4417 BROOKS ST NE
WASHINGTON DC 20019-4649
USA

Dual Addressing

Dual addressing refers to the practice of putting both the addressee's physical location and mailing address on the mail item. CPC discourages dual addressing. However, if the administrative assistant is requested to use dual addressing, it is imperative that the delivery address information, municipality, province, and postal code be on the last two or three lines of the address. For example:

SKYLINE CABLEVISION LTD
1810 ST. LAURENT BLVD
PO BOX 9708 STN T
OTTAWA ON K1G 0N2

Bilingual Addressing

Bilingual addressing is the use of address information in both English and French. The standard bilingual format is two side-by-side address blocks: the left block in French, the right block in English. The address blocks should be separated by a solid black line at least 0.7 mm thick. The following sample illustrates bilingual addressing.

MASTER CARD	MASTER CARD
BANQUE DE MONTREAL	BANK OF MONTREAL
CP 6044 SUCC A	PO BOX 6044 STN A
MONTREAL QC H3C 3X2	MONTREAL QC H3C 3X2

Return Address

A mail item should display a return address that includes postal code. The return address should appear in the upper left-hand corner of the face of the mail item. The same rules regarding components and format of the mailing address apply to the return address. Sender's name, address information, municipality, province, and postal code lines are mandatory.

Metered Mail

Many organizations use in-house postage meters. Metered mail need not be cancelled when it reaches the post office; however, it must be turned in at a postal outlet counter and not simply dropped into a mailbox. Metered mail is sent directly for sorting, since it does not need cancelling by CPC. **Cancelling mail** refers to the process of printing bars over the stamps, as well as printing the date, time, and municipality where mail processing has occurred. This process prevents a person from reusing the postage; more importantly, it also allows the receiver to track the actual time, date, and place where processing occurred.

Since properly prepared metered mail can go directly to the sorting machine in the postal centre, it may be dispatched slightly sooner than mail that must be cancelled. However, the real advantage to the user is the convenience of not using stamps, not waiting in line at the postal outlet, and being able to apply whatever amount of postage is needed.

Postage meter machines vary in size from lightweight desk models to fully automatic models that feed, seal, and stack envelopes in addition to printing the postage, the postmark, and the date of mailing.

Manufacturers of postage meter machines must have the approval of CPC before distributing the machines. The meter impression die is the property of CPC. Only an authorized representative of CPC may set, lock, and seal a postage meter.

The user of a basic postage meter must take the meter to the post office and pay for a specified amount of postage. The meter dials are then set for this amount by a CPC agent. Each time an envelope is imprinted with an amount of postage, the unused balance on the meter is decreased by that amount. When the unused balance runs low, the meter must be taken to the post office to be reset.

Most offices use a computerized postage machine that provides real efficiency. Refer to Figure 6-22. These machines have a number of features, including electronic weighing, metering, and sealing. Computerized postage machines are leased from an authorized dealer such as Pitney Bowes. They are designed so that you can buy postage electronically without having to go to CPC. Because the service is computerized, you can purchase postage at any time, even when the leasing agents are closed. The postage is purchased electronically from the leasing agent, over the telephone. This process, referred to as *Postage by Phone*, may be accessed by calling 1-800-387-4660.

If you use a postage meter, check the manual dials or electronic readout to make sure the correct postage will be printed on the mail. Also check the date to be certain it is the correct date of mailing, not the previous day's date.

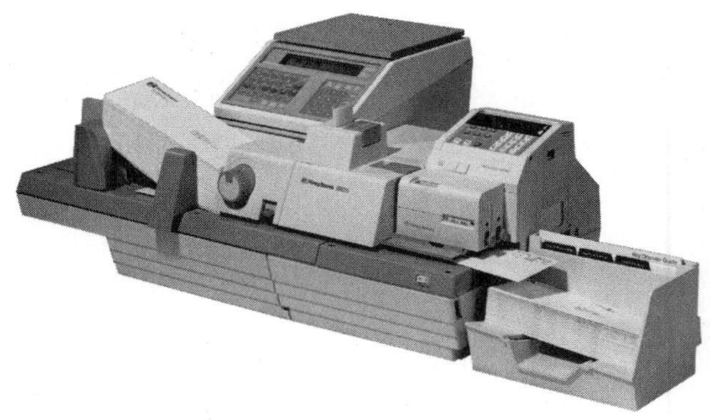

Figure 6-22 Computerized mailing system.
Courtesy of Pitney Bowes

In order to work efficiently, group your mail and stamp all mail requiring the same denomination in one batch. Put pieces of mail requiring irregular amounts of postage aside until the rest of the mail is stamped.

After you have processed all the mail, reset the machine so that the next user will not waste postage because the meter was set for the wrong amount.

Try to avoid making mistakes when stamping mail. But if you do make a mistake, you can request credit from the leasing agent. When complete and legible meter stamps cannot be used because of misprints, spoiled envelopes or cards, and the like, the agent will credit the postage. You should note that in order to receive a credit, you must supply the complete envelope as proof, not just the meter impression.

Other Delivery Options

Courier Services

Courier service is available for sending documents or packages across town or across the world. It guarantees expeditious delivery; however, the cost of this service is high relative to that of CPC's Priority Courier. Courier services are privately owned and represent strong competition for CPC.

Many courier services offer one-hour pickup and delivery in the same city, overnight delivery to all major cities in Canada and the United States, and door-to-door delivery of sensitive packages and business documents. See Figure 6-23. When an administrative assistant is responsible for having an item delivered within a very short time, a courier service is often the best option.

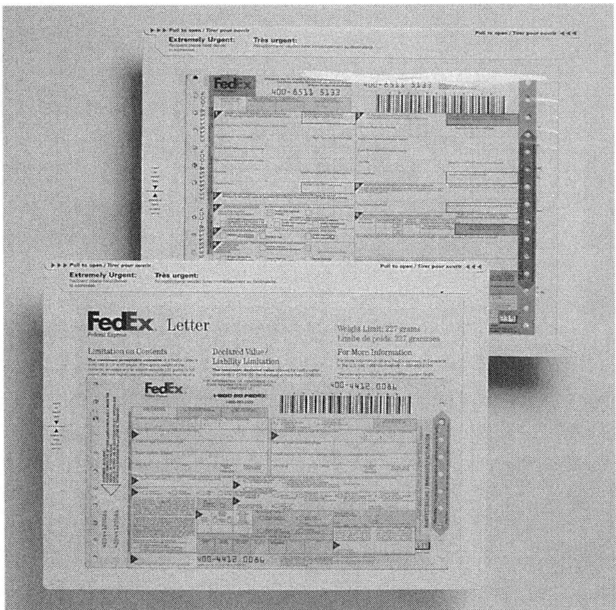

Figure 6-23 Courier service provides expeditious delivery to international and domestic locations.
Courtesy of Federal Express Canada Ltd.

Airline Services

Canada's airlines offer a competitive delivery service between all destinations they serve. If urgency of delivery is not the major factor, you may ship documents and goods via air cargo services. This service will transport almost any size of cargo, and pickup and delivery are available. Shipments are guaranteed to move on the first available flight. This service is much more economical than express services.

However, if you wish to ensure that your shipments arrive the next business day, you should use the airline express or priority services. Of course, these services cost more.

Bus Express

The most rapid means of delivering a package to a small town in your geographic area (or to more distant points not served by an airport) may be *bus express*. Most bus companies offer a shipping service on a round-the-clock basis, including Sundays and holidays. Packages often get same-day or next-day delivery. Call the local offices of bus companies for information on rates, restrictions, and schedules. Also inquire about pickup and delivery services.

Freight Shipments

Freight service is used for sending heavy, bulky goods in large quantities. Carriers include railway companies, trucking companies, and shipping lines. Airline transport is not as economical but is more expeditious. If the decision to ship goods by freight is based on economics alone, the sender will likely choose the railway, trucking, or shipping lines.

EXCEPTIONS

The mail does not always go through without problems. What happens to undelivered mail? Is it possible to recall a piece of mail or to refuse mail? As an administrative assistant, you will encounter these situations, and you will have to make decisions regarding what to do when there is an exception or a change in procedure.

Redirecting Mail

When you receive mail that must be forwarded to a different company or office, as a courtesy to the sender you should make a notation on the envelope indicating the correct company name and address. Once you drop the mail in the mailbox, CPC will return the item to the sender.

Changing an Address

When the organization for which you work changes its address, someone within the organization must notify the local postal outlet of the change. If doing this is your responsibility, ask CPC for a change-of-address kit. Complete the cards with the old and new addresses, including the postal codes, and with the effective date of the change. See Figure 6-24. CPC will redirect your mail for a fee that covers three months of service.

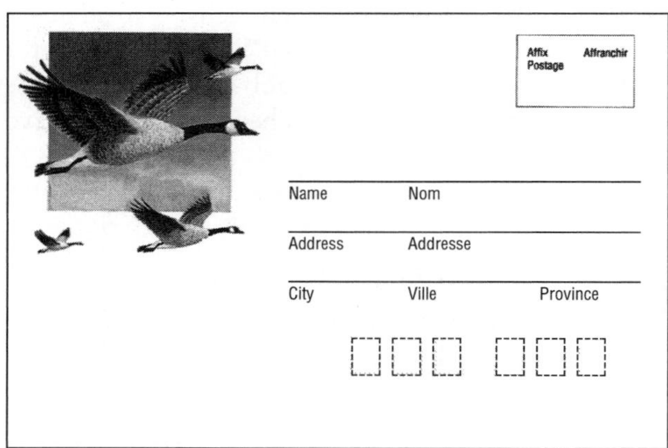

Figure 6-24 Change of Address Kit.
Courtesy of Canada Post Corporation

Returning Undelivered Mail

Keep mailing lists up to date, and address envelopes and labels with absolute accuracy, to avoid the cost and delay involved when mail is returned. A returned letter must be placed in a fresh envelope, correctly addressed, and have the postage repaid.

If the addressee has moved or simply refuses to accept mail; or if there is insufficient postage, or an incorrect or incomplete address; or if for legal reasons the mail cannot be delivered, CPC will return the item to the sender. Where the item is sent as Lettermail and contains a return address, the sender is not charged a fee. However, charges apply to many other types of mail that must be returned to the sender.

Undeliverable items without return addresses are sent to the National Undeliverable Mail Office in Scarborough, Ontario. If necessary, CPC will open the mail to look for an address and, if one is found, return the mail to the sender. If no return address is found, mail with no obvious value is destroyed. If the item contains cash, the money is deposited to the credit of CPC. Saleable merchandise found in the undeliverable items is sold, and again, the monies are deposited to the credit of CPC; merchandise that is not saleable is destroyed. Customers wishing to inquire about undeliverable mail should contact the local customer-service division of CPC.

Refusing Mail

The recipient of unsolicited mail, such as books and other items of some value, is not obligated to pay for the item or to return it. However, if unsolicited mail arrives at your desk and you wish to return it, you may do so without paying postage if you have not opened it. Simply write "Return to Sender" in clear words on the exterior of the item and drop it in the local mailbox. However, often mail becomes solicited without intention. Be certain to read carefully the fine print before agreeing to receive information through the mail. Often when people agree to receive information, they are also agreeing to receive merchandise that has a cost.

Questions for Study and Review

1. What information should a fax transmittal form contain?
2. Explain the meaning of the terms *facsimile automatic redial, facsimile broadcasting*, and *facsimile repository*.
3. What is the oldest form of technology-based mail?
4. List five items that you might employ to make your e-mail more meaningful.
5. When money has been electronically transferred, what information must the collector provide before the money is released to him or her?
6. How would you use a Bulletin Board?
7. How are electronic Lettermail and electronic Admail different from Lettermail and Admail?
8. How does Omnipost use both Lettermail and electronic mail delivery?
9. What is an electronic mailbox?
10. What should you do with a personal letter addressed to a former employee of your department?
11. What are the correct steps to take if you open a letter by mistake?
12. Why is date-time stamping important?
13. What is annotating? Why is it helpful?
14. The recommended methods for placing mail on the executive's desk are to put it in a folder or in an envelope. Why?
15. Give reasons for opening booklets and advertising mail daily.
16. What information should be recorded in a Mail-Expected Record? Why is the follow-up significant?
17. Suggest ways to group mail that has arrived in your manager's absence before presenting it to him or her.
18. State what happens to Lettermail items that are mailed without sufficient postage.
19. Who may send items as Publication Mail?
20. What is another term for Unaddressed Admail?
21. If you wish to include a letter in a parcel, mailed at parcel rates, what must you do?
22. Compare XPRESSPOST to Priority Courier and Lettermail.
23. Can certified mail be put in a street letter box? Or must it be handed in at the post office?
24. Is COD an international service?
25. State five items that would be considered dangerous goods.
26. Where does the attention line go on a properly addressed envelope? Where does the postal code go on a properly addressed envelope?
27. What punctuation is acceptable in the address on an envelope?
28. What is the rule for dual addressing on an envelope?
29. Why do many organizations use electronic postage meters?
30. What advantage does a courier service offer?
31. What would be the most economical and fastest method of sending a bulky parcel to Whitehorse, Yukon?

Spelling Reinforcement

accidentally
acknowledgment/ acknowledgement
annotating
continual
diplomacy
expedite
expeditious
explicit
facsimile
familiar
initials
international
mutilate
parcel
recipient
satisfactory
schedule
separately
sufficient
unsolicited
urgent
warrant
weight

On-the-Job Situations

1. A friend told you that her manager was furious when she admitted that she had been throwing away more than half of the advertising material at the time it arrived, never giving her manager a chance to see it. He discovered this through telephone conversations in which he was told by several different callers that brochures had been mailed to him. Your friend seemed confused about what to do with the booklets and advertising material, and has asked you for advice. Knowing that her manager wants to see all the mail, what guidelines can you give her?
2. Your manager, who is head of the Accounting Department, forwarded a letter to the sales manager requesting that she reply. The situation is difficult to handle. The customer is dissatisfied with a product and threatens to send it back rather than pay for it. Your manager is convinced that the sales manager must handle the problem. Here is the chain of events that follow: The sales manager's administrative assistant immediately sends the letter back to you. You attach an "Action Requested" slip to it and send it right back to the sales manager. The sales manager's administrative assistant calls you on the telephone and says, "We just sent this back to you, and here it is on my desk again." She demands that your manager answer the letter. What should you say to her? What should you do next?
3. As you open the mail, for each of the following what notations would you make and where would you make them?
   a. two enclosures mentioned in the letter, but you received only one
   b. a confirmation of an appointment your manager requested by letter
   c. a reference to a catalogue being sent separately
   d. a memorandum requesting forms that you supply others
   e. a memorandum from your manager's superior, reminding your manager that she wants to approve the final draft of a sales bulletin before she leaves town on Thursday afternoon
   f. a second letter from a customer whose first letter was sent to another department a week ago for a reply
   g. a letter being sent to another department for a reply to one part of it
   h. a letter including a price quotation that you requested by telephone.

Special Reports

1. Obtain a brochure on international rates and fees from CPC or research the Internet.

   Find:
   a. the rates for sending a letter to Mexico, South America, France, and Japan
   b. the cost of sending a parcel weighing 1 kg to Australia, Israel, Spain, Great Britain, and Peru.
2. Using information from CPC, find the cost of the following:
   a. an Acknowledgment of Receipt obtained at the time of mailing
   b. an Acknowledgment of Receipt requested after the item has been mailed
   c. a letter-size XPRESSPOST travelling to a destination 800 km away
   d. insurance for a package valued at $60
   e. registration for an item with a declared value of CDN$2,700
   f. a 2.75 kg parcel mailed within your local postal zone.
3. Interview the person in charge of the mail at your school. Ask about the responsibilities and procedures used for processing the mail.
4. By searching the CPC website, determine the service standards for:
   - Lettermail
   - Addressed Admail
   - Unaddressed Admail
   - Newspapers and Periodicals.

Production Challenges

6-A Processing Incoming Mail

Supplies needed:

- *Notes on Incoming Mail for Monday Morning, July 14, Form 6-A-1, page 402*
- *Mail Expected Record, Form 6-A-2, page 403*
- *Daily Mail Record, Form 6-A-3, page 404*
- *To Do List, Form 6-A-4, page 405*
- *Routing Slips, Forms 6-A-5, 6-A-6, 6-A-7, and 6-A-8, pages 406 and 407*
- *Plain Paper*

Mr. Wilson is out of the office during the week of July 14. You are processing the mail on Monday morning, July 14. Mr. Wilson always wants mail from a region routed to the respective assistant vice-president for the region. However, Mr. Wilson expects you to open the letters and to keep a record of the mail forwarded to the assistant vice-presidents. You route magazines and advertising letters from other organizations to the assistant vice-presidents. On your To Do List, put reminders to yourself and notes about items that you should follow up on. Put the other letters, memoranda, and important items in a folder for Mr. Wilson. For your instructor, make a list of the items you will put in a folder for Mr. Wilson.

6-B Indicating Types of Mail

Supplies needed:

- *List of Outgoing Mail, Form 6-B, page 408*

To reinforce your knowledge of the types of mail, indicate the type of mail for each item listed on Form 6-B.

6-C Checking Postal Services

Supplies needed:

- *Information from CPC*
- *Question Sheet, Form 6-C, page 409*

Collect information from CPC. Read and interpret the information in order to answer the questions on Question Sheet, Form 6-C.

World Wide Websites

A Beginner's Guide to Effective e-mail

www.webfoot.com/advice/email.top.html?Yahoo
This introduction to e-mail focuses on the content of e-mail: how to say what you need to say, page layout, intonation, gestures, and jargon and acronyms.

Pitney Bowes Mail and Messaging Management

www.pitneybowes.com
Pitney Bowes supplies small office products, supplies, and **Postage by Phone** for your Pitney Bowes mailing system.

Western Union Commercial Messaging Services

www.wucs.com/
A comprehensive selection of messaging services including Telegrams and Cash Transfer.

Canada Post Corporation's Guide to Formatting the Postal Code and Address

www.canadapost.ca/CPC2/addrm/pclookup/pcinfo.html
This is where you can find current information about formatting the address for your envelope.

Canada Post

www.canadapost.ca/
Here users may locate rates and postal code information.

Federal Express

www.fedex.com/
Federal Express provides on-line services, free software, tracking, delivery options, What's New, and drop-off locaters.

Purolator

www.purolator.com
Purolator gives users on-line services, drop box locations, and other services.

UPS Package Tracking

www.ups.com/
Check with UPS to find out whether and when your package was delivered, and who signed for it.

WhoWhere?

www.whowhere.lycos.com/
This is a resource for searching for e-mail addresses, phone numbers, home pages, companies on the Internet, and much more.

Information Management

Outline

Learning Outcomes

At the completion of this chapter, the student will be able to:

1. Describe the need for information systems in a professional office environment.
2. Describe the process of organizing information for paper files and electronic filing.
3. Describe the supplies and equipment necessary to manage and store records.
4. Explain how a computer can manage records.
5. Explain the difference between paper, magnetic media, and micrographics in terms of their retention value.
6. Discuss the reality of the "Paperless Office."
7. Index and alphabetize names for the alphabetic filing system.
8. Prepare cross-reference cards for alphabetic filing.
9. Compare alphabetic, subject, geographic, and numeric filing systems.

Filing involves classifying, arranging, and storing materials according to a systematic plan for quick reference, for preservation, and—most important of all—for retrieving an item readily when it is required. Filing is one segment of a broad office function called *information management*.

Some Canadian provinces and territories have legislated a Freedom of Information and Protection of Privacy Act. This legislation has motivated public and private organizations and businesses to

- establish formal information management systems
- set up policies and procedures based on the legislation
- institute training programs to ensure staff familiarity with the new policies.

This new legislation establishes records management as a priority function in the office.

THE NEED FOR INFORMATION SYSTEMS

Materials are stored so they can be used and so they will be protected. Information can be stored in one of several ways: on paper, on electronic media, or on **micrographics**. Electronic media refers to hard disks, floppy disks, and zip disks. Micrographics refers to **microfilm**, **microfiche**, and other microforms of documents placed on film.

A filing system within an organization can be

1. centralized
2. decentralized
3. a combination of centralized and decentralized.

When the system is centralized, the files are located in one central area, are indexed by a central plan, and are made available through data management personnel to all the departments within the organization. Under the decentralized plan, each department or division controls and maintains its respective filing system.

Using a combination of these systems, the records manager develops the central filing procedures for the entire organization. All the files are indexed according to the central plan; however, the files are housed and maintained in each work area.

In the past, all business information was recorded (on paper) in its original form—for example, price lists, purchase orders, sales slips, invoices, statements, cheques, letters, and reports. In the future, paper will be used even less than it is now. However, as long as a sheet of paper serves as the vehicle for the flow of business information, someone within the organization must process and maintain each sheet of paper while it is in use or until it is stored in some other form. Electronic media and micrographics must also be filed.

"Accuracy is the key to having a smooth running department."

Susan Muise, Graduate
Nova Scotia Community College
Burridge Campus

Even when an organization has a centralized filing system, the administrative assistants keep in their offices the active files. It is primarily the administrative assistant who processes correspondence—incoming and outgoing e-mails, letters, memoranda, and reports. This means that administrative assistants need to be skilled in filing procedures so they can quickly and easily find materials in the files; also, in order to use a centralized system effectively, it is important to understand how information is stored under such a system.

GRADUATE PROFILE

Alice Kavanagh
Executive Assistant

Avalon Ford Sales 1996 Limited

College Graduation:
Secretarial Science Program
College of the North Atlantic
St. John's Newfoundland
1992

Alice Kavanagh believes that office professionals should think "outside the box" and not be limited to their job descriptions. In order to keep motivated, Alice says office professionals should continue their education after graduation and become involved in professional organizations. As an example of her own advice, Alice is currently enrolled in evening courses with the goal of achieving her Business Administration Diploma.

In Alice's role as executive assistant, she consults the local ARMA (Association of Records Managers and Administrators) chapter and the provincial and federal tax offices for advice on records management. She has the responsibilities of forms management as well as records disposition and storage, ensuring that all records are properly boxed, indexed, and stored. Alice says that the electronic office has helped with records management productivity as it increases the speed of information being stored and retrieved. She states that sharing information is an important step in both maintaining an efficient office and in creating a positive working environment for the staff.

Alice's philosophy for successful leadership is to be a proactive thinker who participates in long-term planning and to give employee recognition where credit is due. In her position as an office proessional, she believes there is an abundance of leadership opportunities for people who are willing to learn and apply their skills to the best of their ability.

"Information is literally at your fingertips."

The discussion in this chapter centres on what an administrative assistant needs to know about maintaining files in a typical office or work area; the specific topics relate to basic filing procedures, the types of supplies used for maintaining files for correspondence and other active papers, and alphabetic indexing rules.

ORGANIZING INFORMATION

Information management involves much more than placing a sheet of paper in a folder. The administrative assistant's role in filing includes getting papers ready to be filed, placing each paper in the appropriate folder, properly labelling and arranging magnetic media and other items in proper sequence, sending papers to be microimaged, locating an item quickly when it is called for, using the computer to manage records, and returning to the files the items that have been taken out to be used. Managing information is a very comprehensive responsibility and involves a critical set of procedures for the efficient and effective office.

Preparation for Computer-Assisted Retrieval

Computer-assisted retrieval (CAR) is used to locate information that is not stored within the computer but is found on other media, such as microfilm or microfiche. There is usually so much of this archival material that it would take up too much room if stored in a computer. In this situation, the computer's function is to assist the user in locating information through a rapid search-and-locate process.

The first step in preparing papers to be placed on micrographics so that they can be accessed by CAR at a later date is to mark the key words on the papers to be processed. The key words may be the author's name, date, subject, name of the recipient of the document, or other selected descriptors (words). These words will form the reference name for the document.

Next, each document is assigned a sequential reference number. This reference number will indicate the microfilm roll number and the frame number on that roll. When the medium is fiche, the number will indicate the fiche (card) number and the frame number.

The operator uses a machine that is capable of recording documents on photosensitive film in microscopic form. The reference name and number are keyed; the document itself is then fed into the machine, which creates the film or fiche. If the original document is not in a hardcopy (paper) form and is located in the computer's memory, the COM system is used to send the document directly from the computer into microfilm or microfiche form.

Figure 7-1 An administrative assistant locates microfiche stored in a specially designed tray.
Courtesy of Kardex

When the document is required at a later date, the computer's CAR system produces an index of the names and reference numbers for all documents filed on film or fiche. The reference number indicates to the user where that document is located. The user then locates the correct micrographics and uses a microfilm/microfiche reader to view the document.

Figure 7-1 shows an administrative assistant retrieving a sheet of microfiche that is stored in a specially designed tray. Before finding the microfiche, the administrative assistant used the CAR system to establish the exact location.

Preparation of Papers for Conventional Filing

Paper records are often very untidy and disorganized. We have all seen stuffed and worn file folders crammed into overcrowded cabinets. These same files often have handwritten labels, no charge-out system, and redundant information. No wonder the task least enjoyed by many administrative assistants is filing. However, an administrative assistant who follows procedures suggested here will be rewarded with increased efficiency and satisfaction. The procedures to follow, before placing a paper inside a file folder, are

1. inspecting
2. indexing
3. coding
4. cross-referencing
5. sorting.

Inspecting

Inspect each paper among the materials to be filed to establish that it has been released for filing. A **release mark**, usually placed in the upper left corner, denotes that a paper is ready to be filed. The release mark can be your manager's initials, your own initials, a check mark, a diagonal line across the paper, or the word FILE stamped on the paper. You do not need a release mark on a copy or on an incoming letter when a copy of the reply has been attached to the letter.

An incoming letter that is unanswered, or any item that is still in process, should not be filed. Regard the absence of a release mark as a signal *not* to file the paper until you have established that all parts of it have been acted upon.

When you are ready to file, follow these procedures:

1. Carefully inspect any papers that are stapled together to ascertain that they should be filed together.
2. Remove all paper clips; also remove extra staples.
3. Staple together related papers, putting the one with the most recent date on top.
4. Remove small slips of paper that are no longer needed—for instance, a slip marked "Please file" or a routing slip.
5. Keep the routing slip with the document being filed, or copy the names on the routing slip near the top of the first page of the document being filed. You may need to determine later whom the document was circulated to.
6. Use tape to mend any torn pages.
7. If you have a small piece of paper, attach it to a full-size sheet so that the small piece will not crumple beneath the other papers in the same folder. Either staple it securely or use paper cement. Another method is to make a photocopy on a full-size sheet.

Indexing

You must decide where to file each paper. The mental process of determining the key word or number under which a paper will be filed is called *indexing*. Careful indexing is the most important part of the process of filing papers. The key word can be a name, a subject, or a geographic location.

When you are filing correspondence by name, scan the correspondence to decide which name to use.

Anticipate the name your manager will use when he or she calls for that particular piece of correspondence.

Remember:

1. Incoming letters are most often called for by the name of the organization appearing in the letterhead.
2. Outgoing letters are called for by the name of the organization appearing in the inside address.

However, an incoming letter should be filed under the name of the individual who signed the letter if that is the name under which it will be retrieved. In the same way, an outgoing letter may be filed under the name of the individual in the inside address. A name in the body of the letter may also determine how the letter should be filed.

Avoid going through papers hastily. Avoid guessing where papers should be filed. Take time to read and decide.

Know what is in your files. Avoid filing papers that belong together in two different places by two different captions.

The complete process of indexing involves determining

1. indexing units within a name
2. the sequence in which to consider the units.

To do this, learn standardized indexing rules and follow them consistently. These rules are presented in this chapter.

Coding

After you decide how a paper should be filed, mark the indexing caption on the paper. This process is called *coding*. To code by name, underline the name with a coloured pencil.

The code on a paper should be complete enough that you can return the paper to the same folder each time it has been removed. As you study the indexing rules, you will learn how to determine the order of units within a name. To increase your accuracy in filing, you can write the numbers 1, 2, 3, and so on on the paper above the respective units to designate the sequential order.

Cross-Referencing

When a paper is apt to be called for by two different names at different times, you should be able to locate it by looking under either name. To make this possible, file the paper according to the caption (the name arranged in index order) by which it is most likely to be requested and also file a reference to it by a second name. This is referred to as **cross-referencing.**

To make a cross-reference for a card file, use a card of the same size as the cards in the file; you may use a different colour. Notice in Figure 7-2 the two cards

Figure 7-2 Original card; cross-reference card.

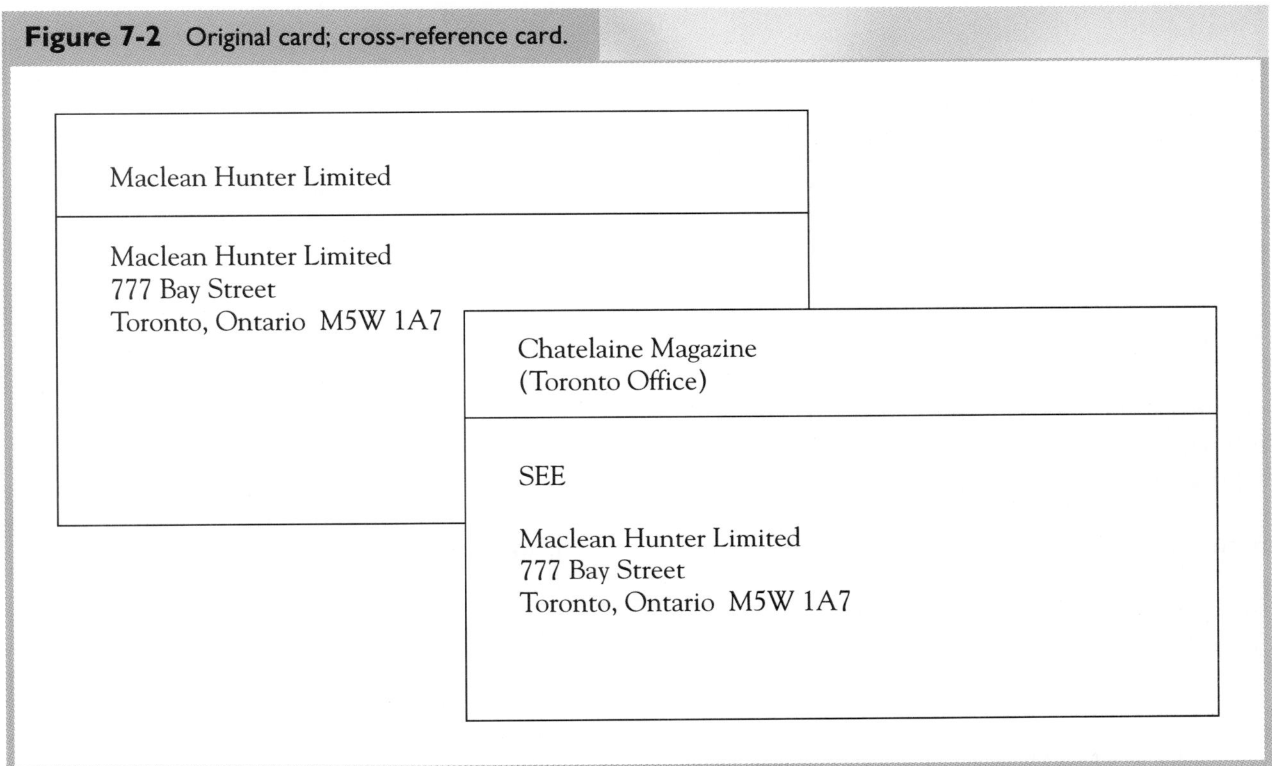

Figure 7-3 Cross-reference sheet.

CROSS-REFERENCE SHEET

NAME OR SUBJECT: Truax Employment Agency **File No.** 2022

Date: 20— 02 22

Remarks: This file holds information on the personnel policies for hiring temporary staff through the Truax Employment Agency.

SEE

Name or Subject: Temporary Help **File No.** 1131

Directions:

- **File this sheet under name or subject at top.**
- **Describe papers under "remarks."**
- **File papers for which this form is to be substituted, under name or subject listed under "see."**

prepared for Maclean Hunter Limited. The information printed below SEE on the cross-reference card is the caption on the original card.

To prepare references for correspondence, use preprinted letter-size cross-reference sheets, similar to the one in Figure 7-3. Make a large X on the actual correspondence in the margin near the name used as a cross-reference; underline the name.

Make two copies of the cross-reference sheet:

1. One copy will be filed in the cross-reference folder. It should be the only piece of paper filed in the folder, since the purpose of the cross-reference sheet is to send you to the correct file. If you have an effective card file system that clearly identifies cross-references, you may eliminate the need for the cross-reference folder and the cross-reference sheet.
2. The second copy will be filed in the actual folder where you want all the correspondence to be placed. This cross-reference sheet will serve as a reminder to you that a cross-reference folder exists. If you are missing information, you may

want to check the cross-reference folder to see whether someone has inadvertently filed documents in the cross-reference folder.

Avoid preparing unnecessary cross-references, but if you are in doubt, make one: it may help you locate a paper when you need it. There are various situations in which cross-referencing is necessary. Consider the following:

1. Correspondence pertaining to individuals may be filed by subject—for example, Temporary Employees.
2. It may be difficult to determine the individual's surname. Consider the name Kent Ross. Is the surname Ross or is it Kent?

   If the surname is Ross, the correct file will read *Ross, Kent* and the cross-reference file label will read *Kent, Ross*. Inside the folder, the cross-reference sheets will read:

   SEE Ross, Kent
3. A married woman may be known by

   a. her maiden name.

   For example, in the name Ms. Heather Ross, the name is indexed as Ross, Heather (Ms.)

   b. her married name.

   For example, in the name Mrs. Heather Whyte the name is indexed as Whyte, Heather (Mrs.).

   c. her husband's name.

   For example, in the name Mrs. Robert Whyte, the name would be indexed as Whyte, Robert (Mrs.)

   A cross-reference will be necessary for two of the three cases. Most commonly, correspondence would be filed under either Ross, Heather (Ms.) or Whyte, Heather (Mrs.). Only one of these files should contain documents; the other two must serve as cross-references only.
4. Subdivisions of a parent company are filed under the name used on their letterhead; they are not filed under the parent company name. However, filing under the parent company name was once a popular method. To avoid confusion, file correctly under the name of the subdivision, but prepare a cross-reference for the name of the parent company. Thus, a subdivision business called Pizza Town with a parent company called Pizza Enterprises would have the correspondence filed as Pizza Town; but a cross-reference sheet would be placed in the Pizza Enterprises folder to send the records manager to the Pizza Town folder.
5. Some organizations are referred to by their acronym because they are better known that way—for example, IAAP (International Association of Administrative Professionals) and CNIB (Canadian National Institute for the Blind). It is acceptable to file the correspondence under either name; however, it is best to check the organization's letterhead or business card to see how the organization refers to itself. Whether you file by the full name or by the popular abbreviation, *consistency must prevail*. A cross-reference will be necessary to keep all the correspondence in the same file.
6. A business name may include several surnames. For Baines, Jones, and Samuelson, file the original by Baines and cross-reference Jones and Samuelson.
7. A company may change its name. File by the new name, and record the date of the change. Retain the old name in the files as a cross-reference only.
8. Names of foreign companies and government agencies are often written in both English and the respective foreign language. For a government agency, file the original paper by the English name, and place a cross-reference sheet in the folder with the foreign spelling.
9. For a foreign company, file the original by the name as it is written, and the cross-reference sheet in the folder under the English translation.
10. When confusion exists concerning a filing rule, alleviate the confusion by making a cross-reference. A cross-reference will send the reader to the correct name of the business.
11. When a department is renamed because of restructuring within the organization, internal correspondence filed by subject is often affected. File the correspondence by the new name; however, retain the old name in the files as a cross-reference.

Sorting

Using the code marks (see "Coding") as a guide, prearrange the papers in the same order in which they will be filed. This preliminary arrangement is called a *sorting*. By sorting the papers carefully, you will eliminate unnecessary shifting back and forth, from drawer to drawer or from shelf to shelf, as you file the papers. As a result, you will be working more efficiently.

Portable vertical sorting trays with dividers and guides are available in a variety of sizes. Use a sorting tray to hold the papers until you file them. If you accumulate a stack of papers in the to-be-filed basket each day and do not have sorting equipment, request it. In the meantime, use the following efficient method of sorting manually.

Sitting at your desk or a table, first divide the papers into manageable groups. For example, if you are sorting by name, first stack the papers in groups A-E, F-J, K-P, Q-T, and U-Z. Next, arrange the papers in the first group in A, B, C, D, and E stacks, and then assemble the papers in each stack in alphabetical order. Sort the remaining groups in the same way. Remember, where two pieces of correspondence share the same name, the most recent document is placed on top.

Techniques for Putting Away Papers

A second meaning of the word *filing* is the actual placing of papers in folders. Allow at least 30 minutes a day in your schedule for this type of filing.

Many administrative assistants rate filing as their most disliked duty. When unfiled papers stack up, a simple task becomes a burden. You will spend more time locating a paper in an unarranged stack than in one that is properly organized. Note also that you run the risk of losing papers when they are disorganized. It is crucial that you keep up with your filing on a daily basis.

With the aid of a sorting tray, you can sort papers at intervals throughout the day, thereby reducing the time you will need late in the afternoon to finish filing.

Automated sorting systems are available. Figure 7-4 shows an administrative assistant sorting documents. By means of a computerized control panel, the slots required are brought in front of the operator. This eliminates unnecessary movements, which in turn reduces sorting time.

Figure 7-4 Automated sorting system.
Courtesy of Kardex

"Putting away" is the last operation of every task you perform. Consider filing as the last step of another task, not an isolated one. After you finish transcribing correspondence, take a few minutes to inspect, index, and code the papers released for filing. To eliminate a second handling, arrange the papers in the sorting tray as you code them. Other advantages result from sorting at intervals throughout the day:

1. You can file for a few minutes at a time, using spare moments, because you have the papers arranged in manageable segments.
2. You will know exactly where to locate a paper if your manager calls for it before it is filed.

To place a paper in a regular folder, lift the folder enough that you can align the paper with the other sheets in the folder and that you are certain to have got it inside the folder, not between folders. Handle the folder by its side or by the reinforced top edge (if it has one); be careful not to pull or lift the folder by the tab. Do not remove the folder; obviously, if you do you will increase your filing time as you search for the proper place to reinsert the folder. Insert the paper facing you, with the top edge of the paper at the left of the folder.

To file a paper in a hanging folder, open the folder enough for the paper to drop into place.

In any new office job, you will be placing and locating materials in files that were maintained by your predecessor. If, as a part of your orientation to the job, he or she explains the filing system to you, listen carefully. Ask questions and take notes. If the organization has a central indexing system, learn it as rapidly as you can. Study it, and memorize the rules and procedures that relate directly to your files.

Do not try to reorganize the files in your office until you are familiar with what they contain. Allow yourself several months to learn this.

In the meantime, become thoroughly familiar with the contents of your files. Keep notes about papers that are difficult to locate and about other aspects of the filing system that create problems. Make a list of the papers you searched for and did not find. Write down your suggestions for improving the filing system.

Charge-out Methods

Since materials are kept in active files for use, effective charge-out methods must be followed if you are to keep track of materials that have been borrowed from the files and are to be returned.

Figure 7-5 An administrative assistant checks the status of a file through an electronically controlled system.
Courtesy of Kardex

Charge-out procedures can be electronically controlled. This reduces the time spent searching for files. Figure 7-5 shows an administrative assistant checking a file's status by computer. The software can give her the location of a file whether it is in the filing system or has been charged out.

Manual charge-out systems are very popular, especially where files are decentralized. A manual system uses special cards, folders, and pressboard guides with the word OUT printed on the tabs to substitute for papers and folders that have been taken from the files. When only a few sheets of paper are removed from the files, an OUT card is used; when the entire folder is removed, either an OUT folder or an OUT guide is substituted. Filing departments use two types of guides: one with printed lines on which to write a description of the material removed, the name of the person to whom it was issued, and the date issued; another with a slot or a pocket to hold a card on which the charge-out information has been written. Both types are reusable. The OUT card, folder, or guide remains in the file until the charged-out material is returned.

When you requisition materials from the central files, observe the charge-out methods used by the records manager.

The method you use for keeping up with materials removed from the files you maintain will depend on how much material is removed from your files at one time, how long the material is kept out of the files, and the number of people you work with. Do not substitute OUT cards and guides for material you remove from the files. Instead, make a notation concerning what you removed in the notebook where you list things to do. When you return a paper or folder to the files, cross out the reference to it in your notebook.

If materials are often borrowed from your files by other departments, or if you maintain files for several people use a formal charge-out method so that you can quickly locate any paper that has been removed. If you are spending time searching for materials that are not in the files, review and improve your charge-out methods. Use substitution cards and OUT guides to control the location of the papers released from the files.

Organization of Files on a Disk

Because most organizations depend heavily on electronic filing methods as well as paper filing methods, it is essential that the administrative assistant have an efficient and effective means of locating documents filed on disks.

Many administrative assistants retrieve files by accessing the hard disk. When they wish to store documents they use the hard disk again for storage. In this situation, it becomes essential for the administrative assistant to create a **directory** where his or her documents are filed. A directory is a section of the disk that is allotted to certain files; it is like the administrative assistant having his or her own filing cabinet. Each time a document is stored or retrieved, the name of the directory must be used in order to place or locate the document.

"My career is just beginning. The one thing I need to do in these early stages is to watch and learn."

Chelsea Lynn McGuire, Graduate
New Brunswick Community College
Saint John Campus

Many organizations store documents on floppy disks and not on the system's hard disk; a company that stores all its documents on the hard disk should still back up those documents on floppy disks. An efficient practice is to assign one floppy disk or one directory on the hard disk for each originator of documents or for each separate topic. When the floppy disk is first used, and again when the floppy disk is full, the date should be noted on the disk's label. The name of the originator should also be noted clearly.

Directories are often used on floppy disks; the originator creates directories for different subjects and then stores the documents under the correct subject or directory on the floppy disk. A very common practice is for the administrative assistant to keep separate floppies for separate topics.

An effective method of organizing files is to develop a code for naming documents. As an example, the document named *M-Bla-Bud* might be a *memo* generated by *Mrs. Black* on the subject of the *budget*. When an index of the floppy disk's files is displayed on the computer's screen, it becomes easy to select the correct file.

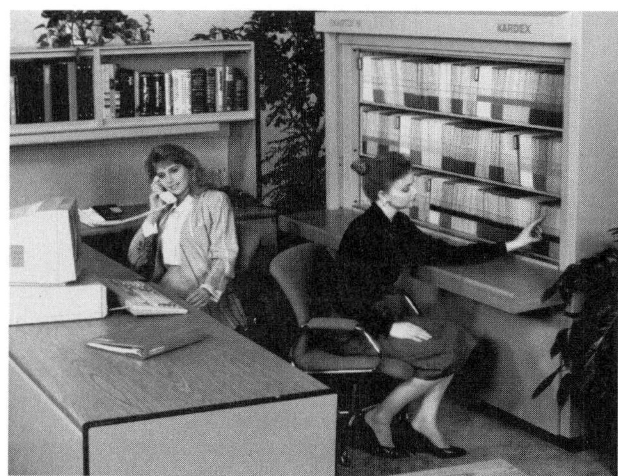

Figure 7-6 An administrative assistant locates a file in an open-shelf filing system.
Courtesy of Kardex

SUPPLIES

Every filing system can be expanded with the proper supplies and equipment. To add to the files, use supplies to match what is already in use. Among the supplies needed for hardcopy (paper) filing of correspondence are guides, folders, and labels. Computerized filing of correspondence will require the administrative assistant to keep a supply of floppy disks and floppy disk labels.

Guides

The dividers in conventional filing drawers or compartments are called *guides*. They usually are made of pressboard, but thin, lightweight aluminum guides are available. Guides serve as signposts, separating the filing space into labelled sections; they also support the folders in an upright position.

The portion of the guide projecting from its edge is called a *tab*. The tab makes the guide easy to locate. Guides with a variety of tabs are available. Some tabs (typically the pressboard ones) are pre-printed with numbers, months, days, or letters of the alphabet; other tabs are of plastic or metal and have slots for inserts.

Guides for open-shelf filing differ from guides for vertical file drawers. Remember to specify how the guide will be used when you place an order. Figure 7-6 shows open-shelf filing. Note that the tabs on the guides are along the side and not on the top, as they would be on vertical files.

Folders

Folders, the containers for holding correspondence and other papers, are made either of plastic or of heavy paper such as Manila or kraft. Folders come in a wide range of colours.

The tab on a folder is described by the width of it, referred to as a *cut*. Often-used cuts are

1. one-third
2. one-fifth
3. two-fifths
4. one-half
5. straight.

The disadvantage of straight-cut folders is that they get lost among other folders. A one-third cut means that the tab extends above the folder for one-third of the width of the top edge of the folder. A one-third cut can be near the left edge, centred, or near the right edge. A one-fifth cut extends above the top edge of the folder for one-fifth of its width, and can be located in one of five positions. In a vertical drawer, the tab near the left edge is in the *first position* (in Figure 7-18, note that the primary guides A, B, and C are in first position).

When you order folders, specify both the cut and the position needed to match the existing folders. See Figure 7-7 for a variety of cut folder styles.

The creases at the bottom of a folder are called *scores*. Do not crease a score until you have enough papers in the folder to fill up the space between the bottom edge of the folder and the first score. If you crease the score when you have inserted only four or five papers, they will slump in the folder. You should crease the first score before the papers begin to ride up in the folder.

Expandable folders are available for oversized files. The folders shown in Figure 7-8 have a gusset instead of a score; gussets allow a folder to expand more than a conventional folder.

Suspension, or hanging, folders are widely used for active files. Hanging folders are suspended by extensions

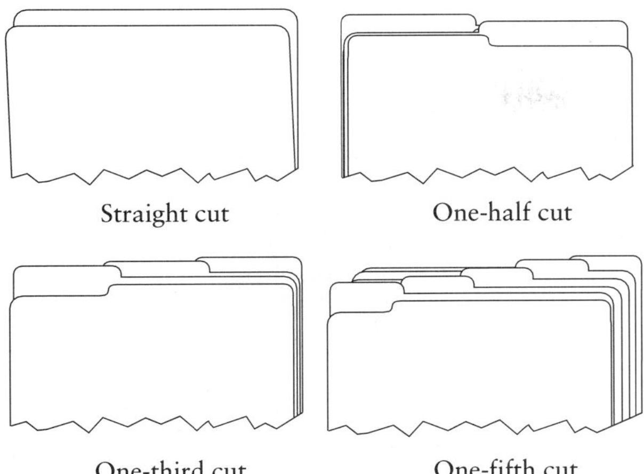

Figure 7-7 Folder cuts.

Figure 7-8 Expandable folders.
Courtesy of Kardex

at their top edges across a metal frame within the file drawer. Refer to Figure 7-9. Suspension folders do not rest on the bottom of the drawer. Materials filed in suspension folders are easily accessible because the folders open wide and slide smoothly on the hanger rail. Attachable tabs are inserted into slots at the top of the folders and are used in place of conventional guides with tabs. Note that the follower block at the back of the drawer is eliminated, allowing extra space for folders.

Labels

Use *labels* to put captions on folders. You will need to label folders when you add a folder for a new correspondent and when you need to open a new volume of an existing folder. The labels you add should match the existing ones.

Labels come in a wide variety of colours; each colour is used to represent a different subdivision in the filing system. If the files you use have labels of different colours, learn what each colour stands for, and then specify colour when you order labels.

Labels are packaged either in continuous strips or on sheets. Always key a label before you separate it from the strip or sheet. Labels are self-adhesive and pressure sensitive. Labels for open-shelf filing should be readable from both front and back.

Key the names on the label in index order. Capitalize the first letter of each word. If you choose, capitalize all the letters in the main word, but not the entire caption, because captions keyed in solid capital letters are difficult to read.

Key the primary caption on the second line from the top of the label. Align the captions two spaces from the left end of the label. Attach the labels to the tabs in perfect alignment with one another. The captions in a file should resemble an aligned list of names, as shown in Figure 7-10.

Label drawers or sections of the files with either open or closed notations. A closed notation indicates the

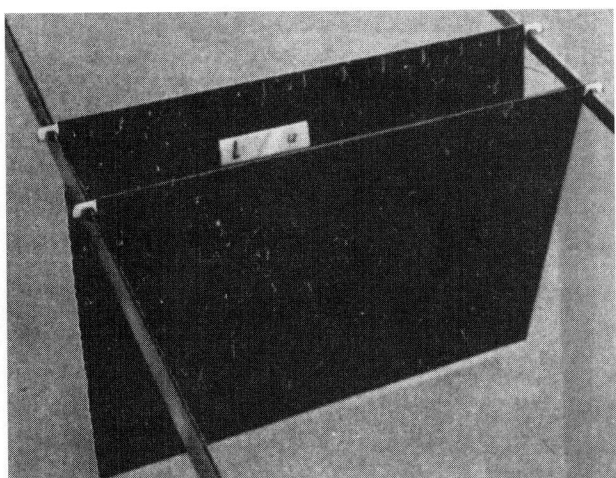

Figure 7-9 Hanging file folder.

Figure 7-10 Aligned labels on folder tabs.

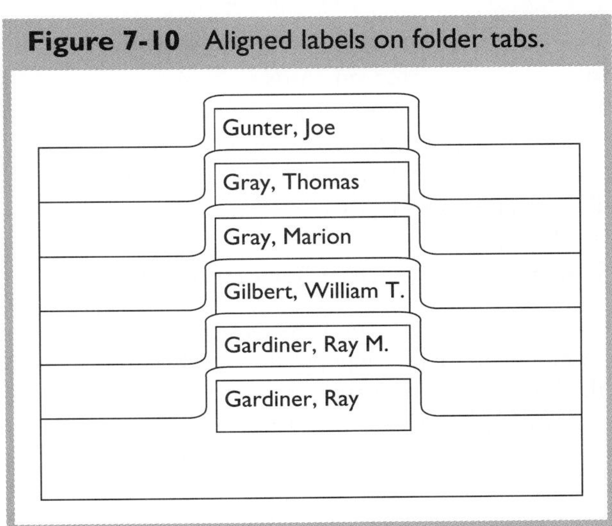

entire span of the contents. A typical example of a closed notation would be:

CORRESPONDENCE
A - H

A typical example of an open notation would be:

CORRESPONDENCE

The office from which the correspondence originates may not keep a paper copy; instead, correspondence may be stored on hard disk, floppy disks or zip disks. In this case, the administrative assistant will need plenty of space on the hard drive, or a supply of floppy disks, or zip disks and disk labels.

Disks

A supply of floppy disks and zip disks will be needed because all administrative assistants will be maintaining at least some electronic files. These disks may be purchased individually or in bulk.

A label that the administrative assistant will complete accompanies each disk. The label should reflect the content of the information stored on the disk. A floppy disk typically holds over 1.4 megabytes of memory. A zip disk stores upwards of 100 megabytes of memory.

EQUIPMENT AND STORAGE

Paper correspondence is usually filed in drawers. Information printed on cards is filed in a variety of ways—in drawers, in trays, on wheels, in panels—to make it easily accessible to the operator. Some filing units are automated, so that the operator can bring the files or cards within easy reach by pressing a button.

Storing Hardcopy Documents

For years paper correspondence has been filed vertically, standing upright and supported by guides and folders in file drawers. Today correspondence and other records are still filed vertically, but the conventional cabinet that pulls out the full depth of the drawer is rapidly being replaced by lateral files. Compare the vertical cabinet in Figure 7-11 to the lateral cabinet in Figure 7-12.

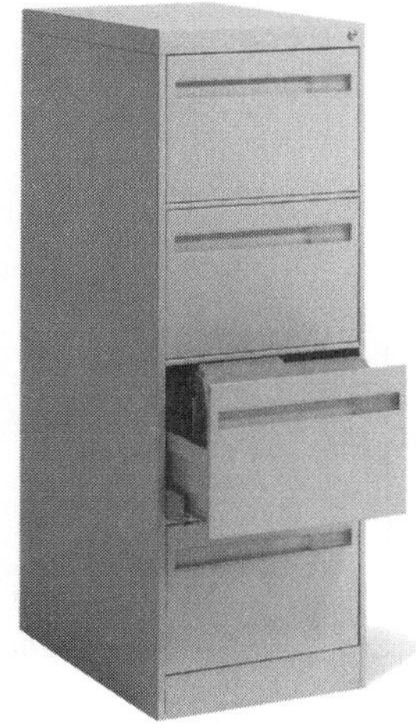

Figure 7-11 Vertical filing cabinet.
Courtesy of Miller Office Group/Corporate Express.

Figure 7-12 Lateral filing cabinet.
Courtesy of Miller Office Group/Corporate Express.

Lateral files were originally designed as components for modular office workstations to be used in landscaped areas. Whether or not they are landscaped, offices equipped with modern furniture will have lateral files.

Lateral files save space because between 25 and 50 percent less aisle space is needed to pull out a lateral file drawer than is needed to pull out a conventional file drawer. Lateral files may be used as single units or may be stacked. They can serve as area dividers. They can be adapted to store almost any kind of records—for example, letters, legal documents, cards, and computer printouts. As well, a lateral file can be adjusted to house microfilm or microfiche along with paper correspondence.

One type of lateral file is open-shelf. This type is used to save floor space, filing and retrieval time, and initial installation costs. For open-shelf filing, the tabs project from the side of the folder. For an illustration of open-shelf filing, refer back to Figure 7-6.

Lateral files are equipped to handle either regular or suspension folders. The folders may be arranged either side by side or from front to back. The tabs are at the top of guides, and the folders are arranged in closed drawers.

A popular device, designed to hold files upright inside the filing drawer, is the wire organizer. See Figure 7-13. With the wire organizer, folders may be placed directly into the file drawer without any suspension folders being used. Folders remain upright, and space is saved. Time is also saved, since duplicate labels for the hanging folders are not needed.

Storing Reference Information

You will need a file for quick reference to names, e-mail and geographic addresses, and telephone and fax numbers of correspondents. Most offices store these types of quick reference files on a database within their computer. However, if you do not use a computer to keep your address lists, key your lists on cards.

Many administrative assistants use portable wheel files that hold cards and guides to arrange information that they need to refer to quickly and often. Slotted cards can be inserted or removed without disturbing the other cards. Wheels are available for different sizes of cards.

Adding a card to a file or replacing an existing card with a new one is easy. When you discover that a correspondent has a new address, telephone number or fax number, key a new card and insert it in place of the old one.

Other types of card files are *vertical visible* and *horizontal visible*. Automated filing equipment is available for both card files and folder files. Motorized filing equipment is constructed so that an operator can bring a shelf of folders or cards assembled in trays within easy reach by pushing a button. Refer to Figure 7-14 to see an administrative assistant accessing files with a control panel.

Figure 7-13 Wire organizer.

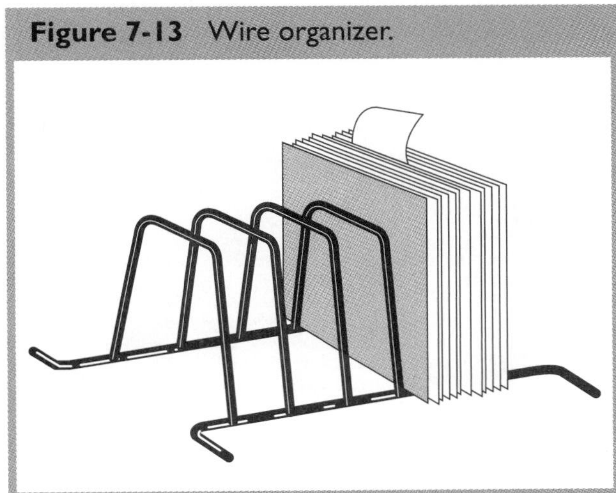

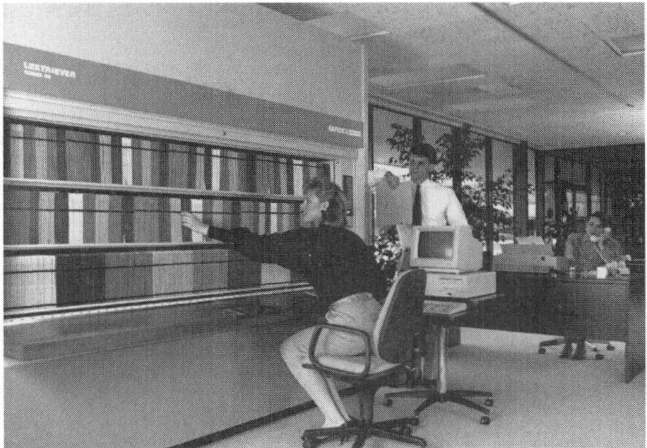

Figure 7-14 An administrative assistant accesses files with a control panel.
Courtesy of Kardex

Storing Magnetic Media

Data generated by computers are stored on floppy disks, zip disks, and hard disks. Hard disks are designed to store large amounts of data while floppy disks and zip disks are portable and are designed to store less information than a hard disk.

A computer can record data directly onto a disk and transfer the data to other disks with ease. Data on auxiliary storage media such as floppy disks or zip disks can be loaded back into the computer by inserting the disk into the disk drive and instructing the computer to read the information on that disk.

Because disks are sensitive to heat, power surges, shocks, and other problems and because so much data can be stored on a single disk, the loss of data on one disk can be a disaster to a business. We depend so heavily on information stored on our computers that the concept of a **Y2K** computer failure or other similar computer crashes is a great concern to some individuals.

One of the greatest enemies of diskettes is electricity. Therefore, disks should be stored in sturdy plastic cases similar to the one shown in Figure 7-15. Many of these cases have an anti-static component to protect the disks from dirt, dust, lint, and static electricity. They should be stored at temperatures between 5° and 32° Celsius. The plastic storage case should have a key lock to control unauthorized access. However, these cases are portable, so although they can be locked, they should be stored overnight in a locked filing cabinet or cupboard to ensure the safety of the disks.

Figure 7-15 Storage case for disks.

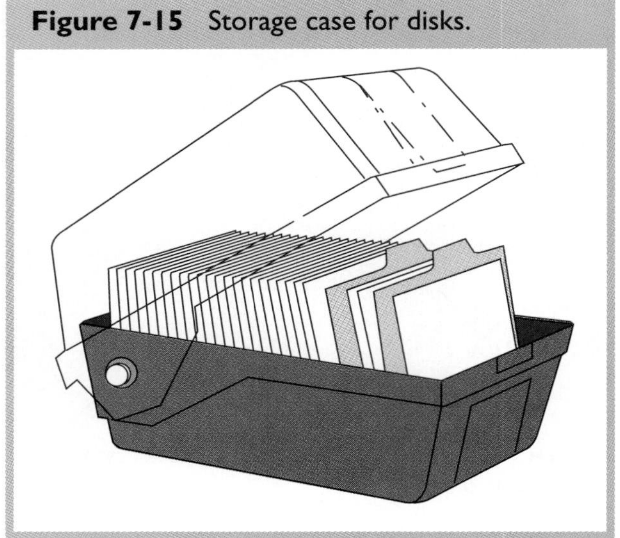

Because magnetic media come in many different shapes and sizes, manufacturers produce multimedia cabinets to store disks, cassettes, and other computer-generated material. Folders are available for storing diskettes with the hard copy.

Although diskettes have a hard plastic cover, they are susceptible to some damage. To provide the utmost protection to diskettes, AVOID the following:

1. leaving diskettes exposed to heat and sunlight
2. eating, drinking, or smoking while handling diskettes.
3. placing a disk under a heavy object
4. using magnetized objects near disks; magnetized objects include telephone answering machines, vacuum cleaners, air conditioners, radios, televisions, electric motors, and many novelty items.

Because we are so dependent on magnetic media, you should always make a backup copy of a disk containing critical information. Store the original and the backup copy away from each other so that the same accident will not destroy both of them.

Storing Micrographics

Micrographics includes microfilm, microfiche, and other microforms produced by cameras and computer output microfilm recorders. Milcrofilming is a photographic process by which documents, printed pages, drawings, and the like are recorded on film in a reduced size for convenience in storage, transportation, and use. Refer to Figure 7-16 for a sample of some micrographic media forms. The film can be viewed directly with the aid of a microfilm reader, and a print the same size as the original can be made from the film with the aid of a reader-printer. When microfilm is printed out on paper it is called a hardcopy.

The advantages of using microfilm are:

1. savings in storage space
2. records protection
3. ease and reduced cost of mailing
4. efficiency of retrieval.

Microfilm can be stored in 2 to 3 percent of the space occupied by the original papers. To increase security, duplicate records can be made on microfilm and stored in a second location.

Figure 7-16 Microfilm media forms.

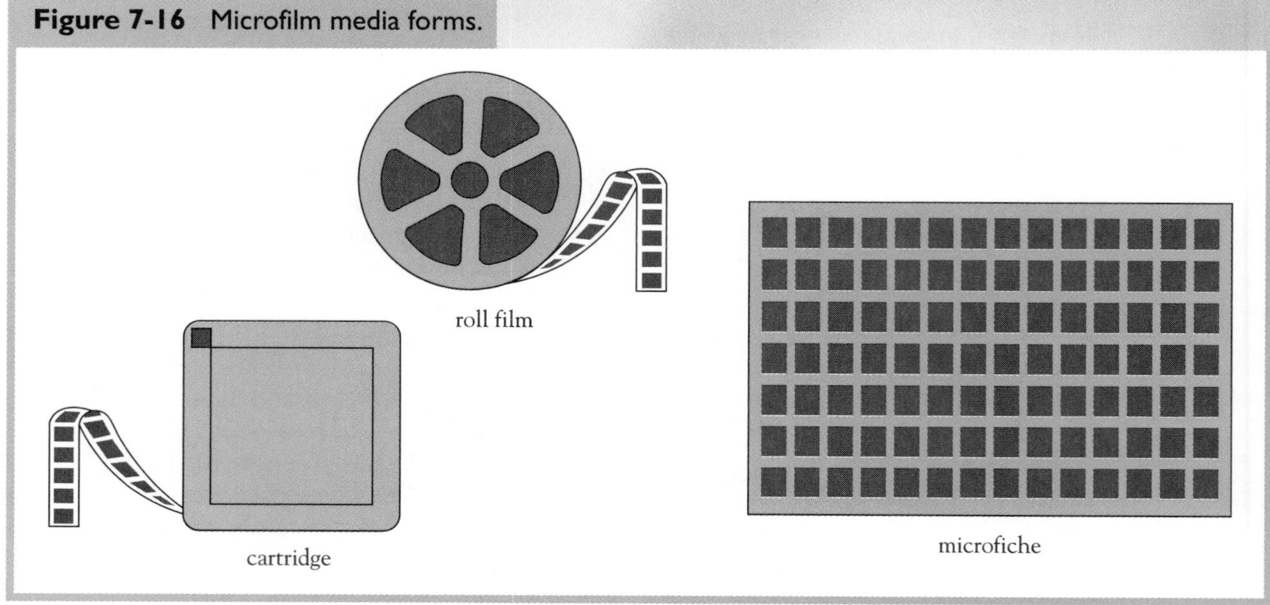

Microfiche (pronounced micro-feesh) is a miniature version of microfilm. It is a transparent sheet of film containing multiple rows of micro-images.

HOW CAN A COMPUTER MANAGE RECORDS?

Computerized records files are an excellent way of storing lists of frequently used names, addresses and numbers as well as inventory items and mailing lists. In fact, computer records lend themselves perfectly to storing and sorting lists of just about anything, including lists of paper files and descriptions of their contents. A variety of computer software is available for creating databases.

The information is entered through scanner or a keyboard. Each letter or number on the keyboard is called a *character*. A name or number, such as a family name, postal code, or telephone number, is called a *field*.

The complete information about one person or one item is called a *record*. An example of a record would be all the information about Harvey Ross.

A collection of records is called a *file*. An example of a file would be all the records of employees in the Finance Department.

A *database* is a set of logically related files. An example would be all the department files for a company.

Records management software can be used to manipulate a database. Such software works with far greater efficiency than does manual records management. Electronic systems (see Figure 7-17)

1. improve accuracy and consistency
2. lower the cost of storing and retrieving information
3. simplify the handling of files
4. incorporate changes rapidly
5. eliminate redundant information.
6. retrieve and store information with speed.

RECORDS RETENTION AND TRANSFER

Some records must be kept permanently. Many records are kept from 3 to 20 years, while some must be held for up to 100 years; others are useful for only a short time and are kept for a year or less. Finally, some records are disposed of without being stored. Records that are kept for longer than a year are usually transferred from the active files to a storage area.

Figure 7-17 Sample information for the Quality Flooring Company illustrates a character, a field, a record, a file, and a database.

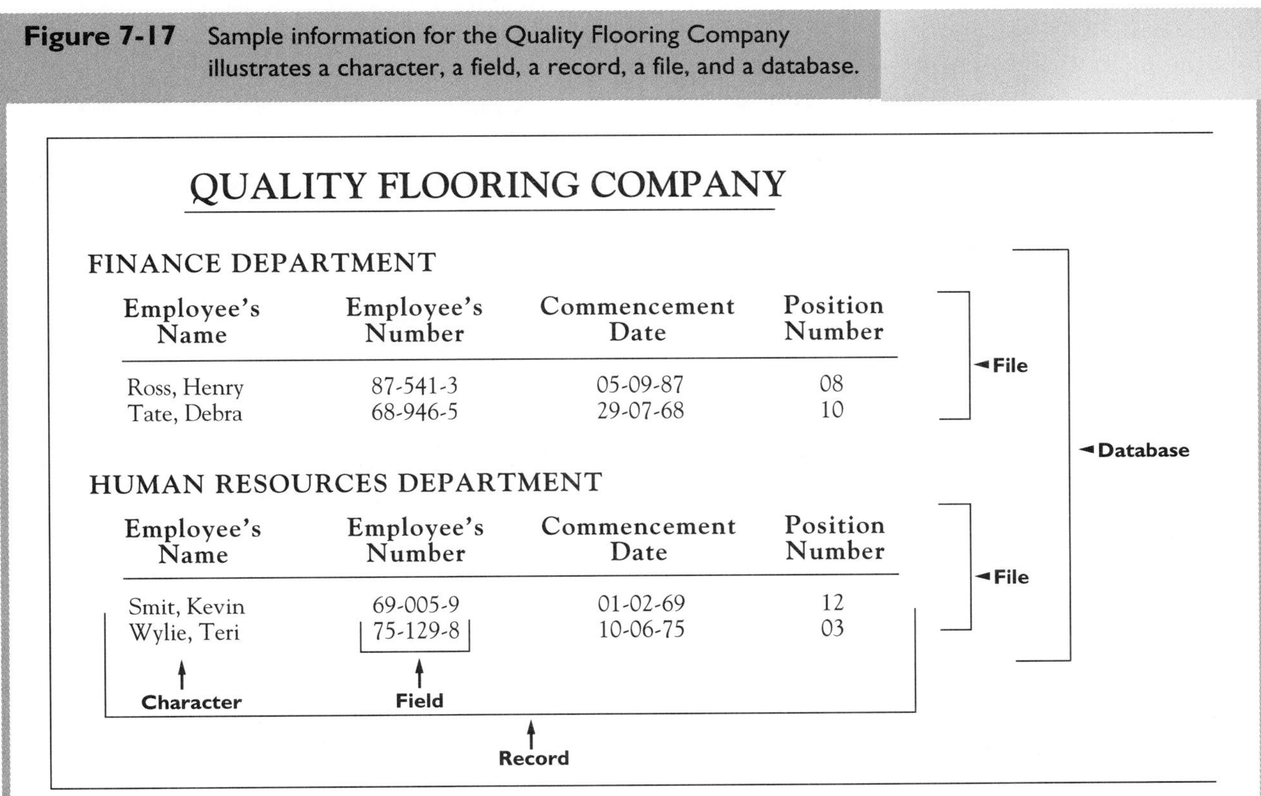

QUALITY FLOORING COMPANY

FINANCE DEPARTMENT

Employee's Name	Employee's Number	Commencement Date	Position Number
Ross, Henry	87-541-3	05-09-87	08
Tate, Debra	68-946-5	29-07-68	10

HUMAN RESOURCES DEPARTMENT

Employee's Name	Employee's Number	Commencement Date	Position Number
Smit, Kevin	69-005-9	01-02-69	12
Wylie, Teri	75-129-8	10-06-75	03

Retention

The following four factors determine how long records must be preserved:

1. the nature of an organization's business operations
2. provincial statutes of limitations
3. regulations of statutes of the federal government
4. regulations of the municipality.

Each province has its own statutes of limitations, specifying the time after which a record cannot be used as evidence in the courts. An organization is subject to the statutes of limitations of the province in which it operates. Among the records affected by provincial statutes of limitations are written contracts, recoveries of land or rent, injury claims, and accident reports.

Banking records, records of employees' taxes, and aircraft operation and maintenance records are examples of records covered by the federal government's regulations and statutes.

Determining which records to keep and for how long is a critical function. An administrative assistant should not dispose of any records or papers from the files without a clear knowledge of retention legislation.

Transfer

The most accessible file space should be used for active files; this means that the less active papers will have to be moved from time to time in order to free up the most accessible space for the current papers. Organizations use two methods of transfer: perpetual and periodic. The discussion here is limited to transferring papers because paper storage consumes much more space than does electronic or micrographic media. However, the concept of perpetual and periodic transfer is also applied to the other media used for storing information.

Perpetual Method

Perpetual transfer is a method of continually transferring papers to inactive storage as a project or case is completed. It is highly applicable for records kept by organizations that handle projects or cases, such as legal firms or construction companies. All the records for one project or case are transferred at the time it is completed.

Periodic Method

The *periodic* method provides for transferring papers to inactive storage at stated intervals such as 6 months, 1 year, or 18 months. Three periodic transfer methods are used: one-period, two-period, and maximum-minimum period.

PRO-LINK

pro-Link

Are you in the Information Management business?

Let's put it another way; are you managing your organization's information and knowledge? If your answer is "yes," then celebrate! Perhaps it's time to advertise the critical nature of your contribution. Consider these moves:

- Produce a newsletter (preferably electronic) on information and knowledge management matters, highlighting developments and services that will help other employees succeed in their work.
- Launch and celebrate new services and developments.
- Hold 'business breakfasts,' 'brown bag lunches,' or evening receptions to demonstrate your service's role in the success of the organization.
- Hold training sessions on new equipment, or 'how to get the most from information.'
- Identify developments in the wider world, which are relevant to your organization.
- Monitor developments and changes within the organization's activity and reflect these in your service strategy.
- Include details of Information Services in new recruits' orientation guide
- Make sure you deliver what you promise.
- Join a professional Information Management Association.

Now you're in the business!

Concept from *Managing Information*, Volume 6, Number 2, March 1999.

When the *one-period* method is employed, all the papers in the active files are transferred to storage at a stated time. No consideration is given to keeping recent papers, which are likely to be needed for reference, in the active files. This method poses one major disadvantage: the administrative assistant, or someone else, must make trips to the storage centre to locate any materials needed.

The *two-period method*, also called the duplicate equipment method, provides matching storage space for inactive files. This space should be adjacent to the active file—either a lower drawer in the same cabinet or a drawer in a nearby cabinet. In addition, space is provided in the storage centre for those papers seldom referred to.

The files are transferred at predetermined intervals. The papers in the inactive file are transferred to the storage centre, and the active papers are transferred to the adjacent file space; this leaves the active file space free to house incoming papers.

Under the *maximum-minimum* plan, all papers are kept in the active files for the minimum time, such as six months, but no papers are kept in the active files beyond the maximum time, such as 18 months. When the transfer is made, the recent papers—all those dated after the minimum cut-off date—are retained in the active files.

Choosing Paper, Magnetic Media, or Micrographics

How does an office professional know when to choose paper, or magnetic media, or micrographics for storage of information?

First, it should be understood that these forms of storage are not mutually exclusive; instead they can be used together for different applications of information management.

The disadvantage of using paper to store documents is that paper requires a significant amount of storage space that results in expense to the company. Paper can be time-consuming to manage. However, every office professional is familiar and comfortable with using paper and so for many it is still the preferred form of media.

Computer magnetic media has many advantages over paper. It can be rapidly retrieved, updated, and stored. As well, it requires minimum storage space compared to paper. The downside of using magnetic media is that it has a limited time period for retention. Also, as computer hardware and software continue to change and advance at incredible speeds, the storage form of old media may not be accessible in the years ahead.

Micrographics has the advantage of needing less storage space than paper. As well, it is suited to very long periods of retention. Because of this, it is the preferred method of storage for documents that may be needed for evidence in the court of law many years in the future. On the other hand, storage and retrieval of micrographics requires specialized equipment not found in most offices; therefore this work is often **out-sourced**.

PAPERLESS OFFICE

Much has been written about the paperless office, but today for most organizations the prospect of a totally paperless office is only a dream. Sales of paper, professionally designed filing systems, and filing equipment provide evidence that paper systems still dominate the information-management field.

Many employees still feel the need to read from a hard copy; this is changing, however, as people become more comfortable with reading and making decisions directly from material presented on a computer screen.

It is true that more and more information that has been stored has never been produced on paper. For an example, consider computer-output microfilm (COM). COM is a means of transferring data directly from the computer to microfilm. However, it is estimated that all the uses of microfilm equal only 5 percent of all business records. And even this estimation is diminishing as legislation and technology provide the means to store data and signatures electronically.

Much of the information generated by computers is never printed because it is stored and readily accessible on magnetic media. As a new generation brought up with using computers and the Internet every day at home and at school enters the professional world, the paperless office becomes more of a reality.

However, for some time to come, until the paperless office is a reality, the administrative assistant will have to know how to manage both magnetic media and paper files.

ALPHABETIC FILING PROCEDURES

All filing systems are based on the alphabet. The main filing systems are alphabetic, geographic, subject, and numeric. The *geographic* system is arranged alphabetically, but geographic locations, such as provinces and cities, provide the primary subdivisions. The primary subdivisions in a *subject* filing system are the functions of the organization; the topics in the subject system are filed alphabetically.

The numeric system is an indirect system. Each person (or topic) is assigned a number, such as a Social Insurance number. The information is filed in sequence by number, but an alphabetic index of the individuals (or topics) to whom numbers have been assigned is also maintained. Several combinations of subject and numeric filing systems have been devised.

The alphabetic system is the arrangement of names or other captions in order from A to Z. Organizations do not follow identical filing rules; however, with few exceptions the names are usually indexed according to the rules presented and explained in the next section of this chapter. (Variations in the rules are explained at the end of this chapter.)

To set up the simplest alphabetic system in strict sequential order for filing correspondence in regular folders, you need

- primary guides—at least one for each letter of the alphabet
- individual name folders
- miscellaneous folders
- special guides
- colour coding (optional).

PERSPECTIVES

The Demise of the Paper Trail

Take a look at the latest advancements in document management. Could the paperless office be just around the corner?

That's the question on everyone's mind these days. And while it seems an admirable goal, we may never get away from paper altogether. Fortunately, technology is helping to drastically cut the amount of paper we use and the time we spend managing files, which is good news when you consider the high premiums on office space and the cost of off-site storage.

Today, paper filing simply is no longer an affordable, cost-effective, or efficient way to manage business records. Regardless of the size of your business, file cabinets waste valuable space, which can cost your company thousands of dollars annually from lost productivity and inefficiency.

But choosing an automated records management system is difficult at best. The wide range of available new technologies—from micrographics to electronic filing—and sophisticated imaging systems can complicate the decision. How do you know what is right for your situation?

Instant access vs. long-term storage

In analyzing the life cycle of a document, for example, first determine how long your documents must be retained. It is important to fully understand the storage and retrieval pattern of documents in your business. Do your primary needs require instant access, long-term storage or a combination of both?

In most office environments the bulk of requests to see a document occur soon—within 90 days—after a document is received (or generated) and filed. Understanding document life cycles and archival and retrieval patterns will help you assess the storage media that is best suited for your operation.

Next, examine why the records are being retained. Are they simply backup documents? Is it an issue of security or disaster recovery? What are your purge schedules? What are the legal considerations—whether document reproductions are admissible in court depends on regulatory restrictions, specific retention laws, the integrity of the document, and your record-keeping operation.

Asking these questions early in the system evaluation process will help you pinpoint solutions that make the most sense.

Long-term retention

Microfilm or microfiche can last forever. Though not as glamorous as the electronic media now available, microfilm is an archival medium that cannot be beat when it comes to long-term records retention—even if your hardware changes in five, 10, or 50 years.

Micrographic technology continues to become more sophisticated. Today's microfilm cameras can capture as many as 10,000 documents an hour, while readers/printers can output up to 20 pages a minute. Current filming equipment can capture documents as much as three times faster than electronic imaging systems and is considerably less expensive. In addition to the long-term benefits, microfilm is the best media for maintaining file integrity and answering legality issues.

Easy access

If easy access is your main requirement, electronic retrieval can be as much as 10 times faster than film retrieval.

"There are a number of advantages for electronic filing systems over paper filing," Gorney said. "First, it provides a very easy way to file and retrieve documents. Second, it minimizes the incidence of misfiles and cuts down on the time it takes to locate files. Third, it greatly reduces the amount of space needed to store documents—one optical disk can hold approximately the same number of documents as a standard four-drawer file cabinet."

More important, it allows for better customer service. Consider the advantages of having instant access to a customer's file. For example, a customer calls to dispute an order or an invoice; with an electronic filing system, the order can be accessed immediately and faxed directly from a PC.

"Electronic filing provides immediate customer response. It eliminates wasted time hunting through file cabinets for paper documents," Gorney said.

The risk, however, is that storage media and system hardware can become obsolete in a few years. It is critical that any electronic system you purchase has an open platform and is flexible for future expansion. Also, while electronic imaging systems are very good at maintaining file integrity, the acceptance of these documents in courts of law still is a concern in some circles. Gorney suggests getting recommendations from your organization's legal department before purchasing a system.

Still, the number of electronic options is growing. Electronic imaging systems are ideal for businesses where quick and easy access is the primary concern.

Each system solves different problems. Your records management and storage needs will change over time. Understanding how to meet those needs is critical to choosing the best system. Ultimately, you, your records manager, and the systems vendors should weigh the cost of paper storage and the quick access versus long-term retention requirements of your documents before selecting an automated system.

Reprinted courtesy of OfficePRO.

Primary Guides

Primary guides divide a file into alphabetic sections. A guide is placed at the beginning of each section. Guides direct the eye to the section of the file in which the folder being sought is located; guides also protect the folders as they are moved back and forth.

Guides are not needed with hanging folders, as the folders are supported from a metal frame and the guide tabs are attached directly to the folders. When guides are used, the correspondence is filed in either individual or miscellaneous folders placed behind the guides.

Individual Name Folders

When you accumulate at least five papers for one correspondent, or when you determine from the current letter that much communication will take place between the correspondent and your manager, prepare an individual folder with the full name of the correspondent keyed in indexed order in the caption.

Arrange individual folders in alphabetical order immediately following the appropriate primary guide, as shown in Figure 7-18. File correspondence within individual folders in chronological order, so that the correspondence bearing the most recent date is placed at the front of the folder. Recent correspondence is usually referred to most often.

Miscellaneous Folders

For every primary guide in your file there should be a miscellaneous folder with a caption corresponding to the caption on the primary guide. Miscellaneous folders belong *behind* individual folders. File in the miscellaneous folders the papers to and from all correspondents for whom you do not have individual name folders.

Figure 7-18 Arrangement of guides and folders in alphabetic correspondence.

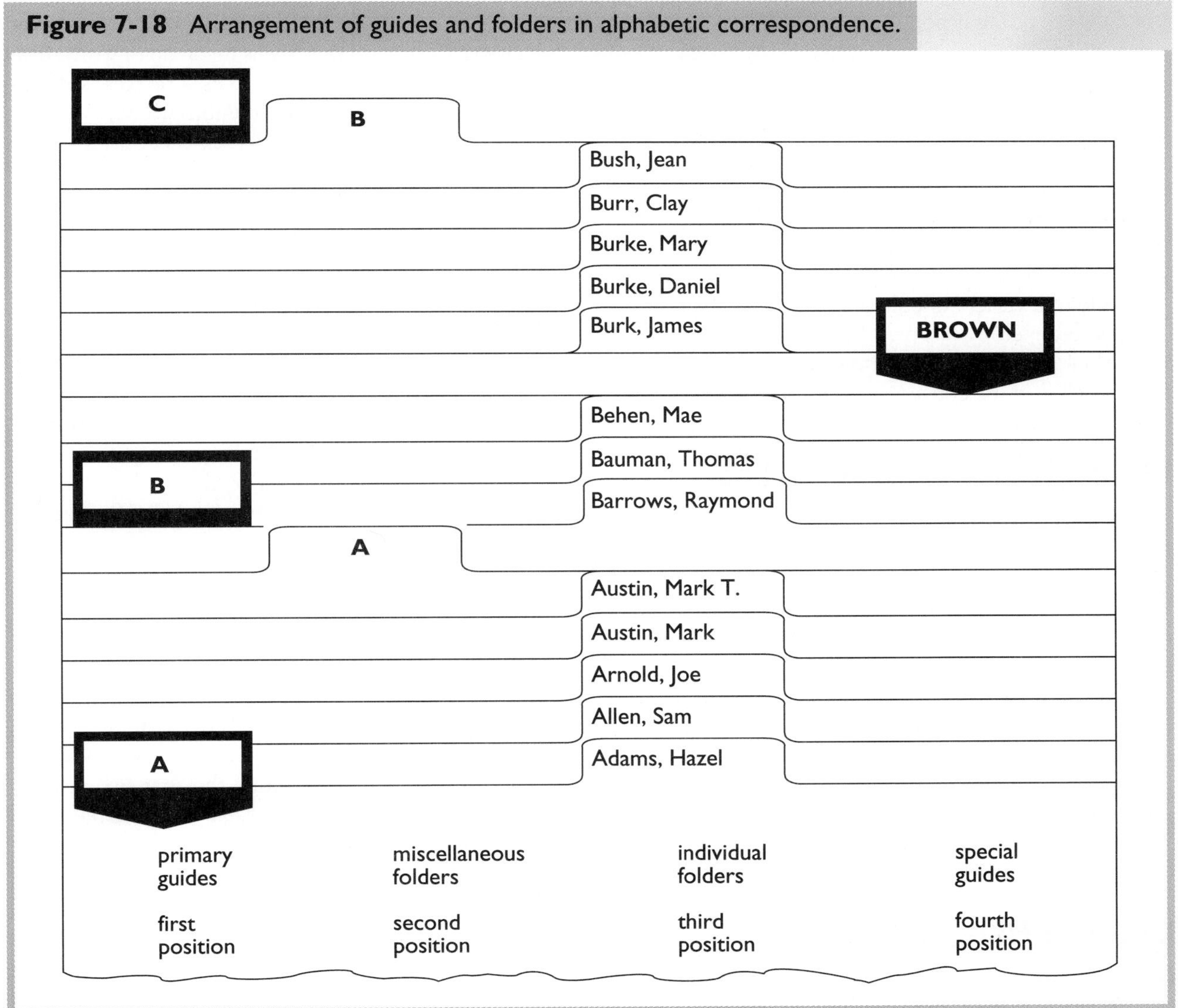

Within a miscellaneous folder, arrange the papers in alphabetical order by name. When you have two or more papers for one correspondent, arrange them in chronological order, so that the one with the most recent date will be in front of the others. Staple related papers together to increase the ease of locating them.

Special Guides

Special guides direct the eye to individual folders that are used frequently. Special guides are also used for subdivisions of the alphabet, or to mark the section of a file containing individual folders for several correspondents with the same surname, such as Smith.

Colour Coding

Colour coding can be applied to any filing sequence — alphabetic, numeric, geographic, subject, or chronological. Furthermore, colour coding can be added without changing the sequence of the existing system.

Colour coding is popular because

1. it provides easy identification for sorting, filing, and finding
2. it confirms that the folders have been filed in the right places.

A misfiled colour-coded folder will break the colour pattern and will stand out as being out of place.

Colour coding is not new, but it is being used in an increasing number of ways. All types of filing supplies are available in a variety of colours.

If you develop your own filing system, you should use colour. First determine how you are going to use colour and then be consistent in following your plan.

ALPHABETIC FILING RULES

Standardization of alphabetic filing rules is very important; it allows office procedures to be consistent and efficient. The Association of Records Managers and Administrators (ARMA), recognizing the need for standardization, published its first standardized rules for alphabetic filing in 1960.

The alphabetic rules presented in this chapter are the standardized rules suggested by ARMA, current at the time this textbook was published. For further information about ARMA or the rules, contact a local ARMA representative or the ARMA headquarters in Prairie Village, Kansas (telephone 913-341-3808; fax 913-341-3742) or visit their website at www.arma.org/hq.

Order of Filing Units

Before you begin any filing process it is important that you understand the following three terms:

Unit. Each part of a name that is used to determine the filing order is called a unit. For example, the name *Steven Andrew Watson* has three units: *Steven*, *Andrew*, *Watson*. The business name *The Wacky Wig Boutique* has four units: *The*, *Wacky*, *Wig*, *Boutique*.

Indexing. Names are not always filed in the same way they are written. In preparation for alphabetic filing, the format and order of a name is often altered. This process of arranging units of a name in order for filing purposes is referred to as *indexing*. An example of indexing is where *Steven Andrew Watson* has his name indexed as *Watson Steven Andrew*. Indexing always precedes alphabetizing.

Alphabetizing. Placing names in an A-to-Z sequence is considered alphabetizing. This process is necessary to maintain an alphabetic filing system. For example, placing the name *Adamson* before the name *Boulton* is alphabetizing.

This process appears relatively simple; however, because the English language is made up of words from other languages, word derivatives, prefixes, suffixes, compound words, and other combinations, the filing process may become complicated and inconsistent unless rules are applied. With that in mind, this text will discuss the simplified alphabetic filing rules as recommended by ARMA.

Before working with the rules, there are some basic principles to remember:

1. Alphabetize by comparing names unit by unit and letter by letter. When first units are identical, move on to compare the second units; when second units are identical, compare third units; and so on. For example, in comparing the indexed names you would need to make the distinction in the third unit, since the first and second units are identical.

Unit 1	Unit 2	Unit 3
Black	Jeff	Peter
Black	Jeff	Robert

2. Nothing comes before something. Thus, in comparing the following indexed names you would file *Ross William* first, since the first two units are identical and *Ross William* does not have a third unit. Nothing is filed before something (*Robert*).

Unit 1	Unit 2	Unit 3
Ross	William	
Ross	William	Robert

Another example of this principle would be

Unit 1	Unit 2	Unit 3
Chatham	Bus	Depot
Chatham	Business	College

In this case, *Bus* would come before *Business* under the principle that nothing comes before something.

3. All punctuation marks should be ignored when indexing. Examples of punctuation marks found in names include periods, quotation marks, apostrophes, hyphens, dashes, and accent marks. Where words have been separated by a hyphen or dash, consider them together as one indexing unit.
4. When the name of a person or business is known in more than one format, file it in the way that is most common. Then prepare a cross-reference. Refer to the discussion on cross-referencing in this chapter for further details on this process.

The following are simplified filing rules as recognized by ARMA. They have been organized into four categories: personal names; business and organization names; government names; and addresses.

Rules for Filing Names of Individuals

Rule 1—Names of Individuals

Names of individuals are transposed. The surname is the first filing unit, followed by the first name or initial, and then the middle name or initial. Because nothing comes before something, initials (such a M) are filed before a name (such as Martha) that begins with the same letter.

AS WRITTEN	AS FILED		
	Unit 1	Unit 2	Unit 3
M. Appleton	Appleton	M	
M.A. Appleton	Appleton	M	A
Martha Appleton	Appleton	Martha	
Martha A. Appleton	Appleton	Martha	A
Martha Ann Appleton	Appleton	Martha	Ann

Rule 2—Abbreviations in Names of Individuals

Abbreviated and shortened personal names are indexed as they are written. Do not spell out the short form of the name.

AS WRITTEN	AS FILED		
	Unit 1	Unit 2	Unit 3
Ed Kaye	Kaye	Ed	
Edward G. Kaye	Kaye	Edward	G
Geo. Little	Little	Geo	
Chas. McKay	McKay	Chas	
Thomas Neilson	Neilson	Thomas	
Tom L. Neilson	Neilson	Tom	L
Wm. Porter	Porter	Wm	
Bob N. Ross	Ross	Bob	N
Robt. Ross	Ross	Robt	
Bill Watson	Watson	Bill	

Rule 3—Prefixes in Names of Individuals

Names of individuals with prefixed surnames, such as De, Des, Du, La, Les, Mac, Mc, O', Van, Vonder, Vander, St., and the like, are filed with the surname as one unit, regardless of whether the surname is written as one word or two. Ignore apostrophes and spaces that follow the prefix.

AS WRITTEN	AS FILED		
	Unit 1	Unit 2	Unit 3
Agnes Lasalle	Lasalle	Agnes	
Paul R. La Salle	LaSalle	Paul	R
David MacNaughton	MacNaughton	David	
Lorene Mason	Mason	Lorene	
A.R. McNitt	McNitt	A	R
Louis St. Denis	St Denis	Louis	
Adam Vandermallie	Vandermallie	Adam	
John Vander Mallie	VanderMallie	John	
Ray L. Van der Mallie	VanderMallie	Ray	L

NOTE: When many names begin with a particular prefix, the current trend is to treat that prefix as a separate group and to file the prefix group preceding the basic listing; for example, *Mac* and *Mc* could be filed before the other M names.

Rule 4—Hyphens in Names of Individuals

Hyphenated names, whether surnames or first or middle names, are treated as one filing unit. The hyphen is ignored during filing, and the two words are placed together as one unit.

AS WRITTEN	AS FILED		
	Unit 1	Unit 2	Unit 3
Jennifer Daleraven	Daleraven	Jennifer	
Irene Dale-Scott	DaleScott	Irene	
Sara Laura-Lee Wilkes	Wilkes	Sara	LauraLee
Sara Lauralie Wilkes	Wilkes	Sara	Lauralie

Rule 5—Titles, Designations, and Degrees in Personal Names

When titles, designations, or degrees are written before or after a name, they are used as indexing units at the end of the name. Punctuation is disregarded.

AS WRITTEN	AS FILED		
	Unit 1	Unit 2	Unit 3
Diana Hart, I	Hart	Diana	I
Diana Hart, II	Hart	Diana	II
Diana Hart, CPS	Hart	Diana	CPS
Reverend Edward Kaye	Kaye	Edward	Reverend
Major Joseph Reimer	Reimer	Joseph	Major
Joseph Reimer, Sr.	Reimer	Joseph	Sr
Ms. Eleanor Vaugh	Vaugh	Eleanor	Ms
Eleanor Vaugh, PhD	Vaugh	Eleanor	PhD

Rules for Filing Names of Businesses and Organizations

Rule 6—Names of Businesses and Organizations

Names of businesses and organizations are indexed in a similar fashion to the names of individuals. However, names of businesses and organizations should be indexed in the order they are written by the business or organization. Therefore, a surname is not necessarily the first unit. If you are unsure of the correct wording or format, refer to the company's letterhead or business card, or make a telephone call to the organization's receptionist.

When the name begins with *The*, place it at the end as the last indexing unit.

AS WRITTEN	AS FILED		
	Unit 1	Unit 2	Unit 3
A Catered Affair	A	Catered	Affair
Chinese Baptist Church	Chinese	Baptist	Church
D. Chow Services	D	Chow	Services
El Toro Mexican Foods	ElToro	Mexican	Foods
The Ice Delights	Ice	Delights	The
Kent Sanatorium	Kent	Sanatorium	
Keyano College	Keyano	College	
Lacy of Linwood	Lacy	of	Linwood
Mr. Submarine	Mr	Submarine	
Play the Game	Play	the	Game
Salvation Army Church	Salvation	Army	Church
The Sock Shop	Sock	Shop	The
Stony Plain Hospital	Stony	Plain	Hospital
Tim Tucker Trucking	Tim	Tucker	Trucking

Rule 7—Punctuation in Names of Businesses and Organizations

Treat punctuation that appears in business and organization names the same way you would for personal names. Ignore all punctuation marks. Where a hyphen separates two words, disregard the hyphen and index the two words as one unit.

AS WRITTEN	AS FILED			
	Unit 1	Unit 2	Unit 3	Unit 4
Marty Allen's Beauty School	Marty	Allens	Beauty	School
Fab-Abs Gym	FabAbs	Gym		
Who's Coming to Dinner?	Whos	Coming	to	Dinner
"Dots" and "Spots"	Dots	and	Spots	
Mr. Lube	Mr	Lube		
When (Pink) Pigs Fly!	When	Pink	Pigs	Fly

Rule 8—Numbers in Names of Businesses and Organizations

Names using either Arabic numerals (7, 54) or Roman numerals (IV, X) are filed in numeric order before the alphabetic characters. Arabic numbers are filed before Roman numerals. The complete numeral is considered as one unit and is not spelled out. Of course, if the company writes out the number in words, such as One Hour Cleaners, the number is spelled out and filed alphabetically after the numerals are filed.

Where a number is hyphenated, such as in 7-11 Convenience Store, only the number before the hyphen (7) is considered; the number that follows the hyphen (11) is ignored.

When a digit contains a suffix (st, d, th) ignore the suffix and index only the number itself. Thus, 1st is indexed as 1, 2d is indexed as 2, 3d as 3, 4th as 4, and so on.

When a number is spelled out and hyphenated—for example, Seventy-Seven Sunset Shop—the hyphen is ignored and the two numbers become one unit (SeventySeven). When a numeral is separated from a word by a hyphen, as in 2-Much Fun Shoppe, the hyphen is ignored and the number joins the word to become one unit (2Much Fun Shop).

AS WRITTEN	AS FILED			
	Unit 1	Unit 2	Unit 3	Unit 4
1st Street Bistro	1	Street	Bistro	
4 J's Barber Shoppe	4	Js	Barber	Shoppe
4–By–4 Sales	4By4	Sales		
7–11 Convenience Store	7	Convenience	Store	
24 Hour Videos	24	Hour	Videos	
101 Parking Lot	101	Parking	Lot	
XXI Century Designs	XXI	Century	Designs	
AA Advertising	AA	Advertising		
Forty-Two Hundred Club	FortyTwo	Hundred	Club	
Fat Fred's 50s Club	Fat	Freds	50s	Club
Koffee Kafe	Koffee	Kafe		
One Hour Martinizing	One	Hour	Martinizing	
Salon on 5th	Salon	on	5	
Twelve Corners Service Centre	Twelve	Corners	Service	Centre

Rule 9—Symbols in Names of Businesses and Organizations

Symbols should be indexed in the way they are pronounced. Examples of such symbols include:

AS WRITTEN	AS INDEXED
$	dollar/s
#	pound or number
&	and
¢	cent/s
%	percent
+	plus

The following examples demonstrate how the symbols appear within the indexed name.

AS WRITTEN	AS FILED			
	Unit 1	Unit 2	Unit 3	Unit 4
The 100% Team	100	Percent	Team	The
Million $ Baby	Million	Dollar	Baby	
#1 Theatre Productions	Number 1	Theatre	Productions	
Reitman & Copp Intl.	Reitman	And	Copp	Intl
We Make ¢	We	Make	Cents	

Rule 10—Abbreviations in Names of Businesses and Organizations

When abbreviations are used in business names, they should be filed as they are written. They are spelled out only when the organization writes them that way. Remember, initials in a person's name are separate units.

To determine whether initials should be separate units, check to see if they have been separated by spaces or periods. If they have been, write them as separate units.

AS WRITTEN	AS FILED				
	Unit 1	Unit 2	Unit 3	Unit 4	Unit 5
ABC Moving Co.	ABC	Moving	Co		
C.P. Bell Travel Agency	C	P	Bell	Travel	Agency
CROC Radio	CROC	Radio			
MSS Inc.	MSS	Inc			

Rules for Filing Names of Governments

Rule 11—Government Names

Government names include civic, municipal, provincial/territorial, federal, and foreign agencies, departments, commissions, and so on.

11A. Local and Provincial/Territorial Governments

When filing local or provincial/territorial government names, the first indexing unit should be that of the province/territory or municipality that has control over the government department. The next indexing unit is that of the most distinctive name in the department, agency or ministry. Indexing government names can be a confusing task if you aren't sure which level of government has jurisdiction over the department. When in doubt, check the local telephone directory's government listings.

AS WRITTEN	UNDER JURISDICTION OF	AS FILED				
		Unit 1	Unit 2	Unit 3	Unit 4	Unit 5
Department of Bylaw Services Winnipeg, Manitoba	City	Winnipeg	Bylaw	Services	Department	of
Department of Social Services Whitehorse, Yukon Territory	Territory	Yukon	Social	Services	Department	of

11B. Federal Government

When the jurisdiction is the federal government, the first two indexing units will be **Canada Government**.

AS WRITTEN	UNDER JURISDICTION OF	AS FILED					
		Unit 1	Unit 2	Unit 3	Unit 4	Unit 5	Unit 6
Health Canada	Country	Canada	Government	Health	Department	of	
National Defence	Country	Canada	Government	National	Defence	Department	of

11C. Foreign Governments

When filing the names of foreign governments, always use the country name as the first unit. The next units will include the most distinctive name of the department; then bureau, commission, or board.

AS WRITTEN	UNDER JURISDICTION OF	AS FILED			
		Unit 1	Unit 2	Unit 3	Unit 4
Ministry of Tourism Bahamas	Foreign Government	Bahamas	Tourism	Ministry	of
Industrial Development Commission Netherlands	Foreign Government	Netherlands	Industrial	Development	Commission

Rules for Filing According to Address

Rule 12—Names and Addresses

At times, two or more names will be identical. In such cases, use the address to determine the filing order. Consider the following elements in this order:

- municipality name
- province/territory name
- street name
- compass directions (N, S, E, W)
- building number

Be certain to spell out in full all elements of the address. This includes names of provinces/territories.

The following is an example of the building number in an address determining the order of filing:

Names and Addresses	Filing order determined by comparing ...
General Assurance Agency Alsask, Saskatchewan	Municipalities
General Assurance Agency Milton, Nova Scotia	Provinces
General Assurance Agency 10 Ashton Avenue Milton, Ontario	Street Names
General Assurance Agency 495 Woodbridge Way North Milton, Ontario	Compass Directions
General Assurance Agency 495 Woodbridge Way South Milton, Ontario	Building Numbers
General Assurance Agency 566 Woodbridge Way South Milton, Ontario	

Variations in Alphabetic Filing Rules

Because conflicts in alphabetic indexing have existed for many years and continue to exist, you need to be aware of the conflicts as well as the standardized rules. When you report for a new work assignment, you will have to retrieve papers that have been filed by someone else. Furthermore, the organization for which you work may have its own rules for indexing and alphabetizing. If so, learn them and apply them so that the files you maintain will be consistent with the other files in the organization.

The variations in filing rules presented here are based on an analysis of published filing rules. Watch for the following variations in indexing and alphabetizing names of individuals:

1. The hyphenated surname of an individual treated as separate units rather than as one filing unit.
2. Names beginning with *Mac* and *Mc* filed before names beginning with M.
3. A nickname used in the signature filed under the true given name, such as *Lawrence* instead of the nickname *Larry*.
4. Numeric seniority designations, such as II and III, filed as spelled out rather than in numeric sequence; also *Sr.* filed before *Jr.*
5. The name of a married woman filed under her husband's name instead of her own name.

There are many variations in the alphabetic filing rules for business establishments, institutions, and other group names. Watch for the following variations:

1. Each part of a hyphenated business name made up of surnames might be indexed as a separate filing unit, instead of the hyphenated name being treated as one filing unit.
2. Each part of a coined business name might be indexed as a separate filing unit, instead of the entire coined word being considered as one filing unit.
3. Geographic names beginning with prefixes might be filed as two separate units rather than one.
4. Words involving more than one compass point (northeast, northwest, southeast, and southwest, and their variations) might be treated as two words instead of being indexed as written in the company name.
5. Geographic names that are spelled as either one or two English words—such as *Mountain View* and *Mountainview*—might be filed inconsistently, with the result that papers pertaining to one business establishment are filed in two different places.
6. Names beginning with numbers expressed in figures, as opposed to written out, might be filed in regular alphabetical sequence with all the numbers spelled out in full rather than filed in strict numeric sequence preceding the entire alphabetic file.
7. The *s* following an apostrophe might be disregarded, so that the word is indexed without the *s*.

OTHER FILING SYSTEMS

Alphabetic filing is a *direct* system for finding filed papers. A document's indexed name, if known, can be located easily by going *directly* to the files, looking through the alphabetized folders for the folder with the appropriate caption, and retrieving the document from this folder. Most offices dealing with individuals and companies use some form of alphabetic name system for filing papers. There are, however, other filing systems that may be more useful for particular types of businesses.

Subject Filing

With subject filing, records are arranged by topics rather than by personal, business, or organization name.

A furniture manufacturer might want to keep documents dealing with tables, chairs, sofas, and beds in separate file folders. In such a case these topics or *subject* headings would be written (coded) on the appropriate documents, and the papers would be put away in folders bearing the same captions.

Care should be taken to choose subject headings that are specific enough that documents are likely to be requested by these headings. A major subject heading should be subdivided into more specific headings if this will make for faster and easier location of papers. If a document deals with more than one subject, cross-reference sheets or photocopies should be placed in the other subject folders.

There are two methods of subject filing. These are

1. the encyclopedic system
2. the dictionary system.

The encyclopedic system is used for both small- and large-volume filing. In this system the major topic is broken down into related subheadings, and folders appear behind each subheading. An example might be:

BEVERAGES	(MAJOR TOPIC)
Coffees	(Subtopic)
• Decaffeinated	(Folder)
• Gourmet	(Folder)
FOOD	(MAJOR TOPIC)
Breads	(Subtopic)
• White	(Folder)
• Brown	(Folder)
• Rye	(Folder)
Vegetables	(Subtopic)
• Potatoes	(Folder)
• Tomatoes	(Folder)

The dictionary system is not effective where a large volume of files exists. Topics are filed alphabetically, with no grouping by related topics—hence the term dictionary system. An example might be:

FOOD	(MAJOR TOPIC)
Brown Bread	(Folder)
Potatoes	(Folder)
Rye Bread	(Folder)
Tea	(Folder)
Tomatoes	(Folder)

Subject filing requires the records manager to refer to an index or list of topics before searching for a folder; for this reason it is considered an indirect access system. The list is called a relative index.

The **relative index** is an alphabetic listing of all topics that appear in the system. Before returning a folder to the system or searching for a folder, the records manager consults the index to establish which topic the folder is kept under. Refer to Figure 7-19 for an example of a relative index.

Geographic Filing

A real estate company may wish to keep its records of houses for sale arranged by street names and numbers. A large organization with many branch offices across the country may wish to file its records by branch office location. The arrangement of files by location is called *geographic filing*.

In geographic filing the largest locations—street, city, province/territory, or country—are used as main divisions, arranged alphabetically by guides. Individual document folders pertaining to these main divisions are arranged behind the division guides, also alphabetically. The system can be as simple or as complex as desired. To meet the needs of customers, office supply companies maintain a wide variety of prearranged geographic, subject, and alphabetic filing systems with guides.

Geographic filing is usually a direct filing system. If the name the document is filed under is known, the document can easily be retrieved by going directly to the files and looking for it in alphabetic order behind the appropriate guide. However, a geographic system in which an index must be consulted before a file can be located is an indirect filing system.

Geographic filing may use either the encyclopedic or the dictionary system (as explained in subject filing). Which one will be determined by the volume of topics.

How a geographic system is divided will depend on the company. One company might find it convenient to use guides with the names of provinces/territories and then further subdivide the filing system by city names. Another company, if it operates in only one city, might use guides that divide the city by districts and then further subdivide the filing system by street names.

Figure 7-19 Relative index.

RELATIVE INDEX FOR RECREATION TOPICS	
TOPIC OF FOLDER	REFER TO THE GUIDE ENTITLED
Bait	Fishing
Boating Registration	Fishing
Competitive Swimming Rules	Swimming
Court Fees	Tennis
Cycle Helmets	Cycling
Golf Clubs	Golfing
Knot Types	Sailing
Mountain Bikes	Cycling
Racquets	Tennis
Reflective Clothing	Running
Shin Splint	Injury
Sun Stroke	Injury
Tacking	Sailing
Tred-Fast	Athletic Shoes

Numeric Filing

Numeric filing is an *indirect* method of storing records. In numeric filing, even if you know the name, subject, or geographic heading of a document, you cannot simply go to the files and find it in its alphabetic order. In numeric filing, each document is given a number and put in a folder with that number on the label. The numbered folders are arranged in the files in sequential order. Refer to Figure 7-20.

To find a document filed under a numeric system, one must first consult a *card index* to ascertain the number assigned to the particular document. The card index may be a box or tray of small index cards arranged alphabetically by name. Refer to Figure 7-21. However, it is far more efficient to use a computerized card system.

Figure 7-20 Numeric filing arrangement.
Courtesy of Kardex

Figure 7-21 Numeric card index.

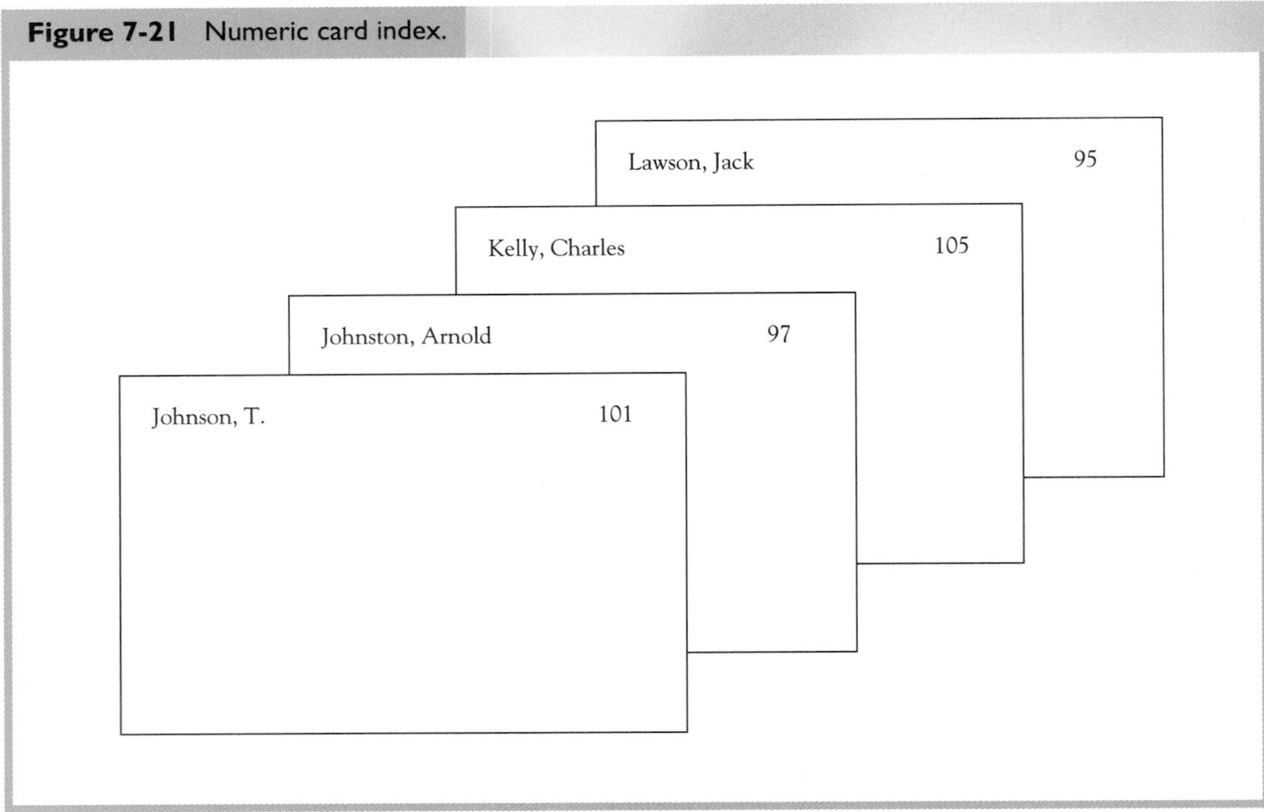

Retrieving and updating information is extremely quick and accurate. Each card shows the number that has been assigned to a name; often, the same card also gives brief information that may be required, such as addresses, and telephone and fax numbers.

Usually, numbers are not assigned to a name until five or more documents bearing that name have accumulated. Until then, the documents are kept in a separate, miscellaneous alphabetic file.

So that there is no question as to what number should be assigned to a name, an accession log is kept. This log keeps track of numbers assigned to files, and of the dates the files were created. This ensures that no file is created with a duplicate number. Refer to Figure 7-22 for an example of an accession log. An accession log kept on a computer is very efficient, because searching and sorting can be performed rapidly and with a high degree of accuracy.

Once the file has been recorded in the accession log, the administrative assistant might prepare an index card. The new folder is now placed numerically in the filing system. The number of the file is coded on all documents that go in this folder. Inside the folder, the documents are filed chronologically, with the most current document on top.

A numeric filing system has four parts:

1. a separate miscellaneous file to store records alphabetically until five or more documents have accumulated under a particular name
2. an accession log to record the numbers assigned to folders
3. an alphabetical card index of names, with the numbers that have been assigned to these names
4. a separate numeric file, in which folders with numeric labels are filed in sequential order.

Why go to so much trouble? While numeric filing may seem cumbersome, it has many advantages over straight alphabetic filing. Three of these are

1. *Time*. Once filed, document folders are faster and easier to find if they are arranged in numeric rather than alphabetic sequence.
2. *Filing expandability*. In an A–Z alphabetic system, if the B section becomes overcrowded all sections behind it must be moved to accommodate the overflow. In a numeric system, because each new name gets the next available number, the file folder is simply added to the end of the files; this does not disarrange the previous file folders.
3. *Privacy of files*. Numeric filing protects the privacy of files, because numbers rather than names are printed on the file folder labels.

Figure 7-22 Accession log.

ACCESSION LOG		
FILE NUMBER	NAME OF CORRESPONDENT	DATE OF CREATION
243	Valerie Kylo, CPS	June 10, 20 –
244	Milton Petruk, PhD	June 10, 20 –
245	Peter R. Joiner	June 11, 20 –
246	Nancy R. Scholtes	June 13, 20 –
247	Theodore Demster, MBA	June 20, 20 –
248	Joan Holm, CPS	June 21, 20 –
249	Patricia Edwards	June 21, 20 –
250	Rebecca George	June 25, 20 –
251	Grace M. NcNally	June 25, 20 –
252	Sara Riives, MEd	June 29, 20 –
253	Rev. Peter Lang, PhD	June 30, 20 –
254	Dr. Sharon Dawson	June 30, 20 –
255	Sylvia Vocaturo	July 3, 20 –
256	Karene Ursulak, CMA	July 3, 20 –
257		
258		
259		
260		
261		
262		
263		
264		
265		
266		

There are many different numeric filing systems. The ones most commonly found in offices are

1. straight numeric
2. middle-digit numeric
3. terminal-digit numeric.

Straight Numeric

In this system the files are arranged consecutively in ascending order. In other words, the file with the lowest number appears first and the one with the highest number appears last.

Middle-digit numeric

In this system the files are located by their middle digits. If these are identical for two files, the next most important digits are those on the left and the least important digits are those on the right.

Consider the following example **M49 - 4 - 07**:

- The middle digit (4) represents the drawer or shelf number.
- The left digit (49) represents the guide number.
- The right digit (07) represents the folder number.

Terminal-digit numeric

This system is considered the most efficient of all numeric systems. Numbers are read from right to left. The digits on the extreme right are the primary digits, the middle digits are the secondary digits, and the digits on the left are the final digits.

Consider the following example **M26 - 14 - 108**:

- The terminal digit (108) represents the drawer or shelf number.
- The middle digit (14) represents the guide number.
- The left digit (26) represents the folder number.

There are advantages and disadvantages to each of these three numeric systems. Your choice of numeric system (if you use numeric filing) will depend on the organization's preference, the volume of files needed, and what system already exists in your organization.

Questions for Study and Review

1. Compare a centralized filing system with a decentralized filing system.
2. What do the letters CAR represent in reference to records management?
3. Why is the release mark an important aspect of preparing information for filing?
4. List the steps involved in getting related papers ready to be filed.
5. What is indexing? What is coding?
6. Explain how a cross-reference can be helpful in locating a paper in the files.
7. Name five situations in which cross-references would be needed for locating materials from the files.
8. Describe how to handle a regular folder when placing documents in it.
9. What is the advantage in using electronically controlled charge-out procedures?
10. What is the purpose of setting up a directory on a disk?
11. What is the difference between a guide, a folder, and a label?
12. Why should you specify the cut and the position of the cut when ordering folders?
13. When should the scores at the bottom of a folder be creased?
14. Describe how to key a primary caption on a label.
15. Approximately how much storage is available on a zip disk?
16. What is the difference between vertical and lateral filing cabinets?
17. What is the purpose of a wire organizer in a filing cabinet?
18. State two ways that reference information is usually stored.
19. State five ways a computer disk can become damaged.
20. Why should a backup be made for magnetic data? Where should it be stored?
21. Describe two forms of micrographics.
22. List one advantage and one disadvantage for using each of the following media forms for storage of documents: paper, magnetic media, and micrographics.
23. State three factors that determine how long records must be preserved.
24. Define the following terms: perpetual transfer method and periodic transfer method.

25. Discuss the reality of the paperless office.
26. Why are primary guides used in an alphabetic system?
27. What should be filed in miscellaneous folders? How many miscellaneous folders should be used in an alphabetic filing system?
28. Describe the proper arrangement of papers within a miscellaneous folder.
29. What association has developed the filing rules used in this textbook?
30. In filing rules, what is the meaning of the saying "nothing comes before something"?
31. Compare between the encyclopedic system and the dictionary system of subject filing.
32. What is the purpose of a relative index for subject filing?
33. In geographic filing, what is the first indexing unit?
34. What is the purpose of an accession log?
35. Differentiate between the straight, middle-digit, and terminal-digit numeric filing systems.
36. Which of the three numeric systems is considered the most efficient? Why?
37. A paper that is urgently needed is missing from the correct file folder. Describe how you will find it.

Spelling Reinforcement

accessible	expandability	perpetual	statutes
anticipate	maintenance	predecessor	techniques
approximately	manageable	preliminary	thoroughly
centralized	microfiche	preservation	transferring
description	miscellaneous	retrieving	variety
encyclopedic	motorized	sequence	vehicle

On-the-Job Situations

1. You are an administrative assistant for the Barker Telecommunication Company. One of the sales executives, David Whyte, tells you in confidence that he has recently separated from his wife. One morning, about two weeks after your conversation with David, you arrive at your workstation to see Mrs. Whyte searching through her husband's personal files. Mr. Whyte is out of the office for the day and cannot be reached. What action should you take?
2. You are convinced that your predecessor made up his or her own rules. You have been working for three weeks, and you have extreme difficulty finding anything your predecessor filed. Your office supervisor has asked you to redo the files and to set up your own system. You are eager to set up a better filing system, but this is the peak season for your department. It will be at least two more months before you have time to redo the files. What can you do in the meantime?
3. The four executives for whom you work have been doing their own filing. However, today you were told that you are to maintain the correspondence files for all four of them. Their files will be moved to your area. You are to maintain separate files for each executive. What can you do to make it easier to get the materials in the right file each time?

Special Reports

1. Use the Yellow Pages to find the name of a business that is listed two ways. If you were including the business in a card file, which name would you use? How would you cross-reference it? Using the illustration given in this chapter, prepare two filing cards. On one 7.6 x 12.7 cm card, key the name as you would file it. On the other card, prepare the cross-reference.
2. Visit an office at a local business that uses an alphabetic filing system. Inquire about
   a. types of folders used
   b. types of labels used
   c. how tabs are prepared
   d. the use of cross-references
   e. charge-out methods
   f. how materials are coded before they are filed
   g. in which types of cabinets or shelves materials are housed
   h. types of magnetic media used
   i. types of micrographic formats used
   j. reduction of paper due to magnetic media
   k. electronically controlled paper files.

Production Challenges

7-A Indexing and Filing Names

Supplies needed:

- *35 7.6 cm x 12.7 cm cards*
- *Set of alphabetic guides, A to Z*
- *Answer Sheet for 7-A, Form 7-A, page 410*

You have many names, addresses, and telephone numbers stored on cards. Since the cards are worn, you have decided to make new cards. The names, addresses, and telephone numbers are computer stored. You have requested a new computer printout of address labels for all your cards. Key the names in indexing order at the top of each card. In the upper right corner of each card, key the corresponding number for each name. (You will need the number to record and check your answers.) The first day you worked on this project you keyed thirty-five cards.

After you have keyed Cards 1 to 35, separate the cards into five groups, arrange the cards in alphabetical order, and file them in correct sequence. Complete answer sheet 7-A and check your answers.

Do NOT remove the 35 cards from your file. In 7-B and 7-C you will add more cards to your file.

Here are the names for Cards 1–35:

1. James R. Larsen
2. Bob O'Donald
3. Helen Vandermallie
4. Martha Odell-Ryan
5. Sister Catherine
6. George Harris, Ph.D.
7. Mrs. Georgia Harris
8. Father Jenkins
9. Ty Chen
10. Martha Odellman
11. Allens Swap Shop
12. J. T. Larson
13. Herbert Vander Mallie
14. George Harris, M.D.
15. Mary Allen's Beauty Shop
16. Marshall Field & Company
17. Georgia Harris
18. Allens' Print Shop
19. Trans-Continent Truckers
20. George Harris
21. James Larson
22. Hubert Vander Mallie
23. George E. Harris
24. Cayuga Industries
25. North East Fuel Supply
26. AAA Batteries
27. CHAM Radio
28. Higgins Cleaners
29. Electronics Laboratory, General Electric Company
30. Niagara Office Supply
31. Over-30 Club
32. Prince Arthur's Hair Styling

33. C & H Television Repair
34. First Baptist Church
35. Hotel Isabella

7-B Indexing and Filing Names

Supplies needed:

- *35 7.6 cm x 12.7 cm cards*
- *The card file prepared in 7-A*
- *Answer Sheet for 7-B, Form 7-B, page 411*

The next time you work on your filing project, you key 35 more names in indexing order on cards. (Be sure to key the corresponding number on each card so that you can record and check your answers.)

Here are the 35 names:

36. James Danforth, Jr.
37. Burns Travel Agency
38. Strathcona County Water Department
39. Norton R. Henson
40. Sister Marie
41. The Lone Ranger Riding Supplies
42. The Jefferson Party House
43. El Rancho Inn
44. Cecil Young-Jones
45. RCT Manufacturers
46. Administrative Management Society
47. Hotel Baker
48. Triple-Star Enterprises
49. Miss Robert's Charm School
50. Acadia University, Wolfville, Nova Scotia
51. Bob Guerin
52. William T. Au
53. Thomas Kaplan, M.D.
54. Irene McGregor
55. Arthur P. Van der Linden
56. Ontario Municipal Board
57. John Wilkins Supply Corp.
58. Southwestern Distributors
59. Department of Employment and Immigration
60. Four Corners Answering Service
61. Reliable Answering Service
62. Montgomery Ward & Co.
63. South East Pipeline
64. Webbers' Home for the Aged
65. People's Republic of China
66. Prince Albert Printing Co.
67. The Mercantile Bank of Canada
68. Aero Bolt and Screw Co., Montreal
69. Strong Memorial Hospital
70. Surv-Ur-Self Pastries, Inc.

After you key the names on the cards, separate the cards into five groups, arrange the cards in alphabetical order, and file them with the 35 cards you filed in 7-A. Complete Answer Sheet 7-B and check your answers.

Next, prepare for Finding Test No. 1. If you had a card filed incorrectly, find out why. Before you take Finding Test No. 1, be sure that all 70 cards are arranged in correct alphabetical order.

When you have completed Finding Test No. 1, you are ready for 7-C. Leave the 70 cards in your file in order.

7-C Indexing and Filing Names

Supplies needed:

- *43 7.6 cm x 12.7 cm cards*
- *The card file prepared in 7-A and 7-B*
- *Answer Sheet for 7-C, Form 7-C, page 412*

You key 40 names in indexing order to complete your list of names. Here are the names:

71. Jason Wayne Suppliers
72. Prudential Assurance Co. Ltd., Winnipeg, Manitoba
73. Prince Charles Tea Shoppe
74. Federal Department of Consumer and Corporate Affairs
75. Hank Christian
76. East Avenue Baptist Church
77. CKY Television
78. Maudeen Livingston
79. Jim Waldrop
80. Department of Highways Alberta
81. The Royal Inn
82. Human Rights Commission, British Columbia
83. Ellen Jan Elgin
84. Robert E. Kramer, D.V.M.
85. Robert E. Kramer
86. United Hauling, Ltd.
87. Prince James Portraiture
88. Harold Roberson
89. London-Canada Insurance Co., Toronto, Ontario
90. The Royal Bank of Canada, 24 11 Bellrose Drive, St. Albert, Alberta

91. Harold O. Roberson
92. Maverick
93. Mrs. Maudeen Livingston
94. George Zimmer Corporation
95. Simon Fraser University
96. Rain or Shine Boot Shoppe
97. M. T. Torres
98. Marion Burnett
99. Harold Robertson
100. John R. de Work
101. Del Monte Properties
102. Mason-Dixon Consultants
103. Robert E. Kramer, M.D.
104. La Belle Arti Furniture Manufacturing
105. Camp Edwards
106. Northern Alberta Pipeline
107. Frank T. Forthright
108. Bill Carter Petroleum Corporation
109. London & Midland General Insurance Co., London, Ontario
110. George Johnston Museum, Teslin, Yukon Territory

You anticipate that you may have difficulty finding cards 71, 75, and 79, because they could be called for by different names. Therefore, make cross-reference cards for them. In the upper-right corner of each cross-reference card, key 71, 75, and 79 respectively.

After you have keyed all the names on the cards, including the cross-reference cards, separate the cards into five groups, arrange the cards in alphabetical order, and file them with the 70 cards you filed in 7-A and 7-B. Complete Answer Sheet 7-C and check your answers.

Next, prepare for Finding Test No. 2. If you had a card filed incorrectly, find out why. Before you take Finding Test No. 2, be sure that all the cards are arranged in correct alphabetical order.

World Wide Websites

Institute for Business Technology

www.ibt-pep.com/reso_pg1.htm
This collection of articles about managing information and keeping organized, features titles such as "Get Super-Organized, Get It Done."

Association of Records Managers and Administrators

www.arma.org/hq
The ARMA site provides a list of local chapters, information on upcoming conferences and events, and links to related websites.

Kardex Systems Inc.

www.kardex.com/
Kardex is an information and materials management company; its site includes a section on office systems and products.

CHAPTER 8

Front-Line Reception

Outline

Making Appointments

- Scheduling Appointments
- Using Electronic Calendars
- Using Traditional Calendars
- Making Entries in Traditional Calendars
- Cancelling or Changing Appointments
- Preparing a List of Appointments

Receiving Callers

- *Perspectives:* "Virtual Receptionists"
- Good morning!—Greeting Callers
- It's Over!—Terminating a Meeting
- Excuse Me—Interrupting a Meeting
- Callers without Appointments
- Sorry—Refusing Appointments

Handling Difficult Customers

- Unwanted Callers
- Tips for Success

Learning Outcomes

At the completion of this chapter, the student will be able to:

1. Provide guidelines for scheduling and cancelling office appointments.
2. Describe how an electronic calendar is used for efficiency.
3. Explain techniques for keeping a well-ordered appointment book.
4. Describe the courtesies necessary when receiving office callers.
5. Explain responsibilities regarding appointments in the following areas:
   (a) advance preparation
   (b) interruption of a meeting
   (c) termination of the appointment.
6. Demonstrate how to handle difficult customers.
7. Prepare a daily appointment calendar.
8. Prepare an appointment schedule from a daily calendar.

GRADUATE PROFILE

Joanne S. Jackson
Executive Assistant to the Chairman

Horn Plastics Inc.

College Graduation:
Executive Secretarial Program
Canadore College of Applied Arts & Technology
North Bay, Ontario
1981

With self-confidence and executive-level skills to reply upon, Joanne has just recently channeled her career toward the private sector as the executive assistant to the new chairman of Horn Plastics Inc., one of Durham Region's top employers. Prior to this last career move, Ms. Jackson worked in the Caucus Liaison Unit of the Premier's Office. Her professional history also includes employment in the office of a Member of Provincial Parliament, with Reference Canada and the Canadian Executive Service Organization.

Her unique skills are founded on the professional training she received from Canadore College and on her natural enthusiasm for meeting people. Those things, along with a positive attitude and a willingness to start in an entry-level position, were enough to launch Joanne on a meaningful career.

When asked for advice on success, this graduate's response reflected a holistic approach to work, self, and environment. Joanne recommends lending a hand whenever possible, establishing lasting relationships with colleagues, and projecting a professional attitude. Joanne feels that being bilingual (French and English) has been a definite asset in her career. Upgrading skills at every opportunity and taking the initiative to start new projects is also part of Joanne's career strategy.

"Be confident in your own abilities."

Joanne is a wife and the mother of one child, as well as an avid reader and swimmer; these activities and responsibilities provide balance in her challenging position.

Organizations have public relations departments that devote themselves full-time to creating and maintaining a favourable image of the organization, but public relations does not begin and end with a public relations department. Every employee who deals with people from outside his or her organization is engaged in public relations. A vital aspect of office work is the public relations function.

As an administrative assistant talking with people over the telephone and in person, you represent the organization. To people who deal only with you, you *are* the organization. The first impression and the lasting impression that you make with your voice, your appearance, and your self-expression must be favourable. Your personality must be pleasing to others. You create the atmosphere by the way you respond to people within and outside your organization.

Two important aspects of public relations discussed in this chapter are making appointments and receiving callers. Avoid performing these functions in mechanical fashion. Your job exists because you are performing a function that a machine cannot perform; take pride in the public relations aspect of your job.

Every time you greet people, either over the telephone or in person, focus your complete attention on their reasons for contacting you. Make people feel glad they are dealing with you and your organization. Make them want to return to your organization instead of going to a competitor.

By being knowledgeable about the company you work for, you can promote better public relations. An administrative assistant who can answer questions relating to the company's services and products as well as interpret and carry out company policies is an asset to the organization. These skills will promote the company's image when customers and clients contact the office.

MAKING APPOINTMENTS

Who makes appointments for managers? Both managers and their administrative assistants make these appointments. The freedom that an administrative assistant is given in making appointments will depend on the manager's preference, and the assistant's astuteness in scheduling.

The most important responsibility associated with scheduling is keeping the appointment calendar up to the minute to avoid conflicts in scheduling.

Scheduling Appointments

Use good judgment in scheduling appointments. Begin by learning

1. the manager's preferences for scheduling appointments
2. which appointments should be given priority
3. how much time appointments should take.

Guidelines for Scheduling Appointments

Use the following information as a guide to setting up appointments.

1. Leave Monday mornings free to start on plans for the week and to handle the e-mail and voice mail that has accumulated during the weekend.
2. Avoid scheduling appointments for your manager on his or her first day back after being out of the office for several days.
3. Avoid crowding the manager's schedule with appointments the day before a trip. Preparation for the trip has priority.
4. Schedule appointments so that they will not overlap.
5. Be cognizant of top-priority conferences and allow plenty of time for them.
6. Avoid scheduling a top-priority conference immediately after one of equal significance.
7. Avoid scheduling an appointment in another location immediately after a conference that is likely to run overtime.
8. Schedule unstructured time frames of 15 minutes between appointments at various times throughout the day. This will give the manager a chance to make telephone calls, sign letters, think about the next conference, or just take a break.
9. Schedule appointments late in the afternoon for persons with whom your manager has a close working relationship. These appointments are easy to shift when your manager is not keeping to the schedule.
10. When someone requests an appointment, suggest specific times, giving the person a chance to select a time from at least two choices.
11. Schedule set times for answering the mail and taking care of other daily activities. Consistently reserve the time slots for these activities.
12. When you are arranging an appointment for a short period of time, subtly let the person know the length of the appointment. For example, if you are setting up the appointment for 1200, say tactfully, "From 1200 until 1215."
13. When you arrange for an unexpected caller to see the manager, let the caller know that your manager has another appointment in 15 minutes—if this is the case.
14. Arrange appointments in another part of the city for first thing in the morning or late in the afternoon so that the manager, if he or she chooses, can go directly from home to the early morning appointment or not return to the office after a late-afternoon appointment.

Appointments by Telephone

Appointments that are not requested through an electronic messaging system are usually requested by telephone. When someone calls your office, requesting an appointment, determine the purpose of the appointment and then decide who is the best person for the caller to see.

During the conversation, tell the caller that if there is any change in the arrangements, you will contact him or her with the new information. Follow through by confirming the appointment with the manager and then contacting the caller either through e-mail or by telephone, if the manager is unable to keep the appointment or other details such as location or time must be changed. Check if it is the office policy to confirm all appointments. Many administrative assistants for doctors and dentists confirm every patient's appointment. Although this may become an onerous task, it ensures that the patient does not miss an appointment and a gap is not left in the doctor's schedule.

Make a special effort to ensure that both you and the person seeking the appointment understand the correct time, date, and place. Repeat the date, day, and time and enter these details into the calendar to reduce the chances of a mistake.

If your office is housed in an obscure or difficult to find location, ask the callers if they need directions. And, of course, always get the telephone numbers and e-mail addresses of the callers in the event that you have to change the details for the meeting.

Using Electronic Calendars

If your workplace has a fully integrated electronic network, you will use the computer to schedule appointments for management as well as your own. Large organizations can justify a fully integrated network if they have many people on the network and if it is used to perform many functions. Using the system to check and organize calendars is one network function you will find to be very valuable.

The electronic calendar is used to enter appointments, rearrange schedules, cancel appointments, create accurate and up-to-the-minute schedules, or simply to

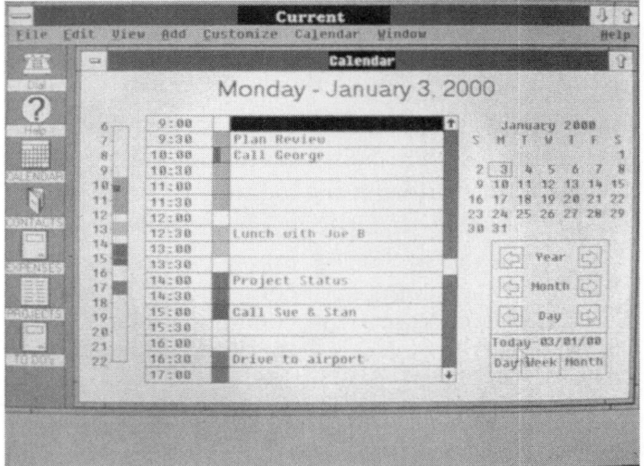

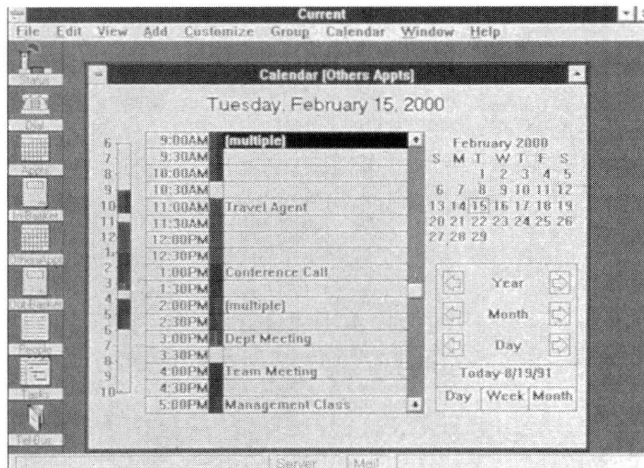

Figure 8-1 Electronic calendar displayed on computer screen.
Courtesy of International Business Machines Corporation. Unauthorized use not permitted.

check and see when other staff are available. You can arrange meetings by comparing the calendars and available time slots of those who make their calendars available on the network. Refer to Figure 8-1.

Advantages of Electronic Calendars

There are many benefits to using electronic calendar systems. Here is a list of some of the advantages of using a networked electronic calendar system as opposed to using a traditional paper calendar system.

1. Electronic calendars can be set to remind you of your up-coming meetings.
2. They will also produce a list of appointments as well as electronic-to-do lists.
3. You can key a full set of details regarding each meeting because you are not working in the small blocks of space found in traditional paper calendars.
4. Cancelling, or editing the details of an appointment in the electronic calendar is as simple as editing a document in word processing software.
5. When you set up a meeting in your electronic calendar, the software gives you the flexibility of creating an invitation list and automatically sending an e-mail to each invitee asking them to decline or accept the meeting. If they accept, the meeting is automatically entered into their electronic calendar. When they accept or decline, a message is automatically sent back to you giving the status of their attendance.
6. With Windows software, you can exit the electronic calendar and then enter other applications software without having to close down applications or insert new disks.

For these reasons, the electronic calendar is always convenient to use as long as you have access to a computer system. For people who spend considerable time out of their office, at meetings or travelling, an **electronic pocket organizer** may be the answer. No bigger than a pocket calculator, the electronic organizer can be easily accessed anywhere or anytime.

One drawback to using an electronic calendar is that unless you have reliable and exclusive access to a notebook computer or an electronic pocket organizer, you will need to back up your electronic calendar with a paper calendar. Being at a meeting without your electronic calendar will be unproductive when you can't refer to dates and times.

Using Traditional Calendars

Select traditional (paper) appointment calendars and yearbooks that meet the needs of the individual. A wide selection is available at stationery stores. They are made in a variety of sizes; some provide a page for each month, others a page for each week, or a page for each day. Office professionals will have their own preference when choosing the right appointment calendar. Preferences are usually based on ease of use, portability, and the number of appointments a person has each day.

People who make commitments months in advance like a full month displayed on one page, with small insert calendars for the preceding and following months. See Figure 8-2. With a monthly calendar they can review engagements without flipping through a lot of pages. People who make several appointments in one day may prefer a daily appointment calendar like the one shown in Figure 8-3. In this sample, each day is divided into 30-minute segments with the time printed in the left column.

20							JANUARY
	SUNDAY	MONDAY	TUESDAY	WEDNESDAY	THURSDAY	FRIDAY	SATURDAY
	NOTES:				1 001	2 002	3 003
20 DECEMBER 20 S M T W T F S 1 2 3 4 5 6 7 8 9 10 11 12 13 14 15 16 17 18 19 20 21 22 23 24 25 26 27 28 29 30 31	4 004	5 005 Manager Meeting Budget Comm.	6 006 Staff Meeting	7 007 Regional Sales Conference	8 008 Regional Sales Conference	9 009 Regional Sales Conference	10 010 Regional Sales Conference
20 JANUARY 20 S M T W T F S 1 2 3 4 5 6 7 8 9 10 11 12 13 14 15 16 17 18 19 20 21 22 23 24 25 26 27 28 29 30 31							
20 FEBRUARY 20 S M T W T F S 1 2 3 4 5 6 7 8 9 10 11 12 13 14 15 16 17 18 19 20 21 22 23 24 25 26 27 28 29	11 011	12 012 Analysis of Year-End Report	13 013 Staff Meeting	14 014	15 015 Lunch with Jack Smith	16 016 Equipment Demonstration	17 017
20 MARCH 20 S M T W T F S 1 2 3 4 5 6 7 8 9 10 11 12 13 14 15 16 17 18 19 20 21 22 23 24 25 26 27 28 29 30 31	18 018	19 019 Managers Meeting	20 020 Staff Meeting	21 021 Speech Chamber of Commerce	22 022	23 023 Annual Meeting	24 024
20 APRIL 20 S M T W T F S 1 2 3 4 5 6 7 8 9 10 11 12 13 14 15 16 17 18 19 20 21 22 23 24 25 26 27 28 29 30 31	25 025	26 026 AMS Seminar	27 027 Staff Meeting	28 028 Employee Appraisal	29 029 Employee Appraisal	30 030 Employee Appraisal	31 031
20 MAY 20 S M T W T F S 1 2 3 4 5 6 7 8 9 10 11 12 13 14 15 16 17 18 19 20 21 22 23/30 24/31 25 26 27 28 29							

Figure 8-2 Monthly calendar.
Courtesy of Sheaffer-Eaton, Division of Textron Inc.

You may find it effective to enter all the manager's appointments in your calendar. This is important if you are responsible for organizing the schedules of management and for reminding managers of their appointments. Use the calendar to prepare a To Do List of activities that the manager must follow through on by the end of the day. Prepare a similar list for your own action items each day.

Making Entries in Traditional Calendars

All appointments even regularly scheduled meetings, whether they are made by telephone, fax, e-mail or in person, should be entered into the calendar. When the days are very busy—and they will be—it is easy to forget even a regularly scheduled meeting. Be consistent and prompt in recording all appointments and commitments in calendars. To ensure that you are, adopt a systematic plan for making the entries and then do not deviate from your plan.

It's much easier to cancel or edit the details of an appointment when you are using an electronic calendar. That's why you should enter appointments in pencil when you are using a desk calendar. Even the firmest commitments can change suddenly. Write small enough that you can put the complete information in the space provided in the calendar. Draw a diagonal line through each entry once the conference is held or the task is completed; this way, you will know whether items have been completed or not.

Because professional commitments are often made outside the office, at social events or recreational events such as games of golf, it becomes imperative for people making these commitments to relay the information back to the office so that administrative assistants can make the appropriate entries into calendars. Where a person carries an electronic pocket organizer, the appointment can be entered even between holes of golf; however, a paper appointment calendar is less likely to accompany people to social and recreational events.

As a result, administrative assistants may have to be persistent with managers to find out about appointments made outside the office. In a situation where managers are remiss in sharing information about appointments that they have made, the administrative assistant should try to get this information once a day. Administrative assistants should try to spend a few minutes with management each morning to discuss the work scheduled for the day. As a general procedure, ask management to send you a voice mail or e-mail, or even leave a brief note on your desk each time they make an appointment that has not been recorded electronically.

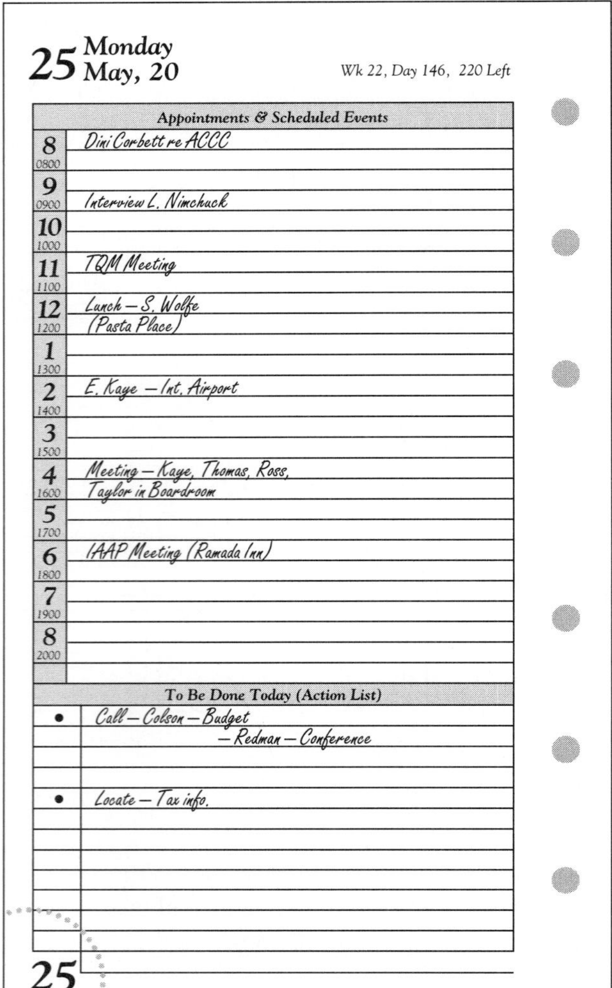

25 Monday May, 20 Wk 22, Day 146, 220 Left

Appointments & Scheduled Events	
8 0800	Dini Corbett re ACCC
9 0900	Interview L. Nimchuck
10 1000	
11 1100	TQM Meeting
12 1200	Lunch – S. Wolfe (Pasta Place)
1 1300	
2 1400	E. Kaye – Int. Airport
3 1500	
4 1600	Meeting – Kaye, Thomas, Ross, Taylor in Boardroom
5 1700	
6 1800	IAAP Meeting (Ramada Inn)
7 1900	
8 2000	

To Be Done Today (Action List)	
•	Call – Colson – Budget – Redman – Conference
•	Locate – Tax info.

25

Figure 8-3 Daily appointment calendar.

Courtesy of Rediform Office Productions, Division of Moore Business Forms, Inc.

As you read incoming e-mail or paper mail, watch for announcements of meetings that managers will be expected to attend or might want to attend. Call attention to them, and make pencil entries about them in the appropriate calendars.

At the end of the day, check the manager's calendar against yours to make sure you have all the correct and comprehensive appointment information. Never turn the page on your calendar until you are confident that all items have been completed. Transfer any items that still need attention to the page for the following business day.

At the time you are clearing your calendar, if you are not sure whether managers have returned telephone calls or kept promises they have made, send e-mails as reminders. Once each week—either on Friday afternoon or on Monday morning—check your follow-up file for the entire week. If you have not already done so, make notations in appropriate calendars concerning work that must be completed by a specified time within the week.

Cancelling or Changing Appointments

When someone calls to cancel an appointment, offer to schedule another one. Be sure to clear the manager's calendar and your own of the cancelled appointment.

When you must cancel an appointment for the manager, let the person whose appointment is being cancelled know at once. Get in touch with the person by telephone or fax.

Use the following guidelines for changing or cancelling an appointment:

1. Express regret on the manager's behalf.
2. Mention that the appointment must be changed.
3. State a reason in general terms, and
4. Offer to schedule another appointment.

Think twice about what explanation you will give for the change. For example, you can say that Ms. Park was called out of town, if she was, but as a general rule do not say where or why. In doing so you might be revealing confidential information. Do not dwell on what the manager cannot do. Quickly shift your conversation to a positive comment, such as, "She is expected back in the office on Monday. Shall I set up another appointment for you early next week?"

Preparing a List of Appointments

Near the end of the day, prepare a list of appointments for the next business day. If you are not using a print off from an electronic calendar system, create a format that is easy to follow. Place a copy on the appropriate managers' desks and keep one for yourself.

When you prepare the list of appointments (see Figure 8-4), indicate the time, name of the caller, affiliation, and purpose of each appointment. Also, include reminders, such as a dinner meeting or a commitment to meet someone at the airport. When an appointment is somewhere other than your office, indicate clearly where it will be.

Some people prefer that the list of appointments be prepared on a 7.6 x 12.7 cm card that can be carried throughout the day as a ready reference.

RECEIVING CALLERS

Receiving office callers is an important part of office work, and one that requires the office professionals to be courteous, gracious, and diplomatic. In your contact with callers, make a special effort to represent your organization favourably. Your duties are twofold:

Figure 8-4 List of appointments.

APPOINTMENTS FOR MONDAY, MAY 25, 20 –	
TIME	APPOINTMENT
0800	Meet with Dini Corbett to discuss ACCC promotions. Remember to take the F.P. Manufacturing folder.
0930	Interview Linda Nimchuck (applicant for Office Manager).
1100	Meet with Total Management Committee - Room 520. Connie Walters should be contacted prior to meeting for info. on the Conference.
1200	Lunch with Sandy Wolfe at the Pasta Place.
1400	Pick up Edward Kaye at the Edmonton International Airport.
1600	Meet with Edward Kaye, Heather Thomas, Ben Ross and Amelia Taylor in the boardroom located on the first floor. Copies of the plan for new equipment purchase are attached. Don't forget to take info. on tax concessions.
1800	Speak at IAAP meeting, Rose Room, Ramada Inn. A copy of the program and your speech are attached. Good Luck!

1. to demonstrate excellent customer relations
2. to help callers accomplish their objective for coming to your office.

In some organizations the administrative assistant serves as the receptionist and is the first person the caller speaks with. Large organizations may have a reception area where all callers check in with the receptionist. The receptionist then calls the appropriate person to announce the caller's arrival. Either the receptionist escorts the caller to the appropriate office or the person, who the appointment is with, comes to the reception area to welcome the caller.

Whether an organization does or does not have a main receptionist, the administrative assistant usually receives the callers before they are admitted to the manager's office. For this reason, you must regard receiving callers as a regular part of your work. As you plan your work, allow time for receiving callers. Never regard a caller's visit as an interruption.

Visitors who come to a professional office may include:

1. callers from outside the organization, some with appointments and some without
2. employees who report directly to the manager
3. other executives and supervisors within the organization, including the manager's superiors
4. friends and family members of office staff.

Find out the manager's policy for seeing callers. What you need to know most of all is who management prefers not to see and where you should direct these callers. Organizations strive to make friends of all callers. Therefore, the policy could be to arrange for all callers, with few exceptions, to see someone within the organization for a few minutes at least.

By turning away callers, you may be harming favourable relationships that already exist, or preventing good ones from developing, and this may create a negative climate in the organization. When you are uncertain, either make an appointment for the caller or ask if the manager will see the caller. It is better to receive too many callers rather than too few.

Your responsibility is to make every caller feel welcome. Be especially courteous to callers you must turn away. How to arrange an appointment for a caller with someone else in the organization, and how to refuse appointments, are discussed later in this chapter.

PERSPECTIVES

Virtual Receptionists

By Erin A. Borick

Electronic assistants can help all kinds of businesses—from a large corporation to a one-person office—better manage their telephone calls and voice-mail messages.

Technology consultant Janet Caswell travels several days a week, and her nine-person firm has no office. Her employees are scattered around the country, linked by computer and Wildfire Gold™ Electronic Assistant. A Wildfire client for two years, Caswell describes the system as "the glue that keeps us together."

Two years ago, the Wildfire Communications Electronic Assistant was the only such system available with the flexibility and features Caswell required. She needed a phone system that would give her clients the impression of a real office, make her company "appear seamless to clients," and allow her to "turn my job on and off," she says.

Caswell also required a system that would allow her the flexibility of being anywhere and still do her job; give her clients access to her any time; and eliminate telephone tag by getting calls the first time, even if away from the office (Wildfire allows you to forward your calls to any phone or pager).

Leslie Anderson, Wildfire's director of corporate communications, also uses Wildfire Gold. "I used to run 30 to 50 voice mails behind. Now I can deal with people in 'real time.'" When she's talking on the phone and a new call comes in, Wildfire Gold announces the call in her ear and she can either respond and accept the call or let it go to voice mail. Important calls aren't missed and calls that can wait, do.

What if your boss is waiting for an important overseas call but you can't tell him because he's on the line talking to someone else. Do you interrupt him? Do you wait to see if he gets off the phone quickly? Do you slip a note under his nose? With Wildfire, the call screening is done for you and the system will pleasantly talk in your boss' ear to let him know that the important call is on the line.

But Wildfire Gold and the digital assistants offered by Webley Systems Inc., Access Point, and others aren't likely to put traditional receptionists out of a job. "Wildfire Gold frees up [office professionals] to do much more valuable and productive things," says Anderson. "They can get out of the loop of announcing and routing calls."

Adding a human touch

Frustrating voice-mail systems, which can trap callers in a voice-mail "black hole" with no way to reach a human being, haven't been meeting the needs for many businesses like Caswell's. And, for small businesses trying to present a more corporate impression or for those businesses that require staff to be out of the office regularly, a reliable, user-friendly answering system is a necessity. That's the niche Wildfire Communications targeted when its product debuted four years ago.

Natural spoken phrases such as "Oh, hi," "What can I do for you," and "Here I am" greet users and callers to this innovative voice-controlled system. Wildfire Gold is entirely voice-driven, meaning users never touch the keypad, unlike traditional voice-mail systems that may require memorizing a variety of one- or two-digit commands to listen to, forward, or erase messages.

Getting comfortable with the system takes some time, however, says Caswell. Wildfire users typically need several weeks to "learn to get their voices going," to understand the cadence and response rate of the Wildfire voice, and mesh the two together, she explains.

How it works

The typical user of the Wildfire system works for a small- to medium-sized, service-oriented business and is out of the office at least 20 percent of the time. The user wants the customer responsiveness of a live assistant and a high level of service to callers for a moderate price.

"These businesses want to give the impression of professionalism, that they are a bigger company than they are, and for callers to feel like they aren't being treated by a machine," says Anderson.

The system is available through local phone companies. Subscribers are assigned a local or 800 number, which they call to check messages or to place calls to others. Subscribers' customers and friends use the same number to place calls to the subscriber. Once connected with Wildfire Gold, simple voice commands such as "find," "dial," "check messages," and "conference" allow users to place a call, hang up, check messages, receive an incoming call, and even conference in another caller on hold—all without hanging up or dialing into the system again.

Calling the system for the first time is startling. Unlike automated voice-mail systems where the computer-generated voice sounds stilted, Wildfire Gold sounds like a friend with its pleasant, familiar, human voice. Nonetheless, Caswell says one of her clients won't use the system. He insists on calling her home number because he doesn't like "talking to a computer."

Humorous touches have been added to Wildfire, such as the following exchange: User: "I'm so depressed." Wildfire: "You're depressed. I live in a box!" It makes you wonder, just for a second, if the person on the other end of the line is real, which is exactly the impression Wildfire Communications' customers want.

"[Wildfire Gold] is a much more productive way to use the phone," Anderson says. And, it's great "for people on the go," Caswell adds.

Reprinted courtesy of OfficePRO.

Good Morning!—Greeting Callers

Callers are influenced by their first impressions of the office and the administrative assistant. A favourable first impression, coupled with your courteous efforts to make callers feel welcome, will create a receptive climate in which you can develop and maintain a good rapport with visitors. The caller's first impression should be that of an efficient administrative assistant working in a well-organized office.

One of your responsibilities will be to keep your own work area and possibly the manager's organized. A busy office does not have to be cluttered. To maintain a well-organized office:

1. Designate and use specific locations for supplies, files, and work-in-progress
2. Remember that completion of each task includes "putting away"; follow through by clearing your desk of materials you are not using.

If you continually put away items you are not using so that nothing accumulates, the few items you have on your desk to continue with your work will enhance the appearance of your office and your efficiency.

As a person who welcomes the public you should look like you belong in a professional office setting. Although many offices have a casual environment, they still want to convey a business-like atmosphere to the public. Your clothing, hairstyle, accessories, and demeanour should convey the message that you are a professional representing the organization where you work. The way you dress should make you feel at ease in the presence of executives and visitors who are usually well dressed.

Immediate Attention

Your job is to make all callers, whether they have appointments or not, feel at ease. When callers come to your office, you should greet them the minute they arrive. As a caller approaches your desk, look at the person directly, smile graciously, and speak immediately. Nobody likes to be ignored, even for a few seconds. To continue keying until you reach the end of the line or paragraph, or to continue reading is extremely rude. To continue chatting with another employee is inexcusable.

"I treat our customers like I have known them for years. I know something about their personal lives, so they know that I am interested in them as people and not just as business."

Joanne Currie Wood, Graduate
Fraser Pacific College

Put your materials out of sight of glancing eyes, but do so discretely. If you keep confidential materials that you are working on in a folder, you can subtly close the folder as a caller nears your desk.

If you are talking on the telephone, the caller probably will hesitate before approaching your desk. Acknowledge the caller by nodding and smiling so that the caller will know you are aware of his or her presence.

Greet an office caller formally by saying, "Good morning" or "Good afternoon." "Hello" or "Hi" is too casual. Use the caller's name whenever you know it. If you are expecting a caller you do not know, but you are sure who he or she is, use the caller's name. The greeting may go something like this: "Good morning, Mr. Slattery, I'm Chris Rogers, Mr. Sung's assistant. Mr. Sung is expecting you." When you receive callers for several executives, do not guess who the callers are. Introduce yourself and ask how you may be of assistance.

Most business callers will introduce themselves immediately. As soon as a stranger does this, repeat the caller's name, introduce yourself, and add whatever statement is appropriate, depending on the circumstances—for instance, "Mr. Sung is expecting you" or "May I help you?"

The atmosphere in most organizations is informal enough that employees call their managers by their first name when visitors are not present. Call your manager by his or her last name until your manager suggests otherwise. Regardless of the informality of your relationship, it may be most appropriate to use your manager's last name in the presence of guests. With experience you will determine how to address management in the presence of guests.

PRO-LINK

pro-Link

An electronic assistant is a telephone application that performs many functions traditionally carried out by administrative assistants. Can an electronic assistant do more than a human office professional? No, it can't—but it can take away some of the routine tasks of the receptionist. An electronic assistant can:

- Answer the telephone with an upbeat greeting.
- Set up a conference call.
- Store and forward faxes.
- Forward calls.
- Respond to simple verbal commands.
- Schedule appointments.
- Record the caller's information such as name and telephone number.
- Receive incoming calls while the user is checking messages.
- Store as many as 150 names, telephone and fax numbers.

Advance Preparation

You will need materials from the files—correspondence and records—to refer to during conferences. Anticipate what materials will be needed and locate them the day before, but do not remove them from the files until the next morning. Always check the contents of a folder to determine that everything that is needed is there and properly arranged.

You may have to compile data or collect information from other departments. Get an early start on these tasks so that you will have the information ready when it is needed. Make sure you give the manager any information you have compiled well enough in advance that it can be reviewed adequately before the meeting.

Anticipate any items the manager will want to take along to meetings and have them ready. These materials might include notes taken during previous committee meetings; printed brochures to be distributed; slides and a projector to supplement a speech your manager is giving; a list of the names, addresses, and affiliation of new members of a professional group; a copy of shipping procedures and proposed revisions, or anything else that is related to the purpose of the meeting.

The Caller Who Has an Appointment

A caller is a guest; make the caller feel comfortable. Indicate to callers where to leave their coats, hats, and briefcases.

Use the caller's name. A caller who has a name that is difficult to pronounce will not mind if you ask him or her to pronounce it for you. When the caller is a stranger, escort the caller to the correct office. Pronounce both the caller's name and your manager's distinctly when you introduce them. Mention the caller's affiliation or the purpose of the visit, and then leave. Say, "Mr. Sung, Mrs. Haines of R.C. Products." Stand to one side, not between the manager and the caller, as you make the introduction, so that it will be easy for the manager to shake hands with the caller.

"Meet your co-workers in the middle .... or a little further if you have to! Attitude sets the pace for success."

Susan Muise, Graduate
Nova Scotia Community College
Burridge Campus

If the manager knows the caller, you can be less formal. As soon as the manager is free, you can invite the caller to go in; or you can open the door, if it is closed, and say, "Mr. Sung, Mrs. Haines." Your manager probably will speak spontaneously to the caller, and you will not have to say anything further.

Invite callers who must wait to have a seat. Locate chairs by a good light and keep current magazines, the morning paper, and other interesting reading material nearby so that callers who must wait for any length of time can read. You are not expected to entertain the caller by carrying on a conversation while the caller is waiting. You should continue with your work.

A caller who arrives early should expect to wait until the time of the appointment. However, as soon as the manager is free, tell the manager that the caller has arrived and ask if he or she is ready to see the caller. Eventually you will learn the manager's preferences about seeing callers ahead of the appointed time. It will usually depend on who the caller is, the purpose of the call, and what tasks your manager must complete between appointments.

A caller who has an appointment should not be kept waiting. Remember, the caller's time is valuable, and asking the caller to wait more than a few minutes is inconsiderate. Nevertheless, an executive who has many appointments in one day may have difficulty keeping to an appointment schedule. This happens even when the executive and the administrative assistant are making a real effort to usher callers in and out in the time allotted. A caller may take twice the expected time, or a top executive may come in unexpectedly. Unfortunately, when this occurs, callers often have to wait. In addition to making the caller feel welcome and comfortable, you should assure the caller that the wait should not be too long. If you say, "Mr. Wilmont should be free in a few minutes," try to sound reassuring. Use this statement only when you anticipate that the ongoing conference is almost over.

The real test of how well you carry out your role as office host lies in what you say and what you do when the wait will be long. First of all, do not let your actions reveal that the day is hectic. When emergencies occur or the day is not going smoothly, regardless of the reason, slow down, put some of your work on tomorrow's list, and approach callers in a very relaxed manner. Give each caller the impression that your only duty at that moment is to meet the caller's needs. Your relaxed manner (or tension) will be contagious.

Be cautious about how you state the reasons for a delay. You can apologize and say that all appointments are running behind schedule, but do not explain why. Avoid statements referring to important business, problems, or inefficiency. The caller is concerned about his or her own schedule and wants to know how long the wait will be. If you know that the manager is involved in a long meeting, tell the caller approximately how long he or she will have to wait. The caller may decide to postpone the appointment.

Do not forget about the caller. Reassure the caller. If you can judge that a conference is ending, turn to the caller and indicate that it is. If a caller whose appointment is delayed cannot wait any longer and tells you he or she must leave, offer to make another appointment and volunteer that your manager will call. Write yourself a note to follow up on your commitment. Remember, this caller has been inconvenienced and deserves special attention.

Introductions

Here is an easy rule for remembering the correct way to make introductions in the office: State the name of the person you want to honour first. Make introductions seem natural; just call each person's name or add "this is." Reserve "may I introduce" and "may I present" for introducing very distinguished people.

Introduce business callers to your manager. Add the person's title or business affiliation, thus: "Mr. Sung, Mr. Jackson of Great Lakes Office Forms," or "Mr. Sung, this is Mr. Jackson of Great Lakes Office Forms."

The business relationship, not the social rule of introducing the man to the woman, the younger to the older person, is the guide for making introductions in business. For example, you would introduce a woman from Temporary Services to your manager in this way: "Mr. Sung, this is Mrs. Cournoyer from Temporary Services, who is here to assist us this week."

Staff Visitors

A difficult aspect of every executive's job relates to maintaining good communication with the employees who report directly to him or her. Whatever an executive's efforts to establish an easy, two-way flow of communication, breakdowns occur and misunderstandings arise; too often, the result is personnel problems that should have been avoided. This is why many executives maintain an "open door" policy for seeing personnel.

According to office protocol, a meeting between a subordinate and a superior is held in the superior's office. Arrange for employees who report to your manager to meet in your manager's office or in a local conference room. When your manager's superior requests a conference, the implied message is that your manager will go to the superior's office unless a specific statement is made to the contrary concerning the place of the meeting.

It's Over!—Terminating a Meeting

Arrange with the manager how you should assist in terminating a meeting.

On those days when the manager's appointment schedule is crowded, watch the time and tactfully interrupt a conference, following predetermined guidelines. One appointment that runs overtime on a busy day can throw all the other appointments off schedule, inconveniencing many callers and giving the impression of inefficient planning. At the manager's request you may have to interrupt to aid in getting rid of callers who overstay their allotted time.

When the second caller arrives promptly for an appointment, and someone is in the manager's office, and you know it is appropriate to interrupt, you can proceed in one of the following ways:

1. Enter the manager's office, apologize for the interruption, and give the manager the caller's name on a slip of paper to indicate that the caller has arrived. Say nothing and exit the office.
2. Enter the manager's office and say, "Excuse me. The visitor for your three o'clock appointment is here. May I tell her how soon you can see her?"
3. Call the manager on the interoffice telephone, especially if you think he or she does not want to rush the first caller. At ten-minute intervals, suggest several times that the conference end, in such a way that the manager can answer "yes" or "no" without further comment.

If you must remind the manager of an appointment outside his or her own office and, in addition, you are using the reminder as a means of terminating a conference, do not reveal where the manager's next conference is, or with whom.

Your interruption, either in person or by telephone, may be all that is needed to prompt the caller to leave. If not, it will be adequate to enable the manager to terminate the conversation.

What should you do when the manager does not have another appointment, but the caller stays and stays, taking up the manager's time unnecessarily? This situation presents a different problem.

Managers need time to plan, to analyze, to make decisions, and to coordinate and direct the work of others. Most executives are skilled at terminating office visits. They thank the callers for coming, stand, and tactfully make statements that let the callers know the conference is over. At times, however, they rely on administrative assistants to rescue them from persistent callers.

Be sure you understand what the manager expects you to do when he or she is having difficulty getting rid of a caller. In what manner does the manager want to be interrupted? You will be able to figure out a tactful and effective way to interrupt if you think about the work the manager should be doing.

You could key a note reminding the manager of work to be done, walk into the manager's office, deliver the note, and say nothing. You could call the manager on the interoffice telephone, giving an opportunity to say, "We are finishing now," or "Yes, in just a few minutes," or a similar comment that will likely prompt the caller to leave. If the manager prefers to continue the conference, the reply could be worded in such a way that you know the conference will last a while longer.

Excuse Me—Interrupting a Meeting

Until you know differently, expect that the manager does not want to be interrupted while someone is in his or her office. Most executives discourage interruptions while they are in conference. The interruptions an executive *will* tolerate are governed by the executive's judgment and personality.

You must arrive at a clear understanding with the manager regarding what conditions are important enough to justify your interrupting a conference. At times the manager may request that you interrupt—say, when an important telephone call comes in. At other times the manager may indicate that there should be no interruptions at all. When you are left to your own judgment and do not know what to do, do not interrupt. An intrusion detracts from the tone of a conference and from the train of thought.

Clearly establish which method the manager prefers you to follow when you must deliver an urgent message. The following method is often used: the administrative assistant keys the message, quietly enters the executive's office, hands the message to the executive or places it face down on the desk, and leaves unless an immediate answer is necessary.

To keep telephone interruptions to a minimum, offer to take a message or to assist the caller yourself. If you cannot complete the call, ask the person telephoning to leave his or her number so that the executive can return the call. Answering a telephone call when someone is in the manager's office places the manager in an awkward position. The manager needs privacy for a telephone conversation and, furthermore, does not want to appear discourteous to the visitor by taking up the visitor's time with a telephone call.

When you receive an urgent telephone call for the manager while someone is in the manager's office, write the name of the person calling and the purpose of the call, hand the note to the manager, and wait for instructions. The executive will either give you a message or take the call.

When you receive a telephone call for a visitor, offer to take a message or to give the visitor the number so that the visitor can return the call. When you do take a message for a visitor, key it. Address the message to the visitor; add your name and the time below the message.

If the person calling insists on speaking to the visitor, let the visitor know. As you enter the office or conference room, apologize for the interruption. Address the visitor, tell the visitor who is calling, and ask if the visitor would like to take the call in your office. When several visitors are in the room, key the message, walk in and hand it to the person addressed, and wait for the reply. Instead of taking the call, the visitor may tell you that he or she will return the call. Give the message to the person calling, ask for the caller's number, and write it on a telephone message blank for the visitor.

Whether or not you interrupt the manager when an unexpected visitor comes to the office will depend on who the person is and the purpose of the visit.

Callers Without Appointments

Be just as pleasant and friendly toward the unexpected visitor as you are toward the caller who has an appointment. Never judge a caller by appearance, for appearance is not indicative of a person's knowledge or contribution to the organization. When you greet visitors, find out their names and the purpose of their visits. When the visitor is a member of the family, a friend, or a business associate, invite the visitor to be seated. If the manager is already engaged with another appointment, you could say, "Mrs. Pollini has someone in her office, but I'll let her know you are here." Either key a note and take it to the manager or call her on the telephone. Friends or family members may prefer that you not interrupt the manager and suggest that they wait. However, business associates have a busy schedule to keep and so you should try not to keep a business associate waiting.

When you interrupt to tell the manager there is a visitor, the manager may step out of the office briefly to speak to the visitor. If the manager does not step out and speak to the visitor, try to reassure the visitor by saying something like "She knows you are here. It shouldn't be long."

Callers may come to your office and decide not to wait when they discover the manager is not immediately available. Always offer to help the person yourself and suggest you set an appointment if the visitor still wishes to see the manager.

When a sales representative calls unexpectedly, find out the purpose of the call to determine if

1. the sales representative should see someone else
2. you should offer to make an appointment for the sales representative
3. you should tell the salesperson the manager is not seeking the product or service.

If the sales representative has been calling, but the manager is no longer involved in purchasing these products or services, tell the representative who the best person to contact would be. Write the name, title, and location of the person you have referenced on a sheet of paper and give this to the representative. Be courteous in explaining to the sales representative how to reach that person's office. If security is a concern in your office, escort the person to the desired office.

Some organizations have policies that restrict sales representatives' visits to certain days of the week, or that limit them in some other way. When management is too busy to see a sales representative or observes strict guidelines for seeing them, offer to make an appointment. Be sure to end the conversation on a positive note. For instance, say, "We will expect you at 2 p.m. on Thursday. Mr. Wilmont will be glad to see you then."

When you are not seeking this particular product or service, graciously tell the sales representative so. The representative may still want an opportunity to convince the manager of the need for the product or service. Invite the sales representative to leave a business card and literature about the product or service and offer to fax the sales representative if the manager is interested in learning more about the product.

Remember that your job, besides running an efficient office, is to make friends for the organization. Give a reason, at least in general terms, before you say "no." Callers who are turned away should feel that they have been dealt with fairly.

Organizations have definite policies, too, about dealing with solicitors. Know what the policies are. If you have been given the authority to handle solicitors, do so assertively but always with courtesy.

What can you do when a caller is overly aggressive or rude? Be gracious; do not engage in an argument with the caller. Speak softly but convincingly. Administrative assistants should be given the names of supervisors or senior employees to call for support when they encounter a difficult situation. If you anticipate that a difficult caller will come back, discuss this with the management and agree on the most appropriate steps to take. Although these situations may at first seem difficult, with practice and perhaps some assertiveness training, you will be able to defuse potentially difficult confrontations without stress.

Sorry—Refusing Appointments

Managers have a lot of work to do in addition to conferring with callers and talking on the telephone. Many managers plan blocks of time in which they hope to work without interruption. At other times an executive will be forced by the pressure of a deadline to devote full time to a task that must be completed.

During periods when the manager is not seeing anyone, simply state that the manager cannot crowd anything more into today's schedule, and then centre the discussion on future arrangements. Handle telephone requests and unexpected office visits in the same way. Indicate when the manager will have time to see the caller. Ask questions such as, "Shall I ask the manager to call you?" or "Would you like to make an appointment?" Your suggestions will vary with the importance of the request.

HANDLING DIFFICULT CUSTOMERS

Every administrative assistant handles difficult customers or clients. Although this situation is undesirable, by learning how to handle it you will be providing benefits to both the company and the customer.

Unwanted Callers

How do you deal with a caller who is obnoxious or one who makes you feel threatened? Many office buildings have security 24 hours per day. If this is the case in your organization, you would call security to have the individual removed. Dealing with unwanted callers is something you need to discuss with your office team. Your colleagues may be able to provide names of people who have an abusive history with your office and are, therefore, not welcome in the office. Your company may have an organizational policy for handling unwanted callers. If so, follow it. If no policy exists, your office team should draft a policy and submit it to management for approval. Every organization wants to provide excellent customer service but customer abuse toward employees should never be tolerated.

Tips for Success

The following are tips for turning an undesirable situation into one that is satisfactory to both parties:

1. *Listen to the customer.* Listen to the spoken words, but also listen to the *unspoken*—that is, to the tone of voice and the body language. Often there is more information in what customers *don't* say than what they do say. Does the body language indicate anger, fear, or frustration? Has the customer omitted an important step in the process he or she is complaining about? If so, is there a reason for this omission?

   Listen quietly and carefully as the customer explains the source of distress. Take notes if necessary and ask questions to ensure clarity.

2. *Apologize if it is appropriate to do so.* Remember that customers are not always right, especially in situations where they have been dishonest or unethical. Where the company is not at fault, an apology might be phrased this way: "We apologize for any inconvenience our company may have caused. However, [company name] has done everything possible to provide you with a quality product [or service]."

   If your company has not performed to the highest of standards, a full apology is in order.

   Remember to use your tone of voice and your body language to reinforce the sincerity of your message.

3. *Show empathy and understanding.* Demonstrate that you have listened carefully and that you understand the customer's reason for distress. Paraphrasing the customer's story may be helpful. Example: "I understand how frustrated you must feel after receiving no response to your voice mail message, where you described the broken part in the product we sold you."
4. *Promise follow-up.* Commit to assisting the person yourself or to having someone else take action. Tell the customer exactly what your action plan will be and when she or he can expect to hear from you. If you do not know what action is necessary, commit to finding out and to calling the customer within a specified time. Now check with the customer to see if your action plan has his or her approval.
5. *Follow through.* Carry out the action plan just as you promised you would. Be certain to keep the customer informed of your progress.
6. *Use common courtesies.* Immediately learn the customer's name and use it along with the appropriate courtesy title (Mrs., Ms., Mr., Dr., or some other). Be sure your tone of voice and body language always convey a positive and sincere message. Most important, do not reciprocate the aggression. It is easy to become defensive and annoyed at a customer who is complaining about your service or product. However, do not personalize the comments of a distressed customer. If you feel the situation is beyond your control and you have been unable to deal effectively with this individual, contact your supervisor for support.

If you adhere to these basic rules, a more satisfactory situation should result.

Questions for Study and Review

1. Explain why appointments should not be scheduled immediately before or after the manager is out of the office for several days.
2. What are the advantages of leaving time frames of 15 to 30 minutes free at intervals during the day?
3. Suggest how you can tactfully let a person know that his or her appointment is for a short segment of time.
4. To avoid conflicts in scheduling, what is the administrative assistant's first step in granting an appointment when one is requested?
5. What are your responsibilities on behalf of a person whose appointment must be confirmed by the manager?
6. State reasons why it is essential to record the telephone number of a person who has requested or confirmed an appointment.
7. Describe how an electronic calendar can be used.
8. When you open the incoming mail, you should enter (in pencil) announcements of meetings into your calendar. What are the advantages of this procedure?
9. Explain why it saves time to prepare notes at the end of the day about items you think the manager has not completed.
10. What entries will you make in your calendar that you will not make in the manager's calendar?
11. What guidelines should you follow when you must cancel an appointment because the manager cannot keep it?
12. What are the administrative assistant's main responsibilities as they relate to receiving office callers?
13. Explain what is meant by giving a caller immediate attention when you are keyboarding, or talking on the telephone.
14. What is an efficient method for locating materials in your files that the manager will need during a conference? for collecting materials from other departments?
15. Explain how to introduce a caller to the manager.
16. Describe the administrative assistant's role in making a caller that must wait, feel comfortable.
17. What should you say if a caller who has an appointment cannot wait and tells you he or she must leave?
18. What is the basic rule for making introductions in business?
19. Why do some managers announce an "open door" policy for seeing personnel?
20. Suggest two ways to help an executive terminate a conference when he or she does not have another appointment soon.
21. What would you do if each of the following visitors did not have an appointment? The CEO of your company? The manager's spouse? The manager's former college friend from out of town? A sales representative your manager wants to keep in touch with but cannot see right now? A sales person representing a product your company does not need? A person soliciting funds? An aggressive and abusive person?
22. Explain six important steps in dealing with a customer who believes she has received an inferior product from your company.

Spelling Reinforcement

adhering	calendar	inconvenienced	reciprocate
affiliation	canceling/cancelling	intrusion	scheduling
aggressive	cognizant	paraphrasing	solicitors
allotted	conferring	personnel	tentative
appointment	coordinated	persuasive	unstructured
atmosphere	definite	protocol	untidiness
brochures	distressed	receiving	volunteer

On-the-Job Situations

1. You work for eight managers. You make appointments for all of them and record their appointments in separate appointment books. Today as you were checking your telephone notebook, you discovered that Mr. Singh had requested an appointment with Mrs. Roberts at 1030 on Wednesday. Inadvertently, you had entered the appointment in Mr. Robbins's appointment calendar. Mrs. Roberts has another appointment at 1030 on Wednesday and will not be in the office on Wednesday afternoon. You do not have Mr. Singh's telephone number. What should you do?
2. Recently Mrs. Garson has made three appointments with your employer, Mr. Stoney. Each time she has cancelled the appointment the day before—once because she was ill, another time because of bad weather, and the last time because she was too busy to keep the appointment. The last time she cancelled the appointment, Mr. Stoney said emphatically, "Please do not grant her another appointment!" This morning Mrs. Garson called requesting another appointment. You told her that Mr. Stoney could not work in another appointment this week and that he would be out of town the following week. Mrs. Garson is furious and insists on talking with Mr. Stoney. What should you do? What will you say to Mrs. Garson?
3. Your manager, Mr. Harper, had a serious heart attack in his office late Tuesday afternoon. Today you are cancelling his appointments for the remainder of this week and next week. You are explaining that the appointments will be rescheduled with someone else. What can you ask in order to judge the urgency of each appointment? How much information can you give about Mr. Harper's illness? What can you say?

Special Reports

1. Have you ever done any kind of office work, either full-time, during the summer, or on a part-time basis while in school? If so, recall what you observed about how office callers were received in the organization in which you worked. Did the organization have a receptionist? Were the callers escorted or directed to the offices of those with whom they had appointments? Were the salespeople's calls restricted? If so, how? What was the caller's first contact with the administrative assistant? Jot down what you recall, and share your ideas with the class. (If you have never worked in an office, ask an administrative assistant you know about how visitors are received in the organization in which he or she works.)
2. Go to a stationery store or to the stationery section of a department store and look at the variety of appointment calendars available. Write down the names of the ones you would select for your own use as an administrative assistant and for the manager's use. Beside the name of each one you select, jot down the features that appeal to you. Share what you learned with the class.

Production Challenges

8-A Scheduling Appointments

Supplies needed:

- *Mr. Wilson's appointment calendar, Form 8-A-1, page 413*
- *Administrative assistant's appointment calendar, Form 8-A-2, page 413*
- *Plain paper*

Mr. Wilson has been scheduling his own appointments. He uses a monthly calendar and crowds the appointments into the spaces. During a discussion with Mr. Wilson on Friday he asked you to schedule his appointments for him.

You decided to use daily appointment calendars—one for Mr. Wilson and one for yourself. Mr. Wilson has no appointments scheduled for Monday and only one for Tuesday. He has the following appointments for Wednesday, August 6, entered in his monthly calendar:

- 0900 Agnes Smith, sales representative for Small Home Appliances, Inc.
- 1000 Pete Rollins, sales representative for Home Gadgets, Inc.
- 1100 Joanna Hansen, Manager of the Eastern Region of Millennium Appliances, Inc., and J.R. Rush, Assistant Vice-President of Marketing, Eastern Region.
- 1200 Lunch with Ms. Hansen and Mr. Rush.
- 1500 Charlene Azam, Assistant Vice-President of Marketing, Western Region, to review marketing plans for fall.

You transfer these appointments to Mr. Wilson's daily calendar and yours.

On Tuesday, August 5, you receive the following telephone calls concerning appointments:

1. From Mrs. Linda Yee, Assistant Vice-President of Marketing, Midwestern Region, saying that she must attend a funeral out of town on Wednesday. She has an appointment on Wednesday at 1500 with O.C. Conners, President of Mapledale Homes, Inc. She asks if Mr. Wilson can see Mr. Conners for her at 1500.

   Here is your response: "I'll try. Mr. Wilson has an appointment with Ms. Azam at 1500. I'll see if I can move Ms. Azam's appointment to 1400. I'll call you and let you know."

   Later you call Mrs. Yee and confirm that Mr. Wilson will see Mr. Conners at 1500.
2. From Pete Rollins's assistant, saying that Mr. Rollins had an automobile accident, is hospitalized, and obviously cannot keep his appointment.
3. From Ray Rogers, co-chairman of the Eastern Region Sales Seminar, asking for an appointment on Wednesday to review plans for the November seminar. You suggest 1000, and Mr. Rogers accepts.
4. From the Personnel Department, asking Mr. Wilson to see a job applicant. You try to postpone this appointment, but the Personnel Department insists that Mr. Wilson will want to meet this applicant while he is in the building on Wednesday. You schedule an appointment for Bill Horvath at 1600.

Before leaving the office on Tuesday, you key Mr. Wilson's appointment schedule for Wednesday, August 6.

On Wednesday at 10:05, Jason Rhodes, a college friend from out of town, comes to the office for a brief visit with Mr. Wilson. You say you will schedule him for a few minutes between appointments at 1045.

On his way to lunch, Mr. Wilson asks you to call the Lakeside Restaurant to tell the manager how many will be in his dinner party Wednesday evening. (Be sure to enter this in the reminder section of your calendar.)

World Wide Websites

Now Software—Time Management Network

now.qualcomm.com/
This site includes Now Software's product information, downloads, calendar, and address book directory.

Day-Timer Store

www.daytimer.com/
This site includes Daytimer's product information, time management tips and web calendar.

Telecommunications in the Office

Outline

Effective Use of the Telephone

Using Telephone Directories
Placing a Local Call
Answering the Telephone
Automatic Answering Services
Placing Long-Distance Calls
Receiving Long-Distance Calls
Placing International Calls

Telephone Equipment, Systems, and Services

Interconnect Equipment
Common Telephone Equipment
Hi-tech Conferences
Telephone Message Systems
Telephone Systems
Telecommunications Services

The Internet

Infrastructure of the Internet
Uses for the Internet
Perspectives: "Cruising the Information Superhighway"
Growth of the Internet
Getting Connected
Internet Connections

Learning Outcomes

At the completion of this chapter, the student will be able to:

1. Use a telephone directory to locate information.
2. Describe the procedures for answering, transferring, and screening office calls.
3. Describe the procedures for placing and receiving long-distance calls.
4. Determine the appropriate time to call offices in other time zones.
5. State the various kinds of long-distance services.
6. Identify office telephone equipment and telephone systems.
7. Describe the advantages and disadvantages of voice mail.
8. Explain how the office professional may use the Internet to improve efficiency in the office.
9. Record telephone messages on telephone message blanks.
10. Plan and record information needed before placing calls.

GRADUATE PROFILE

Gerald Lemay
President

Internet Institute

College Graduation:
Bilingual Executive Secretarial Program
Algonquin College of Applied Arts and Technology
Nepean, Ontario

Algonquin College is particularly proud of Gerald Lemay's success. After graduation, Gerald was hired by the Federal Provincial Relations Office of the Government of Canada, where he organized meetings of first ministers. A year later he was working for the Privy Council Office coordinating briefing books for the transition of power between Prime Ministers Trudeau, Turner, and Mulroney. In 1986 the Treasury Board of Canada hired Gerald as a secretary in the Office of the Comptroller General of Canada. Later he was promoted to the position of Assistant to the Comptroller General; in that position, prior committee experience gave him the tools he needed to lead a team. At the Treasury Board he managed a nationwide electronic bulletin board service to enhance the distribution and retrieval of information. To acknowledge his contributions, Gerald was given the Highest Level of Achievement Award at the Treasury Board.

In 1995, Gerald founded an Internet training company. Gerald's success has been profiled during interviews with CTV National News, CBC Radio, and Fureteur (a French Internet television show). As well, he has been nominated for several business awards.

Gerald says that a graduate, in order to succeed, must be willing to continue professional development after graduation, and must be prepared to enthusiastically undertake new projects, even if they involve working overtime. Gerald advises graduates to improve and practise their communication and leadership skills. Keeping up to date with new trends, which includes studying their feasibility, is another of Gerald's recommendations. Finally, he suggests that graduates read voraciously.

"Find a way you can make a difference in your company."

Every office has a telephone, and it rings and rings and rings. While the telephone is an important instrument in every organization, the value actually gained from it depends on how it is used. The telephone must be used correctly, yet it is the most abused and misused piece of office equipment. Office professionals agree that proper techniques for handling business telephone calls should be emphasized in office technology programs and in-service training sessions.

EFFECTIVE USE OF THE TELEPHONE

Effective telephone techniques involve placing and receiving local and long-distance calls and using related telephone services.

Talking over the telephone at home does not prepare a person for handling business calls. When you are handling business calls, learn and remember effective techniques, and apply them. As you place and receive calls, observe the telephone techniques used by others. Think about the types of telephone calls you have received that could be improved upon, and then be prepared to use an improved technique yourself.

Using Telephone Directories

A local telephone directory is available for every telephone. Directories for other geographic areas may be obtained for a nominal fee, by contacting the telephone company that publishes the directory. Organizations provide their employees with a staff directory for calling other employees within the organization.

An administrative assistant should become skilled at using the alphabetic and classified sections of public telephone directories, and should be thoroughly familiar with the telephoning procedures described in the introductory section of the local directory.

The alphabetic directory, which may be a separate volume or may be bound with the classified directory, contains the name, address, and telephone number of every subscriber in the local calling area (except for those with unlisted numbers). Names of individuals and organizations are listed in alphabetical order.

In most Canadian city directories the municipal, provincial, and federal government listings are found in a section separate from the alphabetic listings. This section often has a different colour than the alphabetic pages.

For the sake of speed, circle new numbers in the alphabetic directory as you look them up. If you do not complete a call on the first attempt, write the number in your telephone notebook so that you won't have to look it up again. If you anticipate that you will be using a number often, transfer the name and number to your telephone card file or computer telephone list. When you are given an unlisted number, be sure to record it in your telephone card file, for you will not be able to look up the number elsewhere. Indicate on your telephone record number that the number is unlisted.

The classified directory, called the *Yellow Pages*, is arranged by subject for products and services. Listings under each subject are then arranged in alphabetical order. To use the Yellow Pages, think of all the possible ways the reference you are seeking might be listed, and search first for the most likely classification. Some Yellow Pages directories offer a *Special Guide* section or a *Quick Reference* section at the beginning of the book; these can save a lot of time.

A more recent innovation to the traditional Yellow Pages is the **Talking Yellow Pages,** a supplemental publication. This service is provided by the local telephone company and small businesses; its purpose is to help the general public locate business information. It is similar to voice mail in two ways:

1. It has business information stored in voice mailboxes.
2. The public accesses those voice mailboxes through numeric instructions.

Refer to the introductory pages of your organization's directory for policies concerning telephone use and procedures to follow when placing calls. In addition to local numbers, an organization's directory will include the telephone numbers of its branch offices, plants, distribution centres, and so on that are located outside the local area.

Placing a Local Call

Before you place a call, assemble the materials you may need to refer to during the telephone conversation. Jot down the questions you want to ask and the comments you want to make. Be sure you have the correct number and name of the person with whom you wish to speak.

If the first person you reach is the receptionist, give the extension number of the person you are calling. If you do not know the extension number, give the receptionist the person's name and department. Receptionists will often say the person's extension number as they look it up; others will give you a number if you request it. Write extension numbers down and add them to your telephone card file.

Give the person ample time to answer. Let the telephone ring at least six times or for a minute.

When the person who answers the telephone is the one with whom you wish to speak, identify yourself immediately. Use an appropriate identification, such as "Good morning, this is Linda McElroy, assistant to Tom Jamison of Millennium Appliances."

If the person who answers is not the one with whom you wish to speak, ask for the person and identify yourself: "May I speak to Ms. Delacroix, please? I'm Linda McElroy, assistant to Tom Jamison of Millennium Appliances." When you do not need to speak to a particular person, make your request of the person who answers.

Managers often place their own calls, but at times you will be expected to get a caller on the line for your manager. When you are placing a call, make sure your manager is ready to talk before you get the other person on the line. Asking the person called to wait is inconsiderate. Call the person by name and add, "Mr. Jamison would like to talk with you." At this point Mr. Jamison should start the conversation.

Answering the Telephone

Every time you answer the telephone, you are projecting the image of your organization. To the caller, you *are* the organization. You must rely on your voice to project a pleasant, businesslike attitude and to give the caller full attention. Be aware of your tone of voice; vary it to be expressive. Both what you say and how you say it are important. Treat every call as if it were the only call of the day.

Answer Promptly

Answer the telephone on the second ring. Avoid surprising the caller by answering too soon, but answer promptly. An unanswered telephone conveys an image of inefficiency. However, do not lift the receiver and let the caller wait while you finish a conversation with someone in the office—this is discourteous.

To be clearly understood, ensure that the transmitter or microphone is close to your lips—between one and two centimetres—and speak directly into it in a normal, conversational tone; use just enough volume for your voice to be pleasant to the listener.

Speak distinctly and at a rate that is neither too fast nor too slow. By speaking at a moderate pace, you will come across as confident and poised. The caller will not be able to understand you if you talk too rapidly, but may become impatient if you talk too slowly.

Give Proper Identification

Let the caller know that the right office has been reached. If the incoming calls are answered by a switch-

Figure 9-1 Your telephone voice must project a pleasant, businesslike attitude.
Courtesy of Northern Telecom (Nortel)

board operator, he or she will say, "Good morning [or good afternoon], Millennium Appliances." When the receptionist rings your telephone, you can say, "Mr. Jamison's office, Linda McElroy speaking," or "Advertising Department, Linda McElroy speaking." Your manager may tell you specifically how the telephone should be answered. If your manager does not tell you, ask. Never answer a business telephone with "Hello." "Hello" is considered far too casual for the business office.

It is courteous to let the caller know who you are. To identify yourself, use both your first and last names. A courtesy title—Miss, Mrs., Ms., Mr.—is not usually necessary; however, follow the procedure that is expected in your organization.

When telephone calls come directly to your office, first let the callers know they have reached the right organization; then add the identification for the particular telephone you are answering, and give your name. Example: "Millennium Appliances, Finance Office, Louisa speaking."

With a Centrex exchange, the administrative assistant may not receive the call first; many calls will go directly to the manager's telephone. If the callers have your manager's Centrex number, which probably will not be listed in the public telephone directory, they will know they have reached the right office as soon as they hear your manager's name or the name of the department. The Centrex system is explained later in this chapter in the section "Telephone Systems, Equipment, and Services."

When you answer the telephone for many managers, code each station on your key-set or switchboard so that you can give proper identification for each person whose telephone you are answering. When you are answering a telephone for a colleague, answer it in a similarly courteous manner, but use your name to let the caller know who is speaking. If you have your own telephone, say, for example, "Linda Lewis speaking."

Be Courteous

Authorities do not agree on whether a greeting, such as "Good morning" or "Good afternoon," should be used when answering the telephone. Nevertheless, a greeting is a necessary courtesy. As well, many callers do not hear the name of the organization if it is the first word spoken when a telephone is answered.

Listen attentively. Listening is an essential element in effective telephone use. If the caller interrupts you, permit the caller to talk. Do not, however, permit the caller to complete a long explanation if the caller has reached the wrong office. You should interrupt by saying, "Excuse me, I believe you should speak to someone in the —— Department. The number for that department is ——. Would you like me to transfer you?"

When you must leave the line to obtain information, explain why and how long it will take. Give the caller a choice. Ask whether:

1. the caller would prefer to wait, or
2. the caller would rather be called back.

If the caller chooses to wait, avoid a wait of more than two minutes. When you return to the caller who is holding, offer your thanks for waiting.

During telephone conversations use "please," "thank you," and other courteous phrases. At appropriate times, use the caller's name.

If you discover that neither you nor your manager can help the caller, redirect the call to someone who can. Do not leave the caller stranded by saying that your department cannot handle the issue. Make a special effort to be helpful. Give the caller the name and number of the appropriate person to call. Let the caller know when you are looking up a number. If the call is from outside the organization, offer to transfer the call. A caller is usually favourably impressed when someone is helpful; your time will have been well spent.

When the caller has dialled the wrong number, be especially courteous. Callers often reach a wrong number because they have looked at the wrong number on a list of frequently called numbers. The caller may be one of your current or future customers.

The person who initiates a telephone call should terminate it. However, you can bring the call to an end by thanking the person for calling, or suggesting that you will give the message to your manager, or whatever is appropriate. When you initiate the call, let the other person know you are going to leave the line. Do not end abruptly.

Take Notes

Keep a small notebook, a pen, and a pad of telephone message blanks by the telephone. Spare yourself the embarrassment of asking a caller to wait while you look for a pen or a pencil.

When you must record the name and the number so that your manager can return the call, write it on the telephone message blank as the caller gives you the information. Always restate the message to assure both yourself and the caller that you have recorded it accurately and in its entirety. Add the caller's business affiliation if the caller is someone your manager does not know. It is important to include the area code when recording the caller's number. Public telephone networks are becoming so congested that telephone companies are subdividing traditional area codes so as to introduce new ones. An example is the introduction of the 780 area code in the traditional 403 region of Northern Alberta.

Record the time of the call. The time of the call is important; if your manager talked with the caller at lunch, he or she needs to know if the call was made before or after lunch.

Write clearly on the first attempt so that you will not waste time later rewriting or keying the information. Key messages only when they involve more than returning the call. Be sure to record the message, and to key it exactly as it was given to you.

Be careful how you explain your manager's absence from the office. Simply say, "Ms. Johnson is away from her desk right now. May I ask her to call you?" or "Ms. Johnson is not in her office at the moment. May I have her call you?" or "She is not here at the moment. May I help you?" Avoid statements such as these:

- "She's playing golf this afternoon."
- "Ms. Johnson is in Ottawa."
- "She is at a doctor's appointment."
- "She's still out for lunch."
- "She's tied up."
- "She has not come in yet."
- "Ms. Johnson is in conference." The conference explanation has been overused and will be received as an excuse. When it is in fact true, you should state in a sincere way that Ms. Johnson is in a meeting, and suggest what time you expect her back in the office.

Transfer Calls Properly

When you are certain that a call should be handled by someone else within the organization, explain to the caller that you are going to transfer the call. Be sure you transfer the call to the right person. Never transfer a call unless absolutely necessary. Offer to transfer a call only when it has been placed from outside the organization.

Give the caller the name and telephone number of the person to whom he or she is being transferred, so that the caller can place the call if he or she is disconnected as you transfer the call. Be sure you know how to transfer a call. The method varies with the telephone system being used.

Before you transfer the call, invite the caller to phone you back if you have not referred him or her to the right person. If the caller does call back, offer to locate the right person and refer the request to that person.

If your department cannot handle the request and you do not know who should handle it, tell the caller so, but offer to:

1. find out who can be of help, or
2. refer the request to that person.

Be sure to follow through on your promise. Doing this will create work for you, but it may result in increased business for your organization.

Callers often find themselves being transferred three or four times. Imagine how frustrating this must be for them: each time they must repeat their story. In addition, three or four people will have been interrupted by calls they cannot handle. When these callers reach you, stop the runaround. Offer to locate someone who *can* help. Never transfer a call on the *speculation* that the person to whom you are transferring the call might be helpful.

Answer the Second Telephone

Many managers have two or more telephone lines into their offices. If two telephones ring at the same time, answer one and ask the caller if you may be excused to answer the other telephone. Do not leave the line until the caller consents. Press the HOLD button and answer the second call. What you do next depends on whether the second call is local or long-distance. In either situation, do not neglect the first caller.

When the second call is a local one, offer to call the second person back, after you have explained why, and return to the first caller. As soon as this conversation ends, dial the second caller.

When the second call is a long-distance call, do not offer to call back. Either ask someone else to take the call or explain to the long-distance caller that you interrupted a local call on another line in order to answer. Excuse yourself long enough to get back to the first caller to say, "I will be with you in a minute." Complete the long-distance call as quickly as possible. Try not to keep the first caller waiting more than a minute. When you get back to the first caller, apologize for the delay and thank the caller for waiting.

Use these same methods if you are talking on the telephone when the second telephone rings.

Know When to Answer

In most organizations, managers answer their own telephone when they are in the office. Alternatively, you may be expected to take *all* telephone calls and immediately put them through to your manager.

Know when to answer the telephone and do a superb job of it. By all means, answer the telephone when someone is in your manager's office. It would be inappropriate for your manager to interrupt a conversation with another person, regardless of who the person is, to talk on the telephone. A person who must sit and wait during a telephone conversation is made to feel unimportant. Furthermore, a telephone interruption can come at the wrong time in a very important conference.

"I always try to go the extra mile for our customers."

Joanne Currie Wood, Graduate
Fraser Pacific College

Do not ask your manager to take a telephone call when your manager has a visitor, unless you have been given specific instructions to interrupt if a particular call comes in or if the call is a long-distance one. Let the caller know that someone is in your manager's office and ask, "May I have Mr. Shea call you?" Be sure to get the caller's name and number. Tell the caller your manager is not free to receive a telephone call *before* you ask who is calling. If you ask who is calling before you let the caller know that your manager has someone in the office or that your manager is not in the office, you give the caller the impression that your manager doesn't want to speak to him or her.

Refer to Chapter 8 for a discussion of how to interrupt your manager when you think a call is urgent enough that you ought to do so.

Not all managers refrain from accepting calls when visitors are in the office. Again, it is best to clarify the desired procedures for different office personnel.

Distribute Messages Promptly

Put telephone messages on your manager's desk or in a designated location in such a way that they will not be covered by papers and overlooked.

Make telephone messages available to office personnel as soon as they are received. However, if your manager is trying to work without interruption, avoid presenting the message immediately. The plan your manager has for addressing messages and returning calls will depend on individual schedules, preferences, and workload. If your manager is expecting a call, and it arrives when your manager is unavailable, call attention to it as soon as your manager returns.

Most managers return telephone calls without being reminded, but some expect their administrative assistant to maintain follow-ups on calls to be returned. Remind your manager by preparing a list each morning of calls to be returned.

If your manager needs to review materials from the files before returning a call, locate the materials and place them on your manager's desk with the telephone message.

Be sure to pass along all telephone messages to your manager. It is up to your manager to decide which calls are of high (or low) priority.

When your manager is unavailable, don't just take messages—take the initiative. Many telephone requests can be satisfied by you or by other employees.

If your manager is away and telephones the office to check on the office activities, never say that nothing is happening. By this comment you are admitting that you are unaware of office activity. You should always be able to provide a brief summary of activities and incoming telephone calls. Remember, the administrative assistant is an information worker. Your job is to collect, use, and provide information.

Screen Calls

Some managers have such heavy demands on their time that their calls must be screened, and many of those calls must be handled by someone else.

If you must screen calls, probe courteously for information. Either respond to the caller yourself or determine what the caller's request is and refer the call to someone else who can help.

Screening calls

1. saves your manager's time
2. assists the caller.

All calls should be handled by someone. The more knowledge you have about the organization, the easier your job of screening calls will be. Never tell a caller "I don't know" and leave the caller wondering what to do next. If you really don't know, it's your responsibility to find out or to solicit the assistance of someone who does know.

Automatic Answering Services

Many large modern offices are equipped with sophisticated telephone systems to handle the deluge of incoming calls and to monitor outgoing calls. Incoming calls are often intercepted by automatic answering services known as

- auto-announcements, or
- Interactive Voice Response.

Auto announcements are similar to answering machines but are only activated when all incoming lines are busy, or after hours when the caller is prompted to leave a message or to call back during business hours.

Interactive Voice Response (IVR) can be programmed to

- respond after a predefined number of rings
- respond between specific times of day
- play different announcements
- prompt the caller through a menu of options to acquire information or leave messages
- repeat messages based on the length of time the caller has been on hold.

Administrative assistants are often called on to help optimize their office's IVR system. When they are, they should involve their local service provider or IVR manufacturer in designing scripts and procedures that appropriately represent the company.

Placing Long-Distance Calls

Long-distance calls are any calls placed outside the local calling area. Canada and the United States are divided into more than one hundred telephone areas. Each of these areas is identified by a three-digit area code. See Figure 9-2 for the Canadian numbering plan. The area code must be used to place all long-distance calls, even within your own area code range. Many international locations do not use a three-digit code; for example, Mexico uses some two-digit area codes. In such cases, however, a country code is used to direct the call first to the country, then the region within the country.

An organization that provides its telephone number in its letterhead includes the area code. Area codes are shown on a map in the front of the telephone directory. North American area code numbers are being expanded each year because of the increasing numbers of users. For this reason, you may have difficulty finding the correct code. If you do, simply dial the operator and ask for the correct code.

Placing and receiving long-distance calls saves not only time but also money and energy. Long-distance calls may be placed either point-to-point or person-to-person.

Point-to-Point Calls

The two kinds of point-to-point calls are

1. direct distance dialling (DDD)—the caller dials the number directly, and no special assistance is needed from the operator

Figure 9-2 Canadian telephone area code map.

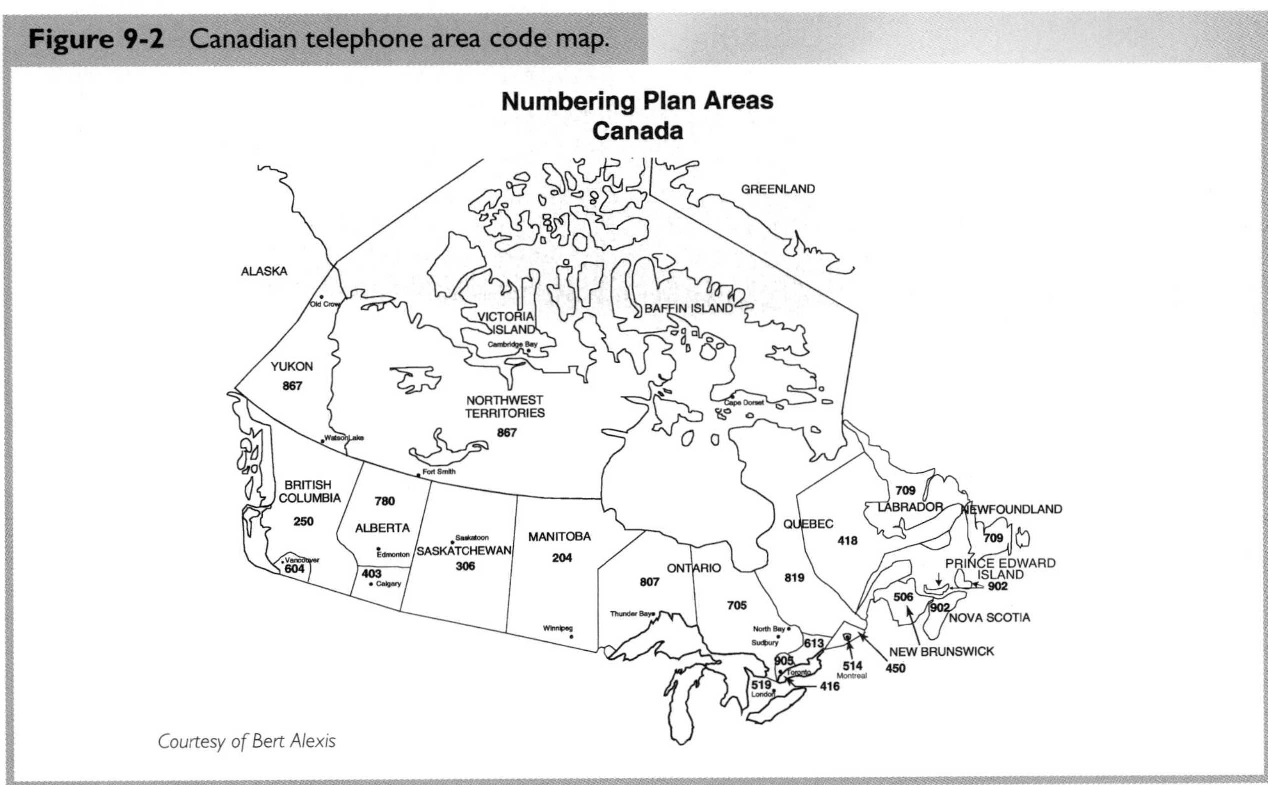

Courtesy of Bert Alexis

2. operator-assisted calls—necessary when calls are
   a. collect
   b. made from pay phones
   c. charged to a credit card
   d. billed to a third party.

Rates for operator-assisted calls are generally higher than rates for comparable DDD calls. A table of rates is provided in the front of all telephone directories.

Calling Card Calls

Telephone **calling cards** may or may not require the assistance of an operator. Many pay phones are now equipped with a magnetic strip reader to accommodate telephone calling cards. When you use this method of placing a call, operator assistance is not required and the charge is automatically billed to your personal or business account. The information stored on the card includes a coded account number.

Prepaid calling cards are the equivalent of a direct debit card. A magnetic stripe on the back of a prepaid card stores the original purchase value of the card and updates (debits) that amount each time a call is made. New pay telephone equipment can read and update a prepaid calling card as the call progresses.

Businesses are finding that calling cards and prepaid calling cards are both convenient and cost-effective.

Rates are lower for point-to-point calls than for person-to-person calls. The charges begin when the called telephone or switchboard is answered. No charge is made, however, when the called telephone is not answered.

Dial point-to-point if you can talk to anyone who answers, or if you anticipate that the person you wish to talk to will be near the telephone.

To place DDD point-to-point calls, dial the access code "1," the area code of the geographic location you are calling, and the seven-digit local number. In most areas the number from which you are calling will be recorded automatically; however, in some areas the operator will intercept to ask for your number.

To place point-to-point calls requiring operator assistance, use the **Zero Plus Dialling** method. Simply dial "0," the area code, and the seven-digit local number. After you have dialled the complete number, a short automated process will start; this is where you have the choice of entering your calling card number, or speaking to a live operator for special services. Give the operator the information essential for completing the call. For instance, to reverse charges to the number being called, say "collect" and give your name; to charge a call to a third number, give the area code and number to which the call is to be charged. When the call is placed from a pay telephone, the operator must check with a person at that third number before allowing the billing. This is necessary because there can be no trace of origin when a call is placed from a pay station. If there is no automated process for calling cards, simply say "calling card call" and give the calling card number.

Person-to-Person Calls

Person-to-person calls require assistance from the operator. For such calls, use the Zero Plus method. Dial 0, the area code, and the seven-digit number. When the operator answers, give the name of the person you are calling. Charges begin when that person answers.

If the person called is not available and you wish your call to be returned, indicate this to the operator. The operator will ask you for the number you wish the call to be returned to, and then will say something like this: "Will you have Tom Jamison call Saskatoon, Saskatchewan, area code 306-382-9012."

Long-distance telephone companies have introduced a computerized operator. If you are placing a long-distance call and wish to reverse the charges, you dial 0–area code–local number. A computer-controlled voice will ask you which service you want and then ask you to clearly state your name. When the call is placed, the computer-controlled voice system announces your name and the fact that it is a person-to-person call. The receiver will accept or refuse the charges either by keying in a response on the telephone pad or by responding to questions with a simple "yes" or "no." All of this takes place without the intervention of a human operator.

Directory Assistance

To obtain a number in order to make a long-distance call, dial "1," the area code of the geographic location you want, and 555-1212. You will reach the information operator, or the automated directory system for the area you are calling . First provide the name of the city or town you want and then the name of the person. Write down the number that is given to you, hang up, and dial "1," the area code, and the seven-digit number. This same procedure is used whether you are dialling inside or outside your own area code.

This service is called long-distance directory assistance. There is a charge for this service whether you request a number inside or outside your area code. (Refer to the introductory pages of your telephone directory to determine how to request local directory assistance.)

You should note that of all the services offered by telephone companies today, those requiring the intervention of a live telephone operator are the most costly. The administrative assistant is advised to become familiar with automated services and to avoid operator assistance wherever possible.

Conference Calling

A conference call is taking place when three or more telephone stations are connected across a network that supports the conversation. Conference calls can be initiated

1. by a prearranged call through a telephone operator, or
2. by using the special "conference" feature on most business telephone sets.

When prearranging a conference call through a telephone operator, you must usually pay a nominal charge. Refer to your local or regional telephone company rate book for the current charge.

The operator will require essential information—cities, names, numbers, and the time of the conference. The operator will call each person involved to obtain acceptance of the time of the conference and will place the call to each participant at the time of the conference.

Some telephone companies are equipped to provide a temporary "bridge," or pass code and temporary number information that participants call at their leisure. This is an automatic process and does not require the intervention of an operator.

No special equipment is needed for conference calls. However, specially designed speaker/microphone conference sets, designed for boardroom use, may be used to enhance the clarity of the conference stations.

One special feature of most business telephone sets is the conference feature. Users can dial a number and ask the receiver of the call to hold while they conference another person into the call. The user simply puts the first caller on hold, presses the conference button, and dials the second number. When the second caller is connected, the user releases the hold button to include the first person, who has been waiting on hold. A three-way conversation is now possible.

Time Zones in Canada

The Canadian provinces and territories are divided into six time zones:

1. Newfoundland
2. Atlantic
3. Eastern
4. Central
5. Mountain
6. Pacific.

From east to west, the time in each zone is one hour earlier than the time in the adjacent zone. An exception is for Newfoundland, which is only half an hour ahead of the Atlantic time zone. The time at the location where the long-distance call originates determines whether day, evening, or night rates apply.

During certain months of the year when daylight-saving time is in effect, the time in each zone will be one hour later.

When you are placing a long-distance call, know the time zone of the city you are calling. For instance, when it is 1530 in Victoria, B.C., you can expect that offices in Quebec City will be closed. When it is 1700 in Quebec City, offices on the West Coast will still be open. Time zones around the world are explained in the following section and are illustrated in Figure 9-3.

Time Zones Around the World

The world is divided into 24 time zones, which are based on degrees of longitude. The zones are one hour apart in time. Greenwich, England, is recognized as the prime meridian of longitude; in other words, standard time is calculated from Greenwich. Basically, each time zone covers 15 degrees of longitude; however, the time zone lines wander to accommodate local geographic regions.

The Greenwich zone is called the *zero zone*, because the difference between standard time and Greenwich Mean Time is zero. Each of the zones in turn is designated by a number representing the number of hours by which the standard time of the zone differs from Greenwich Mean Time.

Zones in east longitude are numbered in sequence from 1 to 12 and labelled *minus;* zones in west longitude are numbered 1 to 12 and labelled *plus*. In each zone the zone number is applied to the standard time in accordance with its plus or minus sign to obtain Greenwich time. For example, Montreal is in the +5 zone, as shown in Figure 9-3. When it is 0900 in Montreal, add five hours to determine that Greenwich time is 1400. Tokyo is in the –9 zone. When it is 1000 in Tokyo, subtract nine hours to determine that Greenwich time is 0100.

If you need to determine time in cities around the globe, get and use a time chart. Time charts similar to the one in Figure 9-4, and more sophisticated ones, are available from the international telegraph companies or from some local cartographers.

The International Date Line is in the twelfth zone. It coincides with the 180th meridian, except that it zigzags so that all of Asia lies to the west of it and all of North America—including the Aleutian Islands—to the east of it. The 180th meridian divides the twelfth zone; therefore, the half in east longitude is *minus* 12 and the half in west longitude is *plus* 12. Each calendar day begins at the International Date Line. When crossing the International Date Line in a westerly direction, *advance* the date by one day; when crossing it in an easterly direction, set the date *back* one day.

Figure 9-3 Standard time zone chart of the world.

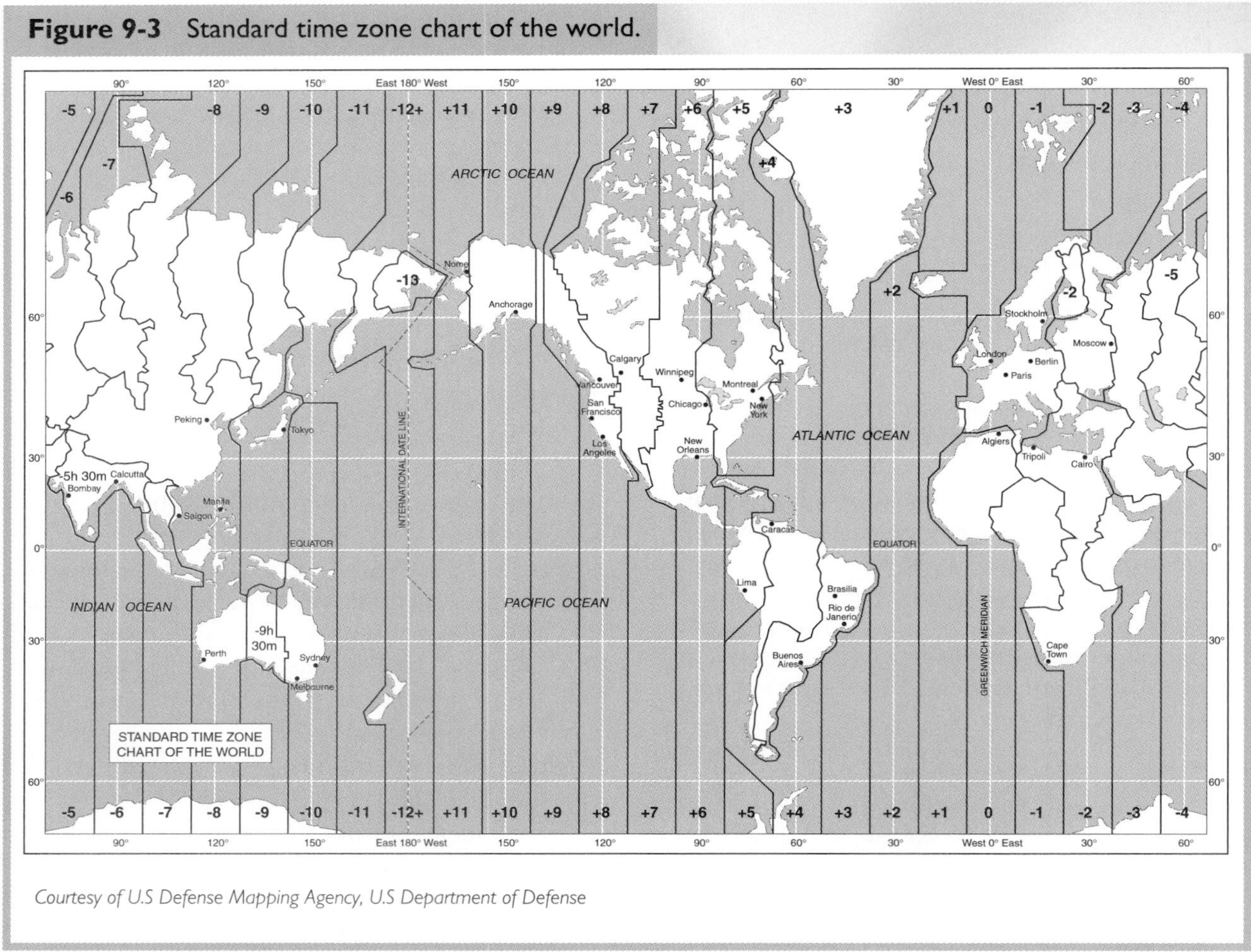

Courtesy of U.S Defense Mapping Agency, U.S Department of Defense

Receiving Long-Distance Calls

When answering a long-distance call that is point-to-point, quickly get someone on the line who can handle the call, or assist the caller yourself and/or take a message. Remember that the caller must pay for the call because the telephone was answered.

Write the message in your telephone notebook and restate it to indicate your understanding of it. Prepare the telephone message immediately and place it on your manager's desk. If you handle the transaction, key a summary of it and give it to your manager.

When the long-distance call is person-to-person and your manager is not there, tell the operator when you expect your manager to return. If the operator asks your manager to return the call, carefully record the call-back information.

You can often help by telling the operator where your manager can be reached. You will have to make a judgment concerning your manager's reaction to taking the call in someone else's office.

Placing International Calls

Calls to the United States, Puerto Rico, the Virgin Islands, Bermuda, and other Caribbean Islands are regular long-distance calls. Each of these places has an assigned area code just like the codes in Canada. Thus, placing a direct-dialled long-distance call to Puerto Rico would require you to dial "1" +"809" (the area code for Puerto Rico) and the local number.

You can dial directly to most other foreign countries as well. To place a direct-dial call, dial "011" (the international long-distance access number), the code for the country being called, the city code if it is required, and the local number. To dial directly to Tokyo, Japan, for example, you would dial "011" + "81" + "3" + the local number. The international country and city codes are given in the front of the White Pages of the local telephone directory. The time differences between each country and the city serviced by the telephone directory are also shown.

You may require operator assistance with your international call if you are making a person-to-person call,

Figure 9-4 How to compute time changes.

COMPUTING TIME			
Add to (+) or subtract from (–) Eastern Standard Time in order to arrive at Standard Time in the following locations. For example, when it is 12:00 noon in Montreal (EST), it is 10:30 p.m. in India.			
Albania	+6	Italy	+6
Argentina	+2	Japan	+14
Austria	+6	Luxembourg	+6
Belgium	+6	Morocco	+5
Bermuda	+1	Netherlands	+6
Bolivia	+1	Newfoundland	+1.5
Borneo	+13	New Zealand	+17
Bulgaria	+7	Nicaragua	–1
Burma	+11.5	Norway	+6
Chile	+1	Paraguay	+1
Colombia	+0	Peru	+0
Cuba	+0	Philippines	+13
Denmark	+6	Poland	+6
Egypt	+7	Portugal	+5
Ethiopia	+8	Puerto Rico	+1
Finland	+7	Spain	+6
France	+6	Sweden	+6
Germany	+6	Switzerland	+6
India	+10.5	Syria	+7
Iran	+8.5	Thailand	+12
Ireland	+5	Turkey	+7
Israel	+7	Vietnam	+12

a credit card call, or a third-party billing call, or are reversing the charges. In these cases, dial "01" + the country code + the routing code + the local number. Example: if dialling London, England, the procedure would be "01"+"44"+"1"+ the local number. At this point the operator would intercept, asking you what special assistance you require.

TELEPHONE EQUIPMENT, SYSTEMS, AND SERVICES

Rapid changes have taken place in telephone equipment, systems, and services since the Canadian Radio-Television and Telecommunications Commission (CRTC) made it legal for companies other than the common carriers to compete with the telephone service.

Interconnect Equipment

Interconnect equipment is the term used to refer to telephone equipment that organizations purchase or lease from suppliers other than the telephone companies.

The manufacturers of telephone interconnect equipment have placed new switchboards and other equipment with hundreds of features on the market.

Most of the new features of modern telephone systems are controlled at the central office. At the central office (which used to be known as the telephone exchange), most mechanical exchanges have been replaced by modern (electronic) digital switches. These digital switches are program-controlled and offer users a variety of services. These services are known as **call management services**. They include:

- Displaying the caller's number on your telephone.
- Forwarding your call to another number when you are busy or away from your desk.
- Having the telephone system monitor a busy number and inform you when that number becomes free.

Other call management features can enhance your telephone effectiveness. For example:

- By touching a predefined button, the administrative assistant can speed-dial a number.
- By pressing a key, you may redial a previously dialed number.
- Most telephone systems provide electronic memory where a list of names and/or numbers is stored.

With the electronic memory feature, frequently used numbers may be recorded and reused for dialing automatically and accurately.

Many more telephone features are gaining popularity as enhancements to productivity: bilingual displays; voice communication over the Internet; and, supplemental features such as lightweight headsets which enable the user to work hands free. See Figure 9-5. New developments include bilingual alphanumeric displays (Figure 9-6) and the provision to check e-mail through the telephone set.

When the personal touch is not necessary, companies often use Interactive Voice Response. When the electronic voice answers a call, it may instruct you to press a code button (such as # or *) or a certain digit sequence to reach the specific person with whom you wish to speak. After a code or digit has been pressed, a recorded voice message of the party you are calling may be heard. It might request that you leave a message. A person wishing to hear the messages received by the electronic system can telephone from a remote location, receive the messages electronically, and dictate a response, which the electronic system can deliver anywhere, anytime. These are a few of the features of **voice mail**, which is discussed in more detail later in this chapter.

We make no attempt here to discuss all the new features that have been introduced by the interconnect industry; instead, we discuss the basic concepts of telephone equipment and systems. If you are using interconnect equipment, study the operator's manual to learn how to operate the special features.

Figure 9-5 A lightweight headset containing a miniaturized mouthpiece allows the administrative assistant to communicate with hands free.
Courtesy of Rogers Cantel Inc.

Figure 9-6 Telephones with advanced features including digital displays.
Courtesy of Northern Telecom (Nortel)

Common Telephone Equipment

The following discussion provides basic information on common telephone equipment.

Touch-tone Telephones

Most regular telephones are touch-tone activated.

The touch-tone telephone provides both regular telephone service and tone transmission of data through a twelve button keypad. Ten buttons represent the numbers 0 through 9 and the alphabet. The other two buttons, showing the # and the * symbols, generate unique tones which access other services. An example of such a service is *repeat dial*, which will redial the last number used. These symbols may be connected to special telephone company services.

The touch-tone telephone provides tone transmissions of data, which can be received and converted by the central office. In this way, you communicate with the central office and access the call management services mentioned earlier in the section "Interconnect Equipment."

Key Telephones

Key telephones, or key-sets, provide flexibility in making and receiving multiple calls simultaneously. Key telephones have multiple buttons, and the buttons on one phone set are the same as those on all the other sets in an office. A number of calls from both inside and outside the office may be made and/or received simultaneously.

The basic key telephone is a regular telephone with push-button keys corresponding to the number of telephone lines terminating in the telephone. The push buttons flash on and off to indicate incoming calls on the lines. To answer a call, push the key that is flashing and lift the receiver. If a second call comes in while the first is in progress, suspend the conversation properly, push the HOLD button, then push the flashing key of the incoming call and answer the call. To suspend this call and get back to the first call, push the HOLD button again, then push the key of the first incoming call. When a push-button key glows steadily, it indicates that the line is in use. Figure 9-7 shows a key telephone with an add-on module that allows more telephone lines to be used.

Wireless Telephones

The wireless telephone service provides mobile communication. This telephone network uses radio waves rather than telephone wires to transmit messages. However, mobile telephone users may communicate with conventional telephone users, since wireless systems interconnect with local and long-distance telephone networks. (See Figure 9-8.)

Wireless telephones are often installed in cars, trucks, and trains; they are also found onboard aircraft. Wireless telephones are often carried in purses and briefcases. Whether for personal or business use, you will find many people in your office will use a wireless telephone.

Wireless telephone users can take advantage of most of the features offered to regular telephone users, including voice mail. With special portable modem and computer equipment, wireless telephones can transmit and receive computer data.

Figure 9-7 Key telephone set with add-on module for additional lines.
Courtesy of Northern Telecom (Nortel)

For those office professionals and management who travel beyond North America, a new generation of wireless telephone may provide the reach and direct access required for calling back to the office. Currently, the **Iridium** wireless telephone will allow its user to call from anywhere in the world provided the telephone signal has a direct line-of-sight to a satellite. From the satellite, the signal is relayed from satellite to satellite to reach its destination.

Hi-tech Conferences

Many companies use telecommunications in the office to conduct electronic meetings, including teleconferences and videoconferences. These forms of meetings reduce travel costs and losses in productivity that result from time spent away from the office.

Depending on the situation, teleconferences and videoconferences can be as effective or more effective than face-to-face meetings because they force people to be prepared. Realizing that every minute costs money, participants are motivated to be organized. However, these types of meetings are less valuable during creative sessions that require personal interaction.

Teleconferences

Teleconferences, also known as **conference calls**, are telecommunication-based meetings that use ordinary telephone lines to bring together three or more people at various locations. Services offered by your local telephone company can connect dozens of people to the same call. Teleconferences can involve local, national, or international calls. Office professionals will often find themselves arranging or participating in a teleconference.

Figure 9-8 Wireless telephone in use.
Courtesy of Rogers Cantel Inc.

To ensure a successful teleconference, always remember that you are part of a meeting involving many people. Here are some specific teleconferencing suggestions:

- If you are a single participant at your location during a teleconference, use a lightweight headset consisting of earphones and a built-in microphone. The headset allows you to move around the room with both hands free as you take notes or search through documents. It also averts fatigue during more lengthy teleconferences
- Identify yourself when speaking and direct your questions or comments to people by name.
- Remember that comments not specifically directed to an individual will be perceived as intended for the entire group.
- Speak naturally as you would during any telephone call but pause for others to comment.

Videoconference

Videoconferences are an important vehicle for collaborative office communication. Videoconferences allow participants in scattered geographic locations to see and hear one another on computer or television monitors (Figure 9-9) by way of images transmitted over telephone lines. This form of meeting can reduce employee travel costs between 20 to 50 percent of the normal cost of bringing people together.

Because videoconferences can connect people in many different locations, participants need special skills to communicate effectively. The following practical guidelines will help office professionals to improve communication during videoconferences. Here are several to consider:

- If your company offers a training session, take advantage of it. Familiarize yourself with the video conference room and its technology before your first meeting.
- Videoconferences transmitted over telephone lines have slight sound delays and images that may appear *choppy*. Participants must be careful listeners because these delays can make the communication more difficult.
- Introduce yourself at the start of a meeting and identify whom you are addressing throughout the conference. Remember that although the meeting may include many participants in various locations, the monitor displays only one location at a time.
- Be more deliberate or restrained in your gestures. Sudden arm and hand movements, for example, may seem exaggerated when transmitted.
- Be aware of body language, just as you are in a face-to-face meeting. Body language that might go unnoticed in a face-to-face meeting is magnified in a videoconference.
- Learn to speak directly to the camera, as if it were a person.
- Because the same microphone that carries your voice will also pick up sounds that you may not want amplified, avoid such distractions as tapping your fingers on the table, or laughing too loudly.

Figure 9-9 Video conference telephone.
Courtesy of Northern Telecom (Nortel)

- Prepare and rehearse anticipated questions by other participants.
- Prepare visual aids using large print sizes, with individual letters no smaller than one-fourth of an inch in height, and bold, simple drawings that contain only the essentials.
- Consider your visual appearance including clothing, grooming, cosmetics, poise, and physical position.

Telephone Message Systems

Organizations often make arrangements for the telephone to be answered after regular business hours or when it is inconvenient for employees to answer the telephone. Commonly used systems are automatic recording machines, answering services, and voice mail.

Automatic Recording Machines

With this system, a user can turn on a recorded message at the end of the business day. The message might tell callers when the office will be open and invite the callers to leave their number or a message. Sometimes customers can place orders at night by means of a recording device.

Answering Services

A telephone answering service is a switchboard attended by an operator who answers subscribers' telephones at designated hours. The operator takes messages, records numbers to be called, and judges whether or not to reach the subscriber during after-business hours. For example, the telephones of many doctors are answered after regular hours by telephone answering services.

If you work for a manager whose telephone is answered when nobody is in the office, one of your early-morning tasks may be to listen to the recording device and transcribe the messages, or to call a telephone answering service for messages.

Just as technology is transforming office administration, it is having a similar impact on telephone messaging. *Voice mail* and *electronic meetings* offer office professionals new tools for conducting more productive conversations and meetings.

Voice Mail

Voice mail is quickly replacing the answering machine as a device for handling telephone messages. **Voice mail** is a computer-based system that processes both incoming and outgoing telephone calls. Special computer chips and software convert the human voice into a digital recording that can be stored on the computer's magnetic storage. The recording can then be retrieved at any time for playback. Today, voice mail is a common method of messaging. Depending on the system, voice mail can help in the following ways:

- Voice mail is ensuring that no telephone calls are missed.
- Messages can be sent regardless of time zones or work schedules.
- Office professionals can leave recorded messages for anyone who has an access code. For example, if you are out of the office and want to leave details of a scheduled meeting, you can give those invited your access code and leave a descriptive voice mail message.
- Voice mail allows messages to be recorded and saved in a mailbox. A voice mail system can also forward messages to another location and/or to other office members.
- Voice mail messages can be sent to a number of people simultaneously.
- Voice mail can also serve as an automated telephone operator by answering calls with a standard recording.

Voice mail also handles telephone messages quickly and efficiently and, if used correctly, may eliminate the annoying practice of **telephone tag**. A caller can leave a detailed message that the receiver can listen to later.

> **PRO-LINK**
>
> ***pro-Link***
>
> Voice mail is both a productivity enhancer and a potential problem! Many companies establish voice mail policies to ask the fundamental question, "Do our customers really need to use voice mail in order to contact us?" Consider these concepts:
>
> - Customers may be uncomfortable speaking to a computer—many are!
> - Customers who still have rotary telephones will be excluded from using your voice mail—voice mail systems require touch-tone service.
> - Callers hear the same message each time they call—keep your greeting messages short.
> - Allow customers to chose an option at any time rather than have to listen to an entire list of choices first.
> - Research tells us that customers prefer to have a human contact first—the human can then ask if the customer wants to be connected to the voice mail system.
>
> What's your experience with voice mail?

However, voice mail has some disadvantages. Callers forced to listen to long messages can find the system annoying. Voice mail also delivers the implicit message that the caller's time is less valuable than the recipient's.

Because voice mail can now be delivered as a public telephone network service, telephone companies can provide many sophisticated voice mail features as a service. For example, voice mail can help employers deal with diversity in the workforce. The local telephone company can provide voice mail services in several different languages. A company's voice mail language of choice will provide workers and customers access to the company's voice mail without encountering a language barrier.

"Always smile and greet co-workers because smiles multiply and we can all use smiles."

Julia Young, Graduate
CompuCollege School of Business
Stephenville

While voice mail lacks the richness of direct communication, there are some fundamental practices that should be considered to improve voice mail interactions:

- Consider stating and changing the date of your greeting message on a daily basis. This provides the caller with information that you are, in fact, in touch with your voice mail system.
- Record an appropriate announcement on your greeting message when leaving for vacation or other extended periods of time when you will not be checking your e-mail for incoming messages.
- When leaving messages for others, state your name and phone number clearly and at a slow enough pace for transcription.
- State your message clearly and succinctly.
- Specify the action you wish to occur.
- Indicate when you will be available to receive a return call.
- Consider your tone of voice and impression that you are leaving with your message.
- Avoid leaving lengthy messages.

Figure 9-10 summarizes the various technologies for office professionals and identifies their primary uses.

Among the disadvantages of voice mail are these:

1. Callers often prefer to talk to a person rather than record a message on a machine.
2. Some users do not check their mailboxes regularly.
3. The recipient does not know that a message has come in unless the system has a signalling feature.

The features and functions of voice mail systems are improving rapidly. It must be noted that unless implemented correctly, the voice mail system will annoy and frustrate callers, with the result that business suffers. It is essential that proper procedures be put in place by any organization that employs voice mail. The following three practices will help minimize caller frustration:

1. Make it possible for the caller to speak to a representative of the company, in addition to being able to leave a message on the voice mail system.
2. Introduce organizational procedures for responding to voice mail in order to resolve the problem of messages not being collected or not being answered.
3. Ensure that all staff are fully trained to use the voice mail message system. When a system fails to meet its objectives, it is often because of inadequate staff training.

Telephone Systems

Organizations that depend upon many telephone calls require the use of an office switchboard. These switch-

Figure 9-10 Conference technology and its application.

Technology	Use
Teleconference	Conference by telephone with three or more participants.
Videoconference	Conference by transmitting video and audio of two or more people in remote locations.
Voice Mail	Manage incoming and outgoing phone calls. Send, receive, and record telephone messages.

boards are known as Private Branch Exchange (PBX), Private Automatic Branch Exchange (PABX), and Centrex. As an administrative assistant, you may never have to operate a large switchboard; even so, knowledge of how calls are handled within your organization will be valuable to you in placing calls rapidly and accurately.

Office Telephone Exchanges

The PBX provides exchange service for calls coming into and going out of the office. It also handles inside calls made between telephone extensions within the office. This type of exchange requires a full-time operator to handle incoming calls and to connect them with extensions within the office. Modern PBXs have a computer appearance and are simple to use.

The PABX provides its users with the ability to directly dial another extension without having to engage the operator. With this system (see Figure 9-11), the telephone user can also dial inside and outside numbers without operator intervention. To dial an outside number, an extension user listens for the dial tone, dials "9," listens for the second dial tone, and then dials the outside number. The PABX is capable of providing many computerized functions to office professionals. They include the following:

1. redialling busy lines automatically
2. redialling the last number that was connected
3. storing up to 30 numbers
4. informing a person that a call is waiting
5. enabling an administrative assistant to answer a telephone at someone else's desk by dialling a code, without leaving his or her desk
6. call forwarding to a preselected phone
7. allowing an administrative assistant to place a call on hold, place a second call to retrieve valuable information needed to complete the first call, and then return to the original caller.

Figure 9-11 Private Automatic Branching Exchange (PABX) attendant console.
Courtesy of Mitel Corporation

Centrex

Central exchange, or *Centrex*, provides direct dialling to an office extension without assistance from an operator. Centrex is used by organizations that have many telephone extensions. The main feature of the Centrex service is *Direct Inward Dialling* (DID).

Both local and long-distance calls can be dialled directly to any Centrex station. In addition to dialling their own internal calls, Centrex station users can dial outside calls, both local and long-distance.

Every telephone within a Centrex system has its own seven-digit number. The extension number for each Centrex telephone forms the last part of the outside number. When you do not know the Centrex number for the person you are calling, dial the organization's number and give the person's name to the operator. When the operator gives you the number of the Centrex station, write it down, because Centrex numbers are not listed in the public telephone directory.

Dial a Centrex number instead of the organization's number to save time. You can also save money on long-distance calls, because your call to a Centrex number is placed point-to-point.

Telecommunications Services

In Canada and the United States, it is not uncommon to find a variety of *telephone services* provided to the office or home. North America is both the leading developer of innovative telecommunications services and the largest consumer of those services. However, no matter how innovative a service may be, all telecommunication services can be categorized as one of the following:

1. voice
2. data
3. wireless.

Voice Services

Probably the most common of services is voice (as it is known in the telecommunications industry). Sophisticated voice networks provide the telephone services we are most familiar with—and possibly take for granted. Voice service is characterized by telephone sets, a dial tone, and the international telephone network, which enables us to talk to other people around the world. Voice services may be as simple as a single, featureless desk telephone, or as complicated as a computerized switching system with every conceivable feature, designed to handle many calls.

Voice services are either *inbound* or *outbound*. Outbound services are originated and paid for by the caller. Each call made from your office or home is an example of an outbound voice call.

Inbound services include calls made by someone calling into your home or office, at your company's expense. These services are commonly known as 1-800 services, or toll-free services. These services are only "toll-free" to the caller; the subscribing company must cover the cost. The use of traditional 1-800 numbers has reached a saturation point; for this reason, telephone companies are now providing a new series of toll-free numbers starting with 1-888.

Inbound, toll-free services are typically employed by companies for customer service, information provision, and help numbers.

The facsimile machine, while not a true voice communication device, can operate on telephone networks designed mainly for voice communications.

Data Services

In addition to the familiar voice services, most offices will have some form of data service connection to their office. Data services are those which are designed to provide a telecommunications network for information you transmit from and receive through your office computer system. While some low-speed data transfer may occur over the voice network, data integrity and reliability is not guaranteed by the telephone companies.

Special telephone lines with data-handling equipment are used for public data networks. These networks may support a single point-to-point computer connection, or they may be the **backbone** of several networks connected together to form a wide area network.

Wireless Services

As the name implies, wireless services are those telecommunication services that are not dependent on terrestrial wires and cables for their main transmission network. Instead, radio waves are used to deliver the services. Wireless services include microwave systems, radio broadcast and reception, wireless telephone services, and direct-to-home television services. Emerging wireless technology has provided us with **personal communications systems** (PCS), and with local area networks that are connected without wires.

THE INTERNET

The most popular method of communicating and researching information is the Internet. The Internet is a public global communications network that enables people to exchange information through a computer.

Infrastructure of the Internet

The popularized Internet is a collection of independent computer networks interconnected by a telecommunications data network. The telecommunications data network employs **routers**, which are devices that route information from one network to another. Routers allow independent networks to function as a large **virtual network** so that users of any network can reach users of any other.

While there are many private commercial computer networks, the Internet is the largest collection of networks in the world. Some examples of Canadian networks that are attached to the Internet are:

- *ACJNet*. This acronym stands for Access to Canadian Justice Network. This particular network provides Canadian justice and legal information and services, including legislation, publications, and discussion forums.
- *Rock Radio Network*. This network is an interactive service that provides the *Rock Report*, *Rockline*, and information on many more radio shows.
- *NetWorks*. NetWorks is a company with information for small and home-based businesses.
- *NewsWorld OnLine*. This network provides text and video clips from the Canadian news network.

Unlike traditional voice or data networks, there is no charge for the long-distance component of the Internet. There is also no charge for exchanging information on the Internet. However, your Internet provider will charge users a fee for the local connection to the Internet.

Uses for the Internet

What can you do with the Internet? Basically, there are five activities that people participate in on the Internet:

1. sending and receiving electronic mail
2. transferring data files
3. joining discussion groups
4. performing remote computing
5. researching topics of interest.

Internet mail is the same as e-mail, which was discussed in Chapter 4. It is electronic text that can be addressed to another Internet user anywhere on the global network.

Data file transfers allow Internet users to access remote computers and retrieve programs or text. Many

PERSPECTIVES

Cruising the Information Superhighway

By Richard G. Ensman Jr.

Take this tour of the Internet and learn how to use tomorrow's technology today.

Pick up any national news magazine these days and you'll read all about the "Information Superhighway." From discussions of sophisticated fiber optic communication networks to the anticipated proliferation of cable television stations to vast electronic libraries, the superhighway seems to be on everyone' lips.

In conceptual terms, the superhighway—at least as presented by many of the world's communications conglomerates and the media—will be a massive electronic network, offering an array of entertainment, shopping, information, and communication services to homes and businesses via computer or some futuristic version of the television set. When will this superhighway be built? It's coming soon, say the communications experts—by 1998, 1999, or early in the next century, they insist.

But, hold on. The Information Superhighway—at least a version of the Superhighway—already exists. It's called the *Internet*, a huge network of computer-based information and communication resources accessible to almost anyone with a computer. Whether the Internet will be the precursor to the Superhighway of tomorrow, or will remain an electronic roadway in its own right, the Internet of today helps us understand what the Information Superhighway will be like.

Paving the road

The Internet wasn't formed as a highly accessible superhighway. It was originally established by the U.S. Defense Department in the late 1960s as a defense research network and a fail-safe communication system that could be fully activated in the event of war or public emergency. The Internet was, and is, nothing more than a collection of huge supercomputers, telephone cable, and satellite transmission systems that relay data to and from thousands of points across the globe.

It's important to remember from the outset that the Internet isn't a "network" in the conventional sense. Rather, it's a "network of networks"; the Internet consists of some 8,000 to 10,000 different computer services and networks, operated by government, industry, and not-for-profit organizations. Just as traditional highways can be accessed by a variety of secondary roads and access ramps, the Internet can be accessed through any of these networks by anyone with a computer, modem, and telephone line. As a consequence, its use has broadened considerably since the late 1960s. Today, educational institutions, business firms, researchers, computer buffs, and people from just about every walk of life use the Internet as a communication and information-retrieval tool.

Traveling the highway

Once you're connected to the Internet, you're part of an electronic community consisting of well over 15 million users. You have access to an estimated 10,000 information sources and databases covering every field of human endeavor. You can, at least in theory, gain access to libraries and experts in more than 50 nations around the globe.

Connect to the Internet, and you'll gain the ability to communicate with other users through electronic mail. You'll have the ability to transfer computer files to other Internet users around the world. You'll be able to search information sources for articles, graphics, and even original research materials—and, frequently, pull the full text of the material into your own computer system with the touch of a few keystrokes. In short, you'll travel today's Information Superhighway—the most powerful information resource known to mankind in the 1990s.

Planning an Internet trip

Because no one "owns" the Internet, you can't obtain an Internet "account" or "subscription." You can't even obtain an official "road map" to this vast superhighway.

For starters, though, all you need for a cruise on the Internet is a computer, a telephone, a modem, and Internet access. "Access" simply means that a network operator—a business, an educational institution, or an online information service such as CompuServe, American Online, or Delphi, for instance—has assigned you an Internet "address," or code, which enables you to send and receive information via the network.

Access is much easier to obtain than you think. If you're affiliated with an educational institution or major corporation, ask if you can obtain an Internet address; you'll probably be able to do so at no charge. Some colleges and universities offer "guest accounts" on their computer systems to community residents for a small fee; these guest accounts usually can be used to access the Internet. Some metropolitan communities offer full or limited Internet access via not-for-profit communication or computing organizations or library systems. Look for a local access source, which will ultimately save you costly long-distance telephone charges.

If you can't find a local organization that will provide you with access, you can easily subscribe to an online service.

Your Internet address will consist of "domains"—a series of numbers and letters that identify you, your host computer, the organization providing you with access, and the national affiliation of the organization. You'll use this address to enter and navigate through the Internet.

Maps and road signs

The Internet, remember, is an amalgamation of thousands of different computers, organizations, and networks. It's not a menu-driven service that provides quick-and-easy access to every destination in the network, and there's no one to call for advice when you get lost on your Internet trip.

You see, no one "governs" the Internet. While the volunteer-driven Internet Society attempts to establish guidelines and protocols for Internet use, it doesn't have the authority or resources to make hard-and-fast rules, approve or disapprove of the content offered by the networks comprising the Internet, or even build up-to-the-minute "road signs," directing casual users to the breath-taking variety of destinations on the superhighway.

So, let's say you have access to the Internet. How do you find your way around? Here are a few suggestions:

- *Use one of the commercially published "Internet guidebooks."* These books list many of the popular Internet destinations and provide the appropriate addresses. But these books can quickly become out of date since Internet offerings and addresses change constantly and no one routinely reports these changes to any central authority.
- *Join an Internet discussion group.* These discussion groups, or "listservs," consist of 100, 200, or even several thousand people who are interested in a particular topic and systematically exchange ideas, data, and chatter with each other through an elaborate computer bulletin board and E-mail system. If you belong to a group on international marketing, for instance, you'll almost certainly hear about a wide variety of Internet destinations that deal with this topic from other members of the group.
- *Navigate with "gophers."* These electronic gateways provide simple menus to sections of the Internet, directing you to your destination quickly and efficiently. Usually set up at specific Internet locations or "nodes," like government offices, universities, or business libraries, they allow you to navigate through topical collections or resources without a lot of guesswork or Internet knowledge. A number of businesses and universities are developing other forms of menu-driven access tools; these will undoubtedly become much more common in the years ahead.

As you become more proficient in navigating the Internet, you'll accumulate a collection of addresses of special interest to you. Besides locating addresses as the result of your own Internet travel, you'll find them in computer publications, professional meetings, and even routine business correspondence. Friends or acquaintances may pass Internet addresses along to you. All of these addresses could—and should—become part of your personal Internet address book. They'll allow you to get to your destination of choice within a matter of seconds.

The Internet is a vast network of electronic roads, boulevards, dead ends, and circles that seemingly take you everywhere—and nowhere. The more addresses you collect, the easier your Internet trips will be.

Reprinted courtesy of OfficePRO.

computers connected to the Internet can access public data files anonymously and copy them free of charge.

A discussion group or newsgroup is a collection of users who exchange news and debate issues of interest. There are many thousands of separate newsgroups on the Internet.

Remote computing can be done by those programmers and scientists who need the power of remote computers, or for those who need to tap large information databases.

Collectively, these functions allow students and business professionals alike to research topics of interest. Clearly, the Internet supplements more familiar resources, such as books and periodicals.

Growth of the Internet

We have experienced rapid growth, faster service, and easier access to seemingly bottomless sources of information. Some futuristic activities are already possible—shopping through electronic malls, placing telephone calls, watching videos, and so on. No doubt these activities will be enhanced in the near future.

The phenomenal success of the Internet is stirring a great deal of discussion. Business users want the Internet to be more financially viable; academics want the Internet to be more intellectually oriented; and each level of government has an interest in regulating the Internet. However, the federal governments of Canada and the United States have recognized the value of the Internet in the delivery of education and social programs, and in regional communications. Both governments have committed themselves, financially and otherwise, to upgrading the telecommunications backbone to allow the mass transfer of data.

Future Internet services may well include high-definition television, 3-D animated graphics, and radio

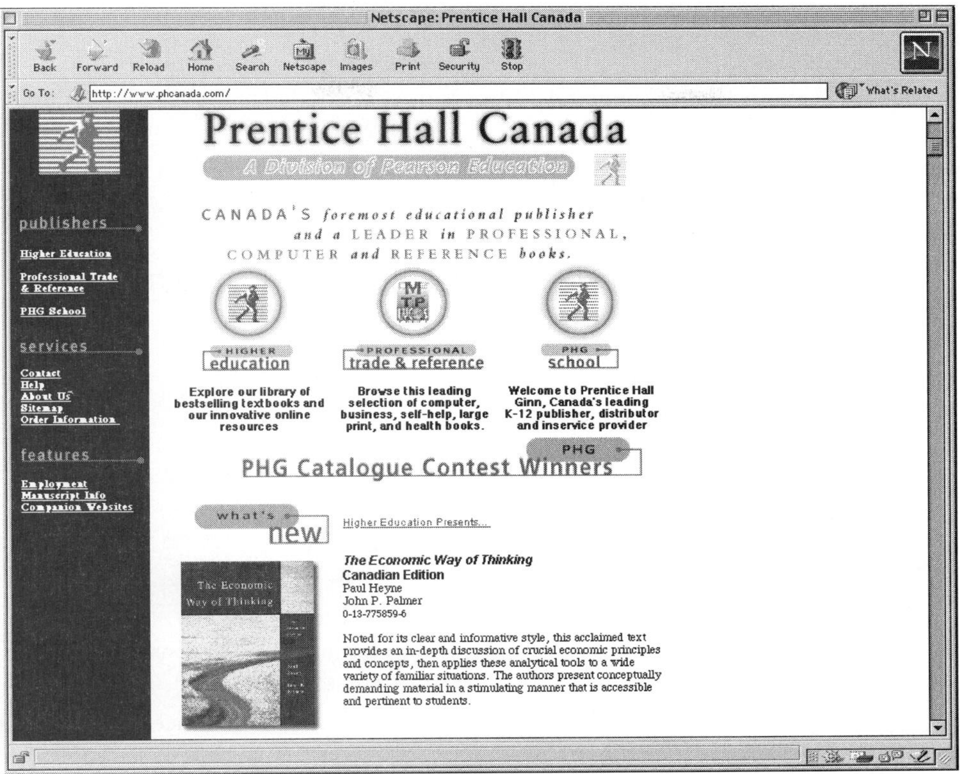

Figure 9-12 Prentice Hall Canada Homepage.

and wireless telephone links to portable computers. As well, the Internet will become more accessible, and part of daily life for more and more people.

Getting Connected

To join the Internet, you need a computer, a modem, and an ordinary voice-quality telephone line. With those, you will be able to establish an e-mail address, join newsgroups, and tap into endless information resources. Your local Internet service provider (ISP) will supply the software you need to use the connection.

Internet Connections

If you need to find out whether a computer site has an Internet connection, there are a number of reliable sources you can consult. Three published directories are:

- *A Directory of Electronic Mail Addressing and Networks* by Donnalyn Frey and Rick Adams
- *The User's Directory of Computer Networks* by Tracy LaQuey
- *The Matrix: Computer Networks and Conferencing Systems Worldwide* by John Quarterman.

World Wide Websites

All-In-One Search Page

www.albany.net/allinone/all1www.html#WWW
Easy access to an enormous number of search engines can be found on this Web page.

Excite's Internet Tours Menu

tours.excite.com/go.webx?14@@/Tours/Computing/
Users take tours of many Internet topics. Included are 11 "New to the Net?" tours on topics such as getting online, choosing an ISP, introduction to e-mail, and what the Web actually is.

Hobbes' Internet Timeline

info.isoc.org/guest/zakon/Internet/History/HIT.html
This timeline gives a history of the Internet.

Internet FAQs and How to Choose an ISP

www.oasisnm.com/isp.html
Visit this site for lots of basic information about the Internet.

Searching for Information on the Internet

www.netskills.ac.uk/resources/searching/search1/search1.html
This article includes many links to search-related topics.

Windows 95 Software Library

www.microsoft.com/windows/software.htm
Shareware and freeware are available on the Internet at this site.

WWW FAQs

www.boutell.com/faq/#intro
Browse frequently asked questions about the World Wide Web, including what it is, what a URL is, and how to access the Web.

More websites can be found on page 198.

Questions for Study and Review

1. How are the Yellow Pages arranged?
2. How are government offices listed in a telephone directory?
3. Where can you find telephoning policies and procedures to be followed within the organization in which you work?
4. What information is essential for adequately identifying yourself when you are placing a telephone call?
5. Why is the time a telephone call was received an important part of a telephone message?
6. Who should terminate a telephone call?
7. Distinguish between telephone messages that should be written in longhand and those that should be keyed.
8. When you are transferring a call, why should you give the caller the name and number of the person to whom the caller is being transferred?
9. Describe what to do when two telephones ring at the same time and you are the only person in the office.
10. Under what conditions would you interrupt your manager to take a telephone call while a visitor is in your manager's office?
11. What is meant by Direct Distance Dialling?
12. For what point-to-point calls is operator assistance needed?
13. Explain how to obtain long-distance directory assistance.
14. Name six ways in which voice mail can enable the administrative assistant to become more efficient in the office.
15. What are your responsibilities when you answer a point-to-point call?
16. Describe how to place an overseas call for which no operator assistance is required. Then describe how to place an overseas call for which operator assistance is required.
17. Why would the key telephone be appropriate for a small business?
18. Where might you see a wireless telephone being used?
19. What is the difference between a telephone recording device and an answering service?
20. Discuss two advantages to an office that employs videoconferencing telephones.
21. Does voice mail eliminate "telephone tag"? Why or why not?
22. State eight ways that voice mail interactions may be improved.
23. Discuss two disadvantages of voice mail.
24. Offer three guidelines for adopting voice mail to ensure that voice mail will be effective and efficient in the office.
25. What do the letters PABX represent? State four features of PABX.
26. What are the three broad categories of telephone services?
27. Describe the main feature of the Centrex service.
28. Discuss a practical application of the Internet that would be used by an office professional.

Spelling Reinforcement

accommodate	determine	implemented	projecting
adjacent	distinctly	initiates	recorded
computerized	document	interconnect	similar
conventional	entirety	international	suppliers
courteous	extension	manufacturers	terminate

On-the-Job Situations

1. During your first job performance appraisal, you were criticized for the way you answer the telephone. You have been asking the caller to state the purpose of the call before you say whether or not your manager is in the office. After you find out who the caller is and the purpose of the call, you say, "Mrs. Burke is not in her office," or "Mrs. Burke is in a meeting." It is true that Mrs. Burke is not in her office when you say this, but apparently the callers are not convinced. What can you do to improve rapport with the callers?
2. You know that your manager, Mr. Perkins, is expecting an important long-distance call. He called Mike Brendl at 0930 and he is expecting Mr. Brendl to return his call. At 1630, Mr. Perkins was called to the president's office. A few minutes after Mr. Perkins left his office, Mr. Brendl calls. You feel that you should not interrupt Mr. Perkins in the president's office. You do not know whether Mr. Perkins will return to his desk before 1700. What should you do? Do you have any alternatives?

Special Reports

1. Use the Yellow Pages of your local telephone directory to determine how the following are classified: educational services (public schools, private schools, colleges and universities), food catering services, medical doctors (general practitioners and specialists), furniture for an office, office stationery, office computers, and airlines. Prepare a list and submit it to your instructor.
2. Refer to the introductory pages of the local telephone directory. Make a list of the information provided in these pages. Submit the list to your instructor.

Production Challenges

9-A Receiving Telephone Calls

Supplies needed:

- *Telephone message blanks*
- *Forms 9-A-1, 9-A-2, 9-A-3, and 9-A-4, page 414*

When your managers are in their offices, they answer their own telephones. Today, August 11, Mr. Wilson, Mr. Rush, and Mr. Levine are not in their offices. You receive the following telephone calls:

0915—for Mr. Rush from Archie Sellars, 683-4750. He wants to know if parts are available for an electric range, Model 1621. Please return his call.

1030—for Mr. Levine from A.L. Wilcox, 442-8761, about a printing order Mr. Levine placed with him. Urgent. Please call.

1100—for Mr. Wilson from Mr. Arnett, 366-8184, a speaker for the November Sales Seminar. He has a business conflict and cannot attend the seminar on Wednesday. Please call.

1115—for Mr. Wilson from Personnel Department, Extension 5738, asking, "When can Mr. Wilson see an applicant?" Please call.

9-B Placing Telephone Calls

Supplies needed:

- *Pages from your telephone notebook*
- *Forms 9-B-1 and 9-B-2, page 415*

Mr. Wilson asked you to place some telephone calls. Here is Mr. Wilson's conversation with you:

"Mr. Arnett, (366-8184), who was scheduled to speak at the November Sales Conference on Wednesday, November 12, at 1000, cannot attend the Sales Seminar on Wednesday. He has an important business conflict. He is substituting for his manager who had a heart attack and will not return to work for at least six months. Mr. Arnett must be in his Toronto office on November 12. He can attend the Seminar on Monday and Tuesday.

"Find a speaker who can trade times with Mr. Arnett. Call James Epstein in Winnipeg, at 690-8699, who is scheduled to talk at 1400 on Monday. If he can't do it, ask Ruth Agway in Vancouver, at 487-3232, who is scheduled to speak at 1100 on Monday. Another possibility is Ray Morris from Margate, in England. Mr. Morris is a special guest on a panel on Tuesday afternoon. He may wish to stay over and speak in place of Mr. Arnett before flying back to England. Mr. Morris's number in England is 01843–386126.

"Be sure to call Mr. Arnett and tell him what arrangements you have made.

"Be sure to make the proper notations in the official copy of the program. It is necessary to write a confirmation letter to the person whose time is changed."

NOTE: When you called Mr. Epstein, he said he could not attend the seminar on Wednesday.

Before you place any calls, use a page or two in your telephone notebook to plan your calls. Record all essential information, such as names, telephone numbers, dates, and times of day. Also jot down reminders about what you need to do after you have found someone who can trade times to speak with Mr. Arnett.

9-C Telephone Services

Supplies needed:

- *A local telephone directory*
- *Questions on telephone services, Forms 9-C-1 and 9-C-2, pages 416 and 417.*

Use a local telephone directory to complete the questions on pages 416 and 417.

World Wide Websites

Big Dummy's Guide to the Internet

http:/nas.com/bdgtti.htm
This guide for beginners includes sections on how to get hooked up, e-mail, usenet, telnet, FTP, and the World Wide Web.

Canadian Internet Service Providers

maplesquare.sympatico.ca/aw/isp-sym.asp
Users gain access to national and provincial lists of Canadian ISPs.

Information Highways Magazine

www.flexnet.com/~infohiwy/
This on-line magazine is dedicated exclusively to helping businesses and professionals take advantage of electronic information, including the Internet.

Maple Square

maplesquare.sympatico.ca/
Canada's Internet directory can be found at Maple Square.

Search.com

www.search.com/
Search.com is a Net-searching megasite.

Yahoo! Canada—Computers and the Internet

www.yahoo.ca/computers_and_internet/internet/
Access links to many topics, including business and economics, communications and networking, electronic mail, magazines, mailing lists, and resources.

Yahoo! Canada—History of the Internet

www.yahoo.ca/computers_and_internet/internet/history/
This site has links to many sites on the history of the Internet.

Travel Arrangements

Outline

Planning the Trip
Internet Travel Services
Travel Department
Travel Agencies
Trip Information Needed

Arranging the Travel
Air Travel
Car Rental Services
Hotel and Motel Reservations
Perspectives: "When in Rome . . ."
Passports
Visas
Immunization Requirements

Following Through
Prior to the Trip
During the Manager's Absence
After the Manager Returns

Learning Outcomes

At the completion of this chapter, the student will be able to:

1. List the services provided by the Internet, travel departments, and travel agencies.
2. Indicate the information needed before contacting a travel agent about a proposed trip.
3. Describe the procedures for making flight, car, and hotel reservations.
4. Interpret a flight schedule.
5. State the requirements for acquiring passports, visas, and immunizations.
6. Outline administrative responsibilities before, during, and after an executive's trip.
7. Make an airline reservation.
8. Prepare and key an itinerary.
9. Prepare a travel fund advance.
10. Prepare a travel expense voucher.

GRADUATE PROFILE

Brian Ellis
Administrative Assistant

Quality Certification Bureau Inc.

College Graduation:
Office Administration Program
Northern Alberta Institute of Technology
Edmonton, Alberta
1997

A strong work ethic, keen administrative skills, and proven leadership qualities are what have contributed to Brian Ellis' success. Being flexible enough to handle a myriad of administrative responsibilities and ready to embrace new challenges makes Brian an excellent office professional.

While at college, he managed to remain on the Dean's Honour Roll, while being President of the Office Administration Association, and leading United Way campaigns. At the same time, he participated in an active life outside school as a jazz musician.

After graduating from the Northern Alberta Institute of Technology, Brian worked with the National Band of the Naval Reserve. As Drum Major, Brian went on tour and led the band at concerts and parades, and was responsible for their discipline, drill, dress, and deportment. He also worked as Inventory Control Manager for a national liquidation company where he managed a multimillion dollar inventory. According to Brian, "Every experience you can get is vital to your career."

Brian's philosophy of work is that you should take your career very seriously; however, he believes that leading an active and happy life is equally important. Having this type of balance in his life, Brian has a positive and optimistic spirit that allows him to provide top-quality customer service at work.

"My future is exciting and promising."

In his time away from his career, Brian continues to be an accomplished musician with the Canadian Armed Forces. He performs with a successful rhythm and blues band, the Chain of Fools, and somehow finds time to play hockey, weight train, and run.

Anyone who works as an administrative assistant will eventually encounter the responsibility of making travel arrangements. If you work for management who travels, you should become thoroughly familiar with the organization's travel policies; know what travel accommodations are available and how to schedule them to meet the executive's preferences; assist the executive in making the best use of her or his time while in the office; and keep the office running smoothly while the executive is away.

PLANNING THE TRIP

Before you proceed to make travel arrangements, ask questions about the policies and procedures followed within the organization. For example:

- Who is responsible for making travel arrangements?
- Is there a travel department?
- Do designated administrative assistants handle the travel arrangements for all the executives of the organization?
- If the services of a travel agency are used, which agency?
- Are the executives expected to fly business class or economy class, or can the executive decide?
- What is the policy concerning the use of private cars and car rental services?
- Does the organization have a preference for a particular airline?
- If so, what are the policies for using it?
- How are payments for reservations handled?
- What is the procedure for getting a cash advance for a traveller?

As soon as you have answers to a few of these questions, you will know whether to turn the arrangements over to someone else or make them yourself. Regardless of who makes the arrangements, request all reservations far enough in advance to ensure that you obtain the accommodations desired.

Internet Travel Services

The Internet offers an abundance of information that will help the administrative assistant plan business trips.

By searching the **website** of a travel service company, the administrative assistant may access information regarding

- the company's background
- customs and immigration
- tourism
- flight schedules
- latest pricing
- telephone numbers
- travel tips
- e-mail, fax, and postal mailing addresses

Some travel companies provide e-mail forms so that the subscriber may communicate with the travel service company directly through the Internet; others offer subscribers the ability to book their own reservations directly through the Internet. At the time, reservations may be made on the Internet. The subscriber pays for the tickets with a credit card number and the ticket voucher is either faxed to the subscriber or the tickets are picked up at a local travel agent or the airport.

Travel Department

Many organizations have a travel department (sometimes called the transportation department) that plans itineraries and makes all types of travel and hotel reservations for the employees. The staff of the travel department works on-line with travel agencies, airline carriers, hotels, and all other travel services.

"The most important factor to having a successful office team is trust in each other."

Jacinthe Lemire, Graduate
CompuCollege School of Business
Fredericton

To request the services of your organization's travel department, call the department and give the date of departure, the destination, the return date, and any special consideration that the manager has indicated. Someone in the travel department will prepare the possible schedules that are available through the carriers and will submit them to you for approval. Always try to deal with the same member of the travel department until the arrangements are completed.

Travel Agencies

If your organization does not have a travel department, you must make the travel arrangements yourself. If the arrangements you are to make involve a nonstop or direct flight and accommodations at a hotel with which you are familiar, you will be able to make the arrangements and obtain the confirmations with a couple of telephone calls—one to the airline and one to the hotel.

If your organization does not have a travel department and the arrangements are complicated, use the services of a travel agent. You will definitely need the services of a travel agent when you make arrangements for international travel; you will find that working through a travel agent is the easiest and best way to make arrangements for domestic travel as well.

Travel agents receive their commissions from the airlines, hotels, and other organizations whose services they sell. The travel agent will not charge your organization for services.

You will have a choice of several local travel agencies. They are listed in the classified section of the telephone directory. If you are concerned about finding a reputable travel agency, call the Better Business Bureau or the Alliance of Canadian Travel Associations (ACTA) in Ottawa, or check the Internet for a listing of ACTA members. ACTA's membership includes travel agents in all major Canadian cities. The standards and the code of ethics of ACTA are both high; the group's members are reliable and efficient. However, not all reputable travel agents are members of ACTA.

Most travel agents are approved by the International Air Transportation Association (IATA). IATA is a conglomerate of international airlines. It grants approval to use its insignia to travel agencies that meet its stringent requirements. An agency seeking IATA's approval must have a solid reputation, as well as the financial backing to ensure its own stability.

Travel agencies maintain up-to-date information on all airline schedules and hotel accommodations. Travel agents, because of their experience, can obtain information faster than an individual, and can often get better service when making reservations.

Figure 10-1 Travel department employee accessing on-line travel information.

Many travel agents refer to the computerized online version of the Official Hotel Guide (OHG). This is a comprehensive international listing and description of accommodation.

A travel agent will plan your manager's trip around the style of accommodations requested and will provide the most satisfactory arrangements possible. The travel agent represents *all* the transportation lines, hotels, and motels, not just certain ones. You, of course, must provide the travel agent with all the details needed. When planning a trip, try to deal with only one person at the agency, and rely on that person to prepare the complete package.

The travel agent will make out the itinerary, procure tickets, make hotel reservations, arrange for car rental, and perform other services related to the trip.

For foreign travel, travel agents perform many other services. They provide information about how much luggage is allowed, furnish guidebooks for the countries being visited, inform you of currency restrictions, and tell you about regulations for bringing foreign purchases through Canadian Customs.

Trip Information Needed

As soon as the manager mentions a trip, start compiling information. Before you contact the travel department, a travel agent, or a carrier, compile the details concerning

1. the destination
2. intermediate stops, either going or returning or both
3. date of departure and date of return
4. date and time of the first business appointment and the time needed between arrival and the appointment
5. preferred time of day for travel
6. method of travel—air, rail, bus, automobile
7. type of service—business class, economy class, and so on
8. hotel preference or the desired location of the hotel within the city
9. need for transportation at the destination or at intermediate stops
10. if car rental is involved, the make of car preferred.

For use in planning future trips, maintain a folder labelled TRIP PREFERENCES. When your employer returns from a trip, make comments about the transportation and hotel accommodations on a copy of the agenda for the trip. Keep in this folder the manager's comments, and all other information that will help you recall preferences when you are planning another trip to the same city or part of the country. If you plan trips for more than one manager, maintain a Trip Preferences folder for each one.

ARRANGING THE TRAVEL

Making transportation arrangements for international travel is similar to making transportation arrangements for domestic travel. An additional factor to take into account when planning international travel is the effect of a long trip through different time zones on the traveller. Refer to Chapter 9 for a discussion of time zones around the world. When planning an overseas trip, allow an adequate rest period following arrival in the country to be visited and following the return home.

To make travel arrangements with ease, you should know about air travel services and other types of transportation, including car rental services; how to make hotel and motel reservations; how to obtain passports and visas; and what is involved in meeting immunization requirements.

Air Travel

Because many managers are required to fly to meetings in different cities, you need to be well informed about air travel services.

Sources of Air Travel Information

You can obtain air travel information about a specific trip by telephoning a local airline. In addition to giving you information over the telephone you can pick up an airline schedule at the office of the airline. All this information is easily accessible on the Internet.

PRO LINK

pro-Link

Dreaming of faraway places? Cruising the Internet to make your arrangements to visit them? It's interesting to know that only a small percentage of businesses rely on booking travel arrangements through the Internet. Why?

- Many offices don't trust the Internet for something as important as booking flights and hotels.
- It's easier to make a single telephone call to a travel agent and let the agent do the rest of the work.

The reluctance by businesses to use the Internet for travel arrangements is not likely to change dramatically until airlines and hotels offer greater incentives such as reduced prices to Internet bookers.

Figure 10-2 General information guide.
Courtesy of Canadian Transportation Agency

As well, the Canadian Transportation Agency has made available a free brochure of general information about air travel. See Figure 10-2.

Types of Flights

Flights that encounter the fewest delays and inconveniences are considered to be the most desirable. Therefore, when making travel arrangements, consider the flights available in this order:

1. a nonstop flight from point of departure to destination
2. a direct flight—regardless of the number of stops en route, the passenger remains on the same plane from departure to destination
3. a flight connecting with another flight of the same airline
4. a flight connecting with another flight of another airline.

When a passenger changes aircraft without changing airlines, the gate for the connecting flight will be near the deplaning gate. The distance between the boarding gates of two different airlines at a major airport can be great, and walking or being shuttled from one gate to another is time-consuming. If the first flight is delayed, the passenger may not have enough time to get to the connecting flight.

Because delays cannot be predicted, use wise judgment when making reservations; if the traveller must make a connection, allow adequate time between the flights. Remember that many cities have two airports. A connection between two different airports in the same city can take two hours, or even longer. Think of the activities involved: deplaning, getting transportation to the second airport, and locating and boarding the next flight.

Commuter flights are short direct flights between two neighbouring cities. These neighbouring cities need not be in the same province, but they must be close enough that significant numbers of travellers use the service as a convenience. There are commuter services between Vancouver and Victoria, Edmonton and Calgary, Toronto and Ottawa, and various other Canadian cities. Many business travellers rely on commuter flights to meet with clients or colleagues in neighbouring cities. These flights leave frequently—often every hour. Although reservations are recommended, they are often not required because of the frequent schedules.

Classes of Service

The services passengers receive aboard the plane—especially where they sit and the food and beverages served—are purchased by class of service. The basic classes of service are business class and economy class. The priority services for business class travelling include expeditious check-in and boarding as well as additional comfort and service during the flight.

Some organizations require their executives to fly business class, because it is considered more prestigious and because it provides wider seats with more leg room and working room—an important consideration on long flights. Other organizations, for obvious financial reasons, require their executives to purchase economy service.

Classes of service are designated by standard reference symbols in the airline schedules and on the tickets. When you make travel arrangements verify the class of service by reading the symbol on the ticket.

Flight Reservations

You can make a flight reservation yourself by telephone, in person, or on-line. Call the airline reservations office or go in person either to the airport terminal office or to the local ticket office of the specific airline. If you book the reservation through your computer, you must still pay for your tickets and receive them either over your fax, through the mail, or by picking them up at your travel agency, the airline office, or the airport.

Before you contact the airline reservations office, collect all the trip information you need for making a flight reservation. The reservations agent will be using a computer system that stores all the reservations. The agent will establish whether the space you want is available. If it is, make the reservation during the initial contact. When the traveller does not know the return date, purchase an **open ticket**. As soon as the traveller knows the return date, call the agent and make the reservation on a particular flight.

If space is not available on the flight you want, proceed with alternative plans. While you are talking with the reservations clerk, inquire about earlier and later flights with the same airline and with other airlines. If you do not select an alternative flight, ask that the manager's name be placed on a waiting list in case there is a cancellation on the flight desired.

Reconfirmation of airline reservations is required on international flights. The traveller should reconfirm reservations for each leg of the trip.

Cost of Tickets and Payment

The fares for all scheduled intra-Canadian airline flights are now deregulated. However, the National Transportation Agency of Canada still evaluates tariffs and monitors competitive economy fares between Canadian destinations. International fares are regulated by IATA based on bilateral agreements between international carriers. Fares may vary minimally between major Canadian airline companies. However, one company may offer a seat sale or an excursion fare. In order to compete, some smaller airline companies are offering *no-frills flights* for reduced prices. Another way to capture savings, is to make reservations well in advance when significant savings can be made.

Only one ticket is issued when more than one airline is involved. The airline with which the flight originates makes out the ticket for the entire trip, including the return trip if it is requested.

However, spontaneous travel plans are more common for business travellers. In this situation the executive does not have time to wait for tickets to arrive via the mail service. The administrative assistant makes the plans directly with the airline or a travel agent, using a credit card to cover the cost. Where speed is important, the administrative assistant can pick the tickets up at the local airline office or travel agency, or have them sent by courier to the company office. The traveller may even pick up the tickets at the airport prior to check-in.

When a passenger must change travel plans or cancel a reservation, the passenger should call the nearest reservations office of the airline at once. Unused airline tickets and unused portions are sometimes redeemable where full fares have been paid.

Timetables

No two airline timetables are identical. Yet timetables are easy to read when you know what to look for. Most carriers publish hardcopies of timetables and update them frequently. Unfortunately, timetables change so often that the printed ones are often inaccurate. This is why on-line timetable information is preferable to a hardcopy version.

If you *do* need to read a printed airline schedule, start by studying the legend. See Figure 10-3. Once you understand the legend, use the schedule to find

1. the departure city and the time zone it is in
2. the destination city and the time zone it is in
3. the time of departure and arrival shown in 24-hour clock time. If a city has more than one airport, a letter following the time will indicate the airport of arrival

Days	Dep	Arr	Flight(s)	Stop
HALIFAX/ DARTMOUTH (Continued)				
CHICAGO (Continued)				
	1440	1810	AC195-AC727	C
X6	1655	2013	AC149-AC729	C
CINCINNATI				
X6	1445	2032	*AC8893*-CO551	C
		5.9◆		
CLEVELAND				
6	0628	1025	AC603-*AC1453*	C
X67	0815	1200	AC605-*AC1453*	C
	1105	1505	AC109-*AC1457*	C
	1440	1835	AC195-*AC1463*	C
X67	1655	2125	AC149-*AC1467*	C
6	1655	2140	AC149-*AC1469*	C
7	1655	2020	AC149-*AC1467*	C
DAYTONA BEACH				
	1445	2244	*AC8893*-CO1197	C
		5.9◆		
DEER LAKE/CORNER BROOK				
X67	1050	1255	*AC8828*	-
67	1050	1230	*AC8880*	-
		5.9◆		
67	1050	1255	*AC8828*	-
◆11.9				
X6	1420	1625	*AC8826*	-
6	1420	1625	*AC8826*	-
		4.9◆		
	1705	1910	*AC8824*	-
X6	2130	2335	*AC8830*	-
		3.9◆		
DENVER				
	1040	1603	*AC8891*-CO215	C
	1445	2005	*AC8893*-CO201	C
		5.9◆		
DETROIT				
	1040	1441	*AC8891*-CO407	C
	1445	2011	*AC8893*-CO779	C
		5.9◆		
EDMONTON				
	0628	1050E	AC603-AC123	C
	1105	1532E	AC109-AC127	C
X6	1440	1918E	AC195-AC159	C
	1655	2114E	AC149-AC135	C
FORT LAUDERDALE				
	1445	2124	*AC8893*-CO1533	C
		5.9◆		
FRANKFURT/FRANCFORT				
	1440	0720+	AC195-AC872	C
FREDERICTON				
X67	0805	0855	*AC8811*	-
X67	1040	1210	*AC8813*	1
7	1040	1210	*AC8813*	1
		5.9◆		
	1405	1535	*AC8815*	1
X6	1435	1525	*AC8877*	-
		5.9◆		
X6	1440	1525	*AC8887*	-
◆6.9				
X6	1700	1750	*AC8817*	-
6	1710	1835	*AC8867*	1
		4.9◆		
GANDER				
X6	1055	1320	*AC8810*	-
6	1055	1320	*AC8810*	-
		4.9◆		
X6	1410	1635	*AC8808*	-

Jours	*Dép.*	*Arr.*	*Vol(s)*	*Esc.*
HALIFAX/ DARTMOUTH (Continued)				
GANDER (Continued)				
6	1425	1650	*AC8810*	-
◆11.9				
X6	1705	2005	*AC8824*	1
6	1705	2005	*AC8824*	1
◆11.9				
X6	1100	1525	*AC8892-AC8831*	C
6	1100	1535	*AC8892-AC8829*	C
		4.9◆		
X6	1420	1850	*AC8894-AC8833*	C
6	1705	2025	*AC8896-AC8808*	C
		4.9◆		
GLASGOW				
2	2135	0910+	AC860	1
5	2135	0910+	AC860	1
		3.9◆		
6	2150	0700+	AC860	-
◆11.9				
GOOSE BAY				
X67	1050	1410	*AC8828*	1
67	1050	1410	*AC8828*	1
◆11.9				
7	1050	1305	*AC8828*	-
		5.9◆		
6	1410	1625	*AC8828*	-
		4.9◆		
6	1705	2020	*AC8824*	1
		4.9◆		
X6	1420	1935	*AC8826-AC8807*	C
GREENSBORO				
	1040	1711	*AC8891*-CO1435	C
X6	1445	1947	*AC8893*-CO484	C
		5.9◆		
HARRISBURG				
	1040	1409	*AC8891*-CO3591	C
HOUSTON				
	0628	1050G	AC603-AC821	C
	1105	1810G	AC109-AC825	C
X6	1310	1810G	AC611-AC825	C
		5.9◆		
X6	1310	1810G	AC125-AC825	C
◆6.9				
INDIANAPOLIS				
	1040	1705	*AC8891*-CO711	C
JACKSONVILLE				
	1040	1728	*AC8891*-CO1701	C
	1445	2228	*AC8893*-CO375	C
		5.9◆		
LAS VEGAS				
	1445	2236	*AC8893*-CO247	C
		5.9◆		
LONDON/LONDRES				
25	2135	0705+	AC860	-
7	2135	0705+	AC860	-
		5.9◆		
67	2150	0910+	AC860	1
◆11.9				
16	2155	0910+	AC860	1
		6.9◆		
34	2155	0910+	AC860	1
LONDON, ON				
X7	0628	0925	AC603-*AC1231*	C
7	0628	0930	AC603-*AC1247*	C
X67	0812	1255	AC113-*AC1353*	C
6	0812	1410	AC113-*AC1347*	C
X67	0815	1130	AC605-*AC1207*	C
	1105	1340	AC109-*AC1211*	C

Days	Dep	Arr	Flight(s)	Stop
HALIFAX/ DARTMOUTH (Continued)				
LONDON, ON (Continued)				
X6	1310	1710	AC125-*AC1217*	C
◆6.9				
X6	1655	1930	AC149-*AC1223*	C
6	1655	1935	AC149-*AC1235*	C
X67	1710	2005	AC139-*AC1491*	C
7	1710	2210	AC139-*AC1357*	C
X56	1910	2150	AC639-*AC1239*	C
5	1910	2210	AC639-*AC1225*	C
LOS ANGELES				
	0628	1110	AC603-AC791	C
	1105	1735	AC109-AC795	C
X6	1310	1735	AC611-AC795	C
		5.9◆		
X6	1310	1735	AC125-AC795	C
◆6.9				
	1655	2110	AC149-AC793	C
MIAMI				
X67	1105	1645	AC109-AC918	C
67	1105	1855	AC109-AC918	C
7	1310	1855	AC611-AC918	C
		5.9◆		
7	1310	1855	AC125-AC918	C
◆12.9				
	1655	2205	AC149-AC914	C
MINNEAPOLIS				
	1040	1704	*AC8891*-CO5023	C
◆24.6				
	1445	2022	*AC8893*-CO1291	C
		5.9◆		
MONCTON				
X67	0815	0850	*AC8851*	-
X6	1105	1140	*AC8842*	-
6	1105	1140	*AC8842*	-
		4.9◆		
X6	1405	1440	*AC8815*	-
6	1415	1450	*AC8835*	-
	1650	1725	*AC8885*	-
X6	1855	1930	*AC8829*	-
MONTEGO BAY				
1	0628	1447	AC603-AC982	C
23	0628	1447	AC603-AC982	C
		1.9◆		
4567	0628	1244	AC603-AC982	C
		5.9◆		
4567	0628	1447	AC603-AC982	C
◆9.9				
MONTRÉAL				
	0810	0841D	AC183	-
X67	1105	1136D	AC619	-
6	1425	1505D	*AC8887*	-
		4.9◆		
6	1425	1505D	*AC8893*	-
◆11.9				
X6	1430	1550D	*AC8887*	1
		5.9◆		
X6	1430	1550D	*AC8893*	1
◆6.9				
	1650	1815D	*AC8885*	1
	1700	1730D	AC155	-
X6	1910	1950D	*AC8897*	-
6	1910	1950D	*AC8897*	-
		4.9◆		
MUNICH				
25	2135	1245+	[illegible]	C

Figure 10-3 Air Canada timetable (not in effect).
Courtesy of Air Canada

4. the flight numbers. When two numbers are given, the second is the number of the connecting flight.
5. the number indicating the total number of en route stops
6. the days of the week the flight operates
7. the beginning and ending dates for flights that do not run for the full period of the published timetable
8. the transfer points, when a flight is not a through flight.

For air travel, the times shown are based on the 24-hour clock. This is to eliminate confusion between a.m. and p.m. Under this system, time begins at one minute past midnight (0001) and continues through the next 24 hours to midnight (2400). Refer to Figure 10-4.

Ground Transportation

Airports are usually located from 6 to 30 (or more) kilometres from cities; for that reason, one or more types of ground transportation—airport limousine, taxi, bus, and car rental—are available at all airports.

The distance and direction of the airport, the travel time needed, the types of ground transportation available, and approximate costs are all listed in the OAG for all destination cities.

To determine what arrangements to make for ground transportation (which here includes air taxi), ask the airline reservations agent or your travel agent.

Limousines and shuttle buses operate on a regular basis between the airport and downtown hotels or the central airport terminal. They leave the designated hotels or the terminal in time to get the passengers to the airport for departing flights, and they meet incoming flights.

Figure 10-4 Time conversion for the 24-hour clock.

1:00 a.m.	=	0100	1.00 p.m.	=	1300
2:00 a.m.	=	0200	2:00 p.m.	=	1400
3:00 a.m.	=	0300	3:00 p.m.	=	1500
4:00 a.m.	=	0400	4:00 p.m.	=	1600
5:00 a.m.	=	0500	5:00 p.m.	=	1700
6:00 a.m.	=	0600	6:00 p.m.	=	1800
7:00 a.m.	=	0700	7:00 p.m.	=	1900
8:00 a.m.	=	0800	8:00 p.m.	=	2000
9:00 a.m.	=	0900	9:00 p.m.	=	2100
10:00 a.m.	=	1000	10:00 p.m.	=	2200
11:00 a.m.	=	1100	11:00 p.m.	=	2300
Noon	=	1200	Midnight	=	2400

Air taxi is a helicopter service available at some airports. Helicopters operate between two airports of a destination city, between an airport and downtown heliports, and/or between the destination airport and an airport not served by jet aircraft. Compared to other types of transportation, air taxi service is expensive, but it does save a traveller's time.

A traveller who must make a connecting flight at an airport may need air taxi service in order to make the connection. On domestic flights, avoid scheduling a connecting flight that involves a second airport. When people travel abroad, they may have to make a connection involving two airports, because the traveller's incoming flight may arrive at one airport and the international flight may depart at another. Before making a reservation for air taxi service, find out about airport limousine or bus service between the central terminals serving the airports involved.

Car Rental Services

The best way to arrange for car rental is to call the local office of the car rental agency and make a reservation.

The largest car rental agencies offer both domestic and international car rental services, publish worldwide directories of their services, and provide toll-free numbers for making reservations.

When you are making arrangements for car rental, specify the following: city, date, and time; the size of the car desired; the location where the car is to be picked up; who will pick up the car; where the car is to be left; the length of time the car will be used; and the method of payment for the charges.

A car can be picked up at the rental agency right at the airport. All the traveller has to do on arrival is go to the airport car rental office, state that there has been a reservation, present a driver's licence, and complete arrangements for payment of the charges.

Charges incurred are payable at the completion of the rental, but the arrangements for payment must be made in advance. Major credit cards are accepted. At the time you are making the reservation, be prepared to give the account number and the expiry date of the credit card to be used for payment. A number of organizations have arrangements with car rental agencies entitling them to a discount. Under this arrangement, the charges are billed to the organization.

Hotel and Motel Reservations

Many hotels provide a toll-free number for making reservations. When you want to make a reservation yourself directly with a hotel, you can obtain the toll-free number by calling 1-800-555-1212.

PERSPECTIVES

When in Rome...

By Blackie Scott

When is dinner served in Spain?

Are handshakes acceptable in Japan?

Which day is off limits for business in the Middle East? Read on and find out.

"When in Rome, do as the Romans do" may be good advice. But, first you need to know what the Romans do and how they do it. In a shrinking world, where more and more business is conducted across oceans, time zones, and national boundaries, it's important for every office professional to have at least a sense of customs and cultures around the globe.

Though not intended as a comprehensive Baedecker on social and business customs abroad, the following overview is designed to provide a basis for a better understanding of people in other parts of the world.

European style

Here are general guidelines for doing business in Europe:

- Gift-giving is expected—candy and flowers are excellent choices.
- Avoid giving chrysanthemums because they are associated with death.
- Avoid giving red roses; they are associated with romance.
- Always give an odd number of flowers—but never 13. Even numbers are considered unlucky.
- Punctuality is appreciated, except in Spain, Greece, and Italy, where it is less important.
- Never take wine to a French home unless you know it to be an excellent vintage.
- The main meal is generally served in the middle of the day.
- Toasting is very important in most countries. A good Swedish toast to remember goes: "Live while you have life to live. Love while you have love to give."
- In Austria and Germany, keeping one's hands in the lap when dining is considered impolite. Keeping one's hands in pockets is also impolite.

In Denmark, Finland, Norway, and Sweden:

- Casual touching is not appreciated.
- "Skoal" is a customary toast.
- People restrict the use of first names.
- And, remember, the "designated driver" concept originated in Norway, where there are strict laws against driving while intoxicated.
- The Dutch in The Netherlands *(not* synonymous with Holland, which is a province), are not prone to touch during social contact.
- Greeks have deep respect for the elderly. They are warm and demonstrative people, and if you admire an object, it may be given to you.
- Greeks smile when they are happy and when they are angry. They may use an up-tilted chin and raised eyebrow to signal "no."
- Though the Spanish may interrupt when you're talking, it is not rudeness, just an indication of their eagerness to respond.
- In Spain, Mr. Carlos Domingas would be addressed as "Mr. Carlos."
- The Spanish take their main meal between 3 p.m. and 4 p.m. and their evening meal at 10 p.m. or later.
- In the British Isles, England is considered generally more formal than Scotland and Wales. Titles and honors are very important there.
- In England, appointments for meetings or social gatherings should be made well in advance.
- The English respect personal privacy.
- It is polite to decline "seconds" when dining in England.
- The English do not usually say, "You're welcome."
- The Irish are not overly conscious about time or punctuality.
- Gift-giving is not a common practice in Ireland.
- In Ireland, one should never refuse a drink or fail to buy a round for others.
- The Italians may use strong and frequent gestures of the hands and the body. They may grasp an elbow when shaking hands.
- In Italy, it is considered rude to talk business during a social occasion.

In the Middle East:

Here are some general rules of thumb for travelling in Middle Eastern countries:

- Friday is a day of rest; business resumes on Saturday.
- Never drink alcohol.
- Pork and pork by-products are forbidden.
- Pointing with one finger is considered impolite; use your open hand instead.
- Eat only with the right hand; the left hand is seen as unclean.
- Give business cards and gifts only with the right hand.
- Never give a gift to an Arab's wife.
- Women usually have second-class status.

- Women do not cross their legs.
- Touching is common and accepted in these cultures.
- Expensive gifts may be given.
- People in the area may use "worry beads" for relaxation.
- Devout Muslims pray five times a day facing the city of Mecca.
- It is considered impolite to sit in any position that will show the soles of your feet.
- Punctuality is important in Persian Gulf countries.

In Israel, specifically:

- People are more formal than North Americans, less formal than Europeans.
- Shake hands when arriving and when leaving.
- Use "shalom" as a greeting and when saying "goodbye."
- Note that Sabbath begins at sunset on Friday and ends at sunset on Saturday.
- Keep in mind that culture and history are good topics for discussion.

Bring jeans

The Commonwealth of Independent States (the former Soviet Union) is becoming a frequent destination for many businesspeople seeking New World opportunities. When travelling there, remember:

- Desirable gifts include pens, books, and jeans; and
- "Bear hugs" and kisses on the cheek are common.

Along the Pacific Rim:

People in Pacific Rim countries have an exquisite sense of politeness and patience. Do absolutely nothing that might embarrass your host or another guest. Style and manner of presentation may be equal to or even more important than substance. Writing (or typing) "thank you" notes is vital following meetings and interviews.

In Hong Kong and the People's Republic of China:

- Nod or bow; your hosts may not shake hands.
- People in Hong Kong do shake hands, due to the country's English influence.
- Seniority and rank are very important when hosting.
- Dual-language business cards are recommended.
- People in these countries use three names—the first is their family name.
- Avoid touching others.
- Toasting is common—many even applaud.
- Gift-giving is common; wrap gifts in soft colors—black and white suggest funerals. Present gifts with both hands, then bow.
- No red or white flowers for hospital patients (red symbolizes blood and white is the color of mourning).
- People here may not communicate "no" directly, as is done in the U.S.

In Japan:

- Western customs are being adopted rapidly.
- Japanese are pleased when a host exhibits their protocol.
- Business cards are exchanged before bowing or shaking hands. A bow is the traditional greeting—the lower the better. Handshakes may be weaker than the customary firm grip in the U.S.
- It is impolite to have long or frequent eye contact.
- First names are rarely used.
- Gift-giving is important.
- Never give 16-petal chrysanthemums; these are reserved for the Imperial Family.
- Phrase questions so that they can be answered with a "yes." Harmony is important—the word "no" is shunned.
- Avoid topics related to World War II or subjects that may cause embarrassment.

In New Zealand:

- Formality may be observed early on, then ease off.
- Avoid loud talking.
- One's rank in business may not be important.
- People here dislike being called Australian.

In Australia, the people:

- Are warm and friendly;
- Offer firm handshakes;
- Speak frankly and directly;
- Dislike class structure and personal distinctions;
- Will not shy away from disagreement;
- Appreciate punctuality; and
- Have a good sense of humor—even in tense situations.

Latin cultures

In Central and South America, people generally:

- Speak Spanish except in Brazil where Portuguese is spoken;
- Have a less than rigid attitude toward time;
- Will stand close when talking—much closer than in the U.S.;
- Touch and expect to be touched;
- May be more interested in you personally than as a representative of your company;
- Eat their main meal at midday;
- Shake hands readily; and
- Expect the host to offer the first toast.

In Mexico specifically:

- Jokes about "Montezuma's revenge" are in poor taste.

- First names are seldom used.
- Titles are important.
- Placing hands on hips suggest aggression.

In the Caribbean:

- Handshakes are common.
- English is the prevailing language.
- Table manners are informal.
- The pace of life is relaxed.
- Punctuality is not critical.
- The main meal is usually taken at midday.
- Business begins with extended social conversation.
- Business cards are important.
- Exchanging gifts is not required.

In Puerto Rico, specifically:

- Standing close to people is customary.
- Backing away during conversation is considered impolite.
- Gifts are exchanged and opened immediately.
- It is polite to decline a gift at first.
- English is spoken freely, but speaking some Spanish phrases is appreciated.

This is intended to whet the appetite of those who may be conducting business with non-Americans. The information presented here is very generalized and does not include several key regions of the world—African countries, for example.

As wise office professionals everywhere know, before you travel to an international destination or host visitors from another country, conduct your own in-depth research. There are many excellent guides to business and social customs in specific countries around the world. Additionally, consult your travel agent, the embassy of the country you'll be visiting, and others within your organization or network of peers who have had similar experiences. You can never be too prepared.

Blackie Scott *is a speaker, consultant, and author with an expertise in corporate etiquette, entertaining, and workplace relationships. She is based in Decatur, Georgia.*

Author's Note: Information used in this article was adapted from the book Do's and Taboos of Hosting International Visitors *by Roger E. Axtell, published by John Wiley & Sons Inc.*

Reprinted courtesy of OfficePRO.

If you are not familiar with the hotels in the destination city, contact a local travel agent. Most international accommodation information changes so rapidly that agents consult on-line computer information, which is updated frequently. Many of the larger hotels and resorts have their own websites so it's very possible to access this information and make your own reservations. Most of these websites provide on-line booking services and toll free telephone numbers. Many of the larger hotels and resorts have their own websites so it is very easy to access this information and make your own reservations. Most of these websites provide toll-free telephone numbers.

Always ask for a confirmation of a hotel reservation. When the operator gives you a confirmation number, be sure to attach it to the itinerary so that the traveller will have it if there is any question about the reservation. Hotels and motels require a deposit when you request that a room be held for late arrival. Make the request and arrange for the deposit if there is the slightest chance that your manager might arrive late. Major credit cards are accepted by hotels; this simplifies the process of making a deposit for a room reservation.

Passports

A passport is a travel document, given to citizens by their own government, granting permission to leave the country and to travel in certain specified foreign countries. A passport serves as proof of citizenship and identity in a foreign country. It asks other countries to allow the bearer free passage within their borders. It entitles the bearer to the protection of her or his own country and that of the countries visited.

Any Canadian citizen who goes abroad must carry a Canadian passport. However, a Canadian citizen is not required by our laws or regulations to have a passport for travel to or in the United States or Mexico. Nevertheless, another country can require that the person travelling to or through the country have a passport or visa. Some countries that do not require a passport *do* require proof of nationality; and, of course, the best proof of nationality is a passport. Inquire at your travel agency or local passport office regarding whether or not a passport is required.

To apply for a passport, a person must complete an application form. The passport application is available free of charge at any post office, or passport office. The Passport Office is an agency of Foreign Affairs and International Trade, Government of Canada. Along with the completed application, the applicant must submit two identical passport photos taken within the previous 12 months and certified on the back by an eligible guarantor. An original document is necessary as proof of Canadian citizenship; a photocopy of a birth certificate is not acceptable. A payment of $60.00 must be made in the form of cash, money order, or a certified cheque made payable to the Receiver General of Canada.

The Passport Office prefers that the application be made in person; however, where this is unreasonable the completed application, photographs, and payment may be mailed to

> Passport Office
> Foreign Affairs and International Trade
> Ottawa, ON K1A 0B3

The processing time for applications made in person at a regional office is five working days. Applicants who submit their passport applications through the mail must expect a wait of approximately three weeks. A Canadian passport is valid for five years and may not be renewed or extended.

Visas

Many countries require foreign travellers to hold a visa. A visa is a stamped permit to travel within a given country for a specified length of time. The visa is stamped inside the passport.

Information on visa requirements can be obtained from the Travel Information Manual (TIM), a supplemental on-line manual provided by a group of international airlines. The TIM includes information on passport and health requirements, taxes, customs, and foreign currency. The TIM is constantly updated to ensure accurate information on medical, visa, and passport requirements. The International Travel Advisory System (ITAS) is another on-line service; it is updated by international governments in an effort to inform travellers of political unrest, threatening health conditions, or other unsafe conditions in various countries.

> *"Aim high. If you want something badly enough, get it!"*
>
> Judy Boone, Graduate
> College of the North Atlantic

Well in advance of departure date, a traveller should check passport and visa requirements with the consulates of the countries to be visited. The traveller should obtain the necessary visas before going abroad. Visas are obtained through consulates and embassies located in Canada. Most foreign consular representatives are located in principal Canadian cities, particularly Ottawa and Toronto. The addresses of foreign consulates in Canada may be obtained by consulting *Diplomatic, Consular and Other Representatives in Canada*, available in public libraries.

After obtaining a passport, the traveller must send it to each consulate involved to obtain visas. The time it takes to process a visa after it reaches a consular office varies. Since travel agents are experienced in obtaining visas, rely on your travel agent for this service.

Immunization Requirements

The International Health Regulations adopted by the World Health Organization (WHO) stipulate that certain vaccinations may be required as a condition of entry to any country. The WHO sends communiqués to local health departments advising them of required and recommended **immunization** for travellers.

For travel to many countries, an International Certificate of Vaccination is not required. If you need one, you can obtain it from the local health clinic. The form must be signed by the doctor who gives the vaccination and stamped by the clinic.

FOLLOWING THROUGH

While administrative assistants can rely on the travel department or a travel agent when planning a trip, they are directly responsible for checking the completeness and the accuracy of the final arrangements.

Prior to the Trip

Just before the manager leaves on a business trip, your main duties will include checking the tickets, getting money for the trip, preparing the itinerary, assembling materials for the trip, getting instructions about special responsibilities you will have in your manager's absence, and perhaps arranging to have new business cards made.

Checking the Tickets

Obtain the tickets in enough time to check them carefully. First compare the information on the tickets with what your boss requested; then thoroughly check each item on the tickets with the itinerary. The information on the tickets and the travel portion of the itinerary should be identical.

Getting Money for the Trip

Credit cards such as American Express, Visa, and MasterCard make it possible to travel without carrying large sums of money. Most people rely on credit cards while travelling.

However, everyone who travels needs some cash. Many organizations provide a cash advance to employees who travel. If this is the policy in your organization, ask the manager how much cash will be needed, complete the required form, and obtain the cash. Figure 10-5 shows a **Travel Fund Advance Form**. Although forms vary, it is important on all forms to fill all appropriate blanks with accurate information. This will help your manager avoid delays in receiving the travel advance.

Whether you are obtaining cash from a bank or from the cashier of your organization, get some coins

Figure 10-5 Travel fund advance.

TRAVEL FUND ADVANCE

Please forward completed forms to: Accounting Department
Millennium Appliances
3431 Bloor Street
Toronto, ON M8X 1G4

Tel (416) 795-2893 Fax (416) 795-3982

Name of Employee Requesting Advance: *Iain Brown*

Date of Request: *25 March, 20xx*

Employee Number: *7 8 4 2 4 4*

Destination: *Vancouver, B.C.*

Reason for Travel: *Meeting with Roe Industries*

Departure Date: *5 April, 20xx* Return Date: *7 April, 20xx*

Date Advance Required: *3 April, 20xx*

Amount Requested:

Accommodation	(Per Diem $120.00)	$ *240.00*
Meals	(Per Diem $39.00)	$ *78.00*
Transportation	(Refer to Policy 432)	$ *50.00*
TOTAL REQUESTED		$ *368.00*

Preferred Method of Payment/Distribution √ Company Cheque ____ Traveller's Cheque

Balance Outstanding (Includes this request) $ *0*

L. Phillips G.M./Marketing *26/3/xx*

Authorization (as per Schedule of Authorities) Date of Authorization

Approval Limits

$ 3000 -Manager
$ 10 000 -Director
$ 10 000+ -President

or small bills for the manager to use for tips and for making telephone calls.

The manager may prefer to carry **traveller's cheques** instead of cash. They must be obtained in person at a bank, or at another company that sells traveller's cheques. An organization cannot supply traveller's cheques to its executives because traveller's cheques must be signed at the time they are purchased by the person who is to use them. For an example of a traveller's cheque, refer to the section "Traveller's Cheques" in Chapter 14.

Preparing the Itinerary

Usually, an **itinerary** is a combined travel/appointment schedule. However, the travel itinerary and the schedule of confirmed appointments can also be prepared as two separate lists. An itinerary shows when, where, and how the traveller will go. It should include

- the day
- the date
- the time of departure
- the name of the airport or station
- the flight numbers
- the time(s) and place(s) for arrival
- the name of the hotel for each overnight stay on the trip.

The itinerary should also include details about confirmed appointments. Examples of such details might be

- the names and titles of the people the traveller will see
- personal notes about people the traveller may see. These comments are intended to aid conversation and familiarity. They may include reminders about family members, recent achievements or personal interests.
- the dates and times of the appointments
- the purpose of the appointments
- software and/or documents required for the appointments.

These details are illustrated in the itinerary in Figure 10-7.

As soon as the travel and hotel accommodations and the appointments have been confirmed, you can prepare the final itinerary. Make a step-by-step plan that is so complete that the manager will know where to go, when, and what materials will be needed by referring to the itinerary.

Preparing an itinerary is time-consuming because you must obtain the information from several different sources. Arrange the papers relating to hotels and appointments in chronological order. Give the itinerary an appropriate heading. Use the days and dates as the major divisions, and list the entries under each division in order according to time. Check the final itinerary more than once to make sure it is 100 percent correct.

You should prepare the itinerary in the style your manager prefers. However, if the travel agent has already prepared a detailed itinerary, instead of rekeying it to add the appointments, prepare a separate schedule of appointments.

Make at least four copies of the final itinerary; one copy

1. for the traveller
2. for the traveller's superior
3. for the traveller to give family members
4. for you

and send it to the traveller on an electronic file so last-minute changes can be made and more copies can be printed.

File your copy as a permanent record of the trip. When changes in the manager's itinerary are necessary, inform everyone who has a copy.

Assembling Materials for the Trip

As you make arrangements for the trip, you should compile a complete list of items the manager will need on the trip. After you have assembled the items that will be needed, your last-minute responsibilities will include numbering them in the order in which they will be used and checking them off your list as you stack them to go in the briefcase.

Figure 10-6 Working en route with a notebook computer.

Courtesy of International Business Machines Corporation. Unauthorized use not permitted.

Figure 10-7 Itinerary.

ITINERARY FOR BENJAMIN EDWARDS

Montreal-Ottawa Regina-Montreal
May 3-May 9, 20xx

<u>Monday, May 3</u>

0905 EDT	Leave Montreal Dorval Airport on AC167 to Ottawa.
0938 EDT	Arrive Ottawa Airport. Chris Bollen will meet you. Chris is our sales representative for Ottawa. She recently received recognition for her contributions to Quality Leadership within our company.
	Reservation at Embassy Hotel. Hotel confirmations are in envelope with airline tickets.
1030 EDT	Appointment with Bob Ross, Manager, Ottawa Branch Office.
1200 EDT	Lunch with Bob Ross and Christine Bollen.
1400 EDT	Conference with Sales Team, Ottawa Branch. This meeting is scheduled to be in the boardroom on the second floor.

<u>Tuesday, May 4</u>

0730 EDT	Leave Ottawa Airport for Toronto on AC 443. Leave Toronto on connecting AC107 for Regina.
1107 CST	Arrive Regina Airport.
	Pick up car from Avis at airport.
	Reservation at Continental Hotel. Hotel confirmations are in envelope with airline tickets.
1300 CST	Appointment with William Mack, Manager, Regina Branch. Mr. Mack wants to introduce you to a new client - Heather Rodden, President of Avanti Products.
1830 CST	Dinner with Mr. and Mrs. Taylor. Their home address is 101-40th Street.

<u>Wednesday, May 5</u>

0830 - 1000 CST	Manufacturing plant tour. Sam Wolfe will meet you at Gate 1 to conduct the tour.
1155 CST	Leave Regina Airport on AC132 for Toronto. Leave Toronto on connecting AC528 for Montreal.
1843 EDT	Arrive Montreal Dorval Airport.

HAVE A PRODUCTIVE TRIP!

Many people now travel with a **notebook computer**. If a notebook computer is one of the items the manager will be taking, make sure he or she takes a fully charged spare power-pack, removable diskettes, and current data for en route work.

Bundle the papers for each appointment in separate envelopes or folders. Number each "bundle" in consecutive order to match the order of appointments. If you use folders, fasten the materials in the folders. A briefcase is private; therefore, do not actually pack the briefcase unless you are asked to do so. But do check to make sure that all papers needed for the trip get into the briefcase.

Make two copies of the list you have compiled of items your manager must take. Staple the list inside Folder #1, or attach it to Envelope #1. Keep one copy for yourself.

Getting Special Instructions

Take notes as the manager gives instructions about what to do in her or his absence. Find out about mail that should be forwarded; materials to be sent to meetings the manager cannot attend; and any special responsibilities you must handle in the manager's absence. Be sure you understand how to follow through on important correspondence and telephone calls.

Printing Business Cards

Here's a suggestion that may improve foreign business relations. If your manager is travelling to a foreign country, before the business trip have new business cards printed. One side should contain the usual information in English; the reverse side should be printed in the foreign language. Foreign business contacts will view this as a courteous gesture.

During the Manager's Absence

Stay at your desk, and work at the same pace while your manager is away as you do when he or she is there.

Some managers want to have their e-mail forwarded to them when they are away from the office for any significant period of time. Most managers who travel will telephone the office to keep in touch. Be ready to report on significant events and important mail and telephone calls. In your notebook, made a summary of what you should discuss, and phrase the questions you need to ask. If the manager keeps in touch with the office through e-mail, you can provide this information on a daily basis and get the manager's feedback immediately.

Sometimes managers plan so much work for their administrative assistants to complete in their absence that the assistants are stressed to complete it. However, if you find you have time to spare, refer to your To Do List and proceed with performing as many of the responsibilities as you can. If possible, plan your schedule so you can spend the first day the manager is back in the office following through on work generated by the trip.

When the manager is away, you will have added responsibilities and may need to allow extra time to handle them. For example, you will want to read the manager's e-mail, postal mail, and faxes, to determine if any of the information is urgent and needs to be handled by the acting manager or by you. Save some time for communicating with the person who has been designated to act in the manager's role. Offer your assistance if you can perform any of these responsibilities. When the manager is away from the office, don't feel that you have extra time and, as a result, delay work that can be completed. Tackle your own work in the usual way. If you have additional time, use it effectively to work on assignments you have been putting off or to assist another employee who needs help.

Schedule appointments for the manager just as you do when the manager is in the office. Try to keep the manager's calendar free of appointments for the first day following the trip. Before the manager returns, key a summary of the appointments you have made. Indicate the date, with whom, and the purpose of each appointment. If the manager uses an electronic calendar, there should be no need to key a list of appointments since the software gives a clear picture of appointments and can print a summary.

After the Manager Returns

Your activities on the manager's first day back after a trip will centre on briefing the manager on what happened during the trip, following up with correspondence, assembling receipts for the expense report, and filing materials your manager brings back.

Report the most significant happenings first. Put on your manager's desk the digest of the mail and the correspondence that arrived in your manager's absence, arranged in folders as explained in Chapter 6; the summary of appointments; a summary of telephone calls; and a list of who came to the office to see him or her.

Early in the day, call attention to anything that requires immediate action.

You should be able to assist the manager with letter writing in two ways. If your manager promised to send materials to others, prepare the materials for mailing and write the accompanying letters. Compose for your manger's signature thank-you letters to those who extended courtesies during the trip. Refer to Chapter 13 for information about writing thank-you letters.

Review your list of the materials the traveller took on the trip that must be returned to the files. Locate these materials and file them. Also file materials your manager acquired during the trip. Copies of materials from the files that your manager took on the trip can be disposed of. First, however, check carefully for notes that may have been made on them.

Travel Expense Voucher

The manager may want you to prepare a **travel expense voucher**, based on receipts obtained during the trip. If you are not sure about your company's policy with regards to expense claims, be certain to consult a policy manual so that your work on the voucher is accurate. Completeness and accuracy are the two necessary ingredients for ensuring a quick return of funds owing to the traveller.

Refer to Figure 10-8 for a sample travel expense voucher. Note that all expenses must have the approval of a senior employee. Although these forms vary from company to company, most require at least the following information:

- the date the expense was incurred
- the location where the expense was incurred
- the number of the work order (if one was involved)
- the "out of pocket" cost of transportation
- the cost of the hotel where the traveller stayed
- the cost and explanation of other business expenses that relate to the trip (including telephone calls, laundry services, or a necessary business item that was purchased)
- the cost of company-related entertaining
- the cost of meals
- the amount of any travel fund advance that may have been received prior to the trip. This amount is deducted from the amount the employee will now receive from the company. Where the form does not provide a designated space for showing a travel advance, and the employee has received one, deduct the amount and make a written explanation.

Figure 10-8 Travel expense voucher.

TRAVEL EXPENSE VOUCHER

CONTROL #: ____________

NAME: *Ian Brown* PIN: *784244*

TITLE: *Sales Manager* DATE: *10 April, 20xx*

Date	Location	Work Order	Transport*	Hotel	Other	Entertain	Meals	Total	Explain Other, Entertain & Meals
05 April	*Vancouver*		*22.50*	*115.00*			— — *19.00*	*156.50*	*Taxi airport—hotel*
06 April	*Vancouver*			*115.00*		*87.50*	*11.00* *12.50* —	*226.00*	*Dinner with A.V. Roe* *Roe Industries Ltd.*
07 April	*Vancouver*		*24.00*				*11.00* — —	*35.00*	*Taxi hotel—airport*
07 April	*Toronto*				*19.80*			*19.80*	*Airport parking* *3 days at $6.60*
EXPENSE TOTAL			*46.50*	*230.00*	*19.80*	*87.50*	*53.50*	*437.30*	
LESS: CASH ADVANCES								*368.00*	TFA DATE:
BALANCE CLAIMED OR RETURNED								*69.30*	LEGEND * Include vehicle from Side 2 (if applicable) ** Enter on Side 2 *** Distribute on Side 2
GST Tax Credit = .0566 x Expense Total			*2.63*	*13.01*	*1.12*	*4.95*	*3.03*	** *24.75*	
Expense Total *** Less Tax Credit			*43.87*	*216.99*	*18.68*	*82.55*	*50.47*	*412.55*	APPROVAL OF EXPENSES *K. Winters* Payment Approved by

CERTIFICATION OF EXPENSES

I certify that I have incurred these expenses.

I. Brown — Employee's Signature

10 April, 20xx — Date

AUDIT

__________ Checked by __________ Date

V.P. Sales — Title

April 16, 20xx — Date

- the GST tax credit. This calculation is often completed by the employee; however, the employee does not receive this amount. The calculation is done for purposes of company expense.

It is common practice for organizations to arrange and pay in advance for air transportation. For convenience, these arrangements are made through the organization's associate travel agent. In such cases the cost of air transportation will not appear on the traveller's travel expense voucher.

Remember that most claimed expenses must be verified by receipts, and must not exceed costs specified by company policy.

These forms are completed by anyone who has a legitimate company expense. This may include any level of employee. If the travel expense voucher form is stored on your computer, you can key the information. If not, it is acceptable to submit these documents in handwritten form.

Questions for Study and Review

1. Organizations have definite policies concerning executive travel. Name some areas where you would expect policies to be clearly stated.
2. How can access to the Internet help the administrative assistant make travel arrangements?
3. What are the functions of a travel department?
4. How are travel agents paid?
5. What services will a travel agent perform for domestic travel? for international travel?
6. What information relating to a trip should an administrative assistant compile before contacting a travel department, travel agency, or carrier?
7. Distinguish between the following:
   a. nonstop flight
   b. direct flight
   c. connecting flight
   d. commuter flight.
8. If the flight space a traveller desires is not available, explain how to proceed to make alternative plans.
9. What is meant by reconfirmation of an airline reservation? When is it necessary?
10. What are the essential items to look for when reading a timetable?
11. What ground transportation is available at airports?
12. What is an air taxi? What is a heliport?
13. Suggest two ways to make hotel reservations.
14. Why should an administrative assistant always ask for a written confirmation of a hotel reservation?
15. What information should an administrative assistant compile before making arrangements for car rental?
16. Using the 24-hour clock, write 6 a.m., 2 p.m., 9 p.m., noon, and midnight.
17. What is a passport?
18. List the items that must be submitted along with a passport application.
19. What is a visa? Who can issue a visa?
20. How would an administrative assistant obtain information about the immunization requirements that the World Health Organization produces?
21. What are an administrative assistant's main responsibilities just prior to the manager's departure on a business trip?
22. How can an administrative assistant avoid delays in receiving a travel advance?
23. What information should be included in an itinerary?
24. Explain how an administrative assistant's time can be used efficiently during the manager's absence.
25. What are the administrative assistant's main responsibilities pertaining to the trip after the manager's return?

Spelling Reinforcement

accommodations
adequate
cancellation
commissions
consular
designated
destination
foreign
helicopter
identity
immunization
itineraries
license/licence
limousine
preferred
shuttle
terminal
traveler/traveller
vaccination
voucher

On-the-Job Situations

1. The manager is planning a business trip to one of the organization's branches located across the country. At the time that the manager asked you to make a reservation for him, all the tickets had been sold for the date he requested and his name was placed on a waiting list for both directions of the trip. Today you receive a telephone call from the airline saying that space is available to the destination city at the time your manager requested but that he still would have to be on a waiting list for the return trip. Should you accept the reservation to the destination city? Explain.
2. When the office manager, Mrs. Orlando, arrived in Saskatoon, she could not find her luggage. Her notes for the talk that she is to give at the conference are in her suitcase. Another copy of the notes is in Mrs. Orlando's desk at the office. Mrs. Orlando calls you at home on Saturday morning and asks you to go to the office, find the notes, and fax them to her. She says the notes are brief and you could read them to her over the telephone. How do you react to this request? Will you comply? What suggestions would you make about packing notes for future talks?
3. You work for three executives. Two of them are planning to attend a national management conference in Toronto, and you have made travel reservations for them. Now the third executive has decided to attend the conference. He has asked you to make travel reservations for him for the same time the other two executives are travelling. You call the airline. A reservation is not available at that time. What should you do while you are talking with the reservations agent?

Special Reports

1. Find a local airline or bus company schedule on the Internet. Select the departure city and a destination city. List the schedules of service available between these two cities.
2. For the following foreign locations (New Delhi, India; Beijing, China; Manila, Philippines) obtain the latest information and prepare a report on one of the following topics:
   a. passport requirements and where passports may be obtained locally
   b. visas regulations and where they can be obtained
   c. immunization requirements
   d. ground transportation to and from the local airport
   e. car rental services.
3. Search the Internet for information on current airline fares. Compare the fares between two major airlines travelling between Calgary and Ottawa. Then compare the fares for the same airlines travelling between Vancouver and Halifax.

Production Challenges

10-A Preparing an Itinerary

Supplies needed:

- *Notes concerning Mr. Wilson's Trip, Form 10-A, pages 418 and 419*
- *Plain paper*

Mr. Wilson will make a business trip to the Midwestern Region during the week of September 11 to 14. He will visit the Midwestern Region Sales Office of Millennium Appliances, Inc., in Regina and the Millennium Appliances Manufacturing plant in Winnipeg. He will speak to the Sales Management Club at Red River Community College.

Prepare Mr. Wilson's itinerary.

10-B Making an Airline Reservation

Supplies needed:

- *Plain paper*

Mr. Wilson asked you to make an airline reservation for him from Toronto to Vancouver on Tuesday, October 10. Since Mr. Wilson does not know how much time he will spend in Vancouver, you are to request an open return ticket. You know that Mr. Wilson prefers to travel in the morning and that he prefers an aisle seat on nonstop and direct flights.

You call the airlines. A nonstop flight is not available. You make a reservation for him with Air Canada. The flight leaves Toronto at 1005, arrives in Winnipeg at 1210, leaves Winnipeg at 1230, and will arrive in Vancouver at 1345. He will be on the same airplane for the entire trip. His tickets will be ready at the counter.

Key Mr. Wilson a note giving him complete information about the airline reservations.

10-C Preparing a Travel Fund Advance

Supplies needed:

- *Travel Fund Advance, Form 10-C, page 420*
- *Working Papers Disk, File 10-C*

Mr. Wilson has requested an advance for his trip to Vancouver. The purpose of this trip is to visit Ms. Singe, Sales Manager. Together they will attend the annual Sales Strategies Seminar. Mr. Wilson will require the advance the day before his departure. He prefers to receive it in the form of a company cheque. The per diem rate is $120.00 for his accommodation and $39.00 for his meals. He estimates that he will remain in Vancouver for three days. The airline tickets will be prepaid by the company; therefore, Mr. Wilson will not be required to claim this as a personal expense. His employee number is 847254. Key the form or complete the form using your most legible handwriting.

10-D Preparing an Open Itinerary

Supplies needed:

- *Plain paper*

Although you do not have complete information for Mr. Wilson's trip to Vancouver, you still need to prepare an itinerary. Use the information provided in 10-B, Making an Airline Reservation, and 10-C, Preparing a Travel Fund Advance, to complete the best open itinerary possible. Do not use the information from 10-E, Preparing a Travel Expense Voucher, since this information is unknown prior to the trip. You will be booking the Bayshore Inn for Mr. Wilson for Tuesday, Wednesday, and Thursday evenings.

10-E Preparing a Travel Expense Voucher

Supplies needed:

- *Travel Expense Voucher, Form 10-E, page 421*
- *Working Papers Disk, File 10-E*

Mr. Wilson returned from Vancouver on Friday, October 13. He has requested that you complete a Travel Expense Voucher on his behalf. He has provided receipts for all his expenses. The receipts give you the following information:

- He stayed at the Bayshore Inn, using the full **per diem rate** each evening.
- Meals for each day were:

Tuesday	–	Dinner = $18.55
Wednesday	–	Breakfast = $8.50
		Lunch= $10.15
		Dinner = $19.25
Thursday	–	Breakfast = $7.25
		Lunch = $9.25
		Dinner = $15.45
Friday	–	Breakfast = $9.50

Please note—charge the per diem amount for the two full days but only the actual expenses incurred for Tuesday and Friday.

- Millennium Appliances have prepaid Mr. Wilson's airfare through their associated travel agent; therefore, this expense will not show up on the travel expense voucher.

- On the day Mr. Wilson arrived in Vancouver, he hired a taxi. The fare was $22.00. The day he left Vancouver he again hired a taxi, for $26.50.
- On Wednesday he rented a car for three days. His receipt shows a total charge of $147.83.
- He had one miscellaneous receipt showing a charge of $30.35 for a portfolio purchased on Wednesday.
- One receipt showed an entertainment expense of $35.50. This was incurred on Thursday, when he bought theatre tickets for Mr. and Mrs. Singe.

Refer to the information in 10-C before completing Form 10-E. Use the Working Papers Disk, File 10-E, to key the form, or use your most legible handwriting on the Travel Expense Voucher, Form 10-E, page 421.

World Wide Websites

Business Travel Online Magazine

www.publish.co.za/bt/
Executive travellers can connect to a world of travel information at this site.

World Time Zones

tycho.usno.navy.mil/tzones.html
Look here for a map of world time zones, and local standard time offset from UTC, with daylight savings time where observed.

Yahoo! Canada—Travel

www.yahoo.ca/recreation/travel/
This site contains indices, and information about flight prices and bookings, currency exchange, health, and travel-related businesses.

Meetings and Conferences

Outline

Informal Business Meetings

Arranging the Meeting
Taking Notes

Formal Business Meetings

Reserving a Room
Planning for Supplies and Equipment
Planning for Refreshments
Sending Notices
Preparing the Agenda
Assembling Materials
Handling Telephone Interruptions
Recording Minutes
Following Up
Preparing Minutes
Correcting Minutes

Team Meetings

Preparation for the Meeting
Roles of Participants
Starting the Meeting
Brainstorming
Nominal Group Technique
Discussion and Solution
Closure

Teleconferencing

Audioconferencing
Videoconferencing
Direct Broadcast Video
Computer Conferencing
Perspectives: "Intimidated by Social Events?"

Learning Outcomes

At the completion of this chapter, the student will be able to:

1. Describe the preliminary arrangements to be made for informal and formal meetings.
2. Explain how to prepare notices and agendas for meetings.
3. Describe the assembly of supportive materials before and after meetings.
4. Outline guidelines for keying minutes of informal and formal meetings.
5. Explain the purpose of conducting a meeting using the TQM process.
6. Describe the roles of participants in team meetings.
7. Describe how a team meeting should be conducted using brainstorming and the nominal group technique.
8. Describe the benefits of teleconferencing.
9. Discuss different forms of teleconferencing that may be used by businesses.
10. Prepare and fax a Notice of Meeting.
11. Compose and key minutes from rough notes.
12. Hold a team meeting that requires Nominal Group Technique voting, a Meeting Log, and Cause and Effect Diagrams.

GRADUATE PROFILE

Dr. Marla Middleton, Ph.D.
Coordinator

Medicine Hat College

College Graduation:
Secretarial Science Program
Olds College
Olds, Alberta
1979

Dr. Marla Middleton is a perfect example of her own philosophy "Believe in yourself! With hard work and perseverance you can achieve whatever goals you set your sight on." After Marla completed her secretarial science certificate from Olds College, she pursued her academic goals by achieving a B.Ed., M.Sc., and finally a Ph.D. These achievements make her a perfect fit for the position of Program Coordinator at Medicine Hat College for the Office Technology and Office Management Programs. Despite her advanced education, Marla says that her secretarial education was invaluable to her career. It not only gave her the background she needed to begin teaching in the office technology area, but it also gave her an excellent start in computer technology and office management.

One of Marla's greatest strengths is her ability to listen. She enjoys chairing meetings where the brainstorming and sharing of ideas result in improved processes. As chairperson, she likes to create an atmosphere where all meeting participants feel comfortable in sharing their input. Marla ensures her meetings are successful by preparing ahead and by sending out agendas and reading materials prior to the meeting. When it comes to meeting preparation, she says, "Agendas should not contain an unrealistic number of items. This just frustrates people."

"If everyone is willing to work toward a common goal, the team will be more effective."

In Marla's leadership position, she strives to be someone with vision who is willing to take calculated risks and accept responsibility for the outcome. She believes that by being fair, honest, and by valuing the work of others you will earn respect from your colleagues.

An administrative assistant may be made responsible for arranging a wide range of meetings. The type of meeting may range from small informal meetings to large conferences. They may be conducted in a boardroom face-to-face, or remotely, using technology such as teleconferencing, or videoconferencing, or a combination of both. This task may involve handling all the preliminary activities—arranging the meeting venue and time, inviting the participants, preparing the agenda, assembling materials needed during the meeting, and arranging for food and accommodation—as well as follow-up activities such as transcribing the minutes and reminding your manager to carry out the commitments made during the meeting.

In addition to handling the preliminary activities and the follow-up, the administrative assistant is often expected to participate during the meeting, making valuable contributions to the decision-making process.

An office team that is skilled in Total Quality Management (refer to Chapter 2) has learned that conducting meetings effectively involves having input from all team members associated with the meeting agenda. It is vital to remember that each team member has something important to contribute. The extent of the contribution will be based on the participant's experience and expertise.

INFORMAL BUSINESS MEETINGS

When a manager calls an informal meeting, an administrative assistant is often expected to perform the following tasks:

1. Invite the participants.
2. Key or assemble materials the manager will need for presentation at the meeting.
3. Duplicate materials for distribution.
4. Take notes during the meeting.
5. Prepare and distribute a summary of the meeting for all the participants.

Arranging the Meeting

Arranging an informal meeting of several people is easy when the following conditions exist:

- The meeting participants in your organization use a computer to keep their calendars.
- Both scheduled time and free time can be identified through the computer.
- The calendars are not classified as private and, therefore, are available to others.

- The executives have electronic mailboxes and/or voice mail.

When you have access to the calendars of those who are to attend the meeting, find a time when all the participants are free, schedule the meeting, and then send the information about the meeting to the electronic mailboxes of the participants.

Using the telephone to find a time when it is convenient for all the participants of an informal conference to meet can become a time-consuming task.

At the time your manager asks you to schedule a meeting or to find out when the other executives are available, your manager should tell you the first and second choices of meeting times and the purpose of the meeting.

Develop an awareness of how much time a meeting on a particular topic should take. Meetings should begin, and end, at the scheduled time.

If you are working with desk calendars, tentatively enter the meeting in pencil for both choices of time in your manager's appointment calendar. Check the electronic calendars of the people the manager wishes to meet with, or leave them a message on their e-mail or voice mail. If these options are not available, then telephone the people who are to be invited to the meeting.

Executive Booking

Although many executives like to schedule their own appointments, some prefer to leave that responsibility to the administrative assistant; therefore, you may be able to deal directly with administrative assistants when you are setting up meetings between executives.

"To set up a successful meeting, I must be organized ahead of time."

Phyllis Thompson, Graduate
Nova Scotia Community College
Springhill Campus

Scheduling a meeting of three or four executives can become complicated, involving many e-mail messages, voice mail messages, or telephone calls, because executives make numerous appointments within a week and also because many of them travel. Let the assistants know that you will respond immediately by electronic mail, voice mail, or telephone if you cannot arrange the meeting as tentatively scheduled.

When you are arranging a meeting for eight or ten executives, you probably will not find a time when all of them are free from previous commitments. Schedule the meeting at a time when most of them—especially the principal members—can attend. At an executive level, corporate politics often determines attendance. It may be important to an executive to attend based on which other executives are attending the meeting. It is important to distribute names of attendees as soon as possible. Notify all of them of the time and place of the meeting. The executive who has the conflict must decide how to resolve it.

As soon as you complete the arrangements, enter the time as a firm commitment in all calendars; clear the calendar of the "extra" meeting time. If the meeting will not be held in your manager's office, reserve a conference room as soon as the time of the meeting is definite.

Last Check

Consider developing a checklist for those last minute activities. Checklists serve not only as a reminder of specific items but also provide consistency as a planning document for future meetings. Consider the following simple checklist as an example of activities you should complete just prior to the meeting:

- ❑ Are meeting materials complete?
- ❑ Are meeting materials in the manager's office or meeting room?
- ❑ Are there enough chairs available?
- ❑ Is there a message pad and pencil by the meeting room telephone?
- ❑ Is the presentation equipment working?
- ❑ Is a spare bulb available for the overhead projector?
- ❑ Do attendees require pads of paper and pencils?
- ❑ Have refreshments been arranged?
- ❑ Has my voice mail been changed to reflect my absence during the meeting?

Complete meeting materials and operational presentation equipment will enhance the most thoroughly planned meeting. Refer to Figure 11-1. However your checklist develops, allow sufficient time to address any of the items prior to the meeting.

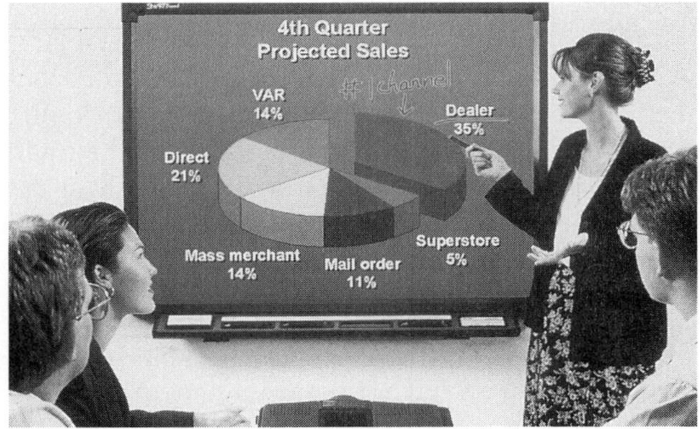

Figure 11-1 An interactive white board acts as an effective presentation tool during a meeting.
Courtesty of Smart Technologies, Calgary, Albera

Taking Notes

When your manager arranges an informal meeting or a conference with another person or several people, the purpose of the meeting is often to reach an agreement that will lead to some type of action. If you are asked to take notes during an informal meeting, record all the essential facts and all the points of the agreement. You are not expected to take the entire conversation verbatim.

When you are confident that you have recorded all the essential information, you may wish to clarify your notes with the members of the meeting. Depending on the type of meeting, you may be able to clarify essential information during (informal) or at the end of a (formal) meeting.

If you use a laptop or notebook computer to record notes during the meeting, your task of preparing a draft will be minimal and no transcription will be required.

If you are to distribute minutes to the participants, prepare them in final form after your manager has approved the draft. Refer to Figure 11-2 for an example of minutes.

FORMAL BUSINESS MEETINGS

Any meeting may be conducted formally; board of directors' meetings and annual meetings of shareholders are (with a few exceptions) formal.

Formality contributes to the smooth conduct of a business meeting when the group is a large one, when sharp disagreement exists among the members, or when a careful record of the proceedings is necessary.

Some groups choose to follow rules of parliamentary procedure in formal meetings in order to:

1. maintain order
2. recognize and protect the rights of each member
3. provide a prescribed pattern for conducting meetings.

A very popular and contemporary method of conducting meetings involves the use of Total Quality Management (TQM) principles, instead of the traditional parliamentary procedures. For more about the TQM meeting procedure, refer to the section "Team Meetings" in this chapter.

When your manager is responsible for a formal meeting, your duties may include:

- reserving a conference or meeting room
- sending notices
- preparing the agenda
- assembling materials
- attending the meeting
- preparing and distributing minutes
- arranging for beverages, light snacks, or lunches
- following through on responsibilities that your manager accepted during the meeting.

Reserving a Room

When you send notices announcing a meeting, begin by reserving the room, for you cannot send notices until you know the meeting place. The type of conference room needed will depend on the size of the group and the equipment required for the presentations. A specially equipped room is needed for a video teleconference.

You can determine the size of room needed by checking the list of participants and the previous minutes to get an estimate of attendance. Also, confer with your manager about the facilities required. Whenever possible, make a special effort to inspect the room in person. Formulas exist for calculating the square footage necessary for meeting space. However, the space required will also depend on the activity during the meeting. Before you determine the size of room necessary, ask the following questions:

- Will the team remain in the same room during coffee or lunch breaks?
- Will the team be required to perform some physical routines, or will the members remain seated throughout the meeting?
- Will the team need to break out into smaller rooms?
- Will special equipment requiring significant space be used?
- Will the meeting be an audio conference or video teleconference?
- Will there be a guest speaker? Does the speaker have special requirements?

Room reservations are often made far in advance of a meeting date. At the time you make the reservation, enter a notation in your calendar reminding you when to prepare and send out notices. Be alert to any changes in meeting dates, and indicate them in your reminder system. You also need a reminder to confirm the room reservation several days before the meeting.

If the meeting or conference has been arranged in an external facility such as a hotel or conference centre, become familiar with the terms and conditions of your booking agreement—particularly the cancellation and refund policy.

Figure 11-2 Minutes.

MINUTES OF THE EXECUTIVE TEAM OF CONTINENTAL TECHNOLOGY INC.

Meeting No. 9 - July 8, 20--

The Executive Team of Continental Technology Inc. met in a regular session at 1030, Wednesday, June 8, 20--, in Conference Room 3. The meeting was adjourned at 1145. The following members were

PRESENT:	Verna Chiasson	(Quality Advisor)
	Penny Handfield	(Guidance Team)
	Maurice Ingram	(Team Member)
	Daniel Lawrence	(Team Member)
	Laura Milton	(Team Leader)
	Betty Noble	(Guidance Team)
	Paul Noel	(Team Member)
	Gregory Patrick	(Recorder)
	Dana Rahn	(Facilitator)
	Michelle Savard	(Team Member)
	Gayle Schmitt	(Team Member)
	Mike Sherman	(Team Member)
ABSENT:	Wendy Scarth	(Team Member)

A motion was made by Maurice Ingram to approve as read the minutes of meeting no. 8. This motion was seconded by Mike Sherman. The following topics were then discussed:

REDUCTION IN ADMINISTRATIVE COSTS:

The ideas presented at the June 10 meeting for cutting administrative costs were revised and the following decisions were made:

Travel. Effective August 1, 20--, all executives of Continental Technology will no longer travel Executive Class; economy fare only will be paid by the company, with the exception of Executive Class fares approved by the Vice-President. Where Continental executives are taking major clients on business trips, the Executive Class will automatically be approved by the Vice-President.

Sales Incentive Trips. The consensus was that the yearly sales incentive trips, given to sales executives reaching their quotas, should be shortened in length. The trips will be shortened from one week to four days. As well, these trips will no longer be to extremely distant points; they will now be to warm weather North American resorts. It was felt that this would reduce both the air fare and accommodation charges considerably. This will be effective May of next year.

EMPLOYEE EVALUATIONS:

Laura Milton circulated copies of a new Employee Performance Evaluation which has been designed to follow TQM principles. The Executive Team votes unanimously in favour of using the new form beginning September 1.

ANNOUNCEMENTS:

Catalogue. A new product catalogue will be available July 25. Copies can be obtained by calling Betty Noble.

New Team Member. Wendy Scarth joined the team as of July 1. However, she is currently on a training course and absent from meeting no. 9. Wendy works in the Marketing Department and was previously employed by CanTech in Montreal.

Next Meeting. The 10th regular meeting will be held in Conference Room 3 at 1030 on Thursday, August 15, 20--.

10 July 20xx — Date

G. Patrick — Gregory Patrick, Secretary

Planning for Supplies and Equipment

The list of meeting supplies and equipment will be different for every meeting. The following list is a general one that could serve as a checklist for any meeting. How many supplies and the type of equipment necessary will depend on the type of meeting, the style of presentations to be given, the level of participants, and the guests who have been invited.

- ❑ notebook computer for presentation hook-up or for notetaking
- ❑ computer disks containing computer presentation
- ❑ professional presentation software, such as PowerPoint from Microsoft or Presentations from Corel
- ❑ projector (data or overhead)
- ❑ transparency sheets for the projector
- ❑ spare bulb for the projector
- ❑ coloured pens for transparency sheets
- ❑ remote control (VCR, or software presentation)
- ❑ projection screen
- ❑ video projector
- ❑ laser pointer for the projection screen
- ❑ manual pointer for the projection screen
- ❑ flip chart paper
- ❑ flip chart tripod or support for paper block
- ❑ coloured markers for flip chart paper
- ❑ name tents or tags, and a marker to write the names
- ❑ scissors
- ❑ adhesive tape or putty to suspend flip chart paper around the meeting room
- ❑ whiteboard markers and eraser
- ❑ writing block for each participant
- ❑ writing pen or pencil for each participant
- ❑ promotional items such as lapel pins, key tags, or pens with company logo

Planning for Refreshments

If you must schedule a luncheon or dinner meeting at a hotel or restaurant, call the banquet or convention manager of the hotel or restaurant. Inquire if there are costs in addition to the cost of the meal plus the gratuity. You may have to guarantee a minimum number of attendees; otherwise, there should be no additional stipulations. If you are asking a hotel or a restaurant for a meeting room only, establish what the cost of the room will be before you work out other details.

Team members can expect to perform at their best when their energy is high; for that reason, it is important to provide beverages and often food at meetings. The type of beverages will depend on the participants and on the time of day. Here are a few guidelines:

1. North Americans are, in general, health-conscious. Keep this in mind when arranging the menu.
2. Most participants enjoy coffee and tea regardless of the hour. Supply some decaffeinated coffee for those who cannot tolerate caffeine.
3. Juices are very popular at morning meetings. Supply both sweetened and unsweetened juices. Many people avoid excess sugar intake.
4. Participants at afternoon breaks often enjoy juice or soft drinks. Remember to provide both regular and unsweetened varieties.
5. Bottled mineral water is appreciated at both morning and afternoon meetings.
6. During a lunch meeting, all of the above choices are acceptable, as is milk. Low-fat white milk (that is, not skim) is the safest choice.
7. The key is to provide some variety. At the very minimum, provide coffee and juices for any of the meeting breaks.
8. At each break you can expect that participants will consume one or two beverages.
9. Ensure that fresh water and glasses are provided throughout the meeting.

When planning for food, think of the energy level and health of the participants. Your intent is not to make people feel sluggish. Rather, the break should provide energy and relieve any stress caused by the meeting. Therefore, provide light foods that provide energy. Some guidelines follow:

1. Remember that some participants will have special-needs diets (such as low-calorie, low-sugar, or low-cholesterol). Don't wait for a participant to identify this ahead of time. Plan enough variety to accommodate differences.
2. Participants enjoy fruit and muffins for morning breaks.
3. Always order food in small, manageable pieces. People generally converse during breaks, and most find that small sandwiches or fruit sections are easier to manage.
4. If you want the team to maintain a high level of energy, stay away from heavy desserts or starchy foods.

5. Never plan for spicy or heavily seasoned foods. These choices cause discomfort to some people, especially when they must sit for long periods of time. Also, not all people find these foods palatable.
6. At lunch, an average participant will consume four small sandwiches, four small pieces of fruit, four to six vegetable pieces, and one small dessert (such as a tart or a piece of cake). Participants usually consume one muffin or one to two small pastries at a coffee break.

At many meetings there will be international guests, and members of various religions and cultures. There may also be vegetarians, and people with special-needs diets. So it is important to include a variety of foods and beverages if you wish to ensure the comfort of all participants.

Sending Notices

Try to determine the best time to send notices of the meeting. Electronic calendars allow you to book the meeting as soon as you know the date and time. Participants with heavy schedules prefer plenty of advance notice.

Figure 11-3 Notice of meeting.

MEETING OF TQM COMMITTEE

PURPOSE:	To Develop a Mission Statement
TIME:	0830–1030
DATE:	Wednesday, June 15, 20--
PLACE:	Conference Room 5th Floor Dominion Tower

Please let Diana Thatcher (tel: 471-8100) know if you are unable to attend. Issues you wish discussed in your absence must be forwarded to Diana prior to the meeting.

See you on June 15!

PD

When composing notices, always specify who, what, when, where, and why. As shown in Figure 11-3, be explicit about when—state the day, date, and hour. Include any other essential information. Store a format for notices on your computer. When a notice is required, simply fill in the variable information using a word processor. Be sure to keep a copy of the notice for the records; in your file copy, include the date the notice was mailed.

Preparing the Agenda

The chairperson or team leader follows a prepared agenda as he or she conducts a meeting. Preparing the agenda is the responsibility of the team leader and/or the administrative assistant.

An agenda is a list of topics to be taken up and acted upon during a meeting, arranged in the order in which the topics will be considered. See Figure 11-4.

When the order of business has not been established by the group, you can use the guideline below, which is generally followed for very formal regular meetings:

1. call to order by presiding officer
2. roll call—either oral or checked by the secretary
3. approval, amendment, or correction of minutes of previous meeting
4. reading of correspondence
5. reports (in this order):
   - officers
   - standing committees
   - special committees
6. unfinished business from previous meetings
7. new business
8. appointment of committees
9. nomination and election of officers—once a year
10. announcements, including the date of the next meeting
11. adjournment.

If your manager is responsible for preparing an agenda, you will be asked to key it and to make copies for distribution; after you've worked in the organization for a while, your manager may ask you to prepare the agenda yourself. How the agenda is distributed depends on the policies of the organization and/or the wishes of the members of the group.

Even for a very informal office meeting, an agenda is often distributed to all the members. Be sure to mail copies of the agenda early enough that the members receive their copies several days before the meeting. This allows members time to prepare, which in turn results in a more productive meeting.

Figure 11-4 Agenda.

AGENDA

MEETING NO. 4

QUALITY CONFERENCE COMMITTEE

DATE:	Wednesday, June 10, 20--
TIME:	1500
PLACE:	Conference Room 3
CHAIRPERSON:	Jeffrey Keaton
RECORDER:	Gina Darroch
COMMITTEE MEMBERS:	Jodi Alford, Satvinder Bhardwaj, Gina Darroch, Gordon McLeod, Chris Dennison, Jeffrey Keaton, Allan Kohut, Kenneth Skoye, Benjamin Ross, Brian Van Bij, Donna Welch, Marian Weston, Edward Woods.

TIME	TOPICS	MEMBER NOTES
1500 - 1510	Adoption of Minutes (Meeting No. 3)	
1510 - 1520	Facilities Report	B. Van Bij
1520 - 1530	Registration Report	A. Kohut
1530 - 1540	Awards Report	C. Dennison
1540 - 1550	Communications Report	G. McLeod
1550 - 1600	Budget Report	S. Bhardwaj
1600 - 1610	Public Relations Report	B. Ross
1610 - 1620	Publications Report	M. Weston
1620 - 1630	Other Business	
1630 - 1640	Announcements	
1640 - 1645	Adjournment	

Members of the group are often asked to submit topics for the agenda. This practice, if followed, should be followed consistently. Requests for items should be made early enough that the administrative assistant has time to prepare a final agenda based on the replies received.

Figure 11-4 illustrates a sample agenda. This particular type of agenda

1. states the topics that will be covered
2. allows the participants to record information regarding decisions and possible follow-up.

Assembling Materials

Before the meeting, assemble the materials your manager will definitely need during the meeting. Arrange them in a folder in the order in which they will be required. Your manager may need

- an agenda
- a list of standing committees
- an up-to-date membership list
- minutes of previous meeting(s)
- other minutes that have not yet been approved
- action items that have not been completed
- documents relating to the agenda items
- copies of materials that have been prepared for distribution

You will be aware that certain supporting materials may be called for during the meeting. Assemble them, but if the meeting is in your manager's office, keep them on your desk. If you attend the meeting, take the folder of supporting materials with you. Do *not* put these papers in with the other materials your manager will take to the meeting. Sorting through papers during the meeting may be disruptive.

If the meeting is out of town, put the supporting materials in 23 x 31 cm envelopes, carefully labelled so that your manager will be able to find them quickly.

As a precaution, never mix file copies with materials to be carried around. Make copies, and leave the originals in the files.

Handling Telephone Interruptions

If you are not attending the meeting and are asked to give a participant a message while the meeting is in progress, key the message, knock lightly on the door, quietly enter, and hand the message to the person who should be the recipient. Your intent should be to enter the room with as little interruption as possible. Above all, make yourself familiar with the office protocol.

If there is a telephone in the meeting room, answer it when it rings. Write the message on a telephone message blank (which you have placed by the telephone before the meeting starts); then hand the message to the recipient. If you must call a participant to the telephone, walk to the person and speak quietly. If the topic being considered at the moment the telephone rings is so important that you cannot stop taking notes, ask someone nearby to answer the telephone.

Recording Minutes

You may be assigned the task of recording and transcribing the minutes of a business meeting. For example, if your manager is chairperson of a committee within your organization, he or she will need your help in preparing a record of the meeting. If your manager is one of the officers of the corporation—particularly the corporate secretary—you may be the one who takes the minutes of the board of directors' meetings.

Using a Tape Recorder

A tape recorder is sometimes used to obtain a verbatim record of a meeting for the purpose of

1. preparing a verbatim transcript
2. assisting the administrative assistant in writing accurate minutes
3. securing a record of discussions on controversial topics.

When you are recording a meeting on tape, you need to be aware of what is *not* being recorded and take essential notes. For instance, when a chairperson acknowledges a speaker, the chairperson does not always call the speaker's name. Likewise, a chairperson does not always restate a motion as it is being voted upon. When members are following distributed materials, reading as the discussion ensues, the section to which the speaker is referring is not always clear from the tape. Use your notes to supplement the recording.

In your notebook record:

- Time and date of meeting
- Place of meeting
- The names of attendees
- References to corrections
- Additions to the minutes
- Who introduced reports and is making motions
- Paragraph and page references to materials being distributed
- The exact statement of each motion (if the chairperson does not state it)

- Who volunteers for follow-up work
- The time of adjournment

and anything else that will be helpful to you in preparing the minutes. If you make a note in your notebook each time a motion is made, you will be able to organize the minutes quickly as you listen to the tape.

Determine the company policy for keeping tapes. Keep each tape until the minutes have been approved, or for a much longer time when the topics are controversial or may become controversial. Some groups keep the minute tapes permanently. Check the company policy before erasing the tape.

Using a Notebook

Taking notes is easiest when parliamentary procedure is followed, because you are not expected to prepare a verbatim transcript: only motions and a few other items must be recorded verbatim. Minutes provide a record of all the action taken during the meeting; they are not a detailed review of what was said. Your job is to record the essential information that will serve as a basis for writing the minutes.

Here are guidelines and suggestions concerning what facts must be included in the minutes:

1. Before the meeting, study the minutes of similar meetings. Become familiar with the form used, and envision what the minutes you write should include.
2. Sit near the chairperson so that you can assist each other.
3. Ask the chairperson to see that you get a copy of all materials read or discussed. These materials are a part of the record and should be attached to the minutes. Do not wait until the end of the meeting to collect them.
4. If you are not using a tape recorder, arrange a signal, such as slightly raising your hand, with the chairperson to let him or her know that you need assistance in getting statements that must be transcribed verbatim.
5. Before the meeting begins, record the name of the group and the date, time, and place of the meeting.
6. Using a list of members that you prepared in advance, place a check mark in the appropriate column to indicate attendance and absence.
7. When minutes are corrected, make the changes with your pen in your copy of the minutes. If the change is not lengthy, carefully draw a line through the words deleted and write in the words to be substituted or added. Jot down a reminder in your notebook that the minutes were corrected, for this action must be described in the minutes of the current meeting. If the change is lengthy or complicated, in your copy of the minutes draw a line through all the words to be deleted; or cross out entire paragraphs and in your notebook write verbatim everything that is to be substituted and added as well as where it is to be inserted.
8. Indicate in your notes the name of the person making the motion.
9. Write the exact words of anyone who asks that his or her view be made a part of the record.
10. Be alert during the informal discussion that sometimes follows the adoption of a main motion. This discussion centres on implementation of the action—the details about who will do what, when, and how. Record each detail as it is suggested. After a detail is agreed upon—this usually is not by vote—write a word such as "agreed" or "yes" beside it. Each of these items must be followed up. Draw a line through suggestions made but not accepted if you have entered them in your notes. Be sure to take copious notes on any obligations your manager assumes during the meeting.
11. While a committee is being appointed, get down the name of the committee, the full names of the members, and who accepted the position of chairperson.
12. When officers are elected, record the names of all the officers—incumbent as well as new—and their respective offices.
13. Make notes on the place, date, and time of the next meeting.
14. Jot down the time of adjournment.
15. As soon as the meeting adjourns, verify any points about which you are doubtful. You may need to ask about a person's title, the full name of a product or a place, the correctness of a technical term with which you are not familiar, or any small details you need in order to prepare complete minutes.

Using a Computer

Technology is improving every aspect of office duties. Recording minutes of meetings is not an exception to this. Transcribing minutes from handwritten notes and a voice recording can be an arduous task. If the administrative assistant uses a notebook computer to record notes during the meeting, the task of transcription will be far simpler; in fact, all that will be required is some reformatting and editing (spelling and grammar) of the text. Refer to Figure 11-5 to see a notebook computer being used during a meeting.

During a meeting, a computer can be used for more than recording notes. A notebook computer may operate from a battery pack, or through an electrical adaptor; also, it may be connected on-line to a local area network (LAN) or to another central processing unit (CPU). All of this provides not only flexibility but also the power to access information needed to make informed decisions during meetings.

Following Up

As soon as you return to your desk, make entries in the appointment calendars, set aside materials to be mailed to members who were absent, and prepare a list reminding your manager of his or her obligations resulting from the meeting. Enter the time of the next meeting in both your manager's calendar and your own. In addition, list any other time commitments your manager made during the meeting.

Figure 11-5 Notebook computer used during a meeting.
Courtesy of International Business Machines Corporation. Unauthorized use not permitted.

Figure 11-6 Computer access is essential for many meetings.
Courtesy of International Business Machines Corporation. Unauthorized use not permitted.

All distributed materials that were introduced and discussed are a part of the minutes and should be referred to in the minutes and attached to them. Everyone who was present already has his or her copy, but you have the added task of mailing copies to members who were absent. Address a large enough envelope (23 x 31 cm or 26 x 33 cm envelopes are usually appropriate) to each absent member and insert the attachments. To simplify your own duties and to extend a courtesy to those who were absent, also mail copies of any materials distributed but not discussed. Since you probably will not refer to these in the minutes, make a longhand notation on each one indicating its status.

> ***"When setting up meetings and conferences, never assume anything and expect the unexpected."***
>
> Kelly Macpherson, Graduate
> Columbia College
> Calgary, AB

Put a copy of everything—agenda, resolutions, reports, and so on—in a folder, ready to be attached to the file copy of the minutes and to be used as reference while you are preparing the minutes. In the upper left corner of each supporting document, write the date and how it was disposed of—adopted, discussed, or postponed.

Keep in mind that the record of a meeting must be meaningful in the future to those who were not present. The record must show that the decisions made actually were carried out. To ensure that there is an understanding of what was agreed upon, and to provide a complete record of transactions, the chairperson writes memoranda to those who are to assist with following up, as well as letters of congratulations to newly elected officers—even if these members were present at the meeting.

After a typical formal meeting, the chairperson will have numerous follow-up tasks. You can help by preparing a To Do List. Each notation can be brief—just a reminder—but your list must be complete. While you are writing the minutes, watch for any item that must be added to the To Do List.

Preparing Minutes

Given adequate information, you can prepare minutes without having attended the meeting yourself. If your manager is recording secretary for a civic or professional organization, he or she will probably do one of the following:

1. dictate the minutes for you to key in final form
2. hand you detailed notes, from which you would transcribe the minutes
3. give you a disk on which the minutes have been keyed and ask you to edit and improve on the format.

You may wonder why preparing minutes for a civic or professional organization is a part of your job. Corporations, institutions such as universities and hospitals, and various types of businesses encourage staff members to participate in civic and professional organizations. Such participation means accepting responsibilities, and providing competent help is the most efficient way to carry out some of these.

Key the minutes immediately following the meeting. When you work from your manager's notes, it is more than likely that you will have to ask questions to gather additional facts, even when you tried to obtain all the information as your manager reviewed the notes with you. Ask any questions while the meeting is fresh in your manager's mind. If you recorded the minutes of the meeting yourself, you will be able to organize the motions and amendments and summarize the discussion much faster if you do these things very soon after the meeting.

Before you prepare a final version, key a rough draft of the minutes, double-spaced, and submit it to your manager for approval. Before you duplicate the minutes, submit the final copy to the organization's secretary or presiding officer for his or her signature.

Your purpose in preparing the minutes is:

1. to include all the essential information as a record that will be meaningful to others in the future
2. to make it easy for the reader to locate a single item.

When a meeting has been conducted so informally that motions were not made and agreement was by consent rather than by voting, include the essential facts about the purpose of the meeting, who attended, and when and where it was held; then summarize the action. For formal meetings, use the following as a guide:

1. Either single- or double-space minutes. Single-spacing saves paper, filing space, and mailing and faxing costs.
2. In all-capital letters, key a heading that fully identifies the meeting: MEETING OF THE PROGRAM PLANNING COMMITTEE, XYZ SOCIETY. Key the date as a subheading a double-space below the heading. Placing the date where the reader can see it at a glance, without reading the opening paragraph, makes it easier to locate information in the future. Repeat the date on each page. If the group holds special meetings, the subheading could read: "Special Meeting, October 22, 20–."
3. Use the past tense, and write complete sentences. In the opening paragraph, state the name of the group, where the meeting was held, both the time and the date, who presided, and whether the meeting was regular or special. When the meeting was "called" (that is, when it was "special"), add the purpose of the meeting, since it was called for an express purpose.
4. State whether the minutes of the previous meeting (mention its date) were "approved as read," "approved as distributed," "approved as corrected," or dispensed with.
5. Use side headings or marginal captions to help the reader locate items. The agenda will be helpful in organizing the minutes.
6. Mention all reports presented by officers, standing committees, and special committees in the order in which they were presented; and say what disposition was made of them. Usually a member of a group moves that the report be accepted; when it is, this action should be reported in the minutes.
7. To make each distributed report a part of the official record, refer to each one in the appropriate section of the minutes. You could say, "The attached report on Revised Plans for Issuing Supplies was distributed by Tamara Yee, chairperson of the Committee on Reducing Office Costs." In the same paragraph, state who made the motion and the action taken.
8. Key verbatim all reports read orally and treat them as quoted material; that is, indent five spaces from the left and the right. This way, the format will reflect the origin of the material. If a report that was read is lengthy and in a form that can be copied, you can say, for example, that "the report on Downtime for Reproduction Equipment, presented by Norman Hanover, was copied and is attached." A participant who reads a report but does not provide copies for the members should present a copy to the secretary. If he or she does not, ask for it.
9. Treat each main motion (and the amendments related to it, if any) as a separate item. Be sure to

include in the minutes all motions made and how they were disposed of. This includes motions framed during the meeting and those submitted in writing; however, it does not include motions that were withdrawn. State each motion verbatim, along with who made it, that it was seconded, whether it was adopted or defeated, and the votes cast for and against it. For some groups, also include the name of the person who seconded the motion.

10. When a motion has been made from the floor, you can begin the paragraph by saying, "Lillie Williamson moved [not made a motion] that ...," or "It was moved by Lillie Williamson and seconded by Raj Falfer that ..."
11. When a motion is amended, give the history of the motion in the minutes. First, state the motion, who made it, and that it was seconded. Next, take up the amendments in the same order as they were made. State each amendment verbatim, who made it, that it was seconded, and the votes cast for and against it. If all the amendments are defeated, the vote is taken on the original motion, and the minutes should reflect this. Since an amended motion is always restated, being voted upon as amended, state an amended motion verbatim; and indicate whether it was adopted or defeated, and the votes cast for and against it.
12. The debate concerning a motion does not have to be included; nevertheless, reasons for a decision are often helpful to the current officers and to others in the future. Therefore, discussion can be included in the minutes. Summarize the debate in broad, concise terms. Try to include all the main ideas—both pros and cons—but do not bog down the minutes with who said what. Write the name of any person who requests that his or her statement be made a part of the record, and then, of course, write the statement verbatim.
13. By allocating extra space to one idea, you are emphasizing it, and thereby overshadowing the other ideas. Avoid this kind of emphasis unless your purpose is to show that one idea is much more significant than the others. Also, avoid using judgment words such as "outstanding" or "excellent."
14. If implementation of the action taken was discussed, write the details of implementation in the paragraph following the statement of the action. State who will do what, when, where, and how. All of these details are important.
15. Motions should appear in the minutes in the same order that they were taken up during the meeting. Minutes shift abruptly from one topic to another. Just separate them with side headings, or triple-space between them when you use marginal captions.
16. An agenda item that has been taken up but not completed becomes unfinished business on the agenda of the next meeting; therefore, indicate with some detail any information that will be helpful when this item is taken up again.
17. Group announcements near the end under the heading "Announcements." Some of the announcements may have been made at the beginning of the meeting or during it, but they can be grouped together.
18. Include the time, place, and date of the next meeting, and the time of adjournment.
19. Minutes that are to be read aloud are signed by the secretary; minutes that are to be distributed are signed by both the chairperson and the secretary. When a group has both a corresponding secretary and a recording secretary, the recording secretary is the one who is responsible for the minutes. When one secretary is responsible for both jobs, the title used is "Secretary." When you act as secretary for a group, your title will be either Secretary or Secretary for the Meeting.
20. Provide a place for the signature and the date of approval, such as

________	____________
Date	Secretary

OR

________	____________
Date	Chairperson
________	____________
Date	Secretary

21. Arrange the file copy of the minutes in chronological order. Arrange all attachments in the order they were introduced in the minutes.

Correcting Minutes

When minutes have been corrected or amended, the changes should be recorded in two places: as an insertion in the minutes being corrected, and in paragraph form in the minutes of the meeting during which the changes were made.

To show corrections and additions in the file copy of the minutes being corrected, add words in longhand

and delete by drawing lines through words. You want the changes to be obvious, so do not erase. In the margin, enter the date of the meeting during which the changes were made. Sometimes the changed material is too lengthy to be inserted in this way. If this is the case, key the corrections and additions on a separate sheet of paper and attach the paper to the end of the minutes; then draw a line through all the material that has been deleted and make a notation that the corrected paragraphs are attached. *Never* rekey minutes to correct them. Make the changes in such a way that anyone reading the minutes can tell what corrections and additions were made, when, and how they were ordered.

If minutes are not regularly approved at the following meeting, you will have the problem of keeping up with which minutes have been approved and which have not. Sometimes the approval of minutes is dispensed with, and then several sets are approved at a later meeting. The place provided for the date of approval usually appears at the end of the minutes. To be able to tell at a glance which minutes have been approved, write "Approved" and the date of approval at the top of the first page of the file copy of each set of minutes immediately after the meeting in which the minutes were approved.

TEAM MEETINGS

The TQM concept of meetings (discussed in Chapter 2) focuses on equal participation; each participant's input is considered to be as significant as all other. The TQM concept is effective because each member is empowered to participate regardless of his or her organizational status. Practitioners of this concept believe that it is effective because of the structure of the team. Teams make decisions at their level of authority. If a decision must be made at a higher level of authority, the team forwards a recommendation to management.

Preparation for the Meeting

A meeting that follows TQM techniques requires the same preparation as any other meeting—a convenient time is established, people are invited, and an agenda is prepared and delivered to participants prior to the meeting.

When TQM techniques are followed, careful attention is given to issues that arise even at the preliminary stages:

- Choosing an appropriate time is important. You want the full attendance and full attention of every team member.
- The people who form the team may be from all levels of the organization. All who are involved in the process (event) to be discussed at the meeting should be invited.
- Each team member carries equal status. No one person is allowed to dominate the meeting. Refer to the section "Roles of Participants" for an understanding of each team member's responsibilities.
- The prepared agenda may be very general, since the actual topics to be discussed should be decided by the team. Refer to the section "Nominal Group Technique."

The agenda is much like that of a more traditional meeting. However, agenda items are often determined at the meeting, so agenda topics may be very general. Refer to Figure 11-7. Every agenda should include the following:

1. meeting date and time, and the number at the meeting
2. venue for the meeting
3. names of the participants
4. agenda topics (even if very general)
5. estimated time guidelines for each agenda item.

Separate from the agenda, design a page for participants to take more detailed notes during the meeting. This meeting log helps the recorder and team members to stay focused during the meeting and to later recall their perception of topics and decisions. Refer to Figure 11-8 for a sample of a TQM meeting log. Often, a meeting log can be used in place of more formal minutes. A complete copy of the meeting log may serve as the record of the meeting; it is filed in the team folder and distributed to all team members as their copy of the minutes.

Roles of Participants

Meetings that follow the TQM principles tend to have a number of participants because all people who are directly or indirectly involved with agenda topics should be present. Part of the TQM philosophy is to get input from people who are actually working within the process. In other words, people who know the most about a process should be at the meeting to discuss it and to make wise recommendations and decisions about it.

Each role in the team is equally important. The following briefly discusses the roles of team participants:

1. ***Team Leader.*** The team leader acts as a chairperson, directing the meeting, moving from one topic to the next, and keeping on schedule.

Figure 11-7 Agenda for a team meeting.

AGENDA

MEETING NO. 1

ADMINISTRATIVE TEAM

DATE:	Wednesday, June 10, 20--
TIME:	1000
PLACE:	Conference Room 3
TEAM LEADER:	Jeffrey Keaton
FACILITATOR:	Jodi Alford
RECORDER:	Gina Darroch
GUIDANCE TEAM:	Kenneth Skoye, Donna Welch
QUALITY ADVISER:	Edward Woods
TEAM MEMBERS:	Jodi Alford, Satvinder Bhardwaj, Gina Darroch, Gordon McLeod, Chris Dennison, Jeffrey Keaton, Allan Kohut, Kenneth Skoye, Benjamin Ross, Brian Van Bij, Donna Welch, Marian Weston.

TIME	TOPICS	NOTES
0830 - 0835	Check-in	
0835 - 0840	State goals of meeting	
0840 - 0845	Review roles of team members	
0845 - 0850	Establish house rules	
0850 - 0930	Brainstorm issues to be discussed	
0930 - 0945	Vote on importance of issues using NGT	
0945 - 1000	Coffee Break	
1000 - 1200	Discussion/recommendations on issues	
1200 - 1300	Lunch	
1300 - 1400	Discussion/recommendations on issues	

Figure 11-8 Meeting log.

<table>
<tr><th colspan="2">MEETING LOG</th></tr>
<tr><td colspan="2">MEETING OF: Quality Team</td></tr>
<tr><td>LOCATION: RW 210</td><td>DATE: May 4, 20— TIME: 1000</td></tr>
<tr><td>MEMBERS PRESENT: J. Alford, S. Bhardwaj, G. Darroch, J. Keaton, A. Kohut, B. Ross, M. Weston</td><td>MEMBERS ABSENT: G. McLeod, C. Dennison, B. Van Bij</td></tr>
<tr><th>PROBLEMS / ISSUES DISCUSSED</th><th>RECORD OF DISCUSSION</th></tr>
<tr><td><u>PROBLEM / ISSUE NO. 1</u>
Topic = Dissatisfaction of customers due to delayed billing.

Follow-up =
1. Gina Darroch will set up meeting with Info. Systems manager.
2. Ben Ross will discuss paperwork with Peter.</td><td>— equip. downtime is high
— messages on telephone not working
— competition is high-tech
— paperwork is slow from sales staff
— work flow is between buildings

Recommendation/s =
1. upgrade hardware & software
2. make paperwork easier for sales staff</td></tr>
<tr><td><u>PROBLEM / ISSUE NO. 2</u>
Topic =

Follow-up =</td><td>

Recommendation/s =</td></tr>
<tr><td><u>PROBLEM / ISSUE NO. 3</u>
Topic =

Follow-up =</td><td>

Recommendation/s =</td></tr>
</table>

2. ***Guidance Team.*** The guidance team should consist of two or more people who are very familiar with the organization. Often these people hold management positions; this enables them to provide information that other members may be unaware of and that will be helpful when team decisions are made. The guidance team members should be people who have the authority to make changes and the clout to put decisions into practice. Where a team has been empowered to make recommendations or decisions, the guidance team does not attend meetings unless requested to do so by the team leader.
3. ***Quality Adviser.*** The responsibility of the quality adviser is to ensure that TQM principles are adhered to. This person is thoroughly trained in the TQM process and, therefore, understands the scientific approach and group dynamics that are necessary to make the meeting successful.

   The quality adviser is necessary in the early stages, when the team is learning these new techniques; there will be little need for this person as the team becomes educated in the new process.
4. ***Project Team Members.*** All members who will take part in the discussions and vote on issues are considered project team members. This includes the team leader but does not include the guidance team or the facilitator. The votes of the project team members are critical to the decision-making process.
5. ***Facilitator.*** The facilitator's responsibility is to make the meeting process flow with ease. Questions are asked of the participants to clarify their ideas, and the wording of comments is manipulated to make them clear.

   The facilitator structures the comments into a simple list, a flowchart, or a cause-and-effect diagram. (Refer to the section "Brainstorming" for more information on cause-and-effect diagrams.) These visual aids make the participants aware of comments that have been presented.

   The facilitator's task is a demanding one; therefore, he or she will often ask a team member to assist by recording the comments on a flip chart or erasable board.

   The facilitator must be completely nonbiased about the topics being discussed. For that reason, the facilitator is often a person from a different department. As well, the facilitator may perform the duties of the quality adviser. Of course, the people in these roles do not participate in voting.
6. ***Recorder.*** The recorder's task is to prepare minutes. Topics discussed, decisions, and follow-up to be made must be a part of the minutes. The recorder is also responsible for forming the priority list of issues after the participants have voted.

   The task of recording is often rotated between team members so that no one team member always has the additional responsibility of taking notes at each meeting. When a team member has the responsibility of taking notes, the attention needed for the task often eliminates her or him from part of the meeting discussion.

   This task is made infinitely easier by the use of a computer and printer at the meeting. A further explanation of this process is found in the section "Nominal Group Technique."

Starting the Meeting

With the TQM process, considerable effort is applied to making meetings productive; it is therefore imperative that meetings commence in an effective manner.

1. ***The team leader starts early.*** He or she should arrive before any of the other participants in order to write the agenda in a place that is visible to all members. A flip chart or an erasable board works well.

   If house rules have been established at a prior meeting, the leader will want to place these rules in an obvious location.

   The leader should make sure the room configuration is conducive to team participation. Perhaps the chairs and tables need to be arranged in a circle. Is there an area for the coffee and juice containers? Does the coffee pot need to be plugged in?

   As each member arrives, the team leader should give him or her a warm welcome in order to establish a friendly environment for sharing information and ideas.
2. ***The meeting begins and ends as scheduled.*** Do not wait for late arrivals. People appreciate a team leader who starts and ends on time. Once late arrivals learn that the meetings begin exactly on schedule, they will try harder to be on time.
3. ***Warm-up.*** If the members do not know each other, the team leader should start the meeting by having all people introduce themselves. This can be considered part of the meeting warm-up. There are many activities that the leader can initiate for team warm-ups. If the members of the team already know each other, the warm-up can be dispensed with.
4. ***Check-in.*** "Checking in" is an opportunity for each team member to express his or her present

state of mind to the whole team. It is not necessary for everyone to check in; however, it is helpful for members to understand the "baggage" that other people have brought with them to the meeting. Most people cannot simply switch off their feelings and become active participants. When possible, it is best to check in with the team.

Checking in may sound something like

- "I am deeply concerned about my son, who is at home and very ill. So if I don't appear to be functioning at my best this morning, you'll all know why."
- "I've been looking forward to getting some of these issues resolved, so I'm very happy to have been invited to this meeting."
- "My desk is loaded with work and I have a paper due for my night school class. If I seem a little stressed, that's why."
- "I've just had a super weekend; my energy has returned and I'm ready to participate."

5. ***Agree on the goals.*** Once the check-in is complete—that is, once all those who wish to check in have done so—the team leader should state the goals of the meeting. Of course, the team members should agree to the goals before moving to the next item.
6. ***Review the roles of the team.*** The roles of the team leader, guidance team, quality adviser, facilitator, and project team members should be reviewed by the team leader. Of course, this will be necessary only for the first or second meeting. Once the team members have exercised their roles, they will know what is expected of them.
7. ***Establish the house rules.*** The next step toward a successful project is establishing the house rules, also referred to as the "ground rules." The team should suggest and agree on some general house rules. When these rules are not adhered to, any team member may point this out and bring the meeting back on track. Suggestions for house rules might be
   - Everyone will be given an equal opportunity to speak.
   - Any person wishing to speak must raise his or her hand.
   - Criticize issue only not the person.
   - Side conversations are not allowed.
   - Each person must focus on the speaker.
   - Expect unfinished business.
   - The meeting will begin and finish on schedule.
   - Everyone will focus on the topic and will not interrupt the team's work for outside reasons.
   - No negative body language is allowed.

Brainstorming

If the agenda is general and the team is expected to provide the issues for discussion, the next step is team **brainstorming**. Even if the topics for discussion have been predetermined, brainstorming is a useful tool to apply now. Brainstorming will help the team develop as many ideas in as short a time as possible.

Brainstorming may be carried out in one of two ways: structured, and unstructured:

1. ***Structured.*** The structured method works well if the point is to avoid having one or two people dominate the meeting. It also works to encourage more introverted members to share their ideas.

   When structured brainstorming is used, every person is given a turn to express opinions, concerns, or ideas. The opportunity to speak rotates participants; people wishing to express their ideas must wait their turn. The rotation of ideas will be repeated until all ideas have been expressed. As each member states a problem he or she would like to deal with at the meeting, that person should also state why it should be considered an issue.

   During the rotation, any member may forfeit the opportunity to share an idea.

   Each of these ideas must be recorded by the facilitator (or the facilitator's assistant) and by the person responsible for preparing the minutes or the meeting log.
2. ***Unstructured.*** The unstructured method of brainstorming has a freer atmosphere; participants are allowed to express their ideas as they think of them. No rotation or waiting for turns is involved. Although this creates a very relaxed atmosphere in which to brainstorm, the problem of domination by one or two members may arise.

Whether the atmosphere is structured or unstructured, the facilitator will work hard to make the ideas clear and relevant and to balance the participation. All ideas must be recorded (by the facilitator or by the facilitator's assistant) where the participants can view them. As well, all team members must agree on the wording.

The recorder remains busy during the brainstorming session, documenting all the problems that the team has identified. These problems are then prioritized by the group according to their importance.

Nominal Group Technique

Once the problems have all been listed, and assuming there are no duplicate problems, the team should establish by vote which issues are most important and need immediate attention.

To ensure that the most vocal or persuasive participants do not dominate the proceedings, the Nominal Group Technique (NGT) should be applied. Without NGT, concerns raised by less forceful participants might never be worked on and resolved.

The recorder should prepare a form similar to the one in Figure 11-9. With this form, each participant can vote on each problem separately. Weighting is based on the following:

3 = The problem is of high priority and should be dealt with now.
2 = The problem is of medium priority and should be dealt with as soon as possible.
1 = The problem is of low priority and should be dealt with when possible.
0 = The issue raised does not affect you or your work.

Once the voting is complete, the facilitator may ask for a show of hands on each issue, or may collect the sheets and do the calculations in private. Once the calculations are complete, the weighting on each listed problem illustrates which issues the team wishes to discuss and resolve. The recorder should sort these weightings on the computer and provide all team members with the revised list. Refer to Figures 11-10 and 11-11.

NGT has helped the team reach a consensus.

Discussion and Solution

The problems that received the highest priority under NGT are now discussed and resolved. To encourage brainstorming, the facilitator might now draw a cause-and-effect diagram.

The cause-and-effect diagram is often referred to as a fishbone diagram. Refer to Figure 11-12. The lines on the diagram (which appear as fishbones) represent the causes of the problem. The facilitator usually starts with four to six major categories such as the ones shown in Figure 11-12 (Equipment and Software, Procedures, People, Sources). These major categories help to get the team thinking. The participants add to the diagram by suggesting more specific causes that fit under these major categories. It is important to use as few words as possible but to make the causes very clear.

The rectangle on the right of the diagram (the fish's "head") represents the *effect*, or the major problem brought on by the causes.

Figure 11-9 Voting sheet.

VOTING SHEET FOR NOMINAL GROUP TECHNIQUE

ITEM NO.	ISSUES FOR DISCUSSION	TOTAL VOTES			
		3	2	1	0
1.	Ticketing of cars parked in the south lot should be reviewed.				
2.	New payment schedule for per diem expenses should be reviewed.				
3.	Criteria for Employee of the Month award should be reviewed.				
4.	Lack of nutritious food in the staff cafeteria should be reviewed.				
5.	Purchase of more voice mail boxes should be reviewed.				
6.	Upgrading of fax machine should be reviewed.				
7.	Purchase of a colour photocopier for the Reprographics Department should be reviewed.				
8.	Extension of LAN services for office support staff should be reviewed.				
9.	Further Total Quality Management training for administrative assistants should be reviewed.				
10.	Dissatisfaction of customers due to delayed billing should be reviewed.				

REMEMBER:
3 = This problem is of high priority and should be dealt with now.
2 = This problem is of medium priority and should be dealt with as soon as possible.
1 = This problem is of low priority and should be dealt with when possible.
0 = This problem does not affect me or my work.

Figure 11-10 Votes have been tallied and weighted.

VOTING SHEET FOR NOMINAL GROUP TECHNIQUE						
ITEM NO.	ISSUES FOR DISCUSSION	TOTAL VOTES				WEIGHTED AVERAGE
		3	2	1	0	
1.	Ticketing of cars parked in the south lot should be reviewed.	7	3	4	1	2.0
2.	New payment schedule for per diem expenses should be reviewed.	12	1	1	1	2.6
3.	Criteria for Employee of the Month award should be reviewed.	10	2	3	0	2.4
4.	Lack of nutritious food in the staff cafeteria should be reviewed.	0	3	9	3	1.0
5.	Purchase of more voice mail boxes should be reviewed.	10	3	2	0	2.5
6.	Upgrading of fax machine should be reviewed.	12	1	1	1	2.6
7.	Purchase of a colour photocopier for the Repro. Dept. should be reviewed.	5	8	1	1	2.11
8.	Extension of LAN services for office support staff should be reviewed.	12	2	1	0	2.7
9.	Further TQM training for administrative assistants should be reviewed.	9	3	3	0	2.4
10.	Dissatisfaction of customers due to delayed billing should be reviewed.	14	1	0	0	2.9

REMEMBER:

3 = This problem is of high priority and should be dealt with now.
2 = This problem is of medium priority and should be dealt with as soon as possible.
1 = This problem is of low priority and should be dealt with when possible.
0 = This problem does not affect me or my work.

CALCULATION OF WEIGHTED AVERAGE:

(3 x No. of Votes in Priority 3)
Plus (2 x No. of Votes in Priority 2)
Plus (No. of Votes in Priority 1)
Divide the sum by total number of votes on the problem

A structured or unstructured brainstorming technique can be used to fill the diagram with all the possible causes of the problem.

Once all the causes have been identified, the team leader leads a discussion in which solutions are sought. The team leader will probably ask the team members why each of the causes happens. No doubt this will encourage discussion.

During the discussion and solution phase, the team must remain respectful of the house rules. Any infraction of the rules should be brought to the attention of the team.

Team members may use their meeting logs to write personal notes while the designated recorder makes a more detailed record of important discussion points, solutions, recommendations, and planned follow-up. The meeting log will form the official record of the meeting.

Closure

Although discussion of the topics has now concluded, it is important to spend a few minutes **debriefing**. The debriefing session allows participants to express their feelings. Each participant is invited to debrief, or "check out"; however, it is not required.

During the debriefing phase you might hear comments such as the following:

- "I feel this was a successful meeting today. The candor of the participants was very helpful in reaching decisions."
- "I feel some scepticism at the decisions made today; however, I am willing to work with these new ideas."
- "Because I'm tired, I was ready to check out some time ago. Although it seemed a long meeting, plenty was accomplished."

Figure 11-11 Issues have been placed in order of priority.

VOTING SHEET FOR NOMINAL GROUP TECHNIQUE						
		TOTAL VOTES				
ITEM NO.	ISSUES FOR DISCUSSION	3	2	1	0	AVERAGE
10.	Dissatisfaction of customers due to delayed billing should be reviewed.	14	1	0	0	2.9
8.	Extension of LAN services for office support staff should be reviewed.	12	2	1	0	2.7
2.	New payment schedule for per diem expenses should be reviewed.	12	1	1	1	2.6
6.	Upgrading of fax machine should be reviewed.	12	1	1	1	2.6
5.	Purchase of more voice mail boxes should be reviewed.	10	3	2	0	2.5
3.	Criteria for Employee of the Month award should be reviewed.	10	2	3	0	2.4
9.	Further TQM training for administrative assistants should be reviewed.	9	3	3	0	2.4
7.	Purchase of a colour photocopier for the Repro. Dept. should be reviewed.	5	8	1	1	2.1
1.	Ticketing of cars parked in the south lot should be reviewed.	7	3	4	1	2.0
4.	Lack of nutritious food in the staff cafeteria should be reviewed.	0	3	9	3	1.0

REMEMBER:

3 = This problem is of high priority and should be dealt with now.

2 = This problem is of medium priority and should be dealt with as soon as possible.

1 = This problem is of low priority and should be dealt with when possible.

0 = This problem does not affect me or my work.

CALCULATION OF WEIGHTED AVERAGE:

(3 x No. of Votes in Priority 3)

Plus (2 x No. of Votes in Priority 2)

Plus (No. of Votes in Priority 1)

Divide the sum by total number of votes on the problem

TELECONFERENCING

Teleconferencing, a time-saving way to conduct meetings, is a powerful tool for decision making and for internal communications. See "Hi Tech Conferences" in Chapter 9. Because executives today have a greater **span of control**, they are constantly seeking ways to spend less time travelling and more time conducting business.

Teleconferencing is a meeting of at least three persons in two or more locations by means of telephones and/or other electronic devices. To save travel time and costs and at the same time maintain effective communications, more and more organizations are using teleconferencing by telephone and video.

The administrative assistant's responsibilities in teleconferencing are similar to those in preparing for other meetings—reserving the conference time, notifying the participants, preparing and assembling materials to be transmitted, taking notes during the conference, and following up on work that needs to be done afterward.

Audioconferencing

Placing conference calls by telephone when the participants are located in different geographic areas is called *audio teleconferencing*. This is the most widely used teleconferencing tool today; it can be used effectively when there is no need for video transmission. The calls are transmitted either with operator assistance or through dedicated lines. Dedicated lines are directly connected to your teleconference destination; this eliminates the need for an operator. For small groups, speakerphones are convenient.

Figure 11-12 Cause-and-effect diagram.

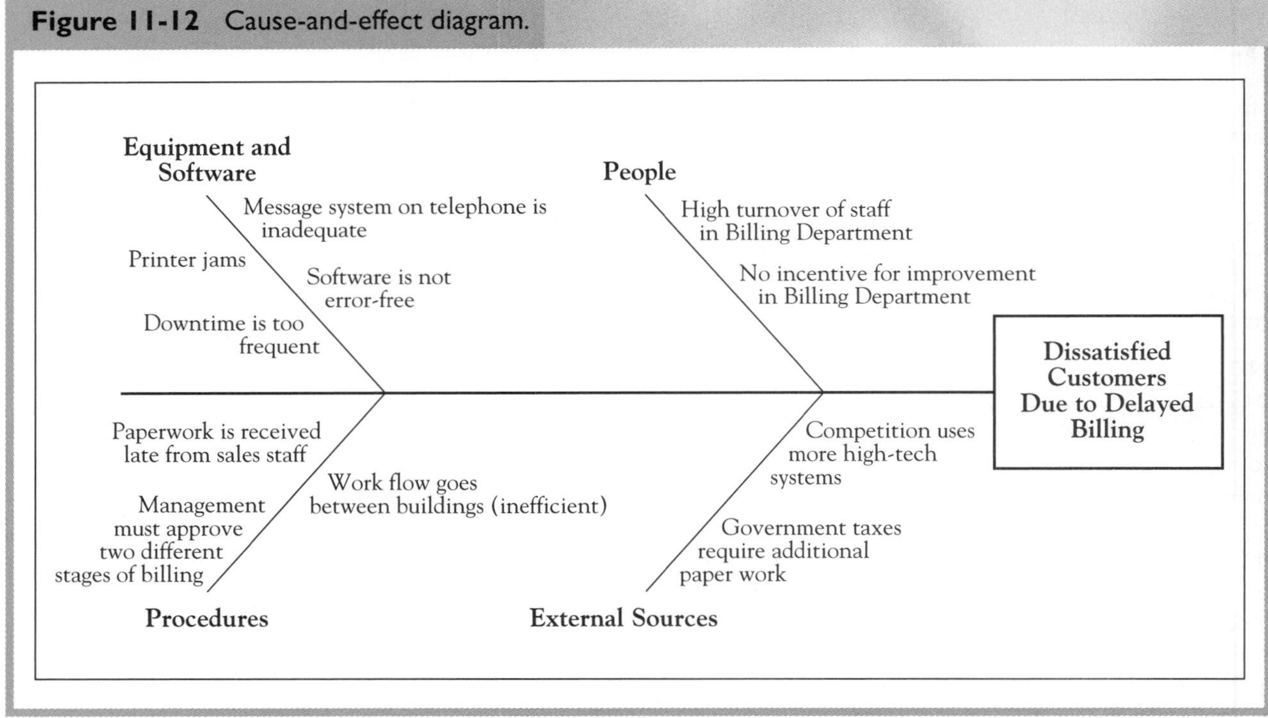

Videoconferencing

A teleconference that combines telephone and video is referred to as a *videoconference*. Videoconference is a relatively expensive method of communicating; however, when compared to the travel expenses that are often involved in conventional long-distance meetings, videoconferencing is relatively affordable.

There are now many privately owned video teleconference studios across Canada. These offer many Canadian businesses an effective alternative to conducting meetings by conventional methods.

Direct Broadcast Video

Direct broadcast video, also called *one-way video*, is video transmission from a single location combined with telephone response from each of the receiving locations. Direct broadcast video is especially helpful in making immediate announcements about new products available throughout the organization, or a corporate-wide announcement by the president.

Computer Conferencing

Organizations can conduct conferences through computer terminals if the terminals are connected to a network. This network may be across the room or across the world, since telephone lines or cable may be used to carry the signals. The use of *computer conferencing* does not allow audio response; the only video response is the message that appears on the computer's screen.

PRO-LINK *pro-Link*

Did you know that there are many behavioural elements that make up the dynamics of a team? Those elements include:

- **Active Listening**—paying attention to the three parts of the message: the nonverbal, the tone, and the words.
- **Creative thinking**—generating and building on the ideas of others to stimulate solutions.
- **Supporting behaviour**—requiring a mind set that there is always merit to someone else's idea or suggestion.
- **Levelling**—the art of being honest with oneself and each other team member.
- **Confronting**—the process of separating the facts, not the people, from assumptions.
- **Consensus decision making**—using team information to make the most informed decision that is accepted by all involved.

Managing these elements is critical to the success of the meeting and the synergy of the team.

PERSPECTIVES

Intimidated by Business Social Events?

By Amy Mills Tunnicliffe

Failure to participate enthusiastically in conferences and meetings can be hazardous to your career. Here's how you can conquer your fears and perfect your schmoozing ability.

National and international conferences, off-site meetings, and company outings allow companies and individuals to achieve multiple goals. These events bring together employees and peers from around the country or around the globe in what is often a relaxed environment focused on motivation, education, and planning. The savvy office professional realizes these meetings also provide an opportunity to reinforce relationships with colleagues and peers, and to make positive impressions on senior management.

Failing to participate enthusiastically, shyly hovering on the periphery, and retreating to your hotel room instead of socializing can be detrimental to your career. A conference is an opportunity to touch base with many people—during required meetings and breakout sessions, as well as during meals and social outings. A lack of social skills, even on the smallest level, reflects poorly on the individual and the company, and ultimately sabotages the career.

Social savvy is crucial at business events and meetings, yet research shows most people experience anxiety at the thought of facing new situations and new people. Once you master the fundamental skills of proper planning and the art of polite, interesting conversation, business functions will become more enjoyable and rewarding, both personally and professionally.

Proper preparation will increase your chance of success. Be prepared with each of the following before the conference and use the information to your advantage:

Know the conference's raison d'etre. Is this an annual state-of-the-union meeting, a reward for a job well done, or an introduction of a new colleague, client, or product? Greet and respond appropriately upon arrival and let the people in charge know you are delighted to be part of the occasion.

- For a job well done, let your host know that you enjoyed being part of the team.
- If the event was planned only for camaraderie, respond by letting your host know you are having fun and enjoying the fellowship.
- If it's to congratulate or welcome, respond by congratulating and welcoming the new employee, client, or those most responsible for introducing a new product or service.

Know who is hosting the event. Conference manners dictate greeting the host and expressing your thanks to him as you exit. Do not leave any event until you have thanked your host.

Get a copy of the guest list. Call the host's assistant and ask for the list of attendees. You might ask for the list by saying: "I'm looking forward to the meeting at the Ritz-Carlton in December. I would like to prepare to meet the employees from headquarters. Would you please send me a guest list?" Study the list and make notes to help you interact with other guests. Think of topics the other person might enjoy based on information you already know about the person.

- Have you met him or her previously?
- Do you have something in common? A shared acquaintance, an alma mater, an interest?
- Follow up on a previous conversation, such as: "The last time we spoke you were preparing for a ski vacation. What did you think of Sun Valley? Have you skied this year?"
- Research as necessary. Ask your colleagues, your manager, or others within the organization about a person with whom you may not be familiar.
- If a guest has a difficult-to-pronounce name, learn in advance how to pronounce it properly—and practice.

Compose an agenda and stick to it.

- Circulate
- Make your way into conversations. "Excuse me. May I introduce myself?" Avoid two people deep in conversation, however. It's easier to approach people in groups of three or more.
- Shake hands with everyone.
- Avoid extra gestures of affection.
- Try to meet everyone at a small gathering. At a large gathering, focus on key people you want to meet.

Converse with ease.

- Be the first to say hello. Introduce yourself to others.
- Show curiosity and interest in others.
- Balance the conversation by both talking and listening.
- Discuss topics that are important to you.
- Listen for key words, facts, and experiences.
- Seek out common interests and details, and remember them.
- Be enthusiastic, friendly, and upbeat.
- Ask open-ended questions that begin with words like how, why, and in what way.

Follow up after the conference. Invest in quality social stationery and use it to write brief, warm notes to the following:

- the host of the conference,
- those who had crucial roles in planning,
- new and old colleagues, and
- key members of management with whom you've conversed.

In today's competitive business climate, it takes more than job skills or the right education to succeed. The socially confident office professional is concerned with the comfort of others and knows how to interact with individuals up and down the corporate ladder. To be an invaluable asset to your company, you must possess the critical social skills that let you easily navigate a business event and ultimately represent your company with poise and polish.

Reprinted by permission of the author.

Questions for Study and Review

1. How can the computer be helpful in arranging meetings?
2. When an administrative assistant is arranging an informal conference by telephone, what is the advantage of starting with two meeting times?
3. When arranging meetings, what preliminary activities can the administrative assistant take full responsibility for?
4. What information does an administrative assistant need before he or she can schedule a conference room for a meeting of a few executives?
5. State five reasons why business meetings might be conducted formally.
6. How can you determine the size of the room needed for a meeting?
7. List 15 supplies or pieces of equipment that may be required for a meeting.
8. State five guidelines to follow when ordering beverages for a meeting. State five guidelines to follow when ordering food for a meeting.
9. What is an agenda? List the order in which business generally is transacted in a formal meeting.
10. Explain how to assemble supporting materials for an out-of-town meeting.
11. Suggest an unobtrusive way to deliver an urgent telephone message to your manager while he or she is holding a conference in the office; and to someone attending a meeting your manager is chairing.
12. What must be recorded verbatim in formal minutes?
13. Corrections and additions (or deletions) to minutes should be recorded in two places. Where should these changes be recorded?
14. What is the purpose of an amendment?
15. A recording on tape must be supplemented with notes. What supplementary information will you need to record in order to write complete and accurate minutes?
16. What functions would a notebook computer serve at a meeting that was following TQM procedures?
17. What information concerning the meeting should you provide to your manager immediately following a meeting that he or she has chaired?
18. If you have booked your meeting at a hotel or conference centre, what two important policies of the booking agreement should you familiarize yourself with? Why?
19. Why should you include either headings or marginal captions in minutes?
20. What information should be included in the first paragraph of minutes?
21. In what order should motions appear in printed minutes? Should motions that were defeated be included? motions that were withdrawn?
22. Explain why you should not erase or rekey minutes to correct them.
23. Suggest a way to mark copies of the minutes for the file in order to determine quickly whether each set of minutes has been approved.
24. What information is recorded on a meeting log?
25. Explain the roles of the following team meeting participants: team leader; guidance team; quality adviser; project team members; facilitator; and recorder.
26. What is the purpose of a warm-up at a team meeting?
27. What is the purpose of a check-in at a team meeting?

28. State five house rules you believe would help make team meetings more productive.
29. Differentiate between structured and unstructured brainstorming.
30. Explain how the Nominal Group Technique is used when an issue must be voted on.
31. What is the purpose of a cause-and-effect diagram?
32. How does debriefing take place at a team meeting?
33. What advantages does the teleconference meeting have over the traditional meeting style?
34. What is videoconferencing?
35. What responsibilities might an administrative assistant have concerning a teleconference?

Spelling Reinforcement

abruptly	closure	facilitates	parliamentary
adjournment	controversial	facilities	proceedings
agenda	convenient	gratuity	society
amendments	corporation	guarantee	supportive
arduous	decaffeinated	implementation	unstructured
chronological	definite	luncheon	verbatim

On-the-Job Situations

1. You receive a long-distance call for Mary Ann Cortelli, who is supposed to be attending a meeting chaired by your manager, Allen Bigby. The meeting is being held near your office. About 75 executives are in attendance. Ms. Cortelli preregistered for the meeting, but she has not picked up her registration badge or her luncheon ticket. You speculate that she is not at the meeting. The telephone call seems urgent. What should you do?
2. Your manager, Ms. Corona, is giving a talk at a national conference in a large city at 1400 tomorrow afternoon. As soon as she arrived at her destination, she called you to say that she does not have the transparencies she needs to illustrate her talk. "Are they there?" she inquires, and sure enough, they are. You forgot to put them in her briefcase. She is certain that the hotel where she is speaking has an overhead projector. She asks you to send the transparencies to her in time for the presentation. You promise to follow through. It is now 1530. What will you do?
3. Your manager, Lee Chung, is the chairperson of a regional group of office managers. The group meets once a month. Today you keyed and duplicated the minutes of the January meeting. Mr. Chung is leaving the office to attend the February meeting, and he plans to take the minutes of the January meeting with him for distribution. As you are looking over the notes of the January meeting, you discover that you omitted a motion that had been voted upon. Mr. Chung does not have time for you to rekey the minutes and duplicate them. Should Mr. Chung take the minutes you have prepared? How can the correction be made?

Special Reports

1. Write to a corporation listed on a major stock exchange, such as the Toronto Stock Exchange or the Montreal Stock Exchange, requesting a copy of the corporation's most recent Report of Annual Meeting to Shareholders. Use a financial publication in your school library to obtain the address of the corporation. Address your letter to the Public Relations department. When you receive the report, notice particularly the section of the report in which the questions raised and the responses are reported verbatim. What constitutes the main part of the report? Envision how the original copy of this report looked.

Production Challenges

11-A Faxing a Notice of Meeting

Supplies needed:

- *Fax Transmittal, Forms 11-A-1, 11-A-2, 11-A-3, and 11-A-4, pages 422 to 425*
- *Working Papers Disk, File 11-A*
- *Plain paper*

The current date is September 3. Mr. Wilson has called a meeting of the Executive Committee of the November Sales Seminar and has asked you to send the notices. The meeting will be held in Mr. Wilson's office at Millennium Appliances, Inc., at 1700 on Wednesday, September 10. The purpose of the meeting is to finalize plans for the November Sales Seminar. The names, addresses, telephone numbers, and fax numbers of the Executive Committee members are:

Mr. Michael Kornachi
Electronic Systems
1509 Speers Road
Oakville, ON L6L 2X5

Tel = (416) 322-5839
Fax = (416) 322-7043

Mr. James Bradford
CanTech Industries
1096 Lansdowne Street W.
Peterborough, ON K9J 1Z9

Tel = (705) 429-7192
Fax = (705) 428-3390

Ms. Louise Witherspoon
City Centre Appliances
94 Royal Oak Drive
St. Catharines, ON L2N 6K8

Tel = (416) 781-6735
Fax = (416) 781-7498

Ms. Lisa Theodorakopoulos
Business Administration Department
Seneca College of Applied Arts and Technology
1750 Finch Avenue East
North York, ON M2N 5T7

Tel = (416) 366-9981
Fax = (416) 366-9811

Ask the committee to fax their replies to:

Mr. William Wilson
Vice President, Market
3431 Bloor Street
Toronto, ON M8X 1G4

Tel = (416) 795-2893
Fax = (416) 795-3982

Mr. Wilson needs to know if each committee member

1. can attend the September 10 meeting
2. has a report to make
3. thinks that an October meeting of the Executive Committee will be necessary.

Phrase your questions carefully.

11-B Composing and Keying Minutes

Supplies needed:

- *Notes on September 10 meeting of the Executive Committee for the November Sales Seminar. Form 11-B, pages 426 to 428*
- *Plain paper*

Mr. Wilson put his notes for the September 10 meeting of the Executive Committee of the November Sales Seminar in your in-basket. The following note was attached: "Please compose and keyboard these minutes."

11-C Holding a Team Meeting

Supplies needed:

- *Voting Sheet Form 11-C-1, page 429*
- *Meeting Log Form 11-C-2, page 430*
- *Cause-and-Effect Diagram Forms 11-C-3, 11-C-4, and 11-C-5 pages 431 to 433*
- *Plain paper*
- *Working Papers Disk, Files 11-C-1 and 11-C-2*

Mr. Wilson asks you to hold a team meeting. The purpose of the meeting is to discuss and make recommendations on the following three issues:

1. Sales brochures are being prepared from an external source. It seems as though there is a problem with the communications between Millennium Appliances and the print shop, since the finished brochure has not matched the intended design on the last two orders.
2. Some employees are abusing the summer working hours. These hours allow employees to begin work at 0700 and finish at 1500. However, reports are being received that employees are not arriving until 0730 or 0745 but are still taking the privilege of leaving at 1500.
3. We are currently placing employee training information on the bulletin board in the staff room. However, a number of employees report that they are missing the brochures either because they do

not read the bulletin board or because the training information is being removed by other employees. Of course, Millennium Appliances wishes to give all employees an equal opportunity to apply for training courses.

Form a team that includes a team leader, recorder, facilitator, guidance team, quality adviser, and other team members. The person on the team who is most knowledgeable about NGT should act as the quality adviser to guide the team members through the correct steps.

The team leader will prepare an agenda on plain paper. The meeting is to be held in Conference Room C at 1030 on June 31, 20—. The meeting will continue until 230. The team leader should remember to include coffee breaks and lunch on the agenda. The team leader must make sure to get an agenda to each team member prior to the meeting.

The team leader should conduct the meeting according to the information in the section "Team Meetings."

The recorder would normally list the issues on the voting sheet (Form 11-C-1, or Working Papers Disk, File 11-C-1), and supply all team members with the form. However, since the three issues are listed here and each team member already has a form, the team leader may instruct the team to key or write the issues onto their forms. The facilitator should ensure that all team members understand the issues and that they record the issues on the voting sheet using the same wording.

The team leader will instruct the team members to vote on the priority of the issues. Each team member may use a vote of 3, 2, or 1 on each issue. (A team member may choose to give all of the issues the same weighting).

The facilitator will then calculate the votes and announce the priority in which the issues will be discussed.

All members will use the meeting log (Form 11-C-2) to take notes and record special comments during the meeting. The recorder must be especially astute to record the details of the discussion, since he or she will use these notes to prepare the minutes after the meeting. The minutes will be prepared from Working Papers Disk, File 11-C-2.

The team leader and facilitator will lead the team members through the cause-and-effect diagrams (Form 11-C-3, 11-C-4 and 11-C-5), starting with the top priority issue. The facilitator may wish to use a blackboard or overhead transparency to guide this discussion. The team members should follow along by filling in their own cause-and-effect diagrams. Recommendations to improve the current problems must be made by the group and recorded on the meeting log.

When the team leader has guided the meeting through closure, the recorder will prepare the minutes on plain paper and provide a copy for all team members.

World Wide Websites

Computer Conferencing

www.soi.city.ac.uk
This site contains a description of computer conferencing, and includes sections on hardware, software, advantages, and disadvantages.

SpeakerSearch

www.speakersearch.com/
SpeakerSearch is an on-line database of speakers for events and conferences.

Successful Meetings Magazine

www.successmtgs.com/
This on-line magazine about planning meetings includes articles, checklists, and links.

Yahoo! Canada—Convention and Visitors Bureaus

www.yahoo.ca/Regional/Countries/Canada/Recreation_and_Sports/Travel/Convention_and_Visitors_Bureaus/
Visit this site for links to Canadian convention and visitor's bureaus.

CHAPTER 12

Reference Resources

Outline

Libraries and Librarians

Titles as Quick Sources of Facts

Reference Databases
Guides to References
Books in Print
Almanacs and Yearbooks
Dictionaries, Encyclopedias, and Atlases
Biographical Information
Financial Information
Etiquette Books and Quotation Sources

Periodical and Newspaper Indexes

Periodical Indexes
Newspaper Indexes

Canadian Government Publications

Directories

Telephone Directories
City Directories
Canadian Almanac and Directory
Canadian Parliamentary Guide
Postal Code Directory
Chamber of Commerce Directories

On-line Computer Search

Procedures Manuals

Perspectives: "Developing a Secretarial Manual"

Learning Outcomes

At the completion of this chapter, the student will be able to:

1. Identify the services provided by libraries.
2. Classify reference titles used in business.
3. Recommend sources to consult to find articles in print.
4. Identify the purpose of different directories.
5. Explain the benefit of an on-line computer search.
6. Develop a procedures manual.

GRADUATE PROFILE

Margo Strong
Administrative Assistant

Keyano College

College Graduation:
Office Administration Diploma Program
Keyano College
Fort McMurray, Alberta
1995

Determination is a Margo Strong point!

While studying for her Office Administration Diploma at Keyano College, Margo resolved to build a career with that venerable institute. By contributing firstly on a part-time basis, she developed a good reputation as a contract employee. But when a temporary full-time opportunity arose with the Keyano College Foundation, Margo quickly accepted the challenge while continuing to provide part-time support to the college. Her continuous effort and reputation coupled with outstanding skills and a positive attitude paid off; she is now a permanent team member of the Research and Planning Office—and loves it!

Margo's main responsibilities are the collection, compilation, and analysis of statistical information required by the government, for funding. It's an essential function that requires working with deans of departments, chairpersons, coordinators, and front-line staff too. She coordinates the timing of data collection by surveyors and departments, then compiles and analyzes the data. When she is not preparing government reports, she provides various reports on graduate outcomes and program and service review data for departments within the college.

As a source of essential information, the Research and Planning Office is accountable for accurate and timely information. "I opted to make our data available from a centralized website," she confesses, "... although the learning curve was a little steep when it came to the design and administration!" Margo overcame the steep learning curve and now her innovative Intranet solution (to the distribution of centralized information) has expanded to accommodate all FOIPPS and training material.

"It is important that we get the critical information to our stakeholders in a timely manner."

So, what does this Office Administrator / Statistician / Web Master do in her spare time? Well, apart from mountain biking and swimming for exercise, Margo is working on her bachelor of general studies degree. "Working at an educational institution has provided me with excellent opportunities on my journey of *lifelong learning*."

The factual information that office professionals use must be accurate and up to date. Searching for facts is an aspect of work for which many researchers need an administrative assistant who knows how to locate information beyond what is contained in reports and manuals developed within the organization. Whether or not an administrative assistant is given this responsibility will depend on the ability to tackle such assignments.

Knowing where to locate facts is more important than actually knowing the facts. The pace at which new knowledge is being discovered is so rapid that we hear it referred to as the "information explosion." Sources of information must be updated frequently. Since facts change so rapidly, any fact that is quoted should be verified by checking the most recent available source.

At a correspondingly rapid pace technology is providing us with an opportunity to search faster and wider than previously possible. Networked computers, CD-ROMs and textual databases have enabled the administrative assistant to use virtual research assistant from the desktop.

Information about the organization for which you work is available from sources within the organization. Other pertinent information is available in libraries, on CD-ROM, and from on-line databases. (On-line databases are discussed later in this chapter.)

Tracking down facts is time consuming. To search effectively, you should know where to look and which sources to rely upon. Many of the sources mentioned in this chapter are in the process of changing from the traditional hardcopy book format to either CD-ROM or an on-line resource. To be sure of the most current reference resource you should consult with a skilled reference librarian.

LIBRARIES AND LIBRARIANS

Thousands of Canadian business organizations maintain their own libraries, which are staffed with professionally trained librarians. If you work for one of these organizations, direct your search for facts to your organization's librarians. If they do not have the information in their library, they will contact other libraries to obtain it.

The Internet provides an important in-house alternative to the organization's librarian. With a good Internet search engine, a broader, less time-consuming search for information can be achieved.

If the organization where you work does not have its own library, use the public library. All public libraries have reference books and many valuable sources that you can use in person. Many libraries maintain a telephone information service and an Internet service provided free of charge to its patrons. If the library is large, it will be divided into departments. To seek assistance by telephone, ask for information service. To use any of the on-line services, including the Internet, the researcher may start by visiting the reference department.

Whether you call by telephone or visit in person, library staff are exceedingly helpful. They want their libraries to be used, and they welcome an opportunity to assist those who truly need help. When you do not know what to ask for, tell the librarian what your need is and depend on the librarian to make suggestions.

"In order to resolve conflict in the office, I feel that preventative measures are the best. Encourage open communication, and clarify any misunderstandings so the situation does not get blown out of proportion."

Laurie Remenda, Graduate
Columbia College

Every library maintains a catalogue of what is housed in the library; this catalogue is a ready reference for users. Most catalogues are available on the computer, which speeds up the retrieval of information.

Many private and special libraries are located in cities and towns throughout Canada. Micromedia publishes the *Directory of Libraries in Canada.* This directory lists federal, university, and special libraries. Private and special libraries are not open to the public. However, it is possible to make special arrangements to borrow materials from them and to get help from their librarians.

Great cooperation exists among public and private libraries. Public libraries, college and university libraries, libraries of business organizations, and private libraries in a given community participate actively in interlibrary loans. They also borrow from libraries in other communities. Through interlibrary loans, you can obtain books and photocopies of articles that your organization's library or the public library do not have. This service is provided for a small charge; some libraries charge only for the photocopying involved. If the organization for which you work does not have a library, make your request through the public library.

Among the private libraries in your community might be:

- a law library in a federal court building or at a college of law
- an industrial library at the local Chamber of Commerce
- a Department of Commerce library, if your city has a regional Department of Commerce office
- a specialized library at an art or historical museum
- a medical library at a hospital or a college of medicine
- a technical library maintained by a professional society
- an international business library at a local or regional International Trade Organization centre.

TITLES AS QUICK SOURCES OF FACTS

Office professionals often consult references such as almanacs, yearbooks, dictionaries, encyclopedias, atlases, biographical publications, and financial directories. You will find some of the titles referred to in this chapter in all public libraries, and nearly all of the titles referred to here in large public libraries.

Some reference sources discussed in this chapter are available from three different sources: on-line, CD-ROM, and hard copy (book form). However, there is a publishing industry trend to move away from the hard-copy form of material to the more cost-effective and environmentally friendlier media of on-line and CD-ROM.

Reference Databases

Most larger libraries have available several reference databases. Refer to Figure 12-1. Using these, you can quickly and easily locate a wide variety of information from periodicals and other sources.

Several years' worth of information may be contained on a database. Databases can easily be searched by subject, title, source, date, or even text abstracts. Once found, search results can often be printed at a nominal cost, or downloaded onto a preformatted diskette.

Figure 12-1 Researcher using CD-ROM for geographical information.

Guides to References

Where can you find the guide to the reference that will lead you to the book or periodical containing the topic you are seeking? Librarians use *Canadian Business and Economics: A Guide to Sources of Information*, edited by Barbara E. Brown (Canadian Library Association). Both English and French titles are included.

A handy paperback list of references is *Sources of Information for Canadian Business* by Brian Land (Canadian Chamber of Commerce). It contains general and government as well as business reference sources. As with most annual references, it is important to seek the current version of each guide to references.

Books in Print

All libraries and many bookstores have up-to-date sources about books that are available from publishers, especially books printed in English. These sources give all the information needed for ordering publications, including the date and the price. Since these sources are used for ordering, they are kept in the catalogue section of the library. One of the sources found in most libraries is *Canadian Books in Print* (University of Toronto Press; includes some French-language titles). This reference source is most often found on CD-ROM but will now be found as an on-line service at most large public libraries. Most Canadian business books are listed in *Canadian Books in Print*, making it a standard reference source. Other, similar sources are *Whitaker's Books in Print*, an authoritative source of information about books available in print from the United Kingdom, with emphasis on publishers, and *Quill & Quire* (Key Publishers; reviews new Canadian books).

Almanacs and Yearbooks

Almanacs and yearbooks contain the latest statistics and facts on all types of human activity. They are updated annually. Most of them are available in both hardcover and paperback, and may be purchased at many local bookstores.

The standard Canadian book of facts is *The Corpus Almanac of Canada*, published annually by Corpus, Don Mills, Ontario.

Canadian Almanac and Directory (Copp Clark), *Whitaker's Almanac* (J. Whitaker & Sons, London), and the *Canada Year Book* (Statistics Canada) are similar to each other, but each contains information not in the others.

An excellent source for locating recent Canadian facts is the *Canadian Global Almanac 20—: A Book of Facts*, published annually. As with all annualized reference sources, ensure that you have the most current issue.

Dictionaries, Encyclopedias, and Atlases

Dictionaries

For your own desk, choose the latest edition of an *abridged* dictionary such as the:

- *New Oxford Canadian Dictionary*
- *Webster's New Collegiate Dictionary*
- *Random House Dictionary of the English Language* (College Edition)
- *Funk & Wagnalls Standard College Dictionary* (available as U.S. only)

Abridged dictionaries are desk-sized and easy to use.

In addition, you should have access to one of the following unabridged dictionaries:

- *The New Oxford Canadian Dictionary*
- *Websters New International Dictionary of the English Language*
- *Funk and Wagnalls New Standard Dictionary* (available as U.S. only)
- *The Random House Dictionary of the English Language*, or
- *The Houghton Mifflin Canadian Dictionary of the English Language*, which features new terms from the fields of business, science, and technology.

Encyclopedias

Encyclopedias are useful for researching a variety of general and nonrelated facts. Available in practically every library is the *Encyclopedia Britannica* (Grolier), an internationally acclaimed source of dependable facts. Also popular is:

- The *Canadian Encyclopedia* (McClelland & Stewart), which is normally updated annually. It is available on-line in most public libraries and can be found in CD-ROM format but updates and new editions are no longer available in book form.
- The *Columbia Encyclopedia*, a single volume with emphasis on names of people and places (mainly American), and
- *Encyclopedia of Management* (Van Nostrand Reinhold), also a single volume, with articles on all aspects of management.

Encyclopedias are also available on **CD-ROM**. (For an explanation of CD-ROM, refer to Chapter 4.) This technology adds a completely new dimension to reference resources; it precludes many of the traditional, laborious methods of research. With a CD-ROM, the researcher

- no longer carries large references books
- has access to more current information
- has faster access to information
- can access information enhanced by sound and graphics.

Atlases

As with most published reference material, atlases are becoming readily available on-line and on CD-ROM format. If your geographic search includes dynamic facts such as migration, climate, or territorial borders, reference to a good on-line or CD-ROM atlas database may provide more current information. The most comprehensive atlas for Canadians is the *National Atlas of Canada* (Macmillan of Canada), which features maps of climate, population, income, forestry, industries, transportation, and trade. Most atlases also contain a gazetteer, which is an index of geographic names and descriptions, alphabetically arranged.

Biographical Information

Many sources have been compiled to provide biographical information about notable people and other people, less prominent, who have made contributions in their respective fields.

Biography Index: A Cumulative Index to Biographical Material in Books and Magazines (H.W.Wilson; published quarterly since 1946) is available on CD-ROM and lists biographical information in books in English and in over 1,500 periodicals.

For information about men and women living today, consult the following:

- *The Canadian Who's Who; Who's Who in Canada.*
- *Directory of Directors* (The Financial Post), which gives information on several thousand Canadian business executives.
- *Who's Who in Canadian Business* (Trans-Canada Press), which includes Canadian business executives.
- *The Blue Book of Canadian Business*, which contains biographies of the chief executive officers of 100 prominent Canadian firms. This book ranks major Canadian companies by their net worth.

For more information about people of earlier times, consult books such as *Webster's Biographical Dictionary*, *Chambers' Biographical Dictionary*, the *Dictionary of National Biography* (British), *Who Was Who*, and biographical dictionaries for other specific countries, as well as encyclopedias.

To locate biographical books, look in the local library catalogue or on-line under the *Subject Guide to Books in Print* using the last name of the person who is the subject of the book.

Financial Information

There are many sources of financial data. The four best-known publishers of financial services are

- Dun & Bradstreet
- The Financial Post Corporation Service
- Moody's Investment Service
- Standard & Poor.

Dun & Bradstreet is widely known for its credit ratings, which are published bimonthly and made available to subscribers only in the *Dun & Bradstreet Reference Book*. In addition to credit and capital ratings, this book gives type of business, address, and a brief history for each listing.

The Financial Post Corporation Service (Combined Communications) deals with Canadian companies whose securities are actively traded on the stock market.

Moody's services to investors are numerous. Among them are *Moody's Manual of Investment, American and Foreign*. Bound annually, it is divided into separate manuals covering the following fields:

- industrials
- transportation
- utilities
- banks, insurance, real estate, and investment trusts
- government and municipal bonds.

These manuals include financial statements, descriptions of plants and products, officers, history, and other pertinent information. Some Moody publications are updated weekly; others are updated semiweekly or monthly. These publications cover foreign companies, including Canadian companies, listed on American stock exchanges.

Among Standard & Poor's publications are *Standard and Poor's Register of Corporations, Directors, and Executives,* listing approximately 34,000 leading American and Canadian corporations.

Two excellent books for obtaining information about Canadian companies are *Canadian Key Businesses* (Dun & Bradstreet) and *V.I.P. Business Contacts* (V.I.P. Business Contacts). Both discuss Canadian businesses, are organized by the name of the company, and are updated annually.

Etiquette Books and Quotation Sources

Other sources of information that an administrative assistant will find useful are books on **etiquette**. If your responsibilities include helping to prepare speeches, oral presentations, or articles, books of quotations will also be useful. The etiquette books are helpful in all areas of gracious living, but they are especially helpful to the administrative assistant in search of suggestions for writing formal invitations, acceptances, and regrets; thank-you letters; and letters of congratulations and condolence. Among the available books are

1. *Behave Yourself: The Working Guide to Business Etiquette,* by Elena Jankowic (Prentice-Hall).
2. *The Blue Book of Broadminded Business Behavior,* by Auren Uris (Fitzhenry & Whiteside).
3. *Emily Post's Etiquette,* by Elizabeth Post (Funk & Wagnalls).
4. *Kiss, Bow, or Shake Hands: How To Do Business In Sixty Countries*, by Terri Morrison (B. Adams, Holbrook, Mass. 1994)

When your manager wants to support his or her ideas with well-known quotations or to add a clever statement, look to a book of quotations. Many such books are available, and every library has some of them. The contents of these books, alphabetized by subject, vary widely, so you may have to consult several to locate the quotation you are seeking. Try these:

1. *Bartlett's Familiar Quotations,* by John Bartlett (Little, Brown).
2. *Colombo's New Canadian Quotations,* by J.R. Colombo (McClelland & Stewart).
3. *The International Thesaurus of Quotations,* compiled by Rhoda Thomas Tripp (Thomas Y. Crowell).

No list of references would be complete without mention of *Robert's Rules of Order* (William Morrow). This book is one of the most popular guides to meeting procedures for businesses, clubs, and organizations. Familiarization with these procedures could be very helpful to an administrative assistant who is called upon to take minutes of formal or informal meetings.

PERIODICAL AND NEWSPAPER INDEXES

Your office will probably subscribe to several professional journals. An effective approach to keeping up with the array of publications will be to either develop and maintain an office library, or to develop a systematic disposal system for the journals after a prescribed period of time. The latter should include an effective recycling process.

If the professional magazines to which your manager subscribes are housed in local libraries, either bound and placed on shelves or stored on microfilm, and if the office staff refers to back issues infrequently, there is no need to keep them.

You may want to save and file the annual indexes to the magazines you dispose of. With many periodicals, once a year one issue contains an index to all the articles it published during the previous year. In addition, before you dispose of technical or specialized magazines, find out if your organization's library or another local library needs extra copies of the magazines you have on hand. Perhaps they would like your office's copies for exchange with other libraries.

The most efficient way to search for magazine and newspaper articles is to consult an index in the reference section of a library. The *Canadian Imperial Index* is a widely used periodical, newspaper, and business index that is available both on-line and CD-ROM format. There are many other indexes besides that one. As the occasion arises, become familiar with the indexes in the libraries that you use.

Periodical Indexes

Administrative assistants who help their managers prepare speeches and articles for publication need to know how to locate articles that have been published on a given subject. The fastest way to locate a magazine or journal article is to consult the appropriate index, of which there are two types: general and specialized. When doing research, consult both types, for articles on popular technical topics appear in general periodicals as well as in specialized journals and periodicals.

Many libraries now have on-line periodical indexes. For example, *Canadian Business and Current Affairs* (Micromedia Ltd.) carries listings for periodical and newspaper articles. A second version of *Canadian Business and Current Affairs* provides the full text of those periodicals being referenced.

To locate business and general periodicals published in other parts of the world and in many languages, consult either *Ulrich's International Periodicals Directory* or *The Serials Directory*. These sources are infrequently used and may not be as well maintained as their North American equivalents.

Consult specialized indexes to locate articles of a technical or specialized nature. The H.W. Wilson Company, which publishes the *Readers' Guide*, also publishes the following on-line indexes to specialized periodicals:

- *Applied Science & Technology Index*
- *Art Index*
- *Biological & Agricultural Index*
- *Business Periodicals Index*
- *Education Index*
- *Index to Legal Periodicals*
- *Social Sciences & Humanities Index*.

Some of these specialized indexes are arranged by subject only; others are arranged by author and subject.

Rarely does one library subscribe to all the specialized indexes. Determine which library in your area would have the specialized index you need, and obtain permission to consult it. Public librarians are usually aware of the holdings of private and special libraries in their geographic area. Your organization's librarian should have the same information.

After you find the articles you want to scan, you have to locate the periodicals. If your organization has a library, inquire there first. If the library does not have the periodical, the librarian will locate it for you. If your organization does not have a library, call the public library or special libraries. Periodical librarians maintain master lists of the periodical holdings of their libraries, and the dates of the available periodicals, and will also be able to tell you whether each periodical is in bound form or is stored on microfilm. You may obtain this information over the telephone.

> *"Develop a winning attitude, confidence, and good work ethic."*
>
> Shannon Mullin, Graduate
> New Brunswick Community College
> Miramichi Campus

The usual procedure is to read the periodicals at the library and take notes. If an entire article or a considerable portion of it will be of value to your manager, you can often make a copy for research purposes. Copying machines are available in libraries. Use a microfilm reader to read an article on microfilm, but rather than taking copious notes, request a hard copy of the article. The charge for copies is by the page, but it is nominal when you think of the time you save.

When making copies, as when taking notes, be sure to obtain the exact title of the article, the source, the date of the source, and the page number. In your notes, place quotation marks around direct quotations to distinguish them from paraphrased material. Take notes in such a way that you will be able to interpret them at a later date. Plan your note-taking carefully. Write on only one side of a card or page. Do not make notes about two topics on the same page.

Newspaper Indexes

Generally, newspaper indexes can be found on the Library Database Network as part of the comprehensive *Canadian Business and Current Affairs* (CBCA) index. CBCA is an excellent broad information source; other sources provide direct and local information.

The Canadian News Index is one means of quickly locating information about news events. It indexes seven major Canadian newspapers:

- *The Globe and Mail*
- *Toronto Star*
- *The Gazette* (Montreal)
- *The Winnipeg Free Press*
- *Vancouver Sun*
- *Calgary Herald*
- *Chronical-Herald* (Halifax).

Libraries in major Canadian cities may have an index solely for the city's own newspaper; or they may have a publicly available facility for searching newspaper articles on-line. Most major newspapers provide on-line information free of charge. Others produce an annually revised CD-ROM that includes the full text. The following newspapers may be found daily on-line, and annually on CD-ROM:

- *The Globe and Mail*
- *Financial Times of Canada*
- *Report on Business Magazine*
- *Times-Colonist* (Victoria)
- *The Winnipeg Free Press*.

Similarly, the full texts of Southam newspapers are available through multimedia databases such as the Internet, CD-ROMs, telephone and other digitized distribution formats. The following short list identifies some of those available:

- *Edmonton Journal*
- *Calgary Herald*
- *Province* (Vancouver)
- *Vancouver Sun*
- *National Post*
- *The Times Colonist*
- *Ottawa Citizen*
- *Sault Star*
- *Windsor Star*
- *Daily News* (Halifax)
- *The Gazette* (Montreal).

Searching for a Specific Newspaper Article

For a comprehensive list of Southam newspapers available in full text, reference the Internet at www. southam. com/newspapers. If you need to search a selection of Canadian newspapers for a specific article go to the Internet at canada.com/newscafe/.

CANADIAN GOVERNMENT PUBLICATIONS

The Canadian government is one of the largest publishers in the country. Many of its publications, which cover nearly all subject areas, are available for a nominal price. All libraries except specialized libraries keep some government publications on file. Some libraries are depository libraries for government publications; that is, they are designated by law to receive all material published by the government in certain broad categories.

Government publications are not usually included in *Canadian Books in Print* or in periodical indexes. A *Weekly Checklist of Canadian Government Publications* is available in hard copy if you wish to review the most recent government publications. The *Selected Titles Catalogue*, published by the Canadian Communications Group (the official publisher for the Government of Canada), provides an on-line catalogue of popular government publications. The Canadian Communications Group may be contacted through:

e-mail:	publishing@ccg-gcc.ca
Telephone:	1-819-956-4800
Fax:	1-819-994-1498

DIRECTORIES

Hundreds of business directories are published in Canada each year. Directories that administrative assistants should not overlook are:

- local and out-of-town telephone directories
- *Canadian Almanac and Directory*
- *Canada's Postal Code Directory*
- directories of chambers of commerce.

Useful to you might be *Scott's Directories* (Southam). These directories list manufacturers in four Canadian geographic areas. As well, an index of trade and occupational magazines and product information ranging from the automotive market to the occupational health and safety market can be found at *http://southam.com/Magazines/index.html*.

Telephone Directories

Telephone directories list the names, addresses, and telephone numbers of subscribers. Because telephone directories are usually published annually, they are useful for verifying addresses. You will find them to be an excellent source for locating a street address when the address you have is incomplete. Because of their tabular form, telephone directories can easily be produced in CD-ROM format. *CanadaPhone* is one such directory; it includes information from both White and Yellow Pages and is updated quarterly. Similar international phone directories are also available.

The business office of the local telephone company, and the local public library, both keep on file telephone directories from a number of other cities in your own and other provinces. Call the public library when you need an address in another city. If the librarian has access to a directory for the city you indicate, the librarian will look up the address and give you the information over the telephone. Large public libraries keep on file a few directories for foreign cities. If you wish to obtain a directory for another city, you may purchase it from the publisher of the directory.

City Directories

City directories include the following:

- a buyer's guide and classified directory
- an alphabetical name directory, which lists residents' names, addresses, and occupations (telephone numbers are given for business names)
- an alphabetical street directory of householders and businesses (street numbers are listed in

consecutive order with the occupant's name and telephone number)
- a numerical telephone directory, which gives the name of the person at each telephone number listed.

One such directory is the *Henderson Directory*, which can be found in the public library.

Canadian Almanac and Directory

Published annually, the *Canadian Almanac and Directory* is one of the standard desk references. It lists alphabetically the names and addresses of banks, trust companies, insurance companies, libraries, book publishers, newspapers, associations, law firms, and federal, provincial, and municipal departments. It also provides a great number of other useful facts and figures.

Canadian Parliamentary Guide

The Canadian Parliamentary Guide, edited by Pierre G. Normandine and published annually in Ottawa, lists the members of the Senate and the House of Commons, of the provincial governments, and of the Supreme Court, as well as other high-ranking public officials. It also contains some biographical material.

Postal Code Directory

You can find the postal code for any address in Canada by referring to *Canada's Postal Code Directory*. It is updated annually and is available by writing or telephoning the National Philatelic Centre, Canada Post Corporation, Station 1, Antigonish, Nova Scotia, B2G 2R8. A toll-free telephone number (1-800-565-4362) may be used if you wish to pay by Visa or MasterCard. Payment may also be made by cheque or money order. The cost is currently $21.95 plus GST and PST.

Chamber of Commerce Directories

Most towns of any size in Canada have an active chamber of commerce. Each local chamber of commerce publishes a list of its members. If your manager is chairing a convention or coordinating a regional sales meeting in another city, the chamber of commerce directory for that city is helpful for locating business personnel who take a special interest in the community. If you wish to obtain information from a chamber of commerce in another city, contact your local chamber of commerce, which will supply the telephone number and address for the chamber of commerce you are requesting.

ON-LINE COMPUTER SEARCH

Most large libraries provide on-line computer-search services. These services give you access to hundreds of commercially supplied databases containing references and documents on many subjects. This method of searching for information is a highly efficient way of obtaining:

- citations from magazines, newspapers, or research reports
- abstracts
- full text documents.

The two main database sources used by Canadian libraries are:

- ***Infomart***, which contains the full text of major Canadian newspapers; company product and trademark information; legal and fax information; and business directories.
- ***Dialog***, which consists of almost 600 databases containing worldwide literature references in categories such as:
  - agriculture
  - business
  - computers
  - education
  - environment
  - energy
  - medicine.

Many libraries offer public and academic *Smart Search* services for a small fee. Reference librarians will conduct an academic or business-focused search for subscribers. On-line searching is usually performed by trained library staff using your search criteria. There will be a charge for this service. Some libraries allow their members access to their databases through subscription or by debit to the member's library account. Charges are based on the length of time of the search. Refer to Figure 12-2.

To access the databases, the user needs a computer, a telephone line, a modem (a device connecting the computer to the telephone), communications software, a subscription to the database, and a printer or screen to receive information.

Many on-line databases may be accessible from a public network such as the Internet. (Refer to Chapter 9.) However, access to specialized databases such as Infomart or Dialog may require permission and a subscription through your library.

Some databases are updated weekly, others monthly. Up-to-the-minute information is available from some

Figure 12-2 Figure 12-2 Subscriber to an on-line database receives information.

pro-Link

So, what's the big deal about a procedures manual?

A well-maintained procedures manual (that is, updated as the organization and its procedures change) is more than a useful productivity enhancement. New office professionals, temporary help, and even some of the office veterans will turn to the manual for guidance or confirmation of a procedure.

Among the many benefits of a manual is the:

- reduced frustration as users have instant answers to their procedural questions
- rapid independence of new office staff as they study and become familiar with procedures
- release of supervisors and peers from time consuming explanations
- cross training as readers learn new skills that enhance their performance
- research and publishing experience of developing and maintaining the manual
- effectiveness of temporary help as they are supported by the manual.

Have the systems department help you put the procedures manual on-line. Make it available to all office staff and see it acknowledged as a definitive communication tool. Yes, it's a big deal!

databases. Most are designed to meet the needs of businesses, but databases are available in fields other than business.

Usually, answers to on-line database queries can be received in a few minutes. The user can save time and money by identifying the precise words that will give the desired information. Keep this in mind when you are obtaining information from an on-line database.

PROCEDURES MANUALS

A critical resource for any office is a procedures manual. If the manual is current, well-organized, and easy to follow, it will assist office staff in performing work correctly and efficiently. Refer to Figure 12-3.

Often it is the responsibility of an administrative assistant to prepare this reference resource. The intent of a procedures manual is to smooth the transition for your successor, and to help the co-workers who cover your temporary absences. When you return to the office there will be less accumulation of incomplete tasks.

The office procedures manual should be available in hard copy, as a desk manual, and also in a softcopy version for ease of maintenance. As well, it should be included, along with other reference information, on your office network.

The list of administrative responsibilities that may require a procedures manual is endless. Some of the tasks for which a manual will be most useful include the following:

- handling the telephone
- receiving and sending fax messages

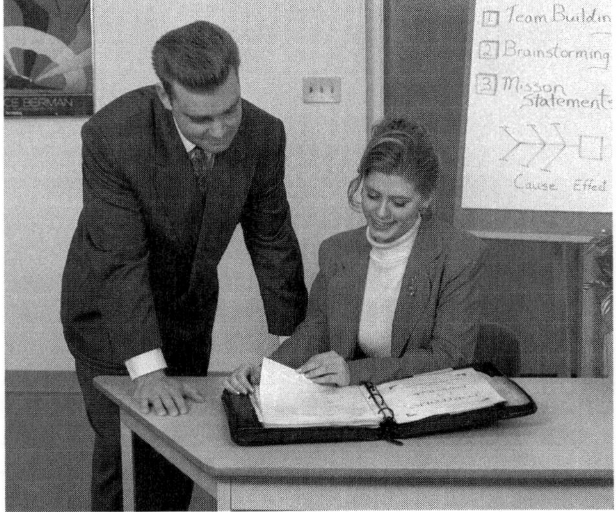

Figure 12-3 An office procedures manual helps office professionals to follow preferred document formats.
Courtesy of Rosina Solylo.

PERSPECTIVES

Developing a Secretarial Manual

By Charlotte E. Humes CPS

Are you looking for a way to make a significant contribution to your company? Are you interested in increasing your own efficiency as well as the effectiveness of other secretaries in your organization?

Here's how: Suggest the publication of a secretarial manual and become involved in its development. The short term inconvenience and extra work will result in a more knowledgeable, capable secretarial staff, and increase the efficiency of the organization many times over.

In a company without a secretarial manual, valuable, accumulated knowledge is lost when a secretary leaves a job. A new secretary or temporaries who are hired to do the job have to search for answers and rely on supervisors and managers for training assistance.

Seeking project approval

To win corporate backing for a secretarial manual project, you've got to be prepared. Develop your facts by anticipating the questions you'll be asked, which will most likely include the following:

- Why does the organization need a secretarial manual?
- How will it benefit your organization and your secretaries?
- What is it going to cost in terms of materials and time?

You won't be able to estimate the cost in actual materials until you've started working on the project and have a feel for how much information will actually end up going into the manual.

The amount of time an individual secretary devotes to the project will vary according to what specific work she's been assigned in the project. You will need to meet as a team for at least one hour a week when the project is getting underway.

Later team meetings will spread out to every two or three weeks depending on the amount of work to be accomplished between meetings. Eventually, when the manual's printed and distributed and you're only dealing with updates, an hourly monthly meeting will most likely be adequate.

- *Who's going to do the work?* Determine in advance how your task force or committee will be structured.

Once you arm yourself with facts, you have to *sell the project.* Clearly show everyone how they can win from the end result of this project: *Higher productivity and quality of work from better equipped secretaries.*

Management's backing and commitment to the project is key. Conflicts can easily arise between bosses and secretaries if both parties have different perceptions about work priorities in juggling routine work with manual assignments.

Common questions

It [the manual] identified the most common questions (listed below) that a new employee would ask and developed a method for finding the answers.

"Who is ...?" An organizational chart and department descriptions help secretaries answer this type of question. Departmental descriptions also provide information about telephone extensions, written directions to the department, hours of operation, services provided and the functions performed by the secretary, and standard secretarial duties (reserves conference rooms, handles audio visual equipment reservations, and so forth).

Department secretaries wrote department descriptions. Their supervisors reviewed the proposed contributions and the task force edited them for uniformity. This process drew on the direct knowledge of that topic's "expert" and it gave the individual secretary an opportunity to be a direct contributor to the manual.

Involving all the secretaries in the writing of departmental descriptions based on direct experience allowed for participation at all levels. These secretaries felt they were a part of the team and the manual project.

"Where can I find ...?" Maps show the location of offices throughout the centre, providing answers to questions about where to locate offices, personnel, and so forth. One map shows an overview of the buildings in the medical centre complex. Individual floor maps of buildings also pinpoint each office location.

"How do I ...?" Several chapters answer this type of question. One chapter on meeting room facilities, for example, discusses size of various conference rooms and identifies the person in charge of taking reservations.

To ensure a uniform secretarial product throughout, a chapter on typing formats gives standard layouts for memoranda and minutes. Another chapter instructs the secretary on how to order office supplies. Still another deals with all forms used by secretaries, giving specific instructions on how to fill out any form a secretary might need to use.

The manual also includes a chapter on policies and procedures that covers basic policies every secretary needs to know as well as the policy control system—how policies are formed, reviewed, and updated.

Finally, reserve space in the manual for each secretary to compile a specific desk manual outlining his or her job responsibilities. Sample forms developed by the task force provide secretaries with a series of questions designed to guide them in preparing their desk manuals.

- preparing correspondence
- processing incoming and outgoing mail
- making appointments
- booking the conference centre
- preparing travel expenses
- ordering office supplies.

This is a very brief list; the choice of tasks to be included in a procedures manual will depend on the range of responsibilities held by the administrative assistant.

The following are some basic rules for creating the manual:

1. Prepare the manual using a simple, step-by-step format. Use easy-to-understand terms and action words.
2. Leave out all extraneous information. Extra information will only confuse the issue. Remember, you are preparing a "how to" list of procedures, not an essay. Nevertheless, be certain that all necessary steps are included.
3. Develop your information by asking yourself and other assistants what specific questions you would want answered if you were learning this new job.
4. Once the procedures are written, test them on another administrative assistant who is unaware of the procedures. Then refine the steps to make them absolutely clear.
5. Since the manual will require continual updating, place it in a ring binder to make replacement pages easy to insert.
6. Use a table of contents and coordinating divider tabs so that the information may be accessed expeditiously.
7. Date the procedures. This will help you keep the manual current.

A current, clear, and comprehensive reference manual is a credit to the administrative assistant who creates it, and proof of a commitment to the company and its goals. For more about preparing office manuals, refer back to the feature article "Developing a Secretarial Manual."

Questions for Study and Review

1. What type of service would it be reasonable to expect from a librarian by telephone?
2. What services are available through interlibrary loans?
3. What source do librarians use to learn about reference books with which they are not familiar?
4. State four ways that multimedia (on-line and CD-ROM) has changed the traditional methods of research.
5. What is the source, other than newspaper indexes, for locating facts appearing in the news within the last two or three weeks?
6. Define atlas, gazetteer, abridged dictionary, and unabridged dictionary.
7. Briefly compare the content of *Who's Who in Canada* and the *Blue Book of Canadian Business*.
8. What useful information, other than financial, can administrative assistants obtain from financial manuals and directories?
9. What should you do with back issues of periodicals that are of no further interest to the office staff?
10. Periodical indexes may be found in two media. Name the two media.
11. Where might you look to find a particular article on business published in England?
12. What department should you call to find out if a library has a specific issue of a magazine you are seeking?
13. How can you quickly obtain a copy of an article from the *Winnipeg Free Press* that was published today?
14. Name three Canadian newspapers that are indexed.
15. What is the source of information for locating or ordering publications of the Canadian government?
16. What is a gazetteer?
17. From what local source can an administrative assistant obtain the telephone number or street address of a person or organization in another town in the same province?
18. What is an on-line database?
19. List seven guidelines for preparing a procedures manual.

Spelling Reinforcement

acquainted	copious	financial	officials
almanac	cumulative	gazetteer	responsibility
alphabetical	directory	language	statistics
assistance	encyclopedia	library	successor
biographical	etiquette	museum	unabridged

On-the-Job Situations

1. Today your manager put three personnel management books on your desk with a note that said, "Are these the latest editions of these three books? I need to know by tomorrow." How will you check on this?
2. Your manager, Mr. Wilson, will be visiting prospective clients in Halifax and Charlottetown. Mr. Wilson has a private pilot's licence and wishes to contact a flying club in each of these cities so that he may rent and fly a plane in his leisure time. How will you get the names and addresses of flying clubs in these cities?
3. Your manager has asked you to find a recent article on interest rates in Australia. How will you begin?

Production Challenges

12-A Selecting Quotations

Supplies needed:

- *Forms 12-A-1 and 12-A-2, page 434*
- *Cards*
- *Working Papers Disk, File 12-A*

Mr. Wilson is giving the keynote address at Career Day for high school seniors. He asked you to find two quotations that will impress high school seniors on the significance of continuing their education. Use the quotation books in the library to select your quotations. Key each quotation verbatim and its source on a 7.6 cm x 12.7 cm card, Forms 12-A-1 and 12-A-2, or File 12-A on your Working Papers Disk.

12-B Finding Information

Supplies needed:

- *Plain paper*

For each of the following activities that you complete, record the source you consulted:

1. Find out if a popular book you are contemplating buying is available in paperback. List the name of the book.
2. You are moving to a city in another province. You want to know the size of the city and the major corporations there. List the city, its size, and five corporations in which you would like to work.
3. Use a periodical index to find three recent articles on a topic of interest to you. Write the titles of the articles, the names of the magazines in which they were published, and the date of publication.
4. Use and name a reference to locate a business administration book that was published before 1980 and is still in print. Find out if a revised edition of it has been published since the first publication of the book. List the name of the book and the most recent date of publication.
5. Use the microfilm reader to look at the advertisements that were published in the *Toronto Star* on the day you were born. Write a paragraph description of the advertisements.
6. Do biographical research on a Canadian whose name is often in the national news. Write three interesting facts about this person.

12-C Developing a Procedures Manual

Supplies needed:

- *Ring binder*
- *Divider tabs*
- *Plain paper*

Using the guidelines discussed in this chapter, develop a procedures manual that covers procedures for two tasks performed in a local office. To do this, you will require training on the tasks. If your school or college has arranged for you to receive work experience, this is an optimum time to complete this task. If your work experience practicum will not be arranged for some time, write a letter to an administrative assistant who is in charge of these tasks and request an appointment to complete this project. You will need hands-on training so that you can write effective procedures. Once the appointment is complete and the procedures have been prepared, send a follow-up thank-you letter and a copy of your work (pages from your procedures manual) to the administrative assistant who trained you.

World Wide Websites

Contents—Canada Site

canada.gc.ca/main_e.html
The Government of Canada's primary site contains links to a government overview, federal organizations, programs and services, a search engine, and other services in English or French.

My Virtual Reference Desk

www.refdesk.com/facts.html
Links to numerous reference sites can be accessed here.

News Café—Canadian Newspapers

www.canada.com/newscafe/
This site provides the facility for a current news article search by story, in English or French. It will also provide headline stories from local newspapers across Canada.

Senators and Members—Government of Canada

www.parl.gc.ca/english/emember.html
An alphabetical list and biographies of members of the Canadian Senate and House of Commons is available at this site.

Yahoo! Canada—Reference

www.yahoo.ca/Reference/
This site provides links to many reference sites relating to almanacs, dictionaries, encyclopedias, libraries, maps, phone numbers, postal information, quotations, thesauri, and so on, and includes the Canadian Geographical Name Server.

13

Business Communication

Outline

Learning Outcomes

At the completion of this chapter, the student will be able to:

1. Describe ways to improve verbal communication.
2. Demonstrate methods of giving and receiving constructive feedback.
3. Discuss ways to be comfortable and effective when giving oral presentations.
4. Explain methods for preventing presentation hazards.
5. Explain appropriate nonverbal communication that relates to image, personal space, eye contact, posture, and facial expressions.
6. Demonstrate ways to improve your listening skills.
7. Describe the qualities of an effective business letter.
8. Compare the techniques for writing favourable, disappointing, and persuasive letters.
9. Differentiate between the following letter styles: full-block, modified-block, and simplified.
10. Discuss the following types of reports: letter, memorandum, informal, and formal.
11. Compare the ordering and formatting of preliminary and supplementary sections of a formal report.
12. Outline the margins and placement of headings and tables in formal reports.
13. State the information that should be included in a letter of transmittal.
14. Compare formal reports written in inductive, deductive, or chronological arrangements.
15. Write and key a letter of request.
16. Key the final draft of a manuscript for corrected copy.
17. Use the Internet in the reference list of a formal report.

Graduate Profile

Wanda Michie
Law Clerk

Oatley, Purser Barristers and Solicitors

College Graduation:
Legal Secretarial Program
Georgian College of Applied Arts & Technology
Barrie, Ontario
1981

Wanda Michie's strategy for moving ahead in her career is to have plenty of initiative and a strong work ethic, be reliable, continue to upgrade skills and education, and pay attention to detail. Wanda recommends having a good mentor who will coach you and share the wealth of experience. She also stresses that it is wise to "take on as much responsibility as you can handle." Wanda states that this is the route to earning respect and a good reputation. With this strategy, Wanda will certainly be successful.

Wanda demonstrates that she is adept at human relations skills by being approachable and by examining office issues without bias. When she is involved in an office conflict, she thinks the problem through and then tries to deal with it in a sensitive manner that does not offend either party. When she witnesses a situation where others are being dealt with unfairly, she deals with the issue directly but diplomatically and once the issue is resolved Wanda moves ahead with a positive attitude.

To improve communication efficiency in the office, Wanda uses technology that includes the Internet, computer networks, e-mail, voice mail, and facsimile machines. As well, she sends communiqués prior to meetings that she arranges to ensure that people are ready to participate.

"Effective communication is important to boosting morale in the office."

Wanda encourages regular meetings where the staff communicates upcoming events and important changes. According to Wanda, "If you keep everyone informed ... this keeps the office grapevine to a minimum."

Effective communication is the responsibility of every person in an organization. As organizations increase their dependence on computers and other electronic equipment, the volume of work that everyone is expected to manage increases. This greater amount of responsibility is accompanied by increased communications, both electronic and personal. As an administrative assistant, you will become involved in verbal, nonverbal, and written communication that requires skills in both electronic and personal domains.

VERBAL COMMUNICATION

Much of the communication in which executives and their assistants are involved is verbal. The best verbal communication takes place in a comfortable atmosphere and on a one-to-one basis.

When communicating verbally with another person, be sensitive to how he or she feels about what you are saying. Listen and watch for verbal and nonverbal feedback. Many factors affect how someone reacts to what you are saying. Among them is past experience—what happened to that person in a similar situation. Choose your words carefully when the topic you are discussing is sensitive or controversial. You may wish to withhold your opinion entirely if you know your view will offend the listener, put the listener on the defensive, or force the listener to disagree with you.

> *"An office cannot function properly without effective communication."*
>
> Lesley Jones, Graduate
> Fanshawe College

Encourage the other person to talk: communication should be two-way. Communication will be open and honest if the person trusts you; it will be restricted if the person does not.

Give the other person your undivided attention. Performing another task while you are talking is distracting and rude. Avoid talking incessantly. Pause often, to give your listener an opportunity to respond.

Communication does not take place until the listener truly understands what you are saying. At the end of a conversation, summarize the important points in logical order and give the listener a chance to ask questions.

Tips for Giving and Receiving Constructive Feedback

One of the best skills an administrative assistant can possess is the ability to give and receive constructive feedback without sounding or appearing to be critical. Giving and receiving constructive feedback requires diplomacy, as well as sensitivity to the needs of other people. It also requires a high degree of professionalism, maturity, and experience.

Giving Constructive Feedback. If you are inexperienced in giving constructive feedback, the following tips will help you to be more effective:

1. If you make a practice of giving positive feedback when appropriate and on a regular basis, the negative feedback will be easier for the listener to accept. Your comments will be more credible if the listener is accustomed to receiving your positive feedback.
2. Phrase your comments as constructive feedback and not as criticism. Be certain to include what the listener has done well and what you see as areas of improvement. Ask the recipient for an opinion on how to improve matters. Perhaps the person will have a better solution than your own.
3. Be certain to describe the context of the problem. Always review the actions that led up to the problem. Just commenting on the problem without providing the details that surround it will lead to confusion and possibly no resolution.
4. Provide constructive feedback only when **you** are capable of doing so. If you are carrying around *personal baggage*, or if your emotions are running high, your chances of being effective are minimal.
5. Provide constructive feedback only when the listener is capable of receiving it. If it is obvious that the recipient is suffering from low self-esteem, perhaps offering friendly assistance is more appropriate than offering constructive feedback at this particular time.
6. Provide the correct environment. Never offer constructive feedback to an individual when there is an audience present. Show respect for the receiver by creating a confidential atmosphere.
7. Describe the facts; do not generalize or exaggerate. If the person has been late five times for your ten team meetings, say "You have been late five times," not "You are late all the time." Ask yourself if your data are accurate. What you don't know for certain should not be promoted as fact.
8. Don't be judgmental. Remember that you are not in the role of an inadequate parent; rather, you are a professional colleague. Judgmental comments such as "That's the worst report I've ever read," tend to belittle others. If your intent is to elicit a mature response, use discretion in

how you choose your words. A better comment would be this: "I have detected five typographical errors and two missing sections in your report."

9. Don't state your impression of the person; instead, describe the problematic actions of that person. For example, if you say "You are lazy," you are likely to receive an angry response. But if you say "You have not completed your last three reports on time," you may get a more cooperative response.
10. Do not be a conduit for other people. Speak only for yourself. Comments such as "Everyone is concerned about ..." are unjust. Rather, say "I feel concerned when you ..."
11. Don't ask the listener a question about her or his behaviour. Instead, state a fact. If you ask "Have you been late for the last five meetings?" you are inviting defensive behaviour and encouraging the listener to lie for the sake of self-preservation. Simply state: "I have observed that you were late for the last five meetings."
12. Use a strategy that expresses how their actions make you feel, and ask for their feedback. Examples:

    "I have observed that you have been late for the last five meetings."

    "When you are late, I feel disappointed because your input at the meetings is valuable."

    Allow the receiver to comment, and leave the door open for a discussion.

    "I would appreciate it if you would attend every meeting on time because, as your team leader, I am depending on your commitment."

    "How do you feel about this?"

    Now, discuss alternatives and a possible compromise.

Receiving Feedback. When your supervisor is giving the feedback, there is no guarantee that it will be constructive. The following tips are designed to help you work through an uncomfortable situation:

1. Attempt to relax. An employee who is being criticized for perceived lack of performance often finds this advice very difficult to follow. Remember to breathe deeply. When we become tense, we often breath shallowly; when we do that, we aren't providing our body with the oxygen it needs to perform at its best.
2. As your supervisor is explaining the problem, listen very carefully. Take notes if possible and appropriate.
3. To clarify the situation, ask your supervisor questions that will help you to understand her or his point of view.
4. If you agree that you have mishandled a piece of work, apologize. Also, acknowledge valid points that are made by your supervisor.
5. Remember, if you feel uncomfortable with your supervisor's comments, you can ask for time before responding. Example: "Thank you for explaining this; however, I feel uncomfortable with this situation. I'd appreciate some time to think about your comments. May we continue discussing this tomorrow?" Use this time to speak to a mentor and, if necessary, to collect facts. Be certain that you have regained your composure before meeting with your supervisor. This is preferable to responding in a way you will later regret.

Be at Ease in the Spotlight

Speaking to an audience is the number one phobia for many people. Some speakers can learn to overcome this fear simply with practice, while others have a great deal of difficulty conquering the phobia. What works for one speaker does not work for the other. Here are some useful suggestions that may help.

- Don's rush to the presentation. Give yourself plenty of time to travel to the location, find the room, and set up. You will need time to lay out your handouts, set up the computer and or projector, flip charts and pens, etc.
- Know your topic inside out and become passionate about it. Your passion should override your nervousness.
- Stand behind a podium if possible. This barrier will help to hide shaky legs and hands.
- Prepare excellent visual aids. These will impress your audience and act as a guide to you for your presentation.
- Prior to the presentation, psyche yourself up. Use music, relaxation exercises, and think of the best highlights of your presentation.

Given time and practice, most people can improve their verbal presentation skills so they can offer informative and entertaining presentations.

Prevent Presentation Frustration

A great presentation requires a lot of planning and organizing of details. Whether you are giving the presentation

pro-Link

What will happen if you forget your words in the middle of an oral presentation? Will you stammer and stutter? Will you look foolish in front of the audience? These are common concerns that presenters often face. Here are some tips to prevent you from becoming speechless.

- Use your computer presentation or overhead transparencies as your guide. These visual aids are not intended just for the audience, they are also for you.
- Keep a set of notes, just in case you need them. If you do, the worst thing that can happen is that you have to read your notes. You will find comfort in knowing you have notes to rely on.
- Know your topic so well that you are the expert—and better, get passionate about the topic so you are the passionate expert.
- Ask yourself what is making you so nervous that you are drawing a blank. If it's a particular person in the audience, stop looking at them. Your eyes can glance around the entire room and still avoid a particular person or location.
- If your presentations are usually peppered by pause words such as "um" and "ah" it may be a habit you need to break. Try attending public speaking classes.

or it's your responsibility to introduce or host the speaker, you want every thing to go without a single hitch. But, the chances are that something may go wrong, especially if you believe in Murphy's Law, "Anything that can go wrong will."

With some serious attention to detail and good preparation, you can improve the odds. Here are some points to prevent presentation frustration.

- If you are introducing the speaker, be sure you have adequate and accurate information to introduce that person.
- Be certain that the speaker arrives in plenty of time. This may include changing air flights or picking up the speaker at the airport. If there is plenty of time there is reduced panic and pressure for both the speaker and the organizer.
- Most presentations require technical equipment and technical equipment leaves plenty of opportunity for mishap. That's why it's imperative to have a backup plan whenever technical equipment is involved. For example, if a speaker is using a computer presentation, you should prepare overhead transparencies and arrange for an overhead projector and extra bulb—just in case! Does the microphone work? How does it work? Does the speaker need a mobile microphone? Does the speaker need a remote control for the computer projector? If you are uncertain about the technical setup, learn all you can about the equipment ahead of time or arrange to have a technician in the room prior to the presentation.
- When you book the presentation room, if you are not familiar with it, visit the room to be certain it will accommodate the presenter, the audience, and the equipment.
- Rooms are full of surprises! You can never depend on the condition that the last group left it in. Chairs and tables may need to be rearranged. Flip chart paper and pens may need to be replaced. Where is the switch that dims the lights? Where is the switch that lowers the projection screen?
- Know the audience. Anticipate their needs, concerns, interests, and questions. If you don't do this research ahead of the presentation, you may be opening yourself or the speaker to a potentially embarrassing situation. Not all audiences are patient and polite.
- If you are the presenter, know where your presentation can be shortened. Presentations often have a delayed start. If you need to stretch your presentation, some well-prepared questions for the audience will extend the presentation without too much extra work.

NONVERBAL COMMUNICATION

Most people are skilled at communicating a message without speaking even one word. Our facial expressions, our body gestures, the decorations in our work space, and the way we dress often express our feelings and opinions better than our spoken words. The adage that actions speak louder than words could not be more true.

However, these subtle nonverbal cues are often misinterpreted by a receiver, so it is imperative that your actions convey a clear meaning—that is, the meaning you intend. Verbal communication can be completely discredited by the nonverbal kind.

Image

It is no surprise that the way we dress sends a message to customers and colleagues. So does the way we decorate our office.

When you wear a business suit, you are conveying the message that you are a professional and want to be taken seriously. Of course, the location of the office,

PERSPECTIVES

The Other International Language

By Elizabeth R. Sphar

Words cannot be used to deceive, but hands and feet tell the truth

Whether you're trying to promote an idea, a product, or yourself, your body language attracts or repels people before you say a word. They judge you by your walk, stance, head tilt, eye contact, gestures, and clothing. Psychologists claim that 60 percent to 90 percent of communication is non-verbal and influences people more than their words. It confirms or contradicts what you say.

Words can be used to deceive, but hands and feet tell the truth. Here's what you're really saying.

- A smile is an important message-sender, especially with strangers, personnel managers, and customers. It shows that you are approachable. Make it a welcoming sign, not a grin or smirk.
- Walk into a room briskly with back straight, head up, and direct eye contact to project purpose and confidence. Enthusiasm makes what you say seem important. Slouching denotes insincerity and disinterest. Swaggering can indicate superiority, contempt, or an effort to cover up fear.
- Direct eye contact is necessary to get your ideas across, but glance away once in awhile so you don't seem to be staring. Shifty eyes give the impression of lack of confidence, even of deception. Eyes wide open shows understanding and acceptance. Raising eyebrows indicates doubt. Squinting means you want something explained.
- Gestures transmit enthusiasm and give power, says Letitia Baldridge in the ***Complete Guide to Executive Manners***. An aggressive person leans towards his listeners, over the desk. Some businesspeople think that being reserved and not using gestures indicates control, but it can seem cold. Every gesture sends a message. Compressing your lips repels people. Clenching facial muscles or hands reveals aggression or anger; open hands, that you have nothing to hide.
- Mannerisms of which you may not be aware define you as an individual, but beware of those that irritate people. Repeatedly glancing at your watch is a turn-off. Jingling keys or coins, twirling bracelets, playing with a pen or paper clip, or doodling takes attention away from your words and breaks your listener's concentration. Do you lick your lips, pull at an earlobe or a lock of hair, or drum on a desk? If so, read your listener's body language to learn if that person is annoyed and is watching your actions instead of listening.
- Your clothing, including accessories, sends messages. Cleanliness and neatness reveal self-respect and respect for others. Dress appropriately for an occasion. Do your handbags and briefcases send the messages you want sent? Are they inappropriate for the office?
- Standing with feet apart, shifting weight from side to side or back and forth, indicates that you feel in control. Overdone, it may seem patronizing. Sitting with legs crossed knee to knee means you are relaxed and willing to listen and negotiate. Sitting erect signifies alertness and being people-oriented. Sitting too erect makes you seem domineering.
- Placing hands on hips makes you look belligerent. Crossing your arms across your chest makes you appear unapproachable. Sweeping with your entire arm signifies that you are anxious to end the discussion. Rubbing your hands together means you are thoughtful, trying to understand an issue.

Newcomers often remark that a town, church, or club is unfriendly. They received that message because most people are reserved with strangers, standing erect with shoulders back and hands at their sides projecting unfriendliness. Space is important; you must not stand too close or too far from people. Your distance from others reveals your relationship with them: intimate, business-like, or antagonistic.

Non-verbal communication can be an indication of status. The boss sits down; the subordinate stands. Equals stand closer than supervisors and workers do. The subordinate looks at the boss often so he can read non-verbal messages. You will be capable of reading others' body language if you have learned how to control your own.

When your body language contradicts your spoken words, you confuse and irritate your listeners and may lose a potential position, sale, or friend. Develop body language that reveals you are a confident, caring, approachable, problem-solving person.

Elizabeth R. Sphar is a professional writer in Green Valley, AZ. She can be reached at 520/648-8291.

Reprinted courtesy of OfficePRO.

the style of management, and the type of industry you work in will all dictate the level of professional dress that is required. There are some highly professional companies where casual clothing is quite appropriate. Where casual clothing is less appropriate, wearing it may give customers the message that you are conducting "casual" business.

It is common practice among many Canadian offices to designate Friday as **casual day**. This policy allows employees to dress in a casual style that is still attractive and presentable. However, customers and clients may be unaware of this convention, and receive the incorrect message that the office is less than professional.

In the same vein, consider carefully how you decorate your office: the things you display, the colours, and the lighting you choose. Are you making a warm, welcoming impression, or a cold and reserved one?

Personal Space

Canadians, like all other nationalities, have expectations about their personal space. This means that when they are engaged in normal conversation, they expect people to stand about one arm's length away. People who stand too close are viewed as aggressive or perhaps too friendly; people who stand farther away are seen as aloof. Our personal space is often violated during an elevator ride. To deal with this discomfort, many people stare down at the floor or up at the floor indicator.

Office professionals should look for communication barriers in the office. Is the arrangement of office furniture such that people cannot violate personal space?

> *"We should be able to laugh at our mistakes, listen to each other's frustrations, and when all else fails, sit down together and share some chocolate."*
>
> Ingrid Lobley, Graduate
> Southern Alberta Institute of Technology

Is there a high, wide counter that separates staff from customers? Does the boss have the office in the back corner with the closed door, while the administrative assistant's area is open to all who pass by? Is personal space for higher-ranking employees more respected? Furniture arrangements, even when intended to be strictly functional, may also be sending a message about the need for personal space.

When the manager holds a meeting, does she sit behind the desk, or sit next to you at a small table? If the former is true, she may be conveying the message of authority. If the latter is correct—that is, if she sits closer to your personal space—she may be conveying a message of teamwork and cooperation.

Eye Contact

It takes confidence to look directly into someone's eyes when you are speaking to them. Eyes are one of our most important nonverbal language tools—we use them to read the other person's body language and in turn they give off our own nonverbal messages. Direct eye contact tells the receiver that you are interested and listening.

However, prolonged eye contact can make people feel uncomfortable, or even threatened. On the other hand, lack of eye contact can send a message of disinterest or even arrogance.

Posture

The way you stand, sit, and walk tells a story. But, it may not be the story you intend to tell, so be cautious about how your body language is perceived.

For example, if you walk rapidly, with your arms moving freely it implies that you have somewhere to go and things to do, you are confident and goal-oriented. Slouching or supporting your head in your hands relays a message of boredom and disinterest. By leaning forward in the chair, you let the receiver know you are paying attention.

When you cross your legs and arms, the receiver may believe you are closed to her or his ideas while uncrossed legs and arms may lead the receiver to believe you are more open to the conversation.

Facial Expressions

The face is capable of many expressions that reflect our attitudes and our emotions. In fact, the face speaks a universal language. When it expresses happiness, fear, anger, and sadness, other cultures share these same expressions. It's common to hear words of congratulations but to see a face expressing envy or to hear words of happiness while the facial expression is that of sadness. You need not speak the foreigner's language to understand what he really feels.

Because nonverbal language is far more powerful than verbal communication, it is imperative that we pay attention to the messages our body language sends.

LISTENING

Few people listen as attentively as they are capable of listening, and those who do have trained themselves to listen. Recognize that listening must be learned, and adopt a plan for improving your listening skills.

Listening is definitely a skill. It involves concentration, as well as the elimination of barriers to listening.

Figure 13-1 Despite the importance of listening many people are poor listeners.
Courtesy of Ben Kilgour.

Barriers actually block out part of what is being said; words are uttered that the listener never hears at all. One of the most prevalent barriers to effective listening is the tendency of our minds to wander in thought because we think at a much faster rate than the speed of the spoken word.

Listeners also tend to concentrate on formulating how they are going to reply; this is another barrier to listening. When we focus on our reply, we single out statements that seem important to us, and concentrate on them rather than on the entire message.

Another barrier to listening is our personal prejudices. We often do not allow ourselves to be totally open-minded to the ideas of others because of our own past experiences and preferences. These personal prejudices, which can cause intolerance and keep us from accepting the validity of new ideas, are clearly a serious barrier to effective communication.

To improve your listening skills, do the following:

1. Concentrate on what is being said and on grasping the meaning of what is said. Avoid saying you understand when you do not.
2. Become aware of your listening barriers and practise eliminating them.
3. Repeat information to ensure complete understanding between you and the other person.
4. Take notes and confirm that they are correct.

BUSINESS LETTERS

The business letter is still one of the main vehicles for transmitting messages to and from customers. An administrative assistant skilled in composing letters may write replies and originate correspondence.

The letters an administrative assistant writes fall into two categories:

1. those the administrative assistant writes for the signature of another person
2. those the administrative assistant writes as a correspondent for the organization.

Whether letter writing becomes one of your major responsibilities will depend on the letter-writing talent you exhibit and on your manager's willingness to delegate the responsibility. Let the manager know that you are interested in writing letters and give the manager a chance to see what you can do. Occasionally, answer a letter that has just arrived in the incoming mail. Key a draft of your letter, attaching it to the letter you are answering, and put it on the manager's desk in the stack of incoming mail. Be certain not to delay the usual letter answering process by hanging onto the incoming letter too long.

By relieving the manager of the task of dealing with correspondence, you are increasing your value to the organization; you are also substituting a challenging administrative responsibility for some of your routine duties.

Writing business letters is a significant endeavour. Think of the business letter as your organization's representative, going out alone to do a job. Keep in mind that communication does not take place until the reader comprehends and responds to the message. Realize that the effectiveness of each letter you write depends on how well you have equipped it to accomplish its task. As you compose a letter, ask yourself this question: Will the letter get the results I am seeking? Although you may learn many guidelines for writing letters, recognize the significance of giving more thought to reactions and to anticipated results than to rigid procedures for writing letters.

The person who writes outstanding business letters has learned to concentrate, weigh each word, anticipate the reader's reaction, and carefully organize every piece of correspondence to accomplish its purpose.

An effective business letter contains the essential facts. The words have been chosen precisely, and the sentences are grammatical and carefully structured. The letter indicates that the writer knows business procedures and policies, and thinks logically. It delivers the message the sender intended.

Letters that convey a favourable message are organized differently from letters that convey an unfavourable message, and persuasive letters are organized in still another way. The basic principles for organizing different classes of letters are discussed as separate topics in this chapter. Certain qualities, however, are

Figure 13-2 Excellent communication is necessary in both electronic and personal formats.
Courtesy of International Business Machines Corporation. No unauthorized use permitted.

common to all effective letters. Incorporate these qualities in all the letters you write.

QUALITIES OF EFFECTIVE LETTERS

An effective business letter

1. centres on a single purpose
2. focuses on the reader
3. conveys a meaningful message completely, correctly, coherently, concisely, and clearly
4. reflects a positive, sincere, and appropriate tone
5. uses natural, vivid, and varied language.

Know Your Purpose

The purpose of a letter may be to inform, to create understanding and acceptance of an idea, to stimulate thought, or to get action.

Isolate the main purpose of the letter you are writing and develop your message around it. Make other points secondary to the main purpose; give the secondary points a subordinate position. Use one letter to do the job when you possibly can, but do not overwork your letter. Sometimes you will need a series of letters to accomplish one purpose. Unrelated topics that require answers should be presented in separate letters.

Focus on the Reader

Keep in mind at all times that you are writing for the reader. Know who your audience is and show consideration for that person. You can do this by putting the reader's needs first, emphasizing words and ideas that will be meaningful and of interest to the reader.

Try to put yourself in the reader's place. Get to know the reader through the letters in your correspondence files, and try to visualize the reader in the reader's type of business. When you are persuading readers to accept ideas or to carry out suggested actions, remember that self-interest is a potent force. In your letter, show the same interest in their needs that you would if you were talking with them in your office or over the telephone.

Convey a Meaningful Message

To ensure that your message will be meaningful to the reader, check it for completeness, correctness, coherence, conciseness, and clarity.

Completeness

For your reply to be complete, you must answer all the questions the reader asked, or discuss all the subtopics mentioned in the reader's letter. When you are making a request, ask all the questions for which you need answers. When you are originating correspondence, always anticipate the background information the reader will need in order to grasp the full meaning of the message. Also, anticipate the questions the reader will have when reading your letter; include the response to these anticipated questions.

Correctness

Correctness means accuracy in every detail: accurate facts and figures in the content, perfect spelling of every word, flawless grammar and punctuation in every sentence, an absence of typographical errors, and an aesthetically pleasing arrangement of the letter on the page. Inaccurate facts will confuse, and possibly irritate, the reader. Furthermore, they will likely delay the response. Always try to eliminate the confusion and extra correspondence generated by inaccurate, incomplete, or vague facts.

You could contend that a letter containing misspellings and incorrect grammar and punctuation can still be meaningful, and you would be correct. However, inaccuracy of any kind reveals carelessness. A customer would be justified in wondering whether an organization that carelessly misspells the customer's name and omits essential punctuation would be equally careless in manufacturing its products or rendering its service. Just as the sales representative must make a good first impression, so must your letter. The only contact the reader has with your organization may be by letter. Give all the letters you send out a chance to make that all-important first impression. Do this by displaying them in an attractive professional format, and by ensuring that they are correct in every detail.

Coherence

Coherence refers to the arrangement of words and ideas in logical order. Words and ideas must be arranged so that they flow naturally within each sentence, within each main paragraph, and in the transitional paragraphs that hold an entire communication together. A coherent communication is woven together so carefully that the reader is always sure of the relationship of the words and ideas. Numerous writing guidelines exist. See the following list of some of the more important guidelines for achieving coherence in writing:

1. **Put modifiers next to the words they modify.**

   WRONG: The rough draft was mailed on May 9 that contains the original specifications in plenty of time for you to revise it.

   RIGHT: The rough draft that contains the original specifications was mailed on May 9, in plenty of time for you to revise it.

2. **Express parallel ideas in parallel form.**

   WRONG: Mary's additional responsibilities this year have been writing letters and to handle travel arrangements.

   RIGHT: Mary's additional responsibilities this year have been writing letters and handling travel arrangements.

3. **Complete comparisons (or eliminate the comparison).**

   WRONG: The prices of the new homes in the Lakeside Addition are much higher than the Southside Addition.

   RIGHT: The prices of the new homes in the Lakeside Addition are much higher than the prices of those in the Southside Addition.

4. **Connect an agent to the right word.**

   WRONG: Before seeking applications for the position, a detailed job description should be written.

   RIGHT: Before seeking applications for the position, you should write a detailed job description.

5. **Place a pronoun close to a definite antecedent.**

   WRONG: Jason and Steve went squirrel hunting, but they were unable to find any.

   RIGHT: Jason and Steve went hunting for squirrels, but they were unable to find any.

6. **Use conjunctions in pairs to connect coordinate ideas.**

   WRONG: Mr. Arnett hoped to be transferred to Victoria or that he would remain in Halifax.

   RIGHT: Mr. Arnett hoped either to be transferred to Victoria or to remain in Halifax.

7. **Hold the same point of view.**

   WRONG: You either may deliver the claim papers to our branch office in Prince Albert, or they may be mailed to our home office in Regina.

   RIGHT: You may either deliver the claim papers to our branch office in Prince Albert or mail them to our home office in Regina.

Conciseness

To write **concise** messages, use all the necessary words, but no more. Send the reader a complete message, but avoid obscuring the thought with needless words. To distinguish between completeness and a profusion of words, watch for irrelevant details, obvious information, and unnecessary repetition of words and ideas, and then eliminate them.

Concise is not the same as *brief*. When you concentrate on brevity, you run the risk of writing a message that is incomplete or curt, or both. A good approach is to write the full message and then stop. Notice the contrast in the following paragraphs:

Wordy: Should any premium which becomes due not be paid before the expiration of the grace period, which in reference to the above-noted premium will be June 15, 20—, said premium automatically will be charged as a loan against the policy in accordance with the automatic premium loan provision contained in your policy.

Concise: If this premium is not paid before the end of the grace period, which is June 15, 20—, it will be automatically charged as a loan against your policy.

Sentences can become loaded with words and phrases that add nothing to the message. Wordiness detracts from the message by slowing down the reader. To write concise sentences, study your phrases and omit the needless words. Compare the phrases in the "wordy" list to the words and phrases in the "concise" list:

Wordy	*Concise*
A cheque in the amount of	A cheque for
At the present time	Now
Decide at a meeting which will be held Tuesday	Decide at a meeting Tuesday
During the year of 1776	In 1776
For the period of a year	For a year
For the purpose of providing	To provide
Give encouragement to	Encourage
In accordance with your request	As requested
Made the announcement that	Announced
Make an inquiry regarding	Inquire about

Wordiness also results from the inclusion of expressions—often called *trite expressions*—that convey no meaning. They are obstacles to concise writing because they are used in place of meaningful words.

For example:

1. **Trite:** It is as plain as the nose on your face.
   Better: It is obvious.
2. **Trite:** Our staff meets once in a blue moon.
   Better: Our staff meets infrequently.

Clarity

Clarity in writing cannot be isolated entirely from completeness, correctness, coherence, and conciseness, but it does involve an added dimension: choice of words. Words have different meanings to different people. Therefore, you must choose words that will have the intended meaning for the reader.

To write a message that can be understood is not enough. You must write a message *that cannot be misunderstood.* Assume that if the message can be misunderstood, it will be; then make an effort to eliminate any chance of misunderstanding. This will force you to learn the precise meanings of words, to use familiar words, to explain technical words, and to avoid colloquialisms, slang, and coined phrases.

Words are symbols; they are tools of thought. Your goal is to choose words that will penetrate the reader's mind and create there the image you want. To do this, you need a vocabulary large enough that you can select the word that will convey your precise meaning. You must understand both the denotation and the connotation of the words you use. *Denotation* is the explicit dictionary meaning of a word. The suggested idea or overtone that a word acquires through association, in addition to its explicit meaning, is called its *connotation*. Avoid any word with a connotation that would be distasteful to the reader.

Write to express an idea, not to impress the reader with your vocabulary. This involves choosing words that are familiar to the reader. Avoid **colloquialisms**, slang, and coined phrases because they may not be familiar. The reader may not know the meaning you give a word or phrase, and may have no way of checking on the meaning you intend.

Use a technical term when it conveys the meaning better than any other word, but write so skillfully that the reader grasps the meaning of the technical term. First use the term, then explain it either in a phrase or in a subsequent sentence or paragraph. The following illustrations of this approach are from newspapers; however, the same techniques for using technical terms well can be applied in writing business letters:

1. **Descriptive Phrase**
   A hypersonic plane *capable of flying 8000 km an hour* was envisioned by the president of the corporation.
2. **Phrase Set Off by Commas**
   On Friday, the country's largest banks boosted to 11 percent their prime, or *minimum*, lending rates to large corporations, making the higher charge almost industrywide.
3. **Phrase Set Off by Dashes**
   The minister underwent a tracheotomy—*a windpipe incision*—yesterday to aid his breathing.
4. **Subsequent Sentence**
   A total of five companies competed for the contract to install a local area network (LAN). *A LAN is a system for communicating electronically between a number of microcomputers located within close proximity.*

Establish an Appropriate Tone

Your attitude toward the reader will have a noticeable effect on the tone of the letter. Even though your attitude is not described in the letter, it has a way of creeping in. Therefore, to set the appropriate tone, examine your feelings toward the reader. Show consideration for the reader. Reflect a sincere attitude.

The tone of each letter must be appropriate for the given situation. Whenever it is appropriate, write informally and radiate a warm, friendly tone. Be courteous and tactful. Do not write sentences or inject words that you will later regret.

One way to achieve tact in business letters is to replace negative words and phrases with words and phrases that are positive in tone. Watch for negative words; do not let them creep into your writing. Compare the tone in the phrases below. The italicized words in the left column are negative in tone. They have been omitted from the phrases in the right column.

Negative	Positive
We are disappointed at your *failure* to include	We had hoped to receive your report
If you would *take the trouble to*	Please
You are probably *ignorant* of the fact	Perhaps you did not know
It is *not* possible for us	We are unable to
We *must* ask that you send us	Please send us

Develop an Interesting Style

Writing style is a distinctive way of expressing ideas. Develop your own style. Give your letters personality. Be natural. Sound like yourself in your letters. Write as naturally as you talk—not exactly as you talk, but with the same naturalness. Trade in stilted and time-worn phrases for natural ones. Compare the phrases in the following list:

Stilted and Time-worn	Natural
As per our telephone conversation	By telephone
At an early date	(Refer to a definite date.)
Enclosed please find	Enclosed is
This will acknowledge receipt of your letter	(Refer to the letter by date.)
Under separate cover	Separately

To make your letters vivid, choose words that give life to what you say. For example:

- Use active verbs, except when you want the statement to be impersonal.
- Make the subject of the sentence a person or a thing.
- Use specific, meaningful words. Use general or abstract words only when a concept has not yet been reduced to specific terms.
- Use familiar words and phrases in place of the unfamiliar.
- Use short words instead of long words. Here are some examples of short words that can be substituted for multisyllabic words:

Multisyllabic	One Syllable
endeavour	try
interrogate	ask
demonstrate	show
encounter	meet
purchase	buy
obtain	get

For variety, mix simple sentences with compound and complex ones. Choose the type of sentence that will most effectively convey the idea.

Increase Readability

Careful writing will contribute to the readability of your message. To increase readability, control the length of the sentences and the arrangement of the letter on the page. Below are some suggestions for increasing readability.

Sentence Length

To change the pace and to increase reader interest, vary the length of your sentences. Write some short sentences and a few long ones. Short sentences are emphatic, but too many short sentences make the letter seem choppy and elementary. A few long sentences are effective, but too many of them will cause the reader to lose interest and will make the letter harder to understand.

Authorities who have studied sentence patterns have found that copy with sentences averaging 17 words in length is highly readable. For business letters, write sentences that average between 17 and 20 words in length. Do not attempt to limit the length of your sentences to 17 or 20 words; be concerned only about the *average* length of all the sentences in one message. Most word processing software programs have built in grammatical checkers and will send a message when the sentence is too long or incomplete.

Arrangement

Arrange the letter on the page so that it is easy to read. Keep the paragraphs short. Try to condense the opening paragraph into four keyboarded lines or less. A one-sentence opening paragraph in a business letter is permissible.

Divide the rest of the letter at the logical points—that is, at the places where there is a change in thought. However, if a paragraph develops into more than seven or eight keyboarded lines, divide it into two paragraphs. Tie the letter together by arranging the ideas in logical order so that one idea naturally follows another.

If possible, vary the arrangement so that all the paragraphs are not the same length. End with a short paragraph. The end of the letter, like the opening, is a place for emphasis.

Allow ample white space around the keyed material. To provide white space:

1. double-space between paragraphs
2. leave at least 2.5 cm margins
3. double-space between enumerations.

Whenever possible, confine the letter to one page. If you often write letters with three or four lines carried over to a second page, improve the conciseness of your writing. A letter requiring two or three full pages is often classified as a letter report. Use subject headings to break up material in letter reports. Letter reports are discussed later in this chapter.

BASIC LETTER-WRITING PRINCIPLES

Most business letters fall into one of three distinct classifications. These are

1. a favourable message
2. a disappointing message
3. a persuasive message.

An effective letter must be planned. The classification of a letter provides clues for organizing it.

In order to supply a "yes" or "no" response, give an explanation, or speak convincingly, you must know what the organization's policies are concerning the topic being discussed. You must be absolutely sure that your reply reflects the current policy, not one followed at an earlier time or one that is being considered but has not yet been approved. If in doubt about a policy, always check to make certain your reply falls within the current policy guidelines of the organization. Correspondents who make statements that are not supported by, or are in disagreement with, the organization's policies can find themselves in embarrassing predicaments.

Incorporate the basic writing principles discussed here in your business letters. Use them as general outlines for organizing favourable, disappointing, and persuasive messages. You should not follow these principles rigidly; you should use them only as guides. You must alter them to fit each individual case, and vary them to emphasize the specific purpose. You will find the favourable letter the easiest to write, for you know at the time you are composing the letter that the reader will be receptive to what you say.

Favourable Letters

Replies that carry a "yes" message, requests that you anticipate will be granted without persuasion, and goodwill letters are classified as favourable. You can use the following guidelines for writing all favourable letters:

1. Begin favourable letters directly. Do not waste words getting the letter started.
2. Make sure the content is complete, correct, and clear.
3. Use a tone that reflects consideration for the reader.
4. When you finish the message, either stop or write an appropriate closing paragraph. Not all favourable letters need a specially prepared closing paragraph. Include one only when it improves the tone of the letter enough to warrant the time you spend composing it.

Replies

When you are writing a reply, establish in the opening that you are doing what the reader has asked you to do. State this in the first sentence, preferably in the first main clause. For example:

> Your antique eight-day clock, which arrived this week, can be repaired and adjusted to keep accurate time. It has been carefully inspected by our service department.

When you are sending something, say so in the opening lines. Thus:

> All 16 rugs that you ordered are on their way. Riverton Truck Lines should deliver them to you on or before March 27.

When you are partially complying with a request, establish in the opening sentence what you are doing; then use the rest of the letter to explain why you are complying with only part of the request.

Do not restate the obvious. "We have received your letter ..."; "This is an answer to ..."; "I am writing this letter to tell you ..."; and "This will acknowledge receipt of your report ..." are not effective openings.

Check carefully that your reply is complete, correct, and clear. If the reader asked questions, answer every question, whether it was direct or implied. Whenever possible, make one letter do the job.

Some replies should end when the explanation is finished. When you write a closing paragraph, always end confidently. Avoid statements such as "I hope that I have answered your questions," or "I trust that this is the information you are asking for." An expression of willingness to comply, when it is used, is much more appropriate in the closing than in the opening. At times an expression of willingness to comply can be used to avoid the possibility of sounding curt.

All replies should be prompt; delay is disappointing and detracts from a favourable situation.

Direct Requests

When you write a request that you anticipate will be granted without persuasion, make your major request in the first line of the letter. Do not hint; write directly. For example:

> Please send me a copy of your booklet, "Tips for Successful Management of a Word Processing Centre," which you offered to those of us who participated in the word processing seminar you conducted in Quebec City on May 15.

If you use a subject line in your letter, do not depend on it to introduce the topic in the body of the letter. Instead, write the letter as though you had not used the subject line.

When you must ask questions, include all the questions to which you want answers and arrange them in logical order. Word your questions to get the information you want. Do not imply that a yes-or-no answer will be adequate when you need a more complete answer. If you have a series of questions, number them so that they can be read quickly. Numbering them will also increase your chances of getting answers to all of them.

Provide the reader with an adequate explanation. If the explanation applies to the request as a whole rather than to a specific question, put it in a separate paragraph either before or after the questions. If, however, the explanation applies to a specific question, put the explanation close to the question it relates to.

When you are asking for confidential information, state that the information will be handled confidentially. Here are two examples:

> We shall appreciate your answering these questions and supplying any other confidential information concerning Mr. Green's managerial qualifications.

> All the information you supply us will be kept confidential.

Your title, plus a statement within the letter, should show that you have a right to be making a confidential inquiry.

In the closing paragraph, express gratitude cordially in first person, future tense: "I would appreciate ..." or "I would be grateful ..." Avoid thanking the reader in advance. It is appropriate to express thanks only after someone has complied with a request. Set a deadline if it is appropriate or if it will expedite the reply. Note the following closing paragraph:

> The 20— directory of the Bridge City Chapter of IAAP is ready to go to press, and we want to include your name on the Education Committee. Please let me know by July 16 that we can count on you to serve on the Education Committee.

Special Goodwill Letters

Thank you notes expressing appreciation for a favour, or for special cooperation; congratulatory notes to a business associate on a promotion, or to an employee on an important anniversary with the organization; and a welcoming note to a newcomer are examples of goodwill letters. These letters should be concise, appropriate in tone, and timely.

The letter must convey that the sender delighted in writing it. The most important single element common to all goodwill letters is timeliness: they must arrive promptly. (Timeliness and appropriate tone are also the two important elements of sympathy letters.) The following letter was used to congratulate a business associate on an important promotion:

> How exciting to read about your promotion in this morning's edition of the *Edmonton Journal*. Congratulations! Those of us who have worked closely with you know how much you deserve this promotion to Executive Vice President. Best wishes for your continued success!

Repetitive Favourable Replies

Save yourself writing time by speeding up the way you handle favourable messages. When giving the same response over and over, stop composing individual letters. The method you choose for replying will depend on the number of replies and the equipment and personnel available. Consider the following ideas:

1. When you are mailing a catalogue or literature about your products or services, either send it without a letter or enclose a pre-printed letter. Make a note on the request that the literature was mailed.

2. Use a form letter, but print it individually for each recipient. Prepare the form letter (primary document) on your word processor. Then merge the date, inside address, salutation, and any other variable information with the primary document. Each form letter will have the appearance of a unique document.
3. Prepare and store form paragraphs. At the time you are answering the letter, compose only the opening and closing paragraphs. Then merge these new paragraphs with the stored paragraphs.
4. Macro functions may be used with word processing software so that merging and printing a letter is a very quick and efficient process. The macro function allows you to program a series of instructions and store them under a single command. The instructions can then be carried out with a few simple keystrokes.

Disappointing Letters

The disappointing letter requires a lot of planning. More words are needed to say "no" than to say "yes."

Use the opening paragraph to get in step with the reader. Reflect a pleasant, cooperative attitude. Perhaps you can agree with the reader on something. Begin closely enough to the subject of the letter for the reader to know that you are answering her or his letter. It often helps to think of a general statement you can use to begin the letter. Never state the refusal in the opening; but at the same time, avoid giving the impression that the answer is favourable. Also, avoid recalling dissatisfaction or stating dissatisfaction any more than is absolutely necessary.

If you are complying with a part of what was requested, either start with a discussion about what you are doing to comply, or include this discussion in the first paragraph.

The opening paragraph, or *buffer paragraph*, should lead naturally into the second paragraph. Your opening paragraph will not be effective if it is not a natural segue to the main content of the letter.

Your explanation should be courteous and convincing. Give at least one reason for the disappointing news before you actually state it. Whenever you can, ferret out reasons that are for the benefit of someone other than yourself or your organization. Make the disappointing news a logical outcome of the reasons you have presented.

Phrase explanations in impersonal terms. For example, say "Your order was incomplete," instead of "You failed to state the size of the sweaters you ordered."

To avoid delaying the disappointing news too long, do not give *all* of the reasons first; provide some of these afterwards. To improve the tone, subordinate the disappointing news; put it in the middle of a paragraph and in a dependent clause.

When you are refusing a request, avoid leaving any room for doubt about the refusal. Do not apologize for the refusal. Eliminate negative words and phrases such as *impossible*, *must refuse*, and *very sorry to tell you that we cannot*. State what you *can* do instead of what you *cannot* do.

If you can suggest an alternative plan, do so at the end of your letter; then provide the reader with information on how to take up the suggestion. Otherwise, use an ending (often unrelated to the problem discussed in the letter) that will provide a pleasant tone.

The following letter was a reply received by a teacher who had requested copies of teaching materials used in office administration courses. It contains

- General opening statement
- Agreement with the reader
- Partial compliance

  You can provide your office administration students additional employment opportunities by offering a specialized program for students interested in becoming executive assistants. I am sending you the associate degree requirements for the executive assistant program at our college and a list of the topics covered and the textbooks used in each of four specialized executive assistant courses.
- Courteous explanation
- Reason before refusal
- Subordinated refusal
- Additional reasons

  The students purchase kits of practice materials that I have prepared for use in the executive assistant courses. Since I am planning to publish these materials, I cannot release them at this time. As the students use the materials in each kit, I make the essential revisions and hope to publish these materials, along with teaching suggestions, in the form in which I actually used them in my classes.
- Pleasant ending

  By all means, submit your proposal for an executive assistant program for approval. If you have specific questions that I might be able to answer about the development of your program, please write to me again.

Persuasive Letters

Persuasive letters are used for selling products, services, and ideas. The informative office memorandum should also be persuasive; that is, it should persuade the recipients to accept the ideas or changes mentioned in the memorandum. When you write a job application letter, be persuasive; after all, you are selling your qualifications for a job. The application letter is presented in Chapter 15.

Letters selling ideas can follow the same plan as a sales presentation:

1. Gain the reader's attention and interest
2. Create a desire
3. Convince
4. Stimulate action.

Instead of beginning a persuasive letter directly, use the opening statements to get the reader interested in what you are saying. Wait until the second paragraph to start explaining your proposal. In the opening paragraph, avoid

1. using a question that can be answered obviously "yes" or "no"
2. depending on an explanation to arouse interest
3. using obvious flattery to win the reader's attention.

Use facts to convince. Give the necessary details to show that your request deserves to be considered and acted upon. Do not phrase the explicit request until most of the reasons leading up to it have been stated. When you do make the request, state it directly; do not hint.

Maintain a tone of positive confidence. Do not apologize for your request, and do not supply excuses that the reader can use to refuse the request. When a negative element is involved, discuss it as a part of the explanation. Omitting any necessary part of an explanation usually results in additional correspondence and delay.

"Take on any experience you can."

Tina Powers, Graduate
Durham College

Close the letter by expressing appreciation and by restating the action you want the reader to take. Establish your appreciation cordially in first person, future tense. The recipient, having finished reading the letter, should know what is expected, how to do it, and the reasons for prompt action. If you have discussed these points at various places throughout the letter, you may need to summarize them in the closing. Discard generalities such as "early reply" and "at your convenience"; cleverly suggest a deadline.

The following letter, about new parking procedures, is persuasive. Before the Miller Company purchased the parking lots, the employees parked on these same lots and paid high daily or weekly rates. Employees could park on any lot where they could find a space. In the letter, the Miller Company is asking each employee to cooperate by using the parking lot designated for him or her. The approach here is to point out the advantages that will accrue to each employee.

- **Gain attention and interest**

  Beginning Monday, June 1, you may park your car near the main office of Miller Company. The Company has purchased seven parking areas near the main office to provide ample parking space for Miller employees.

- **Create a desire to cooperate**

  To assure each of you a parking space near the building entrance close to your work area, we have assigned employee parking by departments. The parking areas have been designated by numbers, and parking area stickers have been distributed to the department heads.

- **Provide ample facts**
- **Make desired action clear**

  To make arrangements to park your car on a company area, obtain a sticker from your department head and present it to the parking lot attendant. He will display it on the lower left side of the windshield of your car.

- **Show benefit of action**

  Using designated parking areas should result in a smooth flow of traffic around the main office of Miller Company and enable you to enter and leave your area with ease.

CORRESPONDENCE FOR THE MANAGER'S SIGNATURE

Writing letters for another person's signature requires a special skill. It is not an easy assignment because the letter must sound as though the person signing the letter actually wrote it. The reader should believe that the letter was written by the manager.

The letter that is the easiest to write for another person's signature is the letter report setting forth a series of facts. This is because the personality of the writer is not so apparent in factual reports. If the message is lengthy, another way to carry out the assignment is for the administrative assistant to write an informal report, to be accompanied by a covering letter actually written by the person over whose signature the information is transmitted.

When you have the assignment of writing letters for your manager's signature, study your manager's letters to become thoroughly familiar with her or his vocabulary and style. Use the same phrases your manager uses; use the same salutation and complimentary close; and organize the letters in the same way your manager does. "Lift" paragraphs, making appropriate changes, from similar letters your manager has written. When feasible, prepare a draft of the letter and ask your manager to review it and make changes before you key the letter in final form. Be tactful; do not advertise that you are writing letters for someone else's signature.

CORRESPONDENCE FOR THE ASSISTANT'S SIGNATURE

From the first day on your job you may be writing correspondence for your manager. As the need arises, you will write correspondence for your own signature.

Correspondence for the Manager

The memorandum is superior to verbal communication as a means of supplying your manager with the bits of information that come to her or his office. Do not put your manager in the situation of having to listen while you recite a series of unrelated happenings. When you write each message down, you will also be freeing yourself from having to remember to tell your manager everything that is happening.

Use the electronic mailbox, voice mail, or a written memorandum to give your manager a reminder, a message, or an update on a particular transaction. Keep each reminder, message, or update separate so that your manager may dispose of it as soon as he or she has acted upon it. Be certain to date each of these pieces of information, and to record the time. Your name or initials should always be given as a part of the information.

If the information is a telephone message, key the message on a message form. For instance, you might relay a telephone message as follows:

> Clyde Barker said that he cancelled the Thursday meeting of the Progress Club because two members of the group cannot attend. He has rescheduled the meeting for Tuesday, June 4, at 12:00 in the Chamber of Commerce dining room. He is expecting you there. I made these changes in your appointment calendar.

Often when someone comes to the office but does not see your manager, you will receive information that you should pass on to your manager. For example:

> Mr. Roberts from the Facilities Department delivered the extra table for your conference room this morning. The table was too large for the space in which it must fit. Mr. Roberts has returned the table to the warehouse and will deliver a smaller table tomorrow morning.

If your manager asks to be reminded of work that he or she must get done, write a memorandum something like this:

> The report for the District 9 sales conference must be ready by November 19. You asked me to remind you to get started on this report at least one week in advance of the time you must present the report. Copies of the report for the previous period and the report for the corresponding period last year are attached.

To a letter that cannot be answered until additional information is received, attach a memorandum that calls attention to what is needed. State what you have done, if anything, to obtain the information. Do not write the obvious. Your message might be stated in this way:

> As soon as I read this letter, I called Ms. Vance and requested the number of overtime hours worked by her department during the past year. Ms. Vance promised to have this figure ready for you by Friday. I believe this is the only additional figure you need to reply to Mr. Cummins' request.

Correspondence with Others

In carrying out your daily work, you may find yourself writing letters that you sign yourself concerning such things as appointments, requests, orders, routine replies, acknowledgments, transmittals, delays, and follow-ups. Use the title "Administrative Assistant to" followed by your manager's name. For your **courtesy title**, use Ms., Miss, Mrs., or Mr. A male should indicate a courtesy title if his name does not reveal his gender—for example, Pat. Use appropriate courtesy titles when you are addressing others. Ms. is a female courtesy title that does not denote marital status. A woman who is sensitive about the use of courtesy titles should always use her courtesy title before her name in the signature block of the letters she writes. When a woman gives you her courtesy title, add it to your address list and use it. Use Ms. for women who prefer it and for women who do not indicate a preference. Do *not* use Ms. when a woman has given you another courtesy title.

Appointments

Appointments are requested, granted, confirmed, changed, cancelled, and sometimes refused as a part of regular business procedure. Typically, appointments are handled entirely by fax, telephone, electronic mail, or voice mail. However, there are occasions where letters are required.

Letters concerning appointments should follow the same guidelines used when appointments are arranged by telephone:

1. Refer to the purpose of the appointment.
2. Clearly set forth the date, day, time, and place.
3. Request a confirmation of the appointment when it is applicable.

When postponing or cancelling an appointment for an indefinite period of time, always express regret and suggest some provision for a future appointment. When you are postponing the appointment, suggest another specific date and ask for a confirmation. The following examples illustrate different situations that arise when appointments are handled by letter:

- **Appointment requested; time suggested**

  Mr. Robert Arnet will be on the West Coast during the week of July 17. He is scheduled to be in Nanaimo on Thursday, July 21, and Friday, July 22.

  Mr. Arnet asked me to set up an appointment with you concerning the production problems you described in your letter of July 7. Will it be convenient for you to meet with Mr. Arnet on Thursday afternoon, July 21, at 1400?

  Sincerely yours,
  Ms. Karen O'Brien
  Administrative Assistant to Mr. Arnet

- **Appointment granted; time suggested**

  Mr. Harrison will be glad to talk with you while you are in Charlottetown during the week of January 24. Will Wednesday, January 26, at 1500 be convenient for you?

  Mr. Harrison is looking forward to seeing you again and to hearing about the plans you have outlined for the Ritter project.

- **Appointment confirmed**

  Mr. Hanson will be expecting you on Thursday, May 15, between 1030 and 1115 in his office, Room 783, to discuss the need for improved shipping containers.

- **Appointment confirmed in manager's absence**

  Before Ms. Wilcox left on an out-of-town trip, she asked me to tell you that she will return on Thursday, June 12, in time to meet with you to discuss the need for temporary help in your area.

- **Change of appointment**

  Ms. Thompson has been called out of town on business and regrets that she must postpone your appointment with her for 0900, Thursday, July 16. Ms. Thompson will be back in the office on Monday. She suggested Tuesday, July 21, from 0900 until 1000 as a time when she can see you.

  Please let me know if July 21 will be satisfactory. When you arrive, come directly to the fourteenth floor and ask the receptionist for Ms. Thompson.

- **Cancellation of appointment**

  Mr. Darnell was suddenly called to our Edmonton office because of the tornado damage to our plant there. He regrets that he cannot keep his appointment with you for this Thursday at 1500.

  When Mr. Darnell returns, I will contact you in order to arrange another appointment that will be mutually convenient.

Routine Requests, Inquiries, and Orders

Use the suggestions presented earlier for writing favourable letters as a guide for writing routine requests and inquiries. Expect that the reply to your letter will be favourable. State the request or inquiry directly, include only essential information, and create a pleasant tone. These letters will be short. If the letter seems curt because it is too brief, add a sentence or two to improve the tone. Observe how these points are achieved in the following letters:

- **Request for a publication**

  Please send me a copy of your booklet, "21 Ideas: Tested Methods to Improve Packing, Shipping and Mail Room Operations." We are continually searching for methods to improve our mailing operations. We look forward to receiving this booklet.

- **Request for information**

  Mr. R.T. Wilson is interested in obtaining information about the notebook computer you have made available to your employees. Please send me the brand name of the computer and the name and address of the company that manufactures it.

- **Inquiry**

  Ms. Jane Williams would like to purchase 125 copies of a booklet recently published by your organization, "Tips on Using Word Processing for Desktop Publishing." Is this booklet available in quantity? If so, what is the charge for 125 copies?

Orders are usually submitted on an order form. If you do not have an order form, include the essential information in a letter. Be sure to give the order number, quantity, an adequate description, the unit price, and the total price. When you are ordering several items, tabulate the information for easy reading. If you do not enclose a cheque, state how payment will be made.

Routine Replies

When a response is favourable, state it in the opening sentence. If you are declining a request, give at least one reason before you state the refusal. The message of a favourable reply carries a favourable tone; for this reason, even a brief message is effective. In a disappointing reply, add a sentence or a paragraph to cushion or soften the message.

When the reply concerns a meeting, repeat the date, day, time, and place. Following are some examples of routine replies:

- **Favourable reply about meeting**

  You can count on Mr. Stephens to attend the Area 5 Board of Directors meeting to be held on Friday, March 24, at the Valhalla Inn, Kitchener, Ontario.

  Mr. Stephens plans to arrive Thursday night and expects to be present at the 0730 breakfast meeting on Friday.

- **Favourable reply; material sent**

  We welcome the opportunity to furnish you with the Right-Way teaching aids you requested. The material will be shipped to you from our Winnipeg warehouse.

  If we may be of further help in your in-service office course, please let us know.

- **Request temporarily declined**

  Because of the heavy demand for the booklet, "Guidelines for Today's Consumer," our supply is exhausted. This booklet is being updated and will be reprinted in quantity.

  I have made a record of your request for eight copies of "Guidelines for Today's Consumer," and will forward them to you as soon as they are available.

  We appreciate your interest in this publication. If we can be of service to you in any other way, please let us know.

Acknowledgments

Most acknowledgments either state or imply that another communication will follow. The administrative assistant often has the responsibility of writing acknowledgments when the manager is away from the office for an extended period of time. Refer to Chapter 6 for further discussion about answering mail in the manager's absence.

Acknowledge correspondence promptly—preferably on the same day it is received. Be cautious about giving away business secrets; make statements about your manager's absence in general terms. Avoid making promises or commitments your manager cannot keep or would prefer not to keep. Make copies of the letters you refer to others and of the letters you forward to your manager.

What you say in an acknowledgment depends on what you are doing about the correspondence. You can acknowledge the letter without answering it, supply the answer yourself, say that you are referring the letter to someone else for reply, or let the reader know that you are forwarding the letter to your manager for reply.

Other uses of acknowledgments are to let the sender know that important business papers have arrived, and to confirm an order when the recipient is not expecting immediate shipment.

Following are examples of the many ways acknowledgment letters can be used:

- **Acknowledgment; letter not answered**

  Mr. Martin will be out of town on business for the next two weeks. Your letter, which arrived this morning, will be given to Mr. Martin for his attention on June 3, the date he is expected to return to his office.

- **Acknowledgment; letter answered**

  Mr. Argyle has set aside every Wednesday afternoon to talk with sales representatives.

  Mr. Argyle is out of town on business, but he plans to return to the office on Friday of this week. He will be glad to see you any Wednesday afternoon that is convenient for you. Please telephone, fax or write me to set up a definite appointment.

- **Acknowledgment; letter referred**

  Your letter, outlining the difficulties with the equipment you recently purchased from us, arrived today.

  Mr. Chung will be out of the office for an indefinite period of time. In his absence, Mr. Walter Barbato, Equipment Specialist, is handling all of Mr. Chung's correspondence concerning equipment. I have referred your letter to Mr. Barbato, and you should hear from him soon.

  If you wish to call Mr. Barbato, his telephone number is 705-555-3501; his fax number is 705-555-3741.

- **Acknowledgment; letter forwarded**

  Ms. Anderson is away on vacation. Since I do not know the title of her talk to be given at the Third Annual Conference of Fashion Designers and because your letter seems urgent, I forwarded it to Ms. Anderson via fax. You should hear from her before your April 10 deadline.

- **Acknowledgment of business papers**

  Today we received the Substitution of Trustee and the Notice of Default in the case of Hamilton Life Insurance Company v. John R. Hilton, along with your confirmation of recording them.

  Thank you for recording these documents and returning them to us.

Covering Letters

Covering letters are actually letters of transmittal. For a detailed discussion of how to write letters of transmittal, refer to the section "Writing the Letter of Transmittal" in this chapter.

A covering letter may be brief. It should, however, state what is being transmitted and who it is from. The covering letter often mentions a focal point or a major highlight of the attached report. Here is an example of a short covering letter.

- **Covering letter**

  Here is your copy of the report "Ten Years Ahead." Mr. Daigle asked me to send each member of the Camp Warwa Committee a copy of this completed report. He requested that all members take special note of the section on fiscal restraint.

Notices of Delay

Because success in business depends on quality of service as well as quality of products, you may be asked to notify a customer whose delivery of merchandise will be delayed. In the letter, include an explanation for the delay and tell the customer what he or she wants to know most—when the merchandise can be expected. Do *not* promise delivery by a date that your organization cannot meet. The following letter was sent when the delay was only 24 hours:

- **Notice of delay**

  Your printing order for 20,000 customer order forms was promised for shipment today.

  Unfortunately, because of a breakdown in equipment and the additional delay of obtaining a part for the machine from Dartmouth, we are 24 hours behind in our printing schedule.

  Our machine is operating this morning. We will ship your order forms tomorrow.

Follow-up Letters

Write a follow-up letter when you have not received something promised or due, or when you have not received a reply to a letter after a certain period of time. Keep a careful record of missing enclosures and other items promised, and write follow-up letters to obtain them. See Chapter 6 for additional suggestions concerning missing enclosures. Write follow-up letters also as reminders.

Be specific about what is being requested. If you are referring to an unanswered letter, send a duplicate of it. Avoid making the reader feel at fault. Notice the content of the follow-up letters below:

- **Follow-up letter; missing enclosure**

  In your letter of May 16 to Mr. Balint, you said you were enclosing a biographical sketch to be used in the brochure for the 47th Annual Conference of RNA. However, your biographical sketch was not enclosed with your letter.

  Since the Conference brochure must be printed by May 22, will you please send your biographical sketch in the next mail.

- **Follow-up letter; order not received**

  On March 12 we ordered 25 copies of your book, *Management Under Stress*. We have not received the books or an acknowledgment of the order.

  Since we need these books for a seminar which begins two weeks from today, please ship us 25 copies of *Management Under Stress* immediately. Mail the invoice to Mr. Arthur Shepherd, Director of Education, who will forward it to the Accounting Department for payment.

- **Reminder**

  Ms. Yates plans to use your report on basic changes in inventory control when she meets with the Executive Committee on March 16. This note is a reminder that Ms. Yates should have the report on March 14 in order to become thoroughly familiar with it before her presentation on March 16.

- **Reminder; lapse of time**

  We have not received your expense report covering the period from October 1 to October 31. As you know, we cannot reimburse any of the sales representatives until all the expense reports for October are approved by the comptroller.

Apparently your October report has gone astray. Please mail us another copy.

- **Reminder to confirm**

  This note is to confirm our meeting, Friday, May 31, at 1200 in the Chamber of Commerce dining room for the purpose of discussing membership activities in the Lethbridge Chapter of CMA for the coming year.

Appreciation Letters

Many situations arise in business for expressing appreciation. Do not neglect writing thank-you letters. Be prompt in sending them, for they lose their effectiveness if delayed.

To let the reader know that the letter was written especially for him or her, be specific, as illustrated below:

- **Thank-you letter**

  Thank you for sending your proposal for needed changes in the contract with dealers. Ms. Wilroy asked me to express her appreciation to you.

  Your proposal arrived in time for Ms. Wilroy to present your ideas to the Executive Committee, which meets this Thursday.

LETTER FORMATS

With the efficiency of e-mail messages fewer letters are being prepared. Further, unless the letter is very formal, contemporary letters usually adapt a basic style. The most popular and recognized formats are the full-block, modified-block, and the simplified letter styles. However, there are many acceptable formats for letters. When you are new to an office position, begin by following the letter style already used in the office. Once you have established some credibility, you may want to introduce one of the following styles.

Full-Block Letter Style

Figure 13-3 illustrates a full-block letter style. Note that:

- Every single line from the date to the initials begins at the left margin.
- Paragraphs are single-spaced.
- A double space separates each paragraph.

Figure 13-3 has used two-point punctuation. This popular punctuation style uses only a colon after the salutation, a comma after the complimentary close, and no other punctuation at the ends of lines outside the body.

Modified-Block Letter Style

Figure 13-4 illustrates a modified-block letter. Note that the format is the same as the full-block style with the exception that:

- The date, complimentary closing, and signature lines begin at the centre and are keyed to the right of centre.
- Although not shown in Figure 13-4, the paragraphs are sometimes indented. However, the preference is to block them at the left.

Simplified Letter Style

Figure 13-5 illustrates a simplified format. Note that:

- There is no salutation.
- There is no complimentary close.
- There is always a subject line that is keyed in all capital letters.
- The subject line is keyed a triple space below the salutation.
- The body appears a triple space below the subject line.
- A simplified letter always uses open punctuation, which means no punctuation is found at the ends of lines outside the body.

The obvious advantage of this letter style is that it can be quickly formatted and that it can be addressed to a company when you don't know whom the reader will be.

CLASSIFICATION OF REPORTS

Reports are used in business primarily

1. to inform
2. to provide decisions and recommendations.

Some reports are prepared merely to keep a record. Much reporting consists of presenting data in statistical form. For the data to be meaningful to the reader, however, someone who understands them must interpret them to determine what they mean and to express their meaning in clear language. Consequently, reports are written for the reader's benefit.

Reports can be classified in many ways. Some reports are classified on the basis of function; others on the basis of form.

Reports that inform without giving conclusions and recommendations are called *informational reports*. Examples of informational reports are personnel booklets

Figure 13-3 Full-block letter style with two-point punctuation.

MA ***Millennium Appliances, Inc.***
3431 Bloor Street, Toronto, ON M8X 1G4
Tel (416) 795-2893 Fax (416) 795-3982 www.millennium.net

05 September 20--

Mr. Samuel Jenkins
Director of Architecture and Design
Abbotsford Contemporary Housing
1000 Mountain View Street
Abbotsford, BC V2T 1W1

Dear Sam:

We were very pleased to read about your recent promotion to Director of Architecture and Design, for Abbotsford Contemporary Housing. No doubt, you will add to the already dynamic team that Abbotsford has been building for the past three years.

Call me once you get settled into your new position. We should have lunch together and discuss a potential business partnership where Millennium Appliances, Inc. can supply you with top-of-the-line home appliances at a wholesale price. Millennium's quality appliances would work well with the very attractive contemporary designs you are putting on your new housing. I am enclosing our latest brochure showing our new kitchen appliances.

Again, congratulations on your promotion and good luck with your new challenges. I look forward to hearing from you.

Sincerely,

C. Azam

Ms. Charlene Azam
Assistant Vice-President of Marketing
Western Region

lr

Enclosure

Figure 13-4 Modified-block letter style.

MA ***Millennium Appliances, Inc.***
3431 Bloor Street, Toronto, ON M8X 1G4
Tel (416) 795-2893 Fax (416) 795-3982 www.millennium.net

05 September 20--

Mr. Samuel Jenkins
Director of Architecture and Design
Abbotsford Contemporary Housing
1000 Mountain View Street
Abbotsford, BC V2T 1W1

Dear Sam:

We were very pleased to read about your recent promotion to Director of Architecture and Design, for Abbotsford Contemporary Housing. No doubt, you will add to the already dynamic team that Abbotsford has been building for the past three years.

Call me once you get settled into your new position. We should have lunch together and discuss a potential business partnership where Millennium Appliances, Inc. can supply you with top-of-the-line home appliances at a wholesale price. Millennium's quality appliances would work well with the very attractive contemporary designs you are putting on your new housing. I am enclosing our latest brochure showing our new kitchen appliances.

Again, congratulations on your promotion and good luck with your new challenges. I look forward to hearing from you.

Sincerely,

C. Azam

Ms. Charlene Azam
Assistant Vice-President of Marketing
Western Region

lr

Enclosure

Figure 13-5 Simplified letter style.

MA ***Millennium Appliances, Inc.***
3431 Bloor Street, Toronto, ON M8X 1G4
Tel (416) 795-2893 Fax (416) 795-3982 www.millennium.net

05 September 20--

Abbotsford Contemporary Housing
1000 Mountain View Street
Abbotsford, BC V2T 1W1

CUSTOMER SERVICE SURVEY

We value your opinion and that is why we are asking for your assistance. Every six months we forward a survey to each of our customers so that we might learn how to improve what we do. That is why your response to the enclosed questionnaire is important to us. We have included a self-addressed and stamped envelope for your convenience. If you prefer, you can locate the same questionnaire at our website, www.millennium.net, where you can simply complete the questionnaire online and forward it directly to my e-mail address. The choice is yours.

The questionnaire is designed so it takes no more than ten minutes to complete. Ten minutes of your time is invaluable to us if it means we can learn your concerns, act on them, and keep you as a valuable customer. It is also important to us to hear what activities we do that meet and exceed your expectations. The questionnaire is designed to capture all your opinions, both positive and negative.

If you would prefer to discuss your concerns and expectations directly with me, I would welcome a visit or telephone call from you. I can be reached by telephone or fax at the above noted numbers or at my e-mail address, azam@millennium.net.

It has been our pleasure to serve you in the past and we hope to be your first choice for appliances in the future.

C. Azam

Ms. Charlene Azam
Assistant Vice-President of Marketing
Western Region

lr

Enclosure

on employee benefits and progress reports on the construction of a new building.

Reports that present an analysis and/or interpretation of data, and that perhaps recommend action as well, are called *analytical reports*. Market surveys and analyses of business conditions are examples of analytical reports.

Some reports are specialized. The annual reports of corporations are financial reports to the shareholders, but in addition these annual reports perform a significant public relations function.

Reports vary in size from a short, one-page memorandum to enough pages to make a thick book. Reports also vary in writing style and format. Some are formal; others are informal. Whether a report is formal or informal depends on the relationship between the reader and the originator, the purpose of the report, and its length. Informal reports, in contrast to formal reports, do not always follow a prescribed format.

As an administrative assistant, you should first learn about the format and organization of reports. Eventually you will compose reports.

INFORMAL REPORTS

An informal report may take the form of

1. a letter
2. a memorandum
3. a short internal report.

Letter Reports

Letter reports are used as both internal and external means of communicating information, analyses of data, and recommendations. They are printed on letterhead stationery, and their layout is the same as that of a letter. They are single-spaced. Letter reports may contain all the parts of a business letter, but sometimes the inside address and the complimentary close are omitted. Letter reports are signed. The name of the originator is keyed at the end of the report, with adequate space allowed for the signature. Reference initials appear on the letter report in the same position as on a letter.

Letter reports differ from business letters in three main ways:

1. Headings are often inserted in the letter report to guide the reader to the different points covered in the report.
2. Tables are often used to summarize data.

Much of the content of a report is factual. The facts should be presented objectively; they should be written without being filtered or influenced by the writer. An objective presentation is stripped of all statements indicating personal opinions or impressions. To achieve objectivity, the writer presents the facts in third person. However, a letter report can contain some statements written in first and second person—for example, "*I* interviewed the managers of the Southern, Western, and Midwestern regions," or "Having studied the facts gleaned from these three managers and presented here, will *you* approve the recommendations contained in this report?"

A **subject line** may be used; if it is, it should appear immediately preceding the body of the report to serve as a title for the text of the report. Double-space before and after the subject line. The subject line may begin flush with the left margin.

The headings within a letter report may be either centred or left-aligned. For emphasis, they should be underscored, keyed in bold, or all-capitals. Triple-space before a heading; double-space after a heading. At least two lines of text should appear after a heading near the bottom of the page. At times you may have to leave additional white space at the bottom of a page to avoid separating a heading from its text.

Both spot tables and formal tables are used in letter reports. Spot tables do not have headings and are not numbered. A spot table is usually introduced by a sentence punctuated with a colon. Note the spot table in Figure 13-6.

Formal tables have titles, called *captions* or *headings*. If more than one formal table appears in the same letter report, the tables should be numbered. The table number, such as TABLE II, may be keyed in either capital or lowercase letters, but the title of the table should be in all-capitals. Sometimes a subtitle is also used. Key a subtitle in lowercase letters with the first letter of each main word capitalized. The table number, main title, and subtitle should be centred. See Figure 13-7.

Arrange the data in the table in columns under appropriate headings. It will often be necessary to show the source of a table. Key the source a double-space below the last line of the table.

When a letter report contains tables, spend some time planning the layout of the letter. Observe the following two rules for inserting tables:

1. When possible, an entire table should appear on the same page.
2. A table should be introduced in the text before it appears.

Use 2.5 cm margins for letter reports. Key the second and subsequent pages on plain paper of the same quality and colour as the letterhead. Key a heading on

Figure 13-6 Spot table in excerpt from letter report.

The number of errors made by the transcriptionists has decreased during the last week. The greatest improvement was made in the reduction of spelling errors. Here is a comparison of the errors made:

Type of Errors Made	Last Week	This Week
Incorrect Punctuation	34	30
Spelling	52	13
Misunderstanding Originator	12	6
Omissions	43	20
Failure to Follow Instructions	10	5

The word orginators should be encouraged to spell proper names and to give instructions at the beginning of the dictation. In the meantime, we will continue our training program and work for a further reduction in transcription errors.

Figure 13-7 Numbered table with subtitle.

Table III COMPARISON OF DISTRICT SALES Information Technology			
District	Dollars This Year	Dollars Last Year	Dollars Increase/Decrease
Northern	300,000	350,000	(50,000)
Western	560,000	500,000	60,000
Eastern	725,000	700,000	25,000
Southern	300,000	345,000	(45,000)

each additional page, using a form acceptable for the heading of the second page of a letter. Indicate the subject of the report, the page number, and the date.

Memorandum Reports

Memorandum reports are used primarily for internal communication. Memorandum reports are often less formal than letter reports; a combination of first-, second- and third-person writing is used for them. The heading of the first page of a memorandum report includes TO, FROM, DATE, and SUBJECT. Memorandum reports may be single- or double-spaced.

Subject headings may be used, and tables may be inserted. To save time in an informal situation, the writer sometimes attaches tables and supporting data in their original form to a covering memorandum; the memorandum is used to refer to the attachments and to state the conclusions and recommendations. Refer to Figure 13-8.

If the memorandum report requires more than one page, the additional pages should begin with appropriate identification—subject, page number, and date.

Memorandum reports are either initialled or signed by the originator, near her or his name, in the heading or just below the last line of the body of the report. The keyboarder's reference initials should be added.

Short Internal Reports

Short reports used within an organization may be written in an informal style. The tone as well as the organization of the report is informal; thus, first-, second- and third-person writing may be used in combination, and the report may be organized in a variety of ways. Informal reports differ from formal reports in length and purpose; however, the text of an informal report can contain the same divisions as the text of a formal report. Usually the preliminary pages used in formal reports—letter of transmittal, cover, title page, letter of authorization, table of contents, list of illustrations, and other items—are not included.

An informal report should have a title and contain at least the following three divisions:

1. An introduction, in which the authorization for the report, its purpose, and the procedures and limitations for compiling the data are stated.
2. A presentation of facts, if the purpose of the report is informational. A presentation of facts *plus* an analysis of them, if the report is analytical.
3. A summary, which may or may not include conclusions and recommendations.

A detailed explanation of these divisions is given in the discussion in the section concerning the divisions of a formal report.

Informal reports are printed on good-quality plain paper, 21.5 x 28 cm. They may be single- or double-spaced, depending on how the reports will be used. The margins are even—2.5 cm on the right and left—because the reports are not bound.

Headings and tables are used to speed up the reader's comprehension of the report. The suggestions given for incorporating tables in letter reports may also be followed when tables are inserted in the text of informal reports. You have more leeway in incorporating tables in informal reports than you do in letter reports. If the tables are long, you can key each table on a separate page and then insert these pages, properly numbered, at the appropriate places in the report. Doing this will save time you otherwise would spend planning the text so that each inserted table comes at the logical point in the text and also fits on the page.

Informal reports often follow a deductive arrangement of ideas. In the basic format of the deductive arrangement, the conclusions and recommendations are presented first and the supporting facts are presented last. In many ways the deductive arrangement is the reverse of the logical arrangement, which is the standard format for a formal report. The ideas in an informal report, however, can be organized according to either the deductive or the inductive (logical) arrangement. Refer to page 302 for a discussion of deductive and inductive arrangements.

FORMAL REPORTS

The format and writing style of a report are determined largely by its purpose and length. Reports moving upward to top management are more likely to be formal than reports moving horizontally between departments. Long reports are easier for the reader to follow when they are arranged according to a prescribed format. Formal reports usually follow a prescribed format. Note here that any report can be presented formally or informally, depending on the preferences of the originator. The following discussion includes guidelines for preparing a formal report, and for the proper arrangement of its parts, as well as suggestions for composing formal reports.

Guidelines for Formatting

Your first encounter with a formal report will be when you key it. Your manager may compose the report, but it will be your responsibility to prepare in final form nearly all—if not all—parts of the text. You may also perform some of the necessary research for the report.

Figure 13-8 Memorandum report.

MEMORANDUM

TO: Ben Norman, Manager
Administrative Services

FROM: Laurie G. Ross, Chairperson
Committee on Employee Turnover

DATE: February 22, 20--

SUBJECT: **Turnover of Assistants in Document Preparation Centre**

The committee assigned to study the problem of turnover of medical transcriptionists in the Document Preparation Centre has completed its investigation. I was assisted in the study by Dini Corbett and Edward Kaye.

We recommend that major changes be made in the assignment of duties in the Document Preparation Centre. Our recommendations are as follows:

1. All employees in the Centre should be assigned a greater variety of tasks. These tasks should include proofreading, document research, and editing on word processing software.
2. No assistant should key correspondence more than four hours a day.
3. Those operators currently handling full word processing responsibilities should be assigned to transcribe correspondence at least two hours a day.
4. All employees of the Document Preparation Centre should be trained on the latest upgrade of Microsoft Word software. This training should take place in-house. Employees should be relieved of their regular responsibilities during training periods so that they may devote their full attention to training.
5. An in-house competition should be held for a Supervisor of the Document Preparation Centre. Also, an assistant supervisory position should be created and filled by the current staff working in the Centre.
6. Equipment changes are also recommended. Three new models are currently being researched and could be brought to the Centre as pilots for employees to test and evaluate. Employees should play a major role in the decision-making process if new equipment is to be purchased.

To conduct this study, we asked the assistants to answer a questionnaire. Edward Kaye talked

Figure 13-8 continued.

Turnover in Document Preparation Centre
Page 2
February 22, 20--

assuring them that the questionnaires were not coded to make it possible to match responses to individuals. The questionnaire contained 40 questions. A copy of this document is attached. Part of the questionnaire asked the assistants to state what they:

1. liked about their jobs
2. disliked about their jobs
3. felt was needed most to improve their positions.

An analysis of their replies shows that 98 percent of the assistants spend the entire day keyboarding. They suggested that their jobs be expanded to include a variety of duties.

Dini Corbett analyzed the reasons the assistants had given during exit interviews for leaving their jobs. All but one mentioned a dislike for keyboarding long hours and lack of variety in the work. Other reasons centred around equipment downtime and frustrations with software.

A table of responses to the questionnaires is attached. As well, graphs representing data that support our recommendations are included.

ivw
Attachments

The material may not resemble a report when your manager first hands it to you. Take time before you begin the report to plan the layout and to itemize what is to be included in the final report.

Preliminary Steps

Read enough of the report to get in mind the overall plan of it. Check all of the following items carefully:

- headings
- tables
- graphics
- accuracy of data
- possible inconsistencies.

Ask questions such as these:

- Does the draft contain all the headings that are to be used in the final copy?
- Are the headings correctly related to one another?
- Are headings at each level constructed in a parallel fashion?

An oversight concerning a heading usually results in the need to reformat more than one page. To avoid an oversight, list the headings in outline form and consider how they relate to one another. Headings of the same level should be of equal importance.

To achieve parallel structure, notice the parts of speech used in the headings. If one secondary heading begins with a participle (an "–ing" word), *every* secondary heading must begin with a participle. If one subheading under a topic is a noun phrase, *every* subheading under this topic must be a noun phrase. However, subheadings under a given topic need to be parallel *only to each other*—not to subheadings used elsewhere in the report.

Before you begin, decide which tables should be inserted on the same page as the text that refers to them, and which should appear on "stand-alone" pages.

Determine whether any graphics (charts, illustrations, drawings, or photos) are being prepared for inclusion in the report. If there are, how many, and where will they be inserted? All visual materials are treated as belonging to the numbered pages and should be numbered. Allow for them as you number the pages of the text. Make a list of them so that you will not overlook a page that is to be inserted as the report is being assembled.

If you have any doubt about the accuracy of the data in either the tables or the text, get verification. Statistical analyses in the text are often based on data provided in tables and charts; this means that one wrong figure in the basic data can affect several pages of analysis.

Word choice and format should be consistent throughout a formal report. Inconsistencies often occur when more than one person is responsible for the writing of the report, and because a number of formats are acceptable. Be alert to shifts from one acceptable format to another. Select one way and be consistent throughout the report. Be alert, too, for poor grammar.

Margins

The margins of a report should be uniform after the report is bound. Allow 2.5 cm margins, exclusive of the part of the page used for binding. Leave extra white space at the top of the first text page. Twelve or so blank lines is the suggested amount.

Always begin a new major section on a new page unless the report is too lengthy. In this case, be certain to number all the sections.

Before you begin, you need to know how the report will be bound. For most reports, a binding allowance of 1.3 cm is adequate. If the report is to be bound at the left, use a 3.8 cm left margin unless you have determined that it should be more. If the report is to be bound at the top, allow at least a 3.8 cm top margin. Also keep in mind that when the report is bound at the left, the margin allowance for binding affects all centred headings. Of course, when word processing is used, the software automatically adjusts for this.

Spacing

Formal reports may be either double- or single-spaced, depending on how the report is to be used and the preference of the author. Reports that are reproduced in quantity are often single-spaced and printed on both sides of the page to save paper and filing space. Reports to be mailed are often single-spaced and printed on both sides of the paper to save mailing costs. A periodic report should be prepared with the same format—including the same spacing—that was used in previous reports.

Double-spacing should be used between the paragraphs of single-spaced material. Single-spacing is used in double-spaced reports to display a list of items.

Even when the report text is double-spaced, single-space the following:

1. Quoted material of more than three lines.
2. An enumeration that occupies two or more lines. Double-space between the items.
3. Spot tables.
4. A bibliographical entry that occupies two or more lines. Double-space between the entries.
5. A two-line notation below a table indicating the source of the data, even when the table is double-spaced.

6. Tables that have headings, unless the table is very short or appears on a page by itself and needs to be expanded to fill the page.
7. A title in the table of contents, in a list of tables, or elsewhere. Exceptions to this guideline are the main title of the report, a chapter, or major section, where the heading is too long to occupy one line.

Paragraph Indention

Indent the paragraphs of a double-spaced report either five or ten spaces to indicate where they begin. Five-space indention is most common.

Since paragraphs in single-spaced reports are separated by double-spacing, paragraph indention in single-spaced reports is optional.

Subject Headings

Headings and subheadings are used to show the reader the organization of the report. They point the reader to where the reader has been and is going. A good heading should indicate clearly the content below it. Headings enable the reader to locate specific sections of the report and to read or reread only those portions of the report that supply the information the reader is seeking.

The form and location of a heading should make its relative importance clear at a glance. Headings for all divisions of equal rank must be in the same format and occupy the same location on the page. Each heading must either be in a different form or occupy a different location from its superior (of which it is a part) and from its inferiors (which are its subdivisions).

Centred headings are superior to side headings in the same format. "All-caps" headings are superior to those with lowercase letters. Headings appearing above the text are superior to those starting on the same line as the text.

Headings should not be depended on as the sole transitional elements in a text. If all the headings were removed, the report should still flow easily from one section to the next.

Here are examples and explanations of headings most frequently used:

FIRST-DEGREE HEADING

The title of the report is the first-degree heading. Since there is only one title, this heading should be written at the highest level, and no other heading should be written in the same form.

Second-Degree Headings

Second-degree headings are used to indicate the major divisions of a report. They are centred horizontally. The first word is always capitalized. So is the first letter of every other word, unless it is an article, or a preposition of four letters or less. The heading is usually underscored or printed in bold type. There should always be at least two second-degree headings.

Third-Degree Headings

Third-degree headings are used as subdivisions under second-degree headings. They are usually formatted exactly like second-degree headings, except that they are placed tight against the left margin.

Fourth-Degree Headings. For further breakdown, fourth-degree headings are used. These are placed at the beginning of the paragraph on the same line with the text. They may be written in the same form as the second- and third-degree headings. They should be separated from the paragraph by a period, and they should be underscored or printed in bold. They are often called run-in headings.

Fifth-degree headings can be handled as a part of the first sentence of the first paragraph about each separate topic, as illustrated by this sentence. The key words at the beginning of the sentence are underscored or printed in bold, but the sentence is written as a regular sentence. Only the first letter of the first word is capitalized.

When any degree of heading is used (that is, beyond the first-degree or title heading), there must be at least two headings. If a section of a report contains only one heading and does not logically divide into two parts, write the entire section without subdivisions. Each section of a report is subdivided independently of the other sections; that is, third-degree headings can be used in one section without being used in the others; fourth- and fifth-degree headings can be used only where they are needed.

Two headings should not appear in a report without intervening text. Often, the discussion between headings of different degrees is a transitional paragraph that tells the reader what to expect next. Transitional paragraphs may be written last; for that reason they are sometimes forgotten. When you are studying the layout of the report and find a heading that is immediately followed by another without intervening text, ask your manager to add the essential paragraphs. Or better, compose them yourself and submit them to your manager for approval.

Page Numbers

Number the pages of the report consecutively with Arabic numbers from the first page of the text through the last page of the supplementary section. Examples of supplementary sections include appendixes and bibliographies. Number the pages in the preliminary section with small Roman numerals.

When the report is bound at the left, the page numbers may be centred horizontally 2.5 cm from the bottom of the page, or placed in the upper right corner so that the number ends flush with the right margin. Where running heads are used, do not print page numbers at the top centre. The number of the first page is usually omitted, but always counted.

When the report is bound at the top, it is best to centre all the page numbers horizontally 2.5 cm from the bottom of the page.

All pages of separate tables and graphic illustrations are counted and should be numbered when it is possible and attractive to do so. More than likely, the report will be collated and bound by someone who is not familiar with the report. Numbering all the pages is a guard against omitting and misplacing pages.

In the preliminary section, count the title page as *i*; but do not print the number. Number the remaining preliminary pages *ii*, *iii*, *iv*, and so on; centre these numbers horizontally 2.5 cm from the bottom of the page.

When a report is reproduced on both sides of the paper (*duplexed*) and bound on the left, it is best to centre page numbers at the bottom of each page. If page numbers appear at the top right on odd-numbered pages, they will appear at the top left on even-numbered pages. When you choose to alternate the page numbers from left to right, remember that this will also alternate the running heads.

Tables

Tables should be inserted in the text immediately following the paragraph in which reference is made to the table. A paragraph should not be divided by a table. A table less than one page in length should not be spread over two pages.

If there is no room on the page for the table to follow the paragraph referring to it, continue the text to the *next* page and insert the table immediately following the *next* paragraph.

A table that requires a full page should follow the page on which the reference to it is made. You can save time and avoid a last-minute rush by printing each table that almost fills a page on a separate sheet of paper. Following are the reasons why:

1. Tables are usually prepared before the report is written. You can prepare many of the tables in final form while you are working on drafts of the report. If you are not sure of the order of the tables at the time you are preparing them, you can number them before you print the final draft.
2. Preparing the text is faster when tables are not inserted on the page with the text.
3. Tables, because they consist of numbers and headings, can be keyed by someone else on different software and still harmonize with the prepared text.

All the tables in the report do not have to conform to the same spacing. That being said, tables usually are single-spaced. Treat each table independently, displaying the data in the most readable and attractive manner possible. A table may be landscaped (placed broadside on the page). When it is, the page should be numbered in the usual way, and the table should be inserted with the top at the left edge of the report.

A table that is too long or too wide to fit on one page should be reduced in size to match the pages in the report. Where this is not practical, a long table may use two successive pages, or a wide table may use a fold-out page.

A table that requires a full page should be centred vertically as well as horizontally on the page. The vertical placement is best at the optical centre, or what is sometimes referred to as the *reading position*. This means that the title of the table begins two spaces above exact vertical centring.

For reports bound at the left, centre the tables and their titles 1.3 cm to the right of the centre of the page to allow for the bound margin. Word processing software will automatically adjust for binding.

Tables should be numbered or lettered consecutively throughout a report. When there are many tables, Arabic numbers are preferable to Roman numerals because the higher Roman numerals can be difficult to read. Key the table number, such as Table III or TABLE 3, in either lowercase or uppercase letters. Centre it horizontally above the title of the table. Key the title in all-caps above the column headings. If the title contains a subtitle, key the subtitle below the title. The guidelines for arranging titles, subtitles, column headings, and sources in a letter report apply to all formal tables. By using shading and double-lines, and by changing the width of lines, you can create attractive tables. Refer back to Figures 13-6 and 13-7.

Quotations

Short direct quotations of three lines or fewer should be enclosed in double quotation marks and incorporated into the text. The lines should extend from margin to margin. See the following example.

> Alexander Pope was responsible for the famous expression "Fools rush in where angels fear to tread."[1] Pope was born in 1688 and died at the age of 56 in 1744.

Direct quotations longer than three lines should be set off from the text, indented five spaces from both the left and right margins, and single-spaced. A quotation that is set off from the text is not enclosed in quotation marks. Refer to the following example.

> George Bernard Shaw, wishing to describe his fellow Englishmen, wrote
>
> > There is nothing so bad or so good that you will not find Englishmen doing it; but you will never find an Englishman in the wrong. He does everything on principle. He fights you on patriotic principles; he robs you on business principles; he enslaves you on imperial principles; he supports his king on royal principles and cuts off his king's head on republican principles.[2]

To indicate a quotation within a quotation, use single quotation marks if the quoted material is enclosed in double quotation marks. Where quoted material has been set off from the text and is not enclosed in quotation marks, use double quotation marks.

Occasionally words are omitted from quoted material. This is permitted if the original meaning is not changed. An omission less than one paragraph in length is indicated by an ellipsis, which is three periods in a row. An ellipsis may be "open" (spaces in between the periods), or "tight" (no spaces). However, there is always a space *before* and *after* an ellipsis.

Documentation

Documentation is used to

- give credit to the source of ideas quoted directly or indirectly or paraphrased
- enable the reader to locate the quoted material
- lend authority to a statement not generally accepted.

In business and scientific reports, citations are often placed within the text. Do one of the following:

1. State the facts as naturally as you would if you were presenting them orally.
2. Use the author's name or some other reference to the source at the logical point in the sentence, followed by the documentation in parentheses.
3. Give the citation at the end of the sentence—either state the author, date, and page number in parentheses or refer to a reference list, arranged alphabetically, at the end of the report.

At times you will need to refer to a source named in your reference list. This reference list may be in the form of either endnotes or a bibliography. There are many acceptable ways to credit sources; one of the most effective is to state the author's surname and the page in the source from which the reference is taken. The following is an example of a quotation where the source is given credit.

> "People from other nations may be more attentive listeners." (Smithson, 337)

This tells the reader that the quote was extracted from page 337 of Smithson's book, which is listed in the endnotes or the bibliography.

Preliminary Sections

Key and assemble the preliminaries of the report after you have completed the text of the report. Among the items placed in the preliminary section of a report are the following:

- letter of transmittal
- cover
- title page
- executive summary or **synopsis**
- acknowledgments
- table of contents
- list of tables
- list of illustrations.

Examples of some preliminary pages are shown in Figures 13-9, 13-10, and 13-11.

Supplementary Sections

Materials that add to the report but do not belong in its text are placed in supplementary sections. The pages of the supplements are numbered as a continuation of the page numbers used in the report text. There are any number of sources that explain how to format supplement pages. If you need more detail than provided here, consult a current office reference manual.

Endnotes

Formal footnotes are rarely used. Instead, a more efficient format called *endnotes* is used. The purpose of endnotes is to give credit to the author(s) of works that have been directly quoted.

Endnotes are numbered just like footnotes but appear on a separate page at the end of the report. The reference list and the appendices follow the endnote page. For an example of an endnotes page, refer to Figure 13-12 on page 296.

Figure 13-12 shows one the correct formats for listing quoted materials from both conventional and Internet sources. A quoted reference to the Internet

Figure 13-9 Title page.

MSS BUSINESS SYSTEMS INC.

PROPOSAL FOR

ADVANCED COMMUNICATION TRAINING

Prepared by

Amelia Jane Ross

Director of Training and Recruitment
MSS Business Systems Inc.

February 22, 20--

Figure 13-10 Table of contents.

TABLE OF CONTENTS

APPENDICES

ii

Figure 13-11 List of tables.

LIST OF TABLES

iii

Figure 13-12 Endnotes.

ENDNOTES

1. Jim Corder, *et. al.*, Handbook of Current English, 3rd Can. ed. (Toronto: Gage Publishing Limited, 2000), 204.

2. *Ibid.*

3. *Ibid.*, pp. 206–207.

4. John Winters, "The Best of the Budgets": Journal for Canadian Professionals (May 1999), 7.

5. Kenneth M. Smithson and Linda Wilson, The Strategic Communications Book (Scarborough: Prentice-Hall Canada Inc., 2000), 443.

6. Winters, *loc. cit.*

7. Smithson and Wilson, *op. cit.*, p. 447.

8. Alberta Apprenticeship and Industry Training Board, A Vision for the Future, 1999 (http://www.gov.ab.ca/dept/aecd/divisions/apprenticeship/vision/profile)

Page 49

Figure 13-13 References.

REFERENCES

Adams, William, The Professional's Pocket Guide to Survival. Prentice-Hall Canada Inc., Scarborough, 2000.

Alberta Apprenticeship and Industry Training Board. (1999). A Vision For The Future. (http://www.gov.ab.ca/dept/aecd/divisions/apprenticeship/vision/profile)

Corder, Jim *et al.*, Handbook of Current English, 4th Can. ed., Gage Publishing Limited, Toronto, 1996.

Smithson, Kenneth M. and Linda Wilson, The Strategic Communications Book. Prentice-Hall Canada Inc., Scarborough, 2000.

Winters, John, "The Best of the Budgets," Journal for Canadian Professionals, May 28, 1999, pp 7-11.Page 50

Page 49

Figure 13-14 Appendix cover sheet.

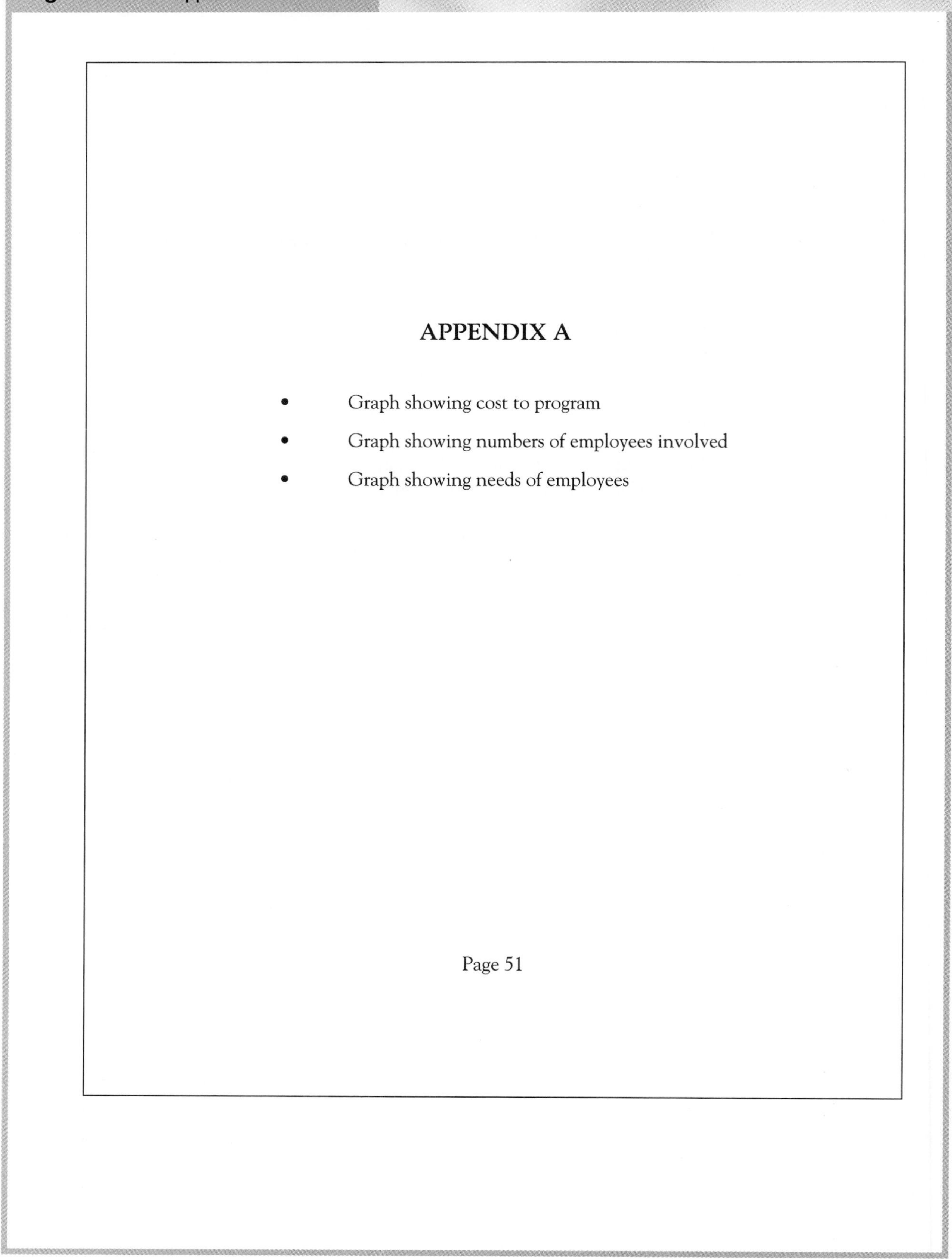

APPENDIX A

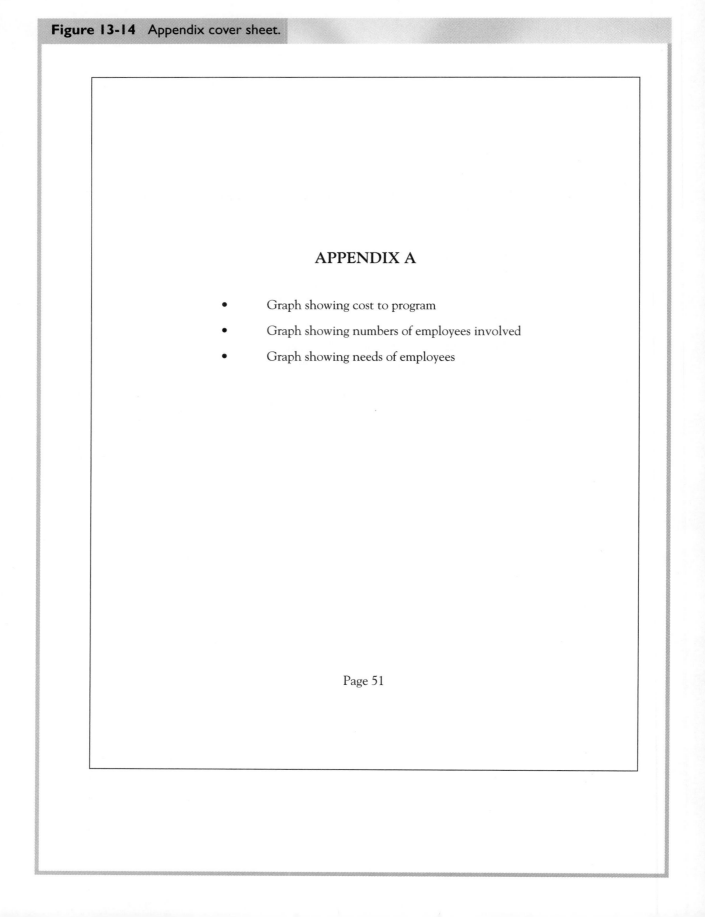

- Graph showing cost to program
- Graph showing numbers of employees involved
- Graph showing needs of employees

Page 51

Figure 13-15 Introduction to a formal report.

A COST ANALYSIS FOR MAINTAINING TERMINALS DURING A THREE-YEAR PERIOD

As authorized by Mrs. Monica Pascini, Manager of Financial Services, MSS Business systems, we have analyzed the cost of repairing terminals at ABC Insurance during a three-year period. The methodology used in this analysis compared the cost of maintaining terminals on a per-call basis with the cost of maintaining the same terminals under a service contract. The results indicate the most cost-effective method of terminal maintenance for ABC Insurance.

Procedures Used for the Analysis

The data on the maintenance cards for the 2063 terminals and the 2263 terminals used in the offices of ABC Insurance were analyzed.

Maintenance Study for the 2063 Terminals

The installation of the 2063 terminals took place in January of 19--; therefore, the study was limited to maintenance during the last three years. Twenty-four 2063 terminals were a part of this study. Terminals that were kept for standby situations were not included. The cost of preventative maintenance was analyzed as a separate item.

The provisions and costs of three service contracts were obtained from three local companies. Copies of these contracts may be found in Appendix A of this report.

In some respects, the study of these workstations was in less detail than the study of the 2263 terminals.

Maintenance Study for the 2263 Terminals

Because the 2263 terminals were installed in March of 19--, we were able to collect more extensive data on these particular workstations.

At this time, there are no 2263 terminals which are considered as standby equipment; therefore, all 2263 terminals were included in the analysis. Fifty-one such terminals are currently in use with this company.

Five service contracts between three different companies were obtained and used for the study. Copies of these reports are included in Appendix B of this report.

should include the same information as that from conventionally published materials (when possible) but it should at least include the full website address with specific link information.

References

The documentary sources used in preparing the report are listed in the **bibliography**, also called a **reference list**. All references cited in the report must be included in the reference list. References which, though not quoted, yield relevant material should also be included in the reference list. A report based entirely on the organization's own data (as numerous business reports are) would not have a reference list.

Materials obtained from the Internet should be noted in the list of references. Just as in the Endnotes, Internet references should include the same information as that from conventionally published materials (when possible) but they should also include the full website address with specific link information. Refer to the Internet entry on the References page in Figure 13-13.

Remember information that is found on the Internet is much more "fluid" than that found in more traditional publications such as books.

The Reference page appears at the end of the manuscript on a separate page or pages. Entries, instead of being numbered, are listed alphabetically by the author's last name. Where the author's name is not available, the name of the publication is considered as the first part of the entry and is used in alphabetical order. Page numbers for reference entries are included only if the material being cited is part of a larger publication. An example of this would be an article from a magazine. Figure 13-13 illustrates these variations.

Appendix

Supporting data that the reader will refer to while reading the report should be incorporated as part of the text; any additional supporting data should be placed in a supplementary section, called an *appendix*, at the end of the report. Examples of items placed in the appendix are

- a copy of a questionnaire used in an investigation
- sample forms and letters
- detailed summaries of data
- graphs and charts.

Not all reports contain appendices. When only one item is appended, its title is APPENDIX. If more than one item is appended, each item should be numbered or lettered under its own heading: APPENDIX A, APPENDIX B, APPENDIX C, and so on.

The appendix begins with a cover sheet stating the appendix number and the contents of the appendix. See Figure 13-14.

The appendices are the final items of the report. They follow the references. Each appendix, along with the page number on which it begins, is listed in the table of contents. See Figure 13-10.

Guidelines for Composing

Your first step in preparing a formal report should be to study the purpose of the report to determine precisely what the expected outcome is. You should be able to state the purpose of a report in one clear sentence.

Next, list the problems that must be solved in order to achieve the purpose of the report. The answers to the problems to be solved will become the main text, or body, of the report.

Do your research thoroughly and accurately. The content presented in the body of the report will be the result of one of the following:

- an analysis of data on the organization's operations
- secondary research, which is information gleaned from published sources
- primary research.

The methods of primary research are

1. observation
2. questionnaire
3. interview
4. experimentation.

In other words, to obtain your facts you may need to carry out an investigation, conduct interviews, confer with a few authorities, send out questionnaires, analyze existing data, and/or do bibliographical research.

Before you begin writing, review the purpose of the report to make sure you have arrived at solutions to all parts of the problem. Those solutions will form your conclusion. Also, check the accuracy of your facts and figures.

Organizing the Report

Give your report a title that is broad enough to encompass all the topics presented in the report. Divide the report into at least three main divisions:

1. Introduction
2. Body
3. Summary.

Next, prepare an outline for the body of the report. Each problem you solve should become a separate division or subdivision of the body. Assign an appropriate heading to each one.

Use a logical arrangement of ideas. State the problem and how the study was conducted. See Figure 13-15. Take the reader step by step, in logical order, through all the procedures you followed to arrive at the conclusion. Use facts to convince the reader. Present all the facts, and use tables and graphics to make it easy for the reader to grasp the facts. Lead the reader logically from the facts to the conclusion or conclusions. Any recommendations you make should be a logical outcome of the conclusions.

Writing the Report

Reports must be factual and impersonal; therefore, they should be written in the third person. Strive for objectivity. Do not let "we," "I," and "you" detract from the objectivity of the report. Another way to achieve objectivity in writing is to report statistical findings, for example:

> Sales in the first quarter of 20— were $77.9 million, a gain of 15 percent over the $67.8 million in last year's first quarter.

Avoid using words or phrases that reflect your reaction to the findings. Instead of saying, "It is interesting to note that the increase in net profit closely parallels the increase in sales," make a direct statement about the relationship between sales and net profit for the period. A more objective way of expressing this would be, "There is a direct relationship between the increase in sales and the increase in net profit."

Write as much of the report as possible in the present tense. A combination of past and present tense may be used. The discussion about how the study, investigation, or analysis was conducted should be expressed in past tense to show the reader that the work is completed, not still in progress. Some business reports must be expressed in the past tense because the facts reported were true only on a given day or for a definite period. Examples of such reports are accounting reports, such as the balance sheet and the profit-and-loss statement.

When describing conditions that definitely have changed since the day the facts were collected, use the past tense. Use the present tense to describe conditions that to a large extent will still exist after the report is finished.

Write first the part of the report that is easiest for you to compose. Consider each main division and each subdivision as a separate topic. Most of the time, you can develop these topics in any order.

Before you begin developing a topic, carefully check all the facts and figures related to that topic. Next list your subtopics in the order that you will present them. Also prepare the tables and graphics you will use to illustrate the topic you are writing about. Carefully label all the columns of your tables and graphics. You can work from a draft or a sketch while these graphic illustrations are being prepared in final form, but keep copies of the illustrations in front of you as you write.

The graphic illustrations belong in the text of the report. Introduce the reader to each illustration before it appears by referring to it in the report. You may want to assign numbers to tables and letters to graphics in order to avoid confusion.

After you introduce a table or graphic, take the reader completely through it, to help the reader understand exactly what is being illustrated. Avoid constructions such as "Table 3 shows ..." or "Chart 4 illustrates ..." Instead, begin sentences with the subject of the table or chart. Example: "A sharp increase in computer sales is illustrated in Chart 4."

Avoid beginning sentences with "There ..." You can strengthen the report by placing the key word of the topic being discussed in a prominent position at the beginning of the sentence. For example: "Telecommunications has made global business a reality."

Write your report so that the reader can grasp the important facts from the written copy without having to study the graphic illustrations. The reader should not have to read the headings to understand the topic. A well-written report will be clear and meaningful even when all the headings and illustrations have been removed.

Interpret data at appropriate points so that they will be meaningful to the reader. Tell the reader what the facts mean in a natural, logical way. For the most significant data, give both the figures and percentages, or other computations. By interpreting the data you will be presenting a picture, not just a string of facts and figures. Present the data to the reader step by step in the same logical order you followed when analyzing them.

Summarize your facts in the final section of the report. If you provided a summary sentence or paragraph as you developed each main topic, restate the content of the interim summaries in the last section of the report. Do not include new facts or new interpretations in the summary section. The conclusions and recommendations, if you write them, belong in the summary section and should be the logical outcome of the facts presented in the report. Make sure the recommendations are based on the conclusions. At the time you are given the assignment, establish whether you are expected to include recommendations. Sometimes when an executive assigns a report to a writer, the executive prefers to write the recommendations.

Usually more than one solution exists for a business problem. In the summarizing section present all the alternatives. Present the most feasible alternative first; then present the others in any order, or in decreasing order of feasibility.

If you require a synopsis at the beginning of the report, write a synopsis and place it in the preliminary section of the report immediately preceding the first page of the text. When you include a synopsis, do not change the summary section; both belong in the report.

The introduction to the report may be written either first or last. The introduction should be brief. Subheadings are optional. Write the purpose of the report and the authorization in the opening paragraph without a heading other than the title of the report. In the paragraphs that follow, describe the methods of collecting the data and the scope and limitations of the study. Using the outline of the text of the report, list the topics in a paragraph in the same order in which they will be discussed in the report.

Read the entire report through from beginning to end at one sitting to examine how all the parts relate to one another. Do you need to add transitional paragraphs or sentences? Transitional paragraphs are guideposts that introduce what is coming next. They give direction to the reader. They may be written after the draft of the report proper is finished; in fact, it often saves time to write them last, because you can compose them more easily when you know precisely what you are introducing.

Writing the Letter of Transmittal

The purposes of the letter of transmittal are to

1. transmit the report
2. refer to the authorization (or request).

The letter of transmittal should indicate why the report was written; for that reason, the subject of the report, the authorization or request, and the date of the authorization or request should be included. These facts can be stated in the opening of the letter. Refer to the following three examples:

1. Here is the report on Internet, television, and radio advertising possibilities that you requested on June 24.
2. In accordance with the authorization given in your letter of May 11, 20—, I have completed the branch plant location survey of Windsor, Ontario, and I am submitting a detailed report of my findings.
3. Following the instructions contained in your letters of July 2, 20—, and August 22, 20—, I am submitting the data you will need for selecting a brand of car to replace the two-year-old models now in the sales fleet.

The letter of transmittal should be factual. It should be written in a direct style because the main message is a positive one. Do not use the letter of transmittal to persuade the reader to accept your conclusions, and do not use it to defend your findings.

You may write in an informal style, using first person, even if the letter accompanies a report written entirely in the third person. You may use the past tense in the letter to show that the report is completed, thus:

> I presented the analysis of the compact cars first because of the cost savings. In the second section of the report I have made a detailed comparison between compact and medium-sized cars.

Letters of transmittal are usually short. Even so, they can also serve the following purposes:

1. Show the purpose of the investigation and of the report
2. Indicate how the facts were collected
3. Give significant findings
4. Orient the reader to the report
5. State the scope and the limitations of the report
6. Point out special problems or special considerations
7. Mention whether the report marks the completion of the investigation or is a progress report
8. State conclusions if it is feasible to do so
9. Call attention to another study or investigation that is needed.

Arranging the Report

Reports may be arranged according to any of the following styles: inductive, deductive, chronological.

The inductive arrangement is used when a report is lengthy, when it is difficult to understand, or when the reader must be convinced of something. The arrangement of ideas is in a logical order. The reader is taken step by step through all phases necessary to arrive at the conclusion. The inductive arrangement was further explained in the preceding discussion on organizing and writing reports.

The deductive arrangement is used when the writer knows that the reader will be receptive to the findings in the report. Executives prefer reports organized by the deductive arrangement because they are easy to read. Because the significant findings appear at the beginning, the executive can read the first part only, or the first part plus selections from the supporting data.

The content of a report is the same whether it is arranged inductively or deductively; only the arrangement of ideas differs. The elements in a deductive arrangement are usually arranged as follows:

1. An introduction, which includes the purpose of the report, the authorization, and how the study was conducted.
2. A summary of the findings and conclusions.
3. The recommendations, if any are given.
4. The supporting data.

Variations of this outline may be used.

Some reports consist mainly of historical background to a problem. When you must refer to situations that occurred at different times over an extended period, the best way to organize the report may be according to the time sequence, using the dates as the subheadings. Chronological reports are easy to write but difficult for the reader to comprehend. The chronological arrangement does not help the reader see how the parts of the report relate to the problem. For this reason, do not use the chronological arrangement when you can organize the data inductively or deductively.

Questions for Study and Review

1. Describe five guidelines for giving constructive feedback and five guidelines for receiving feedback.
2. Explain six guidelines for coping with the fear of giving oral presentations.
3. Discuss seven methods for preventing the frustration caused by presentation hazards.
4. What nonverbal messages are conveyed through the way you dress and the amount of personal space you allow other people?
5. Describe how eye contact can make the receiver feel comfortable or uncomfortable.
6. Why are facial expressions considered a universal language?
7. Discuss how posture can send a message of interest or disinterest.
8. Suggest four ways to improve listening skills.
9. Suggest how an administrative assistant can take initiative in answering correspondence.
10. List the qualities common to all effective letters.
11. Describe the circumstances under which it would be desirable to write two letters instead of one to the same addressee at the same time.
12. When the writer is originating correspondence, what guidelines should be used to check the completeness of the message?
13. What is achieved through coherence in a communication?
14. Compare conciseness with brevity.
15. Compare connotation and denotation.
16. Summarize the techniques for using technical words effectively in business letters.
17. Name six ways to achieve vividness in writing.
18. State the requirement for an effective opening sentence in a favourable reply.
19. What can the writer say to let the reader know that confidential information will be handled properly?
20. What is the most important single element common to all goodwill letters?
21. Describe the opening paragraph of a disappointing letter.
22. When should the request be stated in a persuasive letter? How should the request be phrased?
23. Assume that you have been given the assignment of writing letters for a manager's signature. What can you do to make your composition sound as though the letter were written by the manager?
24. Contrast the following letter styles: full-block, modified-block, and simplified.
25. What are the primary uses of business reports?
26. What determines whether a report is formal or informal?
27. State two writing techniques for presenting facts objectively.
28. How does a spot table differ from a formal table?
29. Where should the source of data contained in a table be indicated?
30. What guidelines concerning parallel structure should you follow when composing headings?
31. State three reasons why reports are often single-spaced.
32. Explain the main differences between fourth- and fifth-degree headings.
33. What guidelines should be followed for keying direct quotations of fewer than three printed lines? of more than three printed lines?

34. Describe the ordering of the supplementary sections in the report.
35. What are the differences between the endnote page and the reference page?
36. State the guidelines a report writer should follow to help the reader understand the tables, charts, and graphs used in a report.
37. What are the main purposes of the letter of transmittal?
38. Compare the inductive and deductive arrangements of reports.

Spelling Reinforcement

achieved	connotation	essential	objectivity
appendixes	convey	expedite	readability
business	deductive	explanation	repetitive
coherence	delegate	ferret	symbols
commitment	dissatisfaction	focus	synopsis
concentrate	endeavor/endeavour	gratitude	technical

On-the-Job Situations

1. You are eager to write letters, and the manager needs help to keep up with the correspondence. This morning as you processed the mail, you selected six letters that you believed you could answer satisfactorily and put them in your desk drawer. At about 1100 a customer called the manager and asked if he had received the letter that the customer had written to him. Your manager asked you about the customer's letter. You had to admit that you were attempting to answer it. What did you do wrong? What would be a better plan for getting an opportunity to write letters?
2. While the manager is away on a three-week vacation, two of his assistants are answering his mail. Today Ms. Wingate, a customer who was displeased with the reply she had received from one of the assistants, called you. The manager will be back in the office in less than one week. What should you do about Ms. Wingate's complaint? What should you say to Ms. Wingate?
3. The manager, Ms. Shapiro, left you an e-mail with an attachment. Her e-mail asks you to have 12 copies of the attached report ready for 0830. tomorrow. The report needs editing and tables inserted. The tables are computer printouts that have been left on your desk. Ms. Shapiro is out of the office for the day. With your normal daily workload—opening the mail, answering the telephone and e-mail, and handling clients—you cannot complete the report before tomorrow morning. What should you do?

Special Reports

1. Request information about an office product advertised in an office technology magazine or over the Internet.
2. Imagine that you are employed in a professional office where the office manager is out of town for two weeks. Before she left, she asked you to acknowledge every fax that is addressed to her. However, you are not to answer the faxes, simply acknowledge them. Draft a fax message you can use as a guide for acknowledging the office manager's faxes in her absence.

Production Challenges

13-A Writing a Letter of Request

Supplies needed:

- *Letterhead for Millennium Appliances, Inc., Form 13-A, page 435*
- *Working Papers Disk, File 13-A*

You want to know more about desktop publishing. Search the current issues of your local city newspaper for advertisements about desktop publishing equipment and/or software. Write a letter to a vendor of desktop publishing software requesting information. Submit the letter to your instructor.

13-B Preparing the Final Draft of a Manuscript

Supplies needed:

- *Draft for Work Improvement Methods, Form 13-B, pages 436 to 443*
- *Working Papers Disk, File 13-B*
- *Plain paper*

Mrs. Yee is preparing an article on work improvement methods for publication in the company magazine. Open File 13-B on your Working Papers Disk and use the edits indicated on Form 13-B to make the corrections on the screen. Watch for all formatting, grammatical, and spelling errors. Use double-spacing; print one copy for Mrs. Yee's files. Note: There are more error and formatting corrections required than those indicated by Mrs. Yee and you are responsible to make the article error-free.

World Wide Websites

Editors' Association of Canada

www.web.net/eac-acr
The Editors' Association of Canada resource page on English style and usage includes grammar and style notes, grammar hotline directory, Keith Ivey's English Usage Page, and On-Line English Grammar.

Elements of Style

www.cc.columbia.edu/acis/bartleby/strunk/
Peruse William Strunk's classic on writing well.

Writing Business Letters and Addressing Envelopes

www.ais.msstate.edu/AEE/Tutorial/bus_letters.html
This tutorial gives examples of different letter types and formats.

CHAPTER 14

Banking Transactions and Record Keeping

Outline

Transferring Funds

- Certified Cheque
- Bank Draft
- Bank Money Order
- Traveller's Cheque
- Western Union Money Transfer

Writing Cheques

- Chequebooks and Cheque Forms
- Rules for Writing Cheques
- Stop-Payment Notification
- Cheques Written for Cash Withdrawals

Efficient Banking Practices

- Electronic Funds Transfer
- Magnetic Ink Characters

Endorsing Cheques

- Restrictive Endorsement
- Blank Endorsement
- Full Endorsement

Making Deposits

- Preparing Items for Deposit
- Preparing the Deposit Slip
- Using the Night Depository

Reconciling the Bank Statement with the Chequebook Balance

- Adopt a Consistent Method
- Prepare the Reconciliation Statement
- Search for Errors
- File Cancelled Cheques

Keeping Records

- Petty Cash Fund
- Office Supplies on Hand

Learning Outcomes

At the completion of this chapter, the student will be able to:

1. Define the following: (a) cheque, (b) certified cheque, (c) bank draft, (d) bank money order, (e) traveller's cheque.
2. Describe the two efficient banking practices, EFT and MICR.
3. Prepare currency for deposit and a deposit slip.
4. Prepare cheques.
5. Describe how to stop payment on a cheque.
6. Compare a restrictive endorsement, a blank endorsement, and a full endorsement.
7. Reconcile a bank statement.
8. Key a bank reconciliation statement.
9. List the standard procedures for keeping a petty cash fund.
10. Make out petty cash vouchers.
11. Prepare a petty cash report.
12. Report on the use of technology in commercial banking practices.

GRADUATE PROFILE

Angela Pettipas
Billing Administrator

Lafarge Canada Inc.

College Graduation:
I. W. Akerley Community College
Dartmouth, NS
1995

If the mission of an organization is fiscal responsibility, then one goal must be to control its accounts. Enter Angela! With a positive attitude and a lot of hard work, she maintains a professional eye on the billing cycle of this Nova Scotia organization. She balances responsibilities for critical deadlines and *daily* account changes with the ever-present auditing requirements.

"Open communication is the key to success [of this demanding role]," she says. Angela has learned that skillful communication and networking are essential *building blocks* to developing the cooperation of those that provide inputs to her billing process. As well, she believes that open communication is the key to effective office teams.

With a penchant for getting along with others, Angela strives to improve her strengths at every opportunity. She subscribes to personal power and improvement workshops that support her effectiveness both in and out of the office.

"Volunteer for important tasks to demonstrate initiative and capability."

Handling banking transactions is one of the more typical duties for the administrative assistant who works for a private company or for a small professional office such as a doctor's or dentist's office. This part of the job may include handling payments received, making bank deposits, writing cheques, and preparing the bank reconciliation.

In a large organization, banking transactions are handled by a department designated for that purpose. Depending on the nature of the business, these departments may be called the Finance Department, Accounts Payable, Accounts Receivable, or simply Administration. All incoming cash and cheques are forwarded to that department. After invoices and statements are approved for payment, they are forwarded to the same department for payment. Funds may be transferred by cheque or by electronic funds transfer.

TRANSFERRING FUNDS

A depositor establishes a chequing account at a bank as a convenient means of transferring funds. The instrument used most often for transferring funds is the ordinary cheque, which is defined as *a written order of a depositor upon a commercial bank to pay to the order of a designated party or to a bearer a specified sum of money on demand.*

The parties to a cheque are the *drawer,* the person who draws the cheque on her or his account, the *drawee,* the bank upon which the cheque is drawn, and the *payee,* the person to whom payment is made. See Figure 14-1.

At the time that the depositor opens a chequing account, the depositor places on file with the bank a signature card showing her or his authorized signature. A depositor should always use her or his authorized signature when signing cheques. If you are to sign cheques for your manager, or for the organization where you work, or both, your manager will ask the bank to honour your signature. You will be asked to fill out a signature card, thereby placing your authorized signature on file with the bank.

In addition to the ordinary cheque, the following are used to transfer funds:

- certified cheque
- bank draft
- bank money order
- traveller's cheque
- electronic funds transfer.

Certified Cheque

A *certified cheque* guarantees payment to the payee by the drawee bank. To obtain certification, the depositor completes the cheque in the usual way and then takes it to the bank where the depositor has an account. After ascertaining that sufficient funds are in the depositor's account to cover the amount of the cheque, an officer

Figure 14-1 Cheque with notations.

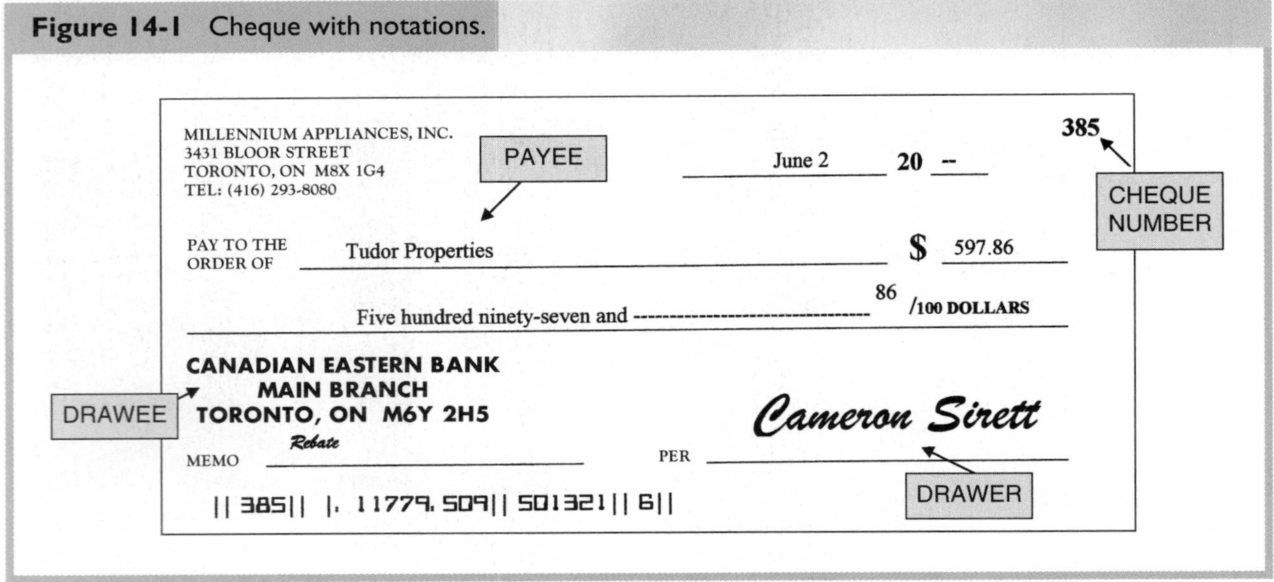

of the bank stamps CERTIFIED, ACCEPTED, or GUARANTEED across the face of the cheque, signs her or his official name, dates the cheque, and immediately charges it to the depositor's account. The "acceptance" written across the face of the cheque is the bank's acknowledgment of its obligation to pay when the cheque is presented for payment. The drawer of a certified cheque cannot stop payment on it.

A depositor whose financial status is unknown to the payee can use a certified cheque as a means of payment. Certified cheques are commonly used when large amounts of money are involved. A certified cheque is required in certain business transactions, such as the purchase of real estate.

An administrative assistant may take the manager's cheque to the bank to be certified. If the certified cheque is not sent to the payee, it should be deposited in the bank, for it has been deducted by the bank from the depositor's account. A certified cheque should never be destroyed.

Bank Draft

A *bank draft* is a cheque drawn by a bank on its own funds (or credit) in another bank. The draft is made payable to a third party, who upon endorsing it may cash it at the bank on which it is drawn.

A bank draft can be used to transfer money to another person or organization in another geographic location within Canada or abroad. A bank draft payable in foreign currency may be purchased.

The process of obtaining a bank draft is quite easy. Simply provide the desired amount of money in the form of cash, a personal cheque, or a business cheque made payable to the bank. The bank will additionally charge a nominal administration fee. In exchange, you will receive a bank draft made payable to the person or organization specified as payee.

Bank Money Order

A *money order,* which is similar to a postal money order, may be obtained from a bank. The service is used mainly by people without chequing accounts to send relatively small amounts of money through the mail.

A bank money order is negotiable, and requires the endorsement of the payee to transfer it. It may be cashed at any bank. The fee for obtaining a bank money order is nominal. The amount for which a single money order may be written is limited, but the number of money orders that may be issued to the same person to be sent to one payee is not restricted.

Traveller's Cheque

Most banks and several companies sell traveller's cheques. Some examples of traveller's cheques are Visa, American Express, Bank of Montreal, and Thomas Cook. Most traveller's cheques are sold in denominations of 10, 20, 50, 100, and 500 Canadian dollars. They may also be purchased in U.S. dollars, British pounds sterling, German marks, French francs, Japanese yen, Swiss francs, and some other currencies. Usually the cost is 1 percent of the face value. There is no time limit on their validity. A traveller who plans an extended stay in a foreign country may find it economically worthwhile to purchase some traveller's cheques in the currency of that particular country. Figure 14-2 is a sample of a traveller's cheque.

Figure 14-2 A sample of a traveler's cheque.

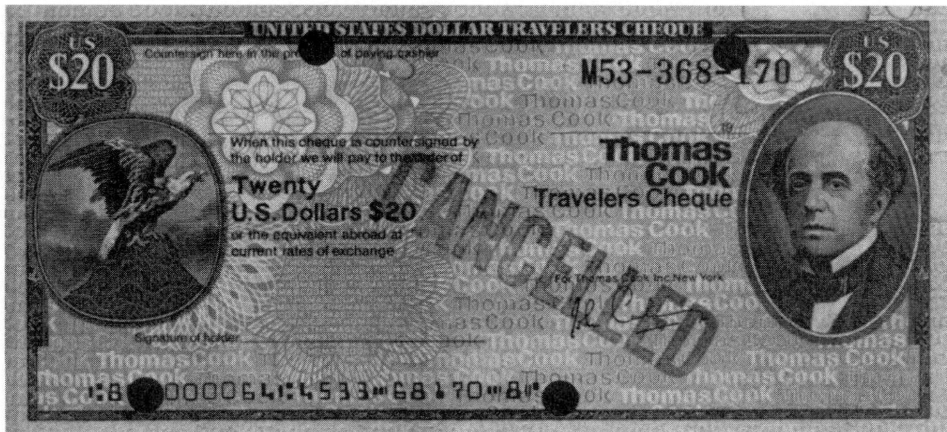

Courtesy of Thomas Cook

The purchaser must obtain traveller's cheques in person because each cheque must be signed in the presence of the agent from whom the cheques are being purchased. The purchaser's signature on each cheque is her or his identification and protection. The purchaser can cash a traveller's cheque at a hotel or bank, at other places of business, or at an office that represents the traveller's cheques he or she is carrying (such as a Thomas Cook or MasterCard office).

"The procedures and organizational skills that I learned at Columbia College are crucial in my career. There is not one thing that I learned in school that I haven't already used in my career."

Laurie Remenda, Graduate
Columbia College

Traveller's cheques are numbered serially. When your manager purchases traveller's cheques, you should prepare a list of the serial numbers on the cheques in duplicate—one for your files and the other for your manager to carry, preferably in a place separate from the traveller's cheques.

When traveller's cheques are lost or stolen, the owner can usually obtain a refund immediately by contacting a representative office of the company whose cheques were purchased.

Western Union Money Transfer

When you wish to transfer money immediately and over a long distance, you may consider contacting a Western Union agency. These agencies are often located in pharmacies and bookstores (see Chapter 6).

You can pay the Western Union agent with cash, certified cheque, or your Visa or MasterCard. When cash or a certified cheque is used, the transfer (even if worldwide) takes only about 15 minutes. Using Visa or MasterCard requires some verification and therefore may take a little longer; regardless, the transaction can be completed within an hour.

Of course, cash is not actually transmitted; one Western Union agency sends an electronic message to another agency, which then pays the receiver.

For further information about electronic money transfers, refer to Chapter 6.

WRITING CHEQUES

Blank cheques are assembled in various forms, but the information to be entered in the cheque does not vary. Follow standard rules for writing cheques.

Today many organizations use computers to prepare cheques. If your organization does not have this facility, you may be asked to prepare them by an alternative method. Cheques may also be prepared with a cheque-writing machine, a computer printer, or a pen. Some businesses use cheque-writing machines as a safety measure against possible alteration of cheques. Others make use of commercially available software for cheque writing such as Intuit's QUICKEN, or SIMPLY ACCOUNTING.

Chequebooks and Cheque Forms

A bank will supply books of single cheques, as well as large books with three cheques to a page. One type has the cheque stub attached to each cheque; another type comes with a separate book for recording information about each cheque written.

Although banks will supply depositors with cheques, an organization may wish to use its own printed forms, called *voucher cheques*. The form of voucher cheques varies. When cheques are written by the computer, attached to the voucher cheque is a perforated form, called a *stub*, for recording the details of the cheque, such as gross payment, type and amount of deductions, and net payment. Some cheques are unbound in multiple copy packs. The carbon copies of the cheques are used within the organization for accounting purposes. Voucher cheques are recorded in numerical order in a cheque register.

Rules for Writing Cheques

Follow these rules when you are writing cheques with a printer or a pen:

1. To make sure that sufficient funds are in the account to cover the cheque, bring the chequebook balance up to date.
2. If you are preparing cheques by computer printer, use a dark-colour ink cartridge whenever possible. If you are preparing cheques by hand, use a pen. (Faintly printed figures and letters are easy to alter. So are handwritten ones.)
3. If the cheque is in a chequebook that contains a stub record, number the stub to agree with the number on the cheque being written.
4. Complete each stub or voucher statement as you write a cheque. Fill in the stub before you write the cheque. When you are paying two invoices with one cheque, show each separately on the stub or voucher statement.
5. Date the cheque as of the day it is being written. Cheques may be dated on Sundays and holidays. Postdating a cheque in anticipation of having additional funds in the bank by the date entered on the cheque could result in an overdraft, because the payee might present the cheque before the date shown and may even be paid. Postdating a cheque is permissible, but doing so should be avoided to protect the financial reputation of the organization. (If you receive a cheque that is not dated, write in the date on which you received it.)
6. Write the name of the payee in full without a title—such as Ms., Mrs., Miss, Mr., or Dr.—preceding the name. Use a married woman's legal name; the name she uses when she endorses the cheque. If the payee is serving as treasurer or chairperson, or in some other capacity, include the official title following her or his name to indicate that the payee is not receiving the money personally. Begin the name at the extreme left.
7. Before entering the amount, verify that the amount of the payment is correct. Take precautions to protect the cheque against alteration. Enter the figures first, placing them as close to the dollar sign and to each other as possible. For even amounts, be sure to fill in the zeros ("00/100") or enter "no/100". Notice how the figures are written in the cheque in Figure 14-3.

Figure 14-3 Keyboarded entries on cheques.

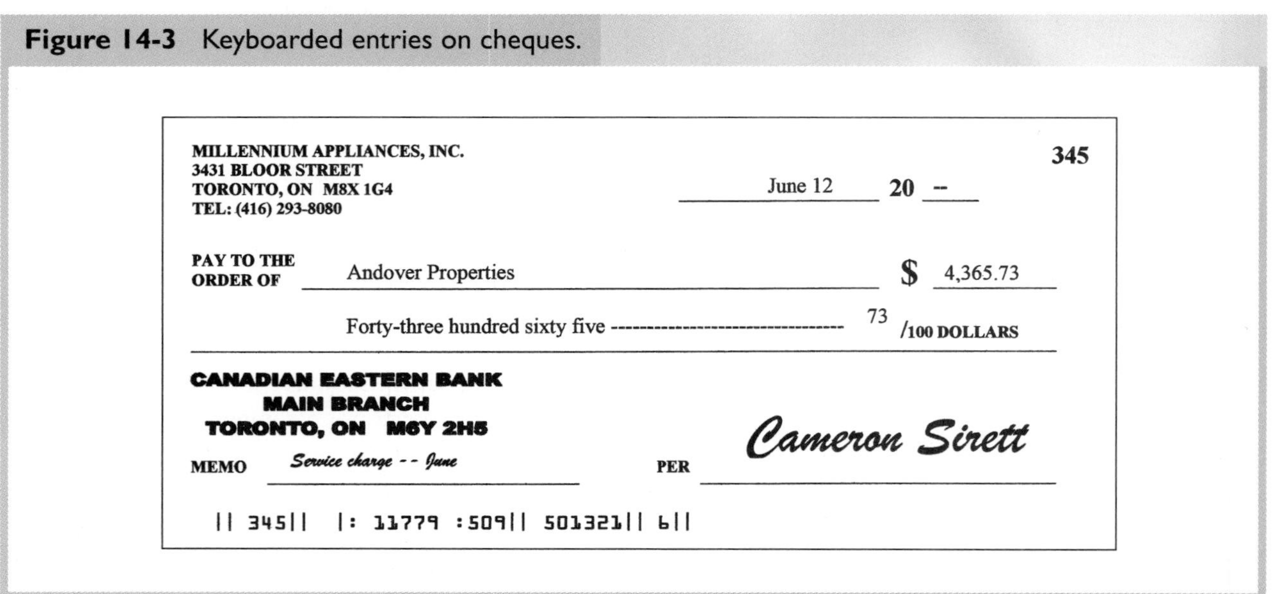
MILLENNIUM APPLIANCES, INC.
3431 BLOOR STREET
TORONTO, ON M8X 1G4
TEL: (416) 293-8080

345

June 12 20 –

PAY TO THE ORDER OF Andover Properties $ 4,365.73

Forty-three hundred sixty five -------------------------------- 73/100 DOLLARS

CANADIAN EASTERN BANK
MAIN BRANCH
TORONTO, ON M6Y 2H5

MEMO Service charge -- June PER Cameron Sirett

|| 345|| |: 11779 :509|| 501321|| 6||

8. Enter the same amount in words. Capitalize only the first word. Begin the words close to the left margin and fill in the space following the words with dashes or a wavy line. Express cents as a fraction of 100. Write large amounts with the fewest number of words. For example, $4,365.73 may be written in the following two ways, but the second example occupies the least space:

   Four thousand three hundred sixty-five and 73/100 ....Dollars

   Forty-three hundred sixty-five and 73/100.......................Dollars

9. Verify that the amount expressed in words agrees with the amount expressed in figures. When the figures and words do not agree, the bank may choose to not cash the cheque.
10. When you must write a cheque for less than $1, circle the figures following the dollar sign. Write "only" before the amount expressed in words and cents following it—for instance, "Only eighty-six cents." Cross out the word "Dollars." See Figure 14-4.
11. If you make a mistake, do not erase or cross out the error. Although some people cross out, correct, and initial their errors, it is better to write VOID across the face of the cheque and the stub. File the voided cheque in numerical order with the cancelled cheques from the bank. Never destroy a voided business cheque.
12. Present the cheques to your manager for your manager's signature. Your manager should sign them in ink *after* they have been filled in. Your manager may prefer to verify that the amounts of payment are correct. If so, provide your manager with the invoices and your calculations for extensions and discounts.

Stop-Payment Notification

At the request of the drawer, a bank will stop payment on a cheque at any time until it has cleared the bank upon which it is drawn. Stopping payment is a safety measure that should be taken when a cheque has been lost or stolen; it may also be taken when a cheque is written for an incorrect amount, when certain conditions of an agreement have not been met, or for other reasons.

As an administrative assistant, you may stop payment of a cheque signed by your manager. To do so, first call the bank and request that payment be stopped. Give the names of the drawer and the payee, the date, number, and amount of the cheque, and the reason why payment must be stopped.

The bank will request a written confirmation of the verbal order to stop payment. The bank will ask you either to complete a stop-payment form or to write a letter of confirmation and fax it to them immediately.

When you are certain that payment has been stopped, write STOPPED PAYMENT across the stub of the cheque and add the amount to the current chequebook balance. Later, if the cheque is returned to you, mark it VOID and file it with the cancelled cheques. Depending on the circumstances, you may need to write a replacement for the cheque on which you stopped payment.

Figure 14-4 Cheque written for less than $1.

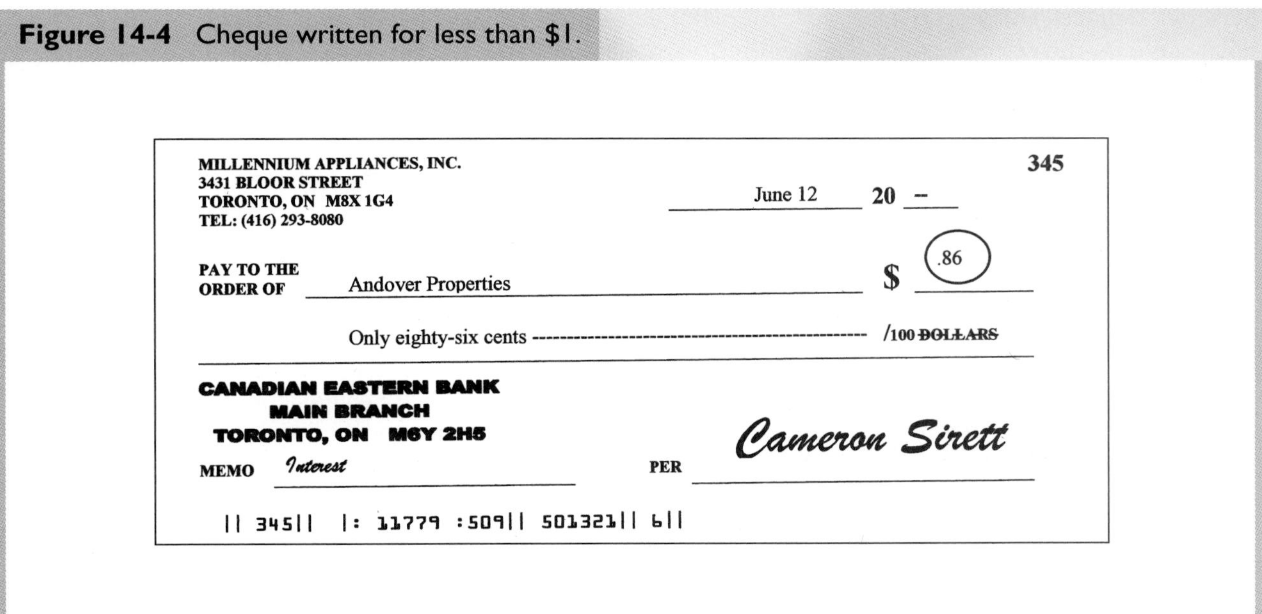

MILLENNIUM APPLIANCES, INC.
3431 BLOOR STREET
TORONTO, ON M8X 1G4
TEL: (416) 293-8080

345

June 12 20 --

PAY TO THE ORDER OF Andover Properties $ .86

Only eighty-six cents -- /100 ~~DOLLARS~~

CANADIAN EASTERN BANK
MAIN BRANCH
TORONTO, ON M6Y 2H5

MEMO Interest PER Cameron Sirett

|| 345|| |: 11779 :509|| 501321|| 6||

Cheques Written for Cash Withdrawals

A depositor can withdraw funds from her or his personal chequing account by writing the word "Cash" on the line provided for the name of the payee, filling in the amount, and signing the cheque. However, since a cheque written in this way is highly negotiable, a depositor should fill in the cheque only when actually at the teller's window ready to receive the money.

One of your responsibilities may be to obtain cash from your manager's personal chequing account. If your manager hands you a cheque made payable to "Cash," be especially careful with it. Anyone who comes in possession of it can cash it.

Handle cash as inconspicuously as possible. Put the cash you obtain for your manager in a sealed envelope. Always keep cash that you obtain for others separate from your own funds.

EFFICIENT BANKING PRACTICES

The Bank Act of 1871 stipulated that a bank must have a parliamentary charter in order to operate. Although this is still the case, Canadian banking practices have changed dramatically since that time. One of the objectives of banking is that it should be an efficient method of handling a person's or a company's money. Interbranch banking, night depositories, drive-in windows, automatic tellers, and banking on the Internet are all practices that have made banking more convenient for the customer.

With a gain in efficiency often comes a loss of personal contact. This is very true of the automatic teller service—the customer's contact is entirely with a banking machine and not with a bank employee.

Two efficient banking practices are electronic funds transfer (EFT) and magnetic ink character recognition (MICR).

Electronic Funds Transfer

By means of computers, financial institutions can carry out many banking transactions without the use of cheques. The main electronic funds transfer (EFT) services are automated teller machines and automated clearing houses. The latter are centres for electronic funds transfer between financial institutions and individuals.

Automated teller machines (ATMs), located at banks, enable customers to obtain cash, make deposits, check the status of their accounts, transfer money between accounts, and pay bills. A simplified version of the ATM—commonly called a cash machine—enables customers to check the balance of their accounts and obtain cash. They are located in shopping malls, supermarkets, gas stations, and other locations. To use an ATM, the customer simply activates the machine with an EFT card and enters a personal identification number (PIN).

"Always be willing to accept change and new challenges."

Pamela Sargent, Graduate
Saskatchewan Institute of Applied Science and Technology

Direct payroll deposit enables an organization to pay its employees without writing cheques. Instead, the organization furnishes the bank with a description of all payroll disbursements to be made to the employees. The bank credits the account of each employee with her or his net pay and withdraws the amount from the account of the employer. The employee receives a statement from her or his employer. The statement shows the gross payment, the types and amounts of deductions, and the net payment. Usually an organization makes arrangements for direct deposit with several banks.

Another type of transfer service is the preauthorized automated transfer of funds for an individual from one account to another within the same financial institution. For example, a customer can transfer funds from a chequing account to a savings account, from a savings account to a chequing account, and from a chequing account to a loan payment.

EFT services are important to the banking industry. Banks encourage their customers to use EFT service, since it is such an efficient method of banking.

While the Internet has grown in popularity for domestic banking, larger commercial applications of Internet banking are still not widely accepted. Occasionally, a small partnership or "domestic-like" organization may depend upon the Internet for its banking but it is not yet considered to be good commercial practice.

Magnetic Ink Characters

Chequing accounts are handled by optical character recognition (OCR) equipment. The OCR equipment sorts the cheques according to the issuing bank and account numbers, computes totals, and posts amounts to depositors' accounts. This is possible through the use of magnetic ink characters printed uniformly at the bottom of cheques.

Banks have adopted a uniform system of magnetic ink character recognition (MICR). This system provides

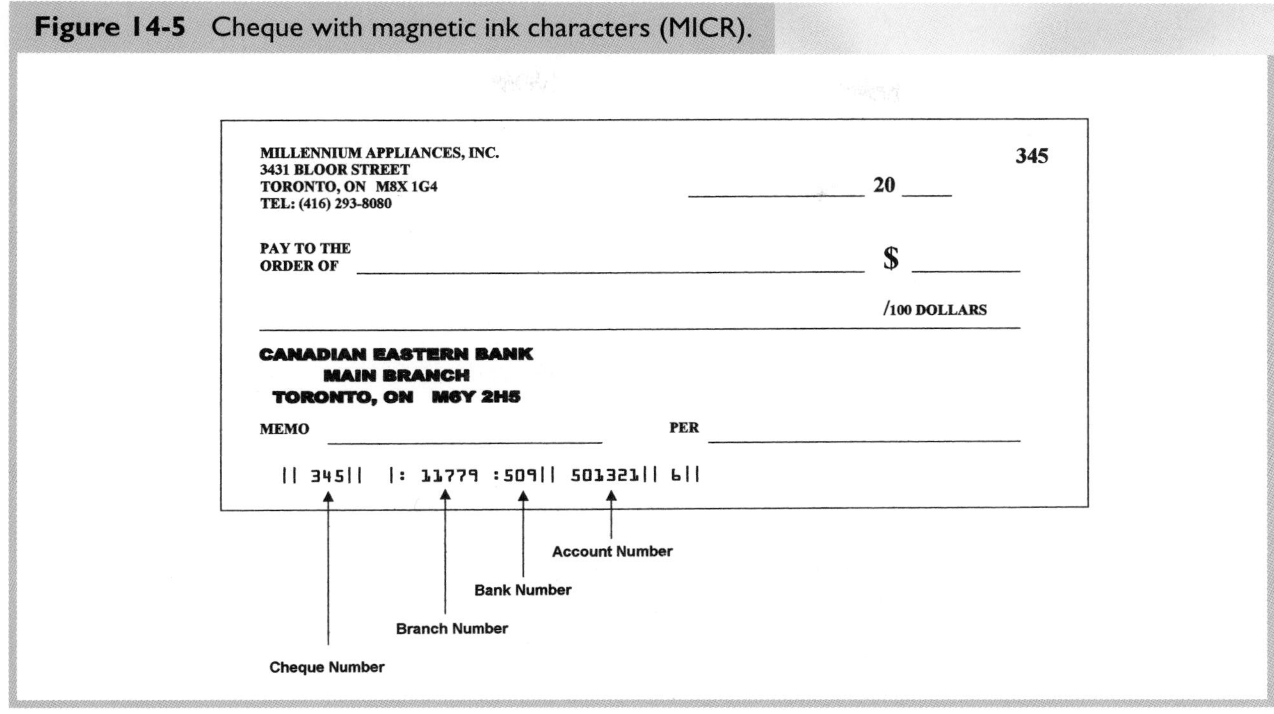

Figure 14-5 Cheque with magnetic ink characters (MICR).

for the pre-printing, in magnetic ink, of the routing symbol, the bank's transit number, and the account number assigned to the depositor by the bank. These numbers in magnetic ink can be read by both people and machines. Refer to Figure 14-5. After the cheque is presented to the bank, the amount of the cheque and other information is added in magnetic ink at the bottom of the cheque.

ENDORSING CHEQUES

A cheque presented for cash or deposit must be signed (endorsed) by the payee on the reverse side of the cheque—preferably at the left end. A bank will accept for deposit cheques that have been endorsed by a representative of the payee. The endorsement may be made with a rubber stamp, or it may be handwritten in ink.

The payee should sign her or his name exactly as the payee's name is carried on the bank account. If the payee's name is written differently on the face of the cheque, it should be endorsed twice—first as it is written and then exactly as the payee's account is carried.

Endorsements are of three types: restrictive, blank, and full. See Figure 14-6.

Restrictive Endorsement

A restrictive endorsement limits the use of a cheque to the purpose stated in the endorsement. Words such as "For deposit only" or "Pay to" are written before the organization's name or the depositor's signature. As a result, further endorsement of the cheque is restricted. A restrictive endorsement should be used when deposits are sent to the bank by mail.

Since most organizations deposit all the cheques they receive, the restrictive endorsement is the most widely used on business cheques. On cheques to be deposited, the endorsement can be made by a rubber stamp. As the endorsement merely transfers the cheque to the depositor's account, a handwritten signature is not usually needed.

Blank Endorsement

A blank endorsement consists only of the signature of the payee. Because a cheque endorsed in blank is payable to the bearer, the holder should use a blank endorsement only when he or she is at the bank depositing or cashing the cheque.

Full Endorsement

A full endorsement transfers a cheque to a specified person or organization. "Pay to the order of" followed by the name of the person or organization to whom the cheque is being transferred is written on the cheque preceding the signature of the endorser.

When a cheque that has been received is forwarded to another person or organization, a full endorsement

Figure 14-6 Endorsements.

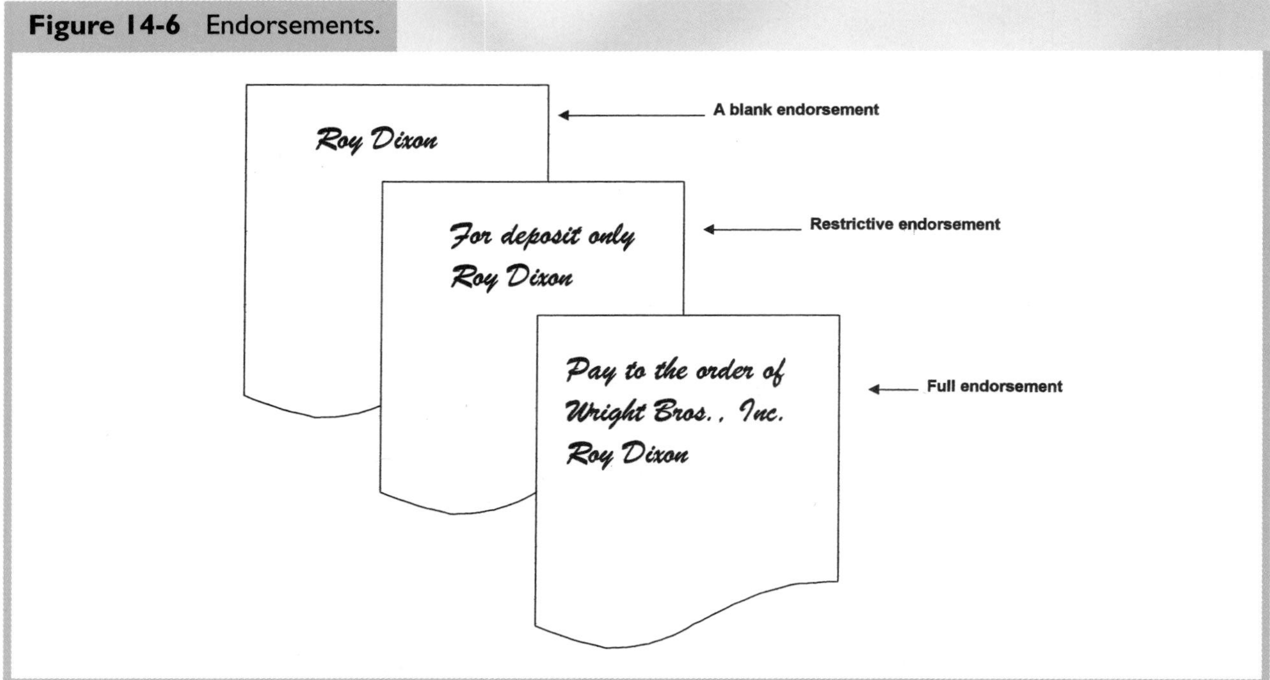

should be used to ensure that only the specified payee can transfer or cash it. To further negotiate the cheque, the endorsee must sign it.

MAKING DEPOSITS

Make bank deposits regularly. In between times, keep the money and cheques in a safe, vault, or other secure place.

Present to the bank teller for deposit, coins, paper currency (bills), cheques, traveller's cheques, money orders, and bank drafts, along with a deposit slip in duplicate listing what is being deposited.

Preparing Items for Deposit

Use coin wrappers supplied by the bank to package a large number of coins in rolls. Write the account name on the outside of each roll. The numbers of coins that can be packaged in different rolls are shown in this table:

Coin	Number in Roll	Value of Roll
Pennies	50	$ 0.50
Nickels	40	2.00
Dimes	50	5.00
Quarters	40	10.00
One Dollar	25	25.00

Put coins insufficient for a roll in a sealed envelope on which you have written the account name and the total value of the coins enclosed.

Stack bills face up according to denominations, and then enclose them in bill wrappers supplied by the bank. Write the account name on each wrapper.

Stack bills of varying denominations face up with the largest denomination on top and the lowest on the bottom. Place a rubber band around them.

Examine each cheque to determine that the amount of the cheque is correct, that the amount written in figures agrees with the amount written in words, and that the cheque is properly signed and not postdated.

Ascertain that the cheques are correctly endorsed either by a rubber-stamp endorsement or by a handwritten signature. Group together all cheques drawn on a given bank. Endorse money orders and bank drafts as though they were cheques.

If your manager is depositing her or his own traveller's cheques, insert your manager's name as the payee on each cheque and have your manager countersign each one. If your manager has accepted a traveller's cheque from someone else, enter your manager's name on the cheque as the payee. Endorse traveller's cheques on the back.

Preparing the Deposit Slip

Keep on hand a supply of deposit slips, which are obtainable from the bank. The deposit slips provided by the bank are multiple-copy sets encoded with the depositor's account number.

Key the current date, the name exactly as it appears in the account, and the address. Add the account number if it is not already on the deposit slip. Some banks require a separate listing of coins and paper currency. See the sample deposit slip in Figure 14-7.

List each cheque by the drawer's name or the drawee's name. Use whatever system works best for your record keeping purposes. Whichever you use, be consistent. When you cannot list all the cheques on one deposit slip, either staple two deposit slips together, or show on the deposit slip the total of the cheques being deposited and attach a separate list of the cheques. Present the cheques to the bank teller in the order in which you list them.

List a money order as "Money order." List a traveller's cheque as "Traveller's cheque."

Make sure that the total shown on the deposit slip is correct.

Figure 14-7 Deposit slip.

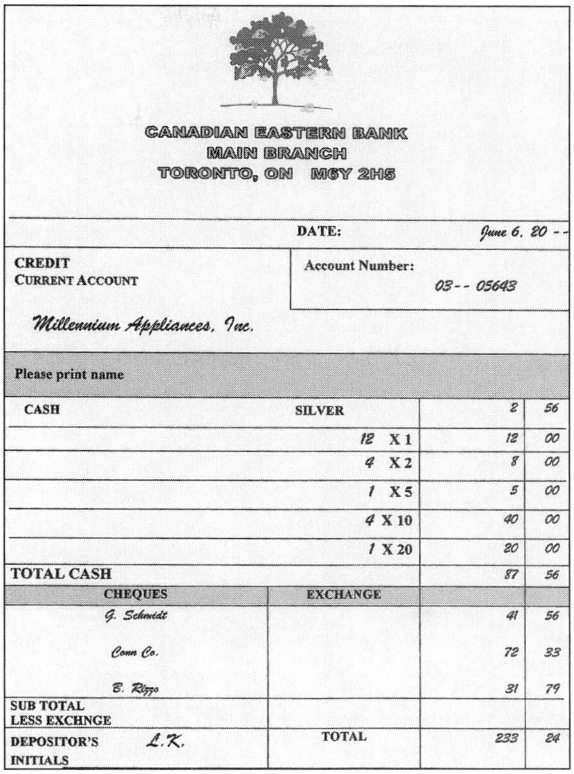

CANADIAN EASTERN BANK
MAIN BRANCH
TORONTO, ON M6Y 2H5

DATE: June 6, 20 - -

CREDIT
CURRENT ACCOUNT

Account Number: 03- - 05643

Millennium Appliances, Inc.

Please print name

CASH	SILVER		
		2	56
	12 X 1	12	00
	4 X 2	8	00
	1 X 5	5	00
	4 X 10	40	00
	1 X 20	20	00
TOTAL CASH		87	56
CHEQUES	EXCHANGE		
G. Schmidt		41	56
Conn Co.		72	33
B. Rizzo		31	79
SUB TOTAL LESS EXCHNGE			
DEPOSITOR'S INITIALS L.K.	TOTAL	233	24

Using the Night Depository

Some organizations that collect cash and cheques after the close of banking hours use the night depository. For this purpose, the bank provides the depositor with a bag with a lock. The depositor places the deposit and deposit slip in the bag, locks it, and takes it to the bank at any time during the night. From the outside of the bank, the depositor drops the bag through a slot that leads into the vault. The next day the deposit is completed in one of two ways:

1. The bank teller unlocks the bag and makes the deposit.
2. The bank leaves the bag locked until the depositor arrives to make the deposit in person.

RECONCILING THE BANK STATEMENT WITH THE CHEQUEBOOK BALANCE

About once a month, the bank returns each depositor's cancelled cheques accompanied by a bank statement (see Figure 14-8). The cancelled cheques are the ones that have been paid by the bank. The statement shows the previous month's balance, deposits made, cheques paid, bank charges, and the ending balance.

Reconcile the bank statement with the chequebook balance as soon as you receive the bank statement and the cancelled cheques. Compare the final balance on the statement and with the balance in the chequebook and then account for the difference. Usually the two balances do not agree, because some cheques that have been written have not been presented for payment, deposits made since the date on the statement are not listed, and automatic subtractions and/or additions may have been made by the bank. For example, if there is a service charge for the account, the bank will deduct the charge. If monthly rental payments or other types of income are deposited directly to the account, the amounts will be added to the statement.

To make the reconciliation statement, assemble

1. the current bank statement and cancelled cheques
2. the bank reconciliation statement for the previous month
3. duplicate deposit slips representing the deposits made since the last one listed on the previous month's reconciliation statement
4. the chequebook or cheque register.

Adopt a Consistent Method

Use the same method each month to prepare the reconciliation statement. By working systematically and checking carefully, you should get the bank balance and the chequebook balance to agree on your first attempt. Here are the steps:

Figure 14-8 Bank statement.

CODE	DESCRIPTION	DEBIT	CREDIT	DAY/MO	BALANCE
CH	Cheque No.66	26.17		04/11	4035.57
LN	Loan Payment	500.20		04/11	3535.57
MB	From Bank 2749-11		2500.00	06/11	6035.57
NS	Cheque Return NSF	200.36			5835.21
SC	Service Charge	10.00		06/11	5825.21
DC	Other Charge — Cheque Print	23.00		07/11	5812.21
IB	InterBank Transfer		8274.92	09/11	14087.13
DD	Direct Deposit		624.25	12/11	14711.38
CH	Cheque No.67	490.00		15/11	14221.38
CH	Cheque No.68	762.60		15/11	13458.78
INC	Interest		56.07	17/11	13514.85
DS	Chargeable Service — Insurance	79.64		18/11	13435.21
SC	Service Charge	3.50		18/11	13431.71
CH	Cheque No.71	4270.50		20/11	9161.21
CH	Cheque No.72	100.00		21/11	9061.21
DD	Direct Deposit		272.82	23/11	9334.03
DC	Other Charge — Cheque Back Fee	5.00		29/11	9329.03
IND	Interest	21.00		30/11	9308.03

No. of Vouchers This Period	0	TOTAL DEBITS	6491.97	TOTAL CREDITS	11728.06

1. While the cancelled cheques are still in the order in which they are listed on the statement, compare the amount of each cheque with the amount on the bank statement. When they agree, make a light pencil mark near the amount on the cheque and by the corresponding amount on the bank statement.
2. Compare the deposit slips with the bank statement to locate any deposits that have not been credited on the statement. As you make this comparison, place a light pencil mark on the deposit slip and by the corresponding amount on the statement.
3. Arrange the cancelled cheques in numerical sequence.
4. Compare the cancelled cheques with the chequebook stubs (or entries in the cheque register). If the amount on the cheque agrees with the amount on the stub or in the register, make a distinctive mark on the stub (or in the register) to show that the cheque has been paid. Next, make a distinctive pencil mark on the cheque—possibly in the upper left corner—to indicate that the cheque stub or register entry has been marked. (Marking the cheque is particularly helpful when several cheques have been paid to the same payee for similar amounts.)
5. On the bank reconciliation statement for the previous month, place a check mark by the outstanding cheques that have now been paid. Doing this will ensure that you locate any cheque from the previous month that still is outstanding. (Make a note on your To Do List to follow up any cheque that has not cleared through the bank within a few weeks of issue.)
6. Prepare the bank reconciliation statement. Either complete the form on the back of the bank statement or key the reconciliation statement on plain paper.
7. Make the adjustments that should be made in the chequebook or register, such as subtracting a service charge or adding interest earned.
8. Mark the cheque stub or cheque register to indicate agreement with the bank statement balance.

Prepare the Reconciliation Statement

To prepare a bank reconciliation statement similar to the one shown in Figure 14-9, proceed in this way:

1. Key an appropriate heading, including the company name, the name of the form (BANK RECONCILIATION), and the date.

2. Enter the chequebook balance and the bank statement balance across the top of the page. In the example, Figure 14-9, the chequebook balance is given as $9,411.62.
3. List any credits to the account that may have been deposited automatically or without your knowledge. An example of an automatic credit is interest earned on your account. Add the credit to your chequebook balance.
4. List and add to the bank statement balance all deposits to the account that are not shown on the previous month's statement. In Figure 14-9, a deposit of $149.00 was made on November 30. This deposit does not appear on the previous bank statement.
5. List, add, and finally deduct the total of all bank charges from your adjusted chequebook balance. These charges would appear on the previous month's statement. Service charges and NSF cheque charges are examples of these deductions.
6. Deduct the sum of all outstanding cheques from the adjusted bank statement balance.
7. Show both the adjusted chequebook balance and the adjusted bank statement balance. They should be equal.

Search for Errors

If the adjusted bank statement balance and the adjusted chequebook balance do not agree, first recheck the figures in the reconciliation statement. Are the figures accurate? Have you added when you should have subtracted?

Next look for omissions of cheques and/or deposits. Have all the cheques written been subtracted from the chequebook balance? Have all the cheques that have not cleared through the bank been listed as outstanding cheques on the reconciliation statement? Have all the deposits been included on the reconciliation statement?

If you still have not located the error, check for an arithmetical mistake in the cheque stubs. When you find one, mark the correction in two places. On the stub where the error occurs, write "Should be" followed by the correct amount. Make the compensating adjustment at the bottom of the last stub used or in the first blank line of the cheque register.

File Cancelled Cheques

Save cancelled cheques. They have legal value as proof of payment.

The system you use for filing cheques will be governed by the frequency with which you must refer to them. File the current bank reconciliation statement so that it will be accessible next month. File the bank statements in chronological order, placing the most recent in front. You can either keep the cancelled cheques inside the folded bank statements or file the cheques separately in numerical order.

The retention period for the cheques and the method of disposing of them will be determined by the

Figure 14-9 Bank reconciliation statement.

BANK RECONCILIATION
Carter Enterprises
12 01 20xx

CHEQUE BOOK BALANCE		$9411.62	BANK STATEMENT BALANCE		$9,308.03
ADD:			ADD:		
Interest Earned	$56.07	$56.07	Deposit of 11/30		$149.00
		$9,467.69			$9,457.03
DEDUCT:			DEDUCT:		
NSF Cheque Plus Service Charge	$210.36		Outstanding Cheques		
Cheque Printing Charge	23.00		No. 69	$180.00	
Interest Charge	21.00		No. 70	72.20	
Cheque Back Fee	5.00				
Service Charge	3.50	$262.86			$252.20
		$9,204.83			$9,204.83

pro-Link

Fraud in the office can be an expensive proposition for any organization. According to the Association of Certified Fraud Examiners (ACFE), small business is the most vulnerable to three main types of fraud and abuse: misappropriation, fraudulent statements, and bribery and corruption.

Here are some preventative tips for *your* office:

- Designate a front-line receptionist to open the mail and systematically list all cheques before passing them on to the accounting department.
- Develop cheque-signing limits. For example, the administrative assistant may sign for $100, the manager $1,000, the executive $10,000, etc.
- Pay attention to your bookkeeping practices. Have your work periodically reviewed by a colleague as a "sanity" check.
- Establish a dual signature practice for cheques but do not sign cheques in advance of your absence.
- If you are about to ask someone new to handle the accounts, make sure they are in good standing with the company—not just qualified to do the work.
- Create an office atmosphere that encourages everyone to be honest, and on the lookout for fraud. Each employee has a vested interest in the well-being of the company.

Can you think of more?

organization's policy. The person in your organization who is responsible for records retention will provide you with information about destroying cheques. Records retention was discussed in Chapter 7.

KEEPING RECORDS

Most organizations keep their accounting records on computer. Accounting is a separate business function, performed by accountants; record keeping occurs wherever a record originates. Consequently, office professionals maintain and assist with various financial records. Some administrative assistants, especially those who work for owners of businesses, help their managers with personal business records.

You can expect to be responsible for a petty cash fund. You may be asked to keep a record of office supplies on hand, or to assist with payroll records.

Petty Cash Fund

When the amount of an office expenditure is small and payment should be made immediately, it may be more convenient to make the payment by cash than by cheque. To provide cash to pay for incidental items, such as **ad hoc** courier service, postage due on a package, and emergency purchases of office supplies, organizations establish a petty cash fund. These funds usually range from $20 to $100 or more, depending on the cash needs for a period of time—perhaps a month. Even though the petty cash is used to make miscellaneous payments, it must still be accounted for.

Generally, the administrative assistant is responsible for handling the petty cash fund. When you are the one who keeps track of petty cash, observe the following standard procedures:

1. Keep the cash and the completed vouchers (see Figure 14-10) in a box or an envelope and put them in a safe place. They should be in a locked desk drawer or file or in an office safe. Balance the petty cash record at least once a week. If the cash and vouchers are left unlocked, balance the record at the end of each day.
2. Prepare a petty cash voucher for each expenditure you make. The voucher, which is a receipt, should show the amount paid, the date, to whom the payment was made, the purpose of the payment, the expense category to which the payment will be charged, and the signature or initials of the person authorizing payment. Some organizations also require the signature or initials of the person receiving payment. Unless the accounting department stipulates that the vouchers be machine

Figure 14-10 Petty cash voucher.

Amount: $4.73   Voucher No.: 31

PETTY CASH VOUCHER

For: Name Tags
Paid to: Ben Ross
Charge to: Supplies
Date: August 15, 20--
Approved by: E. Miller
Comments: - extras for Sept. 8 conference

printed, write them, using a pen; this way, you complete the voucher quickly at the time you are making the payment and without interrupting work you may have in the printer.

3. Keep an accurate petty cash record, using either a petty cash book or a distribution sheet or envelope (see Figure 14-11). For each payment from the petty cash fund, enter the date, the amount, the voucher number, and an explanation in the petty cash report (see Figure 14-12). Total expenditures plus cash on hand should equal the original amount of the petty cash fund.

   Some petty cash books provide columns for expense categories; others do not. The columns and the appropriate headings for the petty cash record can be printed on a sheet of paper or a Manila envelope. Accounting departments often supply Manila envelopes imprinted with columns and headings for the petty cash record, including columns for the distribution of payments.

   A petty cash record with columns for the distribution of payments is shown in Figure 14-11. Posting the expenditures to the columns provided for each predetermined expense category simplifies preparing the summary of expenditures when you need to replenish the petty cash fund.

4. Replenish the petty cash fund soon enough to keep an adequate supply of cash on hand. In some organizations, petty cash is replenished at a predetermined time—for instance, when only one-fourth of the cash is on hand. In other organizations, replenishing the petty cash fund is left to the judgment of the office professional responsible for maintaining the fund.

5. To replenish the petty cash fund, balance the petty cash record, formally request a cheque for the amount needed, and prepare the petty cash report.

   Begin by balancing the petty cash record: Count the cash on hand, total the columns of the petty cash record, determine the amount needed to replenish the petty cash fund to the original amount, and enter the balance in the petty cash record. Verify that the cash on hand plus the total amount of the vouchers equals the original amount of the fund. Also, add the totals of the

Figure 14-11 Petty cash envelope.

PETTY CASH ENVELOPE

Petty Cash Fund		Date	No.	Explanation	Distribution of Payments				
Received	Paid Out				Supplies	Post	Misc.	Del.	Tele.
	4 08	May 3	161	Tape & liquid ppr	4 08				
	8 50	May 3	162	Telepost					8 50
	3 90	May 4	163	Stamps		3 90			
	3 84	May 10	164	Reg. Mail		3 84			
	2 87	May 15	165	Cleaning Supplies			2 87		
	2 50	May 18	166	Flower Delivery				2 50	
	3 64	May 27	167	File Labels	3 64				
	2 79	June 4	168	Reg. Mail		2 79			
	2 75	June 8	169	Messenger				2 75	
	4 96	June 9	170	Pencils	4 96				
	3 75	June 12	171	Parcel Delivery				3 75	
	43 58	—		Totals	12 68	10 53	2 87	9 00	8 50

Figure 14-12 Petty cash report.

MEMORANDUM

TO: Tyler Rivest
Accounting

FROM: Belinda Nixon
Research and Development

DATE: 13 June 20--

SUBJECT: **PETTY CASH REPORT**

The following report is a summary of petty cash paid out from May 3 until June 12.

Petty Cash Report

June 13, 20--

Opening Balance		$50.00
Expenditures		
Supplies	$12.68	
Postage	10.53	
Delivery	9.00	
Telepost	8.50	
Miscellaneous	2.87	43.58
Closing Balance		$ 6.42

Please issue a cheque for $43.58 to replenish the petty cash fund to the original amount of $50.00. Eleven petty cash vouchers are attached.

bn

Attachments (11)

distribution of payment columns as a check that the total amount distributed equals the total amount spent. In the illustration in Figure 14-12, the original petty cash fund was $50. Total expenditures were $43.58; the balance is $6.42. The cash on hand should be $6.42. The amount of the cheque written to replenish the fund should be $43.58.

Request the amount needed to replenish the petty cash fund to its original amount, unless you have been authorized to decrease or increase the fund. In some organizations the person in charge of the fund is expected to write the cheque. If you write the cheque, make it payable to "Petty Cash," and present it to the person who is authorized to sign it.

With the request for cash, submit the records called for by the accounting department. When the accounting department supplies a petty cash distribution envelope, the usual procedure is to submit the envelope with the supporting vouchers enclosed. Before you release an envelope, make a copy for your files. If you keep a petty cash book, submit a petty cash report similar to the one shown in Figure 14-12. Attach the petty cash vouchers.

6. Cash the cheque. Enter the amount and the date in the Received column of the petty cash record. If you are using a new petty cash distribution envelope, transfer the balance of the old envelope to the Received column of the new petty cash envelope, together with the amount of new cash received.

Office Supplies on Hand

Administrative assistants should replenish their office supplies during the time of day or week that they are the least busy. Yet they need to plan well enough that they are not searching for supplies when they are pressed for time to complete a rush job. Sometimes an administrative assistant is responsible for stocking office supplies for an entire floor or a department. To manage this, you need a record, preferably kept in longhand, of supplies on hand.

An easy way to determine supplies needed is to keep an inventory of each item on a 10.2 x 15.2 cm card. These cards, when completed, are known as perpetual inventory cards. When you check supplies out of the main supply department or order them directly, enter the amount of each item received on its card and then add the amount to the figure in the balance column. When you take supplies from the supply cabinet or shelf, enter the amount in the checked-out column and then subtract the amount to show the new balance. Encourage others who check out supplies to follow the same procedure.

By looking at the perpetual inventory cards, you can decide

1. whether or not the item you need is on hand in sufficient quantity
2. when it is time to order additional supplies.

Questions for Study and Review

1. What is a cheque?
2. Explain how an administrative assistant can obtain a certified cheque for the manager.
3. How does a bank draft differ from an ordinary cheque?
4. Summarize the rules that should be followed when writing cheques.
5. Describe the steps an administrative assistant would need to take to stop payment on a cheque.
6. Why should cheques made payable to the order of Cash be given special protection?
7. What role do magnetic ink characters play in cheque processing?
8. When should each of the following endorsements be used: blank, full, restrictive?
9. An administrative assistant or other representative of an organization can endorse the organization's cheques that are being deposited. Explain a time-saving way to make endorsements.
10. Describe how to prepare coins for deposit. Describe how to prepare a large number of bills for deposit.
11. How should money orders and bank drafts be endorsed?
12. Explain how an endorsement should be made on unused traveller's cheques.
13. State how to list cheques on a deposit slip.
14. What are the two plans for completing the deposit when the night depository is used?
15. What information is needed for making a bank reconciliation statement?
16. Why do the bank statement balance and the chequebook balance seldom agree?
17. Summarize the steps involved in making a bank reconciliation statement.
18. When your bank reconciliation statement does not balance, how should you proceed to locate errors?
19. What should be done with cancelled cheques?
20. What do the letters EFT represent?
21. What is the function of EFT?
22. What is the purpose of the petty cash fund?
23. How can you be sure you have kept an accurate petty cash record?
24. When you replenish the petty cash fund, how do you determine the amount of money to request?
25. To show the distribution of expenditures, why should you use categories predetermined by the accounting department rather than your own?

Spelling Reinforcement

certification
character
denomination
endorsement
envelope
expenditure
guaranteed
inconspicuously
negotiate
omission
quantity
receipt
reconciliation
replenish
restrictive
retention
sequence
transaction
treasurer
voucher

On-the-Job Situations

1. You mail a deposit to the bank almost every business day. Today you received a blank envelope from the bank. The deposit slip was missing. What should you do?
2. You work for an investor. Your responsibilities include keeping a record of money received and writing cheques for expenses. When you reconciled the bank statement for March, you had a difference of $550 between the chequebook balance and the bank statement balance. The bank statement was $550 more. You rechecked every entry. You finally remembered that your manager had recently purchased a house to rent and had instructed the renter to mail the rent cheque to the bank. You went through the cheques and other items returned from the bank. There was a deposit slip for $550. What entry should you make in the chequebook?
3. When you reconciled the balance of the bank statement for September with the chequebook balance, the bank statement balance exceeded the chequebook balance by $1,100, a difference for which you had difficulty accounting. You finally discovered that this was the amount of a cheque issued for supplies that were never delivered. The cheque was returned to you by the vendor. What adjustments, if any, would you make to the chequebook balance side of the bank reconciliation statement?

Special Reports

1. Examine some cancelled cheques. How can you tell that the cheques have been paid by the bank? How have the cheques been endorsed? Ascertain which magnetic ink characters near the bottom of the cheques were added after the cheques were presented to the bank. Can you read the information? If you can, what is it? Compare the information on your cheques with the information on the cheques that other members of the class have.
2. Survey four different organizations to determine how extensively they rely upon technology for their banking. Do they use software for maintaining their accounts? Do they generate their own cheques? Do they use EFT? Do they use the Internet for banking? These questions and their answers should be included in a report of your findings.

Production Challenges

14-A Making Deposits

Supplies needed:

- *Deposit slip, Form 14-A-1, page 444*
- *Cheque Register, Form 14-A-2, page 445*
- *Working Papers Disk, File 14-A-2*

Mr. Levine is in charge of registration for the November Sales Seminar, and you are assisting him.

On Tuesday, November 4, you received cheques from four registrants as follows:

Mr. Leroy McGovern, $75.00
Ms. Janet Temple, $75.00
Mr. Kevin Smythe, $75.00
Ms. Laura Cole, $75.00

Make out a deposit ticket for the November Sales Seminar account (by William Wilson) for November 4. The account number is 09-04156. Also, record the amount of the deposit in the cheque register and show the balance. The account has a balance of $360.27.

During the week, you received cheques from the registrants for the following amounts:

Nov. 5	$1,500.00	20 registrants
Nov. 6	3,000.00	40 registrants
Nov. 7	2,250.00	30 registrants

On Monday, November 10, the first day of the seminar, eight more people registered; total amount of cheques was $600.00.

Assume that you made out daily deposit tickets, taken the deposit tickets and the cheques to the bank, and entered the daily amounts in the cheque register. (In an actual situation, you would also make out a receipt and a name tag for each registrant.)

14-B Writing Cheques

Supplies needed:

- *Blank cheques, Forms 14-B-1 through 14-B-12, pages 446 to 451*
- *Cheque Register used in 14-A*

On Thursday, November 13, the November Sales Seminar is over, and you are writing the cheques for the expenses incurred on behalf of the seminar. Mr. Wilson signed the signature card at the bank for the November Sales Seminar account, so Mr. Wilson must sign the cheques.

Prepare cheques for the following expenses:

- Parker's Restaurant for banquet, $1,224.00
- A & R Breakfast House for Tuesday's breakfast, $510.00
- Jane's Pancake House for Wednesday's breakfast, $450.00
- BJ Florist, $96.00
- Ramco Signs, $78.25
- Al's Print Shop, $1,700.00
- City Equipment Rental, $25.00
- William Wilson, reimbursement for postage, $60.00
- Parker's Hostess Service, for coffee and rolls at morning and afternoon breaks, $300.45
- Louise Barclay, keynote speaker, $500.00
- Raymond Clevenger, banquet speaker, $500.00

14-C Reconciling the Bank Statement

Supplies needed:

- *Cheque Register used in 14-A and 14-B*
- *Bank Statement, Form 14-C, page 452*
- *Plain paper*

On November 26 you receive the bank statement for the November Sales Seminar account. Two cheques that you had written had not been paid by the bank. They were: Cheque to Ramco Signs, $78.25 and cheque to BJ Florist, $96.00. On November 23 you received a cheque from Al's Print Shop for $170.00 as a 10 percent discount for paying promptly. You mailed this cheque to the bank, but it is not shown on the bank statement.

Reconcile the bank statement with the cheque register for the November Sales Seminar. Key the bank reconciliation statement.

14-D Handling Petty Cash

Supplies needed:

- *Petty Cash Envelope, Form 14-D-1, page 453*
- *Petty Cash Vouchers, Forms 14-D-2 through 14-D-13, pages 454 to 456*
- *Plain paper*

Mary Higgins, who had been handling petty cash transactions for the marketing division, was transferred to another division, and you were asked to handle petty cash.

You started with a clean petty cash envelope. The balance in the fund was $50.00. Write $50.00 in the Received column.

You paid out cash for the following items:

- December 1 paid Meyers Stationery Store $3.69 for a special drawing pen.
- December 3 paid $3.75 to the post office for stamps.
- December 3 paid $3.12 to post office for postage and insurance for a package.
- December 4 paid City Taxi $3.25 to deliver a package to Airlift Freight office.
- December 5 paid Williams Drugstore $2.50 for two magazines for the reception area.
- December 8 paid BJ Florist $6.50 for plant for Mr. Wilson's office.
- December 8 paid Williams Drugstore $2.29 for fertilizer tablets for plants at the office.
- December 9 paid Rapid Courier $12.50 to deliver a telegram.
- December 9 paid Meyers Stationery Store $6.50 for a set of markers.

Your cash fund is getting low. Record the totals for the Paid Out column and the distribution columns. Carry the balance forward to the Received column but label it as "Balance." On plain paper, key a petty cash report and ask for enough money to bring the petty cash fund to $50.00. Attach the petty cash vouchers to the report. You are authorized to sign the vouchers.

World Wide Websites

Royal Bank Home Page

www.royalbank.com
This site includes sections titled Banking for Business, International Banking, and Library.

Smart Bank

www.bmo.com/business/index.html
The Bank of Montreal website for business.

Toronto Dominion Bank

www.tdbank.ca
TD Bank's Business Banking Centre has information for small, medium, and large businesses, and includes a business library and discussion of business issues.

PART III
THE FUTURE OF THE ADMINSTRATIVE SUPPORT SERVICE

CHAPTER 15

Employment Strategies

Outline

Learning Outcomes

At the completion of this chapter the student will be able to:

1. Suggest methods for searching employment opportunities.
2. Inventory job qualifications.
3. Prepare a personal résumé that gets attention.
4. Prepare an effective letter of application.
5. Complete an employment application form with accuracy.
6. Prepare for and participate in a successful job interview.
7. Develop a portfolio that illustrates accomplishments and skills.
8. Answer behavioural descriptive interview questions.
9. Analyze interview experiences.
10. Prepare employment follow-up letters such as a thank-you, reminders, inquires, acceptance and refusal letters.
11. Use the Internet as a valuable job search and recruitment tool.
12. Prepare a résumé for electronic scanning.
13. Complete an employment application form.

Graduate Profile

Carol Parsons, Q.A.A.
Team Manager

Customer Services Department
Alberta Blue Cross

College Graduation:
Office Administration Program
Northern Alberta Institute of Technology
Edmonton, Alberta
1990

A strong focus on excellent customer service has lead Carol into her current position in Customer Services. She believes that providing quality customer service to both external and internal customers and maintaining a positive attitude are key to any successful career. After graduation, Carol began her career at Alberta Blue Cross as a secretary. She transitioned into increasingly responsible positions resulting in a position as executive assistant to a vice president.

While an executive assistant, Carol earned her Qualified Administrative Assistant (Q.A.A.) designation through the Association of Administrative Assistants. She was an active member at both branch and national levels and held many executive positions in the Edmonton branch.

Carol is the past chairperson of the Office Administration Advisory Committee at the Northern Alberta Institute of Technology and continues to maintain her relationship with that program. She recently completed a term position as an instructor in the Office Administration Program where she enjoyed her interaction with the students and the opportunity to share her professional experiences.

Life-long learning and continuous personal growth are important to Carol. She is currently enrolled in the Supervisory Development Program at a local college as well as the Management Development Program at the University of Alberta. Her advice for career success is to "be the best that you can be." Carol suggests office professionals share their knowledge and experiences with their peers to assist them in reaching their career goals.

"Maintain a positive attitude and be open to change."

Very few administrative assistants' positions are protected from corporate restructuring and job layoffs. Therefore, it is important to plan an effective job campaign.

Search for a job that matches your qualifications, personality, and interests. Your administrative career should be rewarding not only monetarily but also in terms of job satisfaction and opportunities for promotion.

The first part of your job campaign should be your decision about where you want to work—the geographic area and the type of business. Unless you have specialized in the legal or medical field, do not limit yourself to seeking a job in a specific department, such as personnel, accounting, or sales. Remain open to opportunities; often, getting your foot in the door is the first step to gaining experience and eventually getting the position you really want.

Your office technology skills are transferable. Often the same basic skills are required in different departments; therefore, never limit your opportunities by expressing interest in working only for one department—instead, express interest in working for the organization. Let the interviewer know you are flexible and willing to adjust to the needs of the department. The interviewer will strive to match you to a position that will maximize your talents.

Start your job campaign several months before graduation. As soon as you decide where you want to work, make a job prospect list, using the sources listed in this chapter. Next, prepare your self-appraisal inventory and your résumé, write your application letter, and make a list of the qualifications you plan to stress during job interviews. After you launch your job campaign, keep searching until you find the right job for you.

LOCATING JOB PROSPECTS

Some of the sources for job prospects are the college placement office, the Yellow Pages, private and public employment agencies, government service announcements, chambers of commerce, the newspapers, and your network of friends and associates.

Use all of these sources, not just one, to find job leads. Once you begin your job campaign, keep it going. Be persistent in checking up and following through on what is available for someone with your qualifications and interests.

Networking

Put in simple terms, **networking** means exchanging information. Information is the most powerful asset a business professional can have. If you have information and are willing to share it, you will be viewed as a valuable person to have on staff.

During the job hunt, networking is an essential step toward gaining successful employment. Sharing employment information with a network of people is probably one of the most effective methods of obtaining employment. As a student you can begin to build your network by attending functions such as career fairs, where prospective employers will be available to meet students. Attend and participate in seminars and other functions where office administrators and assistants will be present. By expressing your keen desire for employment and by leaving a positive impression, you will be increasing your opportunity to learn about possible employment opportunities.

> *"The transition from college to the workforce is difficult but follow your heart. You should view your first job as the first of many steps that are to come, not as a permanent decision."*
>
> Shannon Mullin, Graduate
> New Brunswick Community College
> Miramichi Campus

The early stages of forming a network should include discussing your employment goal with your instructors and with business friends of the family. Tell your neighbours, relatives, and business contacts that you are actively seeking employment and that you would appreciate their help in finding out about job openings.

When your contacts give you job leads, follow through on them. Then let the person who told you about the lead know the results. This is a simple courtesy and a way of thanking this person for his or her assistance.

Remember that networking is an *exchange* of information, not a one-way effort. The more information you give, the more information you usually get back.

To be a good networker you must be a good listener. By applying your best listening skills you will collect accurate information. This, in the long run, may save you time and effort in your job search.

By listening to the needs of other networkers, you will be able to offer them greater assistance. In this way, you will be viewed as a valuable network partner. As previously stated, the more information you provide others, the more people will reciprocate.

Networking is a developed skill that will help you enhance your life and your career. It will increase your ability to be employed and to advance.

The following are suggestions for improving your networking skills:

1. If you have recently been employed, choose a corporate **mentor**. A corporate mentor usually holds a position at a higher level than yours. This person can offer you information and advice about the organization and give you career direction.
2. Never limit your contacts by missing an opportunity to meet new people. Your network may include business associates, friends, neighbours, past graduates from your college, relatives, and many other groups of people. A network should become a vast chain of information. The more effort you put into networking, the more the network will expand, and the greater your chances of career success will be.
3. Make yourself visible. Becoming a leader of a professional organization or volunteering to serve on a committee will open networking doors.
4. If you haven't already, purchase a telephone message machine. Missed messages may mean lost contacts.
5. Increase your reading of business materials. Remember that information is power and reading will build your information base.
6. Develop an organized database of your contacts. A computer database will be invaluable as the number of contacts expands. You will want to keep a current record of
    - names
    - addresses
    - telephone and fax numbers, and e-mail addresses
    - places of employment
    - job titles
    - personal information that will assist your communications with your contacts.

    Probably the most important information to record is any information your contacts have provided, and how you followed up on the information.
7. Be a giver and not just a taker. Business organizations attempt to hire candidates with a reputation for being contributors to the team, not people who are self-serving. Therefore, don't provide information to your network contacts only because you think you will get some in return.

PERSPECTIVES

Strengthen Your Networking Know-How

By Anne Baber and Lynne Waymon

The most effective networking involves more giving than receiving. Here's why.

Whether you love it or hate it, have the gift of gab or just fake it, networking is a vital organizational and career skill. With a little help from your friends and colleagues, you'll excel in your job, be able to direct your career, and enjoy life to its fullest.

Think back over your life. Hasn't most of the best information you've gotten—a job lead, a great place to vacation, a lead on computer software that helped you redesign an important report—come from *people* not print?

But even if you have successfully used your networks in the past—possibly without realizing that you were networking—you may be uncertain about how and when to network. The following example illustrates how to use networking for help on the job.

Shaking the tree

Sue had worked for her company for 16 years in a variety of positions. She was asked to design and manage an employee survey to gather data on several changes that were in the works. She had never conducted an employee survey before, but was certain somebody she knew had.

She checked with friends, peers, a previous boss, a former employee who had moved to a different organization, a neighbor, and someone she'd met in a training class the month before. Within a few days she had lined up her resources: She had the name of a book suggested by a friend who took a class in designing surveys, a lunch date with the former employee who'd conducted employee surveys for her company and two copies of similar surveys from a neighbor.

That's how it works. You shake your "tree" and the apples fall into your lap. Whatever it is you need to know, somebody you know knows somebody who knows about it—*if you know the three "knows" of networking.*

1. Know what you want and how to ask for it. Ask yourself, "What would I like to learn, find, connect with, have more of in my life?" Put those things on your agenda to talk with people about wherever you go—the cafeteria, a convention, a backyard barbecue, a professional meeting. Rather than seeing all those informal and unstructured moments with people as time to be filled up with small talk about the weather or how much work you have, use that time as a chance to connect with people about the ideas and resources that will enrich your life and your work.

2. Know what you have to give and how to give it. Networking is exchanging information and resources in order to build relationships. It's a life-long process, not a one-time event. In order to get exchanges going you have to be aware of the wealth of information, resources, and referrals *you* have to give. If you are saying, "I don't have anything to give," think again. Start learning and doing so you approach networking with more confidence and more information to share.

   Make a list of all the things you feel excited about and interested in. Become known by what you give away. Whether you want to excel at your current job, recharge your career or try out your entrepreneurial wings, learn what all good networkers know: You have to dig your well before you can drink from it. Look for ways to notice what's on other people's agendas so you can help them make connections by giving your resources, ideas, and expertise. Don't be afraid that this is phony or manipulative. The chance to enrich someone else's life with a magazine article about the new computer software they're learning or the phone number of a day-care center you trust is one of the most satisfying things about networking.

3. Know how to listen and what to listen for. Networking doesn't mean doing all the talking. There's a quiet side to networking called listening. Listen for two kinds of things. First, tune in to clues about what's on the other person's agenda so you can offer resources. If it's not clear, *ask!* And be alert for information that will help you connect with what's on your agenda.

   When you see every chance meeting as an appointment and approach every person as a feature story, networking becomes a way of life. You're in touch with all the resources you need to meet every professional and career challenge.

Anne Baber and Lynne Waymon at 1-800-352-2939 are experts in cultivating business relationships, are professional speakers and are co-authors of Great Connections: Small Talk & Networking for Businesspeople.

College Placement Office

Most postsecondary institutions have a placement office to provide their graduates assistance in making contacts for jobs. At the beginning of your job campaign, register with the placement office at your school. Complete the application form, and provide a résumé, transcript, and any other information required to place your name on the active file with the placement office. Your credentials, when kept on an active file, are available to employers on request.

The placement director and counsellors keep up to date on employment opportunities and provide many employment services to graduates. Often the placement director arranges for company representatives to conduct interviews on campus. The placement director maintains a list of job openings prepared from the requests of personnel managers, who call the placement office in search of prospective employees. The counsellors talk with graduates in group sessions and on a one-to-one basis.

Watch for the announcement of forthcoming campus interviews at your school, and call the placement office to schedule interviews for jobs you are interested in. Campus interviews are discussed later in this chapter.

Get acquainted with the placement director and counsellors. Schedule an appointment with a counsellor to talk about your specific interests, to ask questions, and to seek guidance. Whether your job hunt is simple and quickly successful or difficult and protracted, you will need all the contacts you can get.

Business News Items

Read the business news in the newspaper of the city where you plan to seek employment for at least a month before you actually apply for jobs. Search for news about established organizations that are relocating their offices in your city or opening a branch; established organizations in your city that are moving their offices to new buildings or expanding at their present sites; newly formed organizations; and companies that are merging. Any changes within organizations may indicate career opportunities.

When you find a news item of interest to you, clip it and save it. It should provide you with the complete name, the type of operation, the location, and possibly the opening date of a new office.

The number of administrative assistants who move to another city when an organization relocates is small compared to the number of executives who transfer to the new location. Therefore, you can expect that any organization that has relocated its offices to another city will be hiring administrative assistants.

A local organization often adds new personnel at the time it moves its offices to a new location. Such a move often happens because the organization needs more space to conduct its current operations and cannot add personnel until it can provide space for them. An organization that is expanding its operations often needs additional office personnel.

A new organization will need someone in the office as soon as it opens and will add personnel to keep pace with the organization's growth.

Direct Application

Often, the best jobs are not advertised. Many organizations prefer to select their employees from applicants who have taken the initiative to come to them seeking employment.

Do not wait for a job to come to you; it probably will not. Take the initiative to search for a job. Decide where you want to work, and apply. Call the organization and arrange an appointment with the person in charge of hiring office staff.

Be optimistic. Some of the organizations on your prospective list may not be seeking administrative assistants at this time, but an impressive application and interview may put you in line for a future opportunity. If an opening for the job you are seeking does not currently exist, ask the personnel manager to place your application on file.

If you decide you want to work for a particular business but do not have a specific company in mind, refer to the Yellow Pages, which provides a list of local businesses. For example, if you are interested in working for an advertising company, look up *Advertising*; there you will find the names and addresses of the local advertising companies.

Employment Agencies

Openings for jobs are listed with both private employment agencies and the federal government. Private employment agencies keep information regarding available employment confidential until a candidate is tested, interviewed, and judged as suitable for the position; however, Canada Employment makes employment information readily available to the public.

Federal Government

Canada Employment Centres list openings for all kinds of work—industrial, commercial, technical, and professional. Their services are free to any job seeker and to any employer.

Job information for your region is available from computerized Job Information Centres (JICs). These centres are located in federal government buildings as well as at kiosks in public areas such as some shopping centres. All new job orders are posted at the same time daily. All JICs throughout a city are connected to the same computer terminal; this way, all centres receive the same job information at the same time.

Most positions for employment with the federal government are never posted in the newspapers. Only when the job requires special skills that are difficult to find will the federal government advertise in the newspapers. In all cases, Canadian citizens are given preference when applying for a federal government position in Canada.

The federal government has a website on the Internet that posts job positions within the federal government. It also publishes a telemessage number in the local telephone directory. This message provides a menu of options; among the choices is the current job information selection.

Human Resources Development Canada (HRDC) also has a website. The HRDC website provides information on the labour market and employment insurance. The website has the facility to connect users to their local HRDC service centres, or to other sites within Canada. The following e-mail address connects the user to Human Resources Development Canada:

http://www.culturenet.ca/hrdc/

Private

Most private employment agencies do *not* charge the applicant a fee for the agency's services. They do, however, charge the employer a *markup* to cover the agency's costs. Once the agency has tested, selected, and placed the applicant, the employer pays the agency a rate. From this amount, the agency collects the markup and pays the employee.

You can ask private employment agencies about the services they offer without being obligated to sign a contract. If you do register with a private employment agency, study the contract thoroughly and ask questions before you sign it.

Canadian employment agencies consider it unethical to use a contract that restricts the applicant's right to hold other contracts with other employment agencies.

Private employment agencies give excellent service. They administer tests, scrutinize the appearance of the applicants, conduct thorough interviews, and carry out a complete job hunt for each applicant. Private employment agencies make a sincere effort to refer applicants to jobs for which they are qualified and which they are likely to accept.

Many private employment agencies belong to the Employment and Staffing Services Association of Canada (ESSAC). This national association represents temporary and staffing services throughout Canada. The mission of the ESSAC is to promote the advancement and growth of the employment industry in Canada. This association has adopted rigid standards of ethical practices, which member agencies are required to follow. Membership in the ESSAC ensures that these agencies are reputable.

Newspaper Advertisements

The career sections and help-wanted columns of newspapers are valuable sources for job openings. In these, the jobs will be listed under a variety of headings, such as:

- administrative assistant
- office professional
- secretary
- administrative secretary
- executive secretary
- executive assistant
- word processing operator
- secretary-receptionist.

By studying career sections and help-wanted ads, you will gain valuable information concerning trends in employment opportunities, salary ranges, and qualifications required. Study the ads in newspapers early in your job campaign.

When you answer a help-wanted ad, be prompt. Reply the same day, if possible, or at least by the next day. Remember that newspapers are widely read and that looking in them for available jobs requires less effort than other search techniques. It follows that the competition will be very high for jobs posted in newspapers.

Follow instructions. If a telephone number is given, call for an appointment. If a post office box number is given, submit your résumé. Many advertisements request that applicants submit résumés by mail and clearly state that they do not want applicants to call. If this is the case, follow the instructions. You risk irritating the employer if you ignore the request for no telephone calls. Of course, it's always more proactive and shows a sense of initiative to telephone the employer and to drop off your résumé in person. These techniques should be part of your strategy unless the employer has requested otherwise.

Always study the advertisement carefully to determine all the stated qualifications and then submit an application letter and résumé showing that you meet all the qualifications for the job. Do not overlook any of them. Follow the suggestions for writing a solicited application letter discussed in the section "The Application Letter" later in this chapter.

Newspaper recruitment advertisements either give the name and address of a company or person to contact, or are *blind* advertisements giving a post office box number or a telephone number. When blind ads are used in a legitimate fashion, it is generally because the organization wishes to avoid having to interview a large number of unqualified applicants. Example: say the local NHL hockey team requires an office professional. If the team advertises its name in the newspaper it will get a flood of applicants, many of whom are unqualified but apply because of their desire to work for celebrities. A simple advertisement that lists the responsibilities of the position, the desired qualifications, and a post office box number is more likely to attract those who are legitimately interested in performing the advertised responsibilities.

Scrutinize blind advertisements carefully. Sometimes they are used for purposes other than recruitment for employment, such as preparing a mailing list of prospective purchasers. If you receive a telephone call in response to a reply to a blind advertisement, ask for the name of the company, and ask some questions about the job during the telephone conversation to ascertain that the job opening being advertised is legitimate. See Figure 15-1 for sample newspaper ads.

Prospects in Another Geographic Area

To begin your search for job opportunities in another geographic area, do the following:

1 Conduct research on the Internet by city name or by company name.
2 Ask the career counsellor in your college to help you. The career counsellor will have lots of useful information and tips on how to secure employment and where to look for it.
3. Inquire at the local public library for the telephone directory and newspapers for the city in which you are seeking employment.
4. Write or fax the chamber of commerce in the desired geographic area.

Ask the career counsellor for the most recent copy of *Career Options—The Graduate Recruitment Annual*, published by the Canadian Association of Career Educators and Employers. It provides valuable information regarding your career search, as well as a directory of employers interested in hiring college graduates.

Tell the college career counsellor your employment goal and ask for suggestions. The counsellor may offer to contact the career counsellor at a college in the area where you plan to relocate, in order to find out about work prospects for administrative assistants there.

The telephone directory for the city where you want to locate will be an excellent source of information. Public libraries generally have telephone directories for a number of cities, and large public libraries have telephone directories from all the major cities in Canada. Public libraries also subscribe to many newspapers.

To find out what your public library has on file that will be helpful to you, call the library and ask for Information Service. The librarian will answer your specific questions concerning what telephone directories and newspapers are available. You can also obtain the addresses of a few companies from the librarian by telephone.

When you write to a chamber of commerce, state your employment goal and ask about opportunities in your field in the geographic area. If the chamber of commerce sends you a list of prospective employers, realize that the list is limited to chamber of commerce members.

APPLYING FOR JOBS

The résumé, the application letter, and the job interview are the applicant's direct contacts with prospective employers. The following discussion will provide you with methods of making all three more persuasive and effective.

The Résumé

A résumé, sometimes called a **curriculum vitae**, is a summary of an applicant's qualifications for the job being sought. Your résumé should answer questions concerning

1. who you are
2. the type of job you are seeking
3. the qualifications you have to offer.
4. the experience you have to offer.

The word *résumé* is spelled with accents in standard dictionaries, but is sometimes written without them. Whichever spelling you choose, be consistent.

Résumé Styles

All résumés should be personalized; however, there are a few formats that offer an attractive and easy to read document to the potential employer. The style and benefits of these résumés is listed below. Because the chronological résumé is usually the preferred style by employers, we feature it in Figure 15-2.

Chronological Résumé—The chronological format arranges your work experience, education, and personal history so that the most recent information is first. The

Figure 15-1 Sample newspaper ads.

Office / Clerical Help Wanted

ADMINISTRATIVE ASSISTANT TO THE CITY ENGINEER

Engineering is one of the city's major departments. As Department Head, the City Engineer requires an administrative assistant who has excellent communication and critical thinking skills, is a team player, and who can give support by performing technical and administrative tasks quickly and accurately. The successful candidate will have been trained in Total Quality Management and will have demonstrated commitment to its philosophy.

Duties include preparing for and arranging meetings, taking minutes, composing correspondence, and assisting the City Engineer with administrative tasks. The ability to train junior office workers and to be an office team leader are desirable. There is frequent contact with private executives, professionals, and senior government and other officials. The diverse duties and responsibilities of this position allow considerable latitude for personal initiative and growth.

The successful applicant will have achieved a post-secondary diploma in office administration and will have superior word processing, database management, spreadsheet, and desktop publishing skills. A university degree would be an asset.

Salary will be commensurate with training and experience. A full benefit package is offered.

Please call (506) 363-1893 for an appointment.

RECEPTIONIST / BOOKKEEPER

We need an enthusiastic, energetic, and organized assistant to perform general office duties. Experience and training in bookkeeping is required. Bring your résumé to 1609 Northfield Rd.

C.A. FIRM

Small C.A. firm requires an enthusiastic graduate of an office administration program to key correspondence and financial statements on word processing and spreadsheeting software. Candidate must be able to assume general office duties, including reception and bookkeeping. Salary negotiable. To apply please call Mrs. L. Rossin at 869-0020.

OFFICE ASSISTANT/ BOOKKEEPER

Required by small sales office. Responsibilities include bookkeeping, payroll and keyboarding. Applicants must have experience in accounting and should have good organizational skills and the ability to work with minimum supervision. Reply to Box AM654.

WORD PROCESSING OPERATOR

Trained and experienced operators needed for temp. and perm. positions. Please contact J. Johnson, 598-2306

chronological résumé has many advantages: it is the most preferred résumé for employers because it is easy to follow and shows exactly what the applicant has done, not what the applicant thinks he or she can do. This is certainly the résumé format of choice especially when the applicant has an impressive work or educational history. As well, this résumé works well for recent graduates because it emphasizes their education and also identifies previous work experience responsibilities that relate to the job being sought.

Functional Résumé—The functional résumé is designed to point to the applicant's skills, abilities and accomplishments. If you have never been employed, the functional résumé will work well. A functional résumé will give you an opportunity to point out leadership and organizational experience that indicate you will be a productive employee. A person who has not been employed but has acquired comparable work experience through volunteering and day-to-day living can also prepare a functional résumé. In this style of résumé the experience section is organized by functions, without reference to the time of the performance or to an organization.

Targeted Résumé—This particular format focuses on the applicant's achievements and abilities that relate only to a specific job. The disadvantage of this style is that applicants need new résumés for every job they apply for.

Purpose of the Résumé

The purpose of a résumé is to obtain an interview. It should be mailed or personally delivered with a one-page application letter. As soon as your résumé opens the door for a job interview, it has served its function. Whether or not you are offered the job will depend on your qualifications and how well you project your knowledge, abilities, and personality during the interview.

Administrative assistants with excellent skills in communication, word processing, spreadsheeting, desktop publishing, database management, and public relations are in demand in many areas of Canada. According to many employers of office staff, the most highly desired skill is excellent communication skills; this includes verbal, written, and computer communications. An attractive, informative, and accurate résumé that accents these skills will be partially responsible for getting the employment you desire.

You will deliver a résumé to the place of employment when you respond to the job posting. However, take additional résumés with you to the job interview. Hand one to the interviewer(s) at the beginning of the interview so that it may be referred to during the interview. By bringing along extra copies of your résumé, you will be indicating to the interviewer that you are organized.

Self-Appraisal Inventory

As a preliminary step to preparing a résumé, decide exactly what your qualifications are. Prepare a detailed inventory of your educational background, work experience, and personal qualities and interests so that you will know exactly what assets you have to offer an employer.

To prepare your inventory chart, record all the data you think might help you in your job search. Use separate sheets of paper to list your education, work history, and personal qualities. Include everything as you make your list; record the items in any order and then rearrange them later, deleting any that may not be relevant to the job you seek.

Under education, list the following:

1. The postsecondary institute(s) attended, date(s) of graduation, and degree(s), diploma(s), or certificate(s) attained
2. The high school you attended, and the dates
3. Any special courses that may support your employment hunt
4. Your skills, including computer and software training, and the ability to operate any additional equipment
5. School activities that suggest organizational, team, and leadership skills.

Under Work History, list all your jobs, including part-time, summer, and volunteer work. Do not exclude jobs that were not office jobs. For each job, give the name and address of the organization, your job title, the details of your duties, and the dates of your employment.

Under Personal Qualities, list your strengths, such as initiative, leadership, ability to organize, and willingness to learn and participate in a team. Discuss these when you write your application letter.

Under Interests, list your hobbies and special talents, and the ways you spend your leisure time.

Points of Emphasis

Organize your résumé so that the interviewer will grasp your most important qualifications if he or she reads only the first line of each section of your résumé. Prepare a one-page résumé, or put the most essential data on the first page.

Many authorities on résumés emphasize preparing a brief résumé. Although some advocate a one-page résumé, this is rarely enough space to include the critical facts. As your experience and education expand, so must your résumé. Most applicants for clerical work should have résumés no longer than two pages.

Indicate the type of position you are seeking in the Objective section.

Decide whether your work experience or your education will be most persuasive, and then place that section immediately after the Objective.

To highlight your education, list your most recent college attendance first; after that, list the other schools you attended in reverse chronological order. It is often helpful to display key courses that relate to the employment opportunity. For the administrative assistant this often means software or skills-oriented courses.

Be consistent; just as you listed your education, arrange your work experience by listing the most recent employment first, followed by other employment in reverse chronological order.

Suggested Outline for a Chronological Résumé

The résumés of two applicants should not be identical, but good résumés tend to follow a recognizable pattern. Plan your résumé so that it presents all your qualifications and highlights your strongest points.

A résumé is a list. It is not necessary to write complete sentences. Use lists to describe duties or skills; but remember to be consistent. A common error in résumés is the use of inconsistent verbs. For example:

Inconsistent List

Responsibilities

- Keyboarding documents
- Manage electronic databases
- Plan meetings and conferences

Consistent List

Responsibilities

- Keyboarding documents
- Managing electronic databases
- Planning meetings and conferences

Avoid using "I." A résumé contains facts only. Statements that reveal philosophy or opinion may be used in the application letter but not in the résumé. The suggestions that follow are illustrated in Figure 15-2.

Heading

In the heading, include your name, postal address, telephone number, fax number, and e-mail address. If you have a temporary address, provide a permanent mailing address to ensure that you receive any documentation sent to you. Use a telephone number that has an answering system so you are not missing any important calls from potential employers.

Job Objective

In the Objective, state the type of position you are seeking and the name of the organization with which you are seeking employment. Write the full name of the organization. Using the name of the company in the résumé shows that the résumé was specially prepared.

Education

1. List the date, name, and city of each postsecondary institute and high school attended. Place the most recent school first. If you are still attending school, write *Expected Graduation Date (or EGD) April 20xx*.
2. For each entry, indicate your major area of study, stating the degree, diploma, or certificate obtained.
3. List your skills. Indicate your keyboarding speed only if it is applicable and impressive.
4. List the different types of software you have experience using.
5. List courses you took that you believe will be helpful to you on the job. List them by name, not number.
6. Add school activities that reflect your organizational, supervisory, and team skills.

Experience

In reverse order, list your employment experience. If your work experience has been limited, include part-time, summer, and volunteer work, even when the work was unrelated to office work. Employers place value on experience that is common to all jobs, such as carrying out instructions, being prompt and dependable, working cooperatively with others, and accepting responsibility.

Use a separate entry for each job, and arrange the entries in reverse chronological order. Give the beginning and ending dates (months and years), the name of the employer, the city in which the organization is located, the position held, and the specific duties performed. If the job was part time or voluntary, place this information under the date. To indicate that you are currently working, leave the date blank following the hyphen after the beginning date.

Interests and Activities

Because the Human Rights Codes relating to equal opportunity employment make it illegal for an employer to discriminate on the basis of age, sex, colour, marital status, religion, place of origin, race, or creed, you are not required to include personal data.

However, where you believe that certain personal data may be to your benefit, you should include them.

Figure 15-2 Résumé.

Ms. Dini Lawrence
10507 - 53 Avenue NW
Edmonton, AB T6H 0R6
Tel: (403) 555-1320 Fax: (403) 555-2398 e-mail: dini@z-wave.ca

OBJECTIVE

To become an office professional with a company that is an innovative organization.

SKILLS

With seven years of professional office experience and an Office Administration diploma from the Southern Alberta Institute of Technology, I have learned to be technically efficient in the office. My human relations skills include leadership and cooperation, as well as loyalty and dedication.

EDUCATION

September 1992 - April 1994

- **Southern Alberta Institute of Technology**
  Office Administration
  Calgary
  - Honours Diploma Received
  - Keyboarding Achieved = 70 words per minute
- **Software Training**
  - Microsoft Word
  - Excel
  - Lotus Notes
  - WordPerfect
  - Peoplesoft
  - Power Point
  - Simply Accounting
  - Access
  - Microsoft Project
  - Visio
- **Application Courses Completed**
  - Document Processing
  - Marketing
  - Project Management
  - Business Law
  - Meetings and Conferences
  - Professional Development
  - Office Procedures
  - Report Writing
  - Advanced Keyboarding
  - Records Management
  - Office Supervision
  - Public Relations
  - Accounting
  - Advanced Business Communications
- **School Activities**
  - President of the Office Administration Society
  - Chairperson of the Graduation Planning Committee
  - Participant in Charity Fundraising

September 1989 - June 1992

- **Salisbury Composite High School**
  Senior Matriculation
  Sherwood Park
  - Honours Diploma Earned

Figure 15-2 continued

Résumé of Dini Lawrence *Page 2*

EXPERIENCE

May 1994 - May 20xx

- **Administrative Assistant**
  Coron Industries
  Calgary
- **Responsibilities**
  - superivsing junior staff
  - keyboarding correspondence using word processing software
  - organizing budgets on electronic spreadsheet
  - composing routine correspondence
  - making travel arrangements
  - arranging meetings and conferences
  - researching potential client markets
  - managing electronic databases
  - performing reception duties
  - designing sales brochures using desktop publishing software

July 1993 - September 1994 (Part Time)

- **Sales Assistant**
  Image Plus
  Calgary
- **Responsibilities**
  - assisting customers
  - handling cash
  - logging financial transactions into computer system
  - answering telephone inquiries
  - participating in training programs

INTERESTS AND ACTIVITIES

July 1999
- member of International Association of Administrative Professionals

October 1998
- volunteer for Special Olympics
- enjoy playing tennis, cycling, reading, and attending theatre events

REFERENCES

Mr. Elton Margate
Director Quality Control
Coron Industries
1601 5 Avenue SW
Calgary, AB T2P 4C8
Tel (403) 555-5489
Fax (403) 555-9008
E-mail emargate@caron.com

Mr. Richard Fenwick
Program Head
Office Administration
SAIT
1301 16th Avenue NW
Calgary, AB T2M 0L4
Tel (403) 555-8581
Fax (403) 555-8940
E-mail richard.fenwick@sait.ab.ca

Ms. Sharon Mott
Manager
Image Plus
237 4 Avenue SW
Calgary AB T2P 4P3
Tel (403) 555-5877
Fax (403) 555-4455
E-mail sharonmott@image.com

In this section you may add whatever you believe will support your application, such as honours received, extracurricular activities, hobbies and sports you enjoy, and professional associations you belong to.

References

The question of whether or not to include references is often raised, because employers know that applicants list as references those persons who will give the applicant favourable recommendations. Many employers check with the persons who are listed as references; some do not.

Some résumés say, "References available upon request." However, if the prospective employer contacts references, why not include them as part of your résumé? Employers are busy people; by including the references on the résumé, you are saving the employer the effort of contacting you again to make the references available. And remember, your references may provide the pulling power you need to get the job. The best advice, then, is to include references with the résumé. You may wish to include references with some résumés and not with others. In this case, key your references on a separate page and treat them as a separate section. This way, you can choose to include the references or not.

As references, give three or more former employers or instructors who can provide a specific evaluation of your competence, work habits, and attitude toward work. If you include a character reference, do not give the name of a relative. Ask permission of each person to include his or her name as a reference, and remind the person of the dates you worked for him or her or were in his or her class.

For each reference, give the full name, position held, and complete address, including the postal code. Also include telephone and fax numbers and e-mail addresses. Use a courtesy title before each name. The position held is significant because it will indicate the person's association with you.

When you succeed in getting a job, send your references a thank-you letter or note expressing your appreciation for their assistance. Thank-you letters are discussed in more detail later in this chapter under "Follow-up Letters."

Appearance of the Résumé

Remember that the résumé is a specimen of your work. If you use the appropriate word processing or desktop publishing software features, your résumé will be a higher-quality document.

Print the résumé with a laser printer on 21.5 x 28 cm bond paper. High-quality white paper is very acceptable. Many applicants choose a high-quality lightly coloured paper in order to attract attention to the résumé. The rule, however, is to be conservative. Never use a bright or pastel shade that will detract from the conservative appearance.

Give the résumé plenty of white space, using margins of approximately 2.5 cm. The size of margins will actually depend on the setup and on the usual requirement to fit the résumé on two pages. To avoid a crowded look, use ample white space before and after headings and between entries. Too much white space, however, will suggest inefficient planning.

Print the main heading at the top of the first page. It should be centred, and highlighted in such a way that it is eye-catching and easy to read. Suggestions would be to use bold, enlarged, or italic print. Boxes or lines used in this area will enhance the appearance.

However, always apply the "be conservative" rule. Using too many enhancements will detract from the qualifications your résumé is trying to present.

Side headings should be emphasized but should not detract from the main titles. To this end, use a combination of capital letters, underlining, and bold or italic print. However, be moderate; you do not want to reduce the importance of the main heading.

The second page will require a running head. It should consist of a brief title and the page number.

You must get your résumé noticed in the pile that will be received by the recruiter. Hundreds of résumés are often received for one position. A recruiter will often ask an administrative assistant to sort out the résumés that do not meet the job requirements or that appear unsuitable. When in doubt about a particular résumé, the administrative assistant will probably cut it from the "suitable" pile. These unsuitable résumés will never reach the desk of the recruiter. Follow these simple rules to be sure your résumé is not filtered out:

1. Clearly state your skills that meet the key requirements of the job.
2. Carefully follow instructions. Give precisely what is requested. If the ad states that the company wishes to have résumés dropped off in person, or if it asks for a handwritten cover letter, do exactly that. Not following instructions demonstrates poor judgment and can be frustrating for the recruiter.
3. Concentrate on every detail. A good administrative assistant will catch the smallest error when scrutinizing the résumés. Any typographical or spelling error will mean immediate rejection. No employer will want to interview an applicant for an administrative assistant's position who allows errors in a document as important as a résumé. For that reason, don't rely only on

spell-checking your document with your word processing software—manually proofread the document as well.

4. Many ads request that applicants not telephone the company. This request should be respected. Telephone only when absolutely necessary; otherwise, you risk annoying the receptionist. Remember that the receptionist is often the "keeper of the gate." Leaving a negative impression with the receptionist could mean the end of your application.

Put yourself in the position of the person who must sort through and filter out the résumés, and then in the position of the recruiter. Make their jobs easier by making your résumé attractive, applicable, easy to understand, and flawless. If you follow these suggestions your chances of receiving an interview will increase.

Faxing Your Résumé

If you've spent hours printing your résumé on bond paper of perfect quality and colour, and perhaps have even used coloured ink for just the right amount of accent, then faxing your résumé will seem like an anticlimax. However, it does have the advantage of expediency. Employers will often request that résumés be faxed in order to save time. If you are requested to fax your résumé or simply determine yourself that faxing is appropriate, consider the following:

- A faxed résumé will probably not be confidential. In fact, several people may see it before the designated receiver collects it. You may be able to avoid this disclosure by telephoning the recipient just prior to sending the fax and asking him or her to collect the faxed document.
- A faxed résumé should always include a cover letter, just like the résumé you mail or hand deliver.
- If your résumé is attractive enough to earn you points, mail an original

Résumé Reminders

Before submitting your résumé, use the following checklist to ensure that your document will work for you. Remember that any poor work may cause an employer to send your résumé to File 13!

Appearance

- ❒ The spacing is attractive.
- ❒ You have plenty of white space.
- ❒ You have used quality paper that is white or of a conservative colour.
- ❒ Excessive enhancements have been avoided.
- ❒ A proportional-space font has been used.
- ❒ Your format is consistent throughout.
- ❒ Your headings are emphasized.
- ❒ Your information is in point form and uses bullets.
- ❒ You have followed the format described in this textbook.
- ❒ Your résumé is free of creases or folds.

Content

- ❒ Résumé headings shown in this textbook have been used.
- ❒ Your résumé emphasizes skills and mastery of software.
- ❒ Your résumé shows your most recent education first.
- ❒ Your résumé shows your most recent experience first.
- ❒ You included references on the bottom of your résumé or you prepared a reference sheet that includes three or four former employers and/or educators.
- ❒ Your references are complete (courtesy titles, working titles, company names, full addresses, telephone and fax numbers, and e-mail addresses).
- ❒ The people given as your references will actually promote your chances of gaining employment.

Accuracy

- ❒ There are absolutely no typographical errors in your résumé. It has been proofread repeatedly by you and by someone else who gave you constructive feedback.
- ❒ You have used the spell-check function to ensure your résumé is free of spelling errors.
- ❒ You have checked your résumé for spelling errors that the spell-check function would not detect.
- ❒ Your lists are consistent in wording as well as format.
- ❒ You have stated your expected date of graduation if you have not already graduated.

Other

- ❒ Your résumé has been delivered in an appropriate way.
- ❒ Your résumé has been delivered on time.

The Application Letter

Write an application letter as a covering letter for your résumé. The main purpose of an application letter is to introduce your résumé in the hope of obtaining an interview.

Application letters are either prospecting or solicited. A *prospecting letter* is written by an applicant who does not know that a job opening exists. It is written to express the applicant's interest in working for a particular organization, to call attention to the applicant's qualifications, and to inquire about the possibility of a job opening. A *solicited letter* is written in response to an announcement that a job opening exists. The announcement might be made through an ad in the newspaper, or placed with a private employment agency, or sent to the placement office of a school, or disseminated through other sources. As a college graduate, write prospecting application letters; do not wait until you know that a specific job opening exists.

The Prospecting Letter

An application letter is a sales letter, and the product is *you*. It represents your initial effort at locating an employer seeking the qualifications you have to offer and at convincing the employer to consider your qualifications. You increase your application letter's chances of gaining attention when you submit a résumé along with it. Let the reader know what qualifications you possess so that he or she can compare them with the requirements of the jobs available within the organization.

Organize your application letter around the steps of a sales presentation:

1. An opening that gets the reader's attention and arouses interest in knowing more about your qualifications
2. Emphasis on facts that will convince the prospective employer that you possess qualifications that match the requirements of a job he or she is trying to fill
3. A brief reference to the résumé you are enclosing
4. A closing that requests action, which in most application letters is a request for an interview.

These points are illustrated in the application letter in Figure 15-3.

The Solicited Letter

When you hear or read about a job opening, write a solicited (invited) letter.

A solicited application letter can be more specific than a prospecting letter because the applicant knows that a job opening exists. Use the first paragraph to refer to the job and to reveal how you found out about it. Include a reference to the source. Request in the opening paragraph that you be considered for the job; for example:

> Please consider this résumé as an application for the position of Administrative Assistant as advertised in the May 14 issue of the *Cape Breton Post*. I recently received an honours diploma for Office Technology. Through my studies I mastered numerous office skills including the use of word processing, desktop publishing, and database management software packages. Because I am an energetic graduate who is willing to learn, I am confident I could contribute to your team.

Write a persuasive letter in such a way that you discuss every requirement mentioned in the announcement and show how you meet these qualifications. It will differ from a prospecting letter in that you will include only the key qualifications that you choose to emphasize.

Enclose a résumé and refer to it in the letter. In the résumé highlight all the qualifications and key words mentioned in the announcement, and include others that may contribute to your getting the job.

Close the letter by requesting action, which usually is a request for an interview in which to discuss your qualifications for the job.

Appearance of the Application Letter

Key your application letter on good bond paper 21.5 x 28 cm in size. Use plain paper that matches the quality and shade of the paper used for your résumé. Include your personalized letterhead above the date. Since your application letter could get separated from your résumé, put your complete mailing address on both the letter and the résumé.

Address the letter to a specific person, if possible. Make an effort to find out the name of the employer the letter should be addressed to. This information can be obtained with a single telephone call to the company.

Limit your letter to one page. Since you have organized all your facts in the accompanying résumé, you can limit your application letter to three or four well-written paragraphs. Most letter styles are acceptable. The key factors in appearance are

- keep the font and format conservative
- keep the appearance professional
- keep the information balanced on the page.

Application Letter Reminders

A cover letter is the window to your résumé so it's critical that your cover letter gives the best view of your

Figure 15-3 Prospecting letter of application.

Ms. *Dini Lawrence*

10507 - 53 Avenue NW
Edmonton, AB T6H 0R6
Tel (403) 555-1320 Fax (403) 555-2398

20 May 20xx

Mrs. Mary Karlovsky
Manager, Sales Office
Northwestern Region
Advantage Technology, Ltd.
9129 Jasper Avenue
Edmonton, AB T5H 3Y2

Dear Mrs. Karlovsky:

Re: Administrative Assistant Position

During my two years of study in the Office Administration Program at the Southern Alberta Institute of Technology (SAIT), my goal was to become qualified to work as an administrative assistant for a progressive and rapidly growing company. Because Advantage Technology has the reputation for being an innovative organization I have a keen desire to join your team.

In April of 1994, I graduated from SAIT, became successfully employed in Calgary, and have recently relocated to Edmonton with the desire to become an employee of your company.

The skills and knowledge attained at SAIT and through industry have prepared me to be both effective and efficient as an administrative assistant. Because I key at a rate of 70 words per minute and have excellent communication, word processing, and desktop publishing skills, I can prepare accurate and attractive business communication with ease. As well, studies and experience in supervision of junior office staff have taught me the importance of cooperation and strong leadership. My knowledge and practice of public relations, conference and travel arrangements, and electronic database management, enable me to perform a variety of tasks in a busy executive office. A résumé has been enclosed for your further information.

At your convenience, I would appreciate an appointment to discuss my qualifications for an administrative assistant position with Advantage Technology, Ltd. I look forward to your response.

Sincerely,

D. Lawrence

Ms. Dini Lawrence

Enclosure

skills. Consider your application letter as one of your marketing tools. The following checklist will help you create an application letter that works for you.

Appearance

- ❒ The letter is keyed.
- ❒ You have used high-quality bond paper.
- ❒ Your paper and font match those on the résumé.
- ❒ Your cover letter is stapled to the top of your résumé.
- ❒ The documents have been placed in an envelope large enough that they may lay flat without folding.

Content

- ❒ You have opened with an attention-getting statement.
- ❒ You have demonstrated knowledge of the company.
- ❒ Your letter complimented the company.
- ❒ Key words have been included that were used in the job posting.
- ❒ You have described what would make you valuable to the company.
- ❒ Your background has been summarized.
- ❒ You closed with a call to action.
- ❒ The letter is short.
- ❒ The letter is simple.
- ❒ The letter sounds sincere.
- ❒ The letter sounds enthusiastic.

Accuracy

- ❒ You have proofread the letter several times for typos, grammar, spelling, punctuation, and content.
- ❒ Another reliable person has proofread it and given you feedback on it.
- ❒ The letterhead contains the correct information (full address, telephone and fax numbers, and e-mail address).

The Application Form

During your job campaign you will be asked to complete application forms. When a company requests that you complete an application form, do so; your résumé does not substitute for a completed application form. If you wish, you may attach your résumé to the completed application form; however, be sure to complete each section of the application. If a question on the application form does not apply to you, write "Not Applicable" or "Does Not Apply" in the blank. If a question calls for salary expected and you do not want to state a figure, write "Open to Negotiation," which means you would prefer to discuss salary once an offer of employment is made. If you leave the answer blank, the employer may assume

- you were careless and missed the question
- you did not complete the form, or
- you did not understand the question.

Any of these assumptions will eliminate your form from the stack of successful applications.

Each organization designs its own form for employee recruitment in order to include the specific questions it wants applicants to answer. Nevertheless, most application forms are similar.

Supplying information on the application forms you are requested to complete is a significant part of your job campaign. Follow the instructions carefully and supply the information exactly as it is called for. If the instruction reads, "Please print," do so. Your printing and handwriting must be legible. After all, you want it to stand out in the pile.

Prepare your answers before you write or key on the application form. When you do this, your form will appear neat and organized. A completed application form becomes a part of the permanent record of the applicant who is hired.

Many organizations follow the procedure of handing the applicant an application form as the first step of an interview taking place on the organization's premises. (For campus interviews, the interviewer will use the application form that you gave the placement director.)

Be prepared to complete the application. Do you

- have a pen?
- know the current date?
- have the names, titles, addresses, and telephone and fax numbers for your references?
- have the dates of previous employment?
- have a list of your volunteer activities and the associations you belong to?
- have the dates you attended high school and postsecondary institutes?
- know your social insurance number?
- know the exact title of the job you are applying for?

Complete the form as requested even if you have your résumé with you. It is acceptable to staple a copy of your résumé to the back of the application form.

The Portfolio

A portfolio is one of best marketing tools you can have on a job interview. It is a collection of samples of your best work and should include only perfect work; nothing less than perfect is acceptable. No smudges or writing of any kind should appear on the documents.

The work should be organized into sections such as samples of spreadsheets, tables graphics, minutes of meetings, letters, and reports that you have composed and keyed. You should also include certificates and diplomas earned, as well as transcripts. At least one letter of reference is a strong asset.

"There is always a benefit to starting at the bottom of the ladder. You get more experience."

Debbie Siscoe, Graduate
Nova Scotia Community College
Burridge Campus

A table of contents and title page are necessary to give the portfolio an organized appearance. Plastic sheets should protect all documents. This work should be packaged into an attractive leather (or simulated leather) case with rings to hold the pages. Do not use a binder since a binder doesn't have the professional appearance you need.

During the interview, find an appropriate opportunity to introduce the portfolio and discuss your work with the interviewer. Remember that the portfolio is not intended to be an information tool. It is a sales tool and the product it is promoting is you!

The Job Interview

A job interview gives you the opportunity to convince a prospective employer that you can make a real contribution to the organization. An interviewer can judge your basic qualifications by studying your transcript, application letter, résumé, test results, and completed application form. During the interview the interviewer will evaluate your personality, attitudes, professional appearance, and ability to communicate. An impressive school record and evidence that you possess the necessary office technology skills are pluses, but your success in landing the job you want will hinge on the way you project yourself during the interview.

The purpose of the job interview is twofold:

1. To give the interviewer an opportunity to evaluate the applicant in terms of the needs of the organization.
2. To give the applicant a chance to appraise the job and the organization.

Figure 15-4 The interviewer will review your résumé and ask questions to determine whether you are qualified for the position.
Courtesy of The Image Works

Sometimes getting an interview is extremely difficult. If getting an interview seems impossible, don't become discouraged: this difficulty may reflect the competition for jobs in your area. Even so, examine your documents and compare them with the Résumé and Application Letter Checklists provided in this chapter.

Attempt to schedule several interviews with organizations that you believe will offer the type of work you are seeking. Do not expect to be offered all the jobs for which you apply, and do not set your expectations on one particular job. Becoming overly anxious about getting a particular job can create unnecessary tension that could cause you to be nervous and ineffective during the interview. Nevertheless, you should enter each interview with the attitude that the job you are applying for is precisely the one you want. As you learn more about the job, it may *become* the job you want.

Before the Interview

Prepare thoroughly for each interview. Your preparation should include

- researching the organization with which you have scheduled the interview
- taking a practice run to the location of the interview
- learning what the current salaries are for administrative assistants in the community
- summarizing your own qualifications
- deciding which qualifications to emphasize
- anticipating the interviewer's questions
- formulating your answers to the interviewer's questions

PERSPECTIVES

Record Your Life's Work

By Beth Gibbs CPS

You can create a portfolio of your work and career just like artists and models.

What is the first thing that comes to mind when you think of the word "portfolio"? Models and artists use portfolios to display their work, and you probably have a financial portfolio that includes your securities and investments. Teacher portfolios are integral to a teacher's career as well. But portfolios also can be used by office professionals in their professional growth.

Professional portfolios are not only an activity record of experience; they also indicate how you achieved your goals and what your goals are for the future. With the downsizing of today's workforce, the need for a portfolio has become more important. You may not be looking for a new job, but what about that raise or promotion? With some government and private companies moving to pay for performance, a professional portfolio can play a big part in your evaluations. Your boss may not be aware of all your work accomplishments or may not remember all the things you did to assist him or her with a presentation, or other critical activity. Your portfolio also can be useful to display your activities for Certified Professional Secretary® recertification points.

You may use your portfolio in a variety of ways: as an assessment device, a marketing tool, or a vehicle for self-awareness. To determine how you will use your portfolio, ask yourself the following questions:

- Who is the intended audience or audiences?
- What do they want or need to know?
- Will the portfolio contain your best work samples or will it be a progressive record of growth?

Assembling the pieces

You must be selective when choosing samples to include in your portfolio. Think about how you will convey the portfolio's purpose to the audience and how others might best review the portfolio. The portfolio's meaningfulness is enhanced by the degree to which it reflects your beliefs. Don't just produce a scrapbook. Scrapbooks are treasures, but they don't get the message across for that promotion, evaluation, or job interview.

Some things you might want to put in your portfolio are a personal mission statement, resume, memberships, community service, workshops/seminars attended, awards, evaluations, professional development plan, letters of recommendation, career goals, letter of application, thank-you and job-well-done letters, and descriptions and examples of computer programs and projects. Don't forget to date the samples. The selection of materials and their arrangements will vary depending on your intent.

When considering what to include in your portfolio, it's important to think about your professional goals. Goals define where you want to go and set the stage for how you want to get there. They are also benchmarks by which you can measure your progress.

Setting goals is easier if you follow these steps:

1. Reflect on your professional needs.
2. Think about where you came from, where you are now, and where you want to be.
3. Write down the areas you want to focus on for goal development.
4. Rank the importance of your focus areas.

As an office professional, you have a better chance to achieve your personal goals if they are compatible with the goals of your company. High achievers seize opportunities to make those goals realities. Goal setting involves a master career plan that consists of long-range goals and more immediate short-range objectives.

Another aspect of goal setting is developing a mission statement. Some say you need to develop your mission statement before you set your goals. Others think the goals need to come first for the same reason. It is up to you which you do first.

In her book, *The Path: Creating Your Mission Statement for Work and for Life,* Laurie Beth Jones says: "No tool is as valuable in providing direction as a mission statement—a brief, succinct, and focused statement of purpose that can be used to initiate, evaluate, and refine all of life's activities." Jones' three elements of a good mission statement are that it's:

- no more than a single sentence long,
- easily understood by a 12 year old, and
- can be recited by memory at gunpoint.

All great leaders in history have had mission statements that were no more than a single sentence long. Abraham Lincoln's mission was to preserve the Union. Mother Teresa's mission was to show mercy and compassion for the dying. As you change and grow in your profession, you may want to change your mission statement. A personal mission statement acts as both a harness and a sword—harnessing you to what is true about your life, and cutting away all that is false.

Packaging the information

The physical structure and appearance of the portfolio should complement its purpose. Provide samples of your best work to illustrate your distinctive style.

You've probably collected armloads of information, so you'll have to start eliminating. A summary sheet might be helpful. Use it to write down how you plan to use your portfolio. As you select pieces to include, ask yourself "would anyone really be interested in this information?"

Beth Gibbs CPS is an administrative assistant at the University of Northern Colorado in Greeley, CO, and member of the Union Colony Chapter of PSI. She can be reached at 970/351-2430.

Reprinted courtesy of OfficePRO.

- choosing clothes appropriate for the interview
- scheduling ample time for personal grooming.

Research

Researching the organization with which you are having the interview is crucial. The following are effective research methods:

- using the Internet to study the organization
- exploring the organization in the reference section of the library
- reading the organization's most recent annual report
- asking the placement director for literature that the organization may have provided for distribution to applicants
- calling the organization's receptionist and requesting information.

Learn all you can about the organization. Research

- the organization's products or services
- how profitable the organization is
- the number of employees the organization has
- how long the organization has been operating
- the extent of the company's operations
- any recent expansion the company may have experienced
- any mergers or name changes the company has undergone
- the company's competitive standing in the industry
- the organization's hiring practices.

Many applicants fall short during an interview because they lack knowledge about the organization to which they are applying. The interviewer will tell you about the organization and its employment opportunities, but you will be able to converse with more ease and ask pertinent questions if you have researched the organization. Lack of knowledge could be viewed by the interviewer as lack of interest in the organization. Prepare thoroughly; show your interest in the organization through your knowledge about it.

Before the interview, research the current salary ranges in your geographic area for the job you are seeking. The best way to do this is by reading the want ads for office jobs in the local paper. Statistics Canada publishes a summary of wage rates for all categories of occupations. This material is available in public libraries or by writing to Statistics Canada.

Anticipate Questions

Think about what you have to offer and the qualifications you want to emphasize. Review your résumé before you go to the interview. The interviewer will expect you to discuss your job objective and why you feel qualified for it. You should be prepared to talk about yourself in an organized way without hesitation.

Anticipate the questions the interviewer will ask and know what your answers will be. Realize, too, that you cannot anticipate all the questions the interviewer will ask. You can expect questions such as the following concerning the job:

1. What do you know about this company?
2. What do you know about the position you are applying for?
3. We are looking for someone with extensive experience. Your résumé indicates limited experience as an office professional. How do you expect to compensate for your lack of experience?
4. Why do you think you might like to work for this organization?
5. What do you expect to be doing five years from now?
6. Why did you choose a career as an administrative assistant?
7. Relating to the responsibilities described in the advertisement for this position, what strengths will you bring to our office?
8. Relating to the responsibilities described in the advertisement for this position, what responsibilities do you believe will be your greatest challenges? How do you expect to meet these challenges?
9. Tell me about yourself.

10. How do you rate the education you received? Why?
11. Throughout your training to be an administrative assistant, what courses did you enjoy the most? The least? Why?
12. Describe the qualities of a good leader. Have you encountered a person like this? Where and when?
13. Describe the characteristics of a poor leader. Have you encountered a person like this? Where and when? How did you handle this poor leadership?
14. Do you plan to continue your education? How? In what field? Why is this important to you?
15. If you were a team leader, what type of team members would you pick? If your team members did not meet your expectations, what action would you take?
16. What are your feelings about working overtime?

At the outset of the interview you may be asked some general questions relating to your personal interests; or you may be asked to give your opinion about the latest current events. Some interviewers begin with questions that they think will put the applicant at ease. Answer all questions thoroughly but without rambling. Consider your answers to all questions seriously; the interviewer is searching for qualified employees who will stay with the organization if they are hired.

To gain insight into your personality and to check on your attitude, the interviewer may ask questions such as these:

1. Give an example of how you have displayed initiative.
2. Do you prefer working within a team or by yourself? Explain.
3. How do you spend your leisure time?
4. What personality characteristics do you think are essential for the job you are seeking?
5. How do you accept criticism?
6. Provide an example of a time when you were criticized. Describe the best/worst employer/teacher you have ever had.
7. Explain a stressful situation you encountered and describe how you handled it.
8. Give an example of a humorous situation that you witnessed in a previous job or at school.

Unethical Questions

Interviewers who want information on marital status, age, smoking habits, physical disabilities, race, ancestry, or place of origin must phrase their inquiries very carefully. Many questions relating to these topics are unethical. Basing employment decisions on these factors is usually illegal.

Although most organizations fall under provincial human rights jurisdiction, some are under federal human rights jurisdiction. Those that are federally governed include all federal government departments, federal Crown corporations, federally chartered banks, and national interest organizations (such as transportation and communication companies). Most other organizations fall under provincial human rights authority. Some businesses are subject to both federal and provincial human rights acts. Human rights legislation is subject to change.

If you have concerns about your human rights as they relate to your job search, your best course of action is to contact both the Human Rights Commission for your province and the federal Human Rights Commission.

pro-Link

Did you know that the Canadian Human Rights Commission (CHRC) advises employers how to conduct job interviews without violating the law? Their guidelines for screening and selection are comprehensive but these few examples are for ***your*** record:

- **Gender**: CHRC says avoid asking males or females to complete different applications and don't ask about pregnancy or childbearing plans.

  You may ask the applicant if attendance requirements can be met.
- **Marital Status**: CHRC says avoid asking the applicant whether they are married, single, divorced, or whether an applicant's spouse is employed or subject to transfer.

  You may ask if there are any circumstances that might prevent minimum service commitment.
- **Race or Colour:** CHRC says avoid any inquiry into race or colour, including colour of eyes, skin, or hair.
- **Height and Weight**: CHRC says that the employer can make no inquiry unless there is evidence they are for genuine occupational requirements.
- **Photographs:** CHRC says avoid asking for a photograph of the applicant before the interview. Photographs for security passes or company files can be taken after successful selection.

Figure 15-5 Prohibited grounds of discrimination chart.

Prohibited Grounds	Federal	British Columbia	Alberta	Saskatchewan	Manitoba	Ontario	Quebec	New Brunswick	Prince Edward Island	Nova Scotia	Newfoundland	Northwest Territories	Yukon
Race or colour	●	●	●	●	●	●	●	●	●	●	●	●	●
Religion or creed	●	●	●	●	●	●	●	●	●	●	●	●	●
Age	●	● 19-65	● 18+	● 18-64	●	● 18-65	●	●	●	●	● 19-65	●	●
Gender (incl. pregnancy or childbirth)	●	●	●	●	●[1]	●[2]	●	●	●[3]	●	●[3]	●	●
Marital status	●	●	●	●	●	●	●[4]	●	●	●	●	●	●
Physical/Mental handicap or disability	●	●	●	●	●	●	●	●	●	●	●	●	●
Sexual orientation	●	●	●†	●	●	●	●	●		●	●[3]		●
National or ethnic origin (incl. linguistic background)	●			●[5]	●	●[6]	●	●	●	●	●	●[5]	●
Family status	●	●	●	●[7]	●	●	●[4]			●		●	●
Dependence on alcohol or drug	●	●[3]	●[3]	●[3]	●[3]	●[3]		●[3, 8]	●[3]	●[8]			
Ancestry or place of origin		●	●	●	●	●		●				●	●
Political belief		●			●		●		●	●	●		●
Based on association					●	●		●	●	●			●
Pardoned conviction	●					●	●					●	
Record of criminal conviction		●					●						●
Source of income			●	●[9]	●					●			
Assignment, attachment or seizure of pay											●		
Social condition/origin							●				●		
Language						●[3]	●						

Harassment on any of the prohibited grounds is considered a form of discrimination.

Threatening, intimidating or discriminating against someone who has filed a complaint, or hampering a complaint investigation, is a violation of provincial human rights codes, and at the federal level is a criminal offence.

* Any limitation, exclusion, denial or preference may be permitted if a bona fide occupational requirement can be demonstrated.
† Sexual orientation is now a prohibited ground for discrimination—April 1998.
1) includes gender-determined characteristics
2) Ontario accepts complaints based on a policy related to female genital mutilation in all social areas on the grounds of gender, place of origin and/or handicap
3) complaints accepted based on policy
4) Quebec uses the term "civil status"
5) defined as nationality
6) Ontario's Code includes only "citizenship"
7) defined as being in a parent-child relationship
8) previous dependence only
9) defined as "receipt of public assistance"

Source: Canadian Human Rights Commission, 1996.
Courtesy of Canadian Human Rights Commission.

Refer to Figure 15-5 to show the Prohibited Grounds of Discrimination Chart.

Ask Intelligent Questions

An interviewer will expect you to ask questions too. Some interviews lend themselves to the applicant asking questions periodically throughout the interview while other interviews give the applicant an opportunity at the end of the interview to ask questions. Your research prior to the interview should help you generate a list of appropriate questions. Your questions should not be asking for information that you can collect on the company's website. In fact, you can state that you have an interest in learning more about a particular area and ask if you might be able to get that information on the website. You should choose a selection of questions, key them on your crib sheet, take the sheet to the interview with you, and refer to the crib sheet when you want to ask questions. The following is a list of intelligent questions to ask on an interview.

- To whom would I report? How many people would I report to?
- What personal qualities improve the likelihood for success in this position?
- What is the organization's mission?
- What are the major barriers for this organization to fulfill its mission?
- I read in the .... that you are expanding your .... division. How would that affect the position I am applying for?
- Do you have a human resource development program in your organization?
- What is the organization's plan to increase revenues or capacities?
- How would you describe the corporate culture of this organization?

Your Appearance Makes a Statement

Although first impressions rarely win jobs, your appearance—your clothes, hair, shoes, cosmetics, and jewellery—can certainly cost you the job before you ever open your mouth. Your goal is to look the part of a business professional. Your appearance should make the statement that you are a professional and that you want to be taken seriously. This is true even in companies that have a dress down policy. Companies that encourage their employees to dress casually still expect applicants to dress and act professionally on the interview. Once they are successful and join the staff, they may adopt the dress code of the company.

Spend the extra time it takes to look well groomed. Dress conservatively since you want the interviewer to focus on your answers without being distracted by your appearance. By applying the following checklist to your interview preparation, you may be able to convey the proper message.

- ❒ Your hair should be neat and away from your face.
- ❒ If you wear cosmetics, apply them sparingly.
- ❒ Your nails should be well manicured and clean.
- ❒ Your jewellery should be simple, minimal, and yet complimentary. Since you don't know the nature of the interviewer, it is best to play it safe and wear limited and conservative jewellery.
- ❒ Your professional attire should include a suit jacket.
- ❒ Your clothing should not be revealing; skirts should be of a comfortable length and blouses should never reveal cleavage or camisole.
- ❒ Shoes should be clean, polished, and conventional.
- ❒ White blouses or shirts must be very white. Cuffs or collars that have a gray appearance are a sign that grooming is less than perfect.
- ❒ Ties should complement a suit rather than be flamboyant.
- ❒ Cologne should be avoided. A fragrance that is attractive to you could be offensive to another person.
- ❒ For men, the most appropriate choice of colour is a variation of black, navy, brown, or gray. Acceptable business clothing for women tends to be more colourful than that of their male counterparts, although still conservative.

Whatever you decide will be your image for an interview, consider the strong nonverbal message that your image will send.

Be Punctual

Be sure you know the exact location of the interview. Plan to arrive 10 to 15 minutes early. Avoid rushing before the interview. You can undermine yourself before the interview by becoming stressed because you did not allow yourself enough time. A few days before the interview, travel to the office, and time yourself. On the actual day of the interview, allow more time than is needed to get there.

Never schedule two interviews for the same morning or afternoon. You have no control over the length of the interview, and you will not feel at ease if you are concerned about time.

Park in a location where you do not risk getting a ticket; the last thing you need to worry about is your car.

What to Take to the Interview

For the interview, you will want to have important materials on hand; but you will not want to be encumbered with items you do not need.

You should avoid bringing the following items to an interview. (Although it seems like common sense not to bring them, many employers report that applicants often do.)

- ❒ Never bring packages. Avoid shopping immediately before an interview, unless you can leave all the packages in your car.
- ❒ Women should never carry a large purse. A small handbag with only necessary items will not distract from a professional appearance.
- ❒ Men and women should never carry a briefcase that is oversized or resembles a schoolbag. Keep everything neat and simple and nondistracting.

- Most important of all, never bring another person. Naturally you wouldn't bring another person into the interview; but a number of applicants make plans to meet friends or relatives immediately after the interview.

The applicant needs to concentrate on the interview, not on the friends or relatives waiting in the lobby or reception area. In particular, don't bring children since their behaviour may cause you to worry. Demonstrate that you are an independent person; arrive alone and leave alone.

Now let's discuss what you *should* take to the interview.

- Your portfolio, if prepared to a professional standard, will be one of the best sales tools you have. Bring it to the interview and look for the perfect opportunity to walk through it with the interviewer.
- Always bring along a pen and paper to write down important facts you learn during the interview. Your pen should be attractive and in good condition. One that has been chewed or runs out of ink will not leave the interviewer with the best impression.
- Bring along extra copies of your résumé. Offer copies to the interviewers just as the interview is ready to start. This demonstrates your preparation. You will also need a copy for yourself to refer to throughout the interview.
- If references do not appear on your résumé, you should bring a list of three or more references that includes names, titles, company names, company addresses, and company telephone and fax numbers. This should be attractively keyed on a single sheet. Be prepared to leave this sheet with the interviewer.
- Bring along a keyed version of the job advertisement if one was posted or appeared in the newspaper. Highlight the key responsibilities listed. Don't be afraid to bring the ad out and refer to it during the interview. This shows that you know exactly what type of job you are applying for and that you are prepared for the interview.
- It is very acceptable to prepare a crib sheet and bring it along to the interview. On the crib sheet you can list the responsibilities of the job and for each one cite specific examples of how you have demonstrated competence. Also, on this crib sheet, key any questions you have prepared. Don't be afraid to refer to this sheet during the interview. The sheet should appear neat and organized and, of course, should be keyed.
- With desktop publishing, you can prepare personal business cards that are professional-looking by printing them on cardstock. Or, for a nominal charge, you can have a professional printer produce a small number of business cards. The applicant who leaves a business card leaves a professional statement.

During the Interview

Be courteous, maintain your poise, and act confident during the interview. As you approach the interviewer, smile, greet the interviewer by name, and introduce yourself. Give the interviewer a firm handshake. This will express your confidence. Try to relax. You will probably feel a little nervous because the interview is important to you. If you feel nervous, don't call attention to your nervousness by twisting your hair, tapping your foot, thumping on the table, sitting on the edge of the chair, talking too rapidly, or showing other outward signs.

There may be one interviewer or a panel of interviewers. The interviewers have a job to perform; they must match an applicant to the requirements of the job to be filled.

The initial interview will probably last 30 minutes or more. A good interviewer will allow the interviewee to talk throughout most of the interview.

Some interviewers break the interview into the following segments:

1. Getting acquainted
2. Presenting the organization's opportunities
3. Evaluating the applicant
4. Answering the applicant's questions.

Others begin the interview with one or more broad, open-ended questions, such as "Tell me about yourself," turning the discussion over to the interviewee at once. The interviewer controls the interview by telling the interviewee what he or she wants to hear about. When this interviewing technique is used, the conversation seems spontaneous rather than structured.

While the interviewer is talking, listen intently. Give the interviewer an opportunity to talk; show that you are an active listener.

When you are asked a question, give a full answer, not simply a yes or no. The interviewer will use a question or a comment to introduce a subject you are expected to discuss. Look the interviewer in the eye and answer all questions frankly. Be deliberate; don't start talking before the interviewer completes the question.

Avoid talking too much; keep to the point. Don't attempt to answer a question you do not understand. Either restate the question as you understand it or ask the interviewer to clarify it.

While you are talking, keep your goal in mind, which is to promote yourself. Use every opportunity to emphasize your good points and to relate them to what you can do for the organization. To sound sincere, present facts, not your opinion, about yourself. Don't criticize yourself and never make derogatory remarks about an instructor or a former employer.

As you are talking, the interviewer will strive to evaluate your mental and physical alertness, your ability to communicate, your attitude toward life and toward the organization, and your enthusiasm for work. Some interviewers will give tests in order to evaluate your skill level.

As discussed in the section "Before the Interview," you should prepare questions to ask at the interview. Every interviewer likes to be asked intelligent questions. The questions you prepare must be relevant to the organization or to the job opportunity. If all your prepared questions have been discussed during the interview and you are left without questions to ask, ask the interviewer to elaborate further on a statement or on details given earlier in the interview.

What About Salary?

At the initial interview your questions should not concern salary or benefits. Reserve these questions until you are offered the job. However, if the interviewer asks you about your expected salary, be prepared to state a range. Remember that the figure the interviewer is likely to remember and focus on is the low end of your range.

If you have prepared a personal budget and have researched office salaries in your location, you will know what an appropriate starting salary is for this employment opportunity.

The best time to negotiate salary is after the job offer has been made. However, the employer is in control of the interview; if the employer asks you a salary question during the interview, you must answer it. Employers are busy people and are not prepared to jump around an issue.

Remember that although salary is often a negotiable item, these negotiations must be handled with diplomacy. Although job satisfaction will be achieved mostly through obtaining a challenging and responsible position, don't sell yourself short when salary is discussed. If you have earned college credentials, you have gained bargaining power.

If you are definitely interested in working for the organization, tell the interviewer that you are. Say this near the end of the interview after you have had a chance to sum up what the interviewer has told you about the job.

Closing the Interview

Watch for cues that the interview is coming to an end. The interviewer may thank-you for coming, suggest that you schedule a time to take employment tests, invite you to arrange for a second interview, stand up, tell you that you will hear by a certain date if the organization is interested in your application, or offer you a job.

A good closure to an interview would include the following actions:

- ❒ Firmly shaking hands.
- ❒ Restating your interest in the position. Example: "I hope you will consider me for the job. I feel confident I would make a positive contribution to your organization."
- ❒ Checking the follow-up procedure that will be employed by the organization. Example: "When might I expect to hear from you? If I don't hear from you by that date, may I call you?"
- ❒ Leaving a business card.

If you are offered the job, you are not expected to accept it on the spot. You are making a long-term commitment, and you should be sure that it is the job you want. The interviewer would prefer that you give it enough thought to be absolutely certain. You may accept at once if you have no doubts about it. Otherwise, tactfully say that you would like time to consider it. Ask if you can let the interviewer know in a day or two or at some definite time you can agree upon.

You cannot always accurately judge how you are being rated by an interviewer. Interviewers who rely on the second interview for making a decision are noncommittal during the initial interview. Appear interested and confident as the interview draws to a close. Always express appreciation to the interviewer before leaving.

After the Interview

Make each interview a learning experience. To improve your techniques, analyze how well you performed after each interview. Review what you said, the interviewer's reaction to it, what you might have said but didn't, and what you should have left unsaid.

Ask yourself the following questions to improve your self-promotion techniques:

- ❒ What points did I make that seemed to interest the interviewer?
- ❒ Did I present my qualifications well?

- ❒ Did I overlook any qualifications that are pertinent to the job?
- ❒ Did I learn all I need to know about the job? or did I forget or hesitate to ask about factors that are important to me?
- ❒ Did I talk too much? too little?
- ❒ Did I interview the employer rather than permit the employer to interview me?
- ❒ Was I too tense?
- ❒ Was I too aggressive? not assertive enough?
- ❒ How can I improve my next interview?

The Campus Interview

Organizations that send their representatives to college campuses are actively recruiting college graduates. These representatives visit many campuses.

Schedule campus interviews and prepare thoroughly for them. Your objective during the campus interview is to be invited for a second interview or to take tests. Stress your strong points; listen attentively; in response to the interviewer's questions, relate how you meet the qualifications for the job; project your personality; and ask relevant questions.

Don't expect that because the interview is held on campus that it means you should dress casually. Give the interviewer a chance to see how you would look on the job if the interviewer hired you. You will look mature and capable of accepting responsibility if you dress accordingly. Furthermore, the interviewer will be comparing your appearance with that of administrative assistants who already work for the organization, not with the appearance of other college students.

If, as a result of the campus interview, you are invited for a second interview or to take tests, be sure to get the address of the building where you are to go. Do not assume that you know. Write down the date, time, address, and name of the person to whom you are to report.

Testing

The placement director and your instructors may know which organizations in your area give tests. If you apply for a job with an organization that administers tests, be psychologically prepared to take a keyboarding speed test, a word processing performance test, and perhaps a keyboarding production test in conjunction with the first interview. The tests will either be given then or will be scheduled for a separate session. Tests are usually given in the personnel office of the organization; they are not usually given in conjunction with campus interviews. Private employment agencies always test applicants for office jobs.

Many tests have time limits. Listen carefully to the instructions you receive. If you do not clearly understand what you are expected to do, ask questions. Ask questions before the test begins so that you can spend the full time allotted for the test actually performing the test.

You will be expected to perform at speed levels determined by the organization administering the tests. Test papers are usually evaluated by degree of accuracy.

Personality tests and mental ability tests are popular. It is not possible to prepare for these. The goal of these examinations is to determine which applicants will work well with existing staff members, which applicants will most likely share the company's goals, and which applicants have potential leadership skills.

The Second Interview

You may be invited for more than one interview. During the initial interview, members of the interview team will screen the interviewees. If tests are given as part of the screening, it will probably be the human resources department that administers them and evaluates the results.

A procedure commonly used is this. When human resources staff members discover applicants they are willing to recommend as candidates for specific jobs, they arrange interviews for the applicants with the actual employers. When you are told that you will be interviewed by the person who will be your manager if you are hired, you will know that your chances of getting the job are increasing. The final selection will be made by the person for whom the administrative assistant will work.

The initial interview, the testing, and the second interview may be conducted on separate days, or they may be part of one interviewing session. When you go for an interview, be prepared to follow through on any arrangements the personnel staff member offers to make for you.

The second interview provides you with an opportunity to promote yourself to the person for whom you would work. Emphasize your strong points. Be as relaxed and natural as possible so that the interviewer can detect your true personality. Ask questions about the scope of the job and about the responsibilities that the person performing it would have. Listen carefully, and answer the questions you are asked. When you know you want the job, say so. The interviewer is not just searching for a qualified applicant; the interviewer is searching for a person who is definitely interested in working for the organization.

Behavioural Descriptive Interviews

An applicant can prepare thoroughly for an interview; however, it is impossible to anticipate all possible interview scenarios. Behavioural descriptive interview questions are now commonly used by recruiters to sort facts from exaggerations. These interviews use a "domino" questioning technique, in which each question leads to the next and probes deeper into an experience or scenario described by the applicant. A typical set of behavioural interview questions is:

1. Describe a situation where you were a team leader in a professional environment and conflict arose within the team.
2. Who were the persons involved in the conflict?
3. What did you do to resolve this conflict?
4. What did you learn from this experience?
5. Since the conflict, how have you applied what you learned?
6. Where and when have you applied what you learned?
7. Who has benefited from your ability to resolve conflict?

Some applicants feel threatened and almost interrogated by the probing nature of these questions. However, these questions, if presented in a diplomatic manner, are highly successful in determining the best candidate. Because many people embellish their résumés and then perform well at exaggerating their talents during the interview, the best candidate is not always selected for the job.

Behavioural descriptive questions are not difficult to answer if the candidate has the experience the recruiter is seeking. If you are asked a behavioural descriptive question and simply don't have the experience necessary to answer the question, be honest. The best policy is to tell the interviewer that you have no experience in this particular area. If you have related experience, ask the recruiter if you might refer to a similar situation in a different type of environment.

Follow-up Letters

The letters essential for continuing and finalizing a job campaign fall into five categories: thank-you, reminder, inquiry, job acceptance, and job refusal. Key follow-up letters on the same quality paper you used for the résumé; be sure to include your return address, telephone and fax numbers, and e-mail address. Check them carefully for accuracy. Be sure that the company's name and the interviewer's name are spelled correctly.

Thank-You Letters

Writing a thank-you letter following a job interview is not a requirement but a courtesy. Always write a thank-you letter and send it immediately after the interview. If you want the job for which you were interviewed, you can use a thank-you letter to do far more than express appreciation to the interviewer. Not everyone writes thank-you letters; consequently, when your thank-you letter arrives at the interviewer's desk, it will single you out from other applicants and call attention once more to your application.

Say that you are definitely interested in the job and that you want to be considered seriously for it. When interviewers are considering several applicants with apparently equal qualifications, one of the questions they are trying to answer is, "Which Applicant has the keenest interest in working for our organization?"

Your letter can be short. In the opening paragraph thank the interviewer, mentioning either the day or the date of the interview and the specific job discussed. Use the remainder of the letter to refer to something specific about the interview and to express interest in the job. Close with a statement to let the interviewer know you are waiting for a reply. Refer to Figure 15-6 for an example of a thank-you letter.

Reminders

When you do not receive a response to an application or are told that your application has been placed on file, write another letter after a few weeks have elapsed to remind the personnel manager that you still are interested. You will find reminder letters especially helpful when you plan to move from one region of Canada to another and make inquiries about jobs months in advance of your availability for employment.

Do not assume that your résumé has been kept on file. Send another copy of your résumé with your reminder letter. In the opening paragraph, mention the job you applied for and when. In the body of the letter briefly state your interest in working for that particular organization, express confidence about what you can do for the organization, ask if an opening for the type of job you are seeking exists, and request, in case one does, that you be considered for it. You may be successful with a letter similar to the one in Figure 15-7.

Inquiries

Following a job interview, you can write a letter of inquiry or make a telephone call if you have not heard anything by the time the personnel manager said you would receive a reply. Do not be impatient. Wait a day or two beyond the time you are expecting a reply and, if you do not hear, telephone or write to inquire. If you are told that the job has not been filled, indicate that you definitely are interested.

Job Acceptance Letters

Even when you accept a job offer during an interview or over the telephone, follow up with a letter. You will

Figure 15-6 Thank-you letter.

Janelle Kisteleki

500 Richter Street, Kelowna, BC V1Y 2Z2
Tel 250-555-5555 E-mail: kisteleki@hotmail.com

February 11, 20xx

Mrs. Barbara Marino
1111 Orchard Steet
Kelowna, BC V1Y 2Z2

Dear Mrs. Marino:

Talking with you last Wednesday afternoon about the duties of an administrative assistant with Midwestern Products convinced me that this is exactly the position I am seeking.

I certainly appreciate the time you spent with me, discussing employment opportunities with your company and describing the job requirements for an administrative assistant's position. I feel confident I can meet these requirements, and I am waiting to hear that you also feel I can.

Sincerely,

Ms. Janelle Kisteleki

Ms. Janelle Kisteleki

probably receive a letter offering you a job and suggesting that you call to accept. Respond by telephone, but also send a letter to leave no doubt about your acceptance. The letter offering you the job, plus your written response, should contain all the elements of a contract and, as such, constitute a contract.

In the opening accept the job enthusiastically. Mention the specific job being accepted. If you have received a form for supplying additional information, complete it, enclose it, and refer to it in your letter. Repeat the report-to-work instructions, giving the date, time, and place. In either the beginning or the closing, express appreciation. Keep a copy of the letter of offer and your reply. Please refer to Figure 15-8 for an example of a job acceptance letter.

Job Refusal Letters

If you conduct a thorough job campaign, you may be offered more than one job and will have the problem of having to refuse all but one of them. Be as prompt in refusing as possible. If you have already accepted a job, refuse the second offer at once. This is a courtesy you owe the person who must search elsewhere to fill the job offered you.

Figure 15-7 Reminder letter.

Kristine Kingsley

1111 Wentworth Way
Toronto, ON M4P 1Z1
Tel 416-555-1111 E-mail: kristinek@z-wave.com

01 May 20xx

Mr. Sam Kimji
Human Resources Director
Modern Plastics
555 Bloor Street East
Toronto, ON M4W 2Z2

Dear Mr. Kimji:

Subject: Appointment to Discuss Qualifications

In January, I inquired about employment opportunities for administrative assistants with your company and sent you a résumé detailing my qualifications.

Modern Plastics is a company that has enjoyed rapid growth, and I would like to be a member of its dynamic team.

Next week I am moving to Toronto. May I please have an appointment during the week of May 25 to discuss my qualifications for employment as an administrative assistant with Modern Plastics? Please reply to my new Toronto mailing address or to my e-mail address shown above.

For your convenience, I am enclosing a copy of the cover letter and résumé that I sent to you in January.

I look forward to receiving a positive response. Thank you for your assistance.

Yours sincerely,

Kristine Kingsley

Kristine Kingsley

Enclosure

Figure 15-8 Job acceptance letter.

Chad Aplin

11 Highland Road, Halifax, Nova Scotia B3M 1X1
Tel 902-555-5555 Fax: 902-555-6666 E-mail: chad@hotmail.com

01 June 20xx

Ms. Samantha Valemeer
Director
International Markets Division
Midwestern Products
451 Atlantic Way
Halifax, NS B3M 2R2

Dear Ms. Valemeer:

Subject: Position as Administrative Assistant

As I expressed over the telephone, I am delighted to accept the position of administrative assistant in the International Markets Division of Midwestern Products.

Enclosed are the forms you requested I complete after our conference last week.

I appreciate the opportunity to join your team and am eager to commence work on Monday, June 16. Again, thank you for offering me the opportunity to work with Midwestern Products.

Sincerely,

Chad Aplin

Chad Aplin

Enclosures

Since your letter will be disappointing to the reader, you should organize it in the same way you organize other disappointing letters. Begin by making a favourable statement concerning your contact with the interviewer or about the organization. Express appreciation for the job offer at either the beginning or the end of the letter. Include at least one reason for refusing the job offer. State the refusal tactfully, but make it clear that you are refusing. By making a definite statement about already having accepted a job or about your continuing to search for a particular job, you will be refusing the offer without making a negative statement. Close with a pleasant comment.

Don't burn your bridges—you may want to work for the organization at some point in the future. Check your letter to make sure that the attitude reflected by your statements does not close the door for you. In Figure 15-9, the writer shows appreciation and says that she would be interested in a more senior position.

Figure 15-9 Job refusal letter.

Ms. Sabrina Tang

1010 Carlton Avenue, Toronto, ON M4W 1R1
Tel 416-555-1111 Fax: 416-555-3333 E-mail: stang@home.com

05 September 20xx

Mr. Jeremy Davis
Public Relations Consultant
AT&T Canada Corporation
1111 Bloor Street East
Toronto, ON M4W 3R3

Dear Ms. Davis:

Subject: Receptionist Position

Thank you for the job offer to become receptionist in the Public Relations Division of AT&T Canada Corporation. However, as I mentioned at the time of the interview, I am seeking a position as an administrative assistant. Another company in the city has offered me this level of employment and I have accepted it.

Ms. Davis, I appreciate the offer to work for your company and the interest you have shown in me. In the future, if a more senior position becomes available, I would be very interested in working for AT&T Canada Corporation.

Yours truly,

Sabrina Tang

Sabrina Tang

ELECTRONIC JOB SEARCH

Computers and telecommunications have changed almost every facet of the way we work. In fact, they now play a part in how we *search* for work. The Internet has become a popular tool for searching for available employment and for posting résumés for potential employers to view. Yet another innovation is the computer-scanned résumé; with this technology, specially prepared résumés get the attention of a computer before they attract the attention of an employer.

Using the Internet

The computer is a valuable job-searching tool. Searching the Internet for job opportunities will not eliminate the need to practise traditional job-hunting techniques, but it will add another dimension to your job search.

Job announcement databases are available for browsing. The National Association of Colleges and Employers (NACE) has a **home page** called JobWeb, on which job opportunities are published as well as useful career search information. By browsing through websites you will reach many on-line Canadian job-search facilities, such as

- CACEE (College and Career Educators and Employers)
- CareerBridge
- NetJobs
- JobMatch
- Canadian Job Exchange
- David Aplin & Associates
- WebJobs Nova Scotia.

In the highly competitive search for work, the Internet has become a new job market. The Internet may be used for job searching, but it is also useful for sending your résumé to one of the on-line career services.

Although the Internet may bring about job opportunities, ask yourself if you want your personal information to be so publicly available. At least in the traditional career search you could be selective as to who received your résumé.

Another option is available with some on-line career services. Your résumé is forwarded to the career service; the heading (your name, address, telephone number, fax number, and e-mail address) of the résumé is removed, so that only the body is left for display. Employers search the on-line résumé listings using key words. These words are the key competencies required to perform the job. Examples might be words like *supervisor, team leader, executive assistant, records management, diploma, degree*, and so on. When an employer believes that your credentials match a job opportunity available, the employer will offer to purchase the identifying header. With your permission, the on-line career service will release the header to the paying customer—the potential employer.

The above is a high-tech job search method that still allows you to protect your identity. As a job search tool, the Internet has this advantage: it enables you to reach a vast audience in almost no time at all. As the candidate database grows, more and more companies are subscribing to the Internet as a recruiting tool.

Electronically Scanned Résumés

A growing number of companies are using electronic scanning systems to digitally scan, store, and track résumés and covering letters. In fact, hundreds of résumés can be scanned in only a few minutes. When recruiters wish to retrieve or **short list** a group of appropriate candidates, they supply key words that are essential for the right applicant. These key words will identify expertise, experience, and education. For example, they might include such words as *bilingual, entrepreneur, desktop publishing, total quality management, supervisor, teams*, and so on. The computer software scans the database, and within minutes a list of applicants whose résumés match the stated criteria is brought to the screen.

Electronically scanned résumés save the recruiter an inordinate amount of time. However, an applicant who is unaware that his or her résumé is being electronically scanned may be preparing an ineffective document. Although the applicant may have extensive credentials, those credentials may go unnoticed if the scanner cannot identify them. However, scanning systems are rapidly becoming more advanced. To be certain that all the information on your résumé is collected by the electronic system, follow these tips for maximizing the computer's ability to read your résumé:

1. Use a standard typeface. Do not use italics.
2. Do not bold any of the text.
3. Do not use the underline feature.
4. Describe your personal traits in nouns, not verbs.
5. Use the key words found in the job ad.
6. Use straightforward words to describe your experience. Embellished terms will not be in the list of skills the recruiter is searching for.
7. Use multiple pages if necessary. Unlike humans, computers do not tire of reading.
8. Use common résumé headings such as Objective, Education, Experience, and Interests.

Figure 15-10 Partial résumé prepared for electronic scanning.

Ms. Kimberly Wong
10507 53 Avenue NW
Edmonton AB T6H 0R6
Tel (403) 478-1320
Fax (403) 478-2398
E-mail kimwong@netcom.ca

OBJECTIVE
To earn the position of administrative assistant with a company that has a progressive team spirit.

EDUCATION
September 1992–April 1994
Southern Alberta Institute of Technology
Office Administration Program
Calgary
Honours Diploma
Keyboarding 70 words per minute
Microsoft Word
PowerPoint
Microsoft Project
WordPerfect
Lotus Notes
President Office Administration Society
Team Leader Graduation Planning Committee
Leader Charity Fundraising

EXPERIENCE
May 1995–January 2000
Administrative Assistant
Coron Industries
Calgary
Supervisor of junior staff
Coordinator of budget
Coordinator of conferences and seminars
Designer of brochures and newsletters

May 1994–May 1995
Administrative Assistant
Image Publishers
Calgary
Supervisor of reception desk
Coordinator of media

9. Do not print your résumé on coloured paper.
10. Avoid using tabs.
11. Increase your lists of key words. Include specific software names such as *WordPerfect* and *Microsoft Word*.

Refer to Figure 15-10 for an example of a partial résumé that has been prepared for electronic scanning.

One advantage of an electronic scanning system is that electronic storage takes so much less space than paper storage. This means that résumés may be kept on file for an extended time.

If applicants are not aware of the electronic scanning process and submit attractive yet traditionally formatted résumés, they may not be identified by the computer, no matter how outstanding. The best approach when you do not know whether electronic or human screening will be used is to submit two résumés. The résumé intended for human scrutiny should be printed on attractive paper, using highlighting features, graphic lines, and so on; the résumé destined for electronic scanning should follow the basic format described in the enumerated list above. The reason you have included two résumés should be briefly explained in your cover letter.

Questions for Study and Review

1. Explain the meaning of the term *networking*. State ways you could network to improve your opportunity for employment.
2. What services are generally available to the college graduate through the college placement office?
3. Explain how business news items can be a valuable source of job prospects.
4. What is the advantage of searching for job openings that are not advertised?
5. Compare the services of private and public employment agencies.
6. How can you find out about and apply for a position with the Government of Canada?
7. How does answering a newspaper advertisement for a job differ from using other means of seeking employment?
8. Why might a company place a blind job advertisement in the newspaper?
9. Name the principal sources of information for seeking employment in another geographic area.
10. What is the meaning of the term *curriculum vitae*?
11. What is the main purpose of the résumé?
12. Should you include the names of references on your résumé? Explain.
13. Suggest why a prospective employer would be interested in information about an applicant's work experience unrelated to office work.
14. What is the purpose of the application letter?
15. How does the purpose of the solicited application letter differ from the purpose of the prospecting application letter?
16. Why would an organization request that an applicant fill out its application form when the applicant has already submitted a résumé?
17. If a question on an application form asks what salary you are expecting, how should you complete this question?
18. State six guidelines for being prepared to complete a job application form.
19. What information about an applicant can an interviewer glean from a personal interview that cannot be learned from the applicant's résumé or transcript?
20. Recommend ten guidelines for personal grooming in preparation for an interview.
21. List four items that should not be taken to the interview. List six items that *should* be taken to an interview.
22. Describe the contents of a portfolio you would carry with you on an interview.
23. Suggest three appropriate questions for the applicant to ask at the interview.
24. Prepare answers to the interview questions provided in this chapter.
25. At what stage in an interview should salary range be discussed?
26. How will you know when the interview is over?
27. State four guidelines for effective closure to a job interview.
28. Explain how the purpose of the second interview differs from the purpose of the initial interview.
29. What is the purpose of behavioural descriptive interviews?

30. If you do not have the experience to answer a behavioural descriptive interview question, how should you respond?
31. List two advantages of writing a thank-you letter following a job interview.
32. Why should you write a job acceptance letter in addition to accepting a job by telephone?
33. How might the Internet assist you in getting employment?
34. How can you maintain confidentiality while using the Internet to advertise your credentials for potential employment?
35. State eight guidelines for preparing a résumé to be electronically scanned.
36. Give three reasons why companies might prefer electronically scanned résumés over the traditional method of screening résumés.

Spelling Reinforcement

appraisal	counselor/counsellor	impatient	résumé
associates	credentials	library	scrutinize
campaign	director	prospective	significant
consequently	entrepreneurial	qualifications	solicited

Job-Hunting Situations

1. During the past week you were interviewed by Company A, Company B, and Company C for office positions. At the end of each interview the interviewer said that you had the qualifications being sought and that you would hear from the Personnel Department of the company within a few days. On Thursday of this week you received a telephone call from Company A offering you a job and requesting that you let Company A know by Monday whether or not you will accept the job offer. You feel that Company A is making you a good offer, but you would prefer to work for Company B. You are not sure that you are being considered by Company B. You are beginning to feel nervous because you would like to work for Company A if you do not get a job offer from Company B. What should you do?
2. A job announcement posted on the office technology bulletin board appeals to you. A variety of responsibilities are listed. You believe that you have the qualifications required for the job. The salary is excellent. The address of the company is local, but you have never heard of the company. You would like to know more about the company before you apply. You went to the library to find out about the company. Neither you nor the librarian who helped you could find out anything about the company. What can you do next to become informed about the company?
3. You and your close friend, Laurie, have gone to five campus interviews, all with the same companies. You have been invited to second interviews by two companies. Today Laurie told you that she has her heart set on working for Company E, and that she has not heard from Company E. In fact, Laurie has not heard from any of the companies that interviewed her on campus. Laurie is asking you what to do. Company E is one of the companies that invited you for a second interview. However, you did not tell Laurie that you had heard from Company E. You want the job with Company E if it is offered to you. What should you do? What should you say to Laurie?

Special Reports

1. Research the Internet for on-line career centres. Make a list of web pages and their e-mail addresses. Share this information with your fellow students through a class presentation.
2. Find an ad in a current newspaper that you are interested in answering. Write the opening paragraph of the letter you would send in response to the ad. Submit the paragraph to your instructor for approval.
3. Assume that you have been offered a job that you do not want to accept. Write a job refusal letter. Submit the letter to your instructor for approval.

Production Challenges

15–A Personal Inventory

Supplies needed:

- *Personal Inventory Form, Forms 15-A-1 and 15-A-2, pages 457 and 458 and Working Papers Disk, File 15-A.*

Completing a personal inventory is a useful step in developing a successful résumé. Attempt to make exhaustive lists when you work through the Personal Inventory Form. Share the results of your form with a family member and again with a fellow student. These people will probably be able to help you add to your list. When your Personal Inventory Form is complete, show your instructor.

15–B Electronically Scanned Resume

Supplies needed:

- *Personal Inventory Forms 15-A-1 and 15-A-2, completed in Challenge 15-A*
- *Plain bond paper*

Use the Personal Inventory Form, completed in 15-A, and the information in this chapter to prepare an attractive résumé for human scanning. Then prepare one for electronic scanning. Write a cover letter for an unsolicited job as an administrative assistant for Millennium Appliances. Your letter must explain why you are submitting two résumés.

15-C Your Job Campaign

Supplies needed:

- *Checklist for Your Job Campaign, Form 15-C-1, page 459 and Working Papers Disk, File 15-C*
- *Application for Employment, Forms 15-C-2 and 15-C-3, pages 460 and 461*
- *Plain bond paper*

All thirteen activities in 15-C are real. They provide guidelines for conducting your own job campaign.

Planning and conducting your own job campaign should be an exciting part of your office procedures course. Possessing office administration skills, knowledge of the business world, and a desire to work in an office are assets in your favour. However, today's job market is competitive. To land the job you have prepared for, you must conduct a successful job campaign.

Start your job campaign at the beginning of the semester in which you are seeking full-time employment. Continue your job campaign throughout the semester or until you land a job.

Your instructor will assist you in planning your job campaign and will suggest the dates on which you should complete many of the job campaign activities. Enter the due dates on Form 15-C-1.

Employment-Campaign Activities

1. Using the suggestions given in Chapter 15, prepare a self-appraisal inventory. Use Form 15-A. It should be helpful to you in determining which qualifications to emphasize during an interview and in preparing your résumé.
2. Look up a local corporation in a financial manual or directory available either at your college or in the public library. Prepare a concise report on the corporation and submit the report to your instructor. Refer to Chapter 12 for information on financial publications.
3. Obtain, from the placement office of your college, literature that may be helpful to you in your job campaign. Read the literature and then file it for ready reference in a job campaign file that you create.
4. Join a committee of peers to study employment opportunities for administrative assistants in your community. Separate committees should be organized on the basis of where the members of the class plan to seek employment—for instance, corporations,

small companies, law firms, medical offices, hospitals, financial institutions, government offices, and other broad classifications. Consult several sources to study one organization. Obtain literature made available to prospective employees, ask corporations for annual reports and brochures, confer with friends and former graduates who work in the various types of offices being studied. Share your findings with the members of your committee and other classmates.

5. Prepare for a job interview. Key a list of qualifications you plan to emphasize during the interview. Anticipate the questions you will be asked and list them. Also key a list of questions you may ask the interviewer. Submit a copy of your qualifications and of your questions to your instructor.
6. Prepare a résumé for employment with a specific organization. Use the example and suggested outline for preparing a résumé presented in Chapter 15. Submit your résumé to your instructor.
7. Write a prospecting job application letter (or a solicited one). Review the suggestions given in Chapter 15. Use the letter to sell yourself to a prospective employer.
8. As soon as your instructor returns your résumé, incorporate the suggestions that your instructor made and print copies of your résumé for use in your job campaign. Take your résumé with you to your job interviews. If you mail a job application letter to a prospective employer, enclose a copy of your résumé.
9. Build a portfolio displaying samples of your perfect work. Remember that the portfolio must be organized with a table of contents. Tabs and dividers are also useful for keeping the portfolio organized. Review the discussion on portfolios in this chapter to see that you have included the correct items.
10. For several weeks, study the help-wanted ads in the newspaper published in the community in which you are seeking employment. Circle the ads that reflect employment opportunities for administrative assistants. Analyze the ads to obtain information about job trends, qualifications sought, salary, and so on. Put the help-wanted pages in your job campaign portfolio.
11. Using the questions presented in Chapter 15, write an evaluation of your performance during an early job interview. Make suggestions that should be helpful to you during your next interview. List both what you think you did well and what you believe you should improve. Share what you have learned about job interviews with the members of your class.
12. To gain confidence in completing an application form neatly and accurately, complete the application form provided. Study the form carefully, and then key your answers in the spaces provided. (Key an application form when it is possible to do so; however, if you are handed an application form immediately before a job interview, you may be expected to complete it in longhand.)
13. When you accept a job, write a job acceptance letter. Submit a copy of your job acceptance letter and of a job refusal letter, if you write one, to your instructor.

World Wide Websites

Career Management and Job Search Help

www.careerlab.com/jobmenu.htm
This page is designed to help you manage your career and includes sections on career counselling, résumés and cover letters, and job search essentials.

Strive—The Career Guide to the New Economy

www.strivemag.com/
This magazine is about excelling in your career.

Wired Hired

www.wiredhired.com

GO Career Resources

infoseek.go.com/Topic/Careers?sv=M1
This page has links to resumé-writing pages.

Professional Development

Outline

Eliminate the Stereotype
Professional Image

Prepare for Advancement
Advancing by Education
Joining a Professional Association
Increasing Technical Certification
Becoming a Supervisor
Becoming an Office Manager
Perspectives: "Defining the True Professional"

Continue to Develop Professionally

Learning Outcomes

At the completion of this chapter the student will be able to:

1. Recommend ways of eliminating the office stereotype.
2. Describe the professional image that challenges the stereotype.
3. Identify methods for job advancement.
4. Describe the educational programs offered by professional associations.
5. Explain how the position of administrative assistant is excellent training for management.
6. Develop a strategy for professional development.

GRADUATE PROFILE

Linda O'Connor Palasz, B.A., B.Ed.
Teacher

Beaufort-Delta Education Council
Inuvik, Northwest Territories

College Graduation:
Computer Applications Diploma
MICAN Business College
Ottawa, Ontario
1998

"There is plenty of untapped talent in offices."

When Linda O'Connor Palasz is not in the classroom, you might find her researching and collecting local Native art or even testing her gourmet talents in the kitchen—cooking caribou, muskox, and char are her new challenges!

As a teacher of high-risk / high-needs students, she works hard to stay current on this topic by researching and consulting with the excellent resources available in Inuvik. Linda's caring and dedicated spirit is evident by her approach to teaching. In fact, her decision to become a teacher was predicated by her desire to bring stability into the lives of students who might be potential future clients of Canada's correctional facilities.

Although Linda is currently a teacher, she spent many years as an administrative assistant, and therefore, remains sensitive to the importance of support staff in the office. Linda explains that the school administrative assistant "is the first person to deal with many, many issues in a day: the late student, the sick student, the irate parent, ... the upset teacher, the overburdened vice principal ... the supplier, the caretaker, the repairman ..." Everyone wants the administrative assistant's attention and help too.

Linda is grateful for her training in office administration and emphasizes that it was invaluable when she continued her studies in criminology, then education, and most recently computer applications. She firmly believes that "Anyone who is in office administration, and wants to teach, would find studying made immeasurably easier while pursuing the necessary degrees, and would find those office skills to be extremely valuable time-savers in all the administrative work teachers have to do."

As a professional, Linda respects and supports her leaders because she understands the challenge in being an effective team leader. When a situation is genuinely wrong, she addresses it through the proper channels and does not make it a matter for public discussion. In keeping with her respect for others, Linda refuses to participate in staff room gossip and to engage in complaints against other staff members. If she recognizes a potentially explosive circumstance, she likes to defuse it and help to negotiate a settlement. As an effective team member, Linda recommends that when you are called upon to work cooperatively, you must trust yourself to be a professional with expertise worth sharing.

A common scenario for a Canadian family is one in which both adults are wage earners *and* parents. Few adults can expect to work at a *job* for only a limited time and then be supported by another adult. Typically, Canadian adults now plan to have more than one career, several jobs, greater responsibilities, and more years of work than previous generations.

An administrative assistant's career is often a stepping stone to other types of careers, including ones that involve supervision and management. Women and men who initially select a career as an administrative assistant should mentally prepare themselves for advancement, and for greater challenges and responsibilities.

Although women have dominated the clerical field for many years, the earliest office clerks and typists were almost always men. The administrative assistant's role has become broader and more diversified, demanding thorough knowledge of computers and software, as well as strong problem-solving and critical thinking skills. Because this career requires people who have technical expertise as well as excellent human relations skills, it is now attracting competent people from both genders, various age groups, and diverse backgrounds.

ELIMINATE THE STEREOTYPE

The attitude that someone is "just a secretary" has no place in the contemporary office. This stereotype developed at a time when women were encouraged to "just get a job." It was perceived that serious positions in the workforce should be held by men, since men were to be providers for the family.

This scenario is, of course, no longer accurate or valid. The stereotype of an office worker who typed, filed, took shorthand, did only routine tasks, and was too emotional has been replaced by a new professional image.

Professional Image

The new professional image reflects

- an educated and skilled employee
- a team player who is expected to contribute valuable ideas
- a polished individual whose appearance and communication style are "professional"
- a person who can problem-solve and integrate ideas
- a person who takes pride in each piece of work he or she produces
- an employee who works for the betterment of the organization and is not self-serving
- a person who takes pride in the career of administrative assistant and who has aspirations for the future
- an employee who manages assignments by applying quality standards
- an employee who is willing to work hard and accept new and more challenging responsibilities.

The best way to eliminate the stereotypical view is for men and women in this profession to initiate the change themselves. By living up to the new professional image of an administrative assistant, they will replace the old stereotype.

The best way to develop the professional image of an administrative assistant is to

1. set short- and long-term goals that are obtainable
2. develop desired strategies for achieving these goals
3. set time lines for each step in the strategies
4. begin to carry out the steps immediately.

To accomplish these goals, you may need support and resources from management. If so, select a person in management whom you can rely on for assistance and with whom you can develop a **mentor** relationship.

PREPARE FOR ADVANCEMENT

When you are comfortably settled in your first job, your initial reaction may be to take it easy. Do not coast. Many opportunities for advancement are available in business, but advancement comes only to those who are prepared to accept additional responsibilities.

Federal legislation barring discrimination in employment on the basis of gender has opened up new opportunities for both men and women at the managerial level. Many organizations are committed to being equal opportunity employers.

"Never stop looking for ways to further your education and develop your skills."

Shannon Mullin, Graduate
New Brunswick Community College
Miramichi Campus

Consequently, women have more opportunity for advancement today than ever before. Yet neither men nor women can advance to higher-level positions unless they are prepared to accept the responsibilities that go with those positions. Many women advance to managerial positions, but only a small percentage advance to the *top* managerial positions. To change this, women must prepare for advancement by improving their credentials.

During your first year of employment, set a professional goal for yourself. Do you want to become an executive assistant, a supervisor, or a manager? Once you have decided on your goal, study to provide yourself with the background necessary to achieve that goal. And once you achieve that goal, set another one.

Advancing by Education

A college diploma or university degree is very useful in advancing to a higher-level office position. In fact, any additional education will prove helpful. When you have an efficient and effective performance record, additional education may provide the competitive edge you need to get ahead.

Many organizations offer in-house training. These courses usually are of short duration and do not carry college or university credit. Talk with your supervisor to find out what is available. Express an interest in taking courses that will help you perform your job or advance in your career. If you successfully complete enough courses, they will become an impressive part of your employment record and will support your efforts toward promotion.

Most large organizations have educational benefits. Some organizations will pay all or part of the tuition for job-related courses that are successfully completed. Ask your supervisor about educational benefits; express your interest in taking job-related courses. Consider courses in these areas:

- project management
- team building

- communication
- time management
- business administration
- software applications
- organizational behaviour
- office supervision/management.

The emphasis in education today is on continuing education. By committing yourself to lifelong learning, you will be increasing your opportunities for promotion and enriching your personal life. Employees who believe in and practise continuous education are more likely to survive during periods of company **right-sizing** and recession.

As an administrative assistant, you choose either to have a job or to have a professional career. This is determined in large part by your attitude. If you have a strong desire to advance and to earn a reputation for being a professional who contributes to the organization and produces only quality work, you will seek ways to achieve professional recognition.

pro-Link

Why is there a **Professional Secretaries Week®**? Should there be one? Here are some facts that will help you to answer these questions.

- Professional Secretaries Week® is observed internationally every year in April.
- The International Association of Administrative Professionals (IAAP) was the first organizer of this special event.
- IAAP is the sole official sponsor of Professional Secretaries Week®.
- The observance of this week is designed to educate the public, and especially business leaders, about the critical contribution made by office administrators and the need for continuous upgrading and education in this profession.
- There are approximately 400,000 office professionals employed in Canada.
- In Canada, common forms of recognition during this week are: gifts, time off, flowers, and complimentary lunches.
- Many Canadian administrative professionals report that being sponsored for a professional seminar or course, or receiving a subscription to a professional magazine is the recognition they most prefer.

Joining a Professional Association

Becoming a member of a professional association is an excellent way of gaining educational skills and new credentials in your field. A number of associations that promote office professionalism are available. The following discussion will identify three associations that offer credentials to office professionals willing to study and take the challenge.

If you are interested in joining or establishing a branch of one of these professional associations in your community, write or call the head office for information. Addresses and telephone numbers of registered associations are available in the *Directory of Associations in Canada* or the *Encyclopedia of Associations*. The *Encyclopedia of Associations* lists international associations as well as those active in Canada. Both of these books can be found in public libraries. Of course, information about associations is readily available on the Internet.

Association of Administrative Assistants (AAA)

The Association of Administrative Assistants is a Canadian, chartered, nonprofit organization, formed in 1951. The motto of the AAA is "Professionalism through Education." The association has the mandate of encouraging office professionals to upgrade skills and enhance professionalism. By assisting members to continually develop their skills, knowledge, and professional development, the AAA will meet its mission to enhance employment opportunities and contributions to the workplace and to the community.

It awards the designation of Qualified Administrative Assistant (QAA) to those who meet the criteria. A sample certificate is displayed in Figure 16-1. In order to achieve the QAA, office professionals must complete seven courses either through correspondence or through study at one of 17 Canadian universities that offer the program. The program consists of three compulsory courses and four electives. The compulsory courses are:

- Business Administration
- Organizational Behaviour
- Effective Business English

Examples of elective courses are:

- Marketing
- Economics
- Human Resource Management
- Financial Accounting
- Psychology
- Commercial Law

- Principles and Practices of Supervision
- Interpersonal Communication

These courses help the participants to be valuable team participants and to understand corporate initiatives. The QAA is a recognizable designation and identifies individuals as dedicated office professionals. Earning this designation will no doubt give an applicant a competitive edge when applying on more senior positions. To learn more about the Association of Administrative Assistants and the QAA certification, contact the association through their website at www.aaa.ca.

International Association of Administrative Professionals® (IAAP®)

IAAP® is an association committed to advancing office professionals by promoting high standards and enhancing the image of the profession. This association provides resources and information to help its members enhance their skills so they may contribute to their organizations in an even more effective manner. Not only does it work to improve the professional skills of its members, it also works to educate the public about the value of the office professional.

The educational program of IAAP® includes workshops, seminars, and study courses on administrative topics. This proactive organization holds an international conference each year and publishes a popular magazine called *OFFICEPro®*.

IAAP® has a professional certification program where successful candidates earn their Certified Professional Secretary® (CPS®). Refer to Figure 16-2 for a sample of the CPS® certification. To earn this certification, candidates must pass a comprehensive examination that lasts for one full day. The exam topics are:

- Behavioural Science in Business
- Communication
- Finance
- Office Technology
- Business law

For more information about the IAAP® and the CPS®, contact IAAP® through their website at www.iaap-hq.org.

National Association of Legal Secretaries® (NALS®)

The National Association of Legal Secretaries® is another professional association that provides a testing program and professional certification for administrative

Figure 16-1 QAA Certificate.

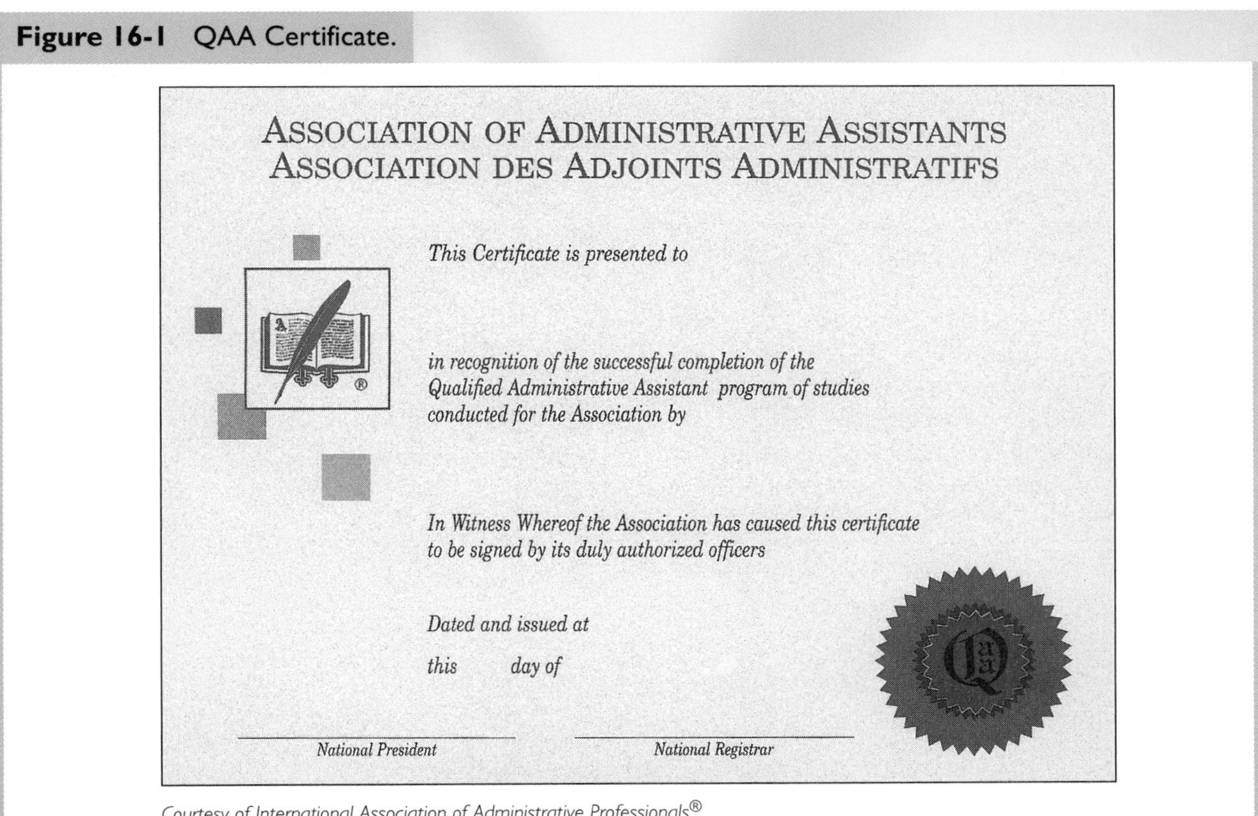

Courtesy of International Association of Administrative Professionals®

Figure 16-2 CPS® Certificate.

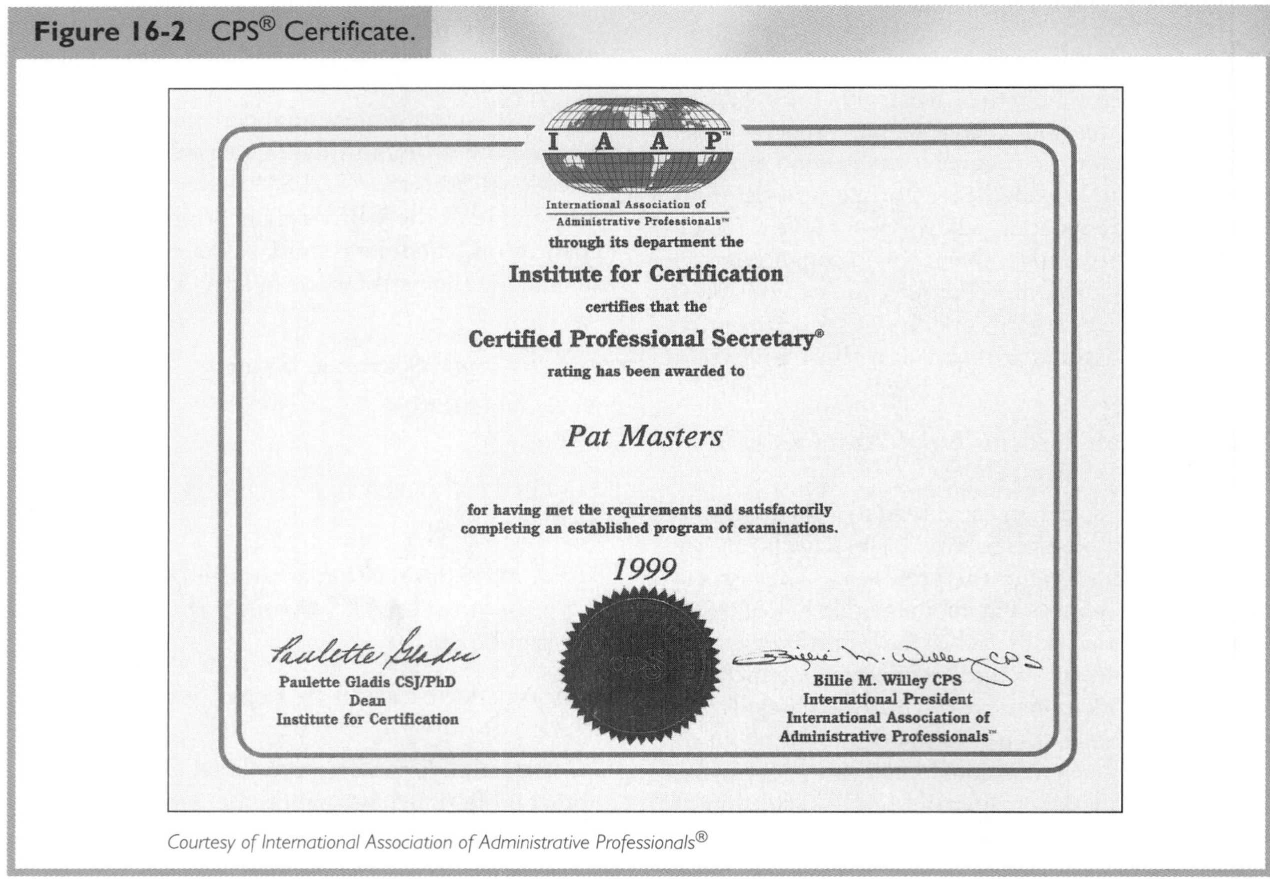

Courtesy of International Association of Administrative Professionals®

assistants. Part of its mandate is to offer continuing legal-education training programs and networking for its members. Office professionals who wish to demonstrate their commitment and aptitude for the legal secretarial profession are encouraged to take the six-hour, three-part examination leading to the Accredited Legal Secretary® (ALS®) certificate. To be eligible for this examination, applicants must have completed either the legal training course offered by NALS®, or an accredited secretarial program, or have completed one year of experience as a legal secretary. However, applicants for this certification need not be members of NALS®.

Those who attain the ALS® are awarded the certificate shown in Figure 16-3. Testing for the ALS® certificate covers the following topics:

- Communication—written, comprehension, and application
- Office administration
- Legal terminology
- Accounting
- Ethics
- Human relations
- Applied office procedures

NALS also offers the Professional Legal Secretary® (PLS®) certification. This designation is for exceptional legal secretaries willing to take the challenge of the two-day, seven-part examination. Applicants must have three years of experience in a legal office but they do not need to be members of NALS®. The three-year requirement may be partially waived if the applicant holds the ALS certification or has post-secondary degrees. The following topics are included in the PLS® examination:

- Office procedures
- Written communication skills
- Ethics
- Legal secretarial skills
- Judgment
- Accounting
- Legal knowledge and procedures

Those applicants who are successful in the examination will earn the PLS® certification shown in Figure 16-3.

If you require more information, contact NALS through their website at www.nals.org.

Figure 16-3 PLS® Certificate.

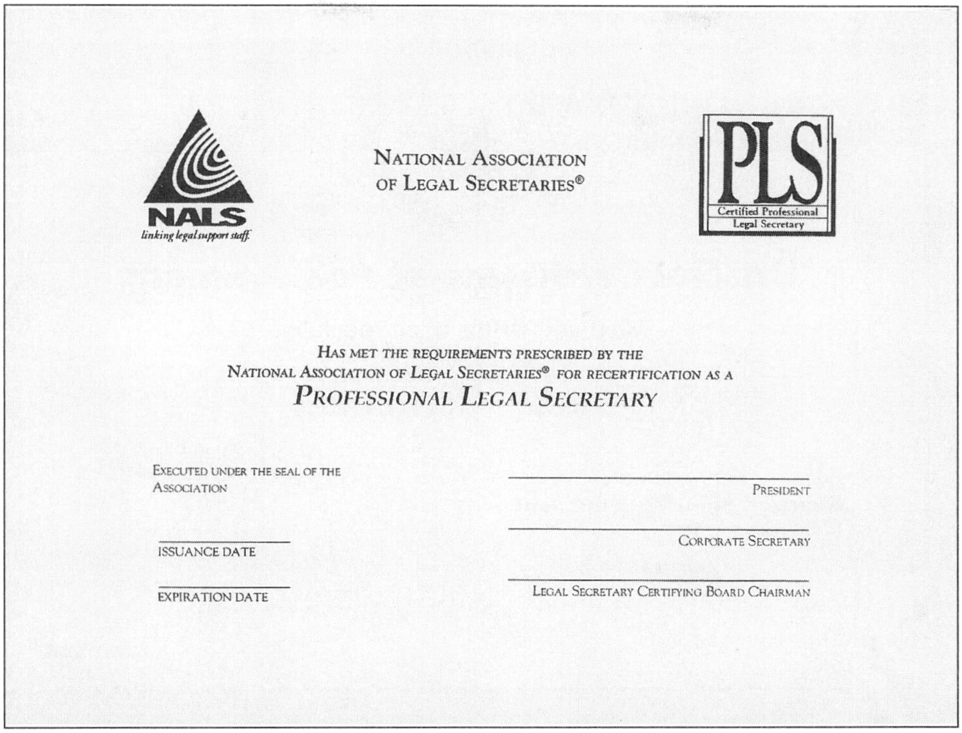

NALS
linking legal support staff

NATIONAL ASSOCIATION
OF LEGAL SECRETARIES®

PLS
Certified Professional
Legal Secretary

HAS MET THE REQUIREMENTS PRESCRIBED BY THE
NATIONAL ASSOCIATION OF LEGAL SECRETARIES® FOR RECERTIFICATION AS A
PROFESSIONAL LEGAL SECRETARY

EXECUTED UNDER THE SEAL OF THE
ASSOCIATION

PRESIDENT

ISSUANCE DATE

CORPORATE SECRETARY

EXPIRATION DATE

LEGAL SECRETARY CERTIFYING BOARD CHAIRMAN

Courtesy of National Association of Legal Secretaries®

Increasing Technical Certification

Technical skills are some of the most highly valued skills of office professionals. By continuing to upgrade technical skills, office professionals can improve their résumés and increase their opportunities for employment and advancement. To validate technical skills, office professionals should earn certification from recognized programs. One of the most recognized and popular types of technical certification is the Microsoft Office User Specialist (MOUS) program.

The MOUS program provides three levels of expertise—Proficient, Expert, and Master. Candidates begin by selecting the Microsoft Office product on which they desire certification. If candidates require training prior to taking the challenge, the MOUS program provides full training packages. Next, candidates determine the level of expertise they wish to challenge. It is not necessary to begin with the Proficient level or to work all the way through the Expert and finally Master levels.

Once the challengers pass the examination, they are awarded certification. The example shown in Figure 16-4 is for a Proficient level of Microsoft Word 97. These certificates, like all professional certification, are excellent items for a portfolio. At the Proficient and Expert levels, candidates are awarded a certificate for each Microsoft Office product exam that they successfully complete. However, the single Master level certificate is reserved only for candidates who successfully complete all the Expert exams for the Microsoft Office products. At the time of printing this book, there were four exams at the Expert level. All four exams would have to be successfully completed in order for a candidate to be awarded the Master level certification.

To learn more about the MOUS certification contact Microsoft at their website www.mous.net.

Becoming a Supervisor

Many supervisors step into the field of supervision without formal training for the position. This acquired position is often the result of seniority, hard work, and success as an employee. Since a supervisory job requires a person who can be effective with both workers and top management, specialized training is a genuine asset.

Your first task in any supervisory role is to become skilled in human relations, so that you can direct work performed by other employees and at the same time provide them with personal satisfaction in their work. Experience in performing your own job, even when you

Figure 16-4 MOUS Certificate.

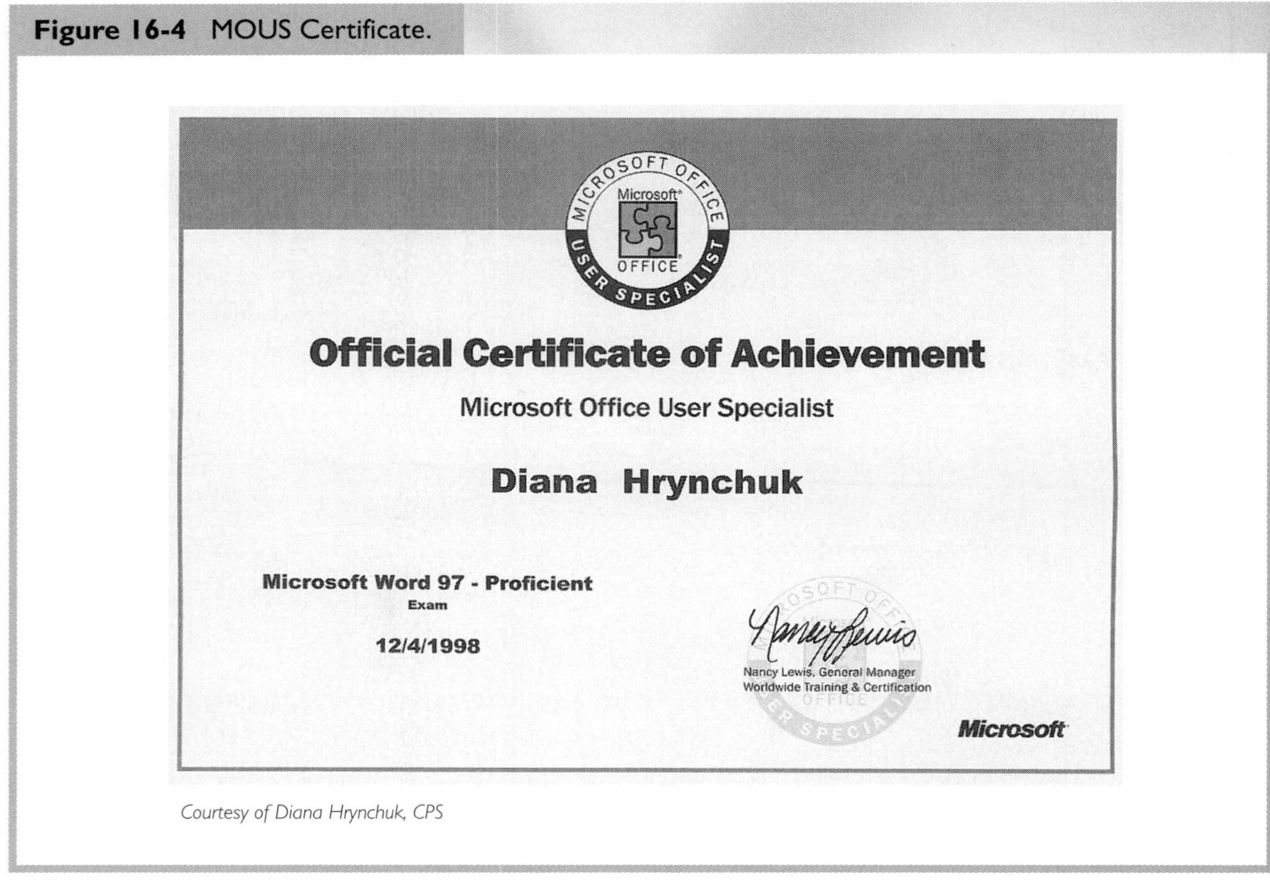

Courtesy of Diana Hrynchuk, CPS

perform it exceptionally well, is not enough to prepare you for leading others.

Being a good supervisor requires actual experience. You can *learn* to accept responsibility as a supervisor and to carry out your function effectively. You can learn from many sources that will be available to you, as well as from experience.

Through discussions with your manager, arrive at an understanding of what your supervisory responsibilities are and what authority you are being given for carrying them out. In addition, those whom you supervise should be told what your role is.

Someone within the Human Resources department will discuss general policies with new employees and provide them with booklets dealing with employee rights and benefits. Nevertheless, one of your ongoing functions will be to interpret personnel policies to employees who have questions. Study the organization's policies until you can answer questions accurately and clearly. Keep your file on changes in policies and procedures up to date. Be able to recall what the changes are if they apply directly to your area of work.

You can learn from your manager. Observe and recall supervisory principles and techniques that your manager uses successfully. Decide if you can apply them in your situation.

Get acquainted with other supervisors and encourage them to share with you their ideas for handling supervisory problems. Be a good listener; learn the "why" as well as the "what" of the problems and solutions being discussed.

Strive to improve your ability to communicate. Much of your success as a supervisor will depend on effective communication.

As a supervisor, self-appraisal is very important. Envision your total job, which could include staffing, planning, organizing, directing, coordinating, reporting, and budgeting. Frequently evaluate your own performance. Think in terms of what you did well and why. Recognize areas in which you need to improve. Concentrate on them until you *do* improve. Build confidence in yourself as a supervisor. As you do, you will become more relaxed; this in turn will enable others to approach you with more ease.

Many books and magazine articles have been published on supervision, personnel management, business psychology, personal relations in business, motivation, communications, and so on. College courses are available on these same topics. Seek materials and/or enroll in courses that will be helpful to you.

Technical know-how is an asset for a supervisor. However, the supervisor's role is to lead and guide. A good supervisor helps the *employees* become the technical experts and relies on their expertise and recommendations to improve and enhance current processes.

You will be directing the work of people who are producing products and services; thus, it will be a benefit to learn about equipment, supplies, and methods that will enable employees to perform their jobs more economically and effectively. Keep up to date on the technical aspects of your job by reading periodicals on office products and methods and by making inquiries of suppliers. You can earn respect by being knowledgable about the hardware and software your employees are using, and by empowering employees to make recommendations and decisions on matters that directly affect their work.

Along with your staff, examine methods to improve the work you are supervising. Brainstorm with your office team in an effort to find the best solutions. Do not be discouraged if management does not readily accept the recommendations of your office team. Management must be convinced that your new methods will benefit the company and be cost-effective.

Becoming an Office Manager

If you aspire to be an office manager, your chances of reaching your goal are much greater than those of your predecessors. In the past, an administrative assistant who reached a management position usually did so after many years of service. Today, more management positions are available to administrative assistants who have educational credentials, regardless of length of service.

Although an academic degree is not always required, the competition for management jobs is intense. If you are currently working toward a diploma in office technology, you may be interested in pursuing a bachelor's degree in business administration (B.B.A.) as your next step.

There is no prescribed method or guaranteed success strategy for becoming a manager. Much of your success will be based on your ability to market your skills and to demonstrate competence in leadership. Volunteering to lead committees and projects is an excellent way to practise your leadership skills, demonstrate your commitment to the organization, learn more about the organization, and gain recognition as a potential manager.

Reading management journals and joining a management association are progressive steps toward a career in office management. Information about a variety of management societies is available on the Internet. The BB&C Association Management Services is actually

Figure 16-5 The ability to relate to clients and co-workers is essential for professional growth.

an *association of associations*. It was established to provide quality leadership and support for business associations. The website provides information on its services and benefits as well as a directory of Canadian business associations. If you are interested in joining a management/business association, you may wish to contact BB&C at this e-mail address:

www.bbandc.com/

The role of Administrative Assistant is an excellent one for managerial training. In fact, the administrative assistant is constantly making decisions and managing projects, people, and time. The following are examples of how the administrative assistant acts as a manager.

Manager of Communications

One of the most important functions of the administrative assistant is to create and edit office documentation. As well, it is the administrative assistant who is the expert on communication equipment (computers, faxes, telephone systems, photocopiers, etc.) in the office.

Manager of Crises

A skilled office professional will be able to remain calm, maintain office efficiency, and handle people with diplomacy even through an office crisis.

Manager of Records and Information

Controlling paper and electronic files is usually the responsibility of the administrative assistant. The administrative assistant develops the system for organizing, finding, retrieving, and storing information.

Manager of Public Relations

The administrative assistant is the first person in the organization that the public sees and speaks to. The image that administrative assistants project will reflect on the organization they represent. Administrative assistants must manage the reception area and the public.

PERSPECTIVES

Defining the True Professional

By Charlene Ashborn

Consider your performance from your supervisor's perspective. Your version of what is "professional" may differ from your boss'.

You're a professional right? After all, you go to the office every day and do the work required of you. You've got the paycheck to prove it. But, does your supervisor consider you to be a professional or just another office drone, clocking time until the nex payday?

How many of us have ever looked at our work lives from the perspective of our supervisors? Probably not too many. Oh, we get our annual evaluation with areas of improvement noted. However, we all know that these often are formalities designed to satisfy government/corporate regulations. The real evaluations come in the form of pay raises, promotions, and perks such as development/educational opportunities. Think back to the times you saw colleagues receive merit pay increases, a bonus, or written compliments from the supervisor. Maybe you asked yourself why they got the reward when you worked just as hard. Apparently, your supervisor doesn't share your viewpoint or you'd be on the receiving end of these rewards.

Consider some possible reasons why your version of "professional" may not coincide with your supervisors.'

1. **Punctuality.** While this seems pretty basic, are you truly punctual or do you arrive a few minutes late every day? Are you routinely late returning from lunch or your breaks? Sure, your boss claims not to mind, but you can be sure your habits are noted.

2. **Respect.** Do you respect your boss' position and that of other executives within your company? This isn't a question of whether you like your boss. You may consider your boss completely inept, but try not to show it. After all, someone must have thought this person had the necessary skills to get the job done. Remember, your boss is the one who has your career, and paycheck, in his or her hands. Respecting your company's hierrachy falls under this category. Just because you can now e-mail your company's CEO doesn't mean you should. The respect you extend to your supervisor also should be shown to everyone you come in contact with.

3. **Quality of work.** Is your work of top-notch quality? There are always going to be occasional typos, but is the final copy perfect?

4. **Dress appropriately**. Some workplaces have no formal dress code. However, most office staff employ common sense when getting dressed in the morning. Wear jeans and run the risk of being asked to go home and change. Make sure your clothes are clean and pressed and appropriate for work. Remember, there may be a time when your boss unexpectedly asks you to attend a function in her place. The more appropriately you're dressed, the more you'll fit in and be a better representative for your department.

5. **Be accountable.** When you're assigned a task, do it. More importantly, take responsibility for the outcome, whether positive or negative.

6. **Assert yourself.** Don't be afraid to ask questions or inform your supervisor of previous priorities. The latter is especially important not that more office staff have multiple supervisors. Don't meekly accept work knowing that you won't be able to complete it. Your supervisor won't appreciate the fact that you tried, but will remember the fact that you failed to get it done. Part of being assertive means being able to ask for additional training, if necessary.

7. **Avoid stagnation.** Don't allow yourself to be defined by your job description. Like the flu, the "it's not my job" syndrome is easy to acquire but difficult to eradicate. In many instances, requests may fall under another colleague's jurisdiction, especially if you work in a highly structured environment such as the government. However, even within tightly defined job descriptions, there's room to learn or apply new skills. With the emphasis on being a team player, refusing to move outside the confines of your present duties doesn't look like conformity to corporate regulations; rather, it appears to be a sign of inflexibility and inability to work with others—two very important traits of all office professionals.

8. **Take initiative.** To make your job more interesting, look for ways you can implement other frequently used skills while benefiting your department. Your boss may become aware of hidden talents. Who knows where it could lead in terms of future job opportunities.

Charlene Ashburn is the publicity chair for the Pomona Chapter of IAAP in Walnut, CA. She can be reached at 909/869-3948 or via e-mail at caashborn@csupomona.edu.

Reprinted courtesy of OfficePRO.

Manager of Planning

It is the administrative assistant who keeps track of meetings, schedules, deadlines, and the whereabouts of the office staff.

Manager of Policies and Procedures

Office policies and procedures need to be interpreted, updated, and organized. Of course, the administrative assistant manages these responsibilities.

Manager of Inventory

Maintaining control of inventory, ordering new stock, and selecting the best product for the best price are just some of the responsibilities of the administrative assistant in the role of inventory manager.

CONTINUE TO DEVELOP PROFESSIONALLY

As you read this chapter, you may conclude that preparation for a successful career is endless. Your conclusion is correct.

Continue to increase both your general knowledge of office procedures and your special skills. The ability to relate well to customers, clients, and co-workers is essential. A working knowledge of computer software—for word processing, spreadsheets, project management, graphics, desktop publishing, electronic messaging and calendaring, database management, and so on—is essential. Computer technology and software is changing at a rapid pace. Develop an affinity for new equipment and learn the new applications.

"I've learned that when one door closes, another opens. Always be open to new opportunities."

Heather Edwards, Graduate
Sault College of Applied Arts and Technology

To advance in your career, you need a broad, general education. An understanding of how to deal with all types of people and business and management concepts is a valuable asset. Organizations are looking for employees who are critical thinkers and problem solvers.

If you wish to advance professionally, make decisions and carry them out. Then take responsibility for both your successes and your failures. Procrastination and the inability to make decisions will be viewed as weaknesses and will prevent opportunities for promotion.

To continue to grow professionally, you should

- subscribe to and read professional magazines
- listen to motivational or informational tapes while you drive to work
- read office bulletins and newsletters to remain up to date on corporate affairs
- attend seminars, conventions, conferences, and workshops to keep abreast of new technology and procedures
- volunteer to be a committee member or chairperson for special events
- apply or offer to work on special task forces
- request that you be placed on the office circulation list for all informational and professional materials
- make a point of meeting new people and listening to their ideas
- read the newspaper to follow local and foreign events
- travel to as many locations as possible
- visit libraries and make note of the many resources available to you
- make appointments with the corporate competition to learn more about other companies
- become aware of your company's policies
- make a point of watching documentaries on television and reading or studying new topics
- make learning a lifelong commitment.

Professional growth is stimulating. It has a motivating effect, and your reward will be a successful and enjoyable career.

Questions for Study and Review

1. As an administrative assistant, how can you eliminate the stereotype associated with office workers of the past?
2. Name three associations that provide professional certification for administrative assistants. What are the certifications they award? How can an office professional obtain these certifications?

3. What is required for an office professional to gain Microsoft certification? What levels of certification are available? How could this certification be useful to the office professional?
4. Why does a supervisor need to increase his or her skills in human relations? How can a supervisor do this?
5. Name three ways to learn supervision skills on the job.
6. Describe five ways that the position of administrative assistant is excellent training for management.
7. Suggest ten ways to grow professionally once you are already employed.

Spelling Reinforcement

certification	implemented	personnel	responsibility
concentrate	initiative	premises	stereotype
discrimination	integrate	professional	supervisor
eligible	modification	pursue	technology
emphasis	orientation	recommendations	tremendous

On-the-Job Situations

1. You have been employed by a large organization as an administrative assistant for five years. You aspire to become a supervisor. At least one supervisor in your area has been appointed during each of the five years. Recently you built up your hopes that you might be appointed to a supervisory position, but you were not. You feel that you definitely were overlooked and are so depressed that you want to quit your job. What questions should you ask yourself to logically analyze what is happening? Also list what you think you could do to be considered for the next supervisory position. Submit your questions and list to your instructor.
2. You supervise a temporary employee, Karen, who assists you with your work. It is Friday afternoon, and she is keying a multipage report. Your manager is waiting for the report and intends to send it to the head office by facsimile as soon as it is finished. Karen volunteered to stay after 5:00 p.m. to finish the report; you leave. As soon as Karen finishes the report, she prints it, hands it to the manager, and leaves the office. Early Monday morning the manager calls you to her office to explain that she could not send the report because it contained errors. Why is she discussing this with you? What should you have done?
3. You supervise two full-time office workers. One of them told you she was ill and asked to go home at noon. You insisted that deadlines had to be met and asked that she stay to finish her work if she possibly could. About two o'clock this employee passed out and had to be rushed to the hospital. You realize that you have made a mistake. What can you do now? Suggest alternatives you could have pursued to get the employee's work finished.

Special Reports

1. Use the Internet to find current information on office supervision. List the website and the author. Summarize what you have read and verbally share this information with your instructor and other class members.
2. Find articles and tips from current issues of *OFFICEPro®* magazine that discuss professional growth. Summarize the tips into a brief report. Share this information with your instructor and other class members.

Working Papers

Vacation Requests

Charlene Azam

Mon., June 9 through Fri., June 13

Mon, Aug. 18 through Fri., Aug. 22

Mon., Dec. 22 through Tues., Dec. 30

Sid Levine

Mon., July 7 through Fri., July 11

Mon., Aug 18 through Fri., Aug 22

Mon., Sept. 8 through Fri., Sept. 12

J.R. Rush

Mon., Aug 25 through Fri., Aug 29

Mon., Oct. 13 through Fri., Oct. 17

Mon., Oct. 20 through Fri., Oct 24

Linda Yee

Mon., Dec. 9 through Fri., Dec. 12

Mon., Dec. 15 through Fri., Dec. 19

Mon., Dec. 22 through Tues., Dec. 30

William Wilson

Mon., July 14 through Fri., July 18

MILLENNIUM REQUISITION FOR SUPPLIES		
REQUESTED BY:		REQUISITION NO.:
LOCATION:		DATE:
QUANTITY	UNIT	DESCRIPTION
SIGNATURE:		

Form In-B-1

MILLENNIUM REQUISITION FOR SUPPLIES		
REQUESTED BY:		REQUISITION NO.:
LOCATION:		DATE:
QUANTITY	UNIT	DESCRIPTION
SIGNATURE:		

Form In-B-2

LETTER FOR CORRECTION

Mr. Roy Baines ______________________

Office Equiptment Supply ______________________

2331 Princess St. ______________________

Kingston, ON K7m-3G1 ______________________

SUBJECT: TRAINING ______________________

Dear Mr. Bainis, ______________________

Thank you for instaling our new office ______________________

equipment so promptly. The decorater putt the ______________________

finishing touchs on our offices tody. ______________________

Based on what you told us last weak, ______________________

training on the microcomputer can start ______________________

immediatly. Since both unites have been ______________________

instaled, can you start our training sessions ______________________

on Monday? ______________________

Mr. Bains, you gave us helpfull advise, ______________________

and we appreciate it. we are looking foreward ______________________

to working with the training directer next ______________________

weak. ______________________

Sincerely Yours, ______________________

NAME:

TIME DISTRIBUTION CHART

DATE:

Major Activities	Wilson	Hrs.	Azam	Hrs.	Levine	Hrs.	Rush	Hrs.	Yee	Hrs.	For Group	Hrs.	TOTAL
TOTAL													

Form 1-A-1

Notes on Time Spent, May 19–23

Mon.		
May 19	Processing postal mail	1 1/2 hrs
	Answering e-mail	1 hr
	Handling telephone calls	1 3/4 hrs
	Answering voice mail	3/4 hr
	Revising draft of report for Ms. Azam	2 hrs
	Filing	1/2 hr
	Total	7 1/2 hrs
Tues.		
May 20	Processing postal mail	1/2 hr
	Answering e-mail	1/2 hr
	Handling telephone calls	1 hr
	Answering voice mail	1 hr
	Verifying statistical data using word processor (for Mr. Levine)	2 1/2 hrs
	Revising draft for Mrs. Yee	1 hr
	Filing	1/2 hr
	Replenishing supplies for 5 executives	1/2 hr
	Total	7 1/2 hrs

Wed.		
May 21	Processing postal mail	1 hr
	Answering e-mail	1 hr
	Handling telephone calls	1 1/2 hrs
	Answering voice mail	1/2 hr
	Filing	1/2 hr
	Receiving callers for Mr. Wilson	1/2 hr
	Making final copy	
	of report for Mr. Rush	2 hrs
	Keying data for Mr. Wilson	1/2 hr
	Total	7 1/2 hrs
Thurs.		
May 22	Processing postal mail	1 hrs
	Answering email	1 hr
	Handling telephone calls	2 hrs
	Answering voice mail	1/2 hr
	Revise draft of a report for	
	Mr. Wilson	2 hrs
	Filing	1/2 hr
	Receiving callers for Mr. Wilson	1/2 hr
	Total	7 1/2 hrs

Fri.		
May 23	Processing postal mail	1 hr
	Answering e-mail	1 hr
	Handling telephone calls	1 hr
	Answering voice mail	1/2 hr
	Drafting report for Ms. Azam	2 hrs
	Preparing final copy of report for Mr. Levine	1 hr
	Filing	1/2 hr
	Planning work for following week	1/2 hr
	Total	7 1/2 hrs

Name:	DAILY PLAN CHART	Date:

Rank	Calls to	Phone No.	Notes	Rank	Reminders

Rank	Letters and Memos to	Notes	Rank	Other Tasks

Priority Rank: 1 = Urgent; 2 = Today; 3 = Tomorrow; 4 = This Week

Form 2-A

ALIGNING COPY

Regardless of what you are keyboarding, display it on the page so that it will be pleasing to the eye. Proper alignment and balanced use of white space enhances error-free copy. The centring and automatic tabulation features make horizontal alignment easy. Follow the rules and guidelines illustrated here to align copy correctly.

Columns of Figures and Words

Align columns of Arabic numbers on the right; align columns of words on the left. A column of Roman Numerals is sometimes aligned on the left, but in outlines and tables roman numerals are aligned on the right.

5	V	Five
18	XVIII	Eighteen
1	I	One
37	XXXVI	Thirty seven
6	VI	Six

Align a column of figures containing decimals at the decimal point:

33.27
6,428.07
1.15
84.00

When a name, title or other item in an address, tabulated column, or signature block is so long that it must be keyed on two lines, indent the second line two or three spaces to indicate that it is a continuation of the preceeding line:

Mrs. Geneva Amway
Director of Training
and Personnel Services
Computer Software, Inc.
9915 -- 108
   Street
Edmonton, AB
T5K 2G8

Enumerated Sentences

When keyboarding, enumerated sentences that occupy more than one line, align the first word of the second line with the first word of the preceeding line, not the number, thus:

1. A simple-numeric subject method can be designed by using three-digit numbers for the main headings and two-digit numbers for the major divisions.
2. The duplex-numeric subject method provides for an unlimited number of main subject headings, major divisions, and subdivisions.

When it is necessary to save space, begin the second line flush with the number.

Outline

The forms of outlines differ, but all outlines are variations of the following basic form: major divisions, roman numerals; first-order subheadings, capital letters, second-order sub-headings, arabic numerals; subdivisions of second-order subheadings, lower case letters; additional subdivisions, Arabic numbers in parentheses and then lower case letters in parenthesis.

Align the capital letters designating the first order subheadings with the first word of a major subdivision; align the Arabic numbers designating the second-order subheadings with the first word of the first-order subheadings.

ALIGNING COPY

Regardless of what you are keyboarding, display it on the page so that it will be pleasing to the eye. Proper alignment and balanced use of white space enhance error-free copy. The centring and automatic tabulation features make horizontal alignment easy. Follow the rules and guidelines illustrated here to align copy correctly.

Columns of Figures and Words

Align columns of Arabic numbers on the right; align columns of words on the left. A column of Roman numerals is sometimes aligned on the left, but in outlines and tables Roman numerals are aligned on the right.

5	V	Five
18	XVIII	Eighteen
1	I	One
37	XXXVII	Thirty-seven
6	VI	Six

Align a column of figures containing decimals at the decimal point:

33.27
6,428.07
1.15
84.00

When a name, title, or other item in an address, tabulated column, or signature block is so long that it must be typed on two lines, indent the second line two or three spaces to indicate that it is a continuation of the preceding line:

Mrs. Geneva Amway
Director of Training
   and Personnel Services
Computer Software, Inc.
9915 108 Street
Edmonton, AB T5K 2G8

Form 3-B-2

Enumerated Sentences

When keyboarding enumerated sentences that occupy more than one line, align the first word of the second line with the first word of the preceding line, not the number, thus:

1. A simple-numeric subject method can be designed by using three-digit numbers for the main headings and two-digit numbers for the major divisions.

2. The duplex-numeric subject method provides for an unlimited number of main subject headings, major divisions, and subdivisions.

When it is necessary to save space, begin the second line flush with the number.

Outline

The forms of outlines differ, but all outlines are variations of the following basic form: major divisions, Roman numerals; first-order subheadings, capital letters; second-order subheadings, lower case letters; additional subdivisions, Arabic numbers in parentheses and then lower case letters in parentheses.

Align the capital letters designating the first-order subheadings with the first word of a major subdivision; align the Arabic numbers designating the second-order subheadings with the first word of the first-order subheadings.

SUPERVISION

As a supervisor, you must rely on others to accomplish your goals. To perform the human relations aspects of a supervisory job smoothly, develop an awareness of basic principles of supervision and become skilled in applying them.

- insert "you should" before "develop"

Recruiting Employees

Involve your manager and the personnel department in the selection of a new employee whom you will supervise. However, your responsibilities may range from very little responsibility to a major role.

- insert "always" after "should"

When you are recruiting an employee, begin with an up-to-date description of the job to be filled. List the duties to be performed and the qualifications. Rank the qualifications in the order of importance for the job. Consider the applicant's potential for promotion within the organizaton, for an objective of every organization is promotion from within.

- insert "needed to perform the job" at end of second sentence
- delete the third sentence

Use the list during the interview. Learn how to conduct job interviews. Consult references on personal management for techniques to apply. Interview more than one applicant for each job.

In making the final selection, use all the criteria available concerning each applicant. After you have narrowed the selection to two or three prospects, discuss them with your manager. Solicit the questions and comments of your manager.

-change "solicit" to "ask for"

Spend ample time in making the selection. By making the right selection, you can recruit a productive worker who enjoys her job. The wrong selection can result in work problems or personnel problems or both and may eventualy lead to employment termination.

- delete "who enjoys her job"
- insert "and happy" after "productive"

Orienting the Employee

How an employee is treated is an important factor in morale building in any office. Allow time on your schedule for helping the new employee to adjust.

- insert "on the first day" after "treated"

Behave in a friendly way and introduce the new employee to the others in the office with whom she will be closely associated. Explain briefly what each one does.

Go to the work station and identify where to put her personal belongings. Tour the office building, pointing out the rest room or lounge, coffee shop, cafeteria, and building entrances. If parking facilities are provided, show where to make arrangements for parking.

Even though the personnel department may have explained the working hours, discuss starting time and your expectations regarding breaks during the working day. Arrange a lunch with others for the first few days. If your organization does not have a personnel department, provide a brief on all the personnel policies yourself.

Give her an overview of the job and communicate that you expect the new employee to work into the job gradually. Provide a manual or written instructions which apply to the specific tasks. Explain how to use the organization's telephone directory, pointing out names necessary to know. Usually the names of executives and of departments are located in one section of the directory.

As you talk, allow time for questions and comments. And then provide some work. Be considerate and convey the impression that you are considerate. At the end of the first day the new employee should be saying, at least to herself, "I'm going to like this."

– on the last sentence, delete "at least to herself" and the commas

Teaching

One of your main functions will be teaching the new employee to perform the job with a minimum of supervision. Start with a part of the job that will be fairly easy to perform and then gradually provide guidance into the total job. Find out what is already known about the type of work to be performed.

Provide the new hire with written instructions and illustrations. Either issue an office manual or, if one is not available, prepare the instructions yourself. Demonstrate as well as explain.

Leave her to work alone as soon as you can. Check frequently, but do not over supervise. Be willing to answer questions at any time.

Assigning Work Loads

You can pave the way for an employee to experience a feeling of accomplishment by dividing work into batches and giving the employee one batch at a time, perhaps an assignment which can be finished in two hours. Setting subgoals for the employees you supervise will be an important part of your work.

- change "which" to "that"
- after "hours" insert "Nobody likes to face an endless task."

Check the finished work at the time it is submitted to you to assure the employee that it is satisfactory and to spot errors which must be corrected.

Give new employees some repetitive tasks enabling them to work successfully for a period of time without asking for help. However, rotate the work to provide enough variety to keep the employee from becoming bored or experiencing unnecessary fatigue.

Workers experience the greatest job satisfaction from performing the complete job. Therefore, look for ways to change a new employee's assignment from performing a segment of a job to that of beginning a job and following it through to completion.

- at the end of paragraph add "Workers take pride in seeing their work in final form."

Gaining Cooperation and Respect

One way to gain the cooperation of employees is to be cooperative yourself. Cooperation and respect are earned. To be successful as a supervisor, you must earn the respect of those whom you supervise.

Two major factors in gaining cooperation and respect are how the supervisor plans, organizes, and schedules work and the supervisor's attitude toward the employees.

Some supervisors create problems which need not exist because their performance as a supervisor is inadequate.

- change "which" to "that"

A supervisor's attitude toward the employees should reflect respect for them, a recognition of their needs, and a sincere appreciation of their contribution to the objectives of the organization. A successful supervisor will request that work be done. There is no need to destroy morale by demanding or controlling with fear. However, a successful supervisor must be impartial, and this requires being firm and consistent. Rules and regulations must be followed by everyone.

-after request insert ", not demand,"

Personnel Problems

- insert "Handling" at beginning of heading

- move this entire section to before "Gaining Cooperation"

Personnel problems will arise, and each one must be studied carefully and handled as a specific case. Be careful not to show favoritism. You can keep down much resentment by being absolutely impartial.

Before you take action on any problem, get the facts and look for the problem behind the immediate problem; for instance, an employee's absenteeism may be due to lack of interest in the job.

A new supervisor can take problems too seriously. Do not be overly concerned about problems. Do not spend your time on a problem that will correct itself, yet face up to the problems you must handle. A subtle approach may be the best means of tackling certain problems; for example, you can appeal to an employee to dress more appropriately by complimenting appropriate dress; or you can set short-range goals for a worker who lacks perseverance rather than addressing the issue directly.

- make a new paragraph after "handle".

Advising on Personal Problems

Employees who respect you and look to you for leadership on the job may seek your advice concerning personal problems. Do not encourage employees to bring their personal problems to you, but when someone does, listen. Serious personal problems do effect a person's job performance. Knowing an employee's problem will enable you to be sympathetic and understanding.

- insert the last sentence after "listen."
- change "effect" to "affect"

Do not give advice on personal problems. Listen while an employee talks out the problem and help identify choices and the consequences related to each choice.

Be extremely cautious in dealing with personal problems. Proceed cautiously so that an employee who makes the wrong decision cannot and would not blame you for poor advice. A person who has serious difficulties frequently tries to place blame.

- switch second and third sentences

Please make the following global changes.

1. Make "work station" one word.
2. Change "her" or "she" to "the employee".
3. Bold the title and side headings.
4. The title must be in all caps and the side headings in initial caps.
5. Side headings must be underlined.
6. Check for correct spelling.
7. Triple-space before each side heading and double-space after it.
8. Triple-space after the title.

Here are some additional changes (not global).

1. pg. 2, under Orienting the Employee
   a. first paragraph, line 3
      — change "her" to "the"
   b. second paragraph
      — insert "he or" before "she"
   c. third paragraph, line 1
      — make end of sentence read ", and indicate where coats are kept."
   d. third paragraph, lines 4 and 5
      — make end of sentence read "explain the arrangements for parking."
   e. fourth paragraph, line 1
      —change "her" to "the"

2. pg. 3, first paragraph
   a. delete first occurrence of "her"
   b. before "apply" change "which" to "that."
   c. delete "one section of" in the last sentence
3. pg 3, first paragraph under heading "Teaching"
   a. change "which" to "that"
   b. delete "you told her," and insert "was said"
4. pg 6, in sentence above "Advising on Personal Problems"
   a. omit "she is"
   b. delete "with her" at end of sentence
5. pg 6, second paragraph from bottom
   a. change first occurrence of "her" to "the"

MA *Millennium Appliances, Inc.*
3431 Bloor Street, Toronto, ON M8X 1G4
Tel (416) 795-2893 Fax (416) 795-3982

TO: Mr William Wilson

FROM: (YOUR NAME)

DATE: October 10, 20--

SUBJECT: Resevrations for Seminar

Reservations have been con firmed at the Splendid Hotel for a meeting room and a luncheons for Friday Nov. 16, from nine until five o'clock.for the seminar on "Supervising Employees".

The meeting room, called the Rose Garden, will seat 125 people. The room is well lighted, beautifully Decorated, and faces the rose garden. The chairs are comforable.

While I was at the splendid hotel, I asked about parking space anditalked with the banquet mgr. about a lunchoen menu. Parking space isad-equate. Mr. Lawrence, the banquet manager, gave me a choice of menus. the ist of choices available is attached. Do you have a preference? We must give a firm com mitment on the number who will attend the luncheom by ten oclock the day of the luncheon.

MA *Millennium Appliances, Inc.*
3431 Bloor Street, Toronto, ON M8X 1G4
Tel (416) 795-2893 Fax (416) 795-3982

MA *Millennium Appliances, Inc.*
3431 Bloor Street, Toronto, ON M8X 1G4
Tel (416) 795-2893 Fax (416) 795-3982

MA *Millennium Appliances, Inc.*

3431 Bloor Street, Toronto, ON M8X 1G4
Tel (416) 795-2893 Fax (416) 795-3982

Form 5-A-3

MA ***Millennium Appliances, Inc.***

3431 Bloor Street, Toronto, ON M8X 1G4
Tel (416) 795-2893 Fax (416) 795-3982

NOTES ON INCOMING MAIL FOR MONDAY, JULY 14

1. The July issue of Sales and Marketing Management.
2. A personal letter for Charlene Azam.
3. A complaint from a customer in the Midwestern Region. The white shade of the new dishwasher she had installed does not match her other white appliances.
4. A letter to Mr. Wilson asking him to speak at the International Conference of the Administrative Management Society.
5. A letter from Microwave Ovens, Inc. saying that the catalogue Mr. Wilson has requested is out of print and will be mailed as soon as it is off the press.
6. The July issue of Management World.
7. A memorandum from the Personnel Department on new personnel policies for Millennium Appliances, Inc.
8. A letter from the sales office in Edmonton, Alberta, saying that the demand for appliances in almond colour is twice as great as that for appliances in other colours. What can be done to increase the shipments of almond appliances?
9. The August issue of Administrative Management.
10. A letter from a customer in Vancouver complaining that the surface on the hood installed with her new electric range is peeling. Will Millennium Appliances replace the hood?
11. A sales letter from Microwave Ovens, Inc. on the new features of their latest microwave oven.
12. A letter from the manager of the Western Manufacturing Plant offering suggestions for speeding up delivery of appliances after they are manufactured.
13. A letter from the sales office in Fredericton saying that the demand for appliances in almond colour is twice as great as that for appliances in other colours. Send more almond appliances.
14. A letter from the Midwestern Manufacturing Plant saying that the parts ordered are not available and will have to be manufactured.
15. A letter from Maybelle Anderson giving the title of her talk for the November Sales Seminar.
16. A complaint from a customer in the Eastern Region. She is dissatisfied with her electric range, which is only two years old, because the element in the oven is burned out. Will Millennium Appliances replace the element?
17. A request from the Executive Vice President asking for a comparative sales report for the past five years.
18. An expiration notice for Administrative Management.
19. A letter from the local Chamber of Commerce asking Mr. Wilson to serve as Chairman of the Community Development Committee.
20. A letter from Jack Winfield cancelling the appointment he has with Mr. Wilson on Friday, August 22.

Form 6-A-1

MAIL-EXPECTED RECORD

EXPECTED FROM	DESCRIPTION OF DOCUMENT	DATE RECEIVED	FOLLOW-UP SENT

Form 6-A-2

DAILY MAIL RECORD

Date Received	Description Of Mail Received	Receiver Of Document	Action To Be Taken	Follow-up Completed

Form 6-A-3

TO DO
TODAY

Date ______________ Completed ☑

______________________________ ☐

______________________________ ☐

______________________________ ☐

______________________________ ☐

______________________________ ☐

______________________________ ☐

______________________________ ☐

______________________________ ☐

______________________________ ☐

Form 6-A-4

ROUTING SLIP			
SEQUENCE	TEAM MEMBER	DATE	INITIAL
	C. Azam		
	S. Levine		
	J. Rush		
	L. Yee		

This routing slip was initiated on ______________________

Please return to W. Wilson by ______________________

Form 6-A-5

ROUTING SLIP			
SEQUENCE	TEAM MEMBER	DATE	INITIAL
	C. Azam		
	S. Levine		
	J. Rush		
	L. Yee		

This routing slip was initiated on ______________________

Please return to W. Wilson by ______________________

Form 6-A-6

ROUTING SLIP			
SEQUENCE	TEAM MEMBER	DATE	INITIAL
	C. Azam		
	S. Levine		
	J. Rush		
	L. Yee		

This routing slip was initiated on ______________________

Please return to W. Wilson by ______________________

Form 6-A-7

ROUTING SLIP			
SEQUENCE	TEAM MEMBER	DATE	INITIAL
	C. Azam		
	S. Levine		
	J. Rush		
	L. Yee		

This routing slip was initiated on ______________________

Please return to W. Wilson by ______________________

Form 6-A-8

LIST OF OUTGOING MAIL

Item	Types of Mail
1. Cheques	
2. Handwritten letter	
3. Keys	
4. Package weighing 26 kg	
5. Business reply cards	
6. Photocopy of a letter	
7. Bulk bills and statements	
8. Postcards	
9. Regularly issued periodicals	
10. Catalogue with 26 bound pages	
11. Film sent to a school	
12. Parcel with an invoice enclosed	
13. Unaddressed magazines	
14. An Excel attachment	

Form 6-B

CHECKING POSTAL SERVICES

Instructions: *Use information collected from CPC to answer the following questions.*

1. What is the fee to send a single letter by Priority Courier to a city in the next province or territory?

2. Explain how the special delivery service works. What is the fee to send an Expedited Parcel weighing 0.6 kg to the next province or territory? A hardcopy signature retrieval is requested when you send the item.

3. What would it cost to insure a ring sent through the mail and costing $375?

4. What are the three services for which CPC will provide Registered Mail?

5. If you sent a letter to another Canadian location, and you wished to register the letter, how much would the service cost you? This letter weighs 35 g. You wish to have a hardcopy signature receipt, which you request when you mail the letter.

6. What would be the postal fee on a COD in Canada where the package was valued at $156.75?

7. If you wish to send a postcard weighing less than 30 g from a Canadian location to Italy, how much postage will you have to pay?

8. For which services can you purchase COD?

9. If you sent a large XPRESSPOST item from Kelowna to Halifax COD, what would be the service delivery time?

Form 6-C

ANSWER SHEET FOR 7-A

A	B	C	D	E	F	G	H	I	J	K	L	M	N	O	P	Q	R	S	T	U	V	W	X	Y	Z

Form 7-A

ANSWER SHEET FOR 7-B

A	B	C	D	E	F	G	H	I	J	K	L	M	N	O	P	Q	R	S	T	U	V	W	X	Y	Z

Form 7-B

ANSWER SHEET FOR 7-C

A	B	C	D	E	F	G	H	I	J	K	L	M	N	O	P	Q	R	S	T	U	V	W	X	Y	Z

Form 7-C

MR. WILSON'S CALENDAR	
DATE	
TIME	APPOINTMENTS
0800	
0820	
0840	
0900	
0920	
0940	
1000	
1020	
1040	
1100	
1120	
1140	
1200	
1220	
1240	
1300	
1320	
1340	
1400	
1420	
1440	
1500	
1520	
1540	
1600	
1620	
1640	
REMINDERS	

Form 8-A-1

ADMIN. ASSISTANT'S CALENDAR	
DATE	
TIME	APPOINTMENTS
0800	
0820	
0840	
0900	
0920	
0940	
1000	
1020	
1040	
1100	
1120	
1140	
1200	
1220	
1240	
1300	
1320	
1340	
1400	
1420	
1440	
1500	
1520	
1540	
1600	
1620	
1640	
REMINDERS	

Form 8-A-2

To ____________________

Date ____________ Time ________

WHILE YOU WERE OUT

M ____________________

of ____________________

Phone No. ____________ Ext. ________

TELEPHONED	☐	PLEASE CALL	☐
CAME TO SEE YOU	☐	WILL CALL AGAIN	☐
WANTS TO SEE YOU	☐	URGENT	☐
		RETURNED YOUR CALL	☐

Message ____________________

Taken by ____________________

Form 9-A-1

To ____________________

Date ____________ Time ________

WHILE YOU WERE OUT

M ____________________

of ____________________

Phone No. ____________ Ext. ________

TELEPHONED	☐	PLEASE CALL	☐
CAME TO SEE YOU	☐	WILL CALL AGAIN	☐
WANTS TO SEE YOU	☐	URGENT	☐
		RETURNED YOUR CALL	☐

Message ____________________

Taken by ____________________

Form 9-A-2

To ____________________

Date ____________ Time ________

WHILE YOU WERE OUT

M ____________________

of ____________________

Phone No. ____________ Ext. ________

TELEPHONED	☐	PLEASE CALL	☐
CAME TO SEE YOU	☐	WILL CALL AGAIN	☐
WANTS TO SEE YOU	☐	URGENT	☐
		RETURNED YOUR CALL	☐

Message ____________________

Taken by ____________________

Form 9-A-3

To ____________________

Date ____________ Time ________

WHILE YOU WERE OUT

M ____________________

of ____________________

Phone No. ____________ Ext. ________

TELEPHONED	☐	PLEASE CALL	☐
CAME TO SEE YOU	☐	WILL CALL AGAIN	☐
WANTS TO SEE YOU	☐	URGENT	☐
		RETURNED YOUR CALL	☐

Message ____________________

Taken by ____________________

Form 9-A-4

Form 9-B-1

Form 9-B-2

TELEPHONE SERVICES

Instructions: Answer the following questions in the space provided. Research for all answers should be gathered from your local telephone directory.

1. List the following emergency numbers.

   a. fire ______________________

   b. police ______________________

   c. your doctor ______________________

   d. hospital closest to home ______________________

   e. ambulance ______________________

2. List the following general information numbers.

   a. gas trouble ______________________

   b. power trouble ______________________

   c. water trouble ______________________

   d. time ______________________

3. List the area codes for the following locations.

   a. Vancouver

   b. Calgary

   c. Saskatoon

   d. Sault Ste. Marie

   e. Montreal

   f. Winnipeg

   g. Edmonton

   h. Seattle

   i. Ottawa

   j. Yellowknife

   k. Whitehorse

   l. Halifax

4. In what part of the telephone directory do you find provincial government listings?

5. What is the telephone number for information on labour standards? (Clue - This deals with a provincial government department.)

6. If you wished to inquire about obtaining a driver's examination, what number would you call? (Clue - This deals with a provincial government department.)

7. In what part of the telephone directory do you find federal government listings?

Form 9-C-1

8. If you wished to receive information about filing your federal income tax return, what number would you call?

9. If you wished to place a complaint with your local division of the Royal Canadian Mounted Police, what number would you call?

10. List the names and telephone numbers for two travel agencies in your town or city.

    a.

    b.

11. List the names and telephone numbers for two general contractors located in your town or city.

    a.

    b.

12. List the names and telephone numbers for two automobile dealers that sell Chevrolet cars in your town or city.

    a.

    b.

13. List the name, address, and telephone number for an office building located in your town or city.

14. List the name, address, and telephone number for a professional moving and storage company located in your town or city.

15. If you place a call when your local time is 1400, what time is it in the offices located in the following cities?

    a. Victoria
    b. Ottawa
    c. Winnipeg
    d. Montreal
    e. Regina
    f. Edmonton
    g. Halifax
    h. Miami
    i. Los Angeles
    j. Calgary
    k. Toronto
    l. Charlottetown

16. If all the offices referred to in question 15 kept office hours of 0900 to 1630, which offices would be open when you placed your call at 1400 your local time?

NOTES ON MR. WILSON'S TRIP TO MIDWESTERN REGION

Appointments:

Wednesday, September 13	At 2000, Mr. Wilson will give a presentation to the Sales Management Club, Red River Community College.
	From 1400 to 1600, Mr. Wilson will meet with Raymond Jones, Plant Manager, Midwestern Region.
Tuesday, September 12	From 1400 to 1500, Mr. Wilson will meet with James Tobacki, Manager of refrigerator sales, Midwestern Region.
	From 0900 to 1100, Mr. Wilson will meet with Art Jocobs, Manager of small appliance sales, Midwestern Region.
	From 1530 to 1630, Mr. Wilson will meet with Agnes Vallesco, Manager of electric sales, Midwestern Region.

Luncheon and dinner engagements:

Tuesday, September 12	Mr. Wilson will have lunch at 1200 with Art Jacobs and John Reddin. Mr. Wilson will have dinner with Mr. and Mrs. Reddin in the Hilton Hotel Revolving Restaurant at 2000.
Wednesday, September 13	At 1200 Mr. Wilson will have lunch with Mr. Matlock and at 1900 he will have dinner at the Sales Management Club banquet at the Red River Community College.

Hotel reservations:

Reservations have been confirmed for the Hilton Hotel in Regina for September 11 and 12. They have also been made for the Best Western Hotel in Winnipeg for September 13. (Hotel confirmations are in the envelope with the airline tickets.)

Travel plans:

Thursday, September 14	Leave Winnipeg Airport at 1130 on Air Canada Flight 192. Arrive in Toronto at 1440 EDT.
Monday, September 11	Leave Pearson Airport, Terminal 2, Toronto, at 1925 EDT, on Air Canada Flight 153. Arrive in Regina at 2045 CST.
Wednesday, September 13	Leave Regina Airport on Air Canada Flight 160 at 0940 CST. Arrive in Winnipeg at 1140 CDT.

Additional notes:

Mr. John Reddin will pick up Mr. Wilson at his hotel on Tuesday morning at 0830 and drive him to the Midwestern Sales Office.

Complimentary limousine service is provided to and from the Regina Airport and downtown hotels.

Mr. Art Jacobs will drive Mr. Wilson back to his hotel after his meetings at the Sales Office on Tuesday.

Mrs. Mabel Wiggins will meet Mr. Wilson at the Best Western Hotel at 1815 and drive him to the Red River Community College for the Sales Management Club banquet. She will also drive him back to his hotel after his talk to the Club.

Mr. Wilson will have to take a taxi from his hotel in Winnipeg to the airport to catch his flight to Toronto on Thursday.

Mr. A.C. Matlock, Vice President in charge of Manufacturing, Midwestern Region, will meet Mr. Wilson at the Winnipeg Airport and take him to the plant for his meeting with Mr. Raymond Jones, Plant Manager. He will drive Mr. Wilson back to his hotel after the meeting.

Form 10-A

MILLENNIUM TRAVEL FUND ADVANCE

Please forward completed forms to:

Accounting Department
Millennium Appliances, Inc.
3431 Bloor Street
Toronto, ON M8X 1G4

Tel (416) 795-2893 Fax (416) 798-3982

Name of Employee Requesting Advance: ______________________

Date of Request: ______________________

Employee Number: ______________________

Destination: ______________________

Reason for Travel: ______________________

Departure Date: ______________________

Return Date: ______________________

Date Advance Required: ______________________

Amount Requested:

Accommodation	(Per Diem $120.00)	$ __________
Meals	(Per Diem $39.00)	$ __________
Transportation	(Refer to Policy 432)	$ __________
TOTAL REQUESTED		$ __________

Preferred Method of Payment/Distribution ____ Company Cheque ____ Traveller's Cheque

Balance Outstanding (includes this request) $ ________

____

Authorization
(as per Schedule of Authorities)

Date of Authorization

Approval Limits

$ 3 000 - Manager
$10 000 - Director
$10 000+ - President

Form 10-C

MILLENNIUM TRAVEL EXPENSE VOUCHER

NAME: ____________ PIN: ________

CONTROL #: ____________ TITLE: ____________ DATE: ________

Date	Location	Work Order	Transport*	Hotel	Other	Entertain	Meals	Total	Explain Other, Entertain & Meals
EXPENSE TOTAL									
LESS: CASH ADVANCE									**TFA DATE:**
BALANCE CLAIMED OR RETURNED									**LEGEND** * Include vehicle from Side 2 (if applicable) ** Enter on Side 2 *** Distribute on Side 2
GST Tax Credit = .0566 x Expense Total								**	
Expense Total *** Less Tax Credit									**APPROVAL OF EXPENSES**

CERTIFICATION OF EXPENSES

I certify that I have incurred these expenses.

Employee's Signature ____________ Date ____________

AUDIT

Checked by ____________ Date ____________

Payment Approved by ____________

Title ____________

Date ____________

Form 10-E

MA **Millennium Appliances, Inc.**
3431 Bloor Street, Toronto, ON M8X 1G4
Tel (416) 795-2893 Fax (416) 795-3982

DATE: **TIME:**

NUMBER OF PAGES TO FOLLOW: ______________________

SENT TO: ______________________
(FAX NUMBER) (Telephone Number)

____
(Name) (Title)

____
(Company)

____
(Address)

____
(City) (Prov./State)

____
(Code) (Country)

SENT FROM: ______________________
(Name) (Title)

MESSAGE: ______________________

____

____

____

____

____

____

____

MA ***Millennium Appliances, Inc.***

3431 Bloor Street, Toronto, ON M8X 1G4
Tel (416) 795-2893 Fax (416) 795-3982

DATE: **TIME:**

NUMBER OF PAGES TO FOLLOW: ______________________

SENT TO: ______________________

(FAX NUMBER) (Telephone Number)

____

(Name) (Title)

____

(Company)

____

(Address)

____

(City) (Prov./State)

____

(Code) (Country)

SENT FROM: ______________________

(Name) (Title)

MESSAGE: ______________________

____

____

____

____

____

____

____

Form 11-A-2

MA *Millennium Appliances, Inc.*
3431 Bloor Street, Toronto, ON M8X 1G4
Tel (416) 795-2893 Fax (416) 795-3982

DATE: TIME:

NUMBER OF PAGES TO FOLLOW: ______________________

SENT TO: ______________________
(FAX NUMBER) (Telephone Number)

____
(Name) (Title)

____
(Company)

____
(Address)

____
(City) (Prov./State)

____
(Code) (Country)

SENT FROM: ______________________
(Name) (Title)

MESSAGE: ______________________

____

____

____

____

____

____

____

Form 11-A-3

MA ***Millennium Appliances, Inc.***
3431 Bloor Street, Toronto, ON M8X 1G4
Tel (416) 795-2893 Fax (416) 795-3982

DATE: **TIME:**

NUMBER OF PAGES TO FOLLOW: ______________________

SENT TO: ______________________

(FAX NUMBER) (Telephone Number)

____

(Name) (Title)

____

(Company)

____

(Address)

____

(City) (Prov./State)

____

(Code) (Country)

SENT FROM: ______________________

(Name) (Title)

MESSAGE: ______________________

____

____

____

____

____

____

____

Meeting of Executive Committee for
November Sales Seminar
Wednesday, Sept. 10, 1700 h
Mr. Wilson's office
All members present

Announcement: Sid Levine has agreed to help with the Nov. Sales Seminar. He will be responsible for registration.

The minutes of the August meeting of the Executive Committee were distributed. One correction was called for. Honorariums will be paid to the keynote speaker and the banquet speaker but not to the luncheon speakers. The minutes were approved as corrected.

James Bradford proposed that the keynote speaker and the banquet speaker each be paid an honorarium of $500. Committee members agreed.

Lisa Rogers reported that James Atwell, who is in charge of working with the hotel on setting up audio-visual equipment, is ill and has asked to be relieved of this responsibility. Whom shall we ask to do this? After some discussion, Mr. Bradford volunteered for the job.

Louise Witherspoon reported that increased attendance at the seminar (over attendance of previous years) is anticipated. Therefore, some of the meeting rooms that have been assigned to the sectional meetings of the Nov. Sales Seminar may be too small. She raised the question, should we ask for larger rooms? The Executive Committee instructed her to check with the hotel to see if larger rooms are available and, if so, to make arrangements to shift the large sectional meetings to larger rooms. Be sure to give the information on room changes to A.C. Rothbaum, who is responsible for having the program printed. He needs the changes by Sept. 20.

Meeting adjourned, 1830 h

W. Wilson

VOTING SHEET FOR NOMINAL GROUP TECHNIQUE

ITEM NO.	ISSUES FOR DISCUSSION	TOTAL VOTES				WEIGHTED AVERAGE
		3	2	1	0	

REMEMBER:

3 = This problem is of high priority and should be dealt with now.

2 = This problem is of medium priority and should be dealt with as soon as possible.

1 = This problem is of low priority and should be dealt with when possible.

0 = This problem does not affect me or my work.

Form 11-C-1

MEETING LOG

MEETING OF:		
LOCATION:	DATE:	TIME:
MEMBERS PRESENT:	MEMBERS ABSENT:	

PROBLEMS / ISSUES DISCUSSED	RECORD OF DISCUSSION
PROBLEM / ISSUE NO. 1 Topic = Follow-up =	Recommendation/s =
PROBLEM / ISSUE NO. 2 Topic = Follow-up =	Recommendation/s =
PROBLEM / ISSUE NO. 3 Topic = Follow-up =	Recommendation/s =

Form 11-C-2

CAUSE-AND-EFFECT DIAGRAM

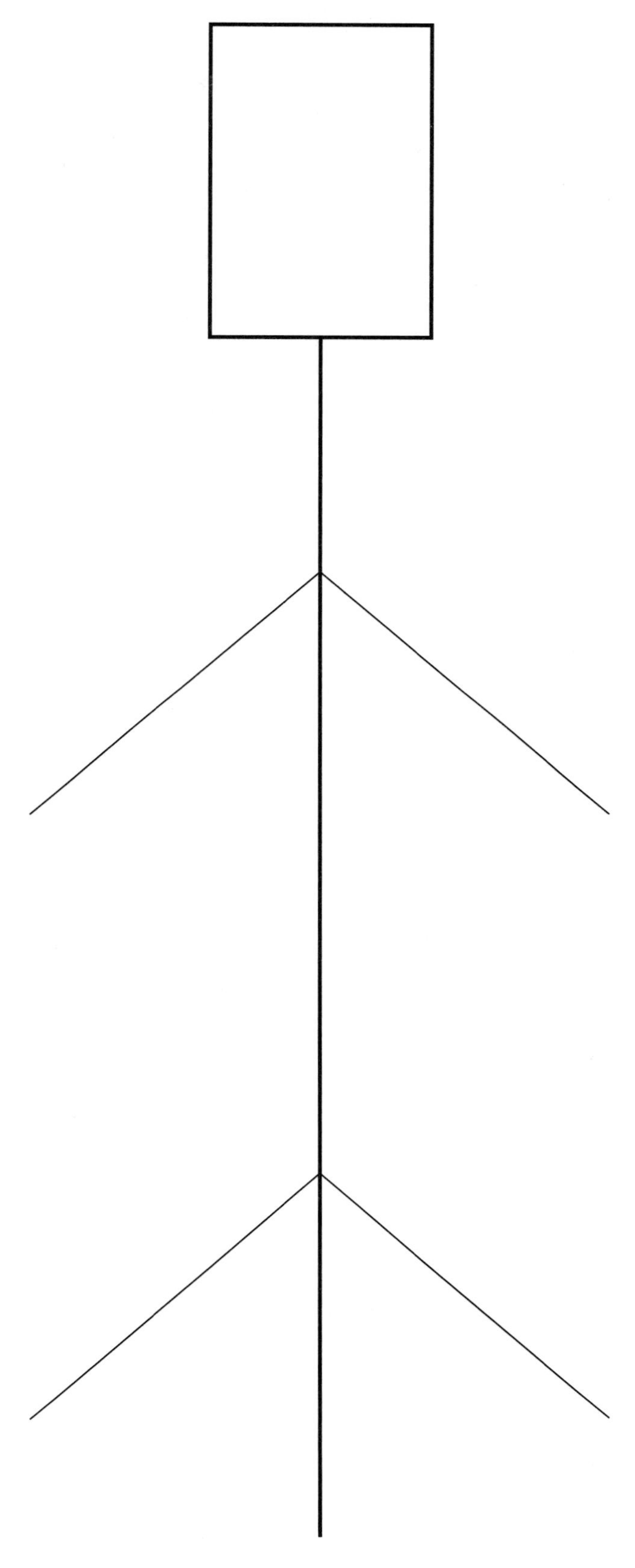

Form 11-C-3

CAUSE-AND-EFFECT DIAGRAM

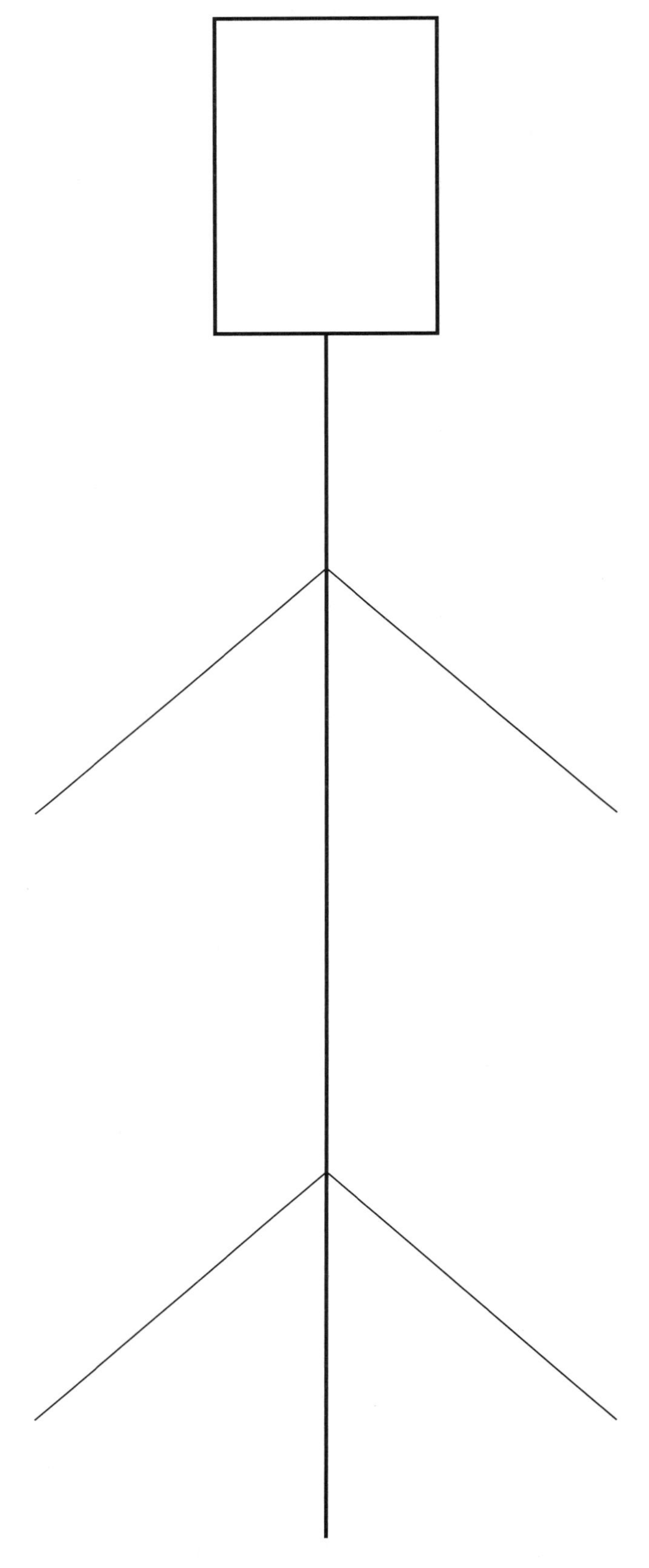

Form 11-C-4

CAUSE-AND-EFFECT DIAGRAM

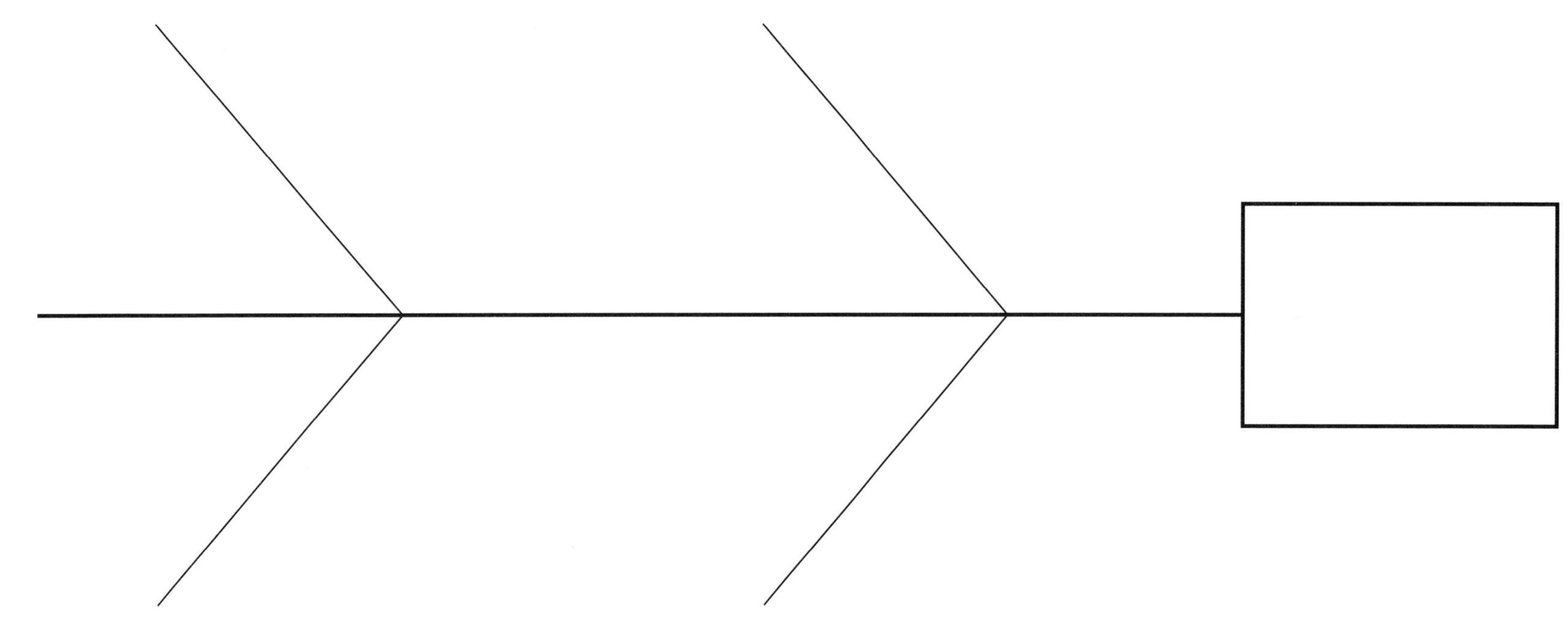

Form 11-C-5

Form 12-A-1

Form 12-A-2

MA *Millennium Appliances, Inc.*
3431 Bloor Street, Toronto, ON M8X 1G4
Tel (416) 795-2893 Fax (416) 795-3982

Work Improvement Methods

The worker who performs a task can contribute ideas for improving that task and, under a work simplification program, is encouraged and trained to do so. Workers become involved to the greatest extent in the aspect of work simplification pertaining to their respective tasks.

The purpose of a work simplification program is to enable workers to perform efficiently and economically. The ultimate goal is improved work, including an increase in the rate of production. This does not mean that the worker will speed up, hurrying thru the steps of a task. When the work simplification approach is applied the unnecessary steps are eliminated, other parts of the task are combined or rearranged, and the necessary parts of the task are simplified. Excessive movement and delays which occur as work moves from 1 work station to another are greatly reduced. The most desirable equipment for performing the job at reduced costs is purchased. After the task is simplified, the worker can improve the quality and increase the quantity of output without a corresponding increase in the amount of energy he expends.

delete

change to energy expended

The tested pattern for improving work includes five steps:

four

1. Select a job to improve.
2. Use a questioning approach to analyze every detail of the job.
3. Obtain all the facts and break

the job down in detail.

4. Apply the new method.

change to either a method or a procedure

These steps may be applied to improve either ~~a procedure or a method.~~ Work analysts use these steps to guide workers thru an analysis of their own tasks in search of ways to improve them. You do not have to wait for your organization to launch a work simplification program in your dept. You can look for ways to work smarter and in turn gain time in which to accept more responsibility. Select only 1 task for improvement at a time.

Move Select . . . time to next para after them

Take the initiative to select a task and analyze it, using the ~~five~~ four steps for work improvement in the same way a work analyst would use them.

Select a Job to Improve

Any job or task can be improved with directed effort, but some can be improved more than others. When you are looking for a job to improve, choose one that has worthwhile improvement possibilities, one that is important enough to warrant the time you will spend studying it.

Recognize that each task consists of three parts: (1) make ready, (2) do, and 3 put away. "Make ready" is the effort and time put into setting up equipment and assembling the necessary materials, "Do" is the actual performance of the work. "Put away" is the storage and clean-up following the actual performance. Scrutinize the "do" operation. If you can eliminate it, you

delete from make ready to actual performance

that

insert paragraphs from pages 6,7

change anyone to those

change his to their

automatically eliminate the "make ready" and "put away" operations which go with it.

Use a Questioning approach

The questioning approach is an attitude. It is essential for anyone searching for ways to improve his job performance. Every detail must be questioned for its necessity, possible combination with other details, and simplification.

Begin by asking why the job is done at all. Next examine each "do" operation and ask why it is necessary. Finally question the necessity of the remaining details — those involving "make ready" and "put away".

After you have separated the essential steps from the nonessential, apply the question test to the essential steps, one by one, in order. For each detail, ask, Where & Why? Who & Why?

When & Why? How & Why? The expanded questions relative to where become, Where is it done? Why is it done there? Where should it be done? For each detail, apply similar questions concerning who, when, and how.

As you question each detail, keep in mind that you are searching for (1) steps to be eliminated, ~~(2)~~ 4 steps to be performed elsewhere, ~~(3)~~ 2 steps to be combined or rearranged, and ~~(4)~~ 3 steps to be simplified.

change numbers as indicated

Obtain All ~~of~~ the Facts; Break~~e~~ the Job Down in Detail

change one to step

move heading and both paragraphs to page 5

Get the facts as the job is being performed. Put each one down detail by detail in the order in which it happens. Get facts, not opinions, and get all the facts. Omissions of facts, excuses, and opinions can lead to wrong conclusions.

To break down the steps of a task as they occur,

prepare a flowchart, the most widely used tool for analyzing work details.

Apply the New Method

After you receive tentative approval from your employer and in turn from management, conduct a trial run of your new method. Ask your employer and others who are knowledgeable about the method to evaluate it and suggest further improvements. Evaluate the new method yourself. Ask, will it work? Will it save time and money? Will it improve quality? Will it increase quantity? Will it be accepted by others who are affected by it?

move heading and paragraphs to page 8

Develop a New Method

Study the answers indicated as you apply the questions What & Why? When & Why? Where and Why? Who & Why? and How & Why? to each detail.

CHEQUE REGISTER								
Cheque No.	Date	Description	Amount of Cheque		Amount of Deposit		Balance	
							360	27

MILLENNIUM APPLIANCES, INC.
3431 BLOOR STREET
TORONTO, ON M8X 1G4
TEL: (416) 293-8080

147

20 ____

PAY TO THE
ORDER OF ______________________ $ ________

/100 DOLLARS

CANADIAN EASTERN BANK
MAIN BRANCH
TORONTO, ON M6Y 2H5

MEMO ____________ PER ____________

|| 147|| |: 11779 :509|| 501321|| 6||

Form 14-B-1

MILLENNIUM APPLIANCES, INC.
3431 BLOOR STREET
TORONTO, ON M8X 1G4
TEL: (416) 293-8080

148

20 ____

PAY TO THE
ORDER OF ______________________ $ ________

/100 DOLLARS

CANADIAN EASTERN BANK
MAIN BRANCH
TORONTO, ON M6Y 2H5

MEMO ____________ PER ____________

|| 148|| |: 11779 :509|| 501321|| 6||

Form 14-B-2

MILLENNIUM APPLIANCES, INC.
3431 BLOOR STREET
TORONTO, ON M8X 1G4
TEL: (416) 293-8080

153

20 ____

PAY TO THE
ORDER OF ______________________ $ ________

/100 DOLLARS

CANADIAN EASTERN BANK
MAIN BRANCH
TORONTO, ON M6Y 2H5

MEMO ____________ PER ____________

|| 153|| |: 11779 :509|| 501321|| 6||

Form 14-B-7

MILLENNIUM APPLIANCES, INC.
3431 BLOOR STREET
TORONTO, ON M8X 1G4
TEL: (416) 293-8080

154

20 ____

PAY TO THE
ORDER OF ______________________ $ ________

/100 DOLLARS

CANADIAN EASTERN BANK
MAIN BRANCH
TORONTO, ON M6Y 2H5

MEMO ____________ PER ____________

|| 154|| |: 11779 :509|| 501321|| 6||

Form 14-B-8

MILLENNIUM APPLIANCES, INC.
3431 BLOOR STREET
TORONTO, ON M8X 1G4
TEL: (416) 293-8080

155

______________ 20 ____

PAY TO THE
ORDER OF ______________________________ $ ________

/100 DOLLARS

CANADIAN EASTERN BANK
MAIN BRANCH
TORONTO, ON M6Y 2H5

MEMO ________________ PER ________________

|| 155|| |: 11779 :509|| 501321|| 6||

Form 14-B-9

MILLENNIUM APPLIANCES, INC.
3431 BLOOR STREET
TORONTO, ON M8X 1G4
TEL: (416) 293-8080

156

______________ 20 ____

PAY TO THE
ORDER OF ______________________________ $ ________

/100 DOLLARS

CANADIAN EASTERN BANK
MAIN BRANCH
TORONTO, ON M6Y 2H5

MEMO ________________ PER ________________

|| 156|| |: 11779 :509|| 501321|| 6||

Form 14-B-10

MILLENNIUM APPLIANCES, INC.
3431 BLOOR STREET
TORONTO, ON M8X 1G4
TEL: (416) 293-8080

157

_______________ 20 ____

PAY TO THE
ORDER OF _______________________________ $ ________

/100 DOLLARS

CANADIAN EASTERN BANK
MAIN BRANCH
TORONTO, ON M6Y 2H5

MEMO ____________________ PER ____________________

|| 157|| |: 11779 :509|| 501321|| 6||

Form 14-B-11

MILLENNIUM APPLIANCES, INC.
3431 BLOOR STREET
TORONTO, ON M8X 1G4
TEL: (416) 293-8080

158

_______________ 20 ____

PAY TO THE
ORDER OF _______________________________ $ ________

/100 DOLLARS

CANADIAN EASTERN BANK
MAIN BRANCH
TORONTO, ON M6Y 2H5

MEMO ____________________ PER ____________________

|| 158|| |: 11779 :509|| 501321|| 6||

Form 14-B-12

BANK STATEMENT

NAME: November Sales Seminar c/o William Wilson 3431 Bloor Street, Toronto, ON		BRANCH: Mississauga Main	
ACCOUNT NO. 08–03261	TRANSIT NO. 3512	BALANCE FORWARD 20xx–11–25	360.27

CODE	DESCRIPTION	DEBIT	CREDIT	DAY/MO	BALANCE
DD	Direct Deposit		300.00	04/11	660.27
DD	Direct Deposit		1500.00	05/11	2160.27
DD	Direct Deposit		3000.00	06/11	5160.27
CH	Cheque No.147	1224.00		07/11	3936.27
CH	Cheque No.151	510.00		08/11	3426.27
CH	Cheque No.150	450.00		08/11	2976.27
DD	Direct Deposit		2250.00	09/11	5226.27
CH	Cheque No.148	1700.00		12/11	3526.27
CH	Cheque No.149	25.00		12/11	3501.27
CH	Cheque No.152	60.00		13/11	3441.27
INC	Interest		17.42	15/11	3458.69
CH	Cheque No.153	300.45		15/11	3158.24
CH	Cheque No.155	500.00		18/11	2658.24
DD	Direct Deposit		600.00	20/11	3258.24
CH	Cheque No.154	500.00		21/11	2758.24

No. of Vouchers This Period	Ø	TOTAL DEBITS	$5269.45	TOTAL CREDITS	$7667.42

Form 14-C

PERSONAL INVENTORY

Answer the following questions in preparation for developing your resume.

PART I: PERSONAL INFORMATION	
Name	
Address	
Residence Telephone	
Business Telephone	

PART II: EMPLOYMENT BACKGROUND

Use action verbs to write sentences that list your work-related accomplishments. Begin your sentences with some of the following verbs.

Earned	Developed	Supervised	Organized
Designed	Improved	Analyzed	Trained
Established	Managed	Prepared	Researched

1.

2.

3.

4.

5.

6.

Think of all the employment you have had, both career related and other. Use reverse chronological order (most recent first) to record your answers.

Working Title	
Company Name	
City Where Company Is Located	
Date Commenced and Ended	
Key Responsibilities	
Working Title	
Company Name	
City Where Company Is Located	
Date Commenced and Ended	
Key Responsibilities	

Form 15-A-1

Continue to record information about your employment.	
Working Title	
Company Name	
City Where Company Is Located	
Date Commenced and Ended	
Key Responsibilities	

PART III: EDUCATION AND TRAINING

Use reverse chronological order to record the following information. Use this area to record post-secondary education (full-time, extension, adult education, etc.)	
Degree/Diploma/Certificate Earned	
Name of Institute	
City Where College Is Located	
Date Commenced and Ended	
Grade Point Average	
Key Courses Completed	

Use this area to record information about your high school education.	
Diploma/Certificate Earned	
Name of Institute	
City Where High School Is Located	
Date Commenced and Ended	
Grade Point Average	

PART IV: INTEREST AND ACTIVITIES

List professional organizations that you have held or currently hold membership in.	1. 2. 3.
List volunteer positions you have held or currently hold in your community.	1. 2. 3.
List sports or hobbies you participate in.	1. 2. 3.

Form 15-A-2

Instructions: Each of the following activities relates to Challenge 15-C. Your instructor may request that you complete all or only a portion of the activities. This form is intended as your personal checklist and organizer. For further details of the activities, refer to the instructions for Challenge 15-C.

CHECKLIST FOR YOUR EMPLOYMENT CAMPAIGN		
Activity	**Date Due**	**Date Submitted**
1. Prepare a self-appraisal inventory.		
2. Use a financial manual or directory, available in either the college or public library, to prepare a statistical report on a local corporation.		
3. From the placement office obtain literature that may be helpful to you in your job campaign.		
4. Join a committee to study employment opportunities for administrative assistants in your community. Obtain literature and share your findings with committee members.		
5. Prepare a list of qualifications you plan to emphasize during job interviews; prepare a list of questions and answers you expect to be asked; prepare a list of questions you wish to ask the interviewer.		
6. Prepare a résumé.		
7. Write either a prospecting job application letter or a solicited job application letter.		
8. Edit your résumé after your instructor has proofread it.		
9. Prepare a portfolio displaying samples of your work.		
10. Study job advertisements. Analyze the advertisements for administrative assistants.		
11. Write an evaluation of your performance during an early job interview.		
12. Complete the job application form (Form 15-C-2).		
13. Prepare a job acceptance letter or a job refusal letter.		

Form 15-C-1

APPLICATION FOR EMPLOYMENT

PERSONAL INFORMATION

Social Insurance No. ____________________

	Last	First	Middle
NAME			

	Street	City	Province	Postal Code
PRESENT ADDRESS				
PERMANENT ADDRESS				

PHONE NO. ____________ REFERRED BY ____________

If related to anyone in our employ, state name and department ____________

TYPE OF EMPLOYMENT DESIRED

POSITION ____________ When can you start? ____________ Salary Desired ____________

Are you employed now? ____________ May we contact your present employer? ____________

EDUCATION	Name and Location of School	Years Attended	Date Graduated	Major Subjects
UNIVERSITY				
COLLEGE				
HIGH SCHOOL				
OTHER				

List specialized courses ____________

What foreign languages do you speak fluently? ____________ Read? ____________ Write? ____________

Form 15-C-2

FORMER EMPLOYERS (List employers, starting with last one first.)

Date Month and Year	Name and Address of Employer	Salary	Position	Reason for Leaving
From				
To				
From				
To				
From				
To				

VOLUNTEER ACTIVITIES (List any community service or volunteer work you have done.)

Position	Name of Organization	Date Commenced and Ended
1		
2		

INTERESTS (List sports that you participate in or other activities you hold an interest in.)

Name of Sport or Activity	Level of Interest or Achievement
1	
2	

MEMBERSHIP (List any professional organization you hold membership in.)

Name of Organization	Position Held
1	
2	

REFERENCES (Give the names of three persons not related to you.)

Name	Address	Business	Years Acquainted
1			
2			
3			

I understand that misrepresentation or omission of facts called for is cause for dismissal. Furthermore, I understand and agree that my employment is for no definite period and may, regardless of the date of payment of my wages and salary, be terminated at any time without previous notice.

Date Signature

Form 15-C-3

Glossary

Abridged Having been shortened by using fewer words while maintaining the main contents

Address The name assigned to a specific location in a computer's memory so that data can be sent to it.

Ad hoc For a specific purpose and not for general application.

Administrative assistant A contemporary secretary whose skill set encompasses office organization, automation, and planning.

Almanac A yearly book or calendar of days, weeks, and months, containing statistical information on many subjects.

Ambient lighting Illumination that surrounds us and is not directly focused on one area as is task lighting.

Annotating The process of making notes on a document for comment or criticism.

Applications program A program or software that performs a collection of related tasks, such as word processing, and that allows the user to specify the data input and output.

Arithmetic unit That part of a microcomputer where all mathematical operations are performed.

Assertiveness Personal characteristic that inclines an individual to be confident and positive.

Automated enquiry system A process where the sender of a registered item of mail may telephone a toll-free number to check the delivery status of the item that has been sent.

Backbone The main communications corridor in a telecommunications network.

Backlog Accumulated work waiting to be processed.

Backup An extra copy often stored in a separate location from the original. The contents of the hard disk are usually backed up using floppy disks; the contents of floppy disks are usually backed up using another set of floppy disks.

Bibliography A list of details about books, their authors and publishers, used or referred to by another author.

Bit A binary digit. The is the smallest possible piece of information. Each bit is represented by a 1 or 0 in the binary system. A sequence of bits forms a byte. (See **byte**.)

Block Adjacent characters, words, sentences, or paragraphs.

Block move A command that enables the operator to remove information from its original location and insert it in another location in the document.

Boldface A feature of printed characters that makes them darker than the other characters on the page.

Booting Using a bootstrap program to initialize a program immediately after turning it on.

Bootstrap A startup program used to initialize the computer.

Brainstorming The unrestrained offering of ideas or suggestions by all members of a conference; the purpose is to find a solution to a problem.

Bulletin board system A computer network–based notice board. It is a location on the network where messages can be written or read by subscribers to the bulletin board.

Buyout The purchase of one company by another company.

Byte A unit of data equivalent to one computer character (see **bit**).

CAD Represents the words *computer-assisted design*. A general term for computer–based application software that allows the user to easily and accurately draw engineering or architectural plans.

Call management service A set of telephone user options provided by the telephone company. (e.g., display of incoming call information, call forwarding).

Calling card Similar in appearance to a credit card, but having a unique number which allows users to remotely bill telephone calls to their personal accounts.

Camera ready The final copy of text and/or graphics ready in both design and quality for camera reproduction.

Canada Postal Guide A publication which gives full details of conditions, facilities, and categories of service provided by Canada Post.

Cancelled mail An envelope that has bars printed over the stamps and that also indicates the date, time, and municipality where the mail was processed.

Casual day A working day designated by management as a day when casual, but respectable, attire may be worn in the office.

Central processing unit The part of a computer where the processing actually occurs.

Clean desk policy A unique office policy which dictates that employees leave their desks clear or tidy when they leave the office.

Coherence The quality of being consistent or intelligible.

Colloquialism A word or expression that is considered informal speech or writing.

Command An instruction that the operator gives to a computer to tell it what function to perform.

Compact disk Smaller version of the optical disk.

Compact Disk Read Only Memory (CD-ROM) A storage medium capable of retaining large quantities of audio, visual, or textual data.

Compatibility The ability of different hardware or software products to function together effectively.

Composure The state of being calm in mind and manner.

Computer-assisted retrieval (CAR) A computer-based index system used to locate information stored on other media.

Computer output microfilm (COM) A system used to produce microfilm or microfiche directly from computer output.

Conference call A meeting or discussion to exchange ideas conducted over the telephone between three or more participants.

Consensus When every team member can support the team decision, the team has reached a consensus. The final decision may not be the choice of each team member; however, all members must agree that they can support it both inside and outside the confines of the meeting.

Concise Brief and to the point.

Conference A meeting or discussion to exchange ideas.

Control unit The section of a computer that controls input, output, processing, and storage of data.

Convenience copier A small, inexpensive photocopier.

Copy A command that enables the operator to keyboard the information once and then repeat it at different locations in the document.

Courtesy title A respectful title to be used in formal address. (e.g., Mr., Ms., Mrs., Miss, Mayor, Vice President, Major)

Credenza A sideboard or cabinet used as an extension of a desk.

Cross-referencing A method of locating a single record from two or more file references.

Curriculum vitae A form of résumé, often referred to as a CV. The actual Latin words mean "course of life." The term describes a document that summarizes a person's history and professional qualifications.

Cursor A symbol (typically a square or underline) that indicates your current location within the document. The movement may be controlled by a mouse or cursor keys.

Debrief To receive information or to recap a meeting or procedure that has been concluded.

Dedicated word processor A computer system that is programmed to function only as a word processor.

Delete To erase. Text may be deleted by the character, line, paragraph, page, or document.

Desktop publishing (DTP) A computer application that enables the user to design and create professional documents that integrate text and graphics.

Directory A designated area of a disk that contains data of common elements.

Disk operating system (DOS) Computer software that controls the disk drives, data loading, and data saving.

Disk drive A device into which the floppy disk is placed when information retrieval from the floppy disk is required.

Diskette Magnetic storage medium consisting of a plastic flexible disk, enclosed in a case.

Display A screen or monitor.

Domestic mail Mailable matter that is transmitted within Canada, which includes the ten provinces, the Yukon, the Northwest Territories, and Nunavut.

Dot matrix printer An impact printer that forms characters from a rectangular array of wires. These wires strike the paper to form the characters.

Effectiveness The practical and productive effect of a procedure on a process.

Efficiency Producing the desired results with the least output of time, but in a capable and competent fashion.

Electronic Bulletin Board A BBS (Bulletin Board System) is a host computer that can be reached by computer modem for the purpose of sharing or exchanging messages or other files.

Electronic calendar A computer-based personal calendar. When computers are networked, calendars may also be used to schedule and plan on behalf of the user.

Electronic Funds Transfer A method of transferring funds via Internet, computer and modem, or other forms of technology.

Electronic mail (e-mail) A computer network-based message routing, storing, and retrieval system.

Electronic mailbox A location in the computer's memory designated as storage space for electronic mail messages.

Electronic pocket organizer A pocket-sized unit no bigger than an electronic calculator that stores addresses and telephone numbers, scheduling, and other organizational facts.

Empowered To be authorized and entrusted to complete a job or task.

Enhancement Improvement. A document can be enhanced with the use of graphics or by the special appearance of text.

Ergonomics The study of efficiency of persons in their working environment.

Etiquette Customs and rules of social or corporate correct behaviour.

Executive A person who manages or directs the business affairs of an institution or organization.

Express money order A foreign currency money order designed to be cashed directly in the foreign country.

Facsimile A device that will copy and transmit, over telephone lines, graphical or textual documents to a corresponding remote facsimile. Also called a fax.

Feature-rich A term used to describe a device or system with many features or options.

Field A field is an area or a location in a unit of data such as a record, message header, or computer instruction. A field can be subdivided into smaller fields.

Flat technology An abbreviation of the term *flat screen technology* which refers to a new design in VDT screens. The characteristic curvature of a VDT screen is eliminated.

Floppy disk See diskette.

Font Complete set of characters that belong to a typeface. They share the same design, size, and style. A font may be purchased in the form of software or as a cartridge used with a printer.

Format The arrangement of text and graphics on a page.

Function key A key that performs special tasks such as deleting, tabbing, bold facing, merging, underlining, and so on.

Gazetteer An index of geographical names.

Gigabyte Approximately one billion bytes.

GIGO An acronym for Garbage In, Garbage Out. The acronym means that poor-quality input to a computer will only result in poor-quality output.

Global Throughout the entire document.

Global Marketplace The worldwide business environment. An international forum in which to conduct business.

Grammar Check A word processing feature that compares the grammar of a keyboarded document with conventional rules.

Grapevine An informal channel of communication within an organization.

Hardware The physical part(s) of a computer system.

Header Text, such as a page number or a date, printed at the top of each page of a multipage document.

Help A feature that allows users to receive on-screen help. When the operator runs into difficulty, he/she may use the Help key to receive detailed instructions on the screen to guide the operator through the procedure.

High-end fax A facsimile device that typically produces excellent copy quality, and is fast, feature-rich, and expensive.

Highlight To emphasize text on the screen.

Home key The key on the keyboard used for returning the cursor to the uppermost left position of the screen.

Home page A screen of graphical information that identifies and provides information about a user or service on the Internet.

Hyphenate A word processing feature that divides words at the ends of lines according to recognized hyphenation rules.

Icon A picture used to represent a computer software function.

Immunization An inoculation that gives immunity to selective infections.

Impact printer A device that produces copy by stamping the character on paper.

Informal organization An organization or group that develops naturally among personnel without direction from the management of the company within which they operate.

Information Age An era in which the timely acquisition, processing, and distribution of information is critical for the growth of business.

Information Highway A concept of worldwide information exchange through a telecommunications network.

Input Data submitted to a computer for processing.

Insert A word processing mode that pushes text to the right while new text is keyed in. Typeover is the opposite mode.

Integrity A personal trait that embodies the quality or state of being honest, sincere, and of good moral principle.

Interface The software and/or hardware that connects one device or system to another, either electronically or physically.

International mail Canadian mail addressed to points of destination outside Canada and the United States of America.

Internet A global network of computer-based information and services.

Itinerary A detailed plan for a journey.

Justified right margin A word processing feature where the right margin is automatically aligned.

Keyboard An input device consisting of an arrangement of keys similar to that on a typewriter.

Kilobyte Approximately one thousand bytes.

Landscaped office An attractive and well-designed open-office plan.

Laser printer A nonimpact printer using a laser beam to form characters.

Line organization An organization structure based on authority. Line authority is hierarchical; the president has ultimate authority and reduced authority is given to others down the line to supervisor.

Line-and-staff organization An organizational structure where line managers have operational positions and staff managers have advisory or administrative positions. Line-and-staff organization structures are often found in large, diverse companies.

Linotype A trademark name for a typesetting machine that sets type in lines of single bars.

Local area network (LAN) Two or more local personal computers or terminals connected together by communication lines in order to share common programs and data.

Log on To send the user's identification to the computer in order to gain access to data and software applications.

Loyalty Faithfulness to a person or organization.

Mail merge The process of combining text (letters/memos) from one file with names and addresses from another file.

Manager A person who is in charge of a specific task or group of people.

Megabyte Approximately one million bytes.

Memory Temporary memory is the place in a computer where programs and data are stored. For permanent memory, see disks.

Mentor In a corporate setting, a mentor is a person who usually holds a position of a higher level than yours. This person can offer you career advice, guidance, and information about the organization.

Menu A list of alternatives displayed on the screen from which the operator can select a command.

Menu pointer A cursor moved by the mouse or cursor keys to point to a selection on the menu. Used with Windows software.

Merger The unification of two or more companies.

Microcomputer A standalone desktop computer used to perform personal or office applications.

Microfiche A transparent sheet of film containing multiple rows of micro images.

Microfilm Micro images on film made by a process that photographs and reduces the size of documents.

Micrographics Format for long-term storage of images. It may include microfilm, microfiche, aperture cards, or other microforms. Cameras and COM readers produce micrographics.

Microprocessor See microprocessor chip.

Microprocessor chip A processing unit miniaturized to fit on a single integrated circuit (chip).

Mnemonic command Use of the first letter of a word to perform a build-in command, like "V" for "view."

Modem A device that converts computer signals to telephone signals and vice versa. It enables communication between computers over telephone lines.

Modular furniture Furniture designed to be used as separate modules or placed together to form larger units.

Monitor Screen output for a computer.

Motivation The inner reason that causes an individual to act.

Mouse Hand-operated input device. It is rolled across a surface to control the movement of a cursor.

Networking 1 Connecting various processors or terminals within the same computer environment.

Networking 2 Informal communications between people, departments, divisions, or organizations for the purpose of sharing information.

Node A communications network routing or distribution hub. Telecommunications signals are received and sent out from the node.

Nonimpact printer A device that produces copy without stamping the character on the paper.

Notebook computer A small-scale personal computer. It has all the functionality of a desktop personal computer but weighs about three kilograms and is the approximate size of this textbook.

Offset printing A printing process in which a rubber cylinder transfers an inked impression from an etched plate to a sheet of paper.

On-line Describing a device connected directly to a computer.

On-line database Computer-based repository of information that is directly available to active users of the computer system.

Open office An office plan or design without conventional walls, corridors, or floor-to-ceiling partitions.

Open ticket A booking arrangement for some forms of transportation where the scheduling details of the return journey are not specified.

Optical disk A storage device using laser technology and capable of storing vast quantities of data.

Optical character recognition (OCR) Computer reading of written or printed characters.

Organization chart A guide to the formal internal structure of an organization.

Outsource Outsourcing is an arrangement in which one company provides a service for another company that could also be or usually have been provided in-house.

Output Information resulting from computer processing.

Pagination A word processing features that allows you to predetermine the number of lines of text per page.

Participatory management A management style that is both permissive and democratic. It involves employees in some aspects of decision making and emphasizes autonomy in work activities.

Per diem rate A daily allowance for expenses. *Per diem* is Latin for *by the day*.

Personal communication system A new wireless telecommunication system where individuals carry a short-range cellular-like telephone bearing one's home or office telephone number.

Personal computer (PC) A microcomputer used for personal applications.

Phototypesetting The process of producing typeset text photographically. This process does not use metal type.

Plotter A device that draws pictures under computer control by moving one or more pens across paper.

Poise Ease and dignity of manner. (Also see **composure.**)

Postal code A unique alphanumeric code used to identify the local destination of a mail item.

Postscript printer Postscript is a programming language that describes the appearance of a printed page. A postscript printer is designed to take advantage of this special language and produce fully enhanced printed pages. The average home laser printer is not a Postscript printer which is somewhat more expensive and more frequently purchased for business use.

Prepaid calling cards Cards that are accepted by the telephone company when the holder makes long-distance calls. The cost of the call is deducted from the current balance or value of the card.

Printer A device that produces copy on paper.

Priorities The assignment of precedence of tasks to be accomplished. Typically the tasks will be ranked in order of importance.

Processing Computer manipulation of data.

Prompt A request on the screen for more information in order to execute a command.

Quality circle A small group of people who meet regularly to identify and solve problems related to the quality of their work. These individuals are directly involved in the problems being discussed and are, therefore, able to offer first-hand information and recommendations.

Random access memory (RAM) A storage location within the computer, containing data or instruction that can be erased. This area of memory is a temporary storage location.

Raw data Source information in its original form.

Read only memory (ROM) A storage location within the computer, containing data or instructions that cannot be erased by overwriting or loss of power.

Reading file A quick reference file of recently completed work.

Release mark A mark or stamp on a document that identifies the document as ready for filing.

Remote access Remote communication with a computer.

Reprographic A term for the hardcopy reproduction process (copying) of text or graphics.

Right-sizing The process of optimizing company resources to achieve efficiency.

Routers Devices that route information from one network to another. Routers allow the independent networks to function as a large virtual nework so that users of any network can reach users of any other.

Scanner An input device that reads printed material and converts it to computer language.

Scroll A feature that allows the user to move the window (screen) over the document in all directions. Since most screens are not large enough for full viewing of the page, this is an important feature for document creation.

Search and replace A word processing feature that allows the user to check through a document in order to find and replace a character, word, or phrase.

Secretary An office worker who handles administrative tasks for a person or organization.

Self-confidence The firm belief in one's own abilities.

Sequential access A method of computer storage that requires data to be retrieved in the same order in which it is stored.

Short list In an employment scenario, this is a list of applicants that has been reduced to the best possible choices.

Sign on A term used to describe the process of starting the computer, entering a password, and ultimately connecting to the application desired.

Sincerity A quality that demonstrates truthfulness and freedom from pretence.

Software The programs, data, or intangible part(s) of a computer system.

Span of control The number of people and functions that one person can supervise.

Spell check A word processing feature that compares each word in a document with the spelling of a built-in dictionary. Words that do not match are highlighted on the screen and changes are suggested.

Spreadsheet A computerized representation of a paper spreadsheet in which data are organized in rows and columns.

Standalone A device that can perform its functions without being connected to another piece of equipment.

Stress A mental or physical state of tension.

Style checker A word processing feature that compares the format of the keyboarded document with conventional rules.

Subject line A line of text, often appearing in memorandums and letters, that identifies the topic of the communication.

Supervisor A person who watches over or controls the work of others.

Synopsis A statement giving a brief, general review or summary.

Talking Yellow Pages A voice mail system that incorporates the Yellow Pages directory and participating businesses. Users can dial numbers and receive recorded commercial information.

Task lighting Directed lighting (illumination) designed to increase the visibility of the assignment being worked on.

Teleconferencing A conference held between remote or distant participants. Typically conducted over telephone facilities.

Telephone tag This is the phenomena occurring when telephone callers continually leave each other messages to return the call.

Tickler file A card index or memorandum book that serves as an automatic reminder to bring matters to timely attention.

Time distribution chart A chart designed to show the distribution of work and time for several workers performing related office tasks.

Time management A skill that enables you to manage time efficiently.

Time-sharing The simultaneous access of a computer by two or more users.

To Do List A simple checklist of things to do. It is intended to serve as a reminder and need not be prioritized.

Toggle A feature that can be turned on or off by striking the same key.

Total Quality Management (TQM) A management philosophy that stresses the delivery of a quality product (the end result of your business), through optimization of the people and processes that produce it.

Transmittal sheet Typically the first page of a facsimile transmission, which provides full details of the originator and intended recipient.

Travel fund advance A cash advance paid to an employee prior to a business trip.

Travel expense voucher (TEV) An official (corporate) form that serves as both a record and a claim for expenses incurred while travelling on company business.

Traveller's cheques A special cheque or draft issued by a bank to a traveller who signs it at issuance and again in the presence of the person cashing it.

Typeface A distinctive design for a family of type. Each member of the family may differ in weight (bold), width of character, and slant. Unlike a font, a typeface cannot be purchased; it is simply a design.

Typeover A word processing mode where existing text is replaced with new text that is being keyed. This is the opposite mode of insert.

Undo A safeguard built into document creation programs to protect the user from deleting the document in error.

USA mail Canadian mail addressed to points of destination within the United States of America.

Video display terminal (VDT) A computer terminal that includes a monitor.

Virtual network A communications connection that may involve routing through several locations and devices. However, it has the appearance and functionality of two computers directly connected with wires.

Voice mail A telephone network-based message routing, storing, and retrieval system.

Voice trained This describes commercial computers that carry out spoken commands and interpret dictation, and are trained to recognize the voice, or voices, of their operators.

Website An addressable location on the World Wide Web, where information or links to other websites can be obtained.

White sound Also known as white noise. A continuous sound formed from many frequencies of equal volume, it has the effect of deadening surrounding sounds.

Wide area network (WAN) Two or more computers and/or local area networks connected together by communications media in order to share programs and data.

Windows A trademarked name for a graphically interfaced operating system that operates on personal computers. Functions are represented through icons and menus.

Word originator The original author of keyboarded or longhand textual material.

Wordwrap A word processing feature that automatically moves a word to the following line if it will not completely fit on the previous line.

Workstation 1 A personal work space, often defined by free-standing partitions.

Workstation 2 A terminal or personal computer.

World Wide Web Often used synonymously with the Internet, the World Wide Web is the user interface for finding, viewing, and making use of the vast amount of information on the Internet.

Y2K A popular short form for the *year 2000*.

Zero-plus dialing A telephone number prefixed with "0" in order that the caller can obtain assistance or special service from the operator.

Appendix

Common Proofreader Marks

Close up	⁀‿
Insert Space	#
Let it stand	stet
Delete	℘
Paragraph	¶
No paragraph	No ¶
Move right	]
Move left	[
Insert	∧
Insert comma	∧ with ,
Insert apostrophe	∨ with '
Transpose	⊓⊔ or tr
Lower	⊔
Raise	⊓
Set in lowercase	lc
Capitalize	Cap or ≡
Align type	//
Spell out	(Sp)
Set in boldface	bf
Underline or italics	___

Index

"*AS IS*" LICENSE AGREEMENT AND LIMITED WARRANTY

READ THIS LICENSE CAREFULLY BEFORE OPENING THIS PACKAGE. BY OPENING THIS PACKAGE, YOU ARE AGREEING TO THE TERMS AND CONDITIONS OF THIS LICENSE. IF YOU DO NOT AGREE, DO NOT OPEN THE PACKAGE. PROMPTLY RETURN THE UNOPENED PACKAGE AND ALL ACCOMPANYING ITEMS TO THE PLACE YOU OBTAINED THEM. *THESE TERMS APPLY TO ALL LICENSED SOFTWARE ON THE DISK EXCEPT THAT THE TERMS FOR USE OF ANY SHAREWARE OR FREEWARE ON THE DISKETTES ARE AS SET FORTH IN THE ELECTRONIC LICENSE LOCATED ON THE DISK:*

1. **GRANT OF LICENSE and OWNERSHIP:** The enclosed computer programs <<and any data>> ("Software") are licensed, not sold, to you by Prentice-Hall Canada Inc. ("We" or the "Company") in consideration of your adoption of the accompanying Company textbooks and/or other materials, and your agreement to these terms. You own only the disk(s) but we and/or our licensors own the Software itself. This license allows instructors and students enrolled in the course using the Company textbook that accompanies this Software (the "Course") to use and display the enclosed copy of the Software for academic use only, so long as you comply with the terms of this Agreement. You may make one copy for back up only. We reserve any rights not granted to you.
2. **USE RESTRICTIONS:** You may <u>not</u> sell or license copies of the Software or the Documentation to others. You may *not* transfer, distribute or make available the Software or the Documentation, except to instructors and students in your school who are users of the adopted Company textbook that accompanies this Software in connection with the course for which the textbook was adopted. You may <u>not</u> reverse engineer, disassemble, decompile, modify, adapt, translate or create derivative works based on the Software or the Documentation. You may be held legally responsible for any copying or copyright infringement which is caused by your failure to abide by the terms of these restrictions.
3. **TERMINATION:** This license is effective until terminated. This license will terminate automatically without notice from the Company if you fail to comply with any provisions or limitations of this license. Upon termination, you shall destroy the Documentation and all copies of the Software. All provisions of this Agreement as to limitation and disclaimer of warranties, limitation of liability, remedies or damages, and our ownership rights shall survive termination.
4. **DISCLAIMER OF WARRANTY: THE COMPANY AND ITS LICENSORS MAKE NO WARRANTIES ABOUT THE SOFTWARE, WHICH IS PROVIDED "*AS-IS*." IF THE DISK IS DEFECTIVE IN MATERIALS OR WORKMANSHIP, YOUR ONLY REMEDY IS TO RETURN IT TO THE COMPANY WITHIN 30 DAYS FOR REPLACEMENT UNLESS THE COMPANY DETERMINES IN GOOD FAITH THAT THE DISK HAS BEEN MISUSED OR IMPROPERLY INSTALLED, REPAIRED, ALTERED OR DAMAGED. THE COMPANY DISCLAIMS ALL WARRANTIES, EXPRESS OR IMPLIED, INCLUDING WITHOUT LIMITATION, THE IMPLIED WARRANTIES OF MERCHANTABILITY AND FITNESS FOR A PARTICULAR PURPOSE. THE COMPANY DOES NOT WARRANT, GUARANTEE OR MAKE ANY REPRESENTATION REGARDING THE ACCURACY, RELIABILITY, CURRENTNESS, USE, OR RESULTS OF USE, OF THE SOFTWARE.**
5. **LIMITATION OF REMEDIES AND DAMAGES: IN NO EVENT, SHALL THE COMPANY OR ITS EMPLOYEES, AGENTS, LICENSORS OR CONTRACTORS BE LIABLE FOR ANY INCIDENTAL, INDIRECT, SPECIAL OR CONSEQUENTIAL DAMAGES ARISING OUT OF OR IN CONNECTION WITH THIS LICENSE OR THE SOFTWARE, INCLUDING, WITHOUT LIMITATION, LOSS OF USE, LOSS OF DATA, LOSS OF INCOME OR PROFIT, OR OTHER LOSSES SUSTAINED AS A RESULT OF INJURY TO ANY PERSON, OR LOSS OF OR DAMAGE TO PROPERTY, OR CLAIMS OF THIRD PARTIES, EVEN IF THE COMPANY OR AN AUTHORIZED REPRESENTATIVE OF THE COMPANY HAS BEEN ADVISED OF THE POSSIBILITY OF SUCH DAMAGES.** SOME JURISDICTIONS DO NOT ALLOW THE LIMITATION OF DAMAGES IN CERTAIN CIRCUMSTANCES, SO THE ABOVE LIMITATIONS MAY NOT ALWAYS APPLY.
6. **GENERAL:** THIS AGREEMENT SHALL BE CONSTRUED AND INTERPRETED ACCORDING TO THE LAWS OF THE PROVINCE OF ONTARIO. This Agreement is the complete and exclusive statement of the agreement between you and the Company and supersedes all proposals, prior agreements, oral or written, and any other communications between you and the company or any of its representatives relating to the subject matter.

Should you have any questions concerning this agreement or if you wish to contact the Company for any reason, please contact in writing: Customer Service, Prentice Hall Canada, 1870 Birchmount Road, Scarborough, Ontario M1P 2J7